*The Consumer Credit and Sales
Legal Practice Series*

FAIR CREDIT REPORTING

2004 Supplement
With CD-Rom

Anthony Rodriguez
Joanne S. Faulkner
Elizabeth De Armond

Contributing Authors: Carolyn L. Carter, Chi Chi Wu

National Consumer Law Center
77 Summer Street, 10th Floor   Boston, MA 02110

www.consumerlaw.org

About NCLC	The National Consumer Law Center, a nonprofit corporation founded in 1969, assists consumers, advocates, and public policy makers nationwide who use the powerful and complex tools of consumer law to ensure justice and fair treatment for all, particularly those whose poverty renders them powerless to demand accountability from the economic marketplace. For more information, go to www.consumerlaw.org.
Ordering NCLC Publications	Order securely online at www.consumerlaw.org, or contact Publications Department, National Consumer Law Center, 77 Summer Street, Boston, MA 02110, (617) 542-9595 x1, FAX: (617) 542-8028, e-mail: publications@nclc.org.
Training and Conferences	NCLC participates in numerous national, regional, and local consumer law trainings. Its annual fall conference is a forum for consumer rights attorneys from legal services programs, private practice, government, and nonprofit organizations to share insights into common problems and explore novel and tested approaches that promote consumer justice in the marketplace. Contact NCLC for more information or see our web site.
Case Consulting	Case analysis, consulting and co-counseling for lawyers representing vulnerable consumers are among NCLC's important activities. Administration on Aging funds allow us to provide free consulting to legal services advocates representing elderly consumers on many types of cases. Massachusetts Legal Assistance Corporation funds permit case assistance to advocates representing low-income Massachusetts consumers. Other funding may allow NCLC to provide very brief consultations to other advocates without charge. More comprehensive case analysis and research is available for a reasonable fee. See our web site for more information at www.consumerlaw.org.
Charitable Donations and Cy Pres Awards	NCLC's work depends in part on the support of private donors. Tax-deductible donations should be made payable to National Consumer Law Center, Inc. For more information, contact Suzanne Cutler of NCLC's Development Office at (617) 542-8010 or scutler@nclc.org. NCLC has also received generous court-approved *cy pres* awards arising from consumer class actions to advance the interests of class members. For more information, contact Robert Hobbs (rhobbs@nclc.org) or Rich Dubois (rdubois@nclc.org) at (617) 542-8010.
Comments and Corrections	Write to the above address to the attention of the Editorial Department or e-mail consumerlaw@nclc.org.
About This Volume	This is the 2004 Supplement to *Fair Credit Reporting* (5th ed. 2002) with a 2004 CD-Rom. Retain the 2002 Fifth Edition, this Supplement, and the 2004 CD-Rom. Discard all prior volumes, supplements, and CDs. Continuing developments can be found in periodic supplements to this volume and in NCLC REPORTS, *Consumer Credit & Usury Edition*.
Cite This Volume As	National Consumer Law Center, Fair Credit Reporting (5th ed. 2002 and Supp.).
Attention	*This publication is designed to provide authoritative information concerning the subject matter covered. Always use the most current edition and supplement, and use other sources for more recent developments or for special rules for individual jurisdictions. This publication cannot substitute for the independent judgment and skills of an attorney or other professional. Non-attorneys are cautioned against using these materials to conduct a lawsuit without advice from an attorney and are cautioned against engaging in the unauthorized practice of law.*
Copyright	© 2004 by National Consumer Law Center, Inc. All Rights Reserved Printed in Canada ISBN 1-931697-59-0 (this Supplement) ISBN 1-931697-27-2 (main volume) ISBN 0-943116-10-4 (Series) Library of Congress Control Number 2002114633

About the Authors

Anthony Rodriguez is an NCLC staff attorney focusing on credit reporting and other consumer law issues. He previously served as the Director of the Massachusetts Attorney General's Disability Rights Project, and also worked as an Assistant Attorney General in the Consumer Protection and Civil Rights Divisions, where he litigated UDAP, telemarketing, credit repair, housing discrimination and public accommodations cases. Before that, he was a legal services attorney in Los Angeles. He is co-author of *Fair Credit Reporting* (5th ed. 2002) and a contributing author to *Credit Discrimination* (3d ed. 2002) and *Consumer Warranty Law's* 2004 Supplement.

Joanne S. Faulkner has a private consumer law practice in New Haven, Connecticut. Previously, she was an attorney at New Haven Legal Assistance for many years and has served as Chair of the Consumer Law Section of the Connecticut Bar Association and as a member of the FRB's Consumer Advisory Council. She has contributed to a number of NCLC publications, including *Fair Credit Reporting* (5th ed. 2002). She is the 2002 recipient of the Vern Countryman Consumer Law Award.

Elizabeth De Armond is on the faculty of Chicago-Kent College of Law. She has been a frequent contributor to NCLC publications and is a contributing author to *Fair Credit Reporting* (5th ed. 2002), *Consumer Warranty Law* (2d ed. 2000), and *Automobile Fraud* (2d ed. 2003). She was in private practice in Texas and a clerk for the Hon. Cornelia Kennedy of the United States Court of Appeals for the Sixth Circuit. She is a member of the Illinois, Massachusetts and Texas bars.

Carolyn L. Carter is of counsel with NCLC, and was formerly co-director of Legal Services, Inc., in Gettysburg, Pennsylvania, and director of the Law Reform Office of the Cleveland Legal Aid Society. She is the editor of *Pennsylvania Consumer Law*, editor of the First Edition of *Ohio Consumer Law*, co-author of *Fair Credit Reporting* (5th ed. 2002), *Consumer Warranty Law* (2d ed. 2001), *Unfair and Deceptive Acts and Practices* (5th ed. 2001), *Repossessions and Foreclosures* (5th ed. 2002), *Automobile Fraud* (2d ed. 2003), contributing author to *Fair Debt Collection* (5th ed. 2004), *Truth in Lending* (1999, 2003) and *The Cost of Credit* (2d ed. 2000), and the 1992 recipient of the Vern Countryman Consumer Award.

Chi Chi Wu is an NCLC staff attorney with a focus on credit discrimination and consumer credit law, with an emphasis on consumer issues affecting domestic violence victims, immigrants, and low-income seniors. She is the co-author of *Credit Discrimination* (3d ed. 2002) and contributing author to *Fair Credit Reporting* (5th ed. 2002), *Truth in Lending* (5th ed. 2003), and *The Cost of Credit* 2004 Supplement. She was formerly an Assistant Attorney General with the Consumer Protection Division of the Massachusetts Attorney General's Office, and an attorney with the Asian Outreach Unit of Greater Boston Legal Services.

Acknowledgments: We are particularly grateful to Denise Lisio for editorial supervision; Emilio Englade for editorial assistance; Shirlron Williams for assistance with cite checking; Shannon Halbrook for production assistance; Xylutions for typesetting services; and to Neil Fogarty of Law Disks for developing the CD-Rom. Thanks to Tom Domonoske, Dick Rubin, Joanne Faulkner, Ian Lynklip, and Len Bennett for their assistance regarding the FACT Act. We also thank Sylvia Antalis Goldsmith, James Fishman, Jim Francis, Ian Lyngklip, John Roddy, Robert Sola, Chris Kitell and Dave Szwak for their substantive contributions, and Mary Kingsley and Allen Agnitti for cite checking, legal research and writing.

What Your Library Should Contain

The Consumer Credit and Sales Legal Practice Series contains 16 titles, updated annually, arranged into four libraries, and designed to be an attorney's primary practice guide and legal resource in all 50 states. Each manual includes a CD-Rom allowing information to be copied into a word processor.

Debtor Rights Library

2000 Sixth Edition, 2003 Supplement, and 2003 CD-Rom, Including Law Disks' Bankruptcy Forms

Consumer Bankruptcy Law and Practice: the definitive personal bankruptcy manual, with step-by-step instructions from initial interview to final discharge, and including consumers' rights as creditors when a merchant or landlord files for bankruptcy. Appendices and CD-Rom contain over 130 annotated pleadings, bankruptcy statutes, rules and fee schedules, an interview questionnaire, a client handout, and software to complete the latest versions of petitions and schedules.

2004 Fifth Edition and 2004 CD-Rom

Fair Debt Collection: the basic reference in the field, covering the Fair Debt Collection Practices Act and common law, state statutory and other federal debt collection protections. Appendices and companion CD-Rom contain sample pleadings and discovery, the FTC's Official Staff Commentary, *all* FTC staff opinion letters, and summaries of reported and unreported cases.

2002 Fifth Edition, 2003 Supplement, and 2003 CD-Rom

Repossessions and Foreclosures: unique guide to VA, FHA and other types of home foreclosures, servicer obligations, car and mobile home repossessions, threatened seizures of household goods, tax and other statutory liens, and automobile lease and rent-to-own default remedies. The CD-Rom reprints relevant UCC provisions and numerous key federal statutes, regulations, and agency letters, summarizes hundreds of state laws, and includes over 150 pleadings covering a wide variety of cases.

2002 Second Edition, 2003 Supplement, and 2003 CD-Rom

Student Loan Law: student loan debt collection and collection fees; discharges based on closed school, false certification, failure to refund, disability, and bankruptcy; tax intercepts, wage garnishment, and offset of social security benefits; repayment plans, consolidation loans, deferments, and non-payment of loan based on school fraud. CD-Rom and appendices contain numerous forms, pleadings, interpretation letters and regulations.

2001 Second Edition, 2003 Supplement, and 2003 CD-Rom

Access to Utility Service: the only examination of consumer rights when dealing with regulated, de-regulated, and unregulated utilities, including telecommunications, terminations, billing errors, low-income payment plans, fuel allowances in subsidized housing, LIHEAP, and weatherization. Includes summaries of state utility regulations.

Credit and Banking Library

2003 Fifth Edition with CD-Rom

Truth in Lending: detailed analysis of *all* aspects of TILA, the Consumer Leasing Act, and the Home Ownership and Equity Protection Act (HOEPA). Appendices and the CD-Rom contain the Acts, Reg. Z, Reg. M, and their Official Staff Commentaries, numerous sample pleadings, rescission notices, and two programs to compute APRs.

National Consumer Law Center ■ 77 Summer Street ■ 10th Floor ■ Boston MA ■ 02110
(617) 542-9595 ■ FAX (617) 542-8028 ■ publications@nclc.org
Order securely online at www.consumerlaw.org

2002 Fifth Edition, 2004 Supplement, and 2004 CD-Rom

Fair Credit Reporting: the key resource for handling any type of credit reporting issue, from cleaning up blemished credit records to suing reporting agencies and creditors for inaccurate reports. Covers credit scoring, privacy issues, identity theft, the FCRA, the new FACT Act, the Credit Repair Organizations Act, state credit reporting and repair statutes, and common law claims.

2002 Second Edition, 2004 Supplement, and 2004 CD-Rom

Consumer Banking and Payments Law: unique analysis of consumer law (and NACHA rules) as to checks, money orders, credit, debit, and stored value cards, and banker's right of setoff. Also extensive treatment of electronic records and signatures, electronic transfer of food stamps, and direct deposits of federal payments. The CD-Rom and appendices reprint relevant agency interpretations and pleadings.

2000 Second Edition, 2004 Supplement, and 2004 CD-Rom

The Cost of Credit: Regulation and Legal Challenges: a one-of-a-kind resource detailing state and federal regulation of consumer credit in all fifty states, federal usury preemption, explaining credit math, and how to challenge excessive credit charges and credit insurance. The CD-Rom includes a credit math program and hard-to-find agency interpretations.

2002 Third Edition, 2004 Supplement, and 2004 CD-Rom

Credit Discrimination: analysis of the Equal Credit Opportunity Act, Fair Housing Act, Civil Rights Acts, and state credit discrimination statutes, including reprints of all relevant federal interpretations, government enforcement actions, and numerous sample pleadings.

Consumer Litigation Library

2003 Third Edition with CD-Rom

Consumer Arbitration Agreements: numerous successful approaches to challenge the enforceability of a binding arbitration agreement, the interrelation of the Federal Arbitration Act and state law, class actions in arbitration, the right to discovery, and other topics. Appendices and CD-Rom include sample discovery, numerous briefs, arbitration service provider rules and affidavits as to arbitrator costs.

2002 Fifth Edition, 2004 Supplement, and 2004 CD-Rom

Consumer Class Actions: A Practical Litigation Guide: makes class action litigation manageable even for small offices, including numerous sample pleadings, class certification memoranda, discovery, class notices, settlement materials, and much more. Includes contributions from seven of the most experienced consumer class action litigators around the country.

2003 CD-Rom with Index Guide: ALL pleadings from ALL NCLC Manuals, including Consumer Law Pleadings Numbers One through Nine

Consumer Law Pleadings on CD-Rom: over 700 notable recent pleadings from all types of consumer cases, including predatory lending, foreclosures, automobile fraud, lemon laws, debt collection, fair credit reporting, home improvement fraud, rent to own, student loans, and lender liability. Finding aids pinpoint the desired pleading in seconds, ready to paste into a word processing program.

Deception and Warranties Library

2001 Fifth Edition, 2003 Supplement, and 2003 CD-Rom

Unfair and Deceptive Acts and Practices: the only practice manual covering all aspects of a deceptive practices case in every state. Special sections on automobile sales, the federal racketeering (RICO) statute, unfair insurance practices, and the FTC Holder Rule.

2003 Second Edition, 2004 Supplement, and 2004 CD-Rom

Automobile Fraud: examination of title law, odometer tampering, lemon laundering, sale of salvage and wrecked cars, undisclosed prior use, prior damage to new cars, numerous sample pleadings, and title search techniques.

2001 Second Edition, 2004 Supplement, and 2004 CD-Rom

Consumer Warranty Law: comprehensive treatment of new and used car lemon laws, the Magnuson-Moss Warranty Act, UCC Articles 2 and 2A, mobile home, new home, and assistive device warranty laws, FTC Used Car Rule, tort theories, car repair and home improvement statutes, service contract and lease laws, with numerous sample pleadings.

National Consumer Law Center ■ 77 Summer Street ■ 10th Floor ■ Boston MA ■ 02110
(617) 542-9595 ■ FAX (617) 542-8028 ■ publications@nclc.org
Order securely online at www.consumerlaw.org

NCLC's CD-Roms

Every NCLC manual comes with a companion CD-Rom featuring pop-up menus, PDF format, Internet-style navigation of appendices, indices, and bonus pleadings, hard-to-find agency interpretations and other practice aids. Documents can be copied into a word processing program. Of special note is *Consumer Law in a Box*:

July 2004 CD-Rom

Consumer Law in a Box: a CD-Rom combining *all* documents and software from 16 other NCLC CD-Roms. Quickly pinpoint a document from thousands found on the CD through keyword searches and Internet-style navigation, links, bookmarks, and other finding aids.

Other NCLC Publications for Lawyers

issued 24 times a year

NCLC REPORTS covers the latest developments and ideas in the practice of consumer law.

2003 First Edition with CD-Rom

The Practice of Consumer Law: Seeking Economic Justice: contains an essential overview to consumer law and explains how to get started in a private or legal services consumer practice. Packed with invaluable sample pleadings and practice pointers for even experienced consumer attorneys.

2002 First Edition with CD-Rom

STOP Predatory Lending: A Guide for Legal Advocates: provides a roadmap and practical legal strategy for litigating predatory lending abuses, from small loans to mortgage loans. The CD-Rom contains a credit math program, pleadings, legislative and administrative materials, and underwriting guidelines.

National Consumer Law Center Guide Series are books designed for consumers, counselors, and attorneys new to consumer law:

2002 Edition

NCLC Guide to Surviving Debt: a great overview of consumer law. Everything a paralegal, new attorney, or client needs to know about debt collectors, managing credit card debt, whether to refinance, credit card problems, home foreclosures, evictions, repossessions, credit reporting, utility terminations, student loans, budgeting, and bankruptcy.

2002 Edition

NCLC Guide to Mobile Homes: what consumers and their advocates need to know about mobile home dealer sales practices and an in-depth look at mobile home quality and defects, with 35 photographs and construction details.

2002 Edition

NCLC Guide to Consumer Rights for Immigrants: an introduction to many of the most critical consumer issues faced by immigrants, including international wires, check cashing and banking, *notario* and immigration consultant fraud, affidavits of support, telephones, utilities, credit history discrimination, high-cost credit, used car fraud, student loans and more.

2000 Edition

Return to Sender: Getting a Refund or Replacement for Your Lemon Car: Find how lemon laws work, what consumers and their lawyers should know to evaluate each other, investigative techniques and discovery tips, how to handle both informal dispute resolution and trials, and more.

Visit **www.consumerlaw.org** to order securely online or for more information on all NCLC manuals and CD-Roms, including the full tables of contents, indices, and listings of CD-Rom contents.

National Consumer Law Center ■ 77 Summer Street ■ 10th Floor ■ Boston MA ■ 02110
(617) 542-9595 ■ FAX (617) 542-8028 ■ publications@nclc.org
Order securely online at www.consumerlaw.org

Finding Aids and Search Tips

The Consumer Credit and Sales Legal Practice Series presently contains sixteen volumes, eleven supplements, and sixteen companion CD-Roms—all constantly being updated. The Series includes over 10,000 pages, over 100 chapters, over 100 appendices, and almost 1000 pleadings, as well as hundreds of documents found on the CD-Roms, but not found in the books. Here are a number of ways to pinpoint in seconds what you need from this array of materials.

Internet-Based Searches

www.consumerlaw.org — **Electronically search every chapter and appendix of all sixteen manuals and their supplements:** go to www.consumerlaw.org/keyword and enter a case name, regulation cite, or other search term. You are instantly given the book names, page numbers, and number of hits on each page in any of the NCLC manuals containing that term.

www.consumerlaw.org — **Current indexes, tables of contents, and CD-Rom contents for all sixteen volumes** are found at www.consumerlaw.org. Just click on *The Consumer Credit and Sales Legal Practice Series* and scroll down to the book you want. Then click on that volume's index, contents, or CD-Rom contents.

Finding Material on NCLC's CD-Roms

Consumer Law in a Box CD-Rom — **Electronically search all sixteen NCLC CD-Roms,** including thousands of agency interpretations, all NCLC appendices and almost 1000 pleadings: use Acrobat's search button* in NCLC's *Consumer Law in a Box CD-Rom* (this CD-Rom is free to set subscribers) to find every instance that a keyword appears on any of our 16 CD-Roms. Then with one click, go to that location to see the full text of the document.

CD-Rom accompanying this volume — **Electronically search the CD-Rom accompanying this volume,** including pleadings, agency interpretations, and regulations. Use Acrobat's search button* to find every instance that a keyword appears on the CD-Rom, and then with one click, go to that location on the CD-Rom. Or just click on subject buttons until you navigate to the document you need.

Finding Pleadings

Consumer Law Pleadings on CD-Rom and Index Guide — **Search five different ways for the right pleading from almost 1000 choices:** use the *Index Guide* accompanying *Consumer Law Pleadings on CD-Rom* to search for pleadings by type, subject, publication title, name of contributor, or contributor's jurisdiction. The guide also provides a summary of the pleading once the right pleading is located. *Consumer Law Pleadings on CD-Rom* and the *Consumer Law in a Box CD-Rom* also let you search for all pleadings electronically by subject, type of pleading, and by publication title, giving you instant access to the full pleading in Word and/or PDF format once you find the pleading you need.

Using This Volume to Find Material in All Sixteen Volumes

This volume — **The Quick Reference** at the back of this volume lets you pinpoint manual sections or appendices where over a 1000 different subject areas are covered.

---

* Users of NCLC CD-Roms should become familiar with "search," a powerful Acrobat tool, distinguished from "find," another Acrobat feature that is far slower and less powerful than "search." The Acrobat 5 "search" icon is a pair of binoculars with paper in the background, while the "find" icon is a pair of binoculars without the paper. Acrobat 6 uses one icon, a pair of binoculars, that brings you to a menu with several search options.

Contents

CD-Rom Contents xxiii

Chapter 1   Introduction

    1.1 About This Manual. 1
        1.1.1 Introduction 1
        1.1.2 Structure of the Manual 1
        1.1.3 Clearinghouse and Other Citations 1
    1.2 About Credit Reporting. 2
    1.3 About the FCRA 2
        1.3.2 Limited Amount of FCRA Litigation 2
        1.3.3 Federal Agency Interpretations of the FCRA 2
    1.4 FCRA Legislative History 2

new subsection   **1.4.9 The Fair and Accurate Credit Transactions Act of 2003** 2
        1.4.9.1 Legislative History 2
        1.4.9.2 Key Provisions 3

Chapter 2   Scope: Consumer Reports and Consumer Reporting Agencies

    2.1 Introduction. 7
    2.3 Is a "Consumer Report" Involved?. 7
        2.3.1 A Consumer Report Compared to a Consumer's File. 7
        2.3.3 Information Must Bear on a Consumer's Creditworthiness, Credit Standing or Capacity, Character, Reputation, Personal Characteristics, or Mode of Living. 7
        2.3.4 Disclosure of "Credit Header" Information 7
        2.3.6 Purposes That Make Information a Consumer Report 7
            2.3.6.1 General 7
            2.3.6.3 Bad Check and Check Approval Lists 7
            2.3.6.4 Reports on Tenants 8
            2.3.6.5 Business Credit and Commercial Reports 8
                2.3.6.5.2 Reports on individuals in their business capacity are not consumer reports. 8
                2.3.6.5.5 Reports used or collected for business purposes can still qualify as consumer reports. 8
            2.3.6.6 Employment Reports. 8
    2.4 Statutory Exemptions to Definition of Consumer Report. 9
        2.4.2 Information Shared by Affiliates. 9
        2.4.5 Conveying Decision to Party Who Requested That Creditor Extend Credit to Consumer. 9
    2.5 The Consumer Reporting Agency. 9
        2.5.7 State and Local Government Agencies 9

Fair Credit Reporting / 2004 Supplement

	2.5.8 "Nationwide" Reporting Agencies	10
2.6	Examples of Consumer Reporting Agencies	10
	2.6.1 Credit Bureaus, Inspection Bureaus, and Medical Information, Tenant Screening, and Check Approval Agencies	10
	2.6.2 Resellers of Consumer Reports	11
	2.6.3 Creditors as Reporting Agencies	11

Chapter 3 — Furnishing Information to Consumer Reporting Agencies

3.1	Introduction	13
3.2	Creditors and Others Who Furnish Information to Consumer Reporting Agencies	13
	3.2.2 Limitations on Who Is a Furnisher	13
	3.2.2.1 Special Rules for Affiliate Sharing	13
	3.2.2.2 Direct Selling of Information Not Covered	14
	3.2.2.3 State Laws Regarding Furnishers Are Preempted	14
3.3	Furnishing Information to Consumer Reporting Agencies	14
	3.3.1 Information Is Usually Furnished Electronically	14
	3.3.2 Metro 2: The Standard Automated Format for Furnishing Information to Consumer Reporting Agencies	14
	3.3.3 The Metro 2 Format Used by Creditors	14
	3.3.3.3 The Base Segment Contains Information About the Consumer and the Debt	14
	3.3.3.7 Common Errors	14
	3.3.3.12 Metro 2 and Bankruptcy	15
	3.3.4 The Furnishing of Disputed Information Is Restricted	15
	3.3.4.2 Debt Collectors Sometimes May Not Furnish Disputed Information and Always Must Note When It Is Disputed	15
new subsection	**3.3.4.2a Debt Collectors Must Notify Creditors of Fraudulent Debt**	15
new subsection	**3.3.4.2b Debt Collectors Must Use Creditor's Date of Account Delinquency**	15
	3.3.5 Other Restrictions on What Information May Be Furnished to a Consumer Reporting Agency	16
	3.3.5.2 Discrimination and Retaliation for Exercising Rights Is Prohibited	16
	3.3.5.4 State Law Restrictions on Public Record Information	16
	3.3.5.4.1 Restrictions reporting cosigners	16
	3.3.5.4.2 Restrictions on child support debts	16
	3.3.5.4.3 Special state requirements	16
3.4	Standards of Accuracy For Furnishers	16
	3.4.1 Introduction	16
	3.4.2 General Duty to Report Accurately	16
replecement subsection	**3.4.3 Accuracy and Integrity Regulations for Furnishers**	17
	3.4.4 Accuracy When Creditor Clearly and Conspicuously Maintains a Special Address for the Consumer to Give Notification of Inaccurate Information	18
new subsection	**3.4.4a Consumers May Dispute Furnished Information Directly with the Furnisher Under the FACTA**	18
	3.4.5 Practical Advice for Informally Disputing Accuracy with Furnisher	19
3.5	Furnishers Have Duty to Correct and Update Furnished Information	19
	3.5.2 Disputing Inaccurate Information With the Creditor	19
	3.5.4 Universal Data Form May Be Used to Make Corrections	19
new section	**3.8a Financial Institution Furnishers Required to Notify Customers of Negative Information Furnished to Agencies**	19
3.9	The Formal Credit Reporting Agency Dispute Process Subjects the Furnisher to Obligations Enforceable by the Consumer	20
3.10	Consumer Reporting Agency Investigation Must Involve Furnisher	21

Contents / 2004 Supplement

	3.11 Furnisher's Duties Upon Notification of Dispute by the Reporting Agency	21
	3.11.1 Furnisher Must Conduct Reasonable Investigation	21
new subsection	**3.11.1a Agencies Must Notify Furnishers of Reinvestigation Results**	**22**
new subsection	**3.11.1b Agency's Reinvestigation Must Be "Reasonable"**	**22**
new subsection	**3.11.1c Agencies Must Reinvestigate upon Notice from Reseller**	**22**
	3.11.2 A Properly Presented Dispute Will Subject a Furnisher to Liability for Conducting an Inadequate Investigation	23
	3.11.3 Furnishers Must Block Unverifiable Information	23
	3.12 Furnisher Must Report Investigation Results	23
	3.12.1 Time for Investigation and Reporting Results Is Limited	23
	3.13 Consumer Reporting Agency Use of Furnisher Report	23
	3.14 Creditor and Furnisher Liability for Information Furnished to Consumer Reporting Agencies	23
	3.14.2 No Private Enforcement of FCRA Obligations to Furnish Accurate and Complete Information	23
	3.14.3 Furnisher Is Liable in Private Suits for Its Reinvestigations	24
	3.14.4 Furnisher Liability for Discrimination and for Retaliating Against a Consumer for Exercising Federal Statutory Rights	24
	3.14.5 Furnisher Liability for Related Torts	24
new section	**3.15 Reinvestigation Requirements Applicable to Resellers**	**27**
new section	**3.16 Furnishers Subject to New Identity Theft Duties and Responsibilities**	**27**

Chapter 4	A Consumer's Right to Learn What Is In File	
	4.2 Information Is Reported on Virtually Every American	29
	4.2.2 Credit Reports Prone to Errors	29
	4.3 Right of Consumer to Know Contents of Own File	30
	4.3.1 Overview	30
	4.3.2 Information Shown to Consumer Often Not What Is Shown to Creditors	31
	4.4 How to Obtain the Contents of a Consumer's File	31
	4.4.1 General	31
	4.4.1.1 Timing of Request and Disclosure	31
	4.4.1.5 Special Rules for Affiliates	31
	4.4.2 Making the Request	31
	4.4.2.1 The Request by the Consumer	31
	4.4.2.2 From Which Agency Should Information Be Requested?	32
	4.4.2.3 How to Get Disclosures From Equifax, Experian, and Trans Union	32
new subsection	**4.4.2.3.a Free reports once a year after FTC issues rules**	32
	4.4.2.4 Time to Respond	32
	4.4.3 Proof of Consumer's Identification or Authorization	33
	4.4.3.1 Information Required to Identify the Consumer	33
	4.4.3.2 Consumer's Written Instructions to Disclose Report to Attorney or Other Third Party	33
	4.4.4 Unreasonable Preconditions or Requests for Information Prior to Disclosure	33
	4.4.5 Consumer Payment for File Disclosure	34
	4.4.5.1 Where FCRA Prohibits Payment	34
	4.4.5.1.2 No charge if consumer believes file is inaccurate due to fraud	34
new subsection	**4.4.5.1.5 No charge for annual report made through centralized source**	34
	4.4.5.2 State Laws Limiting Payment	34
	4.4.5.3 Payment Amounts Where Allowed	34
new subsection	**4.4.5.3a Federal Legislation to Provide for Free Credit Reports**	34

Fair Credit Reporting / 2004 Supplement

	4.5 File Information That Must Be Disclosed	35
	4.5.2 Nearly All Information in the Consumer's File Must Be Disclosed . . .	35
	4.5.2.1 Introduction	35
	4.5.2.2 Disclosure of Previously Reported Information.	35
	4.5.5 Medical Information	35
	4.5.7 Information Which Does Not Have to Be Disclosed	35
replacement heading	**4.5.7.1 FBI Counter-Intelligence and Government Security Clearance Usage May Not Be Disclosed.**	36
replacement heading	**4.5.7.2 Audit Trail and Other Ancillary Information**	36
	4.6 Disclosure Must Include a Summary of Consumer Rights	36
	4.8 Analyzing Information Provided to the Consumer	36
	4.8.1 Form of Disclosure.	36
	4.8.3 How to Use the Information Disclosed	36
	4.8.3.1 Limits on Utility of Information Disclosed	36
Chapter 5	**Furnishing Consumer Reports to Users**	
	5.1 General.	37
	5.1.1 Background.	37
	5.1.2 Reports May Be Released Only for Permissible Purposes.	37
	5.1.4 Agents of the User.	37
	5.1.7 Discovering an Impermissible Use	37
	5.2 Permissible Uses.	38
	5.2.1 In Response to a Court Order.	38
	5.2.2 The Consumer's Written Instructions.	38
	5.2.3 Identifying Information Furnished to the Government	38
	5.2.4 Permissible Use in Connection with Credit.	38
	5.2.4.1 General	38
	5.2.4.2 Collection of Credit Accounts, Judgment Debts	39
	5.2.5 Permissible Use in Connection With Employment	39
	5.2.5.1 Overview.	39
	5.2.5.3 Employer Must Provide Prior Certification	39
	5.2.5.4 Agency Must Enclose Summary of Consumer Rights	39
new subsection	**5.2.5.5 Communications Concerning Employee Investigations for Certain Types of Conduct Not Considered Consumer Reports**. .	40
	5.2.7 Permissible Use in Connection With Government Licenses or Other Benefits.	41
	5.2.9 Permissible Use in Connection With Business Transactions.	41
	5.2.9.1 User's Business Purpose, Where Individual Has a Consumer Purpose	41
	5.2.10 User's Legitimate Business Need to Review a Consumer's Account	41
	5.2.11 Permissible Use by Officials to Determine Child Support Payment Levels.	41
	5.3 Potentially Impermissible Purposes	41
	5.3.1 General.	41
	5.3.4 Use in Civil or Criminal Litigation	41
	5.3.5 Use by Investigators	42
	5.3.6 Use of Reports on the Consumer's Spouse, Relatives, or Other Third Parties	42
	5.3.7 Use in Connection With Insurance Claims	42
	5.3.8 Use of Lists of Consumers, Marketing Research, and Prescreening	42
	5.3.8.4 Prescreening Lists	42
	5.3.8.4.1 Lists allowed for credit and insurance solicitations	42
	5.3.8.4.2 Prescreened lists are a type of consumer report.	43
	5.3.8.4.3 A firm offer is required.	43

Contents / 2004 Supplement

	5.3.8.4.4 Consumers can elect to be excluded from prescreening lists	43
5.4	Agency Procedures Insuring That Only Users with Permissible Purposes Obtain Reports	43
	5.4.2 User Identification and Certifications	43
	5.4.2.2 Blanket Certifications	43
	5.4.3 Agency Verification Procedures	44
	5.4.4 Electronic Communication of Reports	44
5.6	User Liability for Impermissible Purposes	44
	5.6.1 Introduction	44
	5.6.2 Uncertified Uses of a Consumer Report	44
	5.6.3 Knowing Non-Compliance of User	44
	5.6.5 Vicarious Liability of User for Acts of Employees	44

Chapter 6 — Notices Concerning Consumer Reports

6.1	Introduction	47
6.2	Importance and Types of Notices	47
6.3	The Summary of Consumer Rights	47
new section 6.3a	**Summary of Rights for Identity Theft Victims**	48
6.4	When Notice of Adverse Action Is Required	49
	6.4.2 Adverse Action Based on Consumer Reports	49
	6.4.2.3 Where Adverse Use Relates to Credit Purposes	49
	6.4.2.3.1 General	49
	6.4.2.3.2 "Denial" of credit defined	49
new subsection	**6.4.2.3.2a Is there an adverse action if a counteroffer is accepted?**	50
	6.4.2.3.3 Denial of leases	51
	6.4.2.4 When Adverse Use Relates to Employment Purposes	51
	6.4.2.5 When Adverse Use Relates to Insurance Purposes	52
	6.4.2.7 When Adverse Use Relates to Other Purposes	53
	6.4.2.7.2 When adverse action relates to a review of the consumer's account	53
	6.4.4 Notice of Adverse Use of Information Other Than Consumer Report	53
	6.4.4.3 Subsequent Disclosure Rights	53
	6.4.5 ECOA Notices Concerning Adverse Action	53
new section 6.4a	**Users Must Provide Consumers With a Risk-Based Pricing Notice**	54
6.5	Notices Required From Users Prior to a Request for Information	55
replacement subsection	**6.5.1 Importance and Types of Notices**	55
replacement subsection	**6.5.2 Notice from an Employer That It May Obtain a Consumer Report**	56
replacement subsection	**6.5.3 Notice That Medical Information May Be Obtained from a Consumer Reporting Agency**	57
	6.5.4 Notice When Certain Information Is Used by Affiliates	58
6.6	Notices Required When a User Has Requested Information	58
	6.6.2 Public Record Information for Employment Purposes	58
	6.6.2.2 The Nature of the Special FCRA Protection	58
	6.6.4 Notice When Information Is Used for Prescreening Purposes	58
new section	**6.8a Notice of Key Factor in Credit Score**	59
new section	**6.8b Notice in Cases of Fraud Alert That Consumer May Request a Free Copy of the File**	59
new section	**6.8c Notice to Consumer If Agency Refuses to Block Alleged Identity Theft Information**	59
new section	**6.8d Disclosure of Credit Scores and Notice to Home Loan Applicant**	59
new section	**6.8e Notice When Negative Information Provided by Financial Institutions**	59
6.9	Liability for Failure to Provide Required Notice	60

Fair Credit Reporting / 2004 Supplement

Chapter 7 — Inaccurate Consumer Reports

- 7.1 Introduction ... 61
- **7.1a What is Accuracy?** ... 61 *(new section)*
- 7.2 Types of Inaccurate Information ... 62
  - 7.2.1 Introduction ... 62
  - 7.2.3 Errors in Collection of Public Record Information ... 62
  - 7.2.4 Mismerged Files ... 62
  - 7.2.5 Identity Theft ... 63
  - 7.2.7 Illogical Files ... 63
  - 7.2.8 Incomplete Files ... 63
  - 7.2.9 Reporting Agency Refusal to Provide Reports to Litigants ... 63
- 7.3 Reporting Agency Reinvestigation and Correction of Disputed Information ... 63
  - 7.3.2 Consumer Request for Reinvestigation ... 63
    - 7.3.2.1 When a Reporting Agency Must Reinvestigate ... 63
    - 7.3.2.2 Consumer Must Make Request to Reporting Agency ... 64
  - 7.3.4 Nature of the Reinvestigation ... 64
    - 7.3.4.3 Type of Reinvestigation Required ... 64
    - 7.3.4.4 Must Reinvestigation Utilize "Reasonable Procedures to Assure Maximum Possible Accuracy"? ... 65
  - 7.3.5 Agency's Reinvestigation Must Involve the Person Who Furnished the Disputed Information to the Reporting Agency ... 65
    - 7.3.5.1 General ... 65
  - 7.3.6 Deadline for Reporting Agency to Respond ... 65
- 7.4 Corrections as a Result of Reinvestigations of Disputed Information ... 66
  - 7.4.2 Correction or Deletion of Disputed Information ... 66
- 7.5 Reinsertion of Information Previously Deleted from Consumer's File ... 66
- 7.6 Inclusion of Consumer's Statement of Dispute in Consumer's File ... 67
  - 7.6.1 Consumer's Right to File Statement of Dispute ... 67
    - 7.6.1.1 Statement Concerning Incomplete or Inaccurate Items ... 67
  - 7.6.2 Reporting Agency Must Note Consumer's Dispute in Subsequent Reports ... 67
- 7.8 Agency Liability for Reporting Inaccurate Information ... 67
  - 7.8.1 General ... 67
  - 7.8.3 Inaccurate Information: The First Test of Accuracy ... 68
    - 7.8.3.1 General ... 68
    - 7.8.3.2 When Is Incomplete Information Inaccurate? ... 68
  - 7.8.4 Reasonable Procedures: The Second Test of Accuracy ... 68
    - 7.8.4.1 General Standards ... 68
    - 7.8.4.2 Proof Issues ... 68
    - 7.8.4.4 Inaccurate Sources ... 68
    - 7.8.4.5 Public Record Information ... 68
    - 7.8.4.6 Mismerged Information and Wrong Consumer Identification ... 69
    - 7.8.4.7 Identity Theft ... 69
    - 7.8.4.10 Incomplete and Outdated Items in the File ... 70
      - 7.8.4.10.2 Guarantors and reports relating to a bankruptcy ... 70
      - 7.8.4.10.3 Reasonable methods to acquire updated information ... 70
  - 7.8.5 Procedures for Reports of Adverse Public Record Information for Employment Purposes ... 71
    - 7.8.5.3 Election to Establish Strict Procedures for Complete and Up-to-Date Public Record Information ... 71

Chapter 8 — Obsolete Information

- 8.3 Maximum Time Periods to Retain Adverse Information ... 73
  - 8.3.1 Structure of the Act ... 73

Contents / 2004 Supplement

8.3.3 Accounts Placed for Collection or Charged Off.	73
new subsection **8.3.10 Fair and Accurate Credit Transaction Act of 2003**.	73
8.5 Reasonable Procedures Concerning Obsolete Information	74
8.5.1 General.	74

Chapter 9   Investigative Consumer Reports

9.1 What Is an Investigative Consumer Report?	75
9.1.1 Introduction.	75
9.1.2 FCRA Definition.	75
9.1.2.4 Reports Excluded from the Definition; Certain Employee Investigations.	75
9.1.3 Types of Investigative Reports.	76
9.1.3.2 Reports for Employment Purposes.	76
9.1.4 Overview of Additional Obligations Required for an Investigative Consumer Report.	76
9.2 Disclosure to Consumer of Investigative Report's Existence.	77
9.2.4 Users' Reasonable Procedures Defense.	77
9.2.5 Waiver of Consumer Rights.	77
9.3 Consumer Utilization of Investigative Report Notices.	77
9.3.1 Consumer's Permission Not Needed If Permissible Purpose for Employee Investigation Report, Except for Other Employment Investigative Reports.	77

Chapter 10   Litigating Credit Report Disputes

10.1 Introduction.	79
10.2 Fair Credit Reporting Act Claims.	79
10.2.2 FCRA Claims Against Reporting Agencies.	80
10.2.2.1 Claims Relating to Inaccurate Reports.	80
10.2.2.3 Claims Relating to Furnishing Reports for Impermissible Purposes.	81
replacement subsection **10.2.2.4 Claims Relating to Medical Information Reported Without Consumer Consent**.	81
10.2.2.6 Claims Relating to Adverse Public Record Information for Employment Purposes.	81
10.2.2.8 Claims Against Resellers.	82
10.2.3 FCRA Claims Against Creditors and Others Who Furnish Information to Reporting Agencies.	82
10.2.3.1 General.	82
10.2.3.2 Claims Relating to Accuracy and Completeness of Information Furnished to Consumer Reporting Agencies.	82
10.2.3.3 Claims Relating to Agency Reinvestigation of Disputed Information.	82
10.2.3.4 Claims Relating to Information From Affiliated Companies.	83
10.2.4 FCRA Claims Against Users of Consumer Reports.	83
10.2.4.1 Claims Against Those Obtaining Reports Without a Permissible Purpose or Under False Pretenses.	83
10.2.4.3 Claims Against Users for Failing to Comply With Disclosure and Certification Requirements for Investigative Reports.	84
10.3 Common Law Torts.	84
10.3.1 Background.	84
10.3.2 The FCRA's Qualified Immunity.	84
10.3.3 Information Must Be Discovered Exclusively Through FCRA-Required Disclosure.	85
10.3.4 Immunity Applies Only to Certain Tort Actions.	85

Fair Credit Reporting / 2004 Supplement

    10.3.6 No Immunity Where Malice or Willful Intent 85
    10.3.8 Elements of Invasion of Privacy Claim 86
10.4 State Statutory Claims 86
    10.4.2 State Deceptive Practices Statutes 86
new subsection   **10.4.2a State Identity Theft Laws**. 86
    10.4.3 General FCRA Preemption Standard 87
    10.4.4 Specific FCRA Preemptions of State Law. 87
10.5 Other Statutory Claims. 90
10.7 Selecting the Parties 91
    10.7.1 Plaintiffs 91
    10.7.2 Class Actions. 91
    10.7.3 Defendants 91
10.9 Selecting the Court 92
    10.9.3 Personal Jurisdiction 92
    10.9.5 Removal 92
10.10 Statute of Limitations. 92
replacement subsection   **10.10.1 FCRA Limitations Period** 92
10.11 Discovery and Litigation Strategies 93
    10.11.3 Formal Discovery 93
        10.11.3.1 General. 93
        10.11.3.2 Confidentiality Agreements and Protective Orders 93
        10.11.3.3 Consumer Reports and Evidentiary Issues 93
        10.11.3.5 Insurance Coverage for FCRA Liability. 93
    10.11.4 Record Retention 94
10.12 Right to Jury Trial; Jury Instructions 94
10.13 Defenses and Counterclaims 94
10.14 Enforceability of Arbitration Agreements 94

Chapter 11   Private Remedies

11.1 Introduction 95
new section   **11.1a FACTA Limitations on Private Enforcement** 95
    11.1a.1 FACTA Expands FCRA's Qualified Immunity Provision. 95
    11.1a.2 No Private Enforcement of Certain New Furnisher Obligations. 96
    11.1a.3 No Private Enforcement for Certain Other New FACTA
        Requirements 96
11.2 Actual Damages 97
    11.2.2 Damages for Pecuniary Loss 97
    11.2.3 Intangible Damages. 97
        11.2.3.1 Are Intangible Damages Available? 97
        11.2.3.2 Proving Intangible Damages 98
    11.2.4 Nominal Damages. 98
11.4 Punitive Damages 98
    11.4.1 Prerequisites for Punitive Damages 98
        11.4.1.1 Relation to Common Law Standards 98
        11.4.1.2 Proving Willfulness 98
        11.4.1.3 No Need to Prove Actual Damages. 99
    11.4.2 Determining the Amount of Punitive Damages 99
        11.4.2.1 No Upper Limit on Size of Awards 99
        11.4.2.2 Determining the Size of the Award. 99
    11.4.3 Punitive Damages: Decided by Judge or Jury? 99
11.5 Injunctive and Declaratory Relief. 100
11.6 Attorney Fees and Costs. 100
    11.6.1 When Are Fees and Costs Awarded? 100
    11.6.2 Calculating the Size of the Attorney Fee Award. 101

Contents / 2004 Supplement

          11.6.2.1 FCRA Awards Will Be Based on Standards Enunciated in Other Federal Fee-Shifting Statutes 101
          11.6.2.2 Current Federal Fee-Shifting Standards 101
     11.6.3 Maximizing the Chances of an Adequate Fee Award 101
     11.6.4 Preserving Fee Entitlement When Case Is Settled. 101
     11.6.5 Rule 68 and Attorney Fee Awards 101
11.7 Quick Reference to Published Awards. 102

Chapter 12 Public Enforcement

12.2 Federal Trade Commission Enforcement 103
     12.2.1 General FTC Enforcement Powers. 103
     12.2.3 FTC Rulemaking, FTC Commentary, and Opinion Letters; Federal Reserve Board Interpretations 104
12.4 State Enforcement 105
     12.4.2 State Enforcement Powers Against Information Furnishers Are Limited... 105
     12.4.4 State Investigatory Powers 106

Chapter 13 Non-Litigation Solutions for Consumers With Blemished or Insufficient Credit Histories

13.1 Introduction 107
13.2 What Information Is Being Reported on the Consumer? 107
     13.2.1 Examining the Consumer's Credit Record. 107
     13.2.2 Beyond Credit Bureaus: Tenant Screening, Check Cashing, and Other Specialized Reporting Agencies. 107
     13.2.7 Information About Spouse, Former Spouse, or Relatives' Credit History .. 107
          13.2.7.1 What Information Appears in Consumer's File 107
          13.2.7.2 Creditor's Use of Spouse's File 108
               13.2.7.2.1 FCRA limitations 108
               13.2.7.2.2 ECOA limitations 108
     13.2.8 Special Restrictions on Reporting of Information 108
          13.2.8.3 Special Protections for Military Personnel 108
13.5 Disputing Debts with the Creditor and the Reporting Agency. 108
     13.5.2 Disputing Debts with the Creditor 108
          13.5.2.1 The Creditor's Duty of Accuracy When Furnishing Information .. 108
          13.5.2.2 No Adverse Reporting While Dispute Pending 109
     13.5.3 Disputing Debts with the Reporting Agency 109
     13.5.4 Dealing with Credit Reporting Issues When Settling Debt Litigation. 109
          13.5.4.1 Importance of Resolving Credit Reporting Issues 109
          13.5.4.3 Selecting the Correct Settlement Language. 110
     13.5.5 Coping with the Results of Identity Theft 110
          13.5.5.1 Nature of Identity Theft 110
          13.5.5.2 Contacting Credit Reporting Agencies, Creditors, Police, and Government Agencies. 111
          13.5.5.3 Monitoring 111
          13.5.5.4 Filing Suit. 111
13.6 Strategies for Improving a Blemished or Insufficient Credit Rating 113
     13.6.2 Ascertaining the Reasons for Denial of Credit 113
     13.6.4 Adding New Information About Existing or Prior Accounts. 113
          13.6.4.5 Use of Spouse's Credit History. 113
     13.6.5 Establishing New Credit Accounts 113
     13.6.6 Negotiating Repayment Schedules or Catching Up on Loan Payments... 113
     13.6.9 Filing Bankruptcy 114

Fair Credit Reporting / 2004 Supplement

	13.7 Coping with a Blemished Credit Record	114
	13.7.2 Home Mortgages	114
	13.7.2.1 Fannie Mae and Freddie Mac Standards	114
	13.7.4 Utilities	114
new subsection	**13.7.10 Credit Counselors and Debt Consolidators**	114
new section	**13.8 Credit Issues for Immigrants**	117

Chapter 14   Credit Scoring

14.1 Introduction	121
14.2 What Is Credit Scoring?	121
14.2.2 The Variations	121
14.2.2.1 Credit Bureau Score	121
14.2.3 Definition of Credit Scoring in Regulation B	121
14.3 Widespread Use of Credit Scores	122
14.4 Disclosure to Consumers of Credit Score	123
14.4.1 Credit Scores Do Not Have to Be Disclosed Under the FCRA	123
14.4.2 Recent Availability of Credit Scores	124
14.5 How a Credit Score Is Calculated	125
14.5.1 The Black Box	125
14.5.2 How Fair, Isaac Scores Are Developed	125
14.5.2.1 Fair, Isaac's Scoring Factors	125
14.5.4 Ideas on How to Peek into the Black Box	126
14.6 How Consumers Can Improve Their Credit Scores	126
14.6.1 Industry's Advice	126
14.6.2 Additional Advice	127
14.7 Policy Concerns with Credit Scoring Systems	127
14.7.2 Lack of Flexibility	127
14.7.3 Credit Scores, Risk-Based Pricing, and Subprime Loans	128
14.8 Concerns over the Accuracy of Credit Scores	128
14.8.1 Garbage In, Garbage Out: The Effect of Credit Report Inaccuracies on Credit Scores	128
14.8.2 Credit Scores Do Not Allow the FCRA's Dispute Mechanisms to Work as Intended	129
14.8.3 The Effect of Inaccurate, Non-Derogatory Information	129
14.8.4 Unreported Information	130
14.8.5 Lack of Validation and Re-Validation	131
14.8.6 Lender Misuse of Credit Scoring Models	131
14.9 Do Credit Scores Discriminate?	131
14.9.1 Credit Scoring's Disparate Impact	131
14.9.2 Discriminatory Credit Score Thresholds or Overrides	134
14.10 Credit Scores and Insurance	134

Chapter 15   Credit Repair Agencies

15.1 General	137
15.2 Federal Credit Repair Organizations Act	137
15.2.1 Introduction	137
15.2.2 Scope: Who Is a Credit Repair Organization?	137
15.2.2.1 General Definition	137
15.2.2.2 Exceptions	138
15.2.2.3 Credit Repair Services That Are Ancillary to Another Activity	138
15.2.2.4 Attorneys	138
15.2.2.5 Assignees, Purchasers of Debt, and Debt Collectors	138
15.2.2.6 Creditors	138

Contents / 2004 Supplement

            15.2.2.7 Sellers Who Advertise Credit Repair................ 139
     15.2.5 Prohibited Practices.. 139
            15.2.5.2 Misstatements to Consumer Reporting Agencies or Creditors ... 139
            15.2.5.3 Concealment of the Consumer's Identity 139
     15.2.6 Private Remedies 139
            15.2.6.1 Noncomplying Contract Is Void 139
  15.3 State Credit Repair Laws 140
     15.3.1 Introduction 140
     15.3.2 Coverage... 140
     15.3.4 Do State Credit Repair Laws Apply to Retailers Who Arrange Credit for Customers?.. 140
            15.3.4.2 Requirement of Payment of Fee for the Credit Services 140
            15.3.4.4 Legislative Intent 141
     15.3.6 Private Causes of Action 141
  15.4 Federal Telemarketing Statutes and Regulations 141
     15.4.1 Federal Telemarketing and Consumer Fraud and Abuse Prevention Act.. 141
     15.4.3 Telephone Consumer Protection Act............................ 142

Chapter 16   Privacy Protection

  16.1 Overview.. 143
  16.2 Privacy from Governmental Intrusion 143
  16.3 Tort of Invasion of Privacy... 144
  16.4 Statutory Protection of Financial Information............................ 145
     16.4.1 The Gramm-Leach-Bliley Act................................... 145
            16.4.1.1 Overview 145
            16.4.1.2 "Financial Institutions"—Entities That Must Comply with Gramm-Leach-Bliley 146
            16.4.1.4 "Nonpublic Personal Information"—The Information Covered by Gramm-Leach-Bliley 146
            16.4.1.5 Exempt Disclosures 146
            16.4.1.11 Weaknesses of Gramm-Leach-Bliley 147
     16.4.2 Other State and Federal Protections 147
            16.4.2.1 General.. 147
new subsection   **16.4.2.3a The FCRA as Amended by the FACTA** 147
            16.4.2.4 State Statutes..................................... 148
  16.5 Common Law Protection of Financial Information 148
  16.6 Identity Theft 149
     16.6.1 General.. 149
new subsection   **16.6.1a The FCRA's Identity Theft Prevention, Credit Restoration, and Financial Information Integrity & Privacy Provisions**........... 149
            16.6.1a.1 Overview 149
            16.6.1a.2 Fraud Alerts and Active Military Duty Alerts........... 151
                16.6.1a.2.1 General 151
                16.6.1a.2.2 Initial fraud alerts......................... 151
                16.6.1a.2.3 Extended fraud alerts 151
                16.6.1a.2.4 Active military duty alerts................. 152
                16.6.1a.2.5 Effects of alerts 152
            16.6.1a.3 Identity Theft Victim's Access to Information About the Theft... 153
                16.6.1a.3.1 Access to thief's transaction information 153
                16.6.1a.3.2 Debt collectors must provide information to victims................................. 154
            16.6.1a.4 Blocking of Fraudulent Information................ 154
                16.6.1a.4.1 Agency responsibilities.................... 154

xix

Fair Credit Reporting / 2004 Supplement

      16.6.1a.4.2 Furnisher responsibilities 155
    16.6.1a.5 Preventing Theft of Consumer's Identification Information . 155
    16.6.1a.6 Creditor Implementation of Red Flag Guidelines 156
      16.6.1a.6.1 Furnisher obligations regarding information
         accuracy and integrity 156
  16.6.2 Identity Theft and Assumption Deterrence Act 157
  16.6.3 State Identity Theft Statutes 158
16.7 Interests Impeding Legislative Protection of Financial Information 158

Appendix A   Fair Credit Reporting Act, Other Federal Statutes and Regulations

A.2 The Fair Credit Reporting Act 159
  A.2.1 Fair Credit Reporting Act Prior to FACTA 159
new subsections **A.2.2 Redline Version of FCRA Including FACTA** 159
  A.2.3 Fair and Accurate Credit Transactions Act of 2003 200
  A.2.4 Regulation on Effective Date of FACTA Amendments 244
    A.2.4.1 Joint Interim Final Rules 244
    A.2.4.2 Joint Final Rules 247
A.5 Gramm-Leach-Bliley 253
  A.5.2 FTC Rules—Selected Provisions 253
A.6 Federal Standards as to FCRA's Applicability to Affiliate Information Sharing .. 255
  A.6.1 Proposed FTC Interpretations 255

Appendix B   Summary of Federal and State Laws on Consumer Reporting and
replacement appendix   Theft of Identity

B.1 Introduction 257
B.2 Summary of Federal Credit Reporting Laws 257
  B.2.1 Fair Credit Reporting Act 257
  B.2.2 Credit Repair Organizations Act 259
B.3 State-by-State Summaries of Laws on Credit Reports and Identity Theft .. 259

Appendix E   FTC and FRB Model Forms

new sections   **E.5 Sample Opt-Out Notices** 303
   E.6 FTC Identity Theft Affidavit 306

Appendix H   Enforcement Orders Against Consumer Reporting Agencies,
replacement title   Resellers, Credit Repair Agencies, and Users

new sections   **H.6 FTC Consent Order Against Quicken** 316
   **H.7 FTC Enforcement Action Against Minor for Violation of Gramm-Leach-
     Bliley Act** 318
   H.8 United States of America v. Equifax Information Services, Inc. 322

Appendix I   Sample Pleadings and Other Litigation Documents

I.1 Sample Complaints 325
I.2 Sample Interrogatories 325
new subsection   **I.2.4 Interrogatories–Reinvestigation (to Furnisher)** 325
I.3 Sample Requests for Production 329
new subsection   **I.3.3 Request for Production of Documents to Furnisher** 329
I.5 Sample Litigation Documents 333
new subsection   **I.5.6 Transcript of Jury Instructions** 333

Index 339

Quick Reference to Consumer Credit and Sales Legal Practice Series ... 379

About the Companion CD-Rom 399

CD-Rom Contents

How to Use/Help
Text Search
Ten-Second Tutorial on Adobe Acrobat
Two-Minute Tutorial on Adobe Acrobat
Navigation: Bookmarks
Disappearing Bookmarks?
Navigation Links
Navigation Arrows
Navigation: "Back" Arrow
Acrobat Articles
View-Zoom-Magnification: Making Text Larger
Full Screen vs. Bookmark View
Copying Text in Acrobat
How to Copy Only One Column
Word Files
About This CD-Rom
How to Install Acrobat Reader, with Search
Finding Aids for NCLC Manuals: What Is Available in the Books

Federal, State Statutes
Fair Credit Reporting Act
new material — **Redlined Version of FCRA Showing FACT Act Amendments (Appendix A.2.2, 2004 Supplement)**
new material — **FACT Act (Appendix A.2.3, 2004 Supplement)**
new material — **Regulations on Effective Date of FACT Act Amendments (Appendix A.2.5, 2004 Supplement)**
Pre-FACT Act Fair Credit Reporting Act (Appendix A.2 and A.2.1, 2004 Supplement)
FCRA Pre-1996 Amendments (Appendix A.3)
Cross Reference Table: U.S.C. and FCRA Section Numbers (Appendix A.1)
Summary of FCRA (Appendix B.2.1, 2004 Supplement)
State-by-State Summaries of Laws on Credit Reports and Identity Theft (Appendix B.3, 2004 Supplement)

Credit Repair Organizations Act
Federal Act (Appendix A.4)
Credit Repair Organizations Act (Summary) (Appendix B.2.2, 2004 Supplement)
State-by-State Summaries of Laws on Credit Reports and Identity Theft (Appendix B.3, 2004 Supplement)

Gramm-Leach-Bliley
Selected Statutory Provisions (Appendix A.5.1)
Selected FTC Rules (Appendix A.5.2)

Fair Credit Reporting / 2004 Supplement

new material   **Additional Selected FTC Rules (16 CFR 314) (Appendix A.5.2, 2004 Supplement)**
Federal Standards as to FCRA's Applicability to Affiliate Information Sharing
       Proposed FTC Interpretations (Appendix A.6.1)

new material   **Note—FACT Act relationship to Affiliate Information Sharing (Appendix A.6.1, 2004 Supplement)**
       Proposed OCC Regulations (Appendix A.6.2)
State-by-State Summaries of Laws on Credit Reports and Identity Theft (Appendix B.3, 2004 Supplement)

FACT Act Legislative History
House

new material   **"The Importance of the National Credit Reporting System to Consumers and the US Economy," No. 108-26, May 8, 2003**

new material   **"The Fair Credit Reporting Act: How it Functions For Consumers and the Economy," No. 108-33, June 4, 2003**

new material   **"The Role of the FCRA in the Credit Granting Process," No. 108-33, June 12, 2003**

new material   **"Role of FCRA in Employee Background Checks and the Collection of Medical Information," June 17, 2003**

new material   **"Fighting Identity Theft," June 24, 2003**

new material   **H.R. 2622: The Fair and Accurate Credit Transactions Act of 2003, Committee on Financial Services, No. 108-47 (July 9, 2003)**

new material   **Fair and Accurate Credit Transactions Act of 2003: H.R. Rep. 108-263, Committee on Financial Services (Sept 4, 2003)**

new material   **Fair and Accurate Credit Transactions Act of 2003: H.R. Rep. 108-263 (Supplemental Report), House Committee on Financial Services (Sept. 9, 2003)**

Senate

new material   **Amending the Fair Credit Reporting Act, S. Rep. 108-166 (Oct. 17, 2003)**

new material   **Manager's Package on S. 1753 (With Explanations and S. 1753): Senate's Proposed Bill in Response to H.R. 2622 (Sept. 22, 2003)**

new material   **Sen. Bunning's Statement, Cong. Rec. S. 14172 (Nov. 6, 2003)**

new material   **Conference Report on H.R. 2622 (Nov. 21, 2003)**

new material   **Sen. Sarbanes' Statement, Cong. Rec. S.15806–15807 (Nov. 24, 2003)**

FCRA Interpretations
FTC Official Staff Commentary (Appendix C.3)
Supplementary Information to FTC Official Staff Commentary (Appendix C.2)
FTC Official Opinion Letter (Appendix C.4)
Sectional Index to FTC Staff Opinion Letters on FCRA (Appendix D)
Full Text of FTC Staff Opinion Letters on FCRA
    1971–May 3, 1990
    May 4, 1990–2002 (Appendix D)
Federal Standards as to FCRA's Applicability to Affiliate Information Sharing
    Proposed FTC Interpretations (Appendix A.6.1)
    Proposed OCC Regulations (Appendix A.6.2)

CD-Rom Contents / 2004 Supplement

Credit Reporting Forms
Sample Credit Reports
    Equifax (Appendix F.1.1)
    Experian (Appendix F.1.2)
    Trans Union (Appendix F.1.3)

Explanation of Credit Report
    Equifax (Appendix F.2)

Summary of Rights
    FTC Model Form (Appendix E.1)
    Equifax (Appendix F.3.1)
    Experian (Appendix F.3.2)
    Trans Union (Appendix F.3.3)

FRB Model Form: Adverse Action and ECOA (Appendix E.4)
FTC Model Form: User Responsibilities (Appendix E.2)
FTC Model Form: Responsibilities of Furnishers (Appendix E.3)
Sample Opt-Out Notices (Appendix E.5)
Sample FTC Identity Theft Affidavit and Instructions for Filling Out Affidavit (Appendix E.6)

Sample Credit Bureau Contracts
    Experian Subscriber Service Agreement (Appendix G.1.1)
    Trans Union Subscriber Agreement
    Factual Data Corp. and Freddie Mac Agreement for Services (Appendix G.1.2)
    Factual Data Corp. and Equifax Reseller Service Agreement (Appendix G.1.3)
    Factual Data Corp. and Experian Reseller Service Agreement
    Factual Data Corp. and Trans Union Reseller Service Agreement

Universal Data Form (Appendix G.2)

Consumer Information
NCLC's Consumer Guide to Credit Reporting (Appendix J)
Know Your Score—A Brochure from Consumers Federation of America on Credit Scoring
Credit Scores and Implications for Consumers
An Overview of Consumer Data and Credit Data, Federal Reserve Board Bulletin (February 2003)
FTC Tabulation of Consumer Complaints Against Credit Bureaus

Government Enforcement Orders
TRW/Experian
    FTC v. TRW (now Experian) (Appendix H.1.2)
    TRW (now Experian) v. Morales (Appendix H.1.3)
    U.S. v. Experian (Telephone Access) (Appendix H.1.4)

Equifax
    Excerpts from FTC's 1980 Opinion, *In re Equifax* (Appendix H.2.2)
    Equifax Agreement (Appendix H.2.3)
    In re Equifax Credit Info. Serv., Inc. (Consent Order) (Appendix H.2.4.1)
    In re Equifax Credit Info. Serv., Inc. (Analysis of Proposed Consent Order) (Appendix H.2.4.2)
    U.S. v. Equifax (Telephone Access) (Appendix H.2.5)
    In re Equifax (Vermont Attorney General Action) (Appendix H.2.6)
    Motion and Order for Modification of Consent Decree, *U.S. v. Equifax* (Appendix H.8, 2004 Supplement)

new material

Fair Credit Reporting / 2004 Supplement

Trans Union
    In re Trans Union Credit Info. Co. (1983 FTC Opinion) (Appendix H.3.2)
    Alabama v. Trans Union (Appendix H.3.3)
    In re Trans Union Corp. (1994 FTC Opinion) (Appendix H.3.4)
    In re Trans Union (1998 FTC Admin. Law Judge Decision on Targeted Marketing Lists) (Appendix H.3.5)
    In re Trans Union (2000 FTC Opinion on Targeted Marketing Lists) (Appendix H.3.6)
    U.S. v. Trans Union (Consent Decree) (Appendix H.3.7)

Consent Agreements with Resellers of Consumer Reports
    Consent Agreement with Inter-Fact (Appendix H.4.1)
    FTC Analysis of Proposed Consent Agreement with IRSC (Appendix H.4.2)
    First American Real Estate Solutions Consent Agreement (Appendix H.4.3.1)
    First American Real Estate Solutions Analysis of Proposed Consent Agreement (Appendix H.4.3.3)
    First American Real Estate Solutions Complaint (Appendix H.4.3.2)

Consent Agreement with Credit Repair Agency—*FTC v. NCS Credit Network, Inc.* (Appendix H.5)

Consent Agreements with Furnishers of Information
    U.S. v. Performance Capital Management Consent Decree (Inaccurate Delinquency Dates for Accounts; Ignoring or Failing to Reinvestigate Consumer Disputes)
    U.S. v. DC Credit Services—Consent Decree (Furnishing Inaccurate Information; Failing to Promptly Notify CRA of Inaccurate Information; Furnishing Information to CRAs After Consumers Had Previously Disputed Its Accuracy; and Falsely Reporting Date of Delinquency)

Consent Agreement with Information Search Inc. (Procurer of Information, Where Alleged Violation of Gramm-Leach-Bliley by Obtaining Financial Information Under False Pretenses)
    First Amended Complaint for Injunctive Relief and Other Equitable Relief
    Stipulated Judgment and Order for Permanent Injunction and Monetary Relief

FTC Consent Order Against Quicken (Appendix H.6, 2004 Supplement)

new material   **FTC Enforcement Action Against Minor for Violation of Gramm-Leach-Bliley Act (Appendix H.7, 2004 Supplement)**

Pleadings

Sample Request for Consumer's Credit Report
Client Retainer Forms
Demand Letter—Claim for Unauthorized Access to Consumer's Credit Report
Sample Letter—Explaining Damages to Opposing Counsel and the Theories for Asserting Such Damages

Complaints
    Credit Reporting Agencies
        Complaint and Demand for Jury Trial—Failure to Correct Inaccurate Credit Reports That Result from Mixing Credit Data of Different People in an Individual's Credit Reports
        Complaint—Failure to Correct Inaccurate Credit Reports That Result from Mixing Credit Data of Different People in an Individual's Credit Reports
        Complaint and Demand for Jury Trial—Failure to Correct Inaccurate Credit Reports After Learning of an Identity Theft
        Complaint—Claim for Unauthorized Access to Consumer's Credit Report

FCRA Complaint Against Multiple Reporting Agencies
Complaint—Unauthorized Release of Credit Report After Imposter Applied for Credit
Punitive Damage Complaint Against Credit Reporting Agencies and Creditors—Identity Theft
Complaint Against Reporting Agency Under Federal and State Law—Reporting Default on Nonexistent Student Loan
Complaint Against Credit Reporting Agency and Furnisher of Information—Failure to Ensure Accuracy and Investigate Disputed Information
Complaint Against Credit Reporting Agency—Failure to Have Reasonable Procedures to Ensure Accuracy and Failure to Reinvestigate Disputed Accuracy of Information
Complaint Against Credit Reporting Agencies, Creditors, and Furnishers of Information—Theft of Identity, Failure to Use Reasonable Procedures, Failure to Reinvestigate
Complaint Against Credit Reporting Agency and Furnisher—Failure to Have Reasonable Procedures to Ensure Accuracy and Failure to Reinvestigate Accuracy of Information Furnished to Credit Reporting Agency
Sample Complaint—Accuracy (Appendix I.1.3)

Creditors, Furnishers of Information

Original Complaint and Request for Trial by Jury—Continuously Reporting Inaccurate Information to a Credit Reporting Agency After Being Notified of the Error
Complaint and Demand for Jury Trial—Continuously Reporting Inaccurate Information to a Credit Reporting Agency After Being Notified of the Error
First Amended and Restated Complaint and Demand for Jury Trial—Denying Low-Cost Car Insurance Premium on Basis of Credit Report Without Telling the Customer
Complaint Against Information Furnishers—Mistaken Identity (Prior to FCRA 1996 Amendments)
Complaint Against Information Suppliers and Multiple Reporting Agencies (Prior to FCRA 1996 Amendments)
Sample Complaint—Failure to Reinvestigate (Appendix I.1.1)

Impermissible Use

Sample Complaint—Impermissible Purposes (Appendix I.1.2)
Complaint—Unauthorized Use of a Credit Report
Class Action Complaint—Insurance Company Obtains Credit Reports with Impermissible Purposes, Under False Pretenses and Fails to Provide Adverse Action Notice
Class Action Complaint—Impermissible Access

Investigative Reports

Sample Complaint—Investigative Report (Appendix I.1.4)

Credit Repair

Complaint—Violation of Credit Repair Organization Statute Against Car Dealer
Complaint—FCRA Violations in Connection with Home Improvement Scam

Use of Credit Score

Complaint by State Attorney General Against Insurance Company—Improper Use of Credit Scoring
Class Action Complaint Against Insurance Company—Improper Use of Credit Scoring

Fair Credit Reporting / 2004 Supplement

        Complaint Against FNMA—Improper Use of Credit Scoring
    Consumer Notice
        Complaint Against Financing Company—"Spot Delivery" Case for Failure to Provide Adverse Action Notice
  Discovery
    Interrogatories
        Sample Interrogatories—Accuracy (Appendix I.2.1)
        Sample Interrogatories—Metro 2 Format (Appendix I.2.2)
        Sample Interrogatories—Permissible Purposes (Appendix I.2.3)

new material   **Interrogatories—Reinvestigation (to Furnisher) (Appendix I.2.4, 2004 Supplement)**
        Plaintiff's Interrogatories to Creditors
        Plaintiff's Interrogatories to Creditors; Affidavit
        Interrogatories to Credit Reporting Agency; Affidavit
        Interrogatories and Document Requests—Unauthorized Use of Credit Report
        Interrogatories to Multiple Reporting Agencies
        Interrogatories and Document Requests—Case Alleging Car Dealer Violates Credit Repair Organization Statute
        Interrogatories to Home Improvement Contractor—FCRA Violations
        Interrogatories to Home Improvement Contractor's Assignee—FCRA Violations
        Interrogatories—Identity Theft Case
        Interrogatories and Document Requests—Identity Theft Case
        Interrogatories and Document Requests—Case Against Reporting Agency Under Federal and State Law for Reporting Default on Nonexistent Student Loan
        Interrogatories Direct to Creditor
        Interrogatories and Document Requests—Metro 2B Duty to Investigate
        Interrogatories to User—Permissible Purposes
        Interrogatories to Reporting Agency—Permissible Purposes
    Document Requests
        Sample Document Requests—Users (Appendix I.3.1)
        Sample Document Requests—Metro 2 (Appendix I.3.2)

new material   **Request for Production of Documents to Furnisher (Appendix I.2.4, 2004 Supplement)**
        Motion for Production of Documents; Affidavit; Letter—Continuously Reporting Inaccurate Information to a Credit Reporting Agency After Being Notified of the Error
        Requests for Production of Documents to First Defendant; Affidavit
        Requests for Production of Documents to Second Defendant; Affidavit
        Requests for Production of Documents to Credit Reporting Agency; Affidavit
        Document Requests—Multiple Reporting Agencies
        Document Requests, Interrogatories, and Requests for Admissions—Multiple Reporting Agencies and Furnishers of Information (in Case Before 1996 FCRA Amendments)
        Document Requests—Home Improvement Contractor in Case Involving FCRA Violations
        Document Requests—Home Improvement Contractor's Assignee in Case Involving FCRA Violations
        Document Requests—Identity Theft Case
        Document Request—Permissible Purpose

CD-Rom Contents / 2004 Supplement

Subpoenas
Sample Subpoena of Custodian of Records (Appendix I.4.1)
Federal Subpoena Commanding Production of Documents
Subpoena Commanding Production of Documents
Subpoena *Duces Tecum* Issued to Non-Party

Notices of Depositions
Sample Notice of Deposition (Appendix I.4.2)
Sample Notice of Deposition—Fed. R. Civ. Pro. 30(b)(6) (Appendix I.4.3)
Notice of Deposition

Motions to Compel
Opposition to Motion to Compel Arbitration and to Stay Discovery; Affidavit—Continuously Reporting Inaccurate Information to a Credit Reporting Agency After Being Notified of the Error
Motion to Compel Defendant's Responses to Requests for Production
Memorandum in Support of Motion to Compel Defendants' Responses to Requests for Production
Motion to Compel Defendant's Responses
Memorandum in Support of Motion to Compel Defendant's Responses; Affidavit
Motion to Compel Discovery and Brief in Support
Memorandum Opposing Defendant's Discovery Objections—Identity Theft
Decision in *Zahran v. Trans Union*—Denial of Protective Order for Discovery Material
Discovery Order

Requests for Admissions
Plaintiff's First Set of Requests for Admissions
Requests for Admissions—Home Improvement Contractor in Case Involving FCRA Violations
Requests for Admissions—Home Improvement Contractor's Assignee in Case Involving FCRA Violations
Requests for Admissions

Deposition Transcripts
Three Depositions of Trans Union Employees Regarding Reinvestigation Process and Procedures, Including Use of Quotas for Reinvestigating Disputes

Trial Documents
Pretrial Order, Trial Brief, Motion in *Limine* and Memorandum—Identity Theft Case
Trial Transcript—Furnisher Reinvestigation

new material — **Cross-Examination of Trans Union Employee in Case Involving Accuracy and Reinvestigation, Pt. 1**

new material — **Cross-Examination of Trans Union Employee in Case Involving Accuracy and Reinvestigation, Pt. 2**

Sample Direct Testimony—Damages (Appendix I.5.1)

new material — **Closing Argument, Case Involving Accuracy and Reinvestigation**

Plaintiff's Closing Arguments to the Jury (Appendix I.5.2)
Sample Jury Instructions—*Bryant* (Appendix I.5.3)
Sample Jury Instructions—*Jones* (Appendix I.5.4)
Sample Jury Instructions—Furnisher Reinvestigation and Impermissible Purpose (Appendix I.5.5)

new material — **Transcript of Jury Instructions (Appendix I.5.6, 2004 Supplement)**

Sample Jury Instructions—Furnisher Reinvestigation

Fair Credit Reporting / 2004 Supplement

    Jury Instructions—Punitive Damage Claims Against Credit Reporting Agencies and Creditors for Identity Theft
    Jury Instruction—Obtaining Credit Report Without Permissible Purpose (False Pretenses)
    Jury Instructions—Maximum Possible Accuracy, Defamation
    Jury Instructions—Accuracy
    Plaintiff's Brief on Defendant's Motion for Post-Trial Relief—Identity Theft Case
    Special Interrogatories to the Jury—Identity Theft Case
    Sample Confidentiality Order (Appendix I.6)
    Attorney Fee Motion and Memorandum—Punitive Damage Claims Against Credit Reporting Agencies and Creditors for Identity Theft

Settlement Agreement And Release

new material   **Class Action Settlement Where Consumer Who Did Not File Bankruptcy Was Reported as "Included" in Bankruptcy**
    Mutual Settlement Agreement
    FTC Settlement with Credit Repair Organization

Motions, Briefs and Memoranda

    Memo Opposing Defendant's Motion for Summary Judgment—§ 1681s-2(b) (Failure to Conduct Reasonable Reinvestigation) Case
    Memo Opposing Motion for Judgment as Matter of Law—§ 1681s-2(b) (Failure to Conduct Reasonable Reinvestigation) Case
    Memo Opposing Motion to Dismiss—"Spot Delivery" Case
    Plaintiff's Motion for Summary Judgment—"Spot Delivery" Case
    Memo Opposing Motion to Dismiss, Order—Continuously Reporting Inaccurate Information to a Credit Reporting Agency After Being Notified of the Error
    Motion for Leave to File; Order—Denying Low-Cost Car Insurance Premium on Basis of Credit Report Without Telling the Customer
    Motion to Strike the Defendant's Answer; Affidavit
    Memo in Support of Motion to Strike Answer
    Opposition to Implead and Join Imposter; Order
    Opposition to Motion to Dismissal
    Response and Opposition to Motion to Dismiss
    Memo in Opposition to Motion to Dismiss; Order
    Memo in Opposition to Partial Motion to Dismiss; Affidavit
    Response and Opposition to Motion for Partial Summary Judgment
    Statement of Material Fact in Opposition to Motion for Summary Judgment
    Motion for Summary Judgment in Merged Case; Order
    Motion for Summary Judgment on the Issue of Liability
    Memo in Support of Motion for Summary Judgment on the Issue of Liability
    Reply to Defendant's Opposition to Motion for Summary Judgment
    Consumer's Proposal for Joint Pre-Trial Order
    Brief—Unauthorized Release of Credit Report After Imposter Applied for Credit
    Appellant's Reply Brief—Unauthorized Release of Credit Report After Imposter Applied for Credit
    Memo—Applicability of Credit Repair Organization Statute to Car Dealer
    Memo Opposing Alleged Settlement of Credit Reporting Claims
    Response to Motion to Dismiss—Unauthorized Use of Credit Report
    Memo Opposing Motion to Dismiss—Multiple Reporting Agencies
    Post-Trial Motion—Opposition to Motion for JMOL, New Trial and Remittitur

CD-Rom Contents / 2004 Supplement

FCRA-Related Websites (Appendix K)

Fair Credit Reporting Appendices on CD-Rom
 Table of Contents
new material **Appendix A, Fair Credit Reporting Act, Other Federal Statutes and Regulations (and 2004 Supplement)**
 Appendix B, Summary of Federal and State Laws on Consumer Reporting and Theft of Identity (Replacement Appendix, 2004 Supplement)
 Appendix C, FTC Official Staff Commentary
 Appendix D, Text of Selected Federal Trade Commission Informal Staff Opinion Letters with FCRA Sectional Index
 Appendix E, FTC and FRB Model Forms (and 2004 Supplement)
 Appendix F, Sample Credit Reports, Consumer Reporting Agency Forms
 Appendix G, Sample Credit Bureau Contract and Universal Data Form
new material **Appendix H, Enforcement Orders Against Consumer Reporting Agencies, Resellers, Credit Repair Agencies, and Users (and 2004 Supplement)**
new material **Appendix I, Sample Pleadings and Other Litigation Documents (and 2004 Supplement)**
 Appendix J, Consumer's Guide To Credit Reporting
 Appendix K, Fair Credit Reporting Related Websites
 Index
 Quick Reference to *Consumer Credit and Sales Legal Practice Series*
 What Your Library Should Contain

Word Pleadings on CD-Rom
 Complaints
 Discovery
 Deposition Transcripts
 Trial Documents
 Settlement Agreement and Release
 Motions, Briefs, and Memoranda

Contents of NCLC Publications
 Detailed and Summary Tables of Contents for Each Manual
 Short Description of Each Manual's Features with Link to Manual's Detailed Index
 Short Index to Major Topics Covered in the 16-Volume Series
 Descriptions of Other NCLC Books for Lawyers and Consumers
 Features of Consumer Law in a Box (16 CD-Roms Combined into One Master CD-Rom)
 Printer-Friendly 3-Page Description of All NCLC Publications, Latest Supplements
 Printer-Friendly 25-Page Brochure Describing All NCLC Publications
 Printer-Friendly Order Form for All NCLC Publications
 Order Securely Online

Consumer Education Brochures, Books
 Legal and General Audience Books Available to Order from NCLC
  The Practice of Consumer Law, Seeking Economic Justice
  STOP Predatory Lending, A Guide for Legal Advocates, with CD-Rom
  Return to Sender: Getting a Refund or Replacement for Your Lemon Car
  The NCLC Guide to Surviving Debt (2002 ed.)
  The NCLC Guide to Consumer Rights for Immigrants
  The NCLC Guide to Mobile Homes

xxxi

Fair Credit Reporting / 2004 Supplement

        Printer-Friendly Order Form
        Order Securely Online
    Brochures for Consumers on this CD-Rom
        General Consumer Education Brochures
        Consumer Concerns for Older Americans
        Immigrant Justice in the Consumer Marketplace

Order NCLC Publications, CD-Roms
    NCLC Manuals and CD-Roms
    Order Publications Online
    Printer-Friendly Order Form
    Consumer Law in a Box CD-Rom
    Credit Math, *Bankruptcy Forms* Software
    Printer-Friendly Publications Brochure
    NCLC Newsletters
    Case Assistance
    Conferences, Training
    Books for Lawyers, Consumers
    Consumer Education Pamphlets
    Consumer Web Links

About NCLC, About This CD-Rom
    National Consumer Law Center
        Mission Statement
        Contact Information: Boston, Washington offices
        Go to NCLC Website
        What Your Library Should Contain
        Order NCLC Publications Online
        Learn More About NCLC Manuals, CD-Roms,
        Order Form: Order NCLC Publications Via Mail, Phone, Fax
    About This CD-Rom
        What Is Contained on This CD-Rom
        Finding Aids for NCLC Manuals: What Is Available in the Books?
        Disclaimers—Need to Adapt Pleadings; Unauthorized Practice of Law
    License Agreement, Copyrights, Trademarks: Please Read
    Law Disks: CD-Rom Producer, Publisher of *Bankruptcy Forms* Software

Acrobat 6.0 Problem

Acrobat Reader 5 and 6.0.1

Chapter 1 Introduction

1.1 About This Manual

1.1.1 Introduction

Page 1

Add to text before "and privacy" in second-to-last sentence of subsection's first paragraph:

identity theft;

Replace subsection's third paragraph with:

Consumers now face greater challenges when they seek to determine what information is contained in their credit reporting files. These challenges include finding out who has accessed their information, how this information has been used to determine their access to credit or employment, and what they can do to correct any errors and mistakes and to handle resistance by credit reporting agencies or others to clear inaccuracies contained in their reports. In addition, consumers face numerous challenges relating to identify theft and protection of their credit information.

Add after "car loans," in second sentence of subsection's fourth paragraph:

utility services,

Page 2

1.1.2 Structure of the Manual

Replace subsection's first sentence with:

Chapter 1 provides an introduction to the manual, the credit reporting industry, the Fair Credit Reporting Act, the Fair and Accurate Credit Transactions Act of 2003,[1.1] and legislative histories of both Acts.

    1.1   Pub. L. No. 108-159 (2003).

Add to text after "FCRA," in fourth sentence of subsection's second paragraph:

and the FACTA,[1.2]

    1.2   *Id.*

Add to text at end of first sentence of subsection's ninth paragraph:

, the FACTA of 2003, including a redlined version of the FCRA that incorporates the FACTA amendments.

Page 3

1.1.3 Clearinghouse and Other Citations

Replace subsection's final sentence of subsection with:

The easiest way to have interpretations of these statutes at your fingertips is to consult NCLC's *Credit Discrimination* (3d ed. 2002 and Supp.) and *Fair Debt Collection* (4th ed. 2000 and Supp.).

1

§ 1.2 *Fair Credit Reporting / 2004 Supplement*

Page 4

Add to text at end of subsection's fourth paragraph:

1.2 About Credit Reporting

, including protection from identity theft.

Page 5

Delete from sentence containing note 13:

More recently,

1.3 About the FCRA

Page 6

1.3.2 Limited Amount of FCRA Litigation

Replace subsection's third paragraph with:

The FCRA is also full of holes. In some instances, the wrongs suffered by consumers are not addressed by the Act. Furthermore, the Act is so poorly drafted and difficult to understand that courts are sometimes in disagreement over some fundamental questions. In part, the difficulty is caused by the circularity of the Act. For example, the basic definition of a term might refer to another term whose definition is based on the definition of the first term.

Page 7

1.3.3 Federal Agency Interpretations of the FCRA

Add to text after subsection's first paragraph:

In 2003, the FACTA amended the FCRA to grant the FTC and other identified federal agencies authority to prescribe rules in a variety of areas.[28.1]

28.1 *Id.*

Replace first sentence of subsection's second paragraph with:

Prior to the 1996 FCRA amendments, the FTC issued an Official Staff Commentary interpreting many particulars of the Act, and its staff sometimes provided informal opinion letters upon request.

Replace second sentence of subsection's third paragraph with:

It is unclear how much weight the courts will accord the Commentary in light of the rulemaking authority granted to the FTC by the 1996 and 2003 amendments.

Replace second and third sentences of subsection's fourth paragraph with:

By contrast, Congress in 1996 granted the FTC only limited rulemaking authority; not until the FACTA of 1993 did Congress expand the FTC's FCRA rulemaking authority.[31] Consequently, courts need not, but still may, show deference to Commentary interpretations that predate the amendments.[32]

31 Pub. L. No. 106-102 (1999); Pub. L. No. 108-159 (2003).
32 *See* Yonter v. Aetna Fin. Co., 777 F. Supp. 490 (E.D. La. 1991).

1.4 FCRA Legislative History

Page 18

Add new subsection after § 1.4.8.

1.4.9 The Fair and Accurate Credit Transactions Act of 2003

1.4.9.1 Legislative History

In 2003, Congress made significant changes to the FCRA by passing the Fair and Accurate Credit Transactions Act (FACTA).[173] The impetus for the FACTA was the expiration of the FCRA's existing subject-matter-specific preemption provisions.[174] The FCRA's preemption of state laws was due to sunset on January 1, 2004.[175] With the end of preemption looming, and the credit reporting and financial industry concerned about states enacting enhanced consumer protection laws, Congress sought to establish so-called "uniform" standards for the credit reporting industry, thus ensuring that existing preemptions continue.[176] In addition, Congress sought to address the problem of identity theft, viewed as reaching near epidemic proportions.[177] Other issues Congress focused on were accuracy, privacy, furnisher responsibilities, protecting medical information, employee investigations and financial literacy.[178]

Both the House and Senate held several hearings concerning the credit reporting industry and its practices. Many of the documents and testimony produced from these hearings, including Committee Reports, are available on the CD-Rom included with this manual, *infra*. The topics covered by hearings in the House included: fighting identity theft; the role of the FCRA in employee background checks; the collection of medical information; the role of the FCRA in the credit granting process; how the FCRA functions for consumers and the economy; and the importance of the national credit reporting system to consumers and the U.S. economy."[179] On the Senate side, the hearings related to a general overview of the credit reporting system;[180] identity theft;[181] affiliate sharing practices;[182] accuracy of credit report information;[183] consumer awareness and understanding of the credit granting process;[184] and addressing measures to enhance the operation of the FCRA.[185]

Although several bills had been proposed on one or more FCRA issues since 1996, it wass not until the House Committee on Financial Services drafted HR 2622 that Congress began the process of substantially amending the FCRA to address the preemption and identity theft issues that had become predominant. HR 2622 made it clear that the preemption provisions would become permanent. HR 2622 proponents believed it was beneficial to consumers, asserting that it provided consumers with tools to fight identity theft and ensure accuracy. However it really only contained modest measures to protect consumers from identity theft, inaccuracies, and invasions of financial privacy.[186]

The Senate took a more balanced approach to the need for consumer protection and preemption. S. 1753, the National Consumer Credit Reporting System Improvement Act of 2003, was the Senate's response to the House's H.R. 2622. S. 1753 sought to address the needs of consumers while providing for the efficient operation of the national credit markets.[187] The Senate Banking Committee, which oversaw S. 1753, focused on several areas, including accuracy, risk-based pricing practices, identity theft, financial literacy, information use practices, and national standards or preemption.[188]

The subsequent legislative history for the FACTA is not extensive and there was virtually no debate and very little substantive discussion in both the House and Senate. There are very few comments on the Senate floor concerning the FACTA. Only Senator Sarbanes provided meaningful comments.[189] On the House side, many members praised the Act's benefits, but offered littleexplanation of the Act's content.[190] The most extensive comments were made by Congressmen Oxley, who also provided supplemental comments several weeks after the FACTA was passed.[191] On December 4, 2003, the President signed the FACTA.

1.4.9.2 Key Provisions

The FCRA, as amended by the FACTA, sets up a web of communication among consumers, agencies, and furnishers that, if properly implemented and employed, could synchronize consumer reports and purge theft-related information from agencies' and furnishers' files. These communications include various notice requirements to consumers from credit reporting agencies, furnishers, and debt collectors.[192]

The FACTA contains several provisions intended to assist consumers with credit reporting problems. The Act provides for free annual credit reports from the three national credit reporting repositories and newly defined national specialty reporting credit bureaus (that is, tenant screening, insurance, and employment).[193] In addition to permanently extending existing preemption provisions in the FCRA, it added a long list of new preemptions that significantly limit states' abilities to regulate much of the FCRA's subject matter and conduct requirements.[194] The full extent of the preemption and limitation of liability provisions is uncertain and will likely remain this way until courts interpret the various provisions added to the FCRA by the FACTA. To combat identity theft, the FACTA allows consumers to place fraud alerts in their credit files[195] and to block information caused by identity theft or fraud.[196] Active military duty personnel can also add an alert to their files.[197]

The FACTA provided the FTC and other federal regulatory agencies with significant rulemaking authority, something the FTC lacked for many years.[198] In addition, the FACTA requires various studies or reports by the FTC and other agencies and in some cases by credit reporting agencies. Such studies or reports will cover a variety of credit reporting issues, including the effectiveness of a new provision requiring victims to receive identity theft transaction information from businesses that conducted business with an identity thief;[199] complaints received by the three national credit reporting repositories;[200] complaints to the FTC regarding accuracy and completeness of credit reports;[201] reinvestigations of disputed information;[202] the efficacy of increasing the number of points of identifying information for matches before releasing credit reports;[203] the ability of consumers to avoid receiving written offers of credit or insurance in connection with transactions not initiated by the consumer;[204] and the effect of credit scores and credit-based insurance scores on the availability and affordability of financial products.[205]

Congress also created a new right for consumers to receive notices relating to risk-based pricing.[206] Whenever a creditor extends credit on terms "materially less favorable than the most favorable terms available to a substantial proportion of consumers," the creditor must provide to consumers a notice that explains that the terms are based on information in a credit report and that the consumers can request a free copy of the report. This notice requirement will address a current flaw in the FCRA relating to failure by creditors to provide notice to consumers when they charge higher interest, fees, or other amounts based on a consumer's credit report. This flaw was specifically highlighted in testimony by FTC Chairman Timothy Muris.[207]

The FACTA also modified the standard of accuracy for furnishers of information.[208] New duties for furnishers include requirements to prevent the "repollution" of consumer reports.[209] Furnishers must also have reasonable procedures in place to prevent them from refurnishing information that is the result of identity theft.[210]

Under the FACTA, debt collectors are prohibited from selling or transferring for consideration, or placing for collection, a debt that they are on notice for and that is the result of identity theft. Third-party debt collectors, once on notice that a debt may be the result of identity theft, must notify the creditor that the information may be the result of identity theft and, upon the request of the consumer, disclose to the consumer information about the transaction.[211]

The Act also provides for the truncation of credit card numbers and social security numbers. Persons who accept credit cards or debit cards may print no more than the last five digits of the card or the expiration date on any receipt provided at the point of sale. This provision is only applicable to electronically printed receipts.[212] Consumers may also request that credit reporting agencies truncate the consumer's social security number and limit disclosure to the last five numbers of the social security number.[213]

The prior version of the FCRA specifically provided that agencies were not required to disclose credit scores to consumers,[214] though it did not preempt states from requiring their disclosure. The FCRA now requires disclosure of credit scores and will standardize the fees for the disclosure, but it also preempts states from imposing new requirements.[215] Mortgage lenders of loans secured by one to four units of residential real property must also disclose a credit score and related information that the lender obtained from an agency or, if the lender uses an automated underwriting system, must disclose that system's credit score and the score's key factors.[216] Mortgage lenders must also give a prescribed notice to the consumer.[217] Although state laws regarding these disclosures are preempted, several existing state laws are exempt from the preemption.[218] The FCRA now requires agencies to give consumers the FTC's summary of rights to dispute information and obtain credit scores;[219] under the prior version, agencies could substitute their own summary.

Introduction / 2004 Supplement § 1.4.9.2

The FACTA also extends the opt-out period for prescreened offers from two years to five.[220] The FTC is to issue rules for the prescreened offer notice that will ensure that such notices are "simple and easy to understand," and agencies must present the notice in that format and must also include the address and telephone number of the opt-out notification system.[221]

Another important area affected by the FACTA is medical information and how furnishers and credit reporting agencies handle such information. The FCRA was amended to provide for enhanced protection of medical information.[222]

Employee investigation communications was an important issue for Congress. Longstanding concerns over employee misconduct investigations and industry frustrations with FCRA notice requirements led Congress to restrict the rights of employees with respect to certain types of investigations. The FCRA now excludes certain communications related to employers' investigation of employees.[223] The FACTA also amended the FCRA's statute of limitations to now provide that the two-year limitation period dates from the consumer's discovery of the violation, not the date of the violation itself.[224]

The FACTA was signed into law on December 4, 2003, and certain provisions without a designated effective date went into effect on this date. However, the effective dates of most provisions are to be determined by the FTC and other federal agencies, and these agencies have adopted regulations specifying effective dates for these provisions.[225] Still other FACTA provisions do not become effective until the FTC or other federal agencies enact regulations interpreting the provisions.

173 Pub. L. No. 108-159 (2003).
174 15 U.S.C. § 1681t(d).
175 *Id.*
176 H.R. Rep. No. 108-263, at 23–25 (Sept. 4, 2003).
177 H.R. Rep. No. 108-263, at 25 (Sept. 4, 2003).
178 H.R. Rep. 108-263 (Sept. 4, 2003); Sen. Rep. 108-166 (Oct. 17, 2003).
179 *See* http://financialservices.house.gov/hearings.asp?formmode=All.
180 *Available at* http://banking.senate.gov/index.cfm?Fuseaction=Hearings.Detail&HearingID=26;.
181 *Available at* http://banking.senate.gov/index.cfm?Fuseaction=Hearings.Detail&HearingID=43.
182 *Available at* http://banking.senate.gov/index.cfm?Fuseaction=Hearings.Testimony&TestimonyID= 262&HearingID=46.
183 *Available at* http://banking.senate.gov/index.cfm?Fuseaction=Hearings.Detail&HearingID=49.
184 *Available at* http://banking.senate.gov/index.cfm?Fuseaction=Hearings.Detail&HearingID=55.
185 *Available at* http://banking.senate.gov/index.cfm?Fuseaction=Hearings.Detail&HearingID=56.
186 H.R. Rep. No. 108–263 (Sept. 4, 2003).
187 Sen. Rep. No. 108–166, at 2 (Oct. 17, 2003).
188 Sen. Rep. No. 108–166 (Oct. 17, 2003).
189 Cong. Rec. pp. S15806–15807 (Nov. 24, 2003).
190 Cong. Rec. H12198-H12224 (Nov. 21, 2003).
191 *Id. See* Cong. Rec. E2512–2519 (Dec. 9, 2003).
192 *See* §§ 6.4a, 6.5.3, 6.8a, 6.8b, 6.8c, 6.8d, 6.8e, and 16.6.1a, *infra*.
193 15 U.S.C. § 1681j(a)(1)(C), *added by* Pub. L. No. 108-159, § 211(a)(2) (2003). The FTC is to issue regulations to establish a mechanism through which consumers can obtain reports from nationwide specialty consumer reporting agencies. *See* § 2.5.8, *infra*.
194 *See* §§ 10.2 and 10.3, *infra*.
195 15 U.S.C. §§ 1681c-1(a), (b), *added by* Pub. L. No. 108-159, § 112 (2003). This provision will become effective on December 1, 2004. 16 C.F.R. § 602.1(c)(3)(i), *added by* 69 Fed. Reg. 6526 (Feb. 11, 2003). *See* § 16.6.1a, *infra*.
196 15 U.S.C. § 1681c-2, *added by* Pub. L. No. 108-159, § 152 (2003). This provision will become effective on December 1, 2004. 16 C.F.R. § 602.1(c)(3)(v), *added by* 69 Fed. Reg. 6526 (Feb. 11, 2003). *See* § 16.6.1a, *infra*.
197 15 U.S.C. § 1681c-1(c), *added by* Pub. L. No. 108-159, § 112 (2003). This provision will become effective on December 1, 2004. 16 C.F.R. § 602.1(c)(3)(i), *added by* 69 Fed. Reg. 6526 (Feb. 11, 2003).
198 15 U.S.C. §§ 1681b(g)(5)(A), 1681c(h)(2)(A), 1681i(e)(4), 1681m(e), 1681m(h)6), 1681s–2(a)(8)(A), 1681t(e)(1), 1681x, *added by* Pub. L. No. 108-159 (2003).
199 15 U.S.C. § 1681g(e)(13), *added by* Pub. L. No. 108-159, § 151(2003).
200 15 U.S.C. § 1681s(f)3), *added by* Pub. L. No. 108-159, § 153 (2003).
201 15 U.S.C. §§ 1681i(e)(1)(A), *added by* Pub. L. No. 108-159, § 313 (2003). *See also* Pub. L. No. 108-159, § 319 (2003).
202 Pub. L. No. 108-159, § 313(b) (2003).

203 Pub. L. No. 108-159, § 318 (2003).
204 Pub. L. No. 108-159, § 213(e) (2003).
205 Pub. L. No. 108-159, § 215(a).
206 Pub. L. No. 108-159, § 311 (2003), amending 15 U.S.C. § 1681m(h). This provision will become effective on December 1, 2004. 16 C.F.R. § 602.1(c)(3)(xiii), *added by* 69 Fed. Reg. 6526 (Feb. 11, 2003).
207 Housing and Urban Affairs, *Prepared Statement of the Federal Trade Commission on the Fair Credit Reporting Act Before the Senate Committee on Banking* 11-12 (July 10, 2003) (statement of Timothy Muris, FTC Chairma). *See* § 6.4a in this supplement, *infra*.
208 15 U.S.C. § 1681s–2(a), *as amended by* Pub. L. No. 108-159, § 312(b). *See* Ch. 3.4.2 in this supplement, *infra*. This new accuracy provision will become effective December 1, 2004. 16 C.F.R. § 602.1(c)(3)(xiv), *added by* 69 Fed. Reg. 6526 (Feb. 11, 2003).
209 *Id.*
210 *Id. See* § 3.4.3 (Supp), *infra*.
211 15 U.S.C. § 1681m(g), *as amended by* Pub. L. No. 108-159, § 312(d). *See* §§ 3.3.4.2a, 3.3.4.2b (Supp), *infra*. This provision will become effective on December 1, 2004. 16 C.F.R. § 602.1(c)(3)(viii), *added by* 69 Fed. Reg. 6526 (Feb. 11, 2003).
212 15 U.S.C. § 1681c(g), *added by* Pub. L. No. 108-159, § 113 (2003). This provision incorporates staggered effective dates. *Id.*
213 15 U.S.C. § 1681g(a)(1), amended by Pub. L. No. 108-159, § 115 (2003).
214 15 U.S.C. § 1681g(a), *as amended by* Pub. L. No. 108-159, § 211 (2003).
215 15 U.S.C. § 1681g(a), *as amended by* Pub. L. No. 108-159, § 212 (2003).
216 15 U.S.C. § 1681g(a), *as amended by* Pub. L. No. 108-159, § 212 (2003).
217 *Id.*
218 15 U.S.C. § 1681m(b)(3), *added by* Pub. L. No. 108-159, § 212 (2003).
219 15 U.S.C. § 1681g(c), *as amended by* Pub. L. No. 108-159, § 211 (2003).
220 15 U.S.C. § 1681b(e), *as amended by* Pub. L. No. 108-159, § 213 (2003). This provision will become effective on December 1, 2004. 16 C.F.R. § 602.1(c)(3)(xi), *added by* 69 Fed. Reg. 6526 (Feb. 11, 2003).
221 15 U.S.C. § 1681m(d)(2), *as amended by* Pub. L. No. 108-159, § 213 (2003).
222 15 U.S.C. §§ 1681b(g), 1681s–2(a)(9), *as amended by* Pub. L. No. 108-159, §§ 411, 412 (2003). Sections 1681b(g)(1) (agencies to exclude certain medical information from reports) and 1681b(g)(4) (limits on redisclosure of medical information) will become effective on June 1, 2004, Pub. L. No. 108-159, § 411 (2003), while the effective date of § 1681b(g)(2) (limits on creditors' use of medical information) depends on the date set by the FTC's regulations, *id.* at § 412.
223 15 U.S.C. § 1681a(d)(2)(D), (x), amended by Pub. L. No. 108-159, § 611 (2003).
224 15 U.S.C. §1681p, as *amended by* Pub. L. No. 108-159, § 156 (2003).
225 69 Fed. Reg. 6526 (Feb. 11, 2003) (to be codified at 16 C.F.R. Part 602).

Chapter 2 Scope: Consumer Reports and Consumer Reporting Agencies

Page 19

2.1 Introduction

Replace note 1 with:

1   See § 3.9, *infra*.

Add to text end of subsection:

The FACTA of 2003 specifically defined a subclass of consumer reporting agencies. A "nationwide specialty consumer reporting agency" encompasses agencies that, while maintaining files on consumers on a nationwide basis, restrict their files to one of five categories of records: medical records or payments, residential or tenant history, check-writing history, employment history, or insurance claims.[4.1]

4.1   Pub. L. No. 108-159 § 111 (2003), adding FCRA § 603(w), 15 U.S.C. § 1681a(w).

2.3 Is a "Consumer Report" Involved?

2.3.1 A Consumer Report Compared to a Consumer's File

Page 20

Add to text after sentence containing note 12:

Instead, it is a consumer file subject to the FCRA's dispute and reinvestigation procedures.[12.1]

12.1   Thomas v. Gulf Coast Credit Serv., Inc., 214 F. Supp. 2d 1228 (M.D. Ala. 2002).

Page 22

2.3.3 Information Must Bear on a Consumer's Creditworthiness, Credit Standing or Capacity, Character, Reputation, Personal Characteristics, or Mode of Living

Addition to note 35.

35   See § 16.4.1, *infra*.

2.3.4 Disclosure of "Credit Header" Information

Addition to note 38.

38   Remsburg v. Docusearch, Inc., 2002 U.S. Dist. LEXIS 6231 (D.N.H. Apr. 4, 2002) (credit header information is not a consumer report).

2.3.6 Purposes That Make Information a Consumer Report

Page 26

2.3.6.1 General

Addition to note 80.

80   *Replace 15 U.S.C. §§ 1681b(1) and (2) citations with*: 1681b(a)(1) and (a)(2).

Page 29

2.3.6.3 Bad Check and Check Approval Lists

Add to text at end of subsection's second paragraph:

A consumer reporting agency that maintains files on consumers' check-writing histories will now also qualify as a "nationwide specialty consumer reporting agency," a new subclass of agencies added to the FCRA by the FACTA.[104.1]

§ 2.3.6.4 — Fair Credit Reporting / 2004 Supplement

104.1 FCRA § 603(w), 15 U.S.C. § 1681a(w), *added by* Pub. L. No. 108-159 § 111 (2003).

Add to text after sentence containing note 105:

Another variation of a check approval company is TELE-TRACK, a company that specializes in providing information to rent-to-own stores and other sub-prime merchants and lenders. Unlike traditional credit reporting agencies, this company maintains a database containing only negative information. In addition to reporting on those who have written bad checks, it also reports on consumers who purportedly have not paid rent, used false social security numbers, have stolen merchandise or automobiles or have not met terms under finance or service agreements with merchants.[105.1]

105.1 *See* www.teletrack.com.

Page 30

2.3.6.4 Reports on Tenants

Add to text at end of subsection:

Now, a consumer reporting agency that complies and maintains files on consumers on a nationwide basis relating to their residential or tenant history will be a "nationwide specialty consumer reporting agency," a new subclass of agency added to the FCRA by the FACTA.[115.1]

115.1 FCRA § 603(w), 15 U.S.C. § 1681a(w), *added by* Pub. L. No. 108-159 § 111 (2003).

2.3.6.5 Business Credit and Commercial Reports

Page 31

2.3.6.5.2 *Reports on individuals in their business capacity are not consumer reports*

Addition to notes 120, 121.

120 Thomas v. Gulf Coast Credit Serv., Inc., 214 F. Supp. 2d 1228 (M.D. Ala. 2002).
121 Lucchesi v. Experian Info. Solutions, Inc., 2003 WL 21542317 (S.D.N.Y. July 7, 2003).

Page 32

2.3.6.5.5 *Reports used or collected for business purposes can still qualify as consumer reports*

Addition to note 131.

131 *Delete citation to Houghton.*

2.3.6.6 Employment Reports

Addition to notes 137, 144. Page 33

137 See § 9.1.3.2 for a discussion of investigative reports that are prepared for employment purposes.
144 Martinets v. Corning Cable Sys., L.L.C., 237 F. Supp. 2d 717 (N.D. Tex. 2002) (report of results from a breathalyzer test does not constitute a "consumer report" because the results are based on a "transaction or experience" between the employee and the clinic performing the screening).

Add to text after sentence containing note 148:

The 2003 amendments to the FCRA pulled out a large chunk of employment reports from the definition of consumer report.[148.1] Congress, responding to employers' complaints that the FCRA's disclosure provisions hindered investigations of workplace misconduct, amended the Act to provide that certain communications made to an employer will no longer be "consumer reports." To qualify, the communication must be in connection with the investigation of either suspected misconduct by an employee or compliance with federal, state, or local laws and regulations, the rules of a self-regulatory organization, or any preexisting written policies of the employer.[148.2] As a safeguard, the provision requires that, to qualify for the exclusion, the communication must not have been made for the purpose of investigating the employee's credit worthiness, credit standing, or credit capacity, and the communication must not be provided to any person other than the employer, the employer's agent, a governmental agency, or a self-regulatory organization.[148.3] If made for any of those purposes the communication will lose its exemption and remain a consumer report. Furthermore, the FCRA does maintain some regulation over such reports, notwithstanding that they are not "consumer reports"; an employer who takes any adverse action based in whole or in part on the exempted communication must disclose to the consumer a summary of the communication, although the

Scope: Consumer Reports and Consumer Reporting Agencies / 2004 Supplement § 2.5.7

employer need not disclose any sources of information for use in preparing what would be, except for the exception, an investigative consumer report.[148.4]

148.1 Pub. L. No. 108-159 § 611(b) (2003), *amending* FCRA § 603(d)(2)(D), 15 U.S.C. § 1681a(d)(2)(D).
148.2 FCRA § 603(x), 15 U.S.C. § 1681a(x), *added by* Pub. L. No. 108-159 § 611 (2003). Eligible self-regulatory organizations are those within the definition of § 3(a)(26) of the Securities Exchange Act of 1934, 15 U.S.C. § 78a(26), any entity established under title I of the Sarbanes-Oxley Act of 2002, 15 U.S.C. §§ 7211-7218, any board of trade designated by the Commodity Futures Trading Commission, and any futures association registered with such Commission. FCRA § 603(x)(3), 15 U.S.C. § 1681a(x)(3).
148.3 FCRA §§ 603(x)(D)(i)-(iii), 15 U.S.C. §§ 1681a(x)(D)(i)–(iii) The provision further allows for those disclosures required by law and those disclosures to governmental agencies permitted by section 608 (15 U.S.C. § 1681f). *Id.* at §§ 603(x)(iv), (v), 15 U.S.C. §§ 1681a(x)(iv), (v).
148.4 FCRA § 603(x)(2), 15 U.S.C. § 1681a(x)(2).

Add to text at end of subsection:

However, those agencies that qualify as consumer reporting agencies and that compile and maintain files on consumers relating to their employment history will now also qualify as nationwide specialty consumer reporting agencies, a new subclass of agency under the FCRA.[153.1]

153.1 FCRA § 603(w), 15 U.S.C. § 1681a(w), *added by* Pub. L. No. 108-159 § 111 (2003).

2.4 Statutory Exemptions to Definition of Consumer Report

Page 41

2.4.2 Information Shared by Affiliates

Replace sentence containing note 233 with:

However, the 2003 revisions to the FCRA allow consumers to prohibit an affiliate from using information for solicitation for marketing purposes when that information avoids being a consumer report due to the affiliate exception[233] and allowed the right to opt out of such solicitations that lasts for five years and can be renewed.[233.1] However, the new provision dilutes the opt-out right by exempting a number of solicitations, including solicitations by an entity that has a pre-existing business relationship with the consumer, solicitations to facilitate communications to an individual to whom the entity provides employment benefit or similar services, and solicitations to perform services on behalf of an affiliate.[233.2]

233 Pub. L. No. 108-159 § 214(a)(2) (2003), adding § 624. The person must clearly and conspicuously disclose to the consumer that the information may be used for making solicitations and must provide the consumer with an opportunity to opt out and a simple method for doing so. § 624(a)(1).
233.1 FCRA § 624(a)(3).
233.2 § 624(a)(4). However, if using information on behalf of an affiliate, the person may not send solicitations on such affiliate's behalf if the consumer has opted out of marketing solicitations by that affiliate. § 624(a)(4)(C).

Page 43

2.4.5 Conveying Decision to Party Who Requested That Creditor Extend Credit to Consumer

Addition to notes 252, 253.

252 *Replace "15 U.S.C. § 1681a(d)(C)" with*: 15 U.S.C. § 1681a(d)(2)(C).
253 *Replace "15 U.S.C. § 1681a(d)(C)" with*: 15 U.S.C. § 1681a(d)(2)(C).

2.5 The Consumer Reporting Agency

Page 48

2.5.7 State and Local Government Agencies

Add to text at end of subsection:

States and their respective agencies are protected by sovereign immunity. Under the Eleventh Amendment of the U.S. Constitution, states, as sovereigns, are immune from suit in federal court absent consent or a valid abrogation of that immunity by Congress.[309.1] This immunity extends to state agencies as well.[309.2] Since Congress enacted the FCRA under the Commerce Clause, it was not empowered to abrogate a state's Eleventh Amendment immunity through the FCRA.[309.3] As a result, neither a state nor its officers acting in their official capacities may

§ 2.5.8 *Fair Credit Reporting / 2004 Supplement*

be held liable for money damages. However, injunctive relief may be available against state officials when they are sued in their official capacity.[309.4]

309.1 *See* Kimel v. Florida Bd. of Regents, 528 U.S. 62 (2000); O'Diah v. New York City, 2002 WL 1941179 (S.D.N.Y. Aug. 21, 2002).
309.2 Puerto Rico Aqueduct & Sewer Auth. v. Metcalf & Eddy, Inc., 506 U.S. 139 (1993).
309.3 *See* Seminole Tribe of Florida v. Florida, 517 U.S. 44 (1996); O'Diah v. New York City, 2002 WL 1941179 (S.D.N.Y. Aug. 21, 2002)
309.4 *Ex Parte* Young, 209 U.S. 123, 159–160; 28 S. Ct. 441, 52 L. Ed. 714 (1908).

2.5.8 "Nationwide" Reporting Agencies

Add to text at end of subsection's third paragraph:

As revised by the FACTA, the FCRA explicitly defines "resellers"[314.1] and designates specific responsibilities for such agencies.

314.1 Pub. L. No. 108-159 § 111 (2003), adding FCRA § 603(u), 15 U.S.C. § 1681a(u).

Add to text at end of subsection:

The FACTA of 2003 imposed new obligations that are specific to nationwide agencies, including obligations to insert fraud and active military duty alerts to consumer files;[318.1] to refer alerts to other such agencies;[318.2] review complaints of inaccuracy compiled by and transmitted by the FTC,[318.3] provide free annual disclosures of consumer reports to consumers,[318.4] coordinate consumer complaints of identity theft and requesting fraud alerts or blocks,[318.5] and report annually to the FTC on consumer identity theft complaints and fraud alerts.[318.6] Nationwide consumer reporting agencies are now also specifically prohibited from using corporate or technological means to try to circumvent these new responsibilities.[318.7]

The FACTA also created a new category called "nationwide specialty consumer reporting agencies," defined as consumer reporting agencies that compile and maintain files on a nationwide basis relating to consumers' medical records or payments, residential or tenant histories, check-writing histories, employment histories, or insurance claims.[318.8] The significance of being a nationwide specialty consumer reporting agency is that such agencies, like nationwide general consumer reporting agencies,[318.9] must provide a free credit report.[318.10]

318.1 FCRA §§ 605A(a)–(c), *added by* Pub. L. No. 108-159 § 112 (2003). This provision will become effective on December 1, 2004. 16 C.F.R. § 602.1(c)(3)(i), *added by* 69 Fed. Reg. 6526–31 (Feb. 5, 2004).
318.2 FCRA § 605A(e).
318.3 FCRA § 609(e)(3), 15 U.S.C. § 1681g(e)(3), *added by* Pub. L. No. 108-159 § 313(a) (2003). This provision became effective on March 31, 2004. 16 C.F.R. § 602.1(c)(2)(iv), *added by* 69 Fed. Reg. 6526–31 (Feb. 5, 2004). Nationwide specialty consumer reporting agencies must also provide free annual reports. *Id.*
318.4 FCRA § 611(a), 15 U.S.C. § 1681j(a), *as amended by* Pub. L. No. 108-159 § 211(a)(2) (2003).
318.5 FCRA § 621(f)(1), 15 U.S.C. § 1681s(f)(1), *added by* Pub. L. No. 108-159 § 153 (2003). This provision will become effective on December 1, 2004. 16 C.F.R. § 602.1(c)(3)(v), *added by* 69 Fed. Reg. 6526–31 (Feb. 5, 2004).
318.6 *Id.*
318.7 FCRA § 629, *added by* Pub. L. No. 108-159 § 211(b) (2003).
318.8 Pub. L. No. 108-159 § 111 (2003), adding FCRA § 603(w), 15 U.S.C. § 1681a(w).
318.9 FCRA § 603(p), 15 U.S.C. § 1681a(p).
318.10 15 U.S.C. § 1681j(a)(1)(C), *added by* Pub. L. No. 108-159 § 211(a)(2) (2003). The FTC is to issue regulations to establish a mechanism through which consumers can obtain reports from nationwide specialty consumer reporting agencies. *Id.*

2.6 Examples of Consumer Reporting Agencies

Page 49

2.6.1 Credit Bureaus, Inspection Bureaus, and Medical Information, Tenant Screening, and Check Approval Agencies

Add to text at end of subsection:

The 2003 revisions to the FCRA created a new category called "nationwide specialty consumer reporting agencies," defined as consumer reporting agencies that compile and maintain files on a nationwide basis relating to consumers' medical records or payments,

Scope: Consumer Reports and Consumer Reporting Agencies / 2004 Supplement § 2.6.3

residential or tenant histories, check-writing histories, employment histories, or insurance claims.[324.1] The significance of being a nationwide specialty consumer reporting agency is that such agencies, like nationwide general consumer reporting agencies,[324.2] must provide a free credit report.[324.3]

- 324.1 Pub. L. No. 108-159 § 111 (2003), adding FCRA § 603(w), 15 U.S.C. § 1681a(w).
- 324.2 FCRA § 603(p), 15 U.S.C. § 1681a(p).
- 324.3 FCRA § 612(a)(1)(C), 15 U.S.C. § 1681j(a)(1)(C), *added by* Pub. L. No. 108-159 § 211(a)(2) (2003). The FTC is to issue regulations to establish a mechanism through which consumers can obtain reports from nationwide specialty consumer reporting agencies. *Id.*

2.6.2 Resellers of Consumer Reports

Replace last sentence of subsection's first paragraph with:

But to the extent to which these resellers buy and sell a consumer report, they must comply with all relevant FCRA requirements.[325] Resellers are obligated to comply only with provisions applicable to resellers and are not liable for more general duties of accuracy and reinvestigation imposed on consumer reporting agencies.

- 325 *Retain as in main edition.*
  Add: Lewis v. Ohio Prof'l Elec. Network L.L.C., 248 F. Supp. 2d 693 (S.D. Ohio 2003); Myers v. Bennett Law Offices, 238 F. Supp. 2d 1196 (D. Nev. 2002).

Add to text at end of subsection's first paragraph:

Responding to this growing trend, the FACTA of 2003 explicitly defined "reseller"[325.1] and specified those obligations of consumer reporting agencies from which resellers are exempt or for which they have modified responsibilities.

- 325.1 Pub. L. No. 108-159 § 111 (2003), adding FCRA § 603(u), 15 U.S.C. § 1681a(u).

Replace sentence containing note 327 and rest of text in subsection's second paragraph with:

The Act now specifically provides that the general reinvestigation requirements applicable to ordinary consumer reporting agencies do not apply to resellers.[327] Nonetheless, resellers will now have specific reinvestigation responsibilities of their own. A reseller that receives a notice from a consumer about an item in the reseller's report must investigate the item to determine whether or not it is incomplete or inaccurate as a result of some act or omission by the reseller.[328] If the reseller determines that the information was its responsibility, the reseller must correct or delete the information in the consumer's report within twenty days of receiving the original notice of dispute.[329] If, however, the item is the result of someone else's act or omission, the reseller need only convey the consumer's notice of the dispute to the agency that originally provided the information.[329.1] The FCRA extends the responsibility of agencies to reinvestigate consumer information by requiring them to reinvestigate upon notice from a reseller that a consumer has disputed the item.[329.2] The agency must then report the results of its reinvestigation back to the reseller, who must then reconvey the results back to the consumer.[329.3] This provision basically treats the reseller as a consumer for purposes of the agency's reinvestigation responsibilities.

- 327 FCRA § 611(f)(1), 15 U.S.C. § 1681i(f)(1), *added by* Pub. L. No. 108-159, § 316(b) (2003).
- 328 FCRA § 611(f)(2), 15 U.S.C. § 1681i(f)(2), *added by* Pub. L. No. 108-159, § 316(b) (2003); 16 C.F.R. § 602.1(c)(3)(xviii), *added by* 69 Fed. Reg. 6526–31 (Feb. 5, 2004).
- 329 *Id.* at § 611(f)(2)(B)(i), 15 U.S.C. § 1681i(f)(2)(b)(i).
- 329.1 *Id.* at § 611(f)(2)(B)(ii), 15 U.S.C. § 1681i(f)(2)(b)(ii).
- 329.2 FCRA § 611(a), 15 U.S.C. § 1681i(a), *as amended by* Pub. L. No. 108-159, § 316 (2003). This provision will become effective on December 1, 2004. 16 C.F.R. § 602.1(c)(3)(xvii), *added by* 69 Fed. Reg. 6526–31 (Feb. 5, 2004).
- 329.3 FCRA § 611(f), 15 U.S.C. 1681i(f), *added by* Pub. L. No. 108-159, § 316 (2003).

2.6.3 Creditors as Reporting Agencies

Addition to note 342.

- 342 Daniels v. Carter One Bank, 39 Fed. Appx. 223; 2002 WL 1363525 (6th Cir. June 21, 2002).

Chapter 3 Furnishing Information to Consumer Reporting Agencies

Page 53

3.1 Introduction

Add to text after subsection's first sentence:

Many of these standards and duties were modified by the FACTA of 2003.[0.1]

    0.1   Fair and Accurate Credit Transactions Act of 2003, Pub. L. No. 108-159 (2003).

Add to text after subsection's fourth paragraph:

The FACTA of 2003 placed additional duties on furnishers, some of which are completely new and many of which relate to existing duties. Such duties include the duty to reinvestigate certain consumer disputes received directly from consumers (§ 3.4.5a, *infra*), the duty of financial institutions to notify consumers when they submit negative information (§ 3.8a, *infra*), and the duty to block unverifiable information (§ 3.11a, *infra*). Additional duties were placed on furnishers with respect to identity theft. These are discussed in Chapter 16, *infra*.

Replace subsection's sixth paragraph with:

The FACTA amended the FCRA to allow consumers to raise disputes about debts with the creditor directly.[0.2] Consumers could do this prior to the amendments, however there was nothing in the FCRA that required the furnisher to respond. Now, however, forthcoming regulations will require furnishers to reinvestigate information disputed and submitted by a consumer to the furnisher directly and to report the results of that reinvestigation to the consumer. (This is discussed in § 3.5.2, *infra*, and in Chapter 13 at § 13.5.1, *infra*.) Nonetheless, since consumers will not be able to enforce the reinvestigation requirement,[0.3] if a dispute is not resolved satisfactorily, it is only by initiating a dispute with the consumer reporting agency under the preexisting provisions that the consumer will trigger the formal FCRA reinvestigation process that provides for a private right of action under the Act. This process will require the participation of the creditor/furnisher and subject the creditor to potential civil liability for which a consumer may bring a cause of action. Disputing information directly with the furnisher can significantly affect the rights of consumers, and no provision is made for private enforcement. For a discussion of disputing information under the Act, see § 3.9, *infra*.

    0.2   15 U.S.C. § 1681s–2(a)(8), Pub. L. No. 108-159, §312(c) (2003). This provision will become effective on December 1, 2004. 16 C.F.R. § 602.1(c)(3)(xiv), *added by* 69 Fed. Reg. 6526–31 (Feb. 5, 2004).

    0.3   *See* 15 U.S.C. § 1681s–2(c)(1), *as amended by* Pub. L. No. 108-159, § 312(e) (2003).

3.2 Creditors and Others Who Furnish Information to Consumer Reporting Agencies

3.2.2 Limitations on Who Is a Furnisher

Page 54

3.2.2.1 Special Rules for Affiliate Sharing

Add to text after sentence containing note 14:

However, the FACTA of 2003 amended the FCRA to exempt, from the definition of "consumer report," communication of transactions or experiences with consumers that are shared between and among affiliates.[14.1] A consumer may opt out of the use by an affiliate of this exempt information when the information is used to market its products or services.

§ 3.2.2.2 *Fair Credit Reporting / 2004 Supplement*

Affiliates must also notify the consumer both of the possibility that an affiliate may use the consumer's information for marketing and of the consumer's right to opt out of such use.[14.2]

14.1 15 U.S.C. § 1681s-3, *added by* Pub. L. No. 108-159, § 214 (2003). *See* § 2.4.2, *supra*.
14.2 15 U.S.C. § 1681s-3, *added by* Pub. L. No. 108-159, § 214 (2003). Certain exemptions apply. *See* 15 U.S.C. § 1681s-3(a)(4).

Page 55

3.2.2.2 Direct Selling of Information Not Covered

Replace note 17 with:

17 *See* Chapter 16, *infra*.

3.2.2.3 State Laws Regarding Furnishers Are Preempted

Add to text before sentence containing note 18:

This preemption of state laws pertaining to furnishers was extended permanently by the FACTA of 2003.[17.1]

17.1 15 U.S.C, § 1681s–2, *as amended by* Pub. L. No. 108-159 (2003). *See* § 10.4.4, *infra*.

3.3 Furnishing Information to Consumer Reporting Agencies

3.3.1 Information Is Usually Furnished Electronically

Add to text after last sentence of subsection's first paragraph:

The credit reporting agencies report that up to 80 percent of their subscribers or furnishers have converted to the Metro 2 reporting system. However, consumer advocates have questioned whether the 80-percent figure is based on the data being reported and not the percentage of furnishers who submit the data.

Page 56

3.3.2 Metro 2: The Standard Automated Format for Furnishing Information to Consumer Reporting Agencies

Add to text after sentence containing note 26:

CDIA's website also contains valuable information about Metro 2, including instructions on how to access the Metro 2 format and frequently asked questions and answers about Metro 2 reporting.[26.1]

26.1 *See* www.cdiaonline.org/data.cfm.

3.3.3 The Metro 2 Format Used by Creditors

Page 58

3.3.3.3 The Base Segment Contains Information About the Consumer and the Debt

Replace note 33 with:

33 Equal Credit Opportunity Act, 15 U.S.C. §§ 1691–1691f. *See generally* National Consumer Law Center, Credit Discrimination (3d ed. 2002 and Supp.).

Page 60

3.3.3.7 Common Errors

Addition to note 45.

45 *Replace NCLC citation with*: *See generally* National Consumer Law Center, Credit Discrimination § 9.4.2.1 (3d ed. 2002 and Supp.).

Furnishing Information to Consumer Reporting Agencies / 2004 Supplement § 3.3.4.2b

Page 62

3.3.3.12 Metro 2 and Bankruptcy

Add note 51.1 after first sentence in subsection's third paragraph.

51.1 See § 7.8.4.10.2, *supra*, for additional discussion on reports relating to bankruptcy.

3.3.4 The Furnishing of Disputed Information Is Restricted

Page 63

3.3.4.2 Debt Collectors Sometimes May Not Furnish Disputed Information and Always Must Note When It Is Disputed

Addition to notes 54, 57.

54 Delete Remsburg.
57 *Add at end of Sullivan citation*: *aff'd sub nom.* Trans Union, L.L.C. v. FTC, 295 F.3d 42 (D.C. Cir. 2002).

Page 64

Add new subsections after § 3.3.4.2.

3.3.4.2a Debt Collectors Must Notify Creditors of Fraudulent Debt

The FACTA of 2003 imposes new notification responsibilities on debt collectors. As of December 1, 2004, once a consumer notifies a debt collector that a debt may be fraudulent or may have resulted from identity theft, the debt collector must notify the creditor of that allegation and must provide the consumer with all information about the debt to which the consumer would be entitled if the consumer were in fact the liable party.[64.1] It is a provision that appears to require the collector to comply with the debt validation provisions of the Fair Debt Collection Practices Act.[64.2] Consumers may enforce this provision,[64.3] but states are preempted from regulating the required conduct mandated by this provision in the FACTA.[64.4]

3.3.4.2b Debt Collectors Must Use Creditor's Date of Account Delinquency

The FCRA was amended by the FACTA to provide rules regarding the date of an account's delinquency for reporting purposes. It specifies how debt collectors should designate the date to ensure that the date of delinquency precedes the date the creditor placed the account for collection,[64.5] which should curb the reporting of obsolete information. If no date can be determined by these procedures, then the furnisher must establish and follow reasonable procedures to ensure that the date reported precedes the date on which the account is placed for collection, charged to profit or loss, or subjected to any similar action.[64.6] A problem may exist here in that some collectors will claim a stale account was never placed for collection or charged to profit or loss until long after it actually went delinquent. Again, this new date designation requirement only exists under the section of the FCRA (15 U.S.C. § 1681s–2(a)) that is not subject to a private right of action under the FCRA, but the duty should be enforceable against debt collectors regulated by the Fair Debt Collection Practices Act.[64.7] Sates are preempted from regulating the subject matter covered.[64.8]

64.1 15 U.S.C. § 1681m(g), *added by* Pub. L. No. 108-159, § 155 (2003); 16 C.F.R. § 602.1(c)(3)(viii), *added by* 69 Fed. Reg. 6526–31 (Feb. 5, 2004).
64.2 15 U.S.C. § 1692g.
64.3 This is assuming that the limitation of liability provision of the new § 615((h)(8) applies only to that subsection.
64.4 15 U.S.C. § 1681t(b)(5)(F).
64.5 15 U.S.C. § 1681s–2(a)(5), *as amended by* Pub. L. No. 108-159, § 312 (2003).
64.6 *Id. See* National Consumer Law Center, Fair Debt Collection § 5.7 (4th ed. 2000 and Supp.).
64.7 15 U.S.C. § 1681g. *See generally* National Consumer Law Center, Fair Debt Collection Ch. 5 (4th ed. 2000 and Supp.).
64.8 15 U.S.C. § 1681t(b)(1)(F).

§ 3.3.5   *Fair Credit Reporting / 2004 Supplement*

3.3.5 Other Restrictions on What Information May Be Furnished to a Consumer Reporting Agency

Page 65

3.3.5.2 Discrimination and Retaliation for Exercising Rights Is Prohibited

Replace note 88 with:

88   15 U.S.C. § 1691(a); 12 C.F.R. § 202.2(m). *See generally* National Consumer Law Center, Credit Discrimination § 9.4 (3d ed. 2002 and Supp.).

3.3.5.4 State Law Restrictions on Public Record Information

Page 66

3.3.5.4.1 Restrictions reporting cosigners

Replace subsection's second paragraph with:

However, the FACTA of 2003 permanently extended the preemption provisions contained in the 1996 amendments to the FCRA regarding requirements placed on those who furnish information to consumer reporting agencies.[95]

95   15 U.S.C. § 1681t, *as amended by* Pub. L. No. 108-159, § 711(3)(A). The former sunset provision that would have ended preemption of state laws governing furnishers, 15 U.S.C. § 1681t(d)(2), was deleted by the FACTA of 2003. *See* § 10.4.4, *infra*.

96   *Reserved.*
97   *Reserved.*
98   *Reserved.*

3.3.5.4.2 Restrictions on child support debts

Delete subsection's last sentence.

Page 67

3.3.5.4.3 Special state requirements

Replace note 109 with:

109   *See* § 10.4.4, *infra*.

3.4 Standards of Accuracy For Furnishers

3.4.1 Introduction

Replace subsection's first sentence with:

The Fair Credit Reporting Act and the FACTA of 2003 establish minimum standards of accuracy for creditors and other furnishers initially providing information about consumers to consumer reporting agencies.

Add to text after the first sentence:

The FACTA of 2003 amended the accuracy standard for creditors that furnish information to credit reporting agencies.[110.1]

110.1   15 U.S.C. § 1681s–2, *as amended by* Pub. L. No. 108-159, § 312(b) (2003). *See* §§ 3.4.2 and 3.4.3, *infra*.

Addition to note 111.

111   Riley v. General Motors Acceptance Corp., 226 F. Supp. 2d 1316 (S.D. Ala. 2002); Vazquez-Garcia v. Trans Union de Puerto Rico, 222 F. Supp. 2d 150 (D. P.R. 2002); Hasvold v. First USA Bank, N.A., 194 F. Supp. 2d 1228 (D. Wyo. 2002).
     Add before semi-colon: , *as amended by* Pub. L. No. 108-159 (2003).

3.4.2 General Duty to Report Accurately

Replace subsection's first paragraph and first sentence of second paragraph with:

The FCRA previously prohibited a furnisher from furnishing information that the furnisher "knows or consciously avoids knowing is inaccurate."[115] This standard was changed by the FACTA of 2003 to prohibit a furnisher from furnishing information that the furnisher "knows or has reasonable cause to believe" is inaccurate.[115.1] The term "reasonable cause to believe" is defined as "having specific knowledge, other than solely allegations by the consumer, that

Furnishing Information to Consumer Reporting Agencies / 2004 Supplement § 3.4.3

would cause a reasonable person to have substantial doubts about the accuracy of the information."[115.2] This standard, however, is not applicable to furnishers who maintain a special address for notification of inaccuracies.[115.3] The FCRA also prohibits furnishers from furnishing information that is in fact inaccurate, but only if the consumer has complained.[115.4] This provision was not amended by the FACTA.

The two accuracy provisions must also be read in conjunction with the subsection that immediately follows them establishing a duty to promptly correct and update furnished information determined to be incomplete or inaccurate, a provision that also was not amended by the FACTA.[115.5] This duty is applicable to furnishers that regularly and in the ordinary course of business furnish information to credit reporting agencies.[115.6]

115 *Id.*, prior to amendment by Pub. L., No. 108-159, § 312(b) (2003).
115.1 15 U.S.C. § 1681s–2(a)(1)(A), *as amended by* Pub. L. No. 108-159, § 312(b) (2003). This provision will become effective on December 1, 2004. 16 C.F.R. § 602.1(c)(3)(xiv), *added by* 69 Fed. Reg. 6526–31 (Feb. 5, 2004).
115.2 15 U.S.C. § 1681s–2(a)(1)(D), *added by* Pub. L. No. 108-159, § 312(b) (2003).
115.3 15 U.S.C. § 1681s–2(a)(1)(C). *See* § 3.4.4, *infra.*
115.4 15 U.S.C. § 1681s–2.
115.5 15 U.S.C. § 1681s–2(a)(2)(B).
115.6 *Id.*

Page 68

Delete from fourth sentence of subsection's second paragraph:

While the specific standard of care is not stated

Add to text after note 119:

The FACTA also requires furnishers to assist in preventing the reporting of identity-theft-related debts by requiring them to have reasonable procedures to prevent the refurnishing of information that an agency has blocked because it resulted from identity theft[119.1] and by prohibiting furnishers from refurnishing information that a consumer has identified to the furnisher at the address specified by such furnisher as resulting from identity theft.[119.2] These provisions will become effective on December 1, 2004.[119.3]

119.1 15 U.S.C. § 1681s–2(a)(6)(A). *See also* 16.6.1a.2.2, *infra.*
119.2 15 U.S.C. § 1681s–2(a)(6)(B). *See also* 16.6.1a.2.2, *infra.*
119.3 16 C.F.R. § 602.1(c)(3)(vii), *added by* 69 Fed. Reg. 6526–31 (Feb. 5, 2004).

Replace § 3.4.3 with:

3.4.3 Accuracy and Integrity Regulations for Furnishers

The FACTA of 2003 requires federal agencies that enforce the FCRA to establish guidelines for furnishers regarding the "accuracy and integrity" of furnished information. The agencies must also issue regulations requiring furnishers to establish reasonable policies and procedures for implementing those guidelines.[123] It is unclear how the term "integrity" will be interpreted by the agencies and the extent to which it will be supplemental to the completeness duty for furnishers. By definition, integrity should include the soundness and completeness of information.[124] While Congress modified the standard for furnishers with respect to information they provide to credit reporting agencies, it did not provide for private enforcement of these new standards,[125] and states are preempted from regulating the subject matter of the provision.[125.1]

123 15 U.S.C. § 1681s–2(e), *added by* Pub. L. No. 108-159, § 312 (2003). This provision will become effective on December 1, 2004. 16 C.F.R. § 602.1(c)(3)(xiv), *added by* 69 Fed. Reg. 6526–31 (Feb. 5, 2004). *See also* § 16.6.1a.3.2, *infra.*
124 The Merriam-Webster definition of integrity includes "incorruptibility; and unimpaired condition, and the quality of being complete." *See* www.merriam-webster.com/cgi-bin/dictionary?book=Dictionary&va=integrity.
125 15 U.S.C. § 1681s–2(c)(2), *added by* Pub. L. No. 108-159, § 312 (2003). However, consumers may bring an action against furnishers for behavior that independently violates § 623(b). *Id.*
125.1 15 U.S.C. § 1681t(b)(1)(F). *See also* § 3.14.5, *infra.*

§ 3.4.4

Fair Credit Reporting / 2004 Supplement

3.4.4 Accuracy When Creditor Clearly and Conspicuously Maintains a Special Address for the Consumer to Give Notification of Inaccurate Information

Page 69

Replace "it no longer matters whether future reports are 'knowingly' inaccurate" in first sentence of subsection's third paragraph, with:

it no longer matters whether the furnisher "knows or has reason to know" that future reports are inaccurate.[127.1]

127.1 *See* 15 U.S.C. §§ 1681s–2(a)(1)(A), (D), *as amended by* Pub. L. No. 108-159, § 312(b) (2003). This amendment will become effective December 1, 2004. 16 C.F.R. § 602.1(c)(3)(xiv), *added by* 69 Fed. Reg. 6526–31 (Feb. 5, 2004).

Add to text at end of first sentence of subsection's fourth paragraph:

or that the furnisher has reasonable cause to believe is false.[127.2]

127.2 *Id.*

Add to text after § 3.4.4:

3.4.4a Consumers May Dispute Furnished Information Directly with the Furnisher Under the FACTA

The prior version of the FCRA had no provision by which a consumer could formally dispute an inaccurate item of information and request a reinvestigation directly with the furnisher; rather, the consumer had to dispute the item with the agency, which was then required by the FCRA to notify the furnisher.[131.1] The FCRA, prior to amendment by the FACTA, required the furnisher to reinvestigate the item only upon receiving the agency's notice; a notice from the consumer was irrelevant and ineffective.[131.2] Now a consumer may trigger a furnisher's responsibility to reinvestigate by disputing the item directly with the furnisher when the circumstances of the dispute meet the conditions of to-be-prescribed regulations.[131.3] This new provision specifically provides, however, that such a reinvestigation responsibility will not be initiated by a notice from or prepared by a credit repair organization,[131.4] and furnishers need not respond to "frivolous" or "irrelevant" disputes.[131.5] However, if the furnisher considers the dispute frivolous, the furnisher must notify the consumer within five business days of this determination, the reason it considers the dispute frivolous, and what information the consumer must provide to convert the dispute into one that will trigger a reinvestigation.[131.6] The furnisher must investigate the dispute and report the results back to the consumer in the same time frame allowed credit reporting agencies for reinvestigation.[131.7] If the furnisher finds the information to be inaccurate, the furnisher must correct the information with each agency to which the furnisher furnished the information.[131.8] As with the pre-existing reinvestigation responsibilities that arise upon notice from an agency, states are preempted from regulating the subject matter of this provision;[131.9] however, unlike those responsibilities, under this law it appears that consumers may not privately enforce this provision against furnishers.[131.10]

To be safe, consumers, not their lawyers, should send their own disputes. A problem may occur when information has previously been disputed but not properly investigated. The consumer will still need the relief, but the furnisher can consider a second investigation request frivolous and refuse to perform any new investigation. A significant concern is that this requirement only exists under § 1681s–2(a), which has been interpreted to free it from enforcement by any private right of action against furnishers who simply refuse to comply.[131.11] This should, however, not affect private enforcement under § 1681s–2(b). State UDAP laws might also be a source by which to attach a remedy to violations of this duty.

131.1 15 U.S.C. § 1681i(a)(2).
131.2 15 U.S.C. § 1681s–2(b).
131.3 15 U.S.C. § 1681s–2(a)(8), *added by* Pub. L. No. 108-159, § 312 (2003). The effective date for the new regulations is December 1, 2003. 16 C.F.R. § 602.1(c)(3)(xiv), *added by* 69 Fed. Reg. 6526–31 (Feb. 5, 2004).
131.4 15 U.S.C. § 1681s–2(a)(8)(G). Even notices from or prepared by organizations that are not defined to be credit repair organizations under the Credit Repair Organizations Act (16 U.S.C. § 1679a) because of their non-profit status will not trigger a reinvestigation. *Id.*

Furnishing Information to Consumer Reporting Agencies / 2004 Supplement § 3.8a

131.5 Such a determination may arise by reason of the consumer's failure to provide sufficient information to allow the furnisher to investigate the disputed information, 15 U.S.C. § 1681s–2(a)(8)(F)(i)(I), or when the submitted dispute reiterates a dispute made by the consumer to either the furnisher or an agency and which the furnisher has already reinvestigated, 15 U.S.C. § 1681s–2(a)(8)(F)(i)(II).
131.6 15 U.S.C. § 1681t(a)(8)(F).
131.7 15 U.S.C. § 1681t (a)(8)(E), *added by* Pub. L. No. 108-159, § 312 (2003).
131.8 *Id.*
131.9 15 U.S.C. § 1681t (b)(1)(F).
131.10 15 U.S.C. § 1681t (c)(1), *added by* Pub. L. No. 108-159, § 312 (2003).
131.11 Pursuant to the limitation of liability provisions in § 1681s–2(c), *as amended by* Pub. L. No. 108-159, § 312(e) (2003).

Replace subsection heading with:

3.4.5 Practical Advice for Informally Disputing Accuracy with Furnisher

Page 70

Replace "or consciously avoids knowing" in sentence containing note 133 with:

or has reasonable cause to believe[132.1]

132.1 15 U.S.C. §§ 1681s–2(a)(1)(A), (D), *amended by* Pub. L. No. 108-159, § 312(b) (2003). This provision will become effective on December 1, 2004. 16 C.F.R. § 602.1(c)(3)(xiv), *added by* 69 Fed. Reg. 6526–31 (Feb. 5, 2004).

3.5 Furnishers Have Duty to Correct and Update Furnished Information

Page 71

3.5.2 Disputing Inaccurate Information with the Creditor

Add to text at beginning of subsection:

A furnisher of information is liable under the FCRA only after the consumer notifies a reporting agency of the dispute, the dispute is conveyed to the furnisher by the agency, and the furnisher does not conduct a reasonable investigation. The furnisher's knowledge of the dispute does not impose FCRA liability.[136.1]

136.1 Stafford v. Cross Country Bank, 262 F. Supp. 2d 776 (W.D. Ky. 2003); Whisenant v. First Nat'l Bank & Trust Co., 258 F. Supp. 2d 1312 (N.D. Okla. 2003).

Page 72

3.5.4 Universal Data Form May Be Used to Make Corrections

Add to text at end of subsection:

Any settlement agreement in which a creditor must change or delete an account should include a requirement that the creditor use the Universal Data Form to correct or change the incorrect information on the account.[142.1]

142.1 *See* § 13.5.4.4, *infra*.

Page 74

Add new section after § 3.8.

3.8a Financial Institution Furnishers Required to Notify Customers of Negative Information Furnished to Agencies

Beginning December 1, 2004, the FCRA as amended by the FACTA of 2003 will require starting that a financial institution notify a customer that it is furnishing negative information about that customer;[151.1] however, financial institutions may take advantage of a safe harbor provision.[151.2] Once notified about an account, it appears there is no other requirement entitling the consumer to receive further notices when additional negative information is reported about that account.[151.3] The notice must be given within thirty days of reporting negative information.[151.4] The Federal Reserve Board is to provide a model notice not to exceed thirty words.[151.5] A financial institution may provide the notice without submitting the

§ 3.9 Fair Credit Reporting / 2004 Supplement

negative information.[151.6] This is an unusual means of providing notice since it would not be accurate. The notice may not be included with disclosures under § 127 of the Truth In Lending Act.[151.7] This provision appears to be unenforceable by private consumer actions under this law.[151.8]

- 151.1 15 U.S.C. § 1681s–2(a)(7), *added by* Pub. L. No. 108-159, § 217 (2003); 16 C.F.R. § 602.1(c)(3)(xii), *added by* 69 Fed. Reg. 6526–31 (Feb. 5, 2004).
- 151.2 The safe harbor provision protects the institution from liability if it maintained reasonable compliance policies and procedures or reasonably believed that it was prohibited by law from contacting the consumer. 15 U.S.C. § 1681s–2(a)(7)(F).
- 151.3 15 U.S.C. § 1681s–2 (a)(7)(A)(ii).
- 151.4 15 U.S.C. § 1681s–2 (a)(7)(B)(i).
- 151.5 15 U.S.C. § 1681s–2 (a)(7)(A)(ii).
- 151.6 *Id.*
- 151.7 15 U.S.C. § 1681s–2 (a)(7)(D)(i).
- 151.8 15 U.S.C. § 1681s–2 (c)(1), *as amended by* Pub. L. No. 108-159, § 312 (2003).

3.9 The Formal Credit Reporting Agency Dispute Process Subjects the Furnisher to Obligations Enforceable by the Consumer

Addition to notes 156–158.

- 156 Moline v. Trans Union, 2003 WL 21878728 (N.D. Ill. Aug. 7, 2003) (case dismissed based on plaintiff's failure to allege that credit reporting agency informed furnisher that consumer was disputing his credit information).
  Add at end of Banks citation: *aff'd*, 232 F.3d 888 (4th Cir. 2000) (table, text at 2000 WL 1578331).
- 157 *Replace Banks citation with*: 2000 WL 1682979 (M.D.N.C. June 1, 2000), *aff'd*, 232 F.3d 888 (4th Cir. 2000) (table, text at 2000 WL 1578331).
- 158 Young v. Equifax Credit Inf. Serv., Inc., 294 F.3d 631 (5th Cir. 2002); Cook v. Experian Inf. Solutions, Inc., 2002 WL 31718624 (N.D. Ill. 2002).

Add to text at end of section's second paragraph:

Testimony in cases suggests that credit reporting agencies receive tens of thousands of consumer disputes each week (one agency reportedly receives between 35,000 and 50,000 per week). Approximately 80 percent of such complaints are written.[160.1] Some agencies reportedly have procedures that require quotas for the number of consumer disputes agency employees must process. One former credit reporting agency employee testified that employees were required to process one dispute every four minutes in order to meet quotas.[160.2]

Each agency has a different process for handling disputed information, but all three collaborated through CDIA to create an automated on-line reinvestigation processing system: "E-OSCAR,"[160.3] touted by the credit reporting industry as a state-of-the-art solution for processing ACDVs and AUDs. However, it appears that use of this automated system has resulted in a verification, not reinvestigation process, in which written disputes from consumers, often containing a detailed letter and other documentation are translated into a two digit code that the credit reporting agency employee believes best describes the dispute. The code is sent to the furnisher for verification. A more thorough reinvestigation in which documents are reviewed appears to be the exception rather than the rule.

- 160.1 *See* Deposition of Eileen Little, Evantash v. G.E. Capital Mortgage, Civ. Action No. 02-CV-1188 (E.D. Pa. Jan. 25, 2003), reprinted on companion CD-Rom, *infra*.
- 160.2 Deposition of Regina Sorenson, Fleischer v. Trans Union, Civ. Action No. 02-71301 (E.D. Mich. Jan 9, 2002), reprinted on CD-Rom, *infra*.
- 160.3 Online Solution for Complete and Accurate Reporting. *See* www.cdiaonline.org/eoscar/eoscarintro.cfm.

Add to text after first sentence of subsection's third paragraph:

Credit reporting agencies routinely respond to requests for reinvestigations by stating that they have received the request from the consumer and that that they will contact the furnisher or source of the disputed information and send results of the reinvestigation to the consumer. Once the disputed information is purportedly reinvestigated the credit reporting agencies then send generic and uninformative letters stating that an investigation has been made, without including any details as to whom they have contacted and what information was obtained or relied upon for a final determination. This information is not unimportant, however, because it reflects the fact that the credit reporting agency received the dispute, that the dispute was in fact forwarded to the furnisher, and that a decision was made with respect to the accuracy or completeness of the disputed information.

3.10 Consumer Reporting Agency Investigation Must Involve Furnisher

Add to text after second sentence of section's second paragraph:

According to one national credit reporting agency, 52 percent of its data furnishers participate in the Automated Consumer Dispute Verification (ACDV) system.[166.1]

166.1 Statement of Harry Gambill, Chief Executive Officer, Trans Union, L.L.C., before the Subcommittee on Financial Institutions and Consumer Credit, June 4, 2003.

3.11 Furnisher's Duties Upon Notification of Dispute by the Reporting Agency

3.11.1 Furnisher Must Conduct Reasonable Investigation

Add to text after first sentence of subsection's second paragraph:

At least one defendant argued unsuccessfully that a furnisher's duty to "investigate" has no qualitative component to it. Their theory, that "any" investigation is sufficient, no matter how cursory, was rejected by a district court in Virginia in an unpublished opinion.[170.1]

170.1 Johnson v. Equifax Information, Civ. Action No. 3:02CV523 (E.D. Va. Feb. 24, 2003) (unpublished opinion).

Addition to note 172.

172 Johnson v. MBNA Am. Bank, NA, 357 F.3d 426 (4th Cir. 2004); Ayers v. Equifax Inf. Servs., 2003 WL 23142201 (E.D. Va. Dec. 16, 2003); Buxton v. Equifax Info. Servs., 2003 WL 22844245 (N.D. Ill. Dec. 1, 2003) (when furnisher timely changed its records in response to the dispute, investigation was reasonable as a matter of law); Zotta v. Nationscredit Fin. Servs., 297 F. Supp. 2d 1196 (E.D. Mo. 2003); Evantash v. G.E. Capital Mortgage Serv., Inc., 2003 WL 22844198 (E.D. Pa. Nov. 25, 2003); Wade v. Equifax, 2003 WL 22089694 (N.D. Ill. 2003) (when furnisher confirmed to reporting agency that last name on the account it was reporting was not the plaintiff's, investigation was adequate); Betts v. Equifax Credit Info. Servs., Inc., 245 F. Supp. 2d 1130 (W.D. Wash. 2003).

Add to text after note 173:

The 4th Circuit upheld the requirement that the investigation must be reasonable: "We therefore hold that § 1681s–2(b)(1) requires creditors, after receiving notice of a consumer dispute from a credit reporting agency, to conduct a reasonable investigation of their records to determine whether the disputed information can be verified."[173.1]

173.1 Johnson v. MBNA Am. Bank, NA, 357 F.3d 426, 431 (4th Cir. 2003). *See also* Agosta v. Inovision, Inc., 2003 WL 22999213, at *5 (E.D. Pa. Dec. 16, 2003); Buxton v. Equifax Credit Info. Services, Inc., 2003 WL 22844245 (N.D. Ill. Dec. 1, 2003); Wade v. Equifax, 2003 WL 22089694 (N.D. Ill. Sept. 8, 2003); Betts v. Equifax Credit Info. Servs., Inc., 245 F. Supp. 2d 1130 (W.D. Wash. 2003); Olwell v. Med. Info. Bureau, 2003 WL 79035 (D. Minn. Jan. 7, 2003); Kronsted v. Equifax, 2001 WL 44124783 (W.D. Wis. Dec. 14, 2001); Bruce v. First U.S.A. Bank, 103 F. Supp. 2d 1135 (E.D. Mo. 2000).

Add to text at end of subsection:

Some furnishers rely on third parties to both gather information from public sources and conduct the reinvestigations of the gathered information, asserting that their selection of a third party vendor is reasonable. This should not, however, relieve the furnisher of its duty to conduct a reasonable reinvestigation.

It has been reported that some credit reporting agencies reject dispute letters from consumers because they are erroneously believed to come from credit repair companies. Credit reporting agencies usually have rules or protocols for handling disputes from credit repair companies. However, if such rules inappropriately exclude legitimate disputes from consumers, it raises questions about whether the agencies are violating the FCRA requirements with respect to reinvestigations. Some credit reporting agencies send consumers letters suggesting that the agency received a letter from a third party (that is, credit repair company) and therefore do not have to reinvestigate.

Add new subsections after § 3.11.1.

3.11.1a Agencies Must Notify Furnishers of Reinvestigation Results

The FACTA has added a requirement for any consumer reporting agency that reinvestigates an item of information upon a consumer's dispute. The agencies must now notify the furnisher if the agency deletes or modifies the item of information from the consumer's file because the agency found that information to be inaccurate, incomplete, or unverifiable.[180.1] Such a notice should imply "reasonable cause to believe that the information is inaccurate," thus satisfying the new accuracy standard imposed on furnishers by the FACTA. If such is the case, the furnisher must cease furnishing the information.[180.2]

3.11.1b Agency's Reinvestigation Must Be "Reasonable"

The FACTA revised the FCRA's agency reinvestigation provision, effective December 1, 2004, to provide as follows:

> Subject to subsection (f), if the completeness or accuracy of any item of information contained in a consumer's file at a consumer reporting agency is disputed by the consumer and the consumer notifies the agency directly, or indirectly through a reseller, of such dispute, the agency shall, free of charge, conduct a reasonable reinvestigation to determine whether the disputed information is inaccurate and record the current status of the disputed information, or delete the item from the file in accordance with paragraph (5), before the end of the 30-day period beginning on the date on which the agency receives the notice of the dispute from the consumer or reseller.[180.3]

Accordingly, the FCRA now explicitly provides that the credit reporting agency's reinvestigation of information must be reasonable, a standard lower than that found in § 607 (§ 1681d), which requires "reasonable procedures to assure maximum possible accuracy" in the initial preparation of the consumer report.[180.4] This appears to be an improvement, but there questions about its effect on furnisher investigations under § 1681s–2(b) regarding furnisher reinvestigation, in which the FCRA does not explicitly include the "reasonable" language.

3.11.1c Agencies Must Reinvestigate upon Notice from Reseller

The FCRA was amended by the FACTA to extend, effective December 1, 2004, the responsibilities of agencies to reinvestigate consumer information by requiring them to reinvestigate upon notice from a reseller that a consumer has disputed the item.[180.5] The agency must then report the results of its reinvestigation back to the reseller, who must then reconvey the results back to the consumer.[180.6] This provision basically treats the reseller as a consumer for purposes of the agency's reinvestigation responsibilities. States are preempted only from regulating the time requirements set for the agency's actions.[180.7]

180.1 15 U.S.C. § 1681i(a), *as amended by* Pub. L. No. 108-159, § 313 (2003).
180.2 *See* 15 U.S.C. §§ 1681s–2(a)(1)(A), (D), *as amended by* Pub. L. No. 108-159, § 312(b) (2003); § 3.4.2, *supra.*
180.3 15 U.S.C. § 1681i(a)(1)(A), *as amended by* Pub. L. No. 108-159, §§ 316, 317 (2003) (emphasis added); 16 C.F.R. § 602.1(c)(3)(xviii), *added by* 69 Fed. Reg. 6526–31 (Feb. 5, 2004).
180.4 15 U.S.C. § 1681i (a)(1)(A), *as amended by* Pub. L. No. 108-159, § 317 (2003).
180.5 15 U.S.C. § 1681i (a), *as amended by* Pub. L. No. 108-159, § 316 (2003); 16 C.F.R. § 602.1(c)(3)(xvii), *added by* 69 Fed. Reg. 6526–31 (Feb. 5, 2004). "Reseller" is now defined in 15 U.S.C. § 1681a(u), *added by* Pub. L. No. 108-159, § 111 (2003).
180.6 15 U.S.C. § 1681i (f), *added by* Pub. L. No. 108-159, § 316 (2003).
180.7 15 U.S.C. § 1681s–2(b)(1)(B).

Furnishing Information to Consumer Reporting Agencies / 2004 Supplement § 3.14.2

3.11.2 A Properly Presented Dispute Will Subject a Furnisher to Liability for Conducting an Inadequate Investigation

Addition to note 184.

184 Olwell v. Medical Information Bureau, 2003 WL 79035 (D. Minn. Jan. 7, 2003) (a reasonable jury could find that failure to contact outside sources during reinvestigation was unreasonable).

Add note 186.1 to end of subsection's fourth paragraph.

186.1 Betts v. Equifax Credit Info. Servs., Inc., 245 F. Supp. 2d 1130 (W.D. Wash. 2003).

Page 77

Add new subsection after § 3.11.2.

3.11.3 Furnishers Must Block Unverifiable Information

Under the prior version of the FCRA, once an agency notified a furnisher that a consumer disputed information that the furnisher had reported to the agency, the furnisher had to reinvestigate that item and report the results of the investigation back to the agency.[189.1] Now the furnisher must also take steps to modify, delete or block that information to prevent re-reporting of the inaccurate information.[189.2] Nothing in the FACTA appears to preclude consumers from enforcing this provision.

189.1 15 U.S.C. § 1681s–2(b).
189.2 15 U.S.C. § 1681s–2(b), *as amended by* Pub. L. No. 108-159, § 314 (2003).

3.12 Furnisher Must Report Investigation Results

3.12.1 Time for Investigation and Reporting Results Is Limited

Replace note 190 with:

190 15 U.S.C. § 1681i(a)(1), *as amended by* Pub. L. No. 108-159, § 316(b) (2003).

Add to text after second sentence of subsection's first paragraph:

If, however, the consumer discovered the dispute through a report provided free pursuant to § 1681j(a), the agency has forty-five days in which to complete the investigation.[190.1]

190.1 15 U.S.C. § 1681j(a)(2), *added by* Pub. L. No. 108-159, § 211(a).

Page 79

3.13 Consumer Reporting Agency Use of Furnisher Report

Add note 204.1 after third sentence of subsection's first paragraph.

204.1 The FACTA of 2003 added a provision to the FCRA requiring credit reporting agencies to promptly notify the furnisher that information has been modified or deleted from the file of the consumer. 15 U.S.C. § 1681i (a)(5)(A)(ii), *as amended by* Pub. L. 108-159, § 314(a).

3.14 Creditor and Furnisher Liability for Information Furnished to Consumer Reporting Agencies

3.14.2 No Private Enforcement of FCRA Obligations to Furnish Accurate and Complete Information

Addition to note 205.

205 Evantash v. G.E. Capital Mortgage Serv., Inc., 2003 WL 22844198 (E.D. Pa. Nov. 25, 2003); Riley v. General Motors Acceptance Corp., 226 F. Supp. 2d 1316 (S.D. Ala. 2002); Vazquez-Garcia v. Trans Union de Puerto Rico, 222 F. Supp. 2d 150 (D. P.R. 2002); Hasvold v. First USA Bank, N.A., 194 F. Supp. 2d 1228 (D. Wyo. 2002); Redhead v. Winston & Winston, P.C., 2002 WL 31106934 (S.D.N.Y. 2002); O'Diah v. New York City, 2002 WL 1941179 (S.D.N.Y. 2002).
Replace date in Johnson citation with: (D. Minn. Oct. 17, 2000). *Add at end of Banks citation: aff'd*, 232 F.3d 888 (4th Cir. 2000) (table, text at 2000 WL 1578331).

Replace "five" in last sentence of subsection's first paragraph with:

seven

§ 3.14.3   Fair Credit Reporting / 2004 Supplement

Page 80

3.14.3 Furnisher Is Liable in Private Suits for Its Reinvestigations

Addition to note 212.

212   Olwell v. Medical Information Bureau, 2003 WL 779035 (D. Minn. Jan. 7, 2003); Redhead v. Winston & Winston, P.C., 2002 WL 31106934 (S.D.N.Y. Sept. 20, 2003); Yutsler v. Sears Roebuck & Co., 263 F. Supp. 2d 1209 (D. Minn. 2003); Mendoza v. Experian Info. Solutions, Inc., 2003 WL 2005832 (S.D. Tex. Mar. 25, 2003); Sheffer v. Experian Info. Solutions, Inc., 249 F. Supp. 2d 560 (E.D. Pa. 2003); Betts v. Equifax Credit Info. Servs., Inc., 245 F. Supp. 2d 1130 (W.D. Wash. 2003); Carlson v. Trans Union, L.L.C., 259 F. Supp. 2d 517 (N.D. Tex. 2003); Stafford v. Cross Country Bank, 262 F. Supp. 2d 776 (W.D. Ky. 2003); Vasquez-Garcia v. Trans Union de Puerto Rico, 222 F. Supp. 2d 150 (D. P.R. 2002); Hawthorne v. Citicorp Data Systems, 216 F. Supp. 2d 45, 47048 (E.D. N.Y. 2002), *vacated on other grounds*, 219 F.R.D. 47 (E.D.N.Y. 2003); Scott v. AmEx/Centurion, 2001 WL 1645362 (N.D. Tex. Dec. 18, 2001); C. Brinckerhoff, FTC Informal Staff Opinion (June 24, 1999) [Watkins] (§ 1681s-2[b] affords a private right of action); Geeslin v. Nissan Motor Acceptance Corp., 1998 WL 433932 (N.D. Miss. June 3, 1998), *aff'd* 228 F.3d 408 (5th Cir. 2000).

      Add at end of Banks citation: *aff'd*, 232 F.3d 888 (4th Cir. 2000) (table, text at 2000 WL 1578331).

Replace first sentence of subsection's fifth paragraph with:

The FACTA of 2003 revised the FCRA's limitations period to extend to two years after the date of discovery by the plaintiff of the violation, but in no event may the plaintiff bring suit more than five years after the date of the violation.[216]

216   15 U.S.C. § 1681p, *amended by* Pub. L. No. 108-159, § 156.

Addition to note 217.

217   Lawrence v. Trans Union, L.L.C., 296 F. Supp. 2d 582 (E.D. Pa. 2003) (two-year limitation for failure to reinvestigate begins thirty days after reporting agency receives the dispute); Acton v. Bank One Corp., 293 F. Supp. 2d 1092 (D. Ariz. 2003) (same).

Page 81

3.14.4 Furnisher Liability for Discrimination and for Retaliating Against a Consumer for Exercising Federal Statutory Rights

Replace note 219 with:

219   15 U.S.C. § 1691(a). *See generally* National Consumer Law Center, Credit Discrimination Ch. 3 (3d ed. 2002 and Supp.).

Page 82

3.14.5 Furnisher Liability for Related Torts

Add to text after sentence containing note 229:

Several cases have considered the effects of section 1681t's preemption. Two different phrases in section 1681t have caused confusion: the meaning of "requirement or prohibition" and the meaning of "subject matter regulated under . . . § 1681s-2."

A Texas district court interpreted "requirement or prohibition" to include only state statutes, not common law actions, on the reasoning that the two specific state laws exempted from the preemption provision were both credit reporting statutes that specifically referenced furnishers.[229.1] A Kansas district court, however, seems to have assumed that the "requirement or prohibition" language includes common law tort actions, and not just state statutes.[229.2]

In a decision that has subsequently been vacated by the judge who issued it, a Pennsylvania district court held that the supplemental preemption provision preempted *all* actions against furnishers.[229.3] This interpretation carries two flaws. First, it ignores the qualifying language in subsection 1681t(b)(1), which limits the sorts of state laws preempted to those that relate to the "subject matter regulated under . . . § 1681s-2." Second, such an interpretation effectively renders the qualified immunity provision of section 1681h(e) superfluous, as it pertains to furnishers, for if the supplemental preemption provision preempted all state causes of action against furnishers, there would be no need to offer furnishers qualified immunity from the listed tort actions. *Since this decision has been vacated, it should not be cited as precedent.*

More thoughtful analyses have sought to reconcile the two provisions by reading the preemption provision restrictively. For example, a Minnesota district court rejected a furnisher's argument that the immunity and preemption provisions together barred any action based on any matter regulated by § 1681s-2 because that reading would render the general immunity provision superfluous as to furnishers.[229.4] Other courts have also agreed that

Furnishing Information to Consumer Reporting Agencies / 2004 Supplement § 3.14.5

Congress's failure to remove furnishers from section 1681h(e) when it added section 1681t indicated that it did not intend for the new section to preempt all claims against them.[229.5] Another interpretation uses the statutory construction rule that specific provisions prevail over general, and therefore the specific language of section 1681h(e) preserves claims that would otherwise be considered preempted by the more general language of section 1681t.[229.6]

The other phrase that determines the scope of section 1681t's preemption is "subject matter regulated under . . . § 1681s-2."[229.7] The cases discussing whether a claim encompasses such subject matter have more or less fallen into two schools of thought. The first, the before-and-after school, focuses on when the conduct that gave rise to the plaintiff's claim against the furnisher occurred, on the theory that § 1681s-2 regulates furnisher conduct only after a specific event has occurred: the furnisher has reported information with actual knowledge of errors (triggering § 1681s-2(a)(1)(A)); the furnisher has received notice from a consumer that specific information is inaccurate (triggering § 1681s-2(a)(1)(B)); or a consumer reporting agency has notified that furnisher that a reported item is in dispute (triggering § 1681s-2(b)). Under this analysis, claims based on the furnisher's behavior after the furnisher's responsibilities under § 1681s-2 have arisen are barred by the preemption provision.

So, for example, in *Aklagi v. Nationscredit Financial*,[229.8] the court held that any defamation claim based on a furnisher furnishing inaccurate information to a consumer reporting agency after the furnisher received notice that the consumer disputed the information was wholly preempted. This suit was brought by an identity theft victim after the defendant made a mortgage loan to a person posing as the plaintiff, a loan that subsequently defaulted and led to the furnisher damaging the plaintiff's credit record. The court reasoned that the subject matter of the suit was regulated by § 1681s-2(a)(1)(B) and therefore section 1681t(b) preempted the state law claims.[229.9] The court distinguished, in its analysis, the plaintiff's claim based on information furnished by the furnisher after it made the loan but before it received notice of the consumer's dispute, acknowledging that such a time period is not regulated under § 1681s-2, given that there was no evidence that the furnisher had known or consciously avoided knowing that the information was inaccurate, which would have been conduct within the strictures of the Act.[229.10] Accordingly, the supplemental preemption provision did not bar the plaintiff's action, but her victory was brief. The court then ruled that the general qualified immunity provision found in section 1681h(e) *did* bar the action, because the plaintiff had failed to show the malice or willful intent necessary to remove the action from immunity.[229.11] Similarly, a district court in Puerto Rico interpreted the provisions of section 1681t as barring all state actions against a furnisher that are based on conduct *after* the furnisher received the notice from a consumer reporting agency that triggers § 1681s-2(b).[229.12]

Other courts have not focused on when the furnisher received notice of the inaccuracy, but rather have directed their attention towards the elements of the alleged cause of action itself, and how those elements compare with § 1681s-2. In short, this school of thought asks whether the essence of the claim the plaintiff seeks to bring is too similar to the subject matter of § 1681s-2 to escape preemption. So, for example, in another identity theft case, *Carlson v. Trans Union, L.L.C.*,[229.13] the court framed its analysis around the elements of the particular claims, and held that a consumer's defamation claim against a telephone company that had furnished allegedly false reports withstood preemption under 1681t. The court noted that the scope of the preemption provision is limited to those state claims that relate to any "subject matter regulated under" § 1681s-2. Accordingly, while a statutory UDAP claim based on the furnisher's reporting of information to a consumer reporting agency would be preempted, a common law defamation claim was not, because the elements—the "subject matter"—of the two claims were different, notwithstanding that the same underlying acts gave rise to both.[229.14] The court reasoned that a claim under § 1681s-2 would require the plaintiff to show that the defendant violated a duty to thoroughly investigate the plaintiff's claim that his credit record was inaccurate. In contrast, a defamation claim would require proof of publication of a defamatory statement that concerned the plaintiff, made with negligence.[229.15]

Like *Carlson*, an Illinois district court ruled that section 1681t does not preempt state common law tort claims such as negligence, defamation, or invasion of privacy against furnishers, because those torts did not in and of themselves impose any special duty on furnishers that did not apply to the public at large.[229.16] The court further stated that the section would not preempt any claims based on the furnisher's improper opening of an account for the thief, because those would be actions not covered by the FCRA, that is, not "subject matter regulated by" § 1681s-2.[229.17]

The degree of similarity necessary to pull the claim into the preemption provision varies from decision to decision. While *Carlson* focused on the elements of the tort claim as compared with the duties imposed by § 1681s-2, to rule that the plaintiff's defamation claim *was not* preempted, another identity theft case, *Stafford v. Cross Country Bank*,[229.18] focused on the role of the defendant at the time the actionable conduct occurred, and ruled that the plaintiff's defamation claim *was* preempted. The court reasoned that section 1681t preempted *only* those tort claims that implicated conduct falling within § 1681s-2, which the court interpreted to be the conduct involved in the reporting of credit information after receiving notice of a dispute.[229.19] In contrast, those claims that involved the bank's actions "independent of its function as a furnisher of credit information" were not preempted.[229.20] Applying this distinction, the court struck the defamation, slander and UDAP claims, along with certain aspects of an invasion of privacy claim, but allowed other aspects of the invasion of privacy claim along with a harassment claim to proceed.[229.21] In addition, the victim's claim that the bank acted unconscionably in verifying the identity of its applicants was not preempted for it did not go to the bank's furnishing function. Under this analysis, the issue is whether the creditor is wearing its furnisher's hat when it commits the injuring acts, as opposed to its creditor's or banker's hat.

229.1 Carlson v. Trans Union, L.C.C., 259 F. Supp. 2d 517 (N.D. Tex. 2003). *See also* Sheffer v. Experian Info. Solutions, Inc., 249 F. Supp. 2d 560 (E.D. Pa. 2003) (refusing to dismiss plaintiff's defamation claim on grounds that neither § 1681h(e) or § 1681t(b)(1) apply when false information is furnished with malice or willful intent to injure, an interpretation that grafts the qualification of § 1681h(e)'s immunity onto § 1681t, but without thorough analysis).

229.2 *See, e.g.*, Aklagi v. Nationscredit Financial, 196 F. Supp. 2d 1186, 1195 (D. Kan. 2002) (holding defamation action preempted).

229.3 Jaramillo v. Experian Info. Solutions, Inc., 155 F. Supp. 2d 356, 362 (E.D. Pa. 2001), *vacated in relevant part,* Jaramillo v. Experian Information Solutions, Inc., 2001 WL 1762626 (E.D. Pa. June 20, 2001). *See also* Hasvold v. First U.S. Bank, N.A., 194 F. Supp. 2d 1228, 1239 (D. Wyo. 2002) (citing *Jaramillo* with approval, holding that § 1681t barred plaintiff, an identity theft victim, from suing a furnisher for defamation and invasion of privacy).

229.4 Yutsler v. Sears Roebuck & Co., 263 F. Supp. 2d 1209 (D. Minn. 2003) (holding that plaintiff's common law claim for defamation of credit that asserted gross negligence survived both the general immunity and supplemental preemption provisions).

229.5 Mattice v. Equifax, 2003 WL 21391679, at *2 (D. Minn. June 13, 2003) (rejecting furnisher's argument that § 1681t completely subsumed § 1681h(e)); Stafford v. Cross Country Bank, 262 F. Supp. 2d 776 (W.D. Ky. 2003) (provisions must be read together); Vazquez-Garcia v. Trans Union de Puerto Rico, 222 F. Supp. 2d 150 (D. P.R. 2002) (rejecting argument that § 1681t completely bars state actions against furnishers on grounds that such a reading would in fact nullify part of § 1681h(e)).

229.6 Gordon v. Greenpoint Credit, 266 F. Supp. 2d 1007 (S.D. Iowa 2003) (holding that negligence and defamation claims against furnisher were not preempted).

229.7 16 U.S.C. § 1681t(b)(1)(F).

229.8 196 F. Supp. 2d 1186, 1195 (D. Kan. 2002). *See also* Mendoza v. Experian Info. Solutions, Inc., 2003 WL 2005832, at *5 (S.D. Tex. Mar. 25, 2003) (whether cause of action survived depended upon whether consumer reporting agencies fulfilled their responsibilities to notify furnisher of dispute; if they did, state claims were preempted, if they did not, claims could survive because cause of action would not relate to subject matter regulated under § 1681s-2(b)).

229.9 *Id.*
229.10 *Id.*
229.11 *Id.* at 1196.
229.12 Vazquez-Garcia v. Trans Union de Puerto Rico, 222 F. Supp. 2d 150 (D. P.R. 2002). However, the court's construction of § 1681h(e) is itself confusing, in that it held that the qualified immunity provision barred the plaintiff's action based on the furnisher's negligent extension of credit to the identity thief. *Id.* at 163. Though on its face § 1681h(e) only extends qualified immunity for the listed torts "with respect to the reporting of information" that is also "based on information disclosed pursuant to [the FCRA]," the court read these qualifiers right out, quoting the immunity provision as reading "[n]o consumer may bring any action or proceeding in the nature of defamation, invasion of privacy, or negligence . . . against . . . any person who furnished information to a consumer reporting agency . . . except as to false information

Furnishing Information to Consumer Reporting Agencies / 2004 Supplement § **3.16**

furnished with malice or willful intent to injure each consumer" (emphasis omitted). *Id.* Reading the qualified immunity provision as applying the malice or willful intent requirement to every possible action against a furnisher would effectively bar any claim based on the original extension of credit, since it would take a true conspiracy theorist to plead that the furnisher had opened the account for the thief with the intent of doing in the victim. *See also* Mattice v. Equifax, 2003 WL 21391679, at *3 (D. Minn. June 13, 2003) (adopting *Aklagi*'s reasoning in refusing to dismiss claim against furnisher).

229.13 2003 WL 2004413 (N.D. Tex. Apr. 16, 2003).
229.14 *Id.* at *3.
229.15 *Id.* at *3. The court did not employ the elevated standard of section 1681h(e).
229.16 Dornhecker v. Ameritech Corp. 99 F. Supp. 2d 918, 931 (N.D. Ill. 2000).
229.17 *Id. See also* Riley v. Gen. Motors Acceptance Corp., 226 F. Supp. 2d 1316 (S.D. Ala. 2002) (section 1681t preempts all state causes of action against furnishers, both statutory and common law, where the state law claim is based on the same conduct that gives rise to the FCRA claim); Carney v. Experian Info. Solutions, Inc., 57 F. Supp. 2d 496 (W.D. Tenn. 1999) (section 1681t preempted state UDAP claim based on furnisher's failure to provide accurate information after being notified by a consumer of a dispute).
229.18 2003 WL 21058173, at *5 (W.D. Ky. May 8, 2003).
229.19 *Id.* at *8.
229.20 *Id.*
229.21 *Id.*

Add new sections after § 3.14.5.

3.15 Reinvestigation Requirements Applicable to Resellers

In general, resellers are exempt from reinvestigation requirements.[231] However, effective December 1, 2004, if a reseller receives a notice from a consumer of a dispute concerning the completeness or accuracy of any item in a consumer report produced by the reseller, the reseller must, within five business days of receipt of the notice, determine whether the item of information is complete or inaccurate as a result of an act or omission of the reseller. If the reseller determines that the item of information is incomplete or inaccurate as a result of an act or omission on their part, they must correct the information in the consumer report or delete it no later than twenty days after receipt of the notice. If the reseller determines that the information is not incomplete or inaccurate as a result of their act or omission, they are only required to convey the notice of the dispute, together with all relevant information provided by the consumer, to each consumer reporting agency that provided the reseller with the information in dispute, using the notification mechanism specified by the consumer reporting agency for such notices.[232] Consumer reporting agencies that complete reinvestigations based on notice from resellers must notify the consumer through the reseller of the results of the investigation.[233]

3.16 Furnishers Subject to New Identity Theft Duties and Responsibilities

FACTA imposed several new requirements on creditors or furnishers with respect to protecting consumers against identity theft. These requirements are discussed in detail in Chapter 16.[234]

231 15 U.S.C. § 1681i(f)(1), *added by* Pub. L. No. 108-159, § 316(b); 16 C.F.R. § 602.1(c)(3)(xviii), *added by* 69 Fed. Reg. 6526–31 (Feb. 5, 2004).
232 15 U.S.C. § 1681i (f)(1),(2).
233 15 U.S.C. § 1681i (f)(3), *added by* Pub. L. No. 108-159, § 316(b).
234 *See* Ch. 16, *infra*.

Chapter 4 A Consumer's Right to Learn What Is in File

4.2 Information Is Reported on Virtually Every American

Page 84

4.2.2 Credit Reports Prone to Errors

Add to text after sentence containing note 14:

According to the FTC, consumer complaints against the three national credit reporting agencies have steadily increased from 875 in 1997 to more than 14,000 in 2002.[14.1] The majority of complaints concerning the three credit reporting agencies are non-identity theft related (11,158).[14.2]

In 2002 the Consumer Federation of America (CFA) and the National Credit Reporting Association analyzed the credit scores of more than a half million consumers and extensively reviewed the files of more than 1700 individuals. The files were maintained by the three major credit repositories—Equifax, Experian, and Trans Union.[14.3] The report also included an analysis of 51 representative files for consistencies and inconsistencies and found common errors of omission (information not reported by all three credit reporting agencies) and commission (inconsistent information between the three credit reporting agencies). Errors included the failure to report negative and positive information. Negative information included delinquencies or charge offs, whereas positive information included payments on accounts. According to the report, 78 percent of files were missing a revolving account in good standing, while one-third (33 percent) of files were missing a mortgage account that had never been late.[14.4] Serious errors of commission also appeared in a significant portion of files. The report also found that files contain conflicting information on the same accounts regarding how often consumers had been late with payments.[14.5] While the report found that some consumers would be harmed by the inaccuracies and others would benefit, it was clear that substantial economic harm could be caused to those adversely affected by the inaccurate information.[14.6]

The authors of the report acknowledged that a sample of 51 reports is too small to generalize for all files, however they concluded that "tens of millions of consumers are at risk of being penalized by inaccurate credit report information and incorrect credit scores."[14.7]

A report in 2003 by the Federal Reserve Board also found that information in credit reporting files is not complete in all regards and at times contains duplications and ambiguities.[14.8] The Federal Reserve study included a nationally representative sample from one of the three national credit reporting agencies and found that credit limits were not reported on one or more revolving accounts. For accounts with a major derogatory piece of information, almost three-fifths were not currently reported.[14.9] These accounts were likely to have been closed or transferred but were not reported as such. With respect to public records, the Federal Reserve study found that about 40 percent of the consumers with public records had more than one such record, often involving the same event or episode. A similar percentage of those with accounts reported by collection agencies had more than one collection item, however for many of these individuals, the multiple record items appeared to pertain to the same episode.[14.10]

Both the CFA and Federal Reserve Board reports document the need for greater accuracy and completeness in consumer credit reports and both conclude that consumers may be helped or hurt by the inaccurate and incomplete files maintained by the credit reporting agencies.

14.1 Letter and enclosures from Joan E. Fina to Chris Hoofnagle in response to FOIA Request No. 2003-470 (June 23, 2003), *reprinted on* the companion CD-Rom, *infra*.
14.2 *Id.* (3,399 complaints received by the Commission in 2002 pertained to identity theft).
14.3 See § 14.4.2, *infra* for a discussion of the reports findings on credit scores; Consumer Federation of America and National Credit Reporting Association, *Credit Score Accuracy and Implications for Consumers*, December 17, 2002, *available at* www.consumerfed.org/121702CFA_NCRA_Credit_Score_Report_Final.pdf, *reprinted on* the companion CD-Rom, *infra. See also* § 14.4.2, *infra*.
14.4 *Id.* at 29.
14.5 *Id.* at 29.
14.6 *Id.* at 24–25.
14.7 *Id.* at 37.
14.8 Robert Avery, Paul Calem, Glenn Canner, and Raphael Bostin, *An Overview of Consumer Data and Consumer Reporting*, Federal Reserve Bulletin 70 (Feb. 2003).
14.9 *Id.* at 71.
14.10 *Id.*

Replace "One study" in first sentence of subsection's first full paragraph with:

In a 1991 study

4.3 Right of Consumer to Know Contents of Own File

4.3.1 Overview

Replace subsection's first paragraph with:

Upon a consumer's request and proper identification, the consumer reporting agency must clearly and accurately disclose to the consumer all information then in the consumer's file.[20] In addition, as of December 1, 2004, a consumer will have a new right to learn the credit score and the key factors adversely affecting the credit score.[20.1]

20 FCRA § 609, 15 U.S.C. § 1681g, *as amended by* Pub. L. No. 108-159 (2003). Section 1681j also mandates disclosure after a credit denial. Note that the obligation to disclose to the consumer is mandatory. See Pub. L. No. 90-321, § 502 (May 29, 1968), 82 Stat. 146, 147, reported as a note following 15 U.S.C. § 1601 (the Consumer Credit Protection Act), which provides in pertinent part: "(1) The word 'may' is used to indicate that an action either is authorized or is permitted. (2) The word 'shall' is used to indicate that an action is both authorized and required. (3) The phrase 'may not' is used to indicate that an action is both unauthorized and forbidden. (4) Rules of law are stated in the indicative mood."

20.1 15 U.S.C. § 1681g(f), *added by* Pub. L. No. 108-159, § 212 (2003); 16 C.F.R. § 602.1(c)(3)(x), *added by* 69 Fed. Reg. 6526–31 (Feb. 5, 2004). The agency need not disclose more than four key factors that adversely affected the consumer's credit score, with the proviso that if the number of enquiries to the consumer's file was a key factor in the score, that factor must be disclosed and is not counted under the cap. 15 U.S.C. §§ 1681g(f)(1)(C), (f)(9). *See also* § 14.4, *infra*. Under the prior version of the Act, consumers were not entitled to learn their credit scores.

Replace subsection's last paragraph with:

The FACTA of 2003 added a significant provision that allows consumers to learn their credit score, a critical piece of information that many creditors use in lieu of examining a consumer's whole file.[26] However, the credit score the agency provides to the consumer may not necessarily be the same score the agency provides to creditors, since the Act allows the agency to provide either the current credit score or the score most recently calculated by the agency for a credit-related purpose.[27]

26 15 U.S.C. § 1682g(f), *added by* Pub. L. No. 108-159, § 212 (2003). Under the prior version of the Act, consumers were not entitled to learn their credit scores. *See also* § 14.4, *infra*.
27 15 U.S.C. § 1681g(g)(1)(A).
28 *Reserved.*

4.3.2 Information Shown to Consumer Often Not What Is Shown to Creditors

Add to text before the word "address" in sentence containing note 32:

current

4.4 How to Obtain the Contents of a Consumer's File

4.4.1 General

4.4.1.1 Timing of Request and Disclosure

Page 86

Add to text at beginning of subsection's last paragraph:

In contrast, the new provision requiring nationwide consumer reporting agencies to provide consumers with one free annual credit report requires those agencies to provide those reports within fifteen days, so long as the consumer uses the centralized source for making the request.[35.1] An additional avenue to a free report lies in the new extended fraud alert provision,[35.2] through which a consumer may obtain from the agency to which the consumer directs the alert all of the information in the consumer's file.[35.3] The agency must provide the information within three business days of the request, without charge.[35.4]

    35.1 15 U.S.C. § 1681j(a)(2), *added by* Pub. L. No. 108-159, § 211(a) (2003). The agencies that must comply with the free report provision are those described in 15 U.S.C. § 1681a(p). However, requests from nationwide specialty consumer reporting agencies, those defined by 15 U.S.C. § 1681a(w), will not be made through a centralized source but rather pursuant to forthcoming regulations that will require such agencies to provide, at a minimum, a toll-free telephone number for consumers to use to request a free report. 15 U.S.C. § 1681j(a)(C)(i), *added by* Pub. L. No. 108-159, § 211(a) (2003). The free report provision will not apply to consumer reporting agencies that have been furnishing consumer reports to third parties for fewer than twelve months prior to the date of the consumer's request. 15 U.S.C. § 1681j(a)(4). However, with respect to requests for reports from nationwide specialty agencies through forthcoming regulations, or through the extended fraud alert provision,

    35.2 15 U.S.C. § 1681c-1(b), *added by* Pub. L. No. 108-159, § 112 (2003). This provision will become effective on December 1, 2004. 16 C.F.R. § 602.1(c)(3)(i), *added by* 69 Fed. Reg. 6526–31 (Feb. 5, 2004).

    35.3 As allowed by 15 U.S.C. § 1681g, *as amended by* Pub. L. No. 108-159, § 115 (2003).

    35.4 15 U.S.C. § 1681c-1(b), *added by* Pub. L. No. 108-159, § 112 (2003).

Page 88

4.4.1.5 Special Rules for Affiliates

Add to text at end of subsection:

The FACTA of 2003 added a new restriction on the use by affiliates of information not deemed a consumer report because it was obtained from an affiliate or because it pertains solely to transactions or experiences between the consumer and the affiliate making the report.[65.1] Now an affiliate may not use that information to solicit the consumer for marketing purposes unless the affiliate discloses to the consumer that the information may be communicated for that purpose and provides the consumer with an opportunity to opt out of such use.[65.2]

    65.1 15 U.S.C. § 1681s-3, *added by* Pub. L. No. 108-159, § 214(a)(2003) (*citing* 15 U.S.C. §§ 1681a(d)(2)(A)(i)–(iii). *See also* §§ 2.4.1, 2.4.2, *supra*.

    65.2 15 U.S.C. § 1681s-3, *added by* Pub. L. No. 108-159, § 214(a)(2003).

4.4.2 Making the Request

4.4.2.1 The Request by the Consumer

Replace first sentence of subsection with:

The FACTA of 2003 amended the FCRA to provide consumers with the right to one free report per year.[65.3] To obtain such a report from a nationwide consumer reporting agency[65.4] the consumer must make the request through a centralized source that the FTC is to set up

§ 4.4.2.2   *Fair Credit Reporting / 2004 Supplement*

through regulations.[65.5] Requests for reports from nationwide specialty consumer reporting agencies[65.6] will not be made through a centralized source but rather pursuant to forthcoming regulations that will require such agencies to provide, at a minimum, a toll-free telephone number for consumers to use to request a free report.[65.7] The effective date of the free credit report provision may be delayed until December 4, 2004, or even beyond.[65.8] Aside from that provision the Act does not specify any particular manner for the consumer to request disclosure of the information in the consumer's file. Each of the nationwide consumer reporting agencies, Experian, TransUnion, and Equifax, allow consumers to obtain credit reports by following procedures designated on their websites.[65.9]

65.3 15 U.S.C. § 1681j(a), 15 U.S.C. § 1681j(a), *amended by* Pub. L. No. 108-159, § 212(a)(2) (2003).
65.4 Defined in § 603(p), 15 U.S.C. § 1681a(p).
65.5 15 U.S.C. § 1681j(a)(1)(B), *amended by* Pub. L. No. 108-159, § 211 (2003).
65.6 Those defined by 15 U.S.C. § 1681a(w), *added by* Pub. L. No. 108-159, § 111(2003).
65.7 15 U.S.C. § 1681j(a)(C)(i), *added by* Pub. L. No. 108-159, § 211(a) (2003).
65.8 Pub. L. No. 108-159, § 211 (2003). The provision does not apply to a nationwide agency that has not been furnishing consumer reports on a continuing basis for the twelve months preceding a consumer's request. 15 U.S.C. § 1681j(a)(4), *added by* Pub. L. No. 108-159, § 211 (2003). The FACTA provides that the FTC has six months from the effective date of the Act to issue regulations that will create the centralized source through which consumers are to make their requests and the regulations will not become effective until 6 months after they become final. *Id.* However, the FTC's proposed regulations would implement a "cumulative regional roll-out" for the centralized source that would delay complete access to the source to September 1, 2005. 69 Fed. Reg. 13198 (Mar. 19, 2004).
65.9 The websites are www.experian.com, www.transunion.com, and www.equifax.com respectively.

Page 89

Add to text at end of subsection's second sentence:

4.4.2.2 From Which Agency Should Information Be Requested?

Once the FTC issues final regulations establishing a centralized source through which consumers can request a free report, consumers will be entitled to one free credit report annually.[78.1] In addition, there are many specialty consumer reporting agencies that compile information about consumers on a nationwide basis relating to a specific subject, such as medical records, tenant history, check writing history, employment history, or insurance claims.[78.2]

78.1 15 U.S.C. § 1681j(a), *amended by* Pub. L. No. 108-159, § 212 (2003).
78.2 *See* § 2.6.1, *supra*.

4.4.2.3 How to Get Disclosures From Equifax, Experian, and Trans Union

Add new subsection before § 4.4.2.3.1.

4.4.2.3.a Free reports once a year after FTC issues rules

Once the FTC issues final regulations establishing a centralized source through which consumers can request a free report from the nationwide consumer reporting agencies,[83.1] consumers will be able to request a free report from these agencies by using that centralized source.[83.2] Until that time, and even after that time for requests for reports for which the Act, as revised, permits an agency to charge the consumer, consumers can make requests as described below.

83.1 15 U.S.C. § 1681j(a)(1)(B), *amended by* Pub. L. No. 108-159, § 211 (2003).
83.2 15 U.S.C. § 1681j(a)(1)(A), *amended by* Pub. L. No. 108-159, § 212 (2003).

Page 90

4.4.2.4 Time to Respond

Add to text at end of subsection:

Once consumers are able to request free reports from the nationwide consumer reporting agencies,[86.1] the agencies will have to provide the report within fifteen days of the request.[86.2] A consumer who has requested an extended fraud alert under the new provision allowing for such alerts,[86.3] and pursuant to FTC rules, may obtain from the agency to which the consumer directs the alert all of the information in the consumer's file.[86.4] The agency must provide the information within three business days of the request, without charge once the rules become effective.[86.5]

A Consumer's Right to Learn What Is in File / 2004 Supplement § 4.4.4

86.1 The FTC has six months to issue regulations that will create the centralized source through which consumers are to make their requests, and the regulations will not become effective until six months after they become final. Pub. L. No. 108-159, § 211 (2003); 15 U.S.C. § 1681j(a), 15 U.S.C. § 1681j(a), *amended by* Pub. L. No. 108-159, § 212 (2003). However, the FTC's proposed regulations would implement a "cumulative regional roll-out" for the centralized source that would delay complete access to the source to September 1, 2005. 69 Fed. Reg. 13198 (Mar. 19, 2004).
86.2 15 U.S.C. § 1681j(a)(2), *amended by* Pub. L. No. 108-159, § 212 (2003).
86.3 15 U.S.C. § 1681c-1(b), *added by* Pub. L. No. 108-159, § 112 (2003). This provision will become effective on December 1, 2004. 16 C.F.R. § 602.1(c)(3)(i), *added by* 69 Fed. Reg. 6526–31 (Feb. 5, 2004).
86.4 As allowed by 15 U.S.C. 1681g, *as amended by* Pub. L. No. 108-159, § 115 (2003).
86.5 15 U.S.C. § 1681c-1(b), *added by* Pub. L. No. 108-159, § 112 (2003).

4.4.3 Proof of Consumer's Identification or Authorization

Page 91

4.4.3.1 Information Required to Identify the Consumer

Replace note 93 with:

93 National Consumer Law Center, Credit Discrimination §§ 3.3.4, 5.5.5.2.2, 5.5.5.2.3 (3d ed. 2002).

Add note 93.1 to end of first sentence of subsection's fifth paragraph.

93.1 Note that the FACTA of 2003 added a provision requiring the FTC, the federal banking agencies, and the National Credit Union Administration to prescribe regulations, to be known as "red-flag" guidelines, for card issuers to follow to ensure that if a card issuer receives notification of a change of address for an existing account and shortly thereafter receives a request for an additional or replacement card, the issuer will use special procedures to verify the identity of the card requester. 15 U.S.C. § 1681m(e)(1)(C), *added by* Pub. L. No. 108-159, § 111 (2003). *See also* § 16.1a, *infra*.

4.4.3.2 Consumer's Written Instructions to Disclose Report to Attorney or Other Third Party

Add to text after sentence containing note 100:

The FACTA of 2003 added, among other privacy protections, a provision allowing the consumer requesting the report to require the agency to truncate the first five digits of the consumer's social security number from the report, so long as the agency has received adequate proof of the requesting consumer's identity;[100.1] this provision will go into effect December 1, 2004.[100.2]

100.1 15 U.S.C. 1681g(a)(1)(A), *amended by* Pub. L. No. 108-159, § 115 (2003). It is unclear why the Act would explicitly require proof of identity before disclosing the report with a truncated social security number when it does not require such proof to disclose the report with the full social security number.
100.2 16 C.F.R. § 602.1(c)(3)(iii), *added by* 69 Fed. Reg. 6526–31 (Feb. 5, 2004).

Page 92

4.4.4 Unreasonable Preconditions or Requests for Information Prior to Disclosure

Add after sentence containing note 105:

Practitioners report that some credit reporting agencies take consumers "off-line" when the consumers bring suit, precluding the consumers from obtaining their credit reports directly from the reporting agency. While initiation of litigation may raise issues regarding direct communications between the consumer's attorney and employees of the defendant reporting agency, the agency continues to have a legal obligation to produce the file to the consumer pursuant to section 1681g. Failure to comply with an appropriate request from a consumer would likely subject the agency to further claims and liability under the Act. It has also been reported that taking consumer files "off-line" precludes creditors and others with legitimate purposes to access the reports of consumers who have filed suit.

§ 4.4.5   *Fair Credit Reporting / 2004 Supplement*

4.4.5 Consumer Payment for File Disclosure

4.4.5.1 Where FCRA Prohibits Payment

Page 93

Add to text at end of subsection's second paragraph:

4.4.5.1.2 No charge if consumer believes file is inaccurate due to fraud

Continuing concern for identity theft led Congress to add a provision in 2003 allowing an identity theft victim to obtain an expedited free report. A consumer who has requested an extended fraud alert under the new provision allowing for such alerts[121.1] may obtain from the agency to which the consumer directs the alert all of the information in the consumer's file.[121.2] The agency must provide the information within three business days of the request, without charge.[121.3]

121.1   15 U.S.C. § 1681c-1(b), *added by* Pub. L. No. 108-159, § 112 (2003). This provision will become effective on December 1, 2004. 16 C.F.R. § 602.1(c)(3)(i), *added by* 69 Fed. Reg. 6526–31 (Feb. 5, 2004). *See also* § 16.1a, *infra*.
121.2   As allowed by 15 U.S.C. 1681g, *as amended by* Pub. L. No. 108-159, § 115 (2003).
121.3   15 U.S.C. § 1681c-1(b), *added by* Pub. L. No. 108-159, § 112 (2003).

Page 94

Add new subsection after § 4.4.5.1.4.

4.4.5.1.5 No charge for annual report made through centralized source

Once the FTC issues final regulations establishing a centralized source through which consumers can request a free report, consumers will be entitled to one free credit report annually.[125.1] In addition, many specialty consumer reporting agencies compile information about consumers on a nationwide basis relating to a specific subject, such as medical records, tenant history, check writing history, employment history, or insurance claims.[125.2] The Act specifically prohibits agencies from imposing a charge for such a report.[125.3]

125.1   The effective date of this provision allowing consumers a free annual credit report from nationwide consumer reporting agencies may be delayed since the FTC has 6 months to issue regulations that will create the centralized source through which consumers are to make their requests, and the regulations will not become effective until 6 months after they become final. Pub. L. No. 108-159, § 211 (2003); 15 U.S.C. § 1681j(a), *amended by* Pub. L. No. 108-159, § 212 (2003). Furthermore, the FTC's proposed regulations would implement a "cumulative regional roll-out" for the centralized source that would delay complete access to the source to September 1, 2005. 69 Fed. Reg. 13198 (Mar. 19, 2004).
125.2   *See* § 2.6.1, *supra*.
125.3   15 U.S.C. § 1681j(f), *amended by* Pub. L. No. 108-159, § 211(a)(6) (2003). However, the provision does not apply to a nationwide agency that has not been furnishing consumer reports on a continuing basis for the twelve months preceding a consumer's request. 15 U.S.C. § 1681j(a)(4), *added by* Pub. L. No. 108-159, § 211 (2003).

4.4.5.2 State Laws Limiting Payment

Add to text after subsection's first sentence:

The FACTA of 2003 preserved these statutes while preempting any other state laws imposing a right to a free credit report more or less frequently than required by the new provision.[126.1]

126.1   15 U.S.C. § 1681t(b)(4), *added by* Pub. L. No. 108-159, § 212(e)(2) (2003).

4.4.5.3 Payment Amounts Where Allowed

Replace note 130 with:

130   67 Fed. Reg. 77282 (December 17, 2002).

Add new subsection after § 4.4.5.3.

4.4.5.3a Federal Legislation to Provide for Free Credit Reports

In 2003, legislation was proposed that would provide for free credit reports and a free summary of credit scores.[133.1] Consumer advocates have argued that consumers should have free disclosure of credit scores and not only a summary of the scores. It remains to be seen

A Consumer's Right to Learn What Is in File / 2004 Supplement § 4.5.7

whether Congress will adopt a provision that provides for a free credit report and credit score for consumers.

133.1 Amendment in the Nature of a Substitute to H.R. 2622, Offered by Mr. Bachus (Manager's Amendment), available at http://financialservices.house.gov/media/pdf/108fihr2622am1.pdf.

4.5 File Information That Must Be Disclosed

4.5.2 Nearly All Information in the Consumer's File Must Be Disclosed

Page 95

Add to text at end of subsection:

4.5.2.1 Introduction

The FACTA of 2003 added, among other privacy protections, a provision allowing the consumer requesting the report to require the agency to truncate the first five digits of the consumer's social security number from the report, so long as the agency has received adequate proof of the requesting consumer's identity.[143.1] This provision will become effective on December 1, 2004.[143.2]

143.1 15 U.S.C. 1681g(a)(1)(A), *amended by* Pub. L. No. 108-159, § 115 (2003).
143.2 16 C.F.R. § 602.1(c)(3)(i), *added by* 69 Fed. Reg. 6526–31 (Feb. 5, 2004).

4.5.2.2 Disclosure of Previously Reported Information

Replace note 146 with:

146   15 U.S.C. § 1681g(c)(2)(B).

Page 98

4.5.5 Medical Information

Add to text at end of subsection's first paragraph:

The FACTA of 2003 revised the FCRA's definition of "medical information" to remove the requirement that the information have been obtained with the consumer's consent and to remove from the definition information that does not relate to the consumer's physical, mental, or behavioral health or condition.[177.1]

177.1 15 U.S.C. § 1681a(i), *amended by* Pub. L. No. 108-159, § 411(c) (2003). This provision will become effective on June 1, 2004, 180 days after passage of the FACTA. Pub. L. No. 108-159, § 411(d) (2003).

Add to text after sentence containing note 178:

The FACTA of 2003 added significant new restrictions on the disclosure by agencies of medical information without the consumer's consent.[178.1]

178.1 *See* §§ 6.5.3, 10.2.2.4, *infra*.

Add to text at end of subsection's fourth paragraph:

Assuming that the MIB falls within the Act's new definition of nationwide specialty consumer reporting agency,[180.1] eventually consumers will be entitled to a free credit report from MIB, though that right may be delayed until the FTC issues final regulations.[180.2]

180.1 15 U.S.C. § 1681a(c), *added by* Pub. L. No. 108-159, § 111 (2003).
180.2 15 U.S.C. § 1681j(a)(1)(C), *added by* Pub. L. No. 108-159, § 211 (2003). *See also* §§ 4.4.2.1, 4.4.2.2, *supra*.

Page 99

4.5.7 Information Which Does Not Have to Be Disclosed

Delete § 4.5.7.1.

§ 4.5.7.1   *Fair Credit Reporting / 2004 Supplement*

Replace § 4.5.7.2 heading with:

4.5.7.1 FBI Counter-Intelligence and Government Security Clearance Usage May Not Be Disclosed

Replace § 4.5.7.3 heading with:

4.5.7.2 Audit Trail and Other Ancillary Information

Page 100

4.6 Disclosure Must Include a Summary of Consumer Rights

Delete parenthetical from section's first sentence.

Replace note 199 with:

199   15 U.S.C. § 1681g(c), *as amended by* Pub. L. No. 108-159, § 211(c) (2003). The FTC is to issue a revised summary of consumer rights. *Id.* at § 1681g(c)(1)(A). The FACTA of 2003 amended this provision to require agencies to use the FTC's prescribed form starting on December 1, 2004 (16 C.F.R. § 602.1(c)(3)(ix), *added by* 69 Fed. Reg. 6526–31 (Feb. 5, 2004)). Under the previous version of the Act, the agencies could provide their own summary of rights so long as it included the required information. *See also* § 6.3, *infra*.

4.8 Analyzing Information Provided to the Consumer

Page 101

4.8.1 Form of Disclosure

Add to text after subsection's last sentence:

In general, consumer files from the three national credit reporting agency contain information pertaining to personal identification, credit accounts, public records, collections and inquiries.[204.1] Personal identification information includes the consumer's name (and aliases), current and previous addresses, and social security number. Files also contain dates of birth, telephone numbers, spouse's names, number of dependents, income and employment information. Credit account information usually includes account dates, balances, payment performance, and descriptions of accounts, including whether it is an individual or joint account, a close-end or open-end account.[204.2] A more complete description of each of the three major credit reporting agency files is described below.

204.1   *See An Overview of Consumer Data and Credit Reporting*, Robert B. Avery, Paul S. Calem, and Glenn B. Canner, Federal Reserve Board Bulletin (Feb. 2003), available at www.federalreserve.gov/pubs/bulletin/2003/0203/lead.pdf.

204.2   *Id.*

4.8.3 How to Use the Information Disclosed

Page 103

4.8.3.1 Limits on Utility of Information Disclosed

Add to text at end of subsection:

The FACTA of 2003 amended the FCRA, effective December 1, 2004, to allow consumers to request their credit scores and the key factors adversely affecting the credit score.[215.1] However, the credit score the agency provides to the consumer may not necessarily be the same score the agency provides to creditors. The FACTA allows the agency to provide either the current credit score or the score most recently calculated by the agency for a credit-related purpose.[215.2] Nonetheless, the key factors adversely impacting the consumer's score may provide significant information to the consumer.[215.3]

215.1   15 U.S.C. § 1681g(f), *added by* Pub. L. No. 108-159, § 212 (2003); 16 C.F.R. § 602.1(o)(3)(x), *added by* 69 Fed. Reg. 6526–31 (Feb. 5, 2004). Under the prior version of the Act, consumers were not entitled to learn their credit scores. The Act defines "key factors" to mean "all relevant elements or reasons adversely affecting the credit score for the particular individual, listed in the order of their importance based on their effect on the credit score." 15 U.S.C. 1681g(f)(2)(B).

215.2   15 U.S.C. 1681g(g)(1)(A), 15 U.S.C. § 1681g(g)(1)(A).

215.3   The agency need not disclose more than four key factors that adversely affected the consumer's credit score, with the proviso that if the number of enquiries to the consumer's file was a key factor in the score, that factor must be disclosed and is not counted under the cap. 15 U.S.C. §§ 1681g(f)(1)(C), (f)(9). §*See also* § 14.4, *infra*.

Chapter 5 Furnishing Consumer Reports to Users

5.1 General

5.1.1 Background

Page 105

Add to text at end of subsection:

The FCRA was amended by the Fair and Accurate Credit Transactions Act of 2003. Privacy and the protection of consumer financial information from identity theft were two of the major objectives behind many of the amendments.[2.1] Most of these amendments are addressed in other chapters in this manual, however some of the amendments affect the furnishing of information to users of credit reports.

2.1 Fair and Accurate Credit Transactions Act of 2003, Pub. L. No. 108-159 (2003). *See* Ch. 16, *infra*.

5.1.2 Reports May Be Released Only for Permissible Purposes

Add note 3.1 at end of fourth sentence of subsection's first paragraph.

3.1 Soghomonian v. U.S., 278 F. Supp. 2d 1151 (E.D. Cal. 2003) (rejecting argument that "may" is permissive; instead, it is limiting). *See* Pub. L. No. 90-321, § 502 (May 29, 1968), 82 Stat. 146, 147, reported as a note following 15 U.S.C. § 1601 (the Consumer Credit Protection Act), which provides in pertinent part: "(1) The word 'may' is used to indicate that an action either is authorized or is permitted. (2) The word 'shall' is used to indicate that an action is both authorized and required. (3) The phrase 'may not' is used to indicate that an action is both unauthorized and forbidden. (4) Rules of law are stated in the indicative mood."

Add to text after subsection's fifth sentence:

The stated purpose is irrelevant, as long as there is actually a permissible purpose.[3.2]

3.2 Marzluff v. Verizon Wireless, 785 N.E.2d 805 (Ohio Ct. App. 2003).

Addition to notes 8, 12, 13.

8 Adams v. Phillips, 2002 WL 31886737 (W.D. La. 2002) (impostor is user where fraudulent conduct was sole cause of issuance of credit report to retailers).

Page 106

12 *See also* Uhlig v. Berge Ford, Inc., 257 F. Supp. 2d 1228 (D. Ariz. 2003).

13 *Replace NCLC citation with*: National Consumer Law Center, Credit Discrimination §§ 3.4.4, 6.2.2.7 (3d ed. 2002 and Supp.).

Page 107

5.1.4 Agents of the User

Add to text at end of subsection:

A dealer is not vicariously liable if it induces a finance company to impermissibly obtain a report; only the finance company is liable.[33.1]

33.1 Mayberry v. Ememessay Inc., 201 F. Supp. 2d 687 (W.D. Va. 2002); Castro v. Union Nissan, Inc., 2002 WL 1466810 (N.D. Ill. 2002).

Page 108

5.1.7 Discovering an Impermissible Use

Add to text after sentence containing note 44:

It can sometimes be difficult for consumers to determine whether the inquiries are permissible or not because creditors use many different names, some of which may not be familiar to the consumer.

§ 5.2 Fair Credit Reporting / 2004 Supplement

5.2 Permissible Uses

5.2.1 In Response to a Court Order

Page 109

Addition to note 46.

    46   *Replace Etefia citation with*: 628 N.W.2d 577 (Mich. App. Ct. 2001).

Replace sentence containing note 58 with:

Rule 45 of the Federal Rules of Civil Procedure was amended to specifically provide for issuance of subpoenas by attorneys as officers of the court. Defiance of a subpoena, even if issued by an attorney, "is nevertheless an act in defiance of a court order" thereby exposing the recipient to contempt sanctions.[58]

    58   *Retain as in main edition.*
           Replace Etefia citation with: 628 N.W.2d 577 (Mich. App. Ct. 2001).

5.2.2 The Consumer's Written Instructions

Page 110

Add to text after sentence containing note 68:

With incidents of identity theft increasing, creditors should take extra care to be certain that the consumer for whom they seek to pull a credit report is in fact the consumer seeking credit. With the proliferation of consumer credit information and instant access to consumer credit files by computer, the potential for impermissible access to credit reports and invasion of consumer privacy also increases.

5.2.3 Identifying Information Furnished to the Government

Page 111

Addition to note 75.

    75   Soghomonian v. U.S., 278 F. Supp. 2d 1151 (E.D. Cal. 2003) (rejecting argument that "may" is permissive; instead, it is limiting). *See* Pub. L. 90-321, § 502 (May 29, 1968), 82 Stat. 146, 147, reported as a note following 15 U.S.C. § 1601 (the Consumer Credit Protection Act), which provides in pertinent part: "(1) The word 'may' is used to indicate that an action either is authorized or is permitted. (2) The word 'shall' is used to indicate that an action is both authorized and required. (3) The phrase 'may not' is used to indicate that an action is both unauthorized and forbidden. (4) Rules of law are stated in the indicative mood."

5.2.4 Permissible Use in Connection with Credit

5.2.4.1 General

Add to text after sentence containing note 85:

This is a particularly troublesome practice because consumers are often unaware that their credit reports are being accessed by financing companies. In many cases consumers do not receive adverse action notices when they are not granted credit, or they pay higher rates for credit, due to information contained in their credit reports.[85.1] Consumers purchasing automobiles are also often unaware that the dealer is shopping their retail installment contract around for financing.[85.2] Another practice by automobile dealers is to request the driver's license of someone looking at automobiles and taking test drives. The consumer provides no authorization for the dealer to access a credit report, however the dealer does so anyway. This is a clear violation of section 1681b(f). If a key factor that adversely affects a consumer's credit score consists of the number of enquiries made with respect to a consumer report, that factor must be included in the disclosures of a credit score, a new requirement under the FACTA of 2003.[85.3] This requirement is not subject to the disclosure limitation of only four key factors that adversely affect a credit score.[85.4]

    85.1   *See* Ch. 6, *infra*.
    85.2   Castro v. Union Nissan, Inc., 2002 WL 1034048 (N.D. Cal. May 15, 2002)(consumers never filled out credit applications from lending institutions that pulled their credit reports, nor did they authorize dealership to "shop around" their credit report).
    85.3   15 U.S.C. § 1681g(f)(9), *added by* Pub. L. No. 108-159, § 212 (2003).
    85.4   15 U.S.C. § 1681g(f)(1)(C), *added by* Pub. L. No. 108-159, § 212 (2003).

Page 112

Addition to note 90.

90   *Replace FTC v. Citigroup citation with*: 239 F. Supp. 2d 1302 (N.D. Ga. 2001).

Add to text after sentence containing note 90:

, or to rewrite the terms of a concluded transaction.[90.1]

90.1   Smith v. Bob Smith Chevrolet, Inc., 275 F. Supp. 2d 808 (W.D. Ky. 2003); Davis v. Reg'l Acceptance Corp., 300 F. Supp. 2d 377 (E.D. Va. 2003).

5.2.4.2 Collection of Credit Accounts, Judgment Debts

Addition to notes 92, 93, 95, 101.
Page 113

92   Phillips v. Grendahl, 312 F.3d 357 (8th Cir. 2002).
93   Perretta v. Capital Acquisitions & Mgmt. Co., 2003 WL 21383757 (N.D. Cal. May 5, 2003).
95   Sather v. Weintraut, 2003 WL 21692111 (D. Minn. July 10, 2003) (attorney may not obtain report of someone who is not personally liable for the judgment, such as owner or officer of corporation against whom judgment was entered).
101   Hasbun v. County of Los Angeles, 323 F.3d. 801 (9th Cir. 2003) (no need to comply with certification requirements when collecting overdue support).

Add to text after sentence containing note 105:

Account reviews are increasingly relied upon as grounds to access consumer reports. The practice of accessing consumer reports for account reviews takes various forms. Some creditors purportedly conduct account reviews on consumers who have previously discharged their debts in bankruptcy. Others access credit reports even though the statute of limitations period to report the debt has run, asserting that even though the creditor's legal remedies may be barred, the debt is not extinguished.

Add to text at end of subsection:

There is no permissible purpose to obtain a credit report on the basis of a belief that one has the right to claim that a debt exists.[105.1]

105.1   Smith v. Bob Smith Chevrolet, Inc., 275 F. Supp. 2d 808 (W.D. Ky. 2003).

5.2.5 Permissible Use in Connection With Employment

Page 114

5.2.5.1 Overview

Replace "before" in subsection's third sentence with:

However, certain employee investigations are now excluded from the definition of a consumer report.[113.1] Before

113.1   15 U.S.C. § 1681a(d)(2)(D)(x), *added by* Pub. L. No. 108-159, § 111 (2003). *See* § 5.2.5.5, *infra*.

Page 115

5.2.5.3 Employer Must Provide Prior Certification

Add to text after sentence containing note 133:

This requirement applies so long as the report does not fall within the excluded communications provision that was added to the FCRA by the FACTA of 2003.[133.1]

133.1   *See* § 5.2.5.5, *infra*.

Add to text at end of subsection:

In addition, the FACTA of 2003 provides for exceptions for certain communications relating to employer investigation of employees.[137.1]

137.1   15 U.S.C. § 1681a(d)(2)(D)(x), *added by* Pub. L. No. 108-159, § 111 (2003). *See* § 5.2.5.5, *infra*.

5.2.5.4 Agency Must Enclose Summary of Consumer Rights

Add note 137.2 at end of subsection's first sentence.

137.2   The FACTA of 2003 amended the FCRA to require the FTC to revise the model Summary of Rights. 15 U.S.C. § 1681g, *added by* Pub. . No. 108-159, § 211 (2003). *See* § 6.3, *infra*.

Add to text after sentence containing note 139:

However, if the report pertains to an employee investigation that falls outside coverage as a consumer report under the FACTA amendments, the employee is only entitled to a summary of the report if adverse action is taken. They will are not entitled to the Summary of Rights.[139.1]

139.1   15 U.S.C. § 1681a(d)(2)(D)(x), *added by* Pub. L. No. 108-159, § 111 (2003). *See* § 5.2.5.5, *infra*.

§ 5.2.5.5 Fair Credit Reporting / 2004 Supplement

Replace sentence containing note 140 with:

The FACTA of 2003 requires the FTC to substantially revise the content of the Summary of Rights.[140] The FTC and Federal Reserve Board have set December 1, 2004, as the effective date of the new Summary of Rights.[140.1]

140   15 U.S.C. § 1681g(c), *as amended by* Pub. L. No. 108-159, § 211(c) (2003).
140.1   69 Fed. Reg. 6530–6531 (Feb. 11, 2004).

Page 116

Add new subsection after § 5.2.5.4.

5.2.5.5 Communications Concerning Employee Investigations for Certain Types of Conduct Not Considered Consumer Reports

The FACTA of 2003 amended the FCRA to exclude from the definition of consumer reports communications related to employer investigations by third parties of employees for certain conduct.[141.1] To fall within this exclusion the communication must be made to an employer by a third party and must be in connection with an investigation of one of the following:

- suspected misconduct relating to employment;
- compliance with Federal, State or Local laws;
- compliance with the rules of a self-regulatory organization; or
- compliance with any preexisting written policies of the employer.

Furthermore, the communication must not be for the purpose of investigating a consumer's credit worthiness, credit standing, or credit capacity. In other words, the communication must only bear on the employee's character, general reputation, personal characteristics or mode of living. The communication must not be provided to anyone other than the employer or the employer's agent, a governmental authority, or a self-regulatory organization with regulatory authority over the employer.[141.2]

Employees who are the subject of these types of investigations and communications have the right to notification only if adverse action is taken based on the communication resulting from the investigation. The notice thus comes after the adverse action. They also have a right to a summary of the nature and substance of the communications. Prior to the FACTA amendments, such employees would have been entitled to a copy of the actual report, not simply a summary of the nature and substance of the report.[141.3] This provision became effective on March 31, 2004.[141.4]

141.1   15 U.S.C. § 1681a(d)(2)(D)(x), *added by* Pub. L. No. 108-159, § 111 (2003).
141.2   *Id.*
141.3   *See* § 5.2.5.4, *supra*.
141.4   69 Fed. Reg. 6530–6531 (Feb. 11, 2004).

Add to text after sentence containing note 143:

One court has ruled that an actual application for insurance is not necessary as long as the insurer intends to use the report for underwriting.[143.1]

143.1   Scharpf v. AIG Mktg., Inc., 242 F. Supp. 2d 455 (W.D. Ky. 2003) (the adverse action notice provision thus also applies despite absence of an actual application).

Replace note 144 with:

144   *See* Ch. 6, *infra*.

Add to text at end of subsection:

Several states also have passed laws governing the issuance of consumer reports for insurance purposes.[148.1] Many states also require notice to consumers if a credit report is to be used for underwriting purposes. For example, Maine requires users of consumer reports to disclose at the time of application for insurance the fact that it will use credit information. If the insurer takes adverse action, it must explain the reasons to the consumer, and provide notice pursuant to state law and the FCRA.[148.2] Many state laws also prohibit insurers from requesting credit information, including credit scores, based on protected status including race, ethnicity, color, religion, marital status, age, gender and other categories.[148.3]

148.1   *See* Appx. B.3, *infra*.
148.2   Me. Rev. Stat. Ann. tit. 24A, §§ 2169-B. *See* Appx. B.3, *infra*.
148.3   *See* Appx. B.3, *infra*.

Furnishing Consumer Reports to Users / 2004 Supplement § 5.3.4

5.2.7 Permissible Use in Connection with Government Licenses or Other Benefits

Replace note 149 with:

149 15 U.S.C. § 1681b(a)(3)(D).

Page 117

Replace note 160 with:

160 15 U.S.C. § 1681b(a)(3)(D).

5.2.9 Permissible Use in Connection with Business Transactions

Page 118

5.2.9.1 User's Business Purpose, Where Individual Has a Consumer Purpose

Addition to notes 168, 178.

168 Smith v. Bob Smith Chevrolet, Inc., 275 F. Supp. 2d 808 (W.D. Ky. 2003) (dealer cannot obtain post-transaction report).
178 Uhlig v. Berge Ford, Inc., 257 F. Supp. 2d 1228 (D. Ariz. 2003).

Page 119

Add to text at end of paragraph containing note 180:

When the dealer mistakenly wrote up the transaction more favorably to the consumer, the dealer does not have a permissible purpose to obtain the report, even though it thinks the consumer should reimburse the dealer. It had no account to review once the sale was consummated and no actual debt.[180.1]

180.1 Smith v. Bob Smith Chevrolet, Inc., 275 F. Supp. 2d 808 (W.D. Ky. 2003).

Page 120

5.2.10 User's Legitimate Business Need to Review a Consumer's Account

Add to text at end of subsection's second paragraph:

Nor may a dealer obtain a credit report when the transaction has been finalized just because it wrote up the terms more favorably than it meant to.[198.1]

198.1 Smith v. Bob Smith Chevrolet, Inc., 275 F. Supp. 2d 808 (W.D. Ky. 2003).

Addition to note 199.

199 *Replace FTC v. Citigroup citation with*: 239 F. Supp. F 1302 (N.D. Ga. 2001).

5.2.11 Permissible Use by Officials to Determine Child Support Payment Levels

Add note 201.1 to end of first sentence in subsection's second paragraph.

201.1 Hasbun v. County of Los Angeles, 323 F.3d 801 (9th Cir. 2003).

5.3 Potentially Impermissible Purposes

Page 121

5.3.1 General

Add to text at end of subsection:

A user can be liable for either using or obtaining a consumer report impermissibly.[206.1]
206.1 Chester v. Purvis, 260 F. Supp. 2d 711 (S.D. Ind. 2003).

Page 122

5.3.4 Use in Civil or Criminal Litigation

Addition to notes 220, 221, 222, 225.

220 Rodgers v. McCullough, 296 F. Supp. 2d 895 (W.D. Tenn. 2003).
221 Chester v. Purvis, 2003 WL 22454885 (S.D. Ind. Oct. 22, 2003).
222 Chester v. Purvis, 260 F. Supp. 2d 711 (S.D. Ind. 2003).
225 Chester v. Purvis, 2003 WL 22454885 (S.D. Ind. Oct. 22, 2003).

Page 123

§ 5.3.5

Add to text after sentence containing note 226:

An attorney for a collection agency has no immunity from suit under the FCRA simply because he obtained and used a credit report in the course of his duties as a lawyer in the context of litigation.[226.1]

    226.1   Chester v. Purvis, 260 F. Supp. 2d 711 (S.D. Ind. 2003).

Page 124

5.3.5 Use by Investigators

Addition to note 233.

    233   Phillips v. Grendahl, 312 F.3d 357 (8th Cir. 2002) (investigation of boyfriend not permissible purpose).

Page 125

5.3.6 Use of Reports on the Consumer's Spouse, Relatives, or Other Third Parties

Addition to notes 246, 248.

    246   Olson v. Six Rivers Nat'l Bank, 111 Cal. App. 4th 1, 3 Cal. Rptr. 3d 301 (Cal. App. 2003) (community property state; applying parallel state law).

    248   *Replace last sentence of note with*: *See generally* National Consumer Law Center, Credit Discrimination (3d ed. 2002 and Supp.) for a discussion of ECOA Regulation B.

Add to text after sentence containing note 250:

A former spouse has a permissible purpose to obtain a joint credit report of her former husband when the information contained in the report related to the creditworthiness, credit standing and credit capacity of the parties' ability to discharge their parental duties under state law.[250.1] An ex-spouse may access the former spouse's credit report as long as she reasonably believes the former spouse owes her a debt (even if it is not actually owed).[250.2]

    250.1   Spencer v. Spencer, 52 Fed. Appx. 874 (9th Cir. 2002) (local court rules may limit citation to this case). *See* 9th Cir. R. 36-3).

    250.2   Marzluff v. Verizon Wireless, 785 N.E.2d 805 (Ohio Ct. App. 2003).

Page 126

5.3.7 Use in Connection With Insurance Claims

Add to text after sentence containing note 260:

Practitioners also report that insurance companies utilize waivers containing vague but broad language in connection with processing insurance claims. Such waivers are then used as grounds to access consumer reports and gather information on the consumers. This practice undermines the FCRA's protections against accessing consumer reports for impermissible purposes.

5.3.8 Use of Lists of Consumers, Marketing Research, and Prescreening

5.3.8.4 Prescreening Lists

Page 127

5.3.8.4.1 Lists allowed for credit and insurance solicitations

Addition to note 274.

    274   Cole v. U.S. Capital, Inc., 2002 WL 31415736 (N.D. Ill. 2002); Gamble v. Citifinancial, 2002 WL 31643028 (D. Conn. 2002).

Add to text after sentence containing note 274:

In 2000, 3.5 billion prescreened offers were sent to consumers based on lists created by credit reporting agencies.[274.1]

    274.1   Neal Walters, *The Fair Credit Reporting Act: Issues and Policies*, p.2, AARP Public Policy Institute Issue Brief No. 58 (Jan. 2003).

Page 128

Replace note 277 with:

    277   15 U.S.C. § 1681b(c),(e), *as amended by* Pub. L. No. 108-159, § 213(c) (2003). Previously, prescreening was permitted for offers of credit only, not for insurance.

Addition to note 281.

    281   Kennedy v. Chase Manhattan Bank, 2003 WL 21181427 (E.D. La. May 19, 2003).

Furnishing Consumer Reports to Users / 2004 Supplement § 5.4.2.2

Page 129

5.3.8.4.2 Prescreened lists are a type of consumer report

Add to text at end of subsection:

In dissenting from the denial of Trans Union's petition for *certiorari*, Justice Kennedy recognized "Prescreening entails the disclosure of detailed credit performance information, including bill payment history. Release of this information is far more invasive of consumer privacy than release of the names and addresses contained in the petitioner's marketing lists."[295.1]

295.1 Trans Union L.L.C., v. F.T.C., 536 U.S. 915 (2002).

5.3.8.4.3 A firm offer is required

Replace first sentence of subsection's second paragraph with:

A "firm offer" does not have to be very firm or include specific terms, such as interest rate.[295.2]

295.2 Tucker v. Olympia Dodge of Countryside, Inc., 2003 WL 21230604 (N.D. Ill. May 28, 2003) (firm offer is defined in terms of a creditor's intention to honor an offer of credit in accordance with creditor's own undisclosed, predetermined criteria).

Add to text after sentence containing note 296:

As one court noted, "[T]he FCRA has been manipulated such that a 'firm offer' really means a 'firm offer if you meet certain criteria.'"[296.1]

296.1 Tucker v. Olympia Dodge of Countryside, Inc., 2003 WL 21230604 (N.D. Ill. May 28, 2003) (satisfies "firm offer" even though depends on creditor's undisclosed predetermined criteria); Kennedy v. Chase Manhattan Bank, 2003 WL 21181427 (E.D. La. May 19, 2003).

Page 130

5.3.8.4.4 Consumers can elect to be excluded from prescreening lists

Replace second sentence of subsection's third paragraph with:

As of December 1, 2004, the term of the opt-out period will extend from two years to five.[299.1] This right to opt-out of prescreening lists should not be confused with the new right of consumers to opt-out of the use of their information by affiliates for marketing purposes. This right, added by the FACTA, applies to information that falls outside of the FCRA's definition of consumer report pursuant to either the first-hand knowledge exception or the affiliate exception.[299.2] Under the FACTA the FTC must issue rules for the prescreened offer notice. The rules must ensure such notices are "simple and easy to understand." Agencies must present the notice in that format and must also include the address and telephone number of the opt-out notification system.[299.3]

299.1 15 U.S.C. §§ 1681b(e)(3)(A), (e)(4)(B)(1), *amended by* Pub. L. No. 108-159 § 213(c) (2003); 16 C.F.R. § 602.1(c)(3)(xi), *added by* 69 Fed. Reg. 6526–31 (Feb. 5, 2004).
299.2 15 U.S.C. § 1681s-3, *added by* Pub. L. No. 108-159 § 213(c) (2003). See also §§ 2.4.1, 2.4.2, *supra*.
299.3 15 U.S.C. § 1681m(d)(2), *as amended by* Pub. L. No. 108-159, § 213 (2003). See § 6.6.6.4, *infra*.

5.4 Agency Procedures Insuring That Only Users with Permissible Purposes Obtain Reports

5.4.2 User Identification and Certifications

Page 133

5.4.2.2 Blanket Certifications

Add a comma after "statute" in the sentence containing note 341 and add:

prohibiting dealers from requesting, obtaining or reviewing a consumer's credit report in connection with: (1) a test drive; (2) a request for information about pricing or financing; or (3) for negotiating with the consumer, unless the dealer received an application from the consumer to lease or finance or has written authorization from the consumer to obtain or review the credit report.

§ 5.4.3 *Fair Credit Reporting / 2004 Supplement*

Page 134

5.4.3 Agency Verification Procedures

Addition to note 349.

349 *Replace Source One citation with*: 763 N.E.2d 42 (Mass. 2002).

5.4.4 Electronic Communication of Reports

Replace note 357 with:

357 FTC Official Staff Commentary § 607 item 2E [reprinted at Appx. C, *infra*]. *See* National Consumer Law Center, Consumer Law Pleadings, No. 3 § 5.1 (2003 Cumulative CD-Rom and Index Guide).

5.6 User Liability for Impermissible Purposes

Page 135

5.6.1 Introduction

Addition to note 366.

366 Davis v. Reg'l Acceptance Corp., 300 F. Supp. 2d 377 (E.D. Va. 2003) (court overlooked § 1681b(f) in ruling that consumer has no claim against user under § 1681b ruling overruled by appellate recognition of § 1682b(f) cause of action in Ausherman v. Bank of Am. Corp., 352 F.3d 896 (4th Cir. 2003)).
Replace Source One citation with: 763 N.E.2d 42 (Mass. 2002).

Add to text at end of subsection:

One court inexplicably ruled that an individual who passively received a report she did not request did not "use or obtain" a consumer report.[366.1]

366.1 Phillips v. Grendahl, 312 F.3d 357 (8th Cir. 2002).

5.6.2 Uncertified Uses of a Consumer Report

Addition to note 371.

371 *Add before cross reference:* Ausherman v. Bank of Am. Corp., 352 F.3d 896 (4th Cir. 2003) (recognizing § 1681b(f) is now primary source of civil liability rather than § 1681q); Sather v. Weintraut, 2003 WL 21692111 (D. Minn. July 10, 2003) (same).

Page 136

5.6.3 Knowing Non-Compliance of User

Add to text at end of subsection's second paragraph:

Familiarity with the FCRA or general knowledge that reports can be obtained under limited circumstances is sufficient to support an inference of knowingly obtaining a consumer report in conscious disregard of the target's legal rights.[377.1] Repeatedly obtaining a consumer's report after notices that consumer had no account with user is sufficient to defeat a motion to dismiss a claim that the user willfully obtained the consumer's report without a permissible purpose.[377.2]

377.1 Phillips v. Grendahl, 312 F.3d 357 (8th Cir. 2002); Sather v. Weintraut, 2003 WL 21692111 (D. Minn. July 10, 2003).

377.2 Sather v. Weintraut, 2003 WL 21692111 (D. Minn. July 10, 2003); Veno v. A. T.& T. Corp., 297 F. Supp. 2d 379 (D. Mass. 2003).

Page 137

5.6.5 Vicarious Liability of User for Acts of Employees

Addition to notes 392–395.
Page 138

392 *Add to end of Myers parenthetical*: , *on remand*, 238 F. Supp. 2d 1196 (D. Nev. 2002).

393 Myers v. Bennett Law Offices, 238 F. Supp. 2d 1196 (D. Nev. 2002) (employer not subject to negligence liability because §§ 1681m(b) and 1681q require knowing or willful acts). *Contra* Del Amora v. Metro Ford Sales and Service, Inc. 206 F. Supp. 2d 947 (N.D. Ill. 2002); Ausherman v. Bank of Am. Corp., 352 F.3d 896 (4th Cir. 2003) (subscriber cannot be liable for acts of unknown person; access code had been terminated; no proof that an employee was involved in obtaining credit reports).

394 Myers v. Bennett Law Offices, 238 F. Supp. 2d 1196 (D. Nev. 2002); Del Amora v. Metro Ford Sales and Service, Inc. 206 F. Supp. 2d 947 (N.D. Ill. 2002) (violation accomplished by virtue of employment position and access to credit reporting computer).

395 Ashby v. Farmers Group, Inc., 261 F. Supp. 2d 1213 (D. Or. 2003) (normal common law rules of agency apply); Spano v. Safeco Ins. Co., 215 F.R.D. 601 (D. Or. 2003).

Add to text at end of subsection:

However, when the employee is acting without express or implied approval of supervisors and was terminated when the employer learned that she had accessed plaintiff's reports impermissibly and contrary to its guidelines, the employer is not liable for the employee's independent tort.[396]

396 Smith v. Sears, Roebuck & Co., 276 F. Supp. 2d 603 (S.D. Miss. 2003) (rejecting respondeat superior, apparent authority, and aided-in-the-agency analyses of other courts); Graves v. Tubb, 281 F. Supp. 2d 886 (N.D. Miss. 2003) (same; nothing in the FCRA makes employer liable for employees who knowingly obtain reports for impermissible purposes).

Chapter 6 Notices Concerning Consumer Reports

Page 139

6.1 Introduction

Replace last sentence in subsection's first paragraph with:

To shed light on this commerce of information, the FCRA requires a variety of notices be given to consumers. Without such notice, few consumers would ever know of their rights under the Act or that their access to, and cost for, credit may have been adversely affected by information in their credit reports. The FCRA was amended in 2003 by the Fair and Accurate Credit Transactions Act,[0.1] which contains additional notice requirements on a variety of subjects, including identity theft (§ 6.3a in this supplement, *infra*), risk-based pricing (§ 6.4a in this supplement, *infra*), negative information furnished by financial institutions to credit reporting agencies (§§ 3.8a and 6.8e in this supplement, *infra*), key factors in credit scores (§ 6.8a in this supplement, *infra*), fraud alerts (§ 6.8b in this supplement, *infra*), blocks for identity theft information (§ 6.8c in this supplement, *infra*), and credit scores (§§ 6.8d and 14.4 (Supp), *infra*).

   0.1   Fair and Accurate Credit Transactions Act of 2003, Pub. L. No. 108-159 (2003).

Replace section's second paragraph with:

This chapter reviews each of the consumer notices required by the FCRA, including those required by the 2003 amendments. Each notice is important because it alerts the consumer to the fact that private information is being disseminated, collected, and used, often to the detriment of the consumer. Some notices also offer the consumer a limited ability to control the use of personal information. Most importantly, perhaps, all notices can trigger a consumer's inquiry into just what personal information is being reported and what the consumer can do to correct misinformation. The chain of events which leads consumers to seek legal counsel about an FCRA matter often begins with an FCRA-required notice.

6.2 Importance and Types of Notices

Replace subsection's first sentence with:

Prior to the FACTA's amendments, five types of notices were required by the FCRA, and each are discussed in the following sections.

Add to text before last sentence of section's first paragraph:

The FACTA added several other notice requirements that address a variety of credit reporting issues. These are discussed later in this chapter.[8.1]

   8.1   Fair and Accurate Credit Transactions Act of 2003, Pub. L. No. 108-159 (2003).

Add to text after last sentence of section's second paragraph:

The FACTA of 2003 requires the FTC to revise the Summary of Consumer Rights.[9.1] The revision is likely to be final on December 1, 2004.[9.2]

   9.1   15 U.S.C. § 1681g(c), *as amended by* Pub. L. No. 108-159, § 21(c) (2003). See § 6.3, *infra*.
   9.2   See § 6.3, *infra*.

Page 141

6.3 The Summary of Consumer Rights

Add after bulleted list:

The FACTA of 2003[29.1] requires the FTC to revise this summary of rights notice.[29.2] The section of the FCRA amended by the FACTA now refers to this notice as a "Summary of Rights To Obtain and Dispute Information In Consumer Reports and To Obtain Credit Scores." This new summary must include a description of—

- the right of consumers to obtain a copy of their report from each credit reporting agency;
- the frequency and circumstances under which a consumer is entitled to receive a credit report without charge from a nationwide consumer reporting agency;
- the right of a consumer to dispute information in that consumer's file;
- the right of a consumer to obtain a credit score from a consumer reporting agency, and a description of how to obtain a credit score;
- the method by which a consumer can contact, and obtain a consumer report from, a nationwide consumer reporting agency without charge, as provided for by FTC regulations; and
- the method by which a consumer can contact, and obtain a consumer report from, a nationwide specialty credit reporting agency, as provided for by FTC regulations.[29.3]

The FACTA also requires the FTC to actively publicize the availability of the summary, conspicuously post on its website the availability of the summary, and promptly make the summary available to consumers upon request.[29.4] The FTC's prescribed form for the Summary of Rights is required to be used by credit reporting agencies.[29.5] Prior to the FACTA amendments, the agencies could use their own form of summary of rights.

The FACTA amendments further require the newly revised Summary of Rights to be included with each written disclosure to a consumer provided by credit reporting agencies.[29.6] If an agency is a nationwide agency, as defined in § 1681a, the nationwide agency must also disclose its toll-free telephone number, which must be staffed by personnel who are accessible to consumers during normal working hours.[29.7] The revised Summary of Rights to be included with agency disclosures must also include the following:

- a list of all federal agencies responsible for enforcing the FCRA, and the address and phone number of each such agency;
- a statement that the consumer may have additional rights under State law, and that the consumer may wish to contact a state or local consumer protection agency or a State attorney general or the equivalent thereof to learn of those rights; and
- a statement that the consumer reporting agency is not required to remove accurate derogatory information from the file of a consumer, unless the information is outdated under § 1681c or cannot be verified.[29.8] This requirement is only applicable to nationwide credit reporting agencies, and does not appear to be applicable to the newly defined nationwide specialty credit reporting agencies.[29.9]

The FACTA eliminated the requirement that the Summary of Rights include "all of the rights" that the consumer had under the FCRA.

29.1 Pub. L. No. 108-159 (2003).
29.2 *Id.* at § 211(c). The FTC has not published a new notice, however, it has indicated that the effective date for the new Summary of Rights is December 1, 2004. *See* 69 Fed Reg. 13192 (Mar. 19, 2004).
29.3 15 U.S.C. § 1681g(c), *as amended by* Pub. L. No. 108-159, § 211(c) (2003).
29.4 15 U.S.C. § 1681g, *as amended by* Pub. L. No. 108-159, § 211(c) (2003).
29.5 15 U.S.C. S 1681g(c), *as amended by* Pub. L. No. 108-159, S 211(c)(2003).
29.6 *Id.*
29.7 *Id.*
29.8 15 U.S.C. § 1681g(c)(2)(A), *as amended by* Pub. L. No. 108-159, § 211(c) (2003).
29.9 *Id.*

Add new section after § 6.3:

6.3a Summary of Rights for Identity Theft Victims

The FACTA of 2003 amends the FCRA to require the FTC, federal banking agencies, and the National Credit Union Administration to prepare a model summary of rights for identity theft victims.[32.1] This summary should include the rights of consumers with respect to procedures for remedying the effects of fraud or identity theft involving credit, an electronic

Notices Concerning Consumer Reports / 2004 Supplement § 6.4.2.3.2

fund transfer, or an account or transaction at or with a financial institution or other creditor.[32.2] Sixty days after the model summary of rights for identity theft victims becomes final, consumer reporting agencies must provide consumers with the summary when consumers express a belief that they are victims of fraud or identity theft involving credit, an electronic fund transfer, or an account or transaction at or with a financial institution or other creditor. This is in addition to any other action the agency may take.[32.3]

32.1   15 U.S.C. § 1681g(d), *as amended by* Pub. L. No. 108-159, § 151 (2003). *See* § 16.6.1a, *infra*.
32.2   15 U.S.C. § 1681g(d)(1).
32.3   *Id.*

6.4 When Notice of Adverse Action Is Required

6.4.2 Adverse Action Based on Consumer Reports

6.4.2.3 Where Adverse Use Relates to Credit Purposes

Page 144

6.4.2.3.1 General

Replace last sentence of subsection's first paragraph with:

Readers should consider the relevant discussions in National Consumer Law Center, *Credit Discrimination* (3d ed. 2002 and Supp.).

Addition to note 64.

64 Cannon v. Metro Ford, Inc., 239 F. Supp. 2d 1302 (N.D. Ga. 2001) (repossession could be adverse action if based on credit report); Castro v. Union Nissan, Inc., 2002 WL 1466810 (N.D. Ill. 2002) (same).

Add to text at end of subsection's second paragraph:

If a yo-yo car sale is subject to a condition subsequent that the dealer obtain financing, denial based on inability to obtain financing (rather than on the credit report) does not require an adverse action notice under the FCRA (even though it does under the ECOA).[64.1]

64.1   Brand v. Rohr-Ville Motors, Inc., 2003 WL 21078022 (N.D. Ill. May 9, 2003).

Replace note 67 with:

67 National Consumer Law Center, Credit Discrimination § 2.2.2 (3d ed. 2002 and Supp.).

Addition to note 68.

68 Payne v. Ken Dipeholz Ford Lincoln Mercury, Inc., 2004 WL 40631 (N.D. Ill. Jan 5, 2004) (requiring cosigner is adverse action); Brand v. Rohr-Ville Motors, Inc., 2003 WL 21078022 (N.D. Ill. May 9, 2003) (question of fact whether adverse action was based on credit report instead of on third party's refusal to buy the loan).

Page 145

6.4.2.3.2 "Denial" of credit defined

Replace second sentence in subsection's last paragraph with:

Some courts have ruled that there is no denial if the consumer accepts a counteroffer made by the creditor,[76] but such a conclusion is not necessarily controlling and arguments can be made that acceptance of counteroffer terms adverse to the consumer still violate the FCRA. *See* § 6.4.2.3.2A, *infra*.

76 Harper v. Lindsay Chevrolet Oldsmobile, L.L.C., 212 F. Supp. 2d 582 (E.D. Va. 2002); Mayberry v. Ememessay Inc., 201 F. Supp. 2d 687 (W.D. Va. 2002); Austin v. J.C. Penney Co., 162 F. Supp. 2d 495 (E.D. Va. 2001) (without deciding the conflicting authority as to whether a check is a credit instrument, court determines that initial refusal to accept check due to credit report, and acceptance of the check 45 minutes later is adverse action within the meaning of FCRA. Court deems notice burden on merchants too great.); National Consumer Law Center, Credit Discrimination § 10.2.4.2 (3d ed. 2002 and Supp.).

Addition to note 77.

77 There is no denial where a dealer merely submitted credit report to potential lenders and made it clear that without lenders approval there was no sale. Najieb v. Chrysler-Plymouth, 2002 WL 31906466 (N.D. Ill. 2002).

Add new subsection after § 6.4.2.3.2.

6.4.2.3.2a Is there an adverse action if a counteroffer is accepted?

One issue associated with counteroffers is whether acceptance of a counteroffer in a credit transaction initiated by the consumer will trigger the FCRA adverse action notice requirement. For example, automobile dealers and other retailers currently offer "zero percent financing" and other teaser rates, but many consumers do not qualify for such offers because of information in their credit reports. These consumers still enter into the transactions at the higher rate, yet they do not receive adverse action notices and are thus unaware that they are paying higher costs because of their credit report or credit score. Does the FCRA require an adverse action notice under these circumstances? The answer to this question hinges on the interpretation of section 1681a(k)(1)(A) (which incorporates the ECOA definition) and section 1681a(k)(1)(B)(iv) (which includes any action "adverse to the consumer.").

The ECOA defines adverse action as

> a denial or revocation of credit, a change in the terms of an existing credit arrangement, or a refusal to grant credit in substantially the same amount or on substantially the terms requested. Such term does not include a refusal to extend additional credit under an existing credit arrangement where the applicant is delinquent or otherwise in default, or where such additional credit would exceed a previously established credit limit.[77.1]

In addition, Regulation B specifically states that adverse action is a "refusal to grant credit in substantially the terms requested in an application *unless the creditor makes a counteroffer (to grant the credit in a different amount or on other terms) and the applicant uses or expressly accepts the credit offered.*"[77.2] The FRB findings, decisions, commentaries and orders apply to any determination of whether an action constitutes an adverse action.[77.3]

These definitions must be compared to section 1681a(k)(1)(B)(iv) which defines adverse action as "an action taken or determination that is (I) made in connection with an application that was made by, or a transaction that was initiated by, any consumer . . . and (II) *adverse to the interests of the consumer.*"[77.4] This definition must be read as a supplement to section 1681a(k)(1)(A) because of the use of the word "and." Moreover, section 1681a(k)(1)(B)(iv) and other subsections clearly go beyond the more limited ECOA definitions.

The FTC has issued contradictory staff opinion letters relating to this issue. The first FTC staff opinion letter (Brinckerhoff) supports the argument that a counteroffer with adverse terms is the type of action for which the FCRA notice was created.[77.5] The example used in the opinion letter is an applicant for an auto loan who had to pay more to finance an automobile purchase than she would have been charged if her credit record had been better. According to this opinion, the increase in charge triggers the notice required under section 1681m of the FCRA.[77.6] A subsequent FTC staff opinion letter does not address the analysis and conclusion contained in the Brinckerhoff letter and instead simply follows the definition of adverse action contained in Regulation B.[77.7]

A court in Virginia has held that a change in interest rate from 23 percent to 25 percent in an auto financing deal did not constitute adverse action as required by section 1681m.[77.8] The court relied upon FRB's Regulation B definition of adverse action as a basis for its decision. The decision did not include any analysis relating to the broader definition of adverse action contained in section 1681a(k)(1)(B)(iv). Until there are additional cases that rule on this issue or legislation is passes that explicitly requires adverse action notices when counteroffers are accepted, this issue will remain unresolved.

77.1 15 U.S.C. § 1691d(6).
77.2 12 C.F.R. § 2.02(c)(1).
77.3 15 U.S.C. § 1681a(k)(2).
77.4 15 U.S.C. § 1681a(k)(1)(B)(iv)(I) and (II).
77.5 Brinkerhoff, FTC Informal Staff Opinion Letter, May 31, 1996 [found on CD-Rom. *See also* Appx. D, *infra*].
77.6 *Id.*
77.7 Keller, FTC Staff Opinion Letter, July 14, 2000 [found on CD-Rom. *See also* Appx. D, *infra*]; Berger, FTC Staff Opinion Letter, June 28, 2003 [found on CD-Rom. *See also* Appx. D, *infra*].
77.8 Harper v. Lindsay Chevrolet Oldsmobile, L.L.C., 212 F. Supp. 2d 582 (E.D. Va. 2002).

Notices Concerning Consumer Reports / 2004 Supplement § 6.4.2.4

6.4.2.3.3 Denial of leases

Replace subsection's first sentence with:

The issue of whether the denial of a lease is an adverse action should be clear.[78]

78 Retain as in main edition.

Add to text after sentence containing note 79:

However, it is less clear that the ECOA notice is required when a consumer is denied a lease because of a credit report.[79.1]

79.1 *See* National Consumer Law Center, Credit Discrimination § 2.2.2.4.4 (3d ed. 2002 and Supp.); Head v. N. Pier Apartment Tower, 2003 WL 221227885 (N.D. Ill. Sept. 12, 2003) (signing of lease was not an extension of credit for ECOA purposes).

Page 146

6.4.2.4 When Adverse Use Relates to Employment Purposes

Replace subsection's first and second paragraphs up to and including note 88 with:

Prior to the FACTA,[87] notice of adverse action was required whenever adverse employment decisions were based, at least in part, on consumer reports. Additional disclosures prior to the adverse action were required as well. However, the FACTA significantly reduced the circumstances in which adverse action notices will be given to employees.

Before the FACTA, employers were required to give notice of adverse action whenever they made any employment decision that was adverse to the interests of the consumer and which either 1) used the consumer's credit information, or 2) was based on the use of an investigative report to make the decision.[88] These rules applied to both prospective employees applying for jobs and to existing employees being investigated for promotion or for disciplinary action based on suspected misconduct.[88.1] Employers objected to applying these requirements to situations in which they were using third-party investigators to determine whether existing employees had violated laws or company policies. As a result, over the vigorous objections of representatives of workers and consumers, Congress caved in to the demands of employers and in the FACTA[88.2] exempted certain reports about employees from the requirements for consumer reports. Of relevance to the discussion in this section is the application of the new rules to adverse action notices.

The FACTA does not change the requirement that employers provide adverse action notices (or other notices required by the FCRA)[88.3] to 1) consumers who are being investigated for a new position or a new job by a third party hired by the employer for that purpose, or 2) any consumers, whether they are existing employees or not, whom the employer decides to evaluate via a consumer credit report in the employment context. As before, employers are required to disclose their reliance on a consumer report—or a third-party investigative report—any time they deny initial employment, promotion, or job transfer to an employee.[88.4]

However, there are new requirements of the FACTA of 2003 for all adverse actions which are applicable to employers' investigations of existing employees. In response to employers' complaints that the FCRA's disclosure provisions hindered investigations of workplace misconduct, the FACTA provides that certain communications made to an employer will no longer be "consumer reports."[88.5] Because of this new exemption, even if a particular investigation would otherwise be an investigative consumer report, it will fall outside of the definition by virtue of being specifically exempted from the definition of "consumer report."[88.6] To fall within the exclusion the communication must be made to an employer and must be in connection with an investigation of one of the following:

- suspected misconduct relating to employment;
- compliance with federal, state, or local laws;
- compliance with the rules of a self-regulatory organization; or
- compliance with the preexisting written policies of the employer.[88.7]

Accordingly, for investigations that meet the exemption, upon adverse action the employee will not be entitled to the standard adverse action notice of § 1681m. Instead, these employees will have the right to a summary of the report and not to a Summary of Rights.[88.8] In contrast to other employment-related investigations, the employer need not provide any notice

§ 6.4.2.5   Fair Credit Reporting / 2004 Supplement

beforehand.[88.9] The effect of this amendment is to remove all of the FCRA protections for misconduct investigations concerning current employees, leaving the existing notice requirements applicable only to prospective employees who are new applicants and those employees who are subject to transfers or promotions. The remainder of this subsection relates to employment uses of consumer information that do not qualify for the new exemption.

Employers complained that the FCRA unfairly undercut meaningful investigations of employee misconduct by requiring the employer to provide FCRA notices ahead of time, notices that effectively alerted the employee to the employer's suspicions.

Among the Act's requirements that were perceived as impeding such investigations were the following: (1) notice to the consumer (in this case, the employee) of the investigation; (2) the employee's consent prior to the investigation; (3) a description of the nature and scope of the proposed investigation, if the employee requested it; (4) a release of a full, un-redacted investigative report to the employee; and (5) notice to the employee of his or her rights under FCRA prior to taking any adverse employment action. 15 U.S.C. § 1681 b(b). *See* § 5.2.5.5, *supra*.

87   Pub. L. No. 108-159 (2003).
88   Keller, FTC Informal Staff Opinion Letter, April 5, 1999, Appx. F, *infra*.
88.1   15 U.S.C. §§ 1681a and 1681m, *as amended by* Pub. L. No. 108-159 (2003).
88.2   *See* 149 Cong. Rec. H8123 (daily ed. Sept. 10, 2003).
88.3   *See* § 9.1.3 and 9.1.2.4, *infra*.
88.4   *See* 15 U.S.C. § 1681a(h). *See also* Silbergeld, FTC Informal Staff Opinion Letter, April 15, 1971 (reproduced on the accompanying CD-Rom). *See also* Appx. D, *infra*. FTC, Compliance with the Fair Credit Reporting Act 41. *Cf.* Maloney, FTC Staff Opinion Letter, Sept. 4, 1984 (reproduced on the accompanying CD-Rom). *See also* Appx. D, *infra*.
88.5   Pub. L. No. 108-159, § 611(b) (2003), *amending* 15 U.S.C. § 1681a(d)(2)(D).
88.6   15 U.S.C. § 1681a(d)(2)(D), *amended by* Pub. L. No. 108-159, § 611(b) (2003).
88.7   *Id.*
88.8   15 U.S.C. § 1681a(d)(2)(D)(x), *added by* Pub. L. No. 108-159, § 111 (2003). *See* § 5.2.5.5, *infra*.
88.9   *See* 15 U.S.C. § 1681b(b)(3).

Page 147

Replace sentence containing note 89 with:

With respect to security clearances for government contractor's employees, the FTC expanded the definition of employment to cover such contractor's employees.[89]

89   Retain as in main edition.

Replace first sentence of subsection's third paragraph with:

Except for communications excluded by the FACTA amendments, an employer intending to take adverse action based, at least in part, on a consumer report must provide to the consumer/employee beforehand a copy of the report itself and a FTC Summary of Rights.[91]

91   Retain as in main edition.

Page 148

6.4.2.5 When Adverse Use Relates to Insurance Purposes

Addition to note 101.

101   Razilov v. Nationwide Mutual Ins. Co., 242 F. Supp. 2d 977 (D. Or. 2003) (obligation limited to issuer; does not extend to underwriter; only the actual insurer must give notice; affiliates involved in the decision are not subject to the adverse action requirement); Ashby v. Farmers Group, Inc., 261 F. Supp. 2d 1213 (D. Or. 2003); Spano v. Safeco Ins. Co., 215 F.R.D. 601 (D. Or. 2003)).

Add to text after sentence containing note 105:

An Alabama district court certified a class action against an insurer who allegedly raised premiums by fifty percent or more in reliance on information contained in consumer reports and allegedly failed to send adverse action notice pursuant to section 1681m.[105.1] The insurer used Insurance Bureau Codes (ICBs) as one factor in setting the amounts of homeowners' renewal premiums. ICBs are generated by Fair Issac, Inc.[105.2] based on information contained in credit reports.[105.3]

105.1   Braxton v. Farmers Insurance Group, 209 F.R.D. 654 (N.D. Ala. 2002).
105.2   See Ch. 14, *infra*, for a discussion of credit scores.
105.3   Braxton v. Farmers Insurance Group, 209 F.R.D. 654 (N.D. Ala. 2002). *See* § 10.7.2, *infra*.

Notices Concerning Consumer Reports / 2004 Supplement § 6.4.5

Add to text after sentence containing note 106:

One practice reportedly used by insurance companies is accessing credit reports of non-applicants for insurance and making determinations on whether to grant insurance or charge higher premiums for the insurance based on the non-applicant's credit history. This practice raises issues regarding adverse action notices and who is entitled to an adverse action notice when insurance is denied or is granted but only at a higher rate because of the credit report of the non-applicant. Should the applicant receive an adverse action notice, the non-applicant or both? No court has ruled on this issue, but advocates have filed actions complaining of this practice.

6.4.2.7 When Adverse Use Relates to Other Purposes

Page 149

6.4.2.7.2 When adverse action relates to a review of the consumer's account

Add note 114.1 after "factors" in second sentence of subsection's second paragraph.

114.1 Jenifer Bayot, *Surprise Jump in Credit Rates Bring Scrutiny*, New York Times, May 20, 2003, at page 1.

6.4.4 Notice of Adverse Use of Information Other Than Consumer Report

Page 153

6.4.4.3 Subsequent Disclosure Rights

Replace note 165 with:

165 15 U.S.C. § 1691(d); Regulation B, 12 C.F.R. § 202.9 and Appendix C. These requirements are treated more extensively in National Consumer Law Center, Credit Discrimination § 10.2 (3d ed. 2002 and Supp.).

6.4.5 ECOA Notices Concerning Adverse Action

Replace note 170.

170 *See* 12 C.F.R. § 202.9(a). *See also* National Consumer Law Center, Credit Discrimination Ch. 10 (3d ed. 2002 and Supp.).

Add to text after sentence containing note 170:

For purposes of ECOA creditors include "any person who regularly extends, renews, or continues credit; any person who regularly arranges for the extension, renewal or continuation of credit; or any assignee or an original creditor who participates in the decision to extend, renew, or credit."[170.1]

170.1 15 U.S.C. § 1691a(e). *See* Reg. B, 12 C.F.R. § 202, Supp. I, Comm. 202.2(1)-1 (Official Staff Commentary) (creditor also includes an assignee or potential purchaser of the obligation who influences the credit decision by indicating whether or not it will purchase the obligation if the transaction is consummated).

Replace notes 174, 176, 181 with:

174 Regulation B, 12 C.F.R. § 202.9; National Consumer Law Center, Credit Discrimination Ch. 10 (3d ed. 2002 and Supp.).
176 National Consumer Law Center, Credit Discrimination Ch. 10 (3d ed. 2002 and Supp.).
181 *See* National Consumer Law Center, Credit Discrimination Ch. 10 (3d ed. 2002 and Supp.).

Addition to note 183.

183 *Replace NCLC citation with*: National Consumer Law Center, Credit Discrimination Appx. B (3d ed. 2002 and Supp.).

Add to text after sentence containing note 183:

However the required notices under the FCRA and ECOA serve different purposes and separate requirements.[183.1]

183.1 FRB Official Staff Commentary on Reg. B § 202.9(b)(2)-9.

Add note 185.1 to end of subsection's second-to-last paragraph.

185.1 *See* Fischl v. General Motors Acceptance Corp., 708 F.2d 143 (5th Cir. 1983) (notification will enable the consumer to request disclosure from the reporting agency of the nature and scope of information in file).

53

§ 6.4a   *Fair Credit Reporting / 2004 Supplement*

Page 154

Add to text at end of subsection's last sentence:

Finally, Regulation B provides that a creditor that uses a computerized system need not keep a written copy of the adverse action if it can regenerate all pertinent information in a timely manner for examination or other purposes.[186.1] It has been reported that this provision has been misused by some creditors to assert that they do not have to produce copies of ECOA adverse action notices because they are not required to maintain copies of such notices. This position appears to ignore the requirement that the creditor be able to regenerate such notices.

186.1   Reg. B, § 212(b) (FRB Official Staff Commentary).

Add new section after § 6.4.5:

6.4a Users Must Provide Consumers With a Risk-Based Pricing Notice

One problem Congress sought to address with the passage of the FACTA is the frequent occurrences fo creditors reviewing consumers' credit reports and making risk-based adjustments to the terms offered to consumers.[186.2] A typical example is when a car dealer offers a low financing interest rate but a consumers fail to qualify for such a rate because of the information in their credit report. The dealer then offers a higher interest rate or charges other fees which the consumer accepts. In such situations, consumers were not being provided with adverse action notices. This flaw was specifically highlighted in testimony by FTC Chairman Timothy Muris.[186.3]

Industry argued that no adverse action notice requirements were triggered, relying on ECOA's Regulation B which excludes from adverse action a counter offer that is accepted by consumer, notwithstanding arguments by consumer advocates that the FCRA's catch-all provision (§ 1681a(k)(1)(B)(iv)) still required notice to the consumer.[186.4] A more detailed discussion of the interplay between the ECOA and FCRA adverse action requirements can be found at § 6.4.2.3a, *supra*.

Consumers now have a right to a new notice relating to risk-based pricing.[186.5] Whenever a creditor extends credit on terms "materially less favorable than the most favorable terms available to a substantial proportion of consumers," the creditor must provide to consumers a notice that explains that the terms are based on information in a credit report and that the consumers can request a free copy of the report. This notice requirement addresses a current flaw that creditors will use as a basis for arguing that they do not need to provide notice to a consumer when they charge higher-interest fees or other charges based on a credit report. The "risk-based pricing" notice must be given at the time of application or communication of the approval.[186.6] This notice may be given orally, in writing, or electronically.[186.7]

Assuming the new FACTA risk-based pricing notice requirements are enforced, this notice will have tremendous effects throughout the retail credit sale industry. Presently, many in the credit industry ignore the proper definition of adverse action and FCRA notices are not given except in ECOA adverse action situations. This practice is based on the false assumption that the catch-all definition of adverse action in the FCRA (§ 1681a(k)(1)(b)(iv)) does not apply to credit transactions. The new requirements make clear that risk-based pricing notices must be provided even if the consumer is given credit and accepts it and also clearly require FCRA notices even when ECOA notices are not required. These notices to have potentially beneficial effects. Wherever a lender charges a higher rate or prepayment penalty or requires a balloon payment because of a consumer report and such terms are "materially less favorable" than terms generally available to a substantial proportion of other consumers, the affected consumer should be entitled to the notice.

The FTC and the FRB are to jointly promulgate regulations. These regulations will further define the term "materially less favorable," the required content of the notice, when the notice is required, and what rights the notice triggers.[186.8] The true meaning of this new requirement will not be apparent until the FTC/FCRA regulations are available.[186.9]

Notices Concerning Consumer Reports / 2004 Supplement § 6.5.1

A major drawback to the new risk-based pricing notice requirement is that it can only be enforced through federal agencies and officials under § 1681s of the FCRA,[186.10] and states are preempted from regulating the subject matter of the provision.[186.11]

186.2 Sen. Rep. No. 312, at 20 (Oct. 17, 2003).
186.3 Housing and Urban Affairs, Prepared Statement of the Federal Trade Commission on the Fair Credit Reporting Act Before the Senate Banking Committee on Banking 11–12 (July 10, 2003). The initial proposal to address this flaw in the law was in Senate Bill 1753, which proposed that regulatory agencies promulgate rules requiring notice to consumers when they have accepted, by way of a counter offer, terms that are materially less favorable than those generally available because of the consumers' credit reports. This proposal was modified by the Joint Conference Committee of the House and Senate such that the requirement would not be limited only to counter offers.
186.4 *See* § 6.4.2.3.2A, in this supplement, *supra*.
186.5 15 U.S.C. § 1681m(h)(6), *as amended by* Pub. L. No. 108-159, § 311 (2003).
186.6 Pub. L. No. 108-159, § 311 (2003).
186.7 *Id.*
186.8 15 U.S.C. § 1681m(h)(6), *as amended by* Pub. L. No. 108-159, § 311 (2003).
186.9 The risk-based pricing notice is in addition to any other notices that are required under the FCRA. An adverse action required under § 1681m(a) cannot substitute for the risk-based pricing notice. 15 U.S.C. § 1681m(h)4).
186.10 15 U.S.C. § 1681m(h)(8)(A), *added by* Pub. L. No. 108-159, § 311 (2003).
186.11 15 U.S.C. § 1681t(b)(1)(I), *added by* Pub. L. No. 108-159, § 311 (2003).

6.5 Notices Required from Users Prior to a Request for Information

Replace § 6.5.1 with :

6.5.1 Importance and Types of Notices

In four circumstances, a user must notify the consumer that it may or will request a consumer report. This prior notice is important as a warning to the consumer that private information is about to be accessed. The four circumstances are:

- notice from an employer that a consumer report may be obtained for employment purposes (except for cases involving suspected employee misconduct, compliance with federal, state, or local laws and regulations, the rules of a self-regulatory organization, or any preexisting written policies of the employer),[187]
- notice through a request by a potential user for permission to obtain a consumer report containing medical information for employment purposes or in connection with a credit or insurance or direct-marketing transaction,[188]
- notice from a user that information about the consumer may be used by an affiliate of the user,[189] or
- notice from a state or local child support enforcement agency that a consumer report will be obtained.[190]

Before the FACTA, there were two circumstances: those involving an employer's use of a consumer report and those involving access to most reports containing medical information, in which a consumer's permission or authorization was effectively required before a user could obtain a consumer report on the consumer. These two limitations were amended by the FACTA of 2003.[190.1] In a third circumstance, a user may not use information which an affiliate has obtained from outside sources without first offering the consumer the opportunity to object to such information sharing.

Finally, a notice from child support enforcement agencies is a warning of potential enforcement action against the consumer.

187 15 U.S.C. § 1681a(x), *added by* Pub. L. No. 108-159, (2003). Eligible self-regulatory organizations are defined by § 3(a)(26) of the Securities and Exchange Act of 1934, 15 U.S.C. § 78a(26), any entity established under title I of the Sarbanes-Oxley Act of 2002, 15 U.S.C. §§ 7211–7218, any board of trade designated by the Commodity Futures Trading Commission and any futures association registered with such Commission. 15 U.S.C. § 1681a(x)(3). *See* § 6.5.2, *infra*.
188 *See* § 6.5.3, *infra*.

§ 6.5.2   Fair Credit Reporting / 2004 Supplement

189   See § 6.5.4, *infra*.
190   See § 6.5.5, *infra*.
190.1 See §§ 6.5.2 and 6.5.3, *infra*.

Replace § 6.5.2 with:

6.5.2 Notice from an Employer That It May Obtain a Consumer Report

An employer must make two disclosures to an employee prior to requesting a consumer report and, if adverse action is taken, make disclosures again prior to the adverse action. The disclosures, which must be made around the time of adverse action, are described in an earlier section.[191] However, the FACTA of 2003 amended the FCRA to remove certain communications from the definition of consumer report.[192] Communications are not consumer reports if they are made to employers in connection with the investigation of suspected employment-related misconduct or the employee's compliance with federal, state, or local laws and regulations, the rules of a self-regulatory organization, or any preexisting written policies of the employer. Such communications must also not have been made for the purpose of investigating an employee's credit worthiness, credit standing, or credit capacity, and the communication must only have been made to the employer, the employer's agent, a governmental agency, or a self-regulatory organization.[193] This amendment substantially limits situations in which employees will receive notice under the FCRA and the timing of any notice employees will receive, if any, with respect to employment. Only new applicants and employees being subject to transfer or promotion will receive notice prior to any adverse action being taken. Investigations of existing employees for alleged misconduct fall within the exception and do not require prior notice.

If an employer asks an agency to check references or to do a background check for a job applicant or a candidate for transfer or promotion, the report will almost certainly be an investigative consumer report. These types of investigations are not affected by the FACTA amendments described above. The additional requirement that a user of an investigative report disclose to the applicant or candidate that such a report may be required is discussed in a later section.[194]

Unless the communications fall outside the definition of a consumer report pursuant to the FACTA amendments, employers must certify to a reporting agency that they have been authorized by the consumer to obtain the report. Otherwise the reporting agency is not permitted to release the report. This certification process is the source of the disclosure requirements on employers and is discussed in Chapter 4, *supra*.[195] Briefly, the certification is intended to ensure that the employer has taken two steps. First, the employer must provide a clear and conspicuous notice to the consumer, in writing and in a separate document, that it may obtain a consumer report for employment purposes.[196] The notice may be provided any time prior to getting the report and may even be part of the sign-up process for a new employee.[197] Second, the employee must also have provided to the employer, in writing, prior authorization to obtain a consumer report.[198] The authorization need not be contemporaneous. Absent employee authorization, no report should be released or used for employment purposes, including investigative reports.[199] A consumer's authorization that an employer may seek a consumer report is not written permission to obtain a report for otherwise impermissible purposes.[200]

In practice, the two requirements may be met in a single disclosure form. The separate document disclosing that a consumer report may be obtained for employment purposes can also include the employer's authorization[201] and may additionally include the required disclosure that an investigative consumer report may be requested;[202] however, it may not include any other information.[203] If an application for employment or the employment contract itself contains the authorization, then the disclosure form must be provided separately, then or later.[204] The form must be separate, and must be clear and conspicuous, but no particular size or print or language is specified.[205] If a blanket authorization is used, covering future reports that may arise during the course of employment, that fact should be clearly stated.[205.1]

Notices Concerning Consumer Reports / 2004 Supplement § 6.5.3

One group of employers is treated differently. Under the so-called "trucker's amendment," an employer regulated by the Secretary of Transportation or subject to certain state safety regulations may be permitted to make the required disclosure orally and obtain the consumer's authorization orally.[205.2] This exception, commonplace enough in the trucking industry, only arises if all interaction between the consumer and the employer with regards to the application has been in person.

191 See § 6.4.2.4, *supra*.
192 15 U.S.C. § 1681a(d)(2)(D), *as amended by* Pub. L. No. 108-159, § 611(b) (2003).
193 15 U.S.C. § 1681a(x)(D)(i)-(iii), *added by* Pub. L. No. 108-159, § 611 (2003).
194 See §§ 6.6.3, 9.2.1, *infra*.
195 See § 5.2.5.3, *supra*.
196 15 U.S.C. § 1681b(b)(2).
197 Meisinger, FTC Informal Staff Opinion Letter, Aug. 31, 1999 (reproduced on the accompanying CD-Rom). *See also* Appx. D, *infra*.
198 15 U.S.C. § 1681b(b)(3).
199 *Cf.* Haynes, FTC Informal Staff Opinion Letter, Dec. 18, 1997 (reproduced on the accompanying CD-Rom). *See also* Appx. D, *infra*. Investigative reports are discussed at § 6.6.3, *infra*.
200 Grimes, FTC Informal Staff Opinion Letter, July 20, 1992 (reproduced on the accompanying CD-Rom). *See also* Appx. D, *infra*.
201 15 U.S.C. § 1681b(b)(2)(A)(ii); Willner, FTC Informal Staff Opinion Letter, Mar. 25, 1999 (reproduced on the accompanying CD-Rom). *See also* Appx. D, *infra*]. Steer, FTC Informal Staff Opinion Letter, Oct. 21, 1997 (reproduced on the accompanying CD-Rom). *See also* Appx. D, *infra*.
202 Willner, FTC Informal Staff Opinion Letter, Mar. 25, 1999 (reproduced on the accompanying CD-Rom). *See also* Appx. D, *infra*. The disclosure that an investigative consumer report may be requested is discussed at § 9.2.1, *infra*.
203 *Id. But see* Coffey, FTC Informal Staff Opinion Letter, Feb. 11, 1998 (reproduced on the accompanying CD-Rom). *See also* Appx. D, *infra*.
204 Coffey, FTC Informal Staff Opinion Letter, Feb. 11, 1998 (reproduced on the accompanying CD-Rom). *See also* Appx. D, *infra*; Haynes, FTC Informal Staff Opinion Letter, Dec. 18, 1997 (reproduced on the accompanying CD-Rom). *See also* Appx. D, *infra*.
205 Coffey, FTC Informal Staff Opinion Letter, Feb. 11, 1998 (reproduced on the accompanying CD-Rom). *See also* Appx. D, *infra*.
205.1 James, FTC Informal Staff Opinion Letter, Aug. 5, 1998 (reproduced on the accompanying CD-Rom). *See also* Appx. D, *infra*.
205.2 15 U.S.C. § 1681b(b)(2)(B) and (C).

Page 155

Replace § 6.5.3 with:

6.5.3 Notice That Medical Information May Be Obtained from a Consumer Reporting Agency

Consumer reporting agencies sometimes specialize in collecting and disseminating medical information.[206] A consumer receives no special notice when this information is accessed. However, effective notice is provided when the user obtains prior authorization from the consumer.

Even prior to the amendments of the FACTA of 2003, a reporting agency could not release medical information for insurance, employment, or credit purposes, or for prescreening and other direct marking transactions, unless the consumer consented.[207] Unlike the use of consumer reports in the employment context, release of the report was not contingent upon certification by the user that the consumer had authorized use of the report. The Act simply provided that no medical report could be released unless the consumer consented.

The FACTA of 2003 continued the prohibition against agencies furnishing a report for employment purposes or in connection with a credit or insurance transaction that contains medical information without the consent of the consumer.[207.1] Now the consumer's consent to furnishing such a report must be written, must be specific, and must describe the use for which the agency will furnish the information.[207.2] However, an agency may furnish medical information that pertains solely to financial transactions if the agency uses codes so as not to

§ 6.5.4   Fair Credit Reporting / 2004 Supplement

identify, or provide information sufficient to infer, the specific provider of medical services or the nature of such services, products, or devices. The FACTA also reduced consumer protections by providing several exceptions to the general prohibition on the release without consumer consent of a consumer report that includes medical information.[207.3] The federal banking agencies, NCUA, and the FTC have been granted rulemaking authority to make exceptions that are "necessary and appropriate to protect legitimate operational, transactional, risk, consumer, and other needs. . . ."[207.4]

206   See § 4.5.5, *supra*. The FACTA of 2003 revised the FCRA's definition of "medical information" to remove the requirement that the information be obtained with the consumer's consent and to remove from the definition information that does not relate to the consumer's physical, mental, or behavioral health or condition. 15 U.S.C. § 1681a(i), *amended by* Pub. L. No. 108-159, § 411(c) (2003).

207   15 U.S.C. § 1681b(g) (effective on and after Sept. 30, 1997). *See also* Cal. Civ. Code § 1785.13(f) (West) (credit reporting agencies may not include medical information in their files or furnish medical information for employment, insurance, or credit purposes in a consumer credit report without the consumer's consent).

207.1   15 U.S.C. § 1681b, *as amended by* Pub. L. No. 108-159, § 411 (2003).
207.2   15 U.S.C. § 1681b(g)(1)(B)(ii), *added by* Pub. L. No. 108-159, § 412 (2003).
207.3   15 U.S.C. §§ 1681b(g)(1)(A)-(C), *as amended by* Pub. L. No. 108-159, § 411 (2003).
207.4   15 U.S.C. § 1681b(g)(5)(A), *as amended by* Pub. L. No. 108-159, § 411(a) (2003).

Page 156

6.5.4 Notice When Certain Information Is Used by Affiliates

Add to text at end of subsection:

The FACTA amended the FCRA to provide that a consumer may opt out of the use by an affiliate of this exempt information to market its products or services, and affiliates must also notify the consumer both of the possibility that an affiliate may use the consumer's information for marketing and of the consumer's right to opt out of such use.[219.1] The opt-out lasts for five years and consumers may extend it for an additional five years.[219.2] States are preempted from regulating the subject matter of this provision.[219.3]

219.1   15 U.S.C. § 1681s-3, *added by* Pub. L. No. 108-159, § 214 (2003). Certain exemptions apply. 15 U.S.C. § 1681s-3(a)((4).
219.2   15 U.S.C. § 1681s-3(a)(3), *added by* Pub. L. No. 108-159, § 214 (2003).
219.3   15 U.S.C. § 1681t(b)(1)(H), *added by* Pub. L. No. 108-159, § 214 (2003).

6.6 Notices Required When a User Has Requested Information

6.6.2 Public Record Information for Employment Purposes

Page 158

6.6.2.2 The Nature of the Special FCRA Protection

Addition to note 236.

236   Feldman v. Comprehensive Info. Servs., Inc., 2003 WL 22413484 (Conn. Super. Oct. 6, 2003) (procedures are alternative).

Page 159

6.6.4 Notice When Information Is Used for Prescreening Purposes

Add to text after sentence containing note 246:

The disclosures must be "clear and conspicuous," which is ordinarily a question for the court to determine.[246.1] Disclosures on the back of the solicitation, with no reference to them on the front and in much smaller type size than the front of the solicitation, are not clear and conspicuous.[246.2]

246.1   Sampson v. W. Sierra Acceptance Corp., 2003 WL 21785612 (N.D. Ill Aug. 1, 2003); Tucker v. Olympia Dodge of Countryside, Inc., 2003 WL 21230604 (N.D. Ill. May 28, 2003).
246.2   Sampson v. W. Sierra Acceptance Corp., 2003 WL 21785612 (N.D. Ill. Aug. 1, 2003).

Page 160

Add new section after § 6.8.

6.8a Notice of Key Factor in Credit Score

The FACTA amended the FCRA to require the disclosure of enquiries if they are a factor in determining a consumer's credit score. Any consumer reporting agency that furnishes a consumer report containing any credit score or other risk score or predictor must include in the report a clear and conspicuous statement that a key factor (as defined in §1681g(f)(2)(B)) which adversely affected such score or predictor was the number of enquiries, if such a predictor was in fact a key factor that adversely affected such score.[250] This notice requirement does not apply to check services companies which issues authorizations for the purpose of approving or processing checks or other negotiable instruments, electronic transfers, or similar methods of payments, to the extent they are engaged in such activities.[251]

6.8b Notice in Cases of Fraud Alert That Consumer May Request a Free Copy of the File

When credit reporting agencies include a fraud alert in a consumer file, the agency must disclose that the consumer may request two free copies of their file during the twelve-month period beginning on the date on which the fraud alert was included in the file.[252] This notice must include the summary of rights of identity theft victims.[253]

6.8c Notice to Consumer If Agency Refuses to Block Alleged Identity Theft Information

Under amendments by the FACTA, if a credit reporting agency declines or rescinds a block of information alleged to be the result of identity theft, the affected consumer must be notified promptly and in the same manner that consumers are notified when information is reinserted into their file upon certification of accuracy.[254] Consumers must be notified regarding the reinsertion of information within five days of the agency's reinsertion of information. This five-day period should be the same limitation for purposes of notification when a block is declined or rescinded.

Resellers that maintain consumer files must also promptly provide notice to consumers of a decision to block the file relating to identity theft information.[255] Such notice must contain the name, address, and telephone number of each consumer reporting agency from which the consumer information was obtained for resale.[256]

6.8d Disclosure of Credit Scores and Notice to Home Loan Applicant

Under amendments by the FACTA, users of credit reports who make credit or insurance solicitations must also disclose their address and telephone number. The disclosure must be prepared in such format and type as to be reasonably understood, in compliance with rules to be adopted by the FTC, in consultation with federal banking agencies and NCUA.[257]

6.8e Notice When Negative Information Provided by Financial Institutions

The FACTA amended the FCRA to require a one-time consumer notice when a financial institution furnishes negative information about that customer.[258] However, a financial institution may take advantage of a safe-harbor provision if it maintained reasonable

§ 6.9   *Fair Credit Reporting / 2004 Supplement*

compliance policies and procedures or reasonably believed that it was prohibited from contacting the consumer.[259] Once notified about an account, it appears that there is no other requirement entitling the consumer to receive further notices when additional negative information is reported about that account.[260] The notice must be given within thirty days of reporting negative information.[261] The Federal Reserve Board is to provide a model notice not to exceed thirty words.[262] A financial institution may provide the notice without submitting the negative information.[263] This is an unusual means of providing notice since it would not be accurate. The notice may not be included with disclosures under § 127 of the Truth in Lending Act.[264] This provision appears not to be enforceable by private consumers' actions.[265]

250   15 U.S.C. § 1681g(d)(2), *added by* Pub. L. No. 108-159, § 212(d) (2003). *See* § 14.4.1 in this supplement, *infra*. The effective date for this provision is December 1, 2004. 69 Fed. Reg. 6526–6531 (Feb. 11, 2004).
251   *Id.*
252   15 U.S.C. § 1681c-1, *added by* Pub. L. No. 108-159, § 112 (2003). *See* § 16.6.1a, in this supplement, *infra*. The effective date for this requirement is December 1, 2004. 69 Fed. Reg. 6526–6531 (Feb. 11, 2004).
253   *Id.*
254   *See* 15 U.S.C. § 1681i(a)(5)(B). *See* § 16.6.1a in this supplement, *infra*.
255   15 U.S.C. § 1681c-2(d)(3), *added by* Pub. L. No. 108-159, § 112 (2003).
256   *Id.*
257   15 U.S.C. § 1681m(b)(2)(B), *added by* Pub. L. No. 108-159, § (2003). *See* § 14.4.1 in this supplement, *infra*. The effective date for this provision is December 1, 2004. 69 Fed. Reg. 6526–6531 (Feb. 11, 2004).
258   15 U.S.C. § 1681s–2(a)(7), *added by* Pub. L. No. 108-159, § 217 (2003).
259   15 U.S.C. § 1681s–2(a)(7)(F).
260   15 U.S.C. § 1681s–2(a)(7)(A)(ii).
261   15 U.S.C. § 1681s–2(a)(7)(B)(i).
262   15 U.S.C. § 1681s–2(a)(7)(A)(ii).
263   *Id.*
264   15 U.S.C. § 1681s–2(a)(7)(D)(i).
265   15 U.S.C. § 1681s–2(c)(1), *as amended by* Pub. L. No. 108-159, § 312 (2003).

6.9 Liability for Failure to Provide Required Notice

Replace notes 255, 266, 268 with:
Page 161

255   The failure to provide disclosure required by the ECOA can also lead to civil liability. *See* National Consumer Law Center, Credit Discrimination § 10.2 (3d ed. 2002 and Supp.).
266   *See* National Consumer Law Center, Credit Discrimination Ch. 10 (3d ed. 2002 and Supp.).
268   *See* National Consumer Law Center, Credit Discrimination Ch. 10 (3d ed. 2002 and Supp.).

Chapter 7   Inaccurate Consumer Reports

Page 163

Replace first sentence of subsection's second paragraph with:

7.1 Introduction

As discussed elsewhere in this manual, studies have shown that inaccuracies continue to be common in the nation's credit reporting system.[0.1] Inaccurate information is especially troublesome since it can adversely affect whether consumers are granted credit and may cause them to pay more for credit than if the information were accurate.[0.2] Risk based pricing is becoming a more prevalent practice by creditors and consumers are increasingly being asked to pay more for credit based on credit scores that are calculated from information in credit files, information that sometimes is inaccurate.

    0.1   See § 4.2.2, *supra*, and § 7.2.1, *infra*.
    0.2   Consumer Federation of America and National Credit Reporting Association, *Credit Score Accuracy and Implications for Consumers*, December 17, 2002, *available at* www.consumerfed.org/ 121702CFA_NCRA_Credit_Score_Report_Final.pdf, *reprinted on* companion CD-Rom, *infra*.

Add to text after sentence containing note 4:

Following the FACTA of 2003, the agency must also inform the furnisher of the information that the agency has modified the information or deleted it from the consumer's file.[4.1]

    4.1   Pub. L. 108-159, § 314(a) (2003). See also § 7.4.2, *infra*.

Add to text after "role" in section's last sentence:

in monitoring the accuracy and completeness of their credit reports.

Add new section after § 7.1:

7.1a What is Accuracy?

The FCRA contains no definition of accuracy. "The legislative history of the FCRA reveals that it was crafted to protect consumers from the transmission of inaccurate information about them, (citations omitted) and to establish credit reporting practices that utilize accurate, relevant and current information in a confidential and responsible manner."[8.1]

The FCRA requires more than technical or literal accuracy; it requires "maximum possible accuracy of the information concerning the individual about whom the report relates."[8.2] Accuracy "requires congruence between the legal status of a consumer's account and the status a CRA reports."[8.3] Courts agree that even "a technical truth . . . can be as misleading as an outright untruth where it paints a misleading picture."[8.4]

Merely parroting what a creditor reports may not fulfill the "maximum possible accuracy" obligation, justified once a reporting agency is notified of a dispute.[8.5]

    8.1   Guimond v. Trans Union Credit Info. Co., 45 F.3d 1329, 1333 (9th Cir. 1995); Hansen v. Morgan, 582 F.2d 1214, 1220 (9th Cir. 1978).
    8.2   Pinner v. Schmidt, 805 F.2d 1258, 1262–63 (5th Cir. 1986); U.S.C. § 1681e(b); Koropoulos v. Credit Bureau, Inc., 734 F.2d 37, 40, 42 (D. C. Cir. 1984).
    8.3   Crane v. Trans Union, L.L.C., 282 F. Supp. 2d 311 (E.D. Pa. 2003).
    8.4   Dalton v. Capital Associated Indus., Inc., 257 F.3d 409, 415 (4th Cir. 2001); Sepulvado v. CSC Credit Servs., 158 F.3d 890, 895 (5th Cir. 1998); Swoager v. Credit Bureau of Greater St. Petersburg, 608 F. Supp. 972, 977 (M.D. Fla. 1985) (entry misleadingly coded); Alexander v. Moore & Assocs., Inc., 553 F. Supp. 948, 952 (D. Haw. 1982).
    8.5   Crane v. Trans Union, L.L.C., 282 F. Supp. 2d 311 (E.D. Pa. 2003) and cases cited therein.

7.2 Types of Inaccurate Information

7.2.1 Introduction

Page 164

Add to text after sentence containing note 10:

Complaints against the three national credit reporting agencies have steadily increased.[10.1]

    10.1   In 2001, the FTC received over 8000 complaints against the major credit reporting agencies. This number grew to over 14,000 in 2002 (letter and enclosures from Joan E. Fina to Chris Hoofnagle in response to FOIA Request No. 2003-470 (June 23, 2003)), *reprinted on* companion CD-Rom, *infra*.

Add to text before first sentence in subsection's third paragraph:

Recently, two separate studies have highlighted accuracy problems within the credit reporting system. In February 2003, the Federal Reserve Board released a study which found that many consumer credit files contained incomplete or ambiguous information.[13.1] In 2002, the Consumer Federation of America reported that errors in consumer credit files could cost consumers millions of dollars in higher costs for credit.[13.2]

    13.1   Robert Avery, Paul Calem, Glenn Canner, and Raphael Bostic, *An Overview of Consumer Data and Credit Reporting*, Federal Reserve Bulletin, February 2003, at 70–71.

    13.2   Consumer Federation of America and National Credit Reporting Association, *Credit Score Accuracy and Implications for Consumers*, December 17, 2002, available at www.consumerfed.org/121702CFA_NCRA_Credit_Score_Report_Final.pdf, *reprinted on* companion CD-Rom, *infra*.

7.2.3 Errors in Collection of Public Record Information

Page 165

Add to text after sentence containing note 21:

A study by the Federal Reserve found that the degree to which lawsuits are reported is inconsistent. In some cases, there was more than one public record item associated with a single episode.[21.1] For example, there may be both a record of a lawsuit being filed and a judgment relating to the same debt. The report also found that there may be inconsistencies in reporting of public records across plaintiffs and geographic areas. For example, three states (Maryland, New York and Pennsylvania) accounted for two thirds of all individuals with records of lawsuits in the files examined.[21.2] The report further found that some plaintiffs obtain separate judgments for individual unpaid items, while other plaintiffs in similar circumstances may have combined the bills.[21.3]

    21.1   Robert Avery, Paul Calem, Glenn Canner, and Raphael Bostic, *An Overview of Consumer Data and Credit Reporting*, Federal Reserve Bulletin, February 2003, at 68.
    21.2   *Id.*
    21.3   *Id.*

7.2.4 Mismerged Files

Addition to note 23.

    23   *Replace Wilson LEXIS citation with*: 206 F.3d 810 (8th Cir. 2000).

Add to text after sentence containing note 25:

A study of credit scores for mortgage applicants by the Consumer Federation of America and the National Credit Reporting Association found that one in ten files (155 out of 1545) contained at least one, but as many as three additional repository consumer reports and that it was very common for the additional reports to contain a mixture of credit information, some of which belonged to the subject of the report requested and some which did not.[25.1] Common reasons for the additional reports include:

    —Confusion between generations with the same name (Jr., Sr., II, III, etc.).
    —Mixed files with similar names, but different social security numbers.
    —Mixed files with matching social security numbers, but different names.
    —Mixed files that listed accounts recorded under the applicant's name, but with the social security number of the co-applicant.
    —Name variations that appeared to contain transposed first and middle names.
    —Files that appeared to track credit under the applicant's nickname.
    —Spelling errors in the name.
    —Transposing digits on the social security number.[25.2]

25.1 Consumer Federation of America and National Credit Reporting Association, *Credit Score Accuracy and Implications for Consumers*, p.21, December 17, 2002, *available at* www.consumerfed.org/121702CFA_NCRA_Credit_Score_Report_Final.pdf, *reprinted on* companion CD-Rom, *infra*.
25.2 *Id.*

Page 166

7.2.5 Identity Theft

Replace note 28 with:

28 See § 13.5.5, *infra*, for a detailed discussion of identity theft.

Add to text after sentence containing note 35:

Congress has proposed measures that would provide consumers with greater protections against identity theft. These consequences to consumers and their credit reports were a significant force behind the FACTA of 2003.[35.1] That Act creates a variety of new tools for consumers to use both to prevent identity theft and to restore credit records polluted by a thief's transactions. These provisions are discussed in § 16.6.1a, *infra*.

35.1 *See, e.g.*, Explanatory Statement of the Conference Committee, 149 Cong. Rec. H12214 (daily ed. Nov. 21, 2003) ("[w]hile criminal prosecutions and strict fraud detection protocols can curtail identity theft, and punish the wrongdoers, not enough had been done heretofore to aid the real victims of this crime—the consumer whose identity is assumed, and can spend months or years trying to rehabilitate their credit and re-order their affairs.").

Page 167

7.2.7 Illogical Files

Addition to note 36.

36 *Replace Wilson LEXIS citation with*: 206 F.3d 810 (8th Cir. 2000).

7.2.8 Incomplete Files

Add to text after sentence containing note 37:

This practice, which is common among subprime lenders, will result in credit reports that do not accurately reflect the positive payment histories for borrowers, especially high-interest borrowers in the subprime market. The Comptroller of the Currency suggested that legislation may be required in order to ensure that such information is reported and consumers are protected from such incomplete reporting.[37.1]

37.1 Office of the Comptroller of the Currency, *Press Release NR99-51*, June 6, 1999, *available at* www.occ.treas.gov/ftp/release/99-51.wpw.

Addition to note 38.

38 *Replace date in Thompson citation with*: Dec. 14, 2001.

Page 168

7.2.9 Reporting Agency Refusal to Provide Reports to Litigants

Add to text at end of second-to-last sentence of subsection's last paragraph:

or if the consumer is the victim of identity theft.

7.3 Reporting Agency Reinvestigation and Correction of Disputed Information

7.3.2 Consumer Request for Reinvestigation

Page 170

7.3.2.1 When a Reporting Agency Must Reinvestigate

Add to text after sentence containing note 67:

The FACTA of 2003 creates special provisions for resellers.[67.1] Although resellers are exempt from the general reinvestigation requirement,[67.2] as of December 1, 2004, they must investigate a consumer's dispute made to the reseller. If the reseller determines that the information is incomplete or inaccurate as a result of the reseller's act or omission, the reseller must correct or delete the information within twenty days.[67.3] If, however, the reseller does

§ 7.3.2.2   *Fair Credit Reporting / 2004 Supplement*

not find that the alleged inaccuracy resulted from the reseller's act or omission, the reseller must notify the agency from whom the reseller obtained the information, and the agency must then reinvestigate the information.[67.4] Once notified, the providing agency must reinvestigate[67.5] and then report the results of its reinvestigation back to the reseller, who must then reconvey the results back to the consumer.[67.6] This provision basically treats the reseller as a consumer for purposes of the agency's reinvestigation responsibilities.

    67.1   Pub. L. No. 108-159, § 316(b) (2003). As amended, the FCRA defines a reseller to be a consumer reporting agency that meets the following criteria:

> (1) assembles and merges information contained in the database of another consumer reporting agency or multiple consumer reporting agencies concerning any consumer for purposes of furnishing such information to any third party, to the extent of such activities; and (2) does not maintain a database of the assembled or merged information from which new consumer reports are produced.

15 U.S.C. § 1681a(u), *added by* Pub. L. No. 108-159, § 111 (2003).

    67.2   15 U.S.C. § 1681i(f)(1), *added by* Pub. L. No. 108-159, § 316 (2003). *See also* § 2.6.2, *supra*.

    67.3   15 U.S.C. § 1681i(f), *added by* Pub. L. No. 108-159, § 316 (2003); 16 C.F.R. § 602.1(c)(3)(xviii), *added by* 69 Fed. Reg. 6526–31 (Feb. 5, 2004).

    67.4   *Id.*

    67.5   15 U.S.C. § 1681i(a), *as amended by* Pub. L. No. 108-159, § 316 (2003). This provision will become effective on December 1, 2004. 16 C.F.R. § 602.1(c)(3)(xvii), *added by* 69 Fed. Reg. 6526–31 (Feb. 5, 2004).

    67.6   15 U.S.C. § 1681i(f), *added by* Pub. L. No. 108-159, § 316 (2003).

Add to text after sentence containing note 75:

The consumer's dispute that she had never filed bankruptcy, without disclosing that her husband had mistakenly listed the accounts in his bankruptcy, was inadequate to obligate the reporting agency to look behind the public records.[75.1]

    75.1   Kettler v. CSC Credit Serv., Inc., 2003 WL 21975919 (D. Minn. Aug. 12, 2003).

Page 171

7.3.2.2 Consumer Must Make Request to Reporting Agency

Add to text at end of subsection's second paragraph:

The FTC has commented on the difficulties consumers may face when disputing information directly to the reseller and not the big three national credit reporting agencies, noting that resellers have no relationship to the creditors and therefore may be ignored when attempting to reinvestigate a consumer's dispute.[79.1]

    79.1   *See* Testimony of Timothy J. Muris, Chairman, Federal Trade Commission, before the Senate Banking Committee, July 10, 2003.

7.3.4 Nature of the Reinvestigation

Page 174

7.3.4.3 Type of Reinvestigation Required

Addition to note 121.

    121   Curtis v. Trans Union, L.L.C., 2002 WL 31748838 (N.D. Ill. 2002).

Add to text at end of subsection's first paragraph:

Some courts have found that the CDV procedure is an adequate reinvestigation method as a matter of law, due to "the enormous burden (and hence cost) that a general requirement of more detailed follow-up procedures would impose on the system."[122.1]

    122.1   Kettler v. CSC Credit Serv., Inc., 2003 WL 21975919 (D. Minn. Aug. 12, 2003). See discussion in § 3.10, *supra*, of obvious problems with the CDV coding system. *Contra* Evantash v. G.E. Capital Mortgage Serv., Inc., 2003 WL 22844198 (E.D. Pa. Nov. 25, 2003) and cases cited therein.

Addition to note 123.

    123   Evantash v. G.E. Capital Mortgage Serv., Inc., 2003 WL 22844198 (E.D. Pa. Nov. 25, 2003) (agency may not merely parrot information provided to it but may have some duty to go beyond the source, depending on whether the consumer has alerted the agency that the source may be unreliable and on the cost of verification compared with the harm to the consumer); Sheffer v. Experian Info. Solutions, Inc., 2003 WL 21710573 (E.D. Pa. July 24, 2003) (same); Soghomonian v. U.S., 278 F. Supp. 2d 1151 (E.D. Cal. 2003) (cannot defer to outside entity, especially when agency does not consider information provided by consumer); Crane v. Trans Union, L.L.C., 282 F. Supp. 2d 311 (E.D. Pa. 2003) (accuracy "requires congruence between the legal status of a consumer's account and the status a CRA reports"); Olwell v.

Inaccurate Consumer Reports / 2004 Supplement § 7.3.6

Medical Info. Bureau, 2003 WL 79035 (D. Minn. 2003) (failure to contact outside source could be unreasonable investigation); Curtis v. Trans Union, L.L.C., 2002 WL 31748838 (N.D. Ill. 2002).

Add to text at end of subsection's second paragraph:

Before the FACTA of 2003, the FCRA did not specify a standard by which the agency must reinvestigate. As of December 1, 2004, the Act clarifies that the reinvestigation must be "reasonable."[124.1] It does not appear that this new requirement fundamentally alters previous case law and FTC commentary, described below, that addresses the conduct required by the reinvestigation provision.

124.1   15 U.S.C. § 1681i(a), *amended by* Pub. L. No. 108-159, § 317 (2003); 16 C.F.R. § 602.1(c)(3)(xviii), *added by* 69 Fed. Reg. 6526–31 (Feb. 5, 2004).

Addition to note 128.

128   Curtis v. Trans Union, L.L.C., 2002 WL 31748838 (N.D. Ill. 2002).

Page 175

Delete subsection's second and third paragraphs.

7.3.4.4 Must Reinvestigation Utilize "Reasonable Procedures to Assure Maximum Possible Accuracy"?

Replace subsection's first paragraph with:

Prior to the Fair and Accurate Credit Transaction Act of 2003, the FCRA failed to specify the degree to which the agency must reinvestigate; accordingly, the question of whether the standard of "reasonable procedures to assure maximum possible accuracy" applied to reinvestigations was uncertain. Now the Act clarifies that, as of December 1, 2004, the reinvestigation must be "reasonable."[139] However, even before the amendment, the practical import of the difference between "using reasonable procedures to assure maximum possible accuracy" and a "reasonable" reinvestigation was not clear.

139   15 U.S.C. § 1681i(a), *amended by* Pub. L. No. 108-159, § 317 (2003); 16 C.F.R. § 602.1(c)(3)(xviii), *added by* 69 Fed. Reg. 6526–31 (Feb. 5, 2004).
140   *Reserved.*

Addition to note 143.

143   Sheffer v. Experian Info. Solutions, Inc., 2003 WL 21710573 (E.D. Pa. July 24, 2003) (after notice of dispute, reporting agency can be liable under both the investigation and the maximum possible accuracy requirements).

7.3.5 Agency's Reinvestigation Must Involve the Person Who Furnished the Disputed Information to the Reporting Agency

Page 176

7.3.5.1 General

Addition to note 152.

152   Olwell v. Medical Info. Bureau, 2003 WL 79035 (D. Minn. 2003) (reasonable jury could find that failure to contact outside sources was unreasonable investigation); Curtis v. Trans Union, L.L.C., 2002 WL 31748838 (N.D. Ill. 2002).

7.3.6 Deadline for Reporting Agency to Respond

Add to text at beginning of subsection:

The deadline for the consumer reporting agency to respond to the consumer's notification depends upon the process through which the consumer obtained the inaccurate information. The Fair and Accurate Credit Transaction Act of 2003 added a new provision granting every consumer the right to a free annual credit report from nationwide consumer reporting agencies.[156.1] To receive the report from a nationwide agency other than the nationwide specialty consumer reporting agency,[156.2] the consumer must use a centralized source to make the request, a source that the FTC is to create by regulation.[156.3] The FTC will also create a separate process through which consumers may request a free report from nationwide

§ 7.4 Fair Credit Reporting / 2004 Supplement

specialty consumer reporting agencies.[156.4] If a consumer requests a reinvestigation after receiving a free report under the new provision, the agency has forty-five days to complete the reinvestigation.[156.5]

156.1 Pub. L. 108-159, § 211(a) (2003), *amending* 15 U.S.C. § 1681j(a). The agencies that must provide free annual reports are those defined in 15 U.S.C. § 1681a(p). *See also* § 4.4, *supra*.
156.2 These agencies are defined in 15 U.S.C. § 1681a(w), *added by* Pub. L. No. 108-159, § 111 (2003).
156.3 The nationwide credit reporting agency does not have to respond to a request unless the consumer uses the special centralized source to be established by the FTC to make the request. 15 U.S.C. § 1681j(a), *amended by* Pub. L. No. 108-159, § 212 (2003). The FTC has six months to issue regulations that will create the centralized source through which consumers are to make their requests, and the regulations will not become effective until six months after they become final. Pub. L. 108-159, § 211 (2003). The FTC's proposed regulations would implement a "cumulative regional roll-out" for the centralized source that would delay complete national access to the source until September 1, 2005. 69 Fed. Reg. 13198 (Mar. 19, 2004).
156.4 15 U.S.C. § 1681j(a)(1)(C), *amended by* Pub. L. No. 108-159, § 211(a) (2003). The FTC must also establish regulations pertaining to this process within six months. 15 U.S.C. § 1681j(a)(1)(C)(iv)(II), *amended by* Pub. L. No. 108-159, § 211(a) (2003). *See also* 69 Fed. Reg. 13208–13209 (Mar. 19, 2004) (proposing new regulation for nationwide specialty consumer reporting agencies).
156.5 15 U.S.C. § 1681j(a)(3), *added by* Pub. L. No. 108-159, § 211(a) (2003).

Add to end of subsection's first sentence:

if the consumer reporting agency receives information from the consumer during the thirty-day period that is relevant to the reinvestigation.

Replace note 157 with:

157 15 U.S.C. § 1681i(a)(1)(B).

7.4 Corrections as a Result of Reinvestigations of Disputed Information

Page 178

7.4.2 Correction or Deletion of Disputed Information

Addition to note 172.

172 *Add to end of Andrews citation*: rev'd on other grounds, 534 U.S. 19 (2001) (discovery rule not applicable to statute's general two-year statute of limitations).

Add to text before subsection's last paragraph:

The FACTA of 2003 added a provision that requires an agency to not only notify the consumer of the results of the reinvestigation but also the furnisher of the information when the agency corrects or deletes the information as a result of the reinvestigation.[173.1] Such a notice should trigger a separate responsibility of the furnisher—to cease furnishing any information if the furnisher "knows or has reason to believe" the information to be inaccurate[173.2]—since the correction/deletion notice from the agency should serve as reason to believe that the information was inaccurate.

173.1 Pub. L. 108-159, § 314(a) (2003), *amending* 15 U.S.C. § 1681i(a)(5)(A). *See also* § 3.13, *supra*.
173.2 15 U.S.C. § 1681s–2(a)(1)(A), *amended by* Pub. L. No. 108-159, § 312(b) (2003). *See also* § 3.4.2, *supra*. Prior to the revision, the FCRA only prohibited furnishers from furnishing information to a consumer reporting agency that the furnisher knew or "consciously avoided" knowing was inaccurate.

Page 179

7.5 Reinsertion of Information Previously Deleted from Consumer's File

Add to text at end of section's first paragraph:

Another problem with reinserted information concerns the inability of some agencies to prevent cloaked information from reappearing when an account is sold or sent to a collection agency which then reports it anew.

Add to text after sentence containing note 185:

The FACTA of 2003 added another layer of protection against the refurnishing of inaccurate information; as of December 1, 2004, a furnisher who receives notice from a consumer reporting agency that the consumer has disputed an item of information and who finds upon reinvestigation that the information is inaccurate, incomplete, or unverifiable, must modify, delete, or permanently block the information in its files for purposes of reporting to a consumer reporting agency.[185.1]

> 185.1   15 U.S.C. § 1681s–2(b)(1)(E), *added by* Pub. L. No. 108-159, § 314(b) (2003); 16 C.F.R. § 602.1(c)(3)(xv), *added by* 69 Fed. Reg. 6526–31 (Feb. 5, 2004). *See* § 3.12.2a, *supra*.

7.6 Inclusion of Consumer's Statement of Dispute in Consumer's File

7.6.1 Consumer's Right to File Statement of Dispute

Page 180

7.6.1.1 Statement Concerning Incomplete or Inaccurate Items

Add to text after sentence containing note 194:

The FACTA of 2003 gave to consumers a powerful right to add what should be far more effective notices to a file: fraud alerts, extended fraud alerts, and active military duty alerts, a provision that becomes effective on December 1, 2004.[194.1] These alerts, unlike the Statement of Dispute discussed below, impose specific obligations on users of reports that contain such alerts.[194.2] These alerts are discussed in Chapter 16, *supra*.

> 194.1   15 U.S.C. § 1681c-1, *added by* Pub. L. No. 108-159, § 112 (2003); 16 C.F.R. § 602.1(c)(3)(i), *added by* 69 Fed. Reg. 6526–31 (Feb. 5, 2004).
> 194.2   *Id.*

Page 182

7.6.2 Reporting Agency Must Note Consumer's Dispute in Subsequent Reports

Add to text at end of subsection:

Whether the agency had reasonable grounds to believe the statement was frivolous or irrelevant is a question of fact for the jury.[219.1]

> 219.1   Crane v. Trans Union, L.L.C., 282 F. Supp. 2d 311 (E.D. Pa. 2003).

7.8 Agency Liability for Reporting Inaccurate Information

Page 183

7.8.1 General

Add to text at end of subsection's second paragraph:

In addition, the FCRA requires the agency to notify the furnisher of the information that the consumer has disputed it.[242.1] As of December 1, 2004, agencies must also notify the furnisher if the agency corrects or deletes information after reinvestigating its accuracy.[242.2]

> 242.1   15 U.S.C. § 1681i(a)(2). *See* § 7.3.5, *supra*.
> 242.2   15 U.S.C. § 1681i(a)(5)(A)(ii), *added by* Pub. L. No. 108-159, § 314(a) (2003); 16 C.F.R. § 602.1(c)(3)(xv), *added by* 69 Fed. Reg. 6526–31 (Feb. 5, 2004). *See* § 7.4.2, *supra*.

Addition to note 243.

> 243   Sheffer v. Experian Info. Solutions, Inc., 2003 WL 21710573 (E.D. Pa. July 24, 2003).

Add to text after sentence containing note 243:

Prior to the FACTA of 2003, no standard explicitly governed the quality of the agency's obligation to reinvestigate an item of information once a consumer notified the agency that it was inaccurate; as of December 1, 2004, an agency must ensure that its reinvestigation is "reasonable."[243.1]

> 243.1   15 U.S.C. § 1681i(a), *amended by* Pub. L. No. 108-159, § 317 (2003); 16 C.F.R. § 602.1(c)(3)(xviii), *added by* 69 Fed. Reg. 6526–31 (Feb. 5, 2004). *See* § 7.3.4, *supra*.

§ 7.8.3   *Fair Credit Reporting / 2004 Supplement*

7.8.3 Inaccurate Information: The First Test of Accuracy

Page 184

7.8.3.1 General

Addition to note 254.

254   Molton v. Experian Info. Solutions, Inc., 2004 WL 161494 (N.D. Ill. Jan. 21, 2004) (paid charge-off is accurate).
     Replace Cassara citation with: 276 F.3d 1210 (10th Cir. 2002).

Page 185

7.8.3.2 When Is Incomplete Information Inaccurate?

Addition to notes 256, 258, 272.

256   Agosta v. Inovision, Inc., 2003 WL 22999213 (E.D. Pa. Dec. 16, 2003) (misleading or materially incomplete entry is inaccurate). Curtis v. Trans Union, L.L.C., 2002 WL 31748838 (N.D. Ill. 2002).
     Replace Wilson LEXIS citation with: 206 F.3d 810 (8th Cir. 2000). *Add after Alexander citation:* (technical accuracy is not the standard; a consumer report must be accurate to the maximum possible extent).

258   Heupel v. Trans Union, L.L.C., 193 F. Supp. 2d 1234 (N.D. Ala. 2002).

Page 186

272   *Replace Thompson citation with:* 197 F. Supp. 2d 1233 (D. Or. 2002).

7.8.4 Reasonable Procedures: The Second Test of Accuracy

7.8.4.1 General Standards

Addition to notes 274, 281.

274   Thomas v. Trans Union, L.L.C., 197 F. Supp. 2d 1233 (D. Or. 2002); Olwell v. Medical Inf. Bureau, 2003 WL 79035 (D. Minn. 2003).
     Replace Andrews LEXIS citation with: 289 F.3d 600 (9th Cir. 2002).

Page 187

281   *Replace Cassara citation with:* 276 F.3d 1210 (10th Cir. 2002).

Add note 281.1 after first sentence of subsection's fourth paragraph.

281.1   Sheffer v. Experian Info. Solutions, Inc., 2003 WL 21710573 (E.D. Pa. July 24, 2003).

Addition to notes 285, 286, 300.

285   Thomas v. GulfCoast Credit Serv., Inc., 214 F. Supp. 2d 1228 (M.D. Ala. 2002) (blind reliance on furnisher in the face of repeated consumer disputes is not reasonable).

286   *Replace Wilson LEXIS citation with:* 206 F.3d 810 (8th Cir. 2000).

Page 188

300   *But see* Olwell v. Medical Info. Bureau, 2002 WL 79035 (D. Minn. Jan. 7, 2003) (plaintiff must offer specific facts that could allow a reasonable fact-finder to determine that defendant's procedures were not reasonable).

Page 189

7.8.4.2 Proof Issues

Addition to notes 301, 302.

301   Thomas v. Gulf Coast Credit Serv., Inc., 214 F. Supp. 2d 1228 (M.D. Ala. 2002).
     Replace Parker citation with: 124 F. Supp. 2d 1216 (M.D. Ala. 2000).

302   *Replace Barron citation with:* 82 F. Supp. 2d 1288 (M.D. Ala. 2000).

7.8.4.4 Inaccurate Sources

Addition to note 313.

313   Soghomonian v. U.S., 278 F. Supp. 2d 1151 (E.D. Cal. 2003).

Page 190

7.8.4.5 Public Record Information

Add to text after sentence containing note 324:

For example, a credit reporting agency may report that a tax lien was placed on a property by a tax assessor's office, but the report may not reflect a subsequent release of the lien because the assessor's office reported it incorrectly. Some credit reporting agencies have asserted that the fact that the lien was placed is "technically accurate" and therefore may be reported, notwithstanding that the lien was subsequently released. This position highlights the inherent problem with using a "technically accurate" standard for accuracy.

Page 191

Addition to note 327.

327 Kettler v. CSC Credit Serv., Inc., 2003 WL 21975919 (D. Minn. Aug. 12, 2003) (consumer's dispute that she had never filed bankruptcy, without disclosing that her husband had mistakenly listed the accounts in his bankruptcy, was inadequate to obligate the reporting agency to look behind the public records.).

Page 192

7.8.4.6 Mismerged Information and Wrong Consumer Identification

Addition to note 340.

340 *Add to end of Crabill citation*: *aff'd*, 259 F.3d 662 (7th Cir. 2001).

7.8.4.7 Identity Theft

Add to text at end of subsection's first paragraph:

The relationship between the FCRA and identity theft is discussed more fully in Chapter 16, *supra*.

Concerns with identity theft were a primary force behind the FACTA of 2003.[348.1] That Act created a variety of new tools for consumers to use both to prevent identity theft and to restore credit records polluted by a thief's transactions. These provisions are discussed thoroughly in § 16.6.1a, *infra*. The most significant provisions will, as of December 1, 2004, allow consumers who believe that they are or are about to be the victim of fraud, including identity theft, to require an agency to include a ninety-day fraud alert in their files.[348.2] The new alert is called a "one-call" alert because the agency must refer the alert to other nationwide agencies, and all the agencies must not only include the alert in the consumer's file but provide the alert each time they generate that consumer's credit score.[348.3] Agencies must also refer identity theft complaints and fraud alerts to each other.[348.4] The agencies must present to any user a "clear and conspicuous" view of the statement that notifies users of the consumer's report that the consumer may be a victim of fraud, including identity theft.[348.5] Those consumers who supply an agency with an identity theft report can obtain a seven-year fraud alert.[348.6] As of December 1, 2004, a consumer can also require an agency to block fraud related information in the consumer's file; the agency must also notify the original furnisher that the information was blocked and the reason for it.[348.7] By that date, furnishers must have reasonable procedures to respond to such notices to prevent them from refurnishing the blocked information.[348.8] Effective December 1, 2004, the Act will require agencies to notify a user when the user's request for a report contains an address for the consumer different from that in the agency's files,[348.9] requiring the creation of red flag guidelines and regulations to help financial institutions and creditors to identify identity theft,[348.10] requiring debt collectors to notify creditors of fraudulent debts,[348.11] and prohibit the sale or transfer of identity theft debts.[348.12] Forthcoming regulations will establish accuracy and integrity guidelines for furnishers.[348.13] Consumers may obtain certain transaction information from businesses that have done business with an identity thief.[348.14] Finally, the Act requires designated agencies to come up with regulations that will require those who use consumer information from consumer reports to dispose of it properly, which could eventually curb thieves' access to consumer financial information.[348.15]

However, while many of these provisions could assist consumers in preventing identity theft, locating identity thieves, and ultimately restoring their credit reports, Congress correspondingly preempted many provisions of state laws targeting identity theft.[349] State laws with "requirements and prohibitions" with respect to the conduct required by the specific preemptions enumerated are thus preempted.[349.1] However, states should nonetheless be able to enact and enforce identity theft laws with respect to other conduct.

Preexisting provisions of the FCRA can also be used to counter identity theft: the requirement that agencies follow reasonable procedures to ensure maximum possible accuracy,[350] and the provisions requiring that the accuracy of information challenged by consumers be reinvestigated.[351]

348.1 *See, e.g.*, Explanatory Statement of the Conference Committee, 149 Cong. Rec. H12214 (daily ed. Nov. 21, 2003) ("While criminal prosecutions and strict fraud detection protocols can curtail identity theft, and punish the wrongdoers, not enough had been done heretofore to aid the real victims of this crime—the

§ 7.8.4.10 *Fair Credit Reporting / 2004 Supplement*

> consumer whose identity is assumed, and can spend months or years trying to rehabilitate their credit and re-order their affairs.").

348.2 15 U.S.C. § 1681c-1, *added by* Pub. L. No. 108-159, § 112 (2003); 16 C.F.R. § 602.1(c)(3)(i), *added by* 69 Fed. Reg. 6526–31 (Feb. 5, 2004). Active military duty consumers may also place an alert of their status in their files. *Id.* at § 168Ic–1(c). *See also* § 16.6.1a.1.1.3, *infra*.

348.3 *Id.*

348.4 15 U.S.C. § 168Ic–1(e).

348.5 15 U.S.C. § 1681a(q)(2)(B), *added by* Pub. L. No. 108-159, § 111 (2003).

348.6 15 U.S.C. § 168Ic–1(b)(1).

348.7 15 U.S.C. § 1681c-2, *added by* Pub. L. No. 108-159, 152 (2003).

348.8 15 U.S.C. § 1681s–2(a)(6), *added by* Pub. L. No. 108-159, 154 (2003); 16 C.F.R. § 602.1(c)(3)(vii), *added by* 69 Fed. Reg. 6526–31 (Feb. 5, 2004).

348.9 15 U.S.C. § 1681m(e), *added by* Pub. L. No. 108-159, § 114 (2003); 16 C.F.R. § 602.1(c)(3)(ii), *added by* 69 Fed. Reg. 6526–31 (Feb. 5, 2004).

348.10 *Id. See also* § 3.4.3, *supra*.

348.11 15 U.S.C. § 1681m(g), *added by* Pub. L. No. 108-159, § 155 (2003); 16 C.F.R. § 602.1(c)(3)(viii), *added by* 69 Fed. Reg. 6526–31 (Feb. 5, 2004). *See also* § 3.3.4.2a, *supra*.

348.12 15 U.S.C. § 1681m(f), *added by* Pub. L. No. 108-159, § 154 (2003); 16 C.F.R. § 602.1(c)(3)(vii), *added by* 69 Fed. Reg. 6526–31 (Feb. 5, 2004).

348.13 15 U.S.C. § 1681s–2(e), *added by* Pub. L. No. 108-159, § 312 (2003). *See* § 3.4.3, *supra*.

348.14 15 U.S.C. § 1681g(e), *added by* Pub. L. No. 108-159, § (2003); 16 C.F.R. § 602.1(c)(3)(iv), *added by* 69 Fed. Reg. 6526–31 (Feb. 5, 2004).

348.15 15 U.S.C. § 1681w, *added by* Pub. L. No. 108-159, 216.

349 See state identity theft statutes in Appx. B.2, *infra*.

349.1 15 U.S.C. § 1681t(b)(5), *added by* Pub. L. No. 108-159, § 711 (2003).

350 *Retain as in main edition.*

351 *Retain as in main edition.*

Page 193

Add at beginning of subsection's existing fifth paragraph:

As noted above, the FACTA of 2003 provided a number of options for identity theft victims to use in preventing identity theft and restoring credit records damaged by a thief, but other preexisting provisions of the FCRA can assist victims as well.

Page 194

Addition to note 361.

361 Haque v. CompUSA, Inc., 2003 WL 117986 (D. Mass. 2003); Thomas v. GulfCoast Credit Serv., Inc., 214 F. Supp. 2d 1228 (M.D. Ala. 2002); Field v. Trans Union, L.L.C., 2002 WL 849589 (N.D. Ill. May 3, 2002).

Add to text at end of subsection:

The FACTA of 2003 went quite a bit further, giving identity theft victims the ability to block fraudulent information in their files and requiring an agency that unblocks the information to notify the consumer in the same manner as the agency must notify consumers that other information has been reinserted.[362.1]

362.1 15 U.S.C. § 1681c-2, *added by* Pub. L. No. 108-159, § 152 (2003). This provision will become effective on December 1, 2004. 16 C.F.R. § 602.1(c)(3)(v), *added by* 69 Fed. Reg. 6526–31 (Feb. 5, 2004). *See* § 16.6.1a, *infra*.

7.8.4.10 Incomplete and Outdated Items in the File

Page 196

7.8.4.10.2 Guarantors and reports relating to a bankruptcy

Addition to note 389.

389 Heupel v. Trans Union, L.L.C., 193 F. Supp. 2d 1234 (N.D. Ala. 2002) ("included in bankruptcy" technically accurate; entry in single tradeline reduced credit score).
Replace Spellman citation with: 289 F.3d 600 (9th Cir. 2002).

Page 197

7.8.4.10.3 Reasonable methods to acquire updated information

Add to text at end of subsection:

The Metro 2 format, developed by a consortium including Equifax, Experian, and Trans Union, was adopted in 1999. There is no longer any excuse for "included in bankruptcy" to be on the credit file of a consumer who did not file bankruptcy, whether as co-signer or authorized user. The Metro 2 credit reporting format allows a creditor/furnisher to report "bankruptcy" indicators for the specific consumer they relate to when reporting a specific tradeline. Under Metro 2, the information furnished to consumer reporting agencies includes, for each account, a J1 or J2 segment which pertains to associated consumers. Under this segment, a creditor may report account conditions specific to the associated consumer.

Industry standards for reporting to credit bureaus, developed by the "Big Three"—Trans Union, Equifax and Experian—repeatedly mandate that a bankruptcy filing must be shown only on the report of the consumer to whom it relates. The standards, issued by the trade organization Associated Credit Bureaus (now CDIA), appear in the Metro 2 format, which is also incorporated into the bureaus' on-line consumer dispute resolution system, E-Oscar. Following are excerpts from the industry standard:

Metro 2 Manual

Page 5-21: Field 11 of the J1 segment "contains a value that indicates a special condition that applies to the specific consumer."

Page 4-17: Base Segment 38 "contains a value that indicates a special condition of the account that applies to the primary consumer."

Page 4-17: J1 Segment "Contains a value that indicates a special condition of the account that applies to the associated consumer."

Page 6-4: "For joint accounts where only one borrower files bankruptcy, report one Base Segment for the account with the Consumer Information Indicator (CII) set to the appropriate bankruptcy code for the borrower who filed bankruptcy. The CII for the other consumer should be blank. The Account Status (field 17A) should reflect the status of the ongoing account for the consumer who did not file bankruptcy."

E-Oscar Manual

Page 2.14 and 3.15, Bankruptcy Reporting: If an account was included in a bankruptcy, it should appear on the credit bureau report of anyone who was an owner or co-owner of the account, no matter who filed the bankruptcy. It should not appear on the credit bureau of any authorized user on the account. If it does, the tradeline can be deleted. The comment line on the credit bureau of the owner or co-owner who did not file bankruptcy, but was on the account, should read "Account included in Chapter __ bankruptcy of another party."

The consumer reporting agency must follow procedures to "assure maximum possible accuracy of the information concerning the individual about whom the report relates." § 1681e(b) (emphasis added). A common thread throughout the FCRA is that a consumer report relates to the individual consumer. *E.g.*, § 1681q ("information on a consumer"); § 1681r ("concerning an individual"). Someone else's bankruptcy does not bear on an individual's credit worthiness or the other personal characteristics recited in § 1681a(d)(1).

7.8.5 Procedures for Reports of Adverse Public Record Information for Employment Purposes

Page 200

7.8.5.3 Election to Establish Strict Procedures for Complete and Up-to-Date Public Record Information

Addition to notes 435, 437.

435 *Add at end of Obabueki citation: aff'd*, 319 F.3d 87 (2d Cir. 2003).
437 *Add at end of Obabueki citation: aff'd*, 319 F.3d 87 (2d Cir. 2003).

Chapter 8 Obsolete Information

8.3 Maximum Time Periods to Retain Adverse Information

Page 203

8.3.1 Structure of the Act

Add at end of subsection:

The section of the FCRA specifying time frames for the five specialized types of information to become obsolete was as amended by the Fair and Accurate Credit Transactions Act of 2003(FACTA) to also exclude certain types of medical information from being reported.[24.1]

24.1 See § 8.3.10, *infra*.

8.3.3 Accounts Placed for Collection or Charged Off

Addition to notes 30, 33.

30 See § 3.3.3.8, *supra* for a discussion of how debt collectors report collection accounts using the Metro 2 reporting system.

33 Waggoner v. Trans Union, L.L.C., 2003 WL 22220668 (N.D. Tex. July 17, 2003) (applying changed obsolescence period).

Page 204

Add note 37.1 after first sentence in subsection's fifth paragraph.

37.1 See § 3.3.3.8, *supra* for a discussion of reporting requirements for debt collectors.

Add to text after sentence containing note 47:

Even though accounts may be listed as charge offs and may not be reported after the applicable obsolescence period has elapsed, creditors may still attempt to collect on the accounts. Charge offs are mere accounting procedures and creditors or debt collectors may still attempt to collect upon the underlying debt even after the account has become obsolete for credit reporting purposes. Such collection efforts remain subject to the applicable statute of limitations defense, so long as the consumer has not made any payments, which would renew the statute.

Page 207

Add new subsection after § 8.3.9.

8.3.10 Fair and Accurate Credit Transaction Act of 2003

The FCRA was amended by the Fair and Accurate Credit Transactions Act of 2003[79.1] to prohibit consumer reporting agencies from including in consumer reports the furnisher's name, address, and telephone number provided by furnishers of medical information. An exception is provided if such information is restricted or reported using codes that do not identify, or provide information sufficient to infer, the specific provider or the nature of such services, products, or devices to a person other than the customer.[79.2] However, agencies may provide such information in reports to insurance companies for a purpose relating to engaging in the business of insurance other than property and casualty insurance.[79.3] States are preempted from regulating the subject matter of this prohibition.[79.4] The large-scale trans-

§ 8.5 *Fair Credit Reporting / 2004 Supplement*

action exception contained in the FCRA, which allows agencies to include otherwise-to-be-excluded information in reports if the dollar value of the transaction meets or exceeds $150,000, does not apply to the prohibition against identifying medical information furnishers and the coding requirements.[79.5]

This amendment to the FCRA was not intended to prohibit the inclusion in a consumer report of information relating to the consumer's place of employment, but instead is intended to ensure that consumers who have medical transactions in their credit files are protected by requiring that the information be coded so that third parties cannot glean any health implications relating to the consumer.[79.6]

79.1 Fair and Accurate Credit Transactions Act of 2003, Pub. L. No. 108-159 (2003).
79.2 15 U.S.C. § 1681c(a)(6)(A), *added by* Pub. L. No. 108-159, § 412 (2003).
79.3 15 U.S.C. § 1681c(a)(6)(B).
79.4 15 U.S.C. § 1681t(b)(1)(E), *as amended by* Pub. L. No. 108-159, § 214(a)(1).
79.5 15 U.S.C. § 1681c(b), *as amended by* Pub. L. No. 108-159, § 412 (2003). *See* H. Rep. No. 108-263 at 53-54 (2003).
79.6 H. Rep. No. 108-263, at 54 (2003).

8.5 Reasonable Procedures Concerning Obsolete Information

Page 208

8.5.1 General

Add to text after sentence containing note 89:

FTC Commentary also states that consumer reporting agencies should establish procedures with its sources of adverse information that will avoid the risk of reporting obsolete information.[89.1]

89.1 FTC Official Staff Commentary § 607 item 1A [*reprinted at* Appx. C, *infra*].

Addition to note 92.

92 Batdorf v. Trans Union, 2002 WL 1034048 (N.D. Cal. 2002) (Trans Union criticized for reporting when furnisher did not provide a date from which the seven-year period can be calculated).

Chapter 9 Investigative Consumer Reports

9.1 What Is an Investigative Consumer Report?

Page 211

9.1.1 Introduction

Add to text at end of subsection's third paragraph:

The FACTA of 2003 amended the FCRA to exclude certain reports of employee behavior from the definition of "consumer report," and thereby from the definition of "investigative consumer report." Nonetheless, employers must make certain disclosures to benefit from the exclusion; these are discussed previously in the manual.[1.1]

1.1 See § 5.2.5.5, *supra*.

9.1.2 FCRA Definition

Page 213

Replace subsection heading with:

9.1.2.4 Reports Excluded from the Definition; Certain Employee Investigations

Addition to text at end of subsection:

The FACTA of 2003 met a rising demand by employers to exempt certain reports about employees from the requirements for consumer reports.[26.1] Nonetheless the Act still requires employers to disclose certain information to an employee in connection with such a report.[26.2] Because of this new exemption, even if a particular investigation would otherwise be an investigative consumer report, it will fall outside of the definition by virtue of being specifically exempted from the definition of "consumer report."[26.3] To fall within the exclusion the communication must be made to an employer and must be in connection with an investigation of one of the following:

- suspected misconduct relating to employment;
- compliance with federal, state, or local laws;
- compliance with the rules of a self-regulatory organization; or
- compliance with the preexisting written policies of the employer.[26.4]

One concern is that the last of the qualifying reasons is one subject to the employer's control; conceivably an employer could draft very broad written policies in order to expand the breadth of this exception.

To limit the exemption's scope the FACTA further requires that the communication must not be for the purpose of investigating a consumer's creditworthiness, credit standing, or credit capacity (in other words, the communication must only bear on the employee's character, general reputation, personal characteristics, or mode of living) and must not be provided to anyone other than the employer (or the employer's agent), a governmental authority, or a self-regulatory organization with regulatory authority over the employer.[26.5] The FACTA defines a self-regulatory organization to be "any self-regulatory organization (as defined in section 3(a)(26) of the Securities Exchange Act of 1934[15 U.S.C. § 78c(a)(26)]), any entity established under title I of the Sarbanes-Oxley Act of 2002 [15 U.S.C. §§

§ 9.1.3   Fair Credit Reporting / 2004 Supplement

7211-7218], any board of trade designated by the Commodity Futures Trading Commission, and any futures association registered with such Commission."[26.6]

Employees will have a right to a notice containing a summary of the nature and substance of the communications if the employer takes adverse action based on communications resulting from an investigation.[26.7]

26.1   See 149 Cong. Rec. H8123 (daily ed. Sept. 10, 2003). Employers complained that the FCRA unfairly undercut meaningful investigations of employee misconduct by requiring the employer to provide FCRA notices ahead of time, notices that effectively alerted the employee to the employer's suspicions. Rep. Jackson explained the problem as follows:

> [I]t deals with or undermines or did undermine the ability of employers to use experienced, outside organizations or individuals to investigate allegations of drug use or sales, violence, sexual harassment, other types of harassment, employment discrimination, job safety and health violations, as well as criminal activity, including theft, fraud, embezzlement, sabotage or arson, patient or elder abuse, child abuse and other types of misconduct related to employment. This was not the intention of the Fair Credit Reporting Act, but by its interpretation this is what occurred.

Id. Among the Act's requirements that were perceived as impeding such investigations were the following: (1) Notice to the consumer (in this case, the employee) of the investigation; (2) The employee's consent prior to the investigation; (3) A description of the nature and scope of the proposed investigation, if the employee requested it; (4) A release of a full, un-redacted investigative report to the employee; and (5) Notice to the employee of his or her rights under FCRA prior to taking any adverse employment action. 15 U.S.C. § 1681 b(b). See § 5.2.5.5, supra.

26.2   15 U.S.C. § 1681a(x)(D)(v), added by Pub. L. No. 108-159, § 611 (2003). See also § 5.2.5.5, supra.
26.3   15 U.S.C. § 1681a(d)(2)(D), amended by Pub. L. No. 108-159, § 611(b) (2003).
26.4   15 U.S.C. § 1681a(x), added by Pub. L. No. 108-159, § 611(a) (2003).
26.5   15 U.S.C. § 1681a(x)(1)(C).
26.6   Id. at § 1681a(x)(3).
26.7   Id. at § 1681a (x)(2).

9.1.3 Types of Investigative Reports

9.1.3.2 Reports for Employment Purposes

Addition to notes 32, 33.

32   In 2003, as part of the debate over continuing the preemption provisions in the FCRA, employers have renewed their efforts to exempt from FCRA coverage workplace investigative reports. See, e.g., H.R. 2622, 108th Cong. (2003).

Page 214

33   See also Rugg v. HANAC Inc., 2002 WL 31132883 (S.D.N.Y. Sept. 26, 2002) (approving Johnson's criticism of FTC opinion letters, however declining to decide if employer consultant was a "consumer reporting agency" under the FCRA).

Add to text after sentence containing note 41:

As noted in the previous subsection, the recent revisions to the FCRA excluded certain employee investigation reports from the definition of consumer report and accordingly from the definition of investigative consumer report.[41.1] Should information from a particular employee investigation not meet the criteria of an exempt employer report, the employer will have to comply with the requirements discussed below, assuming the report qualifies as an investigative consumer report. Even where an employee investigation report meets the criteria for an exempt report, employees have a right to only to a summary containing the nature and substance of the communication upon which the employer's adverse action is based.[41.2]

41.1   See §§ 5.2.5.5, 6.4.2.4, 6.5.2, 9.2.1.4, supra.
41.2   15 U.S.C. § 1681a(x)(2), added by Pub. L. No. 108-59, § 611(b) (2003).

Page 216

9.1.4 Overview of Additional Obligations Required for an Investigative Consumer Report

Add to text after sentence containing note 58:

As discussed before, however, if a report qualifies as an employee investigation report the report will be exempt from the definition of consumer report and accordingly from the related definition of investigative consumer report.[58.1] In such a case the employer need not comply

Investigative Consumer Reports / 2004 Supplement § 9.3.1

with these requirements, though the employer must comply with the special disclosure provisions imposed on employee investigation reports.[58.2]

58.1   15 U.S.C. § 1681a(d)(2)(D), *amended by* Pub. L. No. 108-159, § 611(b) (2003).
58.2   *See* §§ 5.2.5, 9.1.2.4, *supra*.

9.2 Disclosure to Consumer of Investigative Report's Existence

Page 221

Replace first sentence of subsection's second paragraph with:

9.2.4 Users' Reasonable Procedures Defense

The Act does not specify the types of procedures that must be shown to avoid liability under this section. Ordinarily, the reasonableness of procedures is a question of fact.[134.1]

134.1   Feldman v. Comprehensive Info. Servs., Inc., 2003 WL 22413484 (Conn. Super. Oct. 6, 2003) (unknown to the employer, the reporting agency did not physically inspect the criminal records but the employer required neither a physical inspection in the written contract nor an affidavit that such an inspection had been done).

Page 222

Add to text at end of subsection:

9.2.5 Waiver of Consumer Rights

Waivers are strictly construed against the drafter; preprinted waivers with potential employees of unequal bargaining power demand careful judicial scrutiny when they are "so broad as to afford protection for all conduct no matter how egregious."[137.1]

137.1   Feldman v. Comprehensive Info. Servs., Inc., 2003 WL 22413484 (Conn. Super. Oct. 6, 2003).

9.3 Consumer Utilization of Investigative Report Notices

Replace subsection heading with:

9.3.1 Consumer's Permission Not Needed If Permissible Purpose for Employee Investigation Report, Except for Other Employment Investigative Reports

Replace first sentence of subsection with:

The recent revisions to the FCRA excluded certain employee investigation reports from the definition of consumer report and accordingly from the definition of investigative consumer report.[137.2] This exemption allows an employer to avoid the special requirements applicable to other types of consumer reports used for employment purposes, although the employer must comply with new disclosure requirements.[137.3] If the employer does not qualify for the exemption, however, perhaps because the employer cannot meet one of the qualifying reasons for obtaining an employee investigation report, the employer may not procure a consumer report (investigative or otherwise) for employment purposes without the written permission of the employee.[138]

137.2   *See* §§ 5.2.5.5, 9.2.1.4, *supra*.
137.3   15 U.S.C. § 1681a(x)(2).
138   *Retain as in main edition.*

Chapter 10 Litigating Credit Report Disputes

Page 227

10.1 Introduction

Add at end of section's third paragraph:

Chapter 11 also includes a discussion on limitations of liability, including limitations on private enforcement that arise from the FACTA of 2003.[7.1]

7.1 See § 11.1a (Supp), *infra*.

10.2 Fair Credit Reporting Act Claims

Replace "any requirement" in first sentence of subsection's second paragraph with:

certain requirements

Page 228

Addition to note 22.

22   Thomas v. Trans Union, L.L.C., 197 F. Supp. 2d 1233 (D. Or. 2002) (FCRA is not a strict liability law). *See also* Guimond v. Trans Union Credit Inf. Co., 45 F.3d 1329, 1333 (9th Cir. 1995); Dalton v. Capital Associated Ind., Inc., 257 F.3d 409, 417 (4th Cir. 2001); Olwell v. Medical Inf. Bureau, 2003 WL 79035 (D. Minn. 2003); Curtis v. Trans Union, L.L.C., 2002 WL 31748838 (N.D. Ill. 2002).

Add to text at end of subsection:

One of the most dramatic aspects of the FACTA is that a sizable portion of the new obligations imposed on businesses, creditors, furnishers, and financial institutions are not enforceable under an FCRA private cause of action.[24.1] The new obligations that have no private enforcement include:[24.2]

- The new responsibility of businesses that have transacted with an identity thief to provide the victim, upon the victim's request, with transaction information[24.3]
- The forthcoming obligation of financial institutions or creditors to establish policies to implement the red flag guidelines that appointed agencies will issue to curb identity theft[24.4]
- The new requirement that creditors issue risk-based pricing notices when they offer credit on "material terms that are materially less favorable" than those offered to other consumers[24.5]
- The revised obligation of furnishers to refrain from furnishing information about a consumer to an agency if the furnisher knows or has reason to believe that the information is inaccurate[24.6]
- The new obligation of furnishers not to furnish information if the furnisher has been notified by a consumer that the information is inaccurate and is in fact inaccurate[24.7]
- The furnisher's obligation to correct and update information[24.8]
- The obligation of a furnisher to notify an agency that a consumer has disputed the furnished information[24.9]
- The obligation of certain furnishers to notify an agency that a consumer has voluntarily closed an account[24.10]
- The revised obligation of furnishers to comply with date delinquency provisions when furnishing account delinquency information[24.11]

§ 10.2.2 Fair Credit Reporting / 2004 Supplement

- The new obligation of furnishers to put in place reasonable procedures for responding to a notice from an agency that that agency has blocked furnished information on the grounds that it was the result of fraud or identity theft[24.12]
- The new obligation of financial institution furnishers to notify customers that the institution has furnished negative information about the customer to a nationwide consumer reporting agency[24.13]
- The upcoming obligation of furnishers to reinvestigate the accuracy of information upon consumer's notice that the information is inaccurate[24.14]
- The new obligation of medical information furnishers to notify an agency to which the furnisher furnishes medical information of their status[24.15]

24.1 15 U.S.C. §§ 1681n, 1681o.
24.2 15 U.S.C. § 1681s–2(c)(1), *amended by* Pub. L. No. 108-159, § 312(e) (2003).
24.3 15 U.S.C. § 1681g(e)(6),*added by* Pub. L. No. 108-159, § 151 (2003). *See also* § 16.6.1a., *infra*. This provision will become effective on December 1, 2004. 16 C.F.R. § 602.1(c)(3)(ivs), *added by* 69 Fed. Reg. 6526–31 (Feb. 5, 2004).
24.4 15 U.S.C, § 1681s–2(c)(3), *added by* Pub. L. No. 108-159, § 314(b) (2003). *See also* § 16.6.1a., *infra*.
24.5 15 U.S.C. § 1681m(h)(8)(A), *added by* Pub. L. No. 108-159, § 311 (2003). This provision will become effective on December 1, 2004. 16 C.F.R. § 602.1(c)(3)(xiii), *added by* 69 Fed. Reg. 6526–31 (Feb. 5, 2004). Note that this subsection states that the private action provisions "shall not apply to any failure by any person to comply with this section" and could be read to apply to the entire substance of section 615 and not just subsection 1681m(h). However, such a reading would be an extraordinary curtailment of consumers' ability to pursue abuses by users of consumer reports not justified by any expressed intent by Congress to do so.
24.6 15 U.S.C. § 1681s–2(a)(1)(A), *amended by* Pub. L. No. 108-159, § 312(b) (2003). *See also* § 3.4.2, *supra*.
24.7 15 U.S.C. § 1681s–2(a)(1)(B), *amended by* Pub. L. No. 108-159, § 312(b) (2003).
24.8 15 U.S.C. § 1681s–2(a)(2).
24.9 5 U.S.C. § 1681s–2(a)(3).
24.10 15 U.S.C. § 1681s–2(a)(4).
24.11 15 U.S.C. § 1681s–2(a)(5), *amended by* Pub. L. No. 108-159, § 312(d) (2003). *See also* § 3.3.4.2b, *supra*.
24.12 15 U.S.C. § 1681s–2(a)(6), *added by* Pub. L. No. 108-159, § 154 (2003). This provision will become effective on December 1, 2004. 16 C.F.R. § 602.1(c)(3)(vii), *added by* 69 Fed. Reg. 6526–31 (Feb. 5, 2004). *See also* § 16.6.1a.2.2 *supra*.
24.13 15 U.S.C. § 1681s–2(a)(7), *added by* Pub. L. No. 108-159, § 217 (2003). This provision will become effective on December 1, 2004. 16 C.F.R. § 602.1(c)(3)(xii), *added by* 69 Fed. Reg. 6526–31 (Feb. 5, 2004).
24.14 15 U.S.C. § 1681s–2(a)(8), *added by* Pub. L. No. 108-159, § 312(c) (2003). This provision will become effective on December 1, 2004. 16 C.F.R. § 602.1(c)(3)(xiv), *added by* 69 Fed. Reg. 6526–31 (Feb. 5, 2004). The obligations will not arise until the identified agencies prescribe regulations that identify circumstances under which a furnisher will be required to reinvestigate a dispute made directly by a consumer. 15 U.S.C. § 1681s–2(a)(8)(C). *See also* § 3.4.5a, *supra*.
24.15 15 U.S.C. § 1681s–2(a)(9), *added by* Pub. L. No. 108-159, § 412(a) (2003). This provision does not become effective until March 4, 2005. *Id. See also* § 3.8a, *supra*.

10.2.2 FCRA Claims Against Reporting Agencies

10.2.2.1 Claims Relating to Inaccurate Reports

Add to text at beginning of subsection:

The FCRA contains no definition of accuracy.[24.16]

24.16 *See* § 7.1.2, supra.

Page 229

Addition to notes 41, 42, 48, 49.

41 McCauley v. Trans Union, L.L.C., 2003 WL 22845741 (S.D.N.Y. Nov. 26, 2003); Acton v. Bank One Corp., 293 F. Supp. 2d 1092 (D. Ariz. 2003).
42 Thomas v. Gulf Coast Credit Serv., Inc., 214 F. Supp. 2d 1228 (M.D. Ala. 2002).
48 *E.g.* Heupel v. Trans Union, L.L.C., 193 F. Supp. 2d 1234 (N.D. Ala. 2002).
49 Soghomonian v. U.S., 278 F. Supp. 2d 1151 (E.D. Cal. 2003).

Litigating Credit Report Disputes / 2004 Supplement § 10.2.2.6

Page 230

10.2.2.3 Claims Relating to Furnishing Reports for Impermissible Purposes

Addition to note 59.

59 *Replace Andrews LEXIS citation with*: 289 F.3d 600 (9th Cir. 2002).

Page 231

Replace § 10.2.2.4 with:

10.2.2.4 Claims Relating to Medical Information Reported Without Consumer Consent

Prior to the FACTA, consumer reporting agencies were prohibited from furnishing medical information about consumers for employment purposes, or in connection with credit, insurance or direct marketing transactions without consumer consent.[66] The FACTA continues to prohibit agencies from issuing a report for employment purposes or in connection with a credit or insurance transaction that contains medical information without the consumer's consent.[67]

In addition, as of June 1, 2004, a consumer's consent must be in writing, must be specific, and must describe the use for which the agency will furnish the information.[68] These requirements are applicable if the report is for employment purposes or in connection with a credit or insurance transaction.[68.1] An agency may provide medical information that pertains solely to financial transactions as long as it insures that the information does not disclose a specific provider of medical services or the nature of services.[68.2] The FACTA also prohibits users from re-disclosing such reports.[68.3]

The FACTA also prohibits reporting agencies from including the name, address, and telephone information of medical information furnishers in consumer reports unless the agency formats the information to prevent the disclosure either of the specific provider or the nature of the medical services. However, the agency may provide such information in a report to an insurance agency.[68.4]

Consistent with the FCRA prior to amendment by the FACTA, these requirements are violated if the medical information is negligently reported. There is no "reasonable procedures" defense to the improper furnishing of medical information without the required consumer consent. If medical information is released without such consent, it should create a prima facie case, or at least a rebuttable presumption, of negligence.

66 15 U.S.C. § 1681b(g). *See* § 4.5.5, *supra*.
67 15 U.S.C. § 1681b(g), *added by* Pub. L. No. 108-159, § 411 (2003).
68 Pub. L. No. 108-159, § 411(d) (2003).
68.1 *Id.*
68.2 15 U.S.C. § 1681b(g)(1)(C), *added by* Pub. L. No. 108-159, § 411 (2003). This provision will become effective on June 1, 2004, 180 days after passage of the FACTA. Pub. L. No. 108-159, § 411(d) (2003).
68.3 15 U.S.C. § 1681b(g)(4), *added by* Pub. L. No. 108-159, § 411 (2003). This provision will become effective on June 1, 2004, 180 days after passage of the FACTA. Pub. L. No. 108-159, § 411(d) (2003).
68.4 15 U.S.C. § 1681c(a)(6), *added by* Pub. L. No. 108-159, § 412 (2003).

Page 232

10.2.2.6 Claims Relating to Adverse Public Record Information for Employment Purposes

Add to text at end of subsection:

The FACTA excludes certain employee investigation communications from FCRA requirements.[71.1] To fall within the exclusion, the communication must not be for the purpose of investigating the employee's credit worthiness, credit standing, personal characteristics or mode of living, and must not be provided to anyone other than the employer or employer's agent, a governmental authority, or a self-regulatory organization with regulatory authority over the employer.[71.2] Employees will have the right of notice if the employer takes adverse action based on the communications resulting from the investigation. The notice must only include a summary of the nature and substance of the communications.[71.3]

71.1 *See* § 6.4.2.4, *supra*.
71.2 15 U.S.C. § 1681a(x)(1)(C), *added by* 108-159, § 611 (2003).
71.3 15 U.S.C. § 1681a(x)(D)(v)(2), *amended by* Pub. L. No. 108-59, § 611 (2003).

10.2.2.8 Claims Against Resellers

Add to text at end of subsection's first paragraph:

While resellers fit the definition of a consumer reporting agency, at least one court has ruled that the 1996 amendment applicable to resellers is the only provision with which they must comply.[75.1]

75.1   15 U.S.C. § 1681e(e); Lewis v. Ohio Prof'l Elec. Network L.L.C., 248 F. Supp. 2d 693 (S.D. Ohio 2003).

Page 233

Addition to note 79.

79   Contra Lewis v. Ohio Prof'l Elec. Network L.L.C., 248 F. Supp. 2d 693 (S.D. Ohio 2003).
Add after "(consent agreement)": [reprinted in Appx. H.4.3, infra].

10.2.3 FCRA Claims Against Creditors and Others Who Furnish Information to Reporting Agencies

Page 234

10.2.3.1 General

Add to text at end of subsection's first paragraph:

The FACTA of 2003 also requires the FTC and other agencies to issue accuracy guidelines for furnishers; however, enforcement of these guidelines is limited to federal and state officials.[88.1]

88.1   15 U.S.C. § 15 U.S.C. § 1681s–2(e), *added by* Pub. L. No. 108-159, § 312 (2003).

Replace sentence containing note 90 with:

If a creditor has provided a reporting agency with inaccurate information, the consumer should initiate a reinvestigation directly with the consumer reporting agency. The FACTA of 2003 added the right for consumers to directly dispute inaccurate information directly with a creditor or other furnisher. However, there is no private right to then challenge the furnisher's response to that request.[90]

90   15 U.S.C. § 1681s–2(a)(8), *as amended by* 108-159, § 312 (2003). This provision will become effective on December 1, 2004. 16 C.F.R. § 602.1(c)(3)(xiv), added by 69 Fed. Reg. 6526–31 (Feb. 5, 2004).

10.2.3.2 Claims Relating to Accuracy and Completeness of Information Furnished to Consumer Reporting Agencies

Addition to note 95.

95   *Add at beginning of note*: Beattie v. Nations Credit Fin. Servs. Corp., 69 Fed. Appx. 585 (4th Cir. 2003) (unpublished); Bank One, N.A. v. Colley, 294 F. Supp. 2d 864 (M.D. La. 2003); Burns v. Bank of Am., 2003 WL 22990065 (S.D.N.Y. Dec. 18, 2003); Ayers v. Equifax Info. Servs., 2003 WL 23142201 (E.D. Va. Dec. 16, 2003); Cisneros v. Trans Union, L.L.C., 293 F. Supp. 2d 1156 (D. Haw. 2003); Gordon v. Greenpoint Credit, 266 F. Supp. 2d 1007 (S.D. Iowa 2003); Redhead v. Winston & Winston, P.C., 2002 WL 31106934 (S.D.N.Y. 2002); Thomas v. Trans Union, L.L.C., 197 F. Supp. 2d 1233 (D. Or. 2002).

Page 235

Add to text at end of subsection:

The FACTA of 2003 permanently extends existing FCRA preemption provisions with respect to furnishers. The FACTA also includes provisions that limit liability for new duties and obligations under the Act.[102.1]

102.1   See § 11.1a in this supplement, *supra*.

10.2.3.3 Claims Relating to Agency Reinvestigation of Disputed Information

Addition to notes 104, 107, 109.

104   Beattie v. Nations Credit Fin. Servs. Corp., 69 Fed. Appx. 585 (4th Cir. 2003) (unpublished); Gordon v. Greenpoint Credit, 266 F. Supp. 2d 1007 (S.D. Iowa 2003); Cisneros v. Trans Union, L.L.C., 293 F. Supp. 2d 1156 (D. Haw. 2003); Burns v. Bank of Am., 2003 WL 22990065 (S.D.N.Y. Dec. 18, 2003); Bank One, N.A. v. Colley, 294 F. Supp. 2d 864 (M.D. La. 2003); Agosta v. Inovision, Inc., 2003 WL 22999213 (E.D. Pa. Dec. 16, 2003); Ayers v. Equifax Inf. Servs., 2003 WL 23142201 (E.D. Va. Dec. 16, 2003); Zotta v. Nationscredit Fin. Servs., 297 F. Supp. 2d 1196 (E.D. Mo. 2003); Evantash v. G.E. Capital Mortgage Serv., Inc., 2003 WL 22844198 (E.D. Pa. Nov. 25, 2003); Donley v. Nordic Properties, Inc., 2003 WL 22282523 (N.D. Ill. Sept. 30, 2003); Densmore v. Gen. Motors Acceptance Corp., 2003 WL 22220177 (N.D. Ill.

Litigating Credit Report Disputes / 2004 Supplement § 10.2.4.1

Sept. 25, 2003); Molina v. Experian Credit Inf. Solutions, 2003 WL 21147771 (N.D. Ill. May 14, 2003); Hawthorne v. Citicorp Data Sys., Inc., 216 F. Supp. 2d 45 (E.D.N.Y. 2002), *vacated on other grounds*, 219 F.R.D. 47 (E.D.N.Y. 2003).

Replace Nelson LEXIS citation with: 282 F.3d 1057 (9th Cir. 2002). *Replace Thomasson citation with*: 137 F. Supp. 2d 721 (E.D. La. 2001).

Page 236

107 Beattie v. Nations Credit Fin. Servs. Corp., 69 Fed. Appx. 585 (4th Cir. 2003) (unpublished); Young v. Equifax Credit Inf. Serv., Inc., 294 F.3d 631 (5th Cir. 2002); Gordon v. Greenpoint Credit, 266 F. Supp. 2d 1007 (S.D. Iowa 2003); Cisneros v. Trans Union, L.L.C., 293 F. Supp. 2d 1156 (D. Haw. 2003); Burns v. Bank of Am., 2003 WL 22990065 (S.D.N.Y. Dec. 18, 2003); Bank One, N.A. v. Colley, 294 F. Supp. 2d 864 (M.D. La. 2003); Agosta v. Inovision, Inc., 2003 WL 22999213 (E.D. Pa. Dec. 16, 2003); Ayers v. Equifax Credit Inf. Servs., 2003 WL 23142201 (E.D. Va. Dec. 16, 2003); Zotta v. Nationscredit Fin. Servs., 297 F. Supp. 2d 1196 (E.D. Mo. 2003); Evantash v. G.E. Capital Mortgage Serv., Inc., 2003 WL 22844198 (E.D. Pa. Nov. 25, 2003); Donley v. Nordic Properties, Inc., 2003 WL 22282523 (N.D. Ill. Sept. 30, 2003); Densmore v. Gen. Motors Acceptance Corp., 2003 WL 22220177 (N.D. Ill. Sept. 25, 2003); Molina v. Experian Credit Info. Solutions, 2003 WL 21147771 (N.D. Ill. May 14, 2003); Cook v. Experian Inf. Solutions, Inc., 2002 WL 31718624 (N.D. Ill. 2002).

Replace Parker citation with: 124 F. Supp. 2d 1216 (M.D. Ala. 2000).

109 *Replace NCLC Credit Discrimination citation with*: National Consumer Law Center, Credit Discrimination § 3.4, Ch. 9 (3d ed. 2002 and Supp.).

Add note 109.1 at end of second full paragraph on page.

109.1 Densmore v. Gen. Motors Acceptance Corp., 2003 WL 22220177 (N.D. Ill. Sept. 25, 2003) (court was not aware that the reporting agencies merely parrot the requirements of the FCRA when describing the procedures used to investigate rather than provide information sufficient to allow a factual allegation of notice to the furnisher); Moline v. Trans Union, L.L.C., 2003 WL 21878728 (N.D. Ill. Aug 7, 2003).

Add to text at end of first sentence of fourth full paragraph on page:

Failure to telephone or send a facsimile to the reporting agency, in addition to attempting correction by electronic ACDV, when the consumer continues to dispute, may show negligence.[111.1]

111.1 Evantash v. G.E. Capital Mortgage Serv., Inc., 2003 WL 22844198 (E.D. Pa. Nov. 25, 2003).

Page 238

10.2.3.4 Claims Relating to Information from Affiliated Companies

Add to text after sentence containing note 129:

The FACTA of 2003 requires affiliates to notify consumers both of the possibility that an affiliate may use the consumer's information for marketing and of the consumer's right to opt out of such use.[129.1] States are preempted from regulating in this area; however, it appears that consumers may enforce these requirements against affiliates.[129.2]

129.1 15 U.S.C. § 1681s–2c(b)(1)(H), *added by* Pub. L. No. 108-159, § 214 (2003).
129.2 See § 3.2.2.1 (Supp), *supra*.

10.2.4 FCRA Claims Against Users of Consumer Reports

10.2.4.1 Claims Against Those Obtaining Reports Without a Permissible Purpose or Under False Pretenses

Add to text at end of subsection's first paragraph:

A "user" includes the person who actually requests or obtains the report, the person who is the ultimate destination of the report, and one who fraudulently causes a report to be issued (such as an impostor who applies for credit using someone else's personal identifiers).[133.1]

133.1 Adams v. Phillips, 2002 WL 31886737 (W.D. La. 2002).

Page 239

Addition to notes 139, 142.

139 Myers v. Bennett Law Offices, 238 F. Supp. 2d 1196 (D. Nev. 2002); Del Amora v. Metro Ford Sales and Service, Inc. 206 F. Supp. 2d 947 (N.D. Ill. 2002) (employer liable for rogue employee because of employee's access to computer).

142 Razilov v. Nationwide Mutual Ins. Co., 242 F. Supp. 2d 977 (D. Or. 2003); Ashby v. Farmers Group, Inc., 261 F. Supp. 2d 1213 (D. Or. 2003); Spano v. Safeco Ins. Co., 215 F.R.D. 601 (D. Or. 2003).

§ 10.2.4.3   Fair Credit Reporting / 2004 Supplement

Page 240

10.2.4.3 Claims Against Users for Failing to Comply With Disclosure and Certification Requirements for Investigative Reports

Addition to note 155.

155   Add at end of Obabueki citation: *aff'd*, 319 F.3d 87 (2d Cir. 2003).

10.3 Common Law Torts

Page 241

10.3.1 Background

Add to text after sentence containing note 163:

However, the courts are having difficulty in reconciling the qualified immunity provision of § 1681h(e) with the state law preemption provisions of § 1681t, discussed *infra*.[163.1]

163.1   See § 10.4.4, *infra*.

10.3.2 The FCRA's Qualified Immunity

Addition to note 167.

167   Feldman v. Comprehensive Info. Servs., Inc., 2003 WL 22413484 at *2 (Conn. Super. Ct. Oct. 6, 2003) (qualified immunity provision barred plaintiff's claim for reckless common law libel when plaintiff failed to show evidence of reckless disregard for the truth).

Page 242

Add to text at end of subsection:

Some of the new responsibilities imposed by the FACTA of 2003 may be eligible for qualified immunity protection to the extent that a plaintiff's action is based on information that the defendant disclosed to fulfill the responsibility. While the FACTA did not amend the qualified immunity provision itself, it did amend two of the three sections, 609 (§ 1681g) and 615 (§ 1681m), that benefit from the immunity section's protection. Accordingly, plaintiffs may have to meet the elevated proof requirements when bringing actions based on the failure of a party to comply with any of the following new (or amended) provisions:

- An agency's responsibility, upon the consumer's request, to truncate the first five digits of the consumer's social security number when making a disclosure pursuant to the consumer's request[174.1]
- An agency's new responsibility to disclose to consumers the forthcoming summary, to be prepared by the FTC, of consumer's rights to obtain and dispute information and to obtain credit scores[174.2]
- An agency's new responsibility to provide identity theft victims with a statement of their rights[174.3]
- The new responsibility of businesses that have done business with an identity thief to provide the victim, upon the victim's request, with transaction information (to the extent such a provision is a "disclosure")[174.4]

174.1   15 U.S.C. § 1681g(a)(1)(A), *amended by* Pub. L. No. 108-159, § 115 (2003). This provision will become effective on December 1, 2004. 16 C.F.R. § 602.1(c)(3)(i), *added by* 69 Fed. Reg. 6526–31 (Feb. 5, 2004). See also § 16.6.1a.3.1, *infra*.
174.2   5 U.S.C. § 1681g(c), *added by* Pub. L. No. 108-159, § 211(c) (2003).
174.3   15 U.S.C. § 1681g(e), *added by* Pub. L. No. 108-159, § 151 (2003). 2004). See also § 16.6.1a.1, *infra*.
174.4   15 U.S.C. § 1681g(d), *added by* Pub. L. No. 108-159, § 151 (2003). However, such an action would only have to clear the qualified immunity hurdle to the extent that it was based on information disclosed under the business transaction subsection *and* the action targeted the reporting of that information. Accordingly, an action that was based on the disclosure of business transaction information but did not target the reporting of information, but rather targeted some other action or failure to act—such as the business' failure to properly verify the consumer's identity—should not be subject to qualified immunity. *See also* § 16.6.1a.1.2, *infra*.

10.3.3 Information Must Be Discovered Exclusively Through FCRA-Required Disclosure

Delete parenthetical at end of sentence containing note 177.

Add to text at end of subsection's first paragraph:

A new disclosure provision requires businesses that have done business with an identity thief to disclose transaction information to the thief's victim upon the victim's request.[177.1] Accordingly, the qualified immunity provision may protect the business from suit to the extent that the suit is in the nature of defamation, invasion of privacy, or negligence, but only to the extent that the action is "with respect to the reporting of information."[177.2]

The same reasoning applies to the new responsibilities of debt collectors who are notified that information related to the debt may be fraudulent or the result of identity theft.[177.3] Though the FCRA now requires such collectors to disclose to the consumer all information to which the consumer would be entitled if the consumer were actually the debtor, since an action based on such disclosures would not be with respect to the reporting of information, the qualified immunity provision should not be an obstacle. Similarly, certain creditors will now have to issue risk-based pricing notices when they offer credit on "material terms that are materially less favorable" than those offered to other consumers.[177.4] But actions based on those disclosures should not be subject to qualified immunity if they are not based on the reporting of information.

177.1 15 U.S.C. § 1681(g)(e), *added by* Pub. L. No. 108-159, § 151 (2003). The victim must first adequately establish his or her identity. *Id. See also* § 16.6.1a.1.2, *infra*.
177.2 15 U.S.C. § 1681h(e).
177.3 15 U.S.C. § 1681m(e), *added by* Pub. L. No. 108-159, § 155 (2003). *See also* § 16.6.1a, *infra*.
177.4 15 U.S.C. § 168am(h) *added by* Pub. L. No. 108-159, § 311 (2003).

Add to text after sentence containing note 179:

The FACTA added to FCRA § 615 (§ 1681m) a provision that will eventually require financial institutions or creditors to establish policies to implement the forthcoming red flag guidelines that appointed agencies will issue to prevent identity theft.[179.1] Since this new provision does not require any disclosures, it should not be subject to the qualified immunity provision.

179.1 15 U.S.C, § 1681m(e), *added by* Pub. L. No. 108-159, § 114 (2003). *See also* § 16.6.1a.3.2.1, *infra*.

Page 244

10.3.4 Immunity Applies Only to Certain Tort Actions

Add at end of subsection's first paragraph:

Harassment and invasion of privacy claims unrelated to reporting of information are not preempted.[195.1]

195.1 Stafford v. Cross Country Bank, 262 F. Supp. 2d 776 (W.D. Ky. 2003).

Add to text at end of subsection:

Effective in 1997, Congress adopted an additional immunity from state laws. The courts are having difficulty in reconciling the qualified immunity with the seemingly broader state law immunity.[199.1]

199.1 15 U.S.C. § 1681t, discussed in § 10.4.4, *infra*.

Page 245

10.3.6 No Immunity Where Malice or Willful Intent

Addition to note 203.

203 Borner v. Zale Lipshy Univ. Hosp., 2002 WL 449576 (N.D. Tex. 2002) (false report quickly corrected shows lack of malice).
Replace Blanche citation with: 74 S.W.3d 444 (Tex. App. 2002).

Add to text after sentence containing note 203:

Since negligence is inconsistent with willfulness, courts have dismissed claims of negligence and negligent infliction of emotional distress.[203.1]

203.1 Carlson v. Trans Union, L.L.C., 259 F. Supp. 2d 517 (N.D. Tex. 2003); Socorro v. IMI Data Search, Inc., 2003 WL 1964269 (N.D. Ill. Apr. 28, 2003); Carlson v. Trans Union, L.L.C., 261 F. Supp. 2d 663 (N.D. Tex. 2003).

§ 10.3.8

Fair Credit Reporting / 2004 Supplement

Addition to notes 205, 209.

205 Gordon v. Greenpoint Credit, 266 F. Supp. 2d 1007 (S.D. Iowa 2003); Yutesler v. Sears Roebuck & Co., 263 F. Supp. 2d 1209 (D. Minn. 2003). *But see* McCloud v. Homeside Lending, 2004 WL 585861 (N.D. Ala. Jan. 30, 2004) (citing state statutory definition of malice).

Page 246

209 *See also* McCloud v. Homeside Lending, 2004 WL 585861 at *6 (N.D. Ala. Jan. 30, 2004) (allegations that holder of mortgage acted willfully sufficiently alleged malice as defined by state statute, denying motion to dismiss defamation and invasion of privacy claims).

Page 247

10.3.8 Elements of Invasion of Privacy Claim

Addition to note 223.

223 Agosta v. Inovision, Inc., 2003 WL 22999213 (E.D. Pa. Dec. 16, 2003) (invasion of privacy claims preempted); Davenport v. Farmers Ins. Group, 2003 WL 21975843 (D. Minn. Aug. 12, 2003) (invasion of privacy not preempted, but prima facie case not established; when FCRA authorizes disclosure of credit reports, disclosure cannot be "highly offensive"). *See* § 16.3, *infra*.

Replace note 225 with:

225 See Chapter 6, *supra*, for a discussion of privacy laws and concerns.

10.4 State Statutory Claims

Page 248

10.4.2 State Deceptive Practices Statutes

Addition to notes 234, 238, 240.

234 *Replace Source One citation with*: 763 N.E.2d 42 (Mass. 2002).

Page 249

238 Beattie v. Nations Credit Fin. Servs. Corp., 69 Fed. Appx. 585 (4th Cir. 2003) (unpublished) (not immoral, unethical, or oppressive to falsely report that mortgage is in foreclosure).

240 Agosta v. Inovision, Inc., 2003 WL 22999213 (E.D. Pa. Dec. 16, 2003) (UDAP claim for intentional failure to reinvestigate is preempted).

Add new subsection after § 10.4.2.

10.4.2a State Identity Theft Laws

While Congress added many new tools to fight and remediate identity theft in the FACTA, it simultaneously took away the ability of states to regulate identity theft and its consequences. Many states have enacted criminal and civil laws that target identity theft.[240.1] The FACTA specifically preempts states from imposing any requirement or prohibition with respect to the "conduct required" by many of the following new provisions of the FCRA aimed at preventing and remediating identity theft:

- The new obligation of merchants to truncate credit and debit card numbers on electronic receipts[240.2]
- The new obligations of agencies to include fraud alters, extended fraud alerts, and active military duty alerts in consumer files[240.3]
- The new obligations of users of reports that include a fraud alert, extended fraud alert or active military duty alert to try to verify the identity of an applicant for credit[240.4]
- The new obligation of agencies to provide fraud victims with a free copy of the consumer's report[240.5]
- The new obligations of agencies to block information identified by a consumer as being fraudulent and to notify the furnisher of such information that the agency has blocked the information[240.6]
- The agency's responsibility, upon the consumer's request, to truncate the first five digits of the consumer's social security number when making a disclosure pursuant to the consumer's request[240.7]
- The obligation of identified federal agencies, including the Federal Trade Commission, to issue red flag guidelines for financial institutions and creditors to use to identify and prevent identity theft[240.8]
- The new requirement prohibiting debt collectors and creditors from transferring or selling an identity theft debt that an agency has blocked from the victim's report[240.9]
- The new obligation of a debt collector that has been notified that a debt may be fraudulent

Litigating Credit Report Disputes / 2004 Supplement § 10.4.4

or the result of identity theft to notify the creditor on whose behalf the collector is acting and to provide the victim to whom the debt relates the information to which the victim would be entitled were the victim in fact the debtor and wished to dispute the debt[240.10]
- The new obligations of nationwide consumer reporting agencies to coordinate identity theft complaints and fraud alerts with each other[240.11]
- The new provision prohibiting furnishers from refurnishing information that a consumer has notified the furnisher resulted from identity theft[240.12]

240.1 See § 16.6.3, App. B.3, *infra*.
240.2 15 U.S.C. § 1681t(b)(5)(A) (*citing* § 1681c(g)). See also § 16.6.1a, *infra*.
240.3 15 U.S.C. § 1681t(b)(5)(B) (*citing* § 1681c-1). See also § 16.6.1a, *infra*.
240.4 15 U.S.C. § 1681t(b)(5)(B) (*citing* § 1681c-1). See also § 16.6.1a, *infra*.
240.5 15 U.S.C. § 1681t(b)(5)(B) (*citing* § 1681c-1). See also § 16.6.1a, *infra*.
240.6 15 U.S.C. § 1681t(b)(5)(C) (*citing* § 1681c-2). See also § 16.6.1a, *infra*.
240.7 15 U.S.C. § 1681t(b)(5)(D) (*citing* § 1681g(a)(1)(A)). See also § 16.6.1a, *infra*.
240.8 15 U.S.C. § 1681t(b)(5)(F) (*citing* § 1681m(e)). See also § 16.6.1a *infra*.
240.9 15 U.S.C. § 1681t(b)(5)(F) (*citing* § 1681m(f)). See also § 16.6.1a, *infra*.
240.10 15 U.S.C. § 1681t(b)(5)(F) (*citing* § 1681m(g)). See also § 16.6.1a, *infra*. Note that, while an action based in state law may now be preempted, the provision does not prevent a consumer from seeking to enforce his or her rights under the Fair Debt Collection Practices Act. *See* National Consumer Law Center, *Fair Debt Collection* (4th ed. 2000 and Supp.).
240.11 15 U.S.C. § 1681t(b)(5)(G) (*citing* § 1681s(f)). See § 16.6.1a, *infra*.
240.12 15 U.S.C. § 1681t(b)(5)(I) (*citing* § 1681s–2(a)(6)). See also § 16.6.1a, *infra*.

10.4.3 General FCRA Preemption Standard

Replace extract containing note 241 with:

Except as provided in subsections (b) and (c), this title does not annul, alter, affect, or exempt any person subject to the provisions of this title from complying with the laws of any State with respect to the collection, distribution, or use of any information on consumers or for the prevention or mitigation of identity theft, except to the extent that those laws are inconsistent with any provision of this title, and then only to the extent of the inconsistency.[241]

241 15 U.S.C. § 1681t(a), renumbered by Pub. L. No. 108-159, § 711(1) (2003).

Add to text after sentence containing note 242:

By specifically adding the words "or for the prevention or mitigation of identity theft," Congress evinced a strong presumption in favor of the rights of states to protect their citizens from this crime.

Page 250

Replace "to disclosure" in sentence containing note 252 with:

to disclose

Page 251

10.4.4 Specific FCRA Preemptions of State Law

Add to text at end of subsection's first paragraph:

The FACTA preempts states from governing much of the new territory added to the FCRA. Prior to the FACTA, the FCRA preempted any "requirement or prohibition" of a state with respect to the "subject matter" of identified FCRA provisions.[260.1] The FACTA added additional preemptions, the largest group of which forbids states from regulating the "conduct required by" certain identified FCRA provisions.

Nonetheless, these preemptions should have a much narrower effect than the preexisting (and supplemented) "subject matter" preemption provision since the preemption should not apply to state laws regulating the subject matter of the provision beyond the specific conduct that the provision demands.[260.2] In addition, the Act preempts state laws with respect to the required disclosures of the FCRA rights of identity theft victims,[260.3] to the new provision allowing consumers to opt out of some use by affiliates of consumer information for solicitation purposes,[260.4] and to the new responsibility of creditors to provide risk-based pricing notices to credit applicants when they offer credit on "material terms that are materially less favorable" than those offered to other consumers.[260.5]

§ 10.4.4   Fair Credit Reporting / 2004 Supplement

260.1   15 U.S.C. § 1681t(b).
260.2   15 U.S.C. § 1681t(b)(5), *added by* Pub. L. No. 108-159, § 711(2) (2003).
260.3   15 U.S.C. § 1682t(b)(1)(G), *added by* Pub. L. No. 108-159, § 151(2) (2003).
260.4   15 U.S.C. § 1682t(b)(1)(H), *added by* Pub. L. No. 108-159, § (2003).
260.5   15 U.S.C. § 1682t(b)(1)(H), *added by* Pub. L. No. 108-159, § 214(d)(2)(B) (2003).

Addition to note 262.

262   Kennedy v. Chase Manhattan Bank, 2003 WL 21181427 (E.D. La. May 19, 2003).

Replace second sentence of sixth bulleted paragraph with:

However, certain laws in Massachusetts and California in effect September 30, 1996, are not preempted.[269] For instance, the California law prohibiting any report if the furnisher "knows or should know" is inaccurate (parallel to section 1681s-2(a)) is not preempted, but the California law providing a private right of action to enforce the prohibition is preempted.[269.1]

269   *Retain as in main edition.*
269.1   Lin v. Universal Card Services Corp., 238 F. Supp. 2d 1147 (N.D. Cal. 2002). *See also* Riley v. General Motors Acceptance Corp., 226 F. Supp. 2d 1316 (S.D. Ala. 2002) (cannot assert state law claims for violation of § 1681s-2(a)).

Page 252

Addition to note 271.

271   Bank of Am., N.A. v. City of Daly City, Cal., 279 F. Supp. 2d 1118 (N.D. Cal. 2003) (preempting information-sharing ordinance).

Add to text after sentence containing note 272:

Congress augmented this list of subject matter preemptions in the FACTA, adding state laws with respect to the list of preempted provisions:

- The new obligation of businesses that have transacted with an identity thief to provide the victim, upon the victim's request, with transaction information.[272.1]
- The new right to opt-out of certain affiliate marketing solicitations.[272.2]
- The new requirement of users to disclose credit applicants when they offer credit on "material terms that are materially less favorable" than those offered to other consumers.[272.3]

272.1   15 U.S.C. § 1681g(e), *added by* Pub. L. No. 108-159, § 151 (2003). *See also* § 16.6.1a.1.2, *infra*.
272.2   15 U.S.C. § 1681t(b)(3) (*citing* § 1681g(c)). *See also* § 16.6.1a, *supra*.
272.3   15 U.S.C. § 1682t(b)(1)(H), *added by* Pub. L. No. 108-159, § 214(d)(2)(B) (2003). *See also* § 16.6.1a, *supra*.

Addition to note 273.

273   Sampson v. W. Sierra Acceptance Corp., 2003 WL 21785612 (N.D. Ill. Aug. 1, 2003).

Replace paragraph containing note 274:

Prior to the 2003 revisions, the preemption provisions were due to expire on January 1, 2004.[274] However, Congress removed that sunset clause with the FACTA, not only perpetuating the provisions but even expanding them.

274   15 U.S.C. § 1681t(d) (2000).

Addition to note 277.

277   Gordon v. Greenpoint Credit, 266 F. Supp. 2d 1007 (S.D. Iowa 2003) (more specific preemption clause of § 1681h(e) controls); Yutesler v. Sears Roebuck & Co., 263 F. Supp. 2d 1209 (D. Minn. 2003) (same); Jeffery v. Trans Union, L.L.C., 273 F. Supp. 2d 725 (E.D. Va. 2003) (preempts state statutes only).

Add to text after sentence containing note 277:

However, the courts are having difficulty in reconciling the narrow qualified immunity of § 1681h(e) with the broader state law preemption provisions of § 1681t. The weight of authority is that state common law as well as state statutory claims are preempted.[277.1] Some courts are using a time line to give effect to both sections. Thus, qualified immunity applies only before the consumer gives notice of the dispute to the credit bureaus, while preemption applies thereafter.[277.2] Other courts view the state law immunity as applying only to state statutory claims.[277.3] Still another approach is to limit preemption to claims relating to accuracy of furnisher reports, since the section refers to that "subject matter."[277.4]

277.1   Riley v. Gen. Motors Acceptance Corp., 226 F. Supp. 2d 1316 (S.D. Ala. 2002); Vazquez-Garcia v. Trans Union de Puerto Rico, 222 F. Supp. 2d 150 (D. P.R. 2002); Hasvold v. First USA Bank, N.A., 194 F. Supp. 2d 1228 (D. Wyo. 2002); Aklagi v. Nationscredit Fin., 196 F. Supp. 2d 1186 (D. Kan. 2002). *Contra* Stafford v. Cross Country Bank, 262 F. Supp. 2d 776 (W.D. Ky. 2003).

Litigating Credit Report Disputes / 2004 Supplement § 10.4.4

277.2 Stafford v. Cross Country Bank, 262 F. Supp. 2d 776 (W. D. Ky. 2003); Vazquez-Garcia v. Trans Union de Puerto Rico, 222 F. Supp. 2d 150 (D. P.R. 2002); Aklagi v. Nationscredit Fin., 196 F. Supp. 2d 1186 (D. Kan. 2002).

277.3 Carlson v. Trans Union, L.L.C., 259 F. Supp. 2d 517 (N.D. Tex. 2003).

277.4 Stafford v. Cross Country Bank, 262 F. Supp. 2d 776 (W.D. Ky. 2003) (state law immunity section preempts defamation, slander, and invasion of privacy claims related to reporting of information even if done with malice).

Addition to note 279.

279 *Replace Barron citation with*: 82 F. Supp. 2d 1288 (M.D. Ala. 2000).

Page 253

Add to text after sentence containing note 281:

The FACTA added a new set of preemptions, these much narrower than those discussed above, because they preempt state laws *only* to the extent that the laws relate to the "conduct required by" the specified FCRA provisions and not to any of the provisions' subject matter.[281.1] The provisions preempted are all new additions to the Act and include the following conduct:[281.2]

- The new obligation of merchants to truncate credit and debit card numbers on electronic receipts[281.3]
- The new obligations of agencies to include fraud alerts, extended fraud alerts, and active military duty alerts in consumer files[281.4]
- The new obligations of users of reports that include a fraud alert, extended fraud alert or active military duty alert to try to verify the identity of an applicant for credit[281.5]
- The new obligation of agencies to provide fraud victims with a free copy of the consumer's report[281.6]
- The new obligations of agencies to block information identified by a consumer as being fraudulent and to notify the furnisher of such information that the agency has blocked the information[281.7]
- The agency's responsibility, upon the consumer's request, to truncate the first five digits of the consumer's social security number when making a disclosure pursuant to the consumer's request[281.8]
- The new provision requiring nationwide consumer reporting agencies to provide free annual consumer reports to consumers[281.9]
- The obligation of identified federal agencies, including the Federal Trade Commission, to issue red flag guidelines for financial institutions and creditors to use to identify and prevent identity theft[281.10]
- The new requirement prohibiting debt collectors and creditors from transferring or selling an identity theft debt that an agency has blocked from the victim's report[281.11]
- The new obligation of a debt collector that has been notified that a debt may be fraudulent or the result of identity theft to notify the creditor on whose behalf the collector is acting and to provide the victim to whom the debt relates the information to which the victim would be entitled were the victim in fact the debtor and wished to dispute the debt[281.12]
- The new obligations of nationwide consumer reporting agencies to coordinate identity theft complaints and fraud alerts with each other[281.13]
- The new provision prohibiting furnishers from refurnishing information that a consumer has notified the furnisher resulted from identity theft[281.14]

In addition to the subject matter preemptions and the conduct-required preemptions, the FACTA added two more types of state laws to the list of preemptions, those with respect to the disclosures required to be made under the following new provisions:

- The newly required summary of rights of consumers to obtain and dispute information in credit reports and to obtain credit scores[281.15]
- The requirement of an agency that has been contacted by a consumer who believes that the consumer is a victim of fraud or identity theft to disclose to the consumer the Federal

§ 10.5   *Fair Credit Reporting / 2004 Supplement*

- Trade Commission's summary of rights and to provide the consumer with information on how to contact the commission to obtain more detailed information[281.16]
- The new responsibility of businesses that have transacted with an identity thief to provide the victim, upon the victim's request, with transaction information (to the extent such a provision is a "disclosure")[281.17]
- The new obligation of agencies to disclose credit scores and the key factors of such scores to a consumer[281.18]
- The new obligation of mortgage lenders to disclose credit scores to a loan applicant[281.19]

However, Congress designated some existing state laws as surviving the preemption, including identified existing laws of California[281.20] and Colorado.[281.21] Finally, the FCRA now preempts any state law with respect to the frequency of free disclosures of credit reports, allowed annually under the revised § 612(a), but with exemptions for identified existing laws of Colorado[281.22] and Georgia.[281.23]

281.1   FCRA § 625(b)(5), *added by* Pub. L. No. 108-159, § 711(2) (2003).
281.2   See generally, § 16.6.1a, *infra*.
281.3   FCRA § 625(b)(5)(A), 15 U.S.C. § 1681t(b)(5)(A) (*citing* § 1681c(g)).
281.4   FCRA § 625(b)(5)(B), 15 U.S.C. § 1681t(b)(5)(B) (*citing* § 1681c-1).
281.5   FCRA § 625(b)(5)(B), 15 U.S.C. § 1681t(b)(5)(B) (*citing* § 1681c-1).
281.6   FCRA § 625(b)(5)(B), 15 U.S.C. § 1681t(b)(5)(B) (*citing* § 1681c-1).
281.7   FCRA § 625(b)(5)(C), 15 U.S.C. § 1681t(b)(5)(C) (*citing* § 1681c-2).
281.8   FCRA § 625(b)(5)(D), 15 U.S.C. § 1681t(b)(5)(D) (*citing* §1681g(a)(1)(A)).
281.9   FCRA § 625(b)(5)(E), 15 U.S.C. § 1681t(b)(5)(E) (*citing* §1681j(a)).
281.10 FCRA § 625(b)(5)(F), 15 U.S.C. § 1681t(b)(5)(F) (*citing* § 1681m(e)).
281.11 FCRA § 625(b)(5)(F), 15 U.S.C. § 1681t(b)(5)(F) (*citing* § 1681m(f)).
281.12 15 U.S.C. § 1681t(b)(5)(F), 15 U.S.C. § 1681t(b)(5)(F) (*citing* § 1681m(g)). Note that, while an action based in state law may now be preempted, the provision does not prevent a consumer from seeking to enforce his or her rights under the Fair Debt Collection Practices Act. *See* National Consumer Law Center, *Fair Debt Collection* (4th ed. 2000 and Supp.).
281.13 15 U.S.C. § 1681t (b)(5)(G), 15 U.S.C. § 1681t(b)(5)(G) (*citing* § 621(f)).
281.14 15 U.S.C. § 1681t (b)(5)(I), 15 U.S.C. § 1681t(b)(5)(I) (*citing* § 23(a)(6)).
281.15 15 U.S.C. § 1681t (b)(3), 15 U.S.C. § 1681t(b)(3) (*citing* § 609(c)).
281.16 15 U.S.C. § 1681t (b)(3), 15 U.S.C. § 1681t(b)(3) (*citing* § 609(d)).
281.17 15 U.S.C. § 1681t (b)(3), 15 U.S.C. § 1681t(b)(3) (*citing* § 609(e)).
281.18 15 U.S.C. § 1681t (b)(3), 15 U.S.C. § 1681t(b)(3) (*citing* § 609(f)).
281.19 15 U.S.C. § 1681t (b)(3), 15 U.S.C. § 1681t(b)(3) (*citing* § 609(g)).
281.20 Cal. Civ. Code §§ 1785.10, 1785.15-.15.2, 1785.16, and 1785.20.3.
281.21 Colo. Rev. Stat. §§ 5-3-106(2) and 12-14.3-104.3. Note that the text of the FACTA cites to Colo. Rev. Stat. § 212-14.3-104.3, but this is apparently a typographical error as such a section does not exist, while § 12-14.3-104.3 requires a consumer reporting agency to disclose a consumer's credit score to the consumer in connection with an application for an extension of credit for a consumer purpose that is to be secured by a dwelling.
281.22 Colo. Rev. Stat. § 12-14.3-105(1)(d).
281.23 Ga. Code Ann. § 10-1-(b)(293)(C). Note that the text of the FACTA cites to Ga. Code Ann. § 10-1-393(29)(C), but this is apparently a typographical error as such a section does not exist, while § 10-1-(b)(293)(C) is a provision of Georgia's deceptive trade practices act that requires agencies to issue two free reports a year.

10.5 Other Statutory Claims

Replace sentence containing notes 289 and 290 with:

While a few consumers have alleged RICO claims in addition to FCRA violations,[289] there are no reported cases where a RICO claim has succeeded. It may also be difficult to allege a requisite predicate act under RICO.[290]

289   *See, e.g.*, Hovater v. Equifax, Inc., 823 F.2d 413 (11th Cir. 1987) (affirming summary judgment for defendant on RICO claims, and reversing judgment for plaintiff on RICO claims); Management Info. Techs. v. Alyeska Pipeline Co., 151 F.R.D. 478 (D.D.C. 1993) (does not address substance of claims).
290   *See, e.g.*, Wiggins v. Equifax Servs., 848 F. Supp. 213 (D.D.C. 1993).

10.7 Selecting the Parties

10.7.1 Plaintiffs

Page 254

Addition to note 295.

295   Haque v. CompUSA, Inc., 2003 WL 117986 (D. Mass. 2003); Soghomonian v. U.S., 278 F. Supp. 2d 1151 (E.D. Cal. 2003).

10.7.2 Class Actions

Add to text after sentence containing note 302:

In Alabama, a district court certified a class of homeowners who did not receive adverse action notices when their insurance premiums were raised by fifty percent or more based on information in credit report.[302.1] The insured class representative alleged that the insurer negligently and/or willfully failed to comply with the FCRA's adverse action notice requirements.[302.2] Class certification was sought pursuant to Federal Rule of Civil Procedure 23(b)(3).[302.3] The insurance company claimed that the insured representative did not have standing because he actually received notice, he suspected that his credit report had been accessed and that he was not caused actual damage since he bought replacement coverage at a cheaper premium. However the court found that the insurer misunderstood the insured's claim, which was not that the notice was not sent, but that it had been sent too late to comply with the FCRA. If the insurance company's notice failed to comply with the Act's requirements, and that the failure was negligent or willful the court concluded that the insured would be entitled to an award of damages and thus he had standing.

The court concluded that the class met the numerosity requirement. The court relied on discovery from the insurance company that revealed the company "took adverse action against 5,000 or more" of its customers in Alabama based in whole or in part on consumer reports. Commonality requirements were also met based on the fact that all class members were mailed letters similar to the letter received by the class representative. Thus there was a question of law common to all class members. The court also found that the insured met the typicality requirement, even though the insurance company argued that the insured's claims were not typical because he received notice, suspected his credit had been accessed and changed carriers at a premium savings, but this argument was rejected by the court.[302.4]

No conflicts of interest were found by the court to make the insured an inadequate class representative and the court concluded that common questions of law and fact predominated therefore the class was conditionally certified.[302.5]

302.1   Braxton v. Farmer's Insurance Group, 209 F.R.D. 654 (N.D. Ala. 2002).
302.2   15 U.S.C. § 1681m(a).
302.3   *See* National Consumer Law Center, Consumer Class Actions (5th ed. and 2003 Supp.).
302.4   *Id.* at 659.
302.5   *Id.*

Page 255

Addition to note 307.

307   *Replace NCLC Class Actions citation with*: National Consumer Law Center, Consumer Class Actions: A Practical Litigation Guide (5th ed. 2002 and Supp.).

Add to text at end of subsection:

Class actions for monetary relief which would have the potential for catastrophic damages may be denied.[308.1]

308.1   *In re* Trans Union Corp. Privacy Litigation, 211 F.R.D. 328 (N.D. 2002).

10.7.3 Defendants

Addition to note 317.

317   *But see* Harris v. Trans Union, L.L.C., 197 F. Supp. 2d 200 (E.D. Pa. 2002) (furnisher's failure to mark CDV forms confirming plaintiff's address in forum state and its failure to attempt to collect erroneous debt lead court to conclude that furnisher did not expressly aim its tortious conduct activity in the forum state.).

10.9 Selecting the Court

Page 258 — ### 10.9.3 Personal Jurisdiction

Addition to notes 346, 347.

346 Add to end of Obabueki citation: *aff'd on other grounds*, 319 F.3d 87 (2d Cir. 2003).

347 Screen v. Equifax Info. Sys., L.L.C., __ F. Supp. 2d __, 2004 WL 78207 (D. Md. Jan. 15, 2004) (out-of-state creditor's response to verification requests was not affirmative conduct aimed at forum); Cisneros v. Trans Union, L.L.C., 293 F. Supp. 2d 1156 (D. Haw. 2003) (no personal jurisdiction in state of temporary residence; furnisher did not know of the location, purposefully avail itself of that forum, or aim its conduct there).

Add to end of subsection:

Generally, jurisdicton is proper in the state where the subject of the consumer report resides.[348]

348 Bertolet v. Bray, 277 F. Supp. 2d 835 (S.D. Ohio 2003) (consumer is injured in state of residence by impermissible access to consumer's credit report).

Page 259 — ### 10.9.5 Removal

Addition to note 356.

356 Wells v. Shelter General Ins. Co., 217 F. Supp. 2d 744 (S.D. Miss. 2002).

10.10 Statute of Limitations

Replace § 10.10.1 with: ### 10.10.1 FCRA Limitations Period

The FACTA amended the FCRA's statute of limitations to provide that the two-year limitations period dates from the consumer's discovery of the violation, not the date of the violation itself. This effectively overrules *Andrews v. TRW*,[359] which held that the discovery rule did not apply to the FCRA's limitations period. However, the consumer must bring the action within five years of the date of the violation, regardless of the discovery rule.[360] The effective date for this change to the statute of limitation is March 31, 2004.[361]

359 15 U.S.C. § 1681x, *added by* Pub. L. No. 108-159, § 211 (2003).
360 15 U.S.C. § 1681p, *as amended by* Pub. L. No. 108-159, § 156 (2003).
361 69 Fed. Reg. 6530 (Feb. 11, 2004).
362 *Reserved.*
363 *Reserved.*
364 *Reserved.*
365 *Reserved.*
366 *Reserved.*
367 *Reserved.*
368 *Reserved.*
369 *Reserved.*
370 *Reserved.*
371 *Reserved.*
372 *Reserved.*
373 *Reserved.*
374 *Reserved.*
375 *Reserved.*
376 *Reserved.*
377 *Reserved.*
378 *Reserved.*
379 *Reserved.*

Litigating Credit Report Disputes / 2004 Supplement § 10.11.3.5

10.11 Discovery and Litigation Strategies

10.11.3 Formal Discovery

Page 263

10.11.3.1 General

Addition to note 397.

397 *Replace Young citation with*: 294 F.3d 631 (5th Cir. 2002).

Add to text after last sentence in subsection's fifth paragraph:

Consumers are entitled to all information in their file except credit scores, not only their credit reports.[397.1]

397.1 15 U.S.C. § 1681g(a)(1).

Add to text after sentence containing note 401:

Credit reporting agencies and other defendants may be unwilling to produce information on net worth without a claim for punitive damages. Consumers must thus include an allegation in their complaint that the defendant acted willfully, in violation of section 1681n, in order to establish a claim for punitive damages, justifying the request for information on net worth.

Page 264

Add to text at end of subsection:

Advocates may also have to seek information from third parties who have been "outsourced" to conduct the reinvestigation of disputed information. This practice of outsourcing investigations appears to be an increasing practice by some reporting agencies.

10.11.3.2 Confidentiality Agreements and Protective Orders

Addition to notes 404, 405.

404 *Add to end of Phillips citation: as amended,* 307 F.3d 1206 (9th Cir. 2002).
405 Zahran v. Trans Union Corp., 2002 WL 31010822 (N.D. Ill. 2002) (Trans Union's dispute manuals and subscriber agreements are not confidential).

Add to text at end of subsection:

Some credit reporting agencies have insisted on protective orders to protect the privacy of third-party consumers who may have been linked with the consumer litigant in a credit report. This strategy by credit reporting agencies should not hinder the rights of the litigant to obtain information necessary for them to pursue their FCRA and related claims.

10.11.3.3 Consumer Reports and Evidentiary Issues

Add to text after second sentence of subsection's first paragraph:

For example, credit reporting agencies sometimes assert that tradelines within credit reports are out-of-court statements of third party non-defendants and thus non-admissible hearsay.

Add to text after first sentence of subsection's second paragraph:

Authentication can also be accomplished through requests for admissions. The business records exception also allows hearsay to be admitted unless the source of information or the method or circumstances of preparation indicate lack of trustworthiness.[409.1] This presumption of trustworthiness for business records is especially applicable to credit reports because Congress has set up an elaborate statutory framework to ensure that credit reports are accurate and complete.[409.2] Thus there is a compelling argument that credit reports are reliable and admissible under the business records exception to the hearsay rule.

409.1 Fed. R. Evid. 803(6).
409.2 5 U.S.C. § 1681, *et. seq.*

Page 266

10.11.3.5 Insurance Coverage for FCRA Liability

Replace subsection's last paragraph with:

Sample discovery requests provided by attorneys based on their own experience are available in NCLC's *Consumer Law Pleadings* (2003 Cumulative CD-Rom with Index Guide).

§ 10.11.4   *Fair Credit Reporting / 2004 Supplement*

10.11.4 Record Retention

Add to text after subsection's first sentence:

Credit reporting agencies also tend not to retain important documents. For example, practitioners report that the three national reporting agencies do not retain consumer dispute verification forms or records of the automated dispute verification forms.

Replace note 422 with:

422   See § 6.4.5, *supra*; and especially National Consumer Law Center, Credit Discrimination § 4.4.1.3 (3d ed. 2002 and Supp.).

10.12 Right to Jury Trial; Jury Instructions

Add to text after sentence containing note 424:

Chapter 11, *infra*, includes a list of jury awards in FCRA cases.[424.1]

424.1   See § 11.4.3, *infra*.

Addition to note 431.

431   See § 11.4.3, *infra*. In federal court, all damage issues, including punitive damages, are to be decided by the jury. Feltner v. Columbia Pictures Television, Inc., 523 U.S. 340, 348, 118 S. Ct. 1279 (1998); Kobs v. Arrow Serv. Bureau, Inc., 134 F.3d 893 (7th Cir. 1998); McGuire v. Russell Miller, Inc., 1 F.3d 1306 (2d Cir. 1993); Kampa v. White Consol. Inc., 115 F.3d 585, 586 (8th Cir. 1997).

Page 267

10.13 Defenses and Counterclaims

Addition to notes 437–440.

437   *Replace Thomas citation with*: 197 F. Supp. 2d 1233 (D. Or. 2002).
438   *Replace Obabueki citation with*: 137 F. Supp. 2d 320 (S.D.N.Y. 2001), *aff'd*, 319 F.3d 87 (2d Cir. 2003).
439   *Replace Silver LEXIS citation with*: 251 F.3d 814 (9th Cir. 2001).
440   *Replace Schoendorf LEXIS citation with*: 97 Cal App. 4th 227, 118 Cal. Rptr. 2d 313 (2002).

Add to text after sentence containing note 440:

There is no litigation privilege or immunity for improperly using a report in litigation.[440.1] However, a reporting agency can properly assert a "justification" defense, ordinarily available only for defamation and tortious interference claims, when it seeks to prevent impermissible access by a credit clinic.[440.2]

440.1   Chester v. Purvis, 260 F. Supp. 2d 711 (S.D. Ind. 2003).
440.2   Money Masters, Inc. v. TRW, Inc., 2003 WL 152770 (Tex. App. Jan. 23, 2003).

Delete first sentence in subsection's third paragraph.

441   Reserved.

Addition to note 442.

442   Fields v. Experian Info. Solutions, Inc., 2003 WL 1960010 (N.D. Miss. Apr. 16, 2003) (denying motion to add impostor).

10.14 Enforceability of Arbitration Agreements

Addition to note 444.

444   Green v. Chase Manhattan Automotive Fin. Corp., 2003 WL 22872102 (E.D. La. Dec. 3, 2003); Walton v. Experian, 2003 WL 22110788 (N.D. Ill. Sept. 9, 2003) (First North American National Bank arbitration clause enforced).

Chapter 11 Private Remedies

Page 269

11.1 Introduction

Replace "any FCRA requirement" in first sentence of section's second paragraph with:

most FCRA requirements

Addition to note 4.

 4 *Replace Whiteside citation with*: 2002 WL 1809084 (E.D. La. Aug. 6, 2002).

Add to text after sentence containing note 4:

The FACTA of 2003 does not amend the relevant FCRA provisions that provide for relief when there are negligent or willful FCRA violations. However, the FACTA includes several limitations on liability that preclude private rights of action for certain violations. These are discussed in § 11.1a, *infra*.

Addition to note 7.

 7 *Replace Hawthorne citation with*: 216 F. Supp. 2d 45 (E.D.N.Y. 2002), *vacated on other grounds*, 219 F.R.D. 47 (E.D.N.Y. 2003).

Add to text after sentence containing note 10:

The FACTA of 2003 amends the FCRA by adding several new obligations and standards for credit reporting agencies and users and furnishers of credit information. The FACTA also provides consumers with additional rights, especially with respect to identity theft and restoration of credit information. Unfortunately, the FACTA limits the ability of consumers to privately enforce some of these new rights.[10.1]

 10.1 See § 11.1a, *infra*.

Page 270

Add new section after § 11.1.

11.1a FACTA Limitations on Private Enforcement

11.1a.1 FACTA Expands FCRA's Qualified Immunity Provision

 The FCRA's provides a qualified immunity to any agency, user or furnisher against any state law claim "in the nature of defamation, invasion of privacy, or negligence" based in whole or in part on a consumer report. (This immunity is qualified because these parties are still liable under state law if the consumer shows that the information was furnished with "malice or willful intent to injure.") Under the pre-existing Act, this qualified immunity only applied to claims based on one of the following four actions:

- reporting agency disclosures to consumers, made pursuant to § 1681g ;
- the conditions and forms of disclosures to consumers, pursuant to § 1681h;
- user disclosures to consumers, made pursuant to § 1681m ; or
- disclosures by a user of a consumer report to or for a consumer against whom the user has taken adverse action, when the disclosure is based on the report.[13.1]

 The FACTA adds eight actions, based on new FACTA requirements, that also come under this qualified immunity:

- Requirements that agencies to withhold the last five digits of a consumer's SSN from the disclosure of the consumer's file if the consumer so requests[13.2]
- Requirements that agencies provide certain information with their disclosure of a file to a consumer, including the FTC's summary of consumers' rights to obtain and dispute information in consumer reports and to obtain and dispute credit scores[13.3]
- Requirements for agencies to provide consumers who believe they are or may be the victim of identity theft with an FTC-issued summary of their right to use the FCRA's new procedures for remedying the fraud[13.4]
- Rights for identity theft victims to obtain business transaction information from businesses that have done business with the thief[13.5]
- Requirements for agencies to disclose credit scores and certain related information[13.6]
- Requirements for mortgage lenders to disclose credit scores to loan applicants and to provide them with a designated notice[13.7]
- Requirements that users making credit or insurance solicitations present the required prescreening notice in a format, size, type, and manner to be established by the FTC[13.8]
- Requirements for creditors to issue risk-based pricing notices[13.9]

11.1a.2 No Private Enforcement of Certain New Furnisher Obligations

The following new furnisher obligations,[13.10] are protected from private enforcement[13.11]:

- The requirement that furnishers have procedures for responding to identity theft notifications from agencies and that prohibits furnishers from re-submitting fraudulent information[13.12]
- The requirement that financial institutions notify customers that they are furnishing negative information to agencies about that customer[13.13]
- The requirement that consumers be allowed to dispute information directly with a furnisher and that furnishers must reinvestigate a dispute when it meets certain conditions, complete the investigation within the designated time, and notify each agency to whom the furnisher furnished the information if the furnisher finds that it was inaccurate[13.14]
- The requirement that persons in the business of providing medical services, products, or devices and who furnish information to agencies notify the agencies of their status as medical information furnishers[13.15]

11.1a.3 No Private Enforcement for Certain Other New FACTA Requirements

The FACTA also adds a number of other limitations on private enforcements as to new responsibilities created by the Act. Identity theft victims may not enforce their new rights to business transaction information from businesses that have done business with the thief.[13.16] Consumers may not enforce the new obligations of users to provide risk-based pricing notices.[13.17] Consumers also may not enforce the obligation of the federal banking agencies, the National Credit Union Administration, and the FTC to establish accuracy and integrity guidelines for furnishers and to prescribe regulations requiring furnishers to establish reasonable policies and procedures for implementing those guidelines.[13.18] Finally, consumers may not enforce the obligation of agencies to issue red flag guidelines and regulations.[13.19] Nonetheless, as long as none of these guidelines and regulations apply to other furnisher requirements in which private claims may be brought, consumers should be able to pursue private actions in accordance with the FCRA's willful and negligent liability provisions.[13.20]

13.1   15 U.S.C. § 1681g(e).
13.2   15 U.S.C. § 1681g(a)(1)(A). This provision will become effective on December 1, 2004. 16 C.F.R. § 602.1(c)(3)(i), *added by* 69 Fed. Reg. 6526–31 (Feb. 5, 2004).

Private Remedies / 2004 Supplement § 11.2.3.1

13.3 15 U.S.C. § 1681g(c). This provision will become effective on December 1, 2004. 16 C.F.R. § 602.1(c)(3)(ix), *added by* 69 Fed. Reg. 6526–31 (Feb. 5, 2004).
13.4 15 U.S.C. § 1681g(d).
13.5 15 U.S.C. § 1681g(e).
13.6 15 U.S.C. § 1681g(f). This provision will become effective on December 1, 2004. 16 C.F.R. § 602.1(c)(3)(x), *added by* 69 Fed. Reg. 6526–31 (Feb. 5, 2004).
13.7 15 U.S.C. § 1681g(g).
13.8 15 U.S.C. § 1681m(d)2).
13.9 15 U.S.C. § 1681m(h). This provision will become effective on December 1, 2004. 16 C.F.R. § 602.1(c)(3)(xiii), *added by* 69 Fed. Reg. 6526–31 (Feb. 5, 2004).
13.10 Added to § 1681s–2(a), by Pub. L. No. 108-159, §§ 154, 217, 312, and 412 (2003).
13.11 Pursuant to § 1681s–2(c).
13.12 § 1681s–2(a)(6). This provision will become effective on December 1, 2004. 16 C.F.R. § 602.1(c)(3)(vii), *added by* 69 Fed. Reg. 6526–31 (Feb. 5, 2004).
13.13 15 U.S.C. § 1681s–2(a)(7). This provision will become effective on December 1, 2004. 16 C.F.R. § 602.1(c)(3)(xii), *added by* 69 Fed. Reg. 6526–31 (Feb. 5, 2004).
13.14 § 1681s–2(a)(8). This provision will become effective on December 1, 2004. 16 C.F.R. § 602.1(c)(3)(xiv), *added by* 69 Fed. Reg. 6526–31 (Feb. 5, 2004).
13.15 15 U.S.C. § 1681s–2(a)(9). This provision does not become effective until March 4, 2005. Pub. L. No. 108-159, § 412 (2003).
13.16 § 1681g(e)(6), *added by* Pub. L. No. 108-159, § 151 (2003).
13.17 § 1681m(h)(8), *added by* Pub. L. No. 108-159, § 311 (2003). An argument exists that the new limitation of liability provision in § 1681m(h) limits liability for *any* violation of § 1681m since the provision refers to "any failure by any person to comply with this *section*," whereas other references within the subsection itself refer to "*subsection*." See, *e.g.*, § 1681m(h)(3). However, such an interpretation would drastically constrict consumers' enforcement rights by eliminating civil actions for nearly all the obligations that the FCRA imposes on users and is not supported by the placement of the limitation of liability provision within a subsection as opposed to placing it at the level of other subsections that would be subject to the limitation.
13.18 § 1681s–2(c)(2), *added by* Pub. L. No. 108-159, § 312 (2003).
13.19 *Added by* Pub. L. No. 108-159, § 312 (2003).
13.20 15 U.S.C. §§ 1681n and 1681o.

11.2 Actual Damages

Page 271

11.2.2 Damages for Pecuniary Loss

Addition to notes 24, 27, 29, 33, 34, 36.

24 Thomas v. Gulf Coast Credit Serv., Inc., 214 F. Supp. 2d 1228 (M.D. Ala. 2002) (denial of credit for investment purposes is not covered by the FCRA).
27 Lawrence v. Trans Union, L.L.C., 296 F. Supp. 2d 582 (E.D. Pa. 2003) (loss of credit opportunity); Heupel v. Trans Union, L.L.C., 193 F. Supp. 2d 1234 (N.D. Ala. 2002).
29 *Replace Obabueki citation with*: 236 F. Supp. 2d 278 (S.D.N.Y. 2002), *aff'd*, 319 F.3d 87 (2d Cir. 2003).
  Replace Thomas citation with: 214 F. Supp. 2d 1228 (M.D. Ala. 2002).

Page 272

33 Heupel v. Trans Union, L.L.C., 193 F. Supp. 2d 1234 (N.D. Ala. 2002) (credit score reduced because of notation in one trade line of a chapter 13 bankruptcy). See Chapter 14, *infra*, for a discussion of credit scores.
34 Kettler v. CSC Credit Serv., Inc., 2003 WL 21975919 (D. Minn. Aug. 12, 2003).
  Replace Thomas citation with: 214 F. Supp. 2d 1228 (M.D. Ala. 2002).
36 Soghomonian v. U.S., 278 F. Supp. 2d 1151 (E.D. Cal. 2003).
  Replace Northrop's 2d Cir. citation with: 2001 WL 68 2301, 12 Fed. Appx. 44 (2d Cir. June 14, 2001).

11.2.3 Intangible Damages

Page 274

11.2.3.1 Are Intangible Damages Available?

Addition to notes 48, 50, 52, 53, 54.

48 *Replace Thomas citation with*: 214 F. Supp. 2d 1228 (M.D. Ala. 2002).
50 Field v. Trans Union, L.L.C., 2002 WL 849589 (N.D. Ill. May 3, 2002).
  Replace Thomas citation with: 214 F. Supp. 2d 1228 (M.D. Ala. 2002).
52 Acton v. Bank One Corp., 293 F. Supp. 2d 1092 (D. Ariz. 2003).
  Replace Thomas citation with: 214 F. Supp. 2d 1228 (M.D. Ala. 2002).
53 *Replace Whiteside citation with*: 2002 WL 1809084 (E.D. La. Aug. 6, 2002), *aff'd on other grounds*, 75 Fed. Appx. 972 (5th Cir. 2003) (unpublished).
54 Sheffer v. Experian Info. Solutions, Inc., 2003 WL 21710573 (E.D. Pa. July 24, 2003); Lawrence v. Trans Union, L.L.C., 296 F. Supp. 2d 582 (E.D. Pa. 2003).

§ 11.2.3.2 Fair Credit Reporting / 2004 Supplement

Replace Whiteside citation with: 2002 WL 1809084 (E.D. La. Aug. 6, 2002), aff'd on other grounds, 75 Fed. Appx. 972 (5th Cir. 2003) (unpublished).

Page 275

Replace note 56 with:

56   National Consumer Law Center, Credit Discrimination § 11.6.2.3 (3d ed. 2002 and Supp.).

11.2.3.2 Proving Intangible Damages

Add to text after sentence containing note 62:

Indeed, the weight of authority is that, contrary to the common law, the plaintiff's testimony alone may not suffice to recover for emotional distress damages. Summary judgment has been granted against a plaintiff who does not present sufficient independent evidence of emotional distress.[62.1]

62.1   Nagle v. Experian Info. Solutions, Inc., 297 F.3d 1305 (11th Cir. 2002); Riley v. Gen. Motors Acceptance Corp., 226 F. Supp. 2d 1316 (S.D. Ala. 2002); Thomas v. GulfCoast Credit Serv., Inc., 214 F. Supp. 2d 1228 (M.D. Ala. 2002); Myers v. Bennett Law Offices, 238 F. Supp. 2d 1196 (D. Nev. 2002); Field v. Trans Union, L.L.C., 2002 WL 849589 (N.D. Ill. May 3, 2002).

Page 277

11.2.4 Nominal Damages

Replace to note 85 with:

85   211 F.R.D. 328 (N.D. Ill. 2002).

11.4 Punitive Damages

11.4.1 Prerequisites for Punitive Damages

Page 279

11.4.1.1 Relation to Common Law Standards

Addition to note 114.

114   *Replace Northrop citation with*: 12 Fed. Appx. 44, 2001 WL 682301 (2d Cir. June 14, 2001).

11.4.1.2 Proving Willfulness

Addition to notes 118, 120.
Page 280

118   Rodgers v. McCullough, 296 F. Supp. 2d 895 (W.D. Tenn. 2003).
120   Feldman v. Comprehensive Info. Servs., Inc., 2003 WL 22413484 (Conn. Super. Oct. 6, 2003); Thomas v. GulfCoast Credit Serv., Inc., 214 F. Supp. 2d 1228 (M.D. Ala. 2002).
   Replace Northrop citation with: 12 Fed. Appx. 44, 2001 WL 682301 (2d Cir. June 14, 2001). *Replace Whiteside citation with*: 125 F. Supp. 2d 807 (W.D. La. 2000).

Add to text after sentence containing note 122:

The Eighth Circuit requires "knowing and intentional commission of an act the defendant knows to violate the law." General familiarity with the FCRA's requirements can support an inference of willfulness.[122.1]

122.1   Phillips v. Grendahl, 312 F.3d 357 (8th Cir. 2002).

Page 281

Addition to note 130.

130   Sheffer v. Experian Info. Solutions, Inc., 2003 WL 21710573 (E.D. Pa. July 24, 2003) (systemic errors, not merely human error, and not promptly cured); Soghomonian v. U.S., 278 F. Supp. 2d 1151 (E.D. Cal. 2003) (failure to pick up the phone to find out the status of tax liens until after suit was filed can show willfulness).

Add to text after sentence containing note 130:

Repeatedly obtaining a consumer's credit report despite efforts by a consumer to stop such actions may also constitute willful noncompliance.[130.1]

130.1   Veno v. AT&T Credit Corp., 297 F. Supp. 2d 379 (D. Mass. 2004).

Private Remedies / 2004 Supplement § 11.4.3

Add after "policy that violates the FCRA" in sentence following sentence containing note 131:		when the agency knew that the report was inaccurate,[131.1]
	131.1	Thomas v. GulfCoast Credit Serv., Inc., 214 F. Supp. 2d 1228 (M.D. Ala. 2002).
Addition to note 132.	132	*Replace first "that" in the note with*: that it.
Add note 133.1 after first sentence of paragraph containing notes 134 and 135.	133.1	Evantash v. G.E. Capital Mortgage Serv., Inc., 2003 WL 22844198 (E.D. Pa. Nov. 25, 2003) (policy not to provide consumer's dispute documentation to furnisher; policy to report whatever information creditors provide); Sheffer v. Experian Info. Solutions, Inc., 2003 WL 21710573 (E.D. Pa. July 24, 2003) (same); Lawrence v. Trans Union, L.L.C., 296 F. Supp. 2d 582 (E.D. Pa. 2003) (same); Soghomonian v. U.S., 278 F. Supp. 2d 1151 (E.D. Cal. 2003).

Page 282

Addition to notes 141, 142.	141	*Replace Whiteside citation with*: 125 F. Supp. 2d 807 (W.D. La. 2000). *Replace Thomas citation with*: 214 F. Supp. 2d 1228 (M.D. Ala. 2002).
	142	*Replace Whiteside citation with*: 2002 WL 1809084 (E.D. La. Aug. 6, 2002), *aff'd on other grounds*, 75 Fed. Appx. 972 (5th Cir. 2003) (unpublished).

Page 283

11.4.1.3 No Need to Prove Actual Damages

Addition to note 147.	147	*Replace Northrop citation with*: 12 Fed. Appx. 44, 2001 WL 682301 (2d Cir. June 14, 2001).

11.4.2 Determining the Amount of Punitive Damages

11.4.2.1 No Upper Limit on Size of Awards

Replace note 157 with:	157	15 U.S.C. § 1691e(b). *See* National Consumer Law Center, Credit Discrimination § 11.6.4.3 (3d ed. 2002 and Supp.).

Page 284

11.4.2.2 Determining the Size of the Award

Add to text after sentence containing note 160:

When a court reviews whether the jury's award is excessive, it considers (1) the degree of reprehensibility of the defendant's conduct, such as whether it was part of a larger pattern of misconduct; (2) the relationship between the punitive damages and the harm suffered; and (3) sanctions, such as criminal penalties for similar misconduct.[160.1]

160.1   Adams v. Phillips, 2002 WL 31886737 (W.D. La. 2002).

Addition to note 164.	164	*Replace Northrop's 2d Cir. citation with*: 12 Fed. Appx. 44, 2001 WL 682301 (2d Cir. June 14, 2001).

11.4.3 Punitive Damages: Decided by Judge or Jury?

Replace subsection's first paragraph with:

The FCRA does not address whether consumers have a right to a jury trial, but numerous FCRA cases have gone to juries and punitive damages have been awarded for willful violations of the Act.[167] Courts deciding non-FCRA cases have held that the issue of punitive damage awards historically has been a matter for determination by a jury.[168]

Under the Federal Rules of Civil Procedure, any party may make a timely demand for a jury trial of any issue triable of right by a jury by timely serving upon the other parties a demand in writing. Failure so to do so constitutes a waiver of the right.[169] Defendants may contend that the judge must determine the size of punitive damages because the FCRA states that the consumer reporting agency or user is liable for "such amount of punitive damages as the court may allow."[169.1] Courts have rejected this reasoning of the Act, finding that the phrase "as the court may allow" means only that the court had a duty to review excessive verdicts and to eliminate any elements of emotion and prejudice reflected in the verdict.[169.2]

167   *See* § 11.7, *infra*.

§ 11.5 *Fair Credit Reporting / 2004 Supplement*

168 *See, e.g.,* Hartford Fire Ins. Co. v. First Nat. Bank of Atmore, 198 F. Supp. 2d 1308 (D.C. Ala. 2002) (insured had right to jury trial as to amount of punitive damages on its claim against insurer for bad faith); Todd v. Roadway Express Inc., 178 F. Supp. 2d 1244 (D.C. Ala. 2001) (it is the function of the jury to determine the amount of punitive damages once it has determined that an award of punitive damages is proper and the role of the court, whether trial or appellate, to determine whether the jury has set an amount which is constitutionally excessive). *See* § 10.12, *supra*. In federal court, all damage issues, including punitive damages, are to be decided by the jury. Feltner v. Columbia Pictures Television, Inc., 523 U.S. 340, 348, 118 S. Ct. 1279 (1998); Kobs v. Arrow Service Bureau, Inc., 134 F.3d 893 (7th Cir. 1998); McGuire v. Russell Miller, Inc., 1 F.3d 1306 (2d Cir. 1993); Kampa v. White Consol. Inc., 115 F.3d 585, 586 (8th Cir. 1997).

169 Fed. R. Civ. P. 38; Fed. R. Civ. P. 39.

169.1 15 U.S.C. § 1681n(a)(2).

169.2 Northrup v. Hoffman, 2001 WL 682301 (2d Cir. June 14, 2001); Barron v. Trans Union Corp., 82 F. Supp. 2d (M.D. Ala. 2000) (issue of fact for jury); Russell v. Shelter Financial Services, 604 F. Supp. 201 (W.D. Mo. 1984): Collins v. Retail Credit Co., 410 F. Supp. 924 (E.D. Mich. 1976) (court found congressional history inconclusive on this point).

Page 285

Addition to note 170.

170 Castro v. Union Nissan, 2002 WL 1466810 (N.D. Ill. July 8, 2002).

11.5 Injunctive and Declaratory Relief

Addition to notes 180, 183, 185, 191, 192, 195, 196.
Page 286

180 *Replace Wenger citation with*: 1995 U.S. Dist. LEXIS 22214 (C.D. Cal. Nov. 14, 1995).
183 *Replace Trans Union citation with*: 211 F.R.D. 328 (N.D. Ill. 2002).
185 *Replace Trans Union citation with*: 211 F.R.D. 328, 339, 340 (N.D. Ill. 2002).
191 *See* Appx. B, *infra*.
192 *See, e.g.,* Mass. Gen. Laws ch. 93A, § 4.
195 *Replace Trans Union citation with*: 211 F.R.D. 328, 340 (N.D. Ill. 2002).
196 *Replace citation with*: *Id.* at 340.

11.6 Attorney Fees and Costs

Page 287

11.6.1 When Are Fees and Costs Awarded?

Addition to note 197.

197 15 U.S.C. § 1681o(a)(2); Sheffer v. Experian Info. Solutions, 290 F. Supp. 2d 538 (E.D. Pa. 2003).

Add to text after "motions" in sentence containing note 203:

but costs were not granted for depositions not used at trial.

Addition to notes 208, 209, 211.

208 *Replace citation to Nagle with*: Nagel v. Experian Information Solutions, Inc., 297 F.3d 1305 (11th Cir. 2002). *Replace Crabill citation with*: 259 F.3d 662 (7th Cir. 2001).

209 Menton v. Experian Corp., 2003 WL 21692829 (S.D.N.Y. July 21, 2003).
     Replace Hawthorne citation with: 216 F. Supp. 2d 45 (E.D.N.Y. 2002).

211 Battley v. City Fin. Corp., 2002 WL 1379204 (M.D. La. 2002) (defendant's failure to respond to prelitigation inquiry shows plaintiff acted in good faith).
     Replace River Oaks citation with: 32 Fed. Appx. 929 (9th Cir. 2002).

Page 288

Add to text at end of subsection:

Costs may be awarded to the prevailing defendant under the federal rules.[214.1]

214.1 Waggoner v. Trans Union, L.L.C., 2003 WL 22838718 (N.D. Tex. Nov. 24, 2003) (awarding $6000 in costs to Trans Union).

Private Remedies / 2004 Supplement § 11.6.5

11.6.2 Calculating the Size of the Attorney Fee Award

11.6.2.1 FCRA Awards Will Be Based on Standards Enunciated in Other Federal Fee-Shifting Statutes

Add note 215.1 to end of subsection's first paragraph.

215.1 City of Burlington v. Dague, 505 U.S. 557, 562 (1992) ("[O]ur case law construing what is a 'reasonable' fee applies uniformly to all" fee shifting statutes.).

Addition to notes 216, 217.

216 Sheffer v. Experian Info. Solutions, Inc., 290 F. Supp. 2d 538 (E.D. Pa. 2003).

217 *Add after Riverside citation*: Yohay v. City of Alexandria, 827 F.2d 967 (4th Cir. 1987) (proportionality would discourage vigorous enforcement of the Act). *Replace Northrop's 2d Cir. citation with*: 12 Fed. Appx. 44, 2001 WL 682301 (2d Cir. June 14, 2001).

Page 289

11.6.2.2 Current Federal Fee-Shifting Standards

Addition to note 223.

223 *Replace Mealer citation with*: 22 Fed. Appx. 700 (8th Cir. 2002).

Add to text at end of subsection:

Although the lodestar is presumed to yield a reasonable fee, a court has considerable discretion to adjust the lodestar upward or downward after the opposing party objects to the fee request.[224.1]

224.1 Sheffer v. Experian Info. Solutions, Inc., 290 F. Supp. 2d 538 (E.D. Pa. 2003).

11.6.3 Maximizing the Chances of an Adequate Fee Award

Addition to note 225.

225 Sheffer v. Experian Info. Solutions, Inc. 290 F. Supp. 2d 538 (E.D. Pa. 2003).

Add note 225.1 after first sentence in subsection's third paragraph.

225.1 Sheffer v. Experian Info. Solutions, Inc. 290 F. Supp. 2d 538 (E.D. Pa. 2003) (court determines reasonable hourly rate by assessing the prevailing party's attorneys' experience and skill compared to the market rates in the relevant community for lawyers of reasonably comparable skill, experience, and reputation).

Add to text at end of subsection:

At least one court has held that it is an abuse of discretion to refuse to allow discovery as to defense counsel's hours and fees when defendant is challenging the reasonableness of plaintiff's hours and fees.[226.1] Advocates may also want to highlight recent FCRA jury verdicts or settlements with substantial awards to plaintiffs. This information is useful to support large awards and to inform both opposing counsel and the courts about the potential for large awards associated with FCRA claims.[226.2]

226.1 Henson v. Columbus Bank & Trust Co., 770 F.2d 1566, 1575 (11th Cir. 1985).
226.2 See § 11.7, *infra* for a list of published FCRA damage awards.

11.6.4 Preserving Fee Entitlement When Case Is Settled

Addition to notes 227–229.

227 *Replace citation with*: 532 U.S. 598 (2001).
228 *Replace citation with*: *Id.*, 532 U.S. at 603, n.4.
229 *Replace citation with*: *Id.*, 532 U.S. at 604.

Replace notes 231, 232 with:
Page 290

231 *Buckhannon*, 532 U.S. at 604, n.7.
232 *Buckhannon*, 532 U.S. at 604.

Addition to notes 236, 238.

236 *Replace John T. citation with*: 318 F.3d 545 (3d Cir. 2003) (preliminary injunction insufficient).
238 *Replace Buckhannon citation with*: 532 U.S. at 604, n.7.

Page 291

11.6.5 Rule 68 and Attorney Fee Awards

Add to text at end of section:

If the offer of judgment does not represent everything the plaintiff could possibly have recovered, the case may not be dismissed.[245.1]

245.1 McCauley v. Trans Union, L.L.C., 2003 WL 22845741 (S.D.N.Y. Nov. 26, 2003) (court rejects claim for punitive damages but remote possibility of their recovery at time of Rule 68 offer renders offer ineffectual).

§ 11.7   *Fair Credit Reporting / 2004 Supplement*

11.7 Quick Reference to Published Awards

Add to bulleted list:
- *Adams v. Phillips*, 2002 WL 31886737 (W.D. La. 2002): $225,000 actual damages and $275,000 punitive damages against impostor.
- *Bakker v. McKinnon*, 152 F.3d 1007 (8th Cir. 1998) $500 actual damages; $5000 punitive damages.
- *Boris v. ChoicePoint Servs., Inc.*, 249 F. Supp. 2d 851 (W.D. Ky. 2003): Jury award of $197,000 actual damages remitted to $100,000; $250,000 punitive damages not excessive.
- Sheffer v. Experian Info. Solutions, Inc., 290 F. Supp. 2d 538 (E.D. Pa. 2003): $1000 actual damages, $25,000 fees, $7500 costs.
- *Yohay v. Alexandria Employees Credit Union Inc.*, 827 F.2d 967 (4th Cir. 1987): no actual damages; $10,000 punitive damages.

Page 292

Replace Northrop v. Hoffman citation with: 12 Fed. Appx. 44, 2001 WL 682301 (2d Cir. June 14, 2001).

Chapter 12 Public Enforcement

12.2 Federal Trade Commission Enforcement

12.2.1 General FTC Enforcement Powers

Page 295

Add to text before subsection's last paragraph:

The FTC has also brought an enforcement action against a user of credit reports for failing to provide adverse action notices.[21.1] According to the complaint filed by the FTC,[21.2] the user of credit reports offered loans to consumers over the Internet and invited consumers to submit applications. During the application process the lender would "prequalify" the consumer for a loan based solely on information submitted by the consumer, or "preapprove" the consumer for a loan based on the consumer's credit report as well as the consumer-supplied information. In selecting the preapproval option, consumers were required to click a button next to the statement, "Order my credit report and use it to preapprove me for a loan." By this method, the lender communicated to consumers that by selecting the preapproval option, the consumers were filing applications for preapproval of a loan under Regulation B.[21.3] For consumers who requested preapproval, the lender obtained credit reports and used the reports to evaluate the consumers' creditworthiness. Consumers whom the lender did not preapprove for one of its on-line loan products received an advisory informing them that they have "unique barrowing needs" and inviting them to go to a "Next Step" that would permit an employee of the lender to contact the consumers about other loan products. The lender's message further informed consumers that the consumers' on-line application for preapproval had been denied. Consumers who received this message on-line had no other contact from the lender. According to the FTC, such actions by the lender constituted adverse action against consumers and the lender was required under the FCRA to notify the consumer of the adverse action, including the name, address and telephone number of the consumer reporting agency from which the credit report was obtained; the consumer's right to obtain a free copy of the consumer report; and the consumer's right to dispute the accuracy of the completeness of the information in the credit report.[21.4] The FTC subsequently settled with the lender, requiring adverse action notices to consumers anytime the lender takes an adverse action on a consumer's application based either in whole or in part on information in a credit report.

However, the FTC would not view failure to grant an on-line request for preapproval as an adverse action if certain conditions had been satisfied. Such conditions included a requirement that the lender provide a clear and conspicuous disclosure in close proximity to the preapproval offer that preapproval may be granted on-line or off-line; that the lender determined that it cannot grant preapproval on-line because it needs additional information, and it determines that the request for preapproval has not been denied, but needs additional information from the consumer; and, if the consumer submits the additional information, the lender decides whether to grant the request and informs the consumer of the decision.[21.5]

21.1 *See In the Matter of* Quicken Loans, Inc., Docket No. 9304, (Dec. 30, 2002) (consent decree), *reprinted in* Appx. H.6, *infra*.
21.2 *In the Matter of* Quicken Loans, Inc., Docket No. 9304 (2002).
21.3 13 C.F.R. § 202.2(f).
21.4 *In the Matter of* Quicken Loans, Inc. Docket No. 9304 (2002).
21.5 *See In the Matter of* Quicken Loans, Inc., Docket No. 9304 (Dec. 30, 2002) (consent decree), *reprinted in* Appx. H.6, *infra*.

§ 12.2.3

Replace "Appendix F" in subsection's last sentence with:

Appendix H

Addition to note 22.

22   *Replace citation to Appx. "F" with:* Appx. H.

Add to text at end of subsection:

The limitation also does not apply to the new obligations of furnishers to put in place reasonable procedures for responding to a notice from an agency that that agency has blocked furnished information because it was the result of fraud or identity theft[24.1] Nor does it apply to the upcoming obligation of furnishers to reinvestigate the accuracy of information upon consumer's notice that the information is inaccurate.[24.2] Two new provisions that apply to specific types of furnishers are also free from the limitation: the new obligation of medical information furnishers to notify a credit reporting agency of their status[24.3] and the new obligation of financial institution furnishers to notify customers when they furnish negative information about the customer to a nationwide consumer reporting agency.[24.4]

24.1   15 U.S.C. § 1681s–2(a)(6), added by Pub. L. No. 108-159, § 154 (2003). This provision will become effective on December 1, 2004. 16 C.F.R. § 602.1(c)(3)(vii), added by 69 Fed. Reg. 6526–31 (Feb. 5, 2004).

24.2   15 U.S.C. § 1681s–2(a)(8), added by Pub. L. No. 108-159, § 312(c) (2003). This provision will become effective on December 1, 2004. 16 C.F.R. § 602.1(c)(3)(xiv), added by 69 Fed. Reg. 6526–31 (Feb. 5, 2004). The obligations will not arise until the identified agencies prescribe regulations that identify circumstances under which a furnisher will be required to reinvestigate a dispute made directly by a consumer. 15 U.S.C. § 1681s–2(a)(8)(C).

24.3   15 U.S.C. § 1681s–2(a)(9), added by Pub. L. No. 108-159, § 412(a) (2003). This provision will become effective March 4, 2005. *Id.*

24.4   15 U.S.C. § 1681s–2(a)(7), added by Pub. L. No. 108-159, § 217 (2003). This provision will become effective on December 1, 2004. 16 C.F.R. § 602.1(c)(3)(xii), added by 69 Fed. Reg. 6526–31 (Feb. 5, 2004).

12.2.3 FTC Rulemaking, FTC Commentary, and Opinion Letters; Federal Reserve Board Interpretations

Replace subsection's first two words with:

Congress in 1996

Add to text at end of subsection's first paragraph:

In the 2003 amendments to the Act Congress imposed a number of new rulemaking requirements on the FTC, the National Credit Union Administration, and federal banking agencies.[28.1] The agencies are required to draft:

- regulations that will create the centralized source through which consumers may request a free annual credit report from a nationwide agency (FTC);[28.2]
- regulations about how nationwide specialty consumer reporting agencies are to provide free annual credit reports (FTC);[28.3]
- regulations imposing obligations on users of consumer information to dispose of that information (FTC, NCUA, and federal banking agencies);[28.4]
- regulations implementing the new provision prohibiting nationwide consumer reporting agencies from circumventing their treatment under the FCRA (FTC);[28.5]
- regulations that will allow creditors to obtain or use medical information pertaining to a consumer in connection with a determination of the consumer's eligibility for credit (the federal banking agencies and NCUA);[28.6]
- regulations regarding the policies and procedures that a user of a consumer report that has an address discrepancy must employ (the federal banking agencies, the NCUA, and the FTC);[28.7]
- regulations defining what constitutes appropriate proof of identity for the purposes of 15 U.S.C. § 1681c-1 (identity theft prevention; fraud alerts; and active duty alerts), 15 U.S.C. § 1681c-2 (block of information resulting from identity theft), and 15 U.S.C. § 1681g(a)(1) (requiring an agency to truncate the social security number of a consumer

on a report issued to a consumer) (FTC);[28.8]
- the red-flag guidelines that financial institutions are to follow to prevent and detect identity theft (the federal banking agencies, NCUA, and the FTC);[28.9]
- the model summary of rights to obtain and dispute information in consumer reports and to obtain credit scores (FTC);[28.10]
- regulations with which creditors must comply regarding risk-based pricing notices (the FRB and the FTC);[28.11]
- regulations identifying the circumstances under which a furnisher must reinvestigate information upon a consumer's direct dispute (the federal banking agencies, the NCUA, and the FTC);[28.12]
- guidelines for furnishers to follow regarding the accuracy and integrity of consumer information that they furnish to agencies (the federal banking agencies, the NCUA, and the FTC);[28.13]
- the model disclosure that financial institutions may use to comply with the new requirement that they disclose to a customer that the institution is furnishing negative information about that customer, the use of which will be deemed to comply with the requirement (the Board of Governors of the FRB);[28.14] and
- regulations to implement the new right of consumers to opt out of an affiliate's use of information for marketing solicitations (the federal banking agencies, NCUA, and the FTC).[28.15]

28.1 These agencies are now defined by § 3 of the Federal Deposit Insurance Act, 12 U.S.C. § 1813. 15 U.S.C. § 1681a(s), added by Pub. L. No. 108-159, § 111 (2003). That provision defines federal banking agencies to mean "the Comptroller of the Currency, the Director of the Office of Thrift Supervision, the Board of Governors of the Federal Reserve System, or the Federal Deposit Insurance Corporation." 12 U.S.C. § 1813(z).

28.2 Pub. L. No. 108-159, § 211 (2003). The provision does not apply to a nationwide agency that has not been furnishing consumer reports on a continuing basis for the twelve months preceding a consumer's request. 15 U.S.C. § 1681j(a)(4), added by Pub. L. No. 108-159, § 211 (2003). The FTC has proposed regulations that would implement a "cumulative regional roll-out" for the centralized source that would delay complete access to the source until September 1, 2005. 69 Fed. Reg. 13198 (Mar. 19, 2004).

28.3 15 U.S.C. § 1681j(a)(1)(C), added by Pub. L. No. 108-159, § 211 (2003).
28.4 15 U.S.C. § 1681w(a), added by Pub. L. No. 108-159, § 216 (2003).
28.5 15 U.S.C. § 1681x, added by Pub. L. No. 108-159, § 211 (2003).
28.6 15 U.S.C. § 1681b(g)(5), added by Pub. L. No. 108-159, § 411 (2003). This provision will become effective on June 1, 2004, 180 days after passage of the FACTA. Pub. L. No. 108-159, § 411(d) (2003).
28.7 15 U.S.C. § 1681c(h)(2), added by Pub. L. No. 108-159, § 315 (2003).
28.8 Pub. L. No. 108-159, § 211 (2003), 15 U.S.C. § 1681c-1 note. These provisions will become effective on December 4, 2004. 16 C.F.R. §§ 602.1(c)(3)(i), (iii), (v), added by 69 Fed. Reg. 6526–31 (Feb. 5, 2004).
28.9 15 U.S.C. § 1681m(e), added by Pub. L. No. 108-159, § 114 (2003).
28.10 15 U.S.C. § 1681g(c)(1), added by Pub. L. No. 108-159, § 211 (2003).
28.11 15 U.S.C. § 1681m(h)(6), added by Pub. L. No. 108-159, § 311 (2003).
28.12 15 U.S.C. § 1681s–2(a)(8)(A), added by Pub. L. No. 108-159, § 312 (2003).
28.13 15 U.S.C. § 1681s–2(e), added by Pub. L. No. 108-159, § 312 (2003).
28.14 15 U.S.C. § 1681a(7)(D), added by Pub. L. No. 108-159, § 217 (2003).
28.15 15 U.S.C. § 1681s–3(a), added by Pub. L. No. 108-159, § 214 (2003).

Add to text at end of subsection:

Recently the FTC has stopped issuing informal staff opinion letters on FCRA-related issues. The last FTC informal staff opinion letter was issued on June 28, 2001.

12.4 State Enforcement

Page 296

12.4.2 State Enforcement Powers Against Information Furnishers Are Limited

Replace note 40 with:

40 See §§ 10.2.1, 10.2.3, *supra*.

Replace subsection's second paragraph with:

Generally speaking, the Act as revised by the FACTA sets forth nine duties of furnishers relating to the provision of information to consumer reporting agencies:[44]

§ 12.4.4   Fair Credit Reporting / 2004 Supplement

    1. A limited duty not to report inaccurate information
    2. A duty to correct and update inaccurate information
    3. A duty to provide notice that the accuracy of information has been disputed by a consumer
    4. A duty to provide notice of voluntarily closed accounts
    5. A duty to provide the date of a delinquency on an account commenced
    6. A new duty to put in place reasonable procedures for responding to a notice from an agency that that agency has blocked furnished information on the grounds that it was the result of fraud or identity theft
    7. An upcoming duty on furnishers to reinvestigate the accuracy of information upon consumer's notice that the information is inaccurate
    8. A new duty of medical information furnishers to notify credit reporting agencies of their status as a furnisher of medical information
    9. A new duty of financial institution furnishers to notify customers when they furnish negative information about the customer to a nationwide consumer reporting agency
    44   *See* Ch. 3, *supra*.

Page 297

Add after "limitation" in sentence containing note 47:

, as amended by the FACTA,[46.1]
    46.1   Pub. L. No. 108-159 (2003).

Add to text at end of subsection:

Effective in 1997, state enforcement efforts were further restricted. A state authority is now precluded from imposing requirements or prohibitions on persons who furnish information to consumer reporting agencies.[48.1]
    48.1   15 U.S.C. § 1681t(b)(1)(F); Ameritech Mich. v. Michigan Pub. Servs. Comm'n, 658 N.W.2d 849 (Mich. App. 2003).

12.4.4   State Investigatory Powers

Replace first six words of subsection with:

Nothing in the FCRA's

Chapter 13 Non-Litigation Solutions for Consumers with Blemished or Insufficient Credit Histories

Page 299

13.1 Introduction

Add to text after last sentence in subsection's first paragraph:

Chapter 14, *infra*, discusses what consumer can do to improve credit scores.[0.1]

   0.1   See § 14.6, *infra*.

13.2 What Information Is Being Reported on the Consumer?

Page 300

13.2.1 Examining the Consumer's Credit Record

Add to text after "adults" in last sentence of subsection's third paragraph:

especially immigrants

Page 301

13.2.2 Beyond Credit Bureaus: Tenant Screening, Check Cashing, and Other Specialized Reporting Agencies

Replace note 12 with:

   12   Cotto v. Jenney, 1989 U.S. Dist. LEXIS 11850 (D. Mass. Apr. 14, 1989) (U.S. Magistrate's Report and Recommendation Regarding Plaintiff's Motion for Summary Judgment and Defendant's Motion for Summary Judgment), *related case reported at* 721 F. Supp. 5 (D. Mass. 1989).

13.2.7 Information About Spouse, Former Spouse, or Relatives' Credit History

Page 304

13.2.7.1 What Information Appears in Consumer's File

Replace note 46 with:

   46   *See* 12 C.F.R. § 202.10; § 13.7.3, *infra*; National Consumer Law Center, Credit Discrimination §§ 5.5.5.4, 9.4.2.1 (3d ed. 2002 and Supp.).

Add to text at end of subsection's second paragraph:

A divorce decree mandating that one spouse be responsible for the debt does not alter the contractual relationship with the creditor, who may continue to report the debt as to both obligated spouses.[46.1]

   46.1   Moline v. Experian Info. Solutions, Inc., 289 F. Supp. 2d 956 (N.D. Ill. 2003).

Add to text at end of subsection:

One court has held that liability for state law necessaries can be reported on both spouse's credit files, even if only one spouse has a contractual obligation.[46.2] A consumer who is going through a divorce should make sure that at least the minimum payment is made on joint accounts if possible. Late payments will appear on both parties' credit reports and will impede future attempts to obtain credit. Even if the divorce decree ultimately assigns responsibility for a joint debt to one party, the other party remains responsible unless the creditor agrees to

§ 13.2.7.2 *Fair Credit Reporting / 2004 Supplement*

release that party. It is a good idea to ask joint creditors to reestablish the account in just one party's name, so that that party alone is responsible for future charges.

46.2   Dunn v. Lehigh Valley Center for Sight, P.C., 2003 WL 22288275 (E.D. Pa. Sept. 30, 2003).

13.2.7.2 Creditor's Use of Spouse's File

13.2.7.2.1 FCRA limitations

Replace note 47 with:

47   See § 5.3.6, *supra*.

Addition to note 54.

54   *Replace last sentence of note with*: *See generally* National Consumer Law Center, Credit Discrimination (3d ed. 2002 and Supp.) for a discussion of ECOA Regulation B.

Page 305

13.2.7.2.2 ECOA limitations

Replace note 67 with:

67   12 C.F.R. § 202.3(c) (definition of incidental credit). *See* National Consumer Law Center, Credit Discrimination §§ 2.2.6.3, 2.2.6.6 (3d ed. 2002 and Supp.).

13.2.8 Special Restrictions on Reporting of Information

Page 306

13.2.8.3 Special Protections for Military Personnel

Replace first seven words of subsection's first sentence with:

The Servicemembers' Civil Relief Act (formerly the Soldiers' and Sailors' Civil Relief Act)

Replace "Soldiers' and Sailors' Civil Relief Act" in sentence containing note 78 with:

Servicemembers' Civil Relief Act

13.5 Disputing Debts with the Creditor and the Reporting Agency

13.5.2 Disputing Debts with the Creditor

Page 313

13.5.2.1 The Creditor's Duty of Accuracy When Furnishing Information

Add to text after sentence containing note 140:

The 2003 amendments to the FCRA heightened these duties.[140.1]

140.1   See § 3.4, *supra*.

Replace "knows or consciously avoids knowing" in sentence containing note 143 with:

knows or has reasonable cause to believe

Addition to note 143.

143   *Add at end of note*: The 2003 amendments to the FCRA replaced the former "knows or consciously avoids knowing" standard with "knows or has reasonable cause to believe." Pub. L. No. 108-159 (2003), § 312(b).

Page 314

Add to text after sentence containing note 147:

The 2003 amendments to the FCRA require that the dispute letter identify the specific information that is disputed, explain the basis for the dispute, and include any supporting documentation required by the furnisher.[147.1]

Non-Litigation Solutions / 2004 Supplement   § 13.5.4.1

147.1   15 U.S.C. § 1681s-2(c)(8)(D), *added by* Pub. L. No. 108-159 (2003), § 312(c).

Add to text at end of subsection:

The 2003 amendments to the FCRA provide that, once regulations are issued, creditors will have a duty to reinvestigate information in response to consumer disputes.[151.1] It does not appear that the consumer has a private cause of action to enforce this duty, however, so the advice in the previous paragraph continues to be sound. Upon receiving a dispute, the credit must conduct an investigation, review the information submitted by the consumer, and report the results to the consumer, all within the same thirty-day period (plus a possible fifteen-day extention) as applies when the dispute is initiated through a credit reporting agency.[151.2] If the creditor finds that the information reported was inaccurate, it must notify all the credit reporting agencies to which it furnished the inaccurate information.[151.3] Creditors need not reinvestigate if the dispute is frivolous or irrelevant or is submitted by a credit repair organization.[151.4]

151.1   15 U.S.C. § 1681s-2(c)(8), *added by* Pub. L. No. 108-159 (2003), § 312(c).
151.2   15 U.S.C. § 1681s-2(c)(8)(E), *added by* Pub. L. No. 108-159 (2003), § 312(c).
151.3   15 U.S.C. § 1681s-2(c)(8)(E)(iv), *added by* Pub. L. No. 108-159 (2003), § 312(c).
151.4   15 U.S.C. § 1681s-2(c)(8)(F), (G), *added by* Pub. L. No. 108-159 (2003), § 312(c).

Page 315

13.5.2.2 No Adverse Reporting While Dispute Pending

Addition to note 158.

158   *Replace NCLC citation with*: National Consumer Law Center, Credit Discrimination § 3.3.4 (3d ed. 2002 and Supp.).

Page 316

13.5.3 Disputing Debts with the Reporting Agency

Add to text at end of subsection's fourth paragraph:

Another example is a report on a cosigner that is based on a default of the principal obligor that the cosigner corrected immediately upon learning of it. A dispute letter that explains why the credit report is incomplete and misleading may be effective.

Page 317

Add to text after sentence containing note 181:

Check the credit reporting agency's materials or its website for the current address for disputes, and use certified mail, return receipt requested, to minimize questions about whether the dispute letter was received.

Many attorneys prefer to have consumers write and send dispute letters on their own, using guidelines supplied by the attorney (and possibly reviewed and edited by the attorney). This is less expensive for the client, and it prevents the attorney from being dragged into the case as a fact witness if the mailing or receipt of the letter becomes an issue. On the other hand, some credit reporting agencies may treat dispute letters from attorneys with more care. Regardless of who writes the letter, including a a power of attorney signed by the consumer, allowing the credit reporting agency to discuss the matter with the consumer's attorney, saves time and trouble later on.

13.5.4 Dealing with Credit Reporting Issues When Settling Debt Litigation

13.5.4.1 Importance of Resolving Credit Reporting Issues

Replace "upon the request of a creditor, from the creditor" in sentence containing note 189 with:

upon the request of the creditor

Replace "request" in third sentence of subsection's fourth paragraph with:

requests

109

§ 13.5.4.3

Fair Credit Reporting / 2004 Supplement

Page 318

13.5.4.3 Selecting the Correct Settlement Language

Add to text after sentence containing note 194:

The agreement should address the possibility that the credit reporting agency will not delete the report despite the creditor's request. In that event, the consumer should plan to dispute the debt, and the creditor should agree that it will not verify the debt if it receives a reinvestigation request from a credit reporting agency.

13.5.5 Coping with the Results of Identity Theft

Page 322

13.5.5.1 Nature of Identity Theft

Add to text at end of subsection's second paragraph:

A thief looking for a bigger haul may snatch a business's computer hardware, acquiring all the sensitive client information in its stores.[205.1]

205.1 *See, e.g.,* Matt Mientka, *Theft at Tri-West Exposes Patient Data,* U.S. Medicine (Feb. 2003) (available at www.usmedicine.com/article.cfm?articleID=589&issueID=47) (reporting theft of hard drives containing personal information of more than 562,000 military servicemembers from managed health care contractor).

Addition to note 207.

207 Michelle Delio, *Fraud Case: Greed Bred Sloppiness,* www.wired.com/news/privacy/0,1848,56593,00.html (Nov. 27, 2002) (reporting on criminal defendant who allegedly used his position at a company that provided hardware and software to consumer reporting agencies to access and sell credit records to a ring of identity thieves, who then accessed as many as 30,000 reports and ransacked many accounts).

Replace subsection's fourth paragraph with:

Identity theft is one of the fastest growing financial crimes. In 2002 the Federal Trade Commission received reports from 161,819 victims of identity theft; calls to its hotline increased by nearly 24 percent over the course of the year.[211] One industry analyst recently estimated that banks alone lost one billion dollars to identity theft in 2002.[212] Analysis of the fraud complaints filed with the FTC showed that 42 percent of the victims suffered credit card fraud, and more than half of those involved a thief opening one or more new credit cards in the victim's name.[213] About one-in-five of the complaints reported that the thief had obtained unauthorized telecommunications or utility equipment or services using the stolen identity.[213.1] 17 percent reported frauds performed on a bank account.[213.2] Other common thefts were use of the stolen identity to obtain employment (9 percent), loans (6 percent), or government benefits or documents (4 percent). Alarmingly, 2 percent of the victims–roughly 3200–reported that the thief used their identity to evade legal sanctions and criminal records, leaving the victim's named stained with the false legal record and corrupting the nation's legal and judicial system.[213.3] According to the FTC's clearinghouse, almost 70 percent of the complaints stated that the victim knew some information about the thief, often gleaned from the creditors, collection agencies and other pursuers; 15 percent knew the thief personally.[213.4] Nonetheless, 72 percent of the victims did not know how the thief came by their information.[213.5]

211 Federal Trade Commission, *Information on Identity Theft for Consumers & Victims From January, 2002 Through December, 2002,* www.consumer.gov/idtheft/reports/CY2002ReportFinal.pdf, at 1; Jennifer 8. Lee, *Identity Theft Complaints Double in '02, Continuing Rise,* N.Y. Times A18 (Jan. 23, 2003). The FTC logs complaints into its Identity Theft Data Clearinghouse, which federal, state and local law enforcement agencies can access through the FTC's Consumer Sentinel Network. Fed. Trade Comm'n, Consumer Sentinel, www.consumer.gov/sentinel/idtchart.htm (accessed July 17, 2003).

212 Bob Sullivan, *ID Theft Costs Banks $1 Billion a Year,* www.msnbc.com/news/891186.asp?0cv=TA01 (Mar. 26, 2003) (citing report by TowerGroup Inc., a financial research and advisory firm).

213 Federal Trade Commission, *Information on Identity Theft for Consumers & Victims From January, 2002 Through December, 2002,* www.consumer.gov/idtheft/reports/CY2002ReportFinal.pdf, at 2

213.1 *Id.*
213.2 *Id.*
213.3 *Id.*
213.4 *Id.* at 7.
213.5 *Id.* at 8.

13.5.5.2 Contacting Credit Reporting Agencies, Creditors, Police, and Government Agencies

Page 323

Add to text at end of subsection's first paragraph:

Ironically, those who do read the fraud statement may make the victim's situation even worse by overreacting. Practitioners have reported that some creditors will deny credit out of hand to a consumer with a fraud statement on file, without bothering to determine whether the credit application was in fact legitimate.

Add to text after "Idaho" in sentence containing note 221:

Virginia

Page 324

Addition to note 221.

221   Va. Code Ann. § 18.2-186.3:1.

Add to text after sentence containing note 222:

In Virginia, an identity theft victim can seek an "Identity Theft Passport" from the state attorney general; the document states that the victim's identity has been used by another person who has been charged or arrested for that use.[222.1]

222.1   Va. Code Ann. § 18.2-186.5.

Add to text before sentence containing note 224:

The FTC provides a form identity theft affidavit that a victim can fill out, execute, and provide to consumer reporting agencies and financial institutions that have mistakenly issued credit, made credit reports, or provided goods or services in the victim's name.[223.1]

223.1   The form affidavit can be found at www.consumer.gov/idtheft/affidavit. A copy of the affidavit form can be found at Appx. H, *infra*.

Add to text at end of subsection:

Even if no debts have yet been incurred in the victim's name, a person whose confidential information has been stolen should take steps to prevent its misuse. For example, a person whose social security number has been stolen should register fraud alerts with the credit reporting agencies and all accounts, get his or her credit reports immediately and again in several months, change all account passwords, call the Social Security Administration's fraud hotline, and visit the identity theft websites for further suggestions.

Page 325

13.5.5.3 Monitoring

Add to text after sentence containing note 233:

Each of the big three consumer reporting agencies offers, for a substantial fee, a service that promises to alert a customer to changes to that customer's credit report that may indicate fraud.[233.1]

233.1   Equifax offers Credit Watch™; Experian, Credit Manager; and Trans Union, TrueCredit™. Among the services that can be purchased are daily e-mail alerts of activity, identity theft insurance, personal identity theft victim assistance, and access to an on-line dispute process. Annual fees range from $59 to $131. Given that these fraud-prevention procedures are available, one question that arises is whether it would be reasonable for agencies to use them to assure maximum possible accuracy, required by the FCRA without charge to the consumer. See § 7.8.4, *supra*.

13.5.5.4 Filing Suit

Addition to note 237.

237   See § 3.14, *supra*.

Add to text after sentence containing note 239:

- A claim against a government agency that may have violated privacy laws by providing information to a thief.[239.1]

A creditor who posts a thief's delinquencies to the victim's credit record may be liable for failing to use due care in opening the account. By extending credit or providing goods or services to the thief without properly verifying the thief's identity, the creditor facilitates the conduct that leads to catastrophic consequences to the victim's credit record. This extension necessarily occurs well before the responsibilities imposed on furnishers by section 1681s-2 arise, and therefore an action based on it will not be preempted by section 1681t.[239.2] Several courts have held that credit card issuers have a duty to ensure that card applicants are who they say they are.[239.3] Counsel should carefully identify the precise duty the creditor owes to the victim, and use appropriate evidence to establish the breach of that duty. Victims generally cannot rely on the mere fact that the identity theft occurred to establish that the creditor breached a duty, and may instead need to put on expert testimony to substantiate the creditor's negligence. It has been held that an identity theft victim may not rely on the doctrine of *res ipsa loquitur* to establish that a credit card provider had failed to abide by a standard of care when it issued a card to a thief in the victim's name.[239.4] The court reasoned that the fraud could have occurred even had the provider strictly followed the verification procedures the plaintiff asserted would have been reasonable, therefore the doctrine did not apply.[239.5] The court further found that the plaintiff failed to show that the creditor had not acted in accordance with commercially reasonable practices. The creditor had the practice of verifying credit card applications by comparing the name, address and social security number on the application with information contained in credit reports.[239.6] Where, as in the plaintiff's case, the applicant's address differed from the address given by the applicant, the creditor would call the telephone number listed by the applicant to verify the application information.[239.7] Though it could perhaps be easily foreseen that an identity thief would in fact list his or her own telephone number and thereby be given the opportunity to explain away the discrepancy to the creditor, the court ruled against the victim because she failed to offer expert testimony about whether more thorough verification procedures would have been commercially reasonable.[239.8] That case followed the reasoning of an earlier identity theft case in which the plaintiff sued two credit card companies that had issued cards in his name to his ex-girlfriend, even though the applications were filled with wrong information.[239.9] That court, too, ruled against the use of *res ipsa loquitur*, and held that without expert testimony, the plaintiff simply could not show that the merchants had acted outside the duty of care.[239.10]

However, by offering convincing expert testimony a plaintiff may well succeed on a claim that a bank or creditor failed to act reasonably in ensuring that the person who opened an account was in fact the person they purported to be. For example, the Alabama Supreme Court overturned a summary judgment in favor of a bank on an identity theft victim's claim that the bank had breached its duty of care to her by allowing an impostor to open an account in her name and write $1500 worth of bad checks on it.[239.11] The plaintiff offered the affidavit of a bank security expert who testified that the bank clerk, who opened the account without requiring picture identification, without verifying the offered social security number, and without inquiring why the impostor's signature did not match that on the plaintiff's temporary—and pictureless—driver's license, did not comport with industry fraud-prevention standards.[239.12] As the incidence of identity theft increases, the degree of diligence and standard of care considered reasonable to counteract fraud should rise.

239.1   *See, e.g.*, Smith v. Illinois Sec. of State, 2003 WL 1908020 (N.D. Ill. Apr. 21, 2003) (denying defendant's motion to dismiss plaintiff's claim that defendant had violated the federal Driver's Privacy Protection Act by providing an identity thief with a false Illinois driver's license that bore the plaintiff's name, date of birth and Social Security Number).
239.2   Stafford v. Cross Country Bank, 262 F. Supp. 2d 776 (W.D. Ky. 2003). *See also* § 3.14.5, *supra*.
239.3   Patrick v. Union State Bank, 681 So. 2d 1364 (Ala. 1996); Lechmere Tire & Sales Co. v. Burwick, 277 N.E.2d 503, 507 (Mass. 1972) (credit card issuer has duty to use due care to ensure that the person using the card is its proper holder or authorized user); Bradshaw v. Mich. Natl. Bank, 197 N.W.2d 531, 531 (Mich. Ct. App. 1972) (affirming denial of motion for summary judgment).
239.4   Yelder v. Credit Bureau of Montgomery, L.L.C., 131 F. Supp. 2d 1275, 1285 (M.D. Ala. 2001).
239.5   *Id.* at 1285.
239.6   *Id.* at 1285–86.
239.7   *Id.*
239.8   *Id.* at 1286.
239.9   Beard v. Goodyear Tire & Rubber Co., 587 A.2d 195 (D.C. 1991).
239.10 *Id.* at 199–200. The plaintiff had not shown that any of the merchants had his credit report, which would

have illuminated the discrepancies in the applications, and since the discrepancies were not obvious on the face of the applications, the court ruled that the plaintiff failed to adequately counter the affidavits offered by the defendants that their verification practices met industry standard. *Id.*

239.11 Patrick v. Union State Bank, 681 So. 2d 1364 (Ala. 1996).

239.12 *Id.* at 1367.

13.6 Strategies for Improving a Blemished or Insufficient Credit Rating

Page 326

13.6.2 Ascertaining the Reasons for Denial of Credit

Replace note 254 with:

254 *See* § 5.4.5, *supra*; National Consumer Law Center, Credit Discrimination § 10.2.7 (3d ed. 2002 and Supp.).

13.6.4 Adding New Information About Existing or Prior Accounts

Page 329

13.6.4.5 Use of Spouse's Credit History

Replace notes 282, 283 with:

282 ECOA Reg. B, 12 C.F.R. § 202.3(a)(2)(ii). *See also* National Consumer Law Center, Credit Discrimination § 2.2.6.2 (3d ed. 2002 and Supp.) for a discussion of this exception.

283 ECOA Reg. B, 12 C.F.R. § 202.3(c)(2)(vii). *See also* National Consumer Law Center, Credit Discrimination § 2.2.6.3 (3d ed. 2002 and Supp.) for a discussion of this exception.

Addition to note 284.

284 *Replace last sentence of note with*: *See also* National Consumer Law Center, Credit Discrimination § 2.2.6.5 (3d ed. 2002 and Supp.) for a discussion of this exception.

Replace note 285 with:

285 ECOA Reg. B, 12 C.F.R. § 202.3(b)(2)(vii). *See also* National Consumer Law Center, Credit Discrimination § 2.2.6.6 (3d ed. 2002 and Supp.) for a discussion of this exception.

Page 331

13.6.5 Establishing New Credit Accounts

Add to text after subsection's third paragraph:

Third, when a consumer applies for credit, the potential creditor's inquiry will appear on the consumer's credit report. A large number of inquiries may reduce the consumer's credit score at least temporarily.

Page 332

Add to text at end of subsection:

But the consumer should avoid signing up for a large number of credit cards, as this may reduce the consumer's credit score.

Page 333

13.6.6 Negotiating Repayment Schedules or Catching Up on Loan Payments

Add to text at end of subsection:

The consumer might also want to consider moving credit card balances to cards with lower rates. Transferring balances so that no card has a balance above 50 percent of the available line of credit may also improve a credit score. However, the consumer should be careful of teaser rates. Many credit cards offer what looks to be a lower rate, but the rate goes up after an initial period, or the creditor reserves the right to raise it if the consumer is late on a payment or the consumer's credit rating declines. The consumer should also be aware that having a large number of credit cards in itself can reduce a credit score.

§ 13.6.9   *Fair Credit Reporting / 2004 Supplement*

Page 335

13.6.9 Filing Bankruptcy

Add to text after fourth sentence of subsection's fourth paragraph:

To obtain this benefit, the consumer should send the credit reporting agencies a copy of the time-stamped bankruptcy petition, the schedules of debts, and the discharge. If debts appear on the debtor's credit report that should have been discharged through the bankruptcy but were inadvertently omitted from the schedules, the debtor should consider reopening the bankruptcy to list the omitted debts.[322.1]

[322.1] See National Consumer Law Center, Consumer Bankruptcy Law and Practice § 14.4.3.3 (6th ed. 2000 and Supp.).

Replace second sentence of fifth paragraph with:

But others look at the fact that the consumer cannot receive a second chapter 7 (straight) bankruptcy discharge for another six years, and that fewer debts are now competing for the consumer's stream of income.

Add to text after sentence containing note 324:

It is important to make sure that the credit reporting agency has a copy of the debtor's bankruptcy papers, including the time-stamped petition, the schedules of debts, and the discharge, so that discharged debts do not continue to appear as current obligations.

13.7 Coping with a Blemished Credit Record

13.7.2 Home Mortgages

Page 339

13.7.2.1 Fannie Mae and Freddie Mac Standards

Add to text after sentence containing note 369:

It is important to make sure that the credit reporting agency has a copy of the debtor's bankruptcy papers, including the time-stamped petition, the schedules of debts, and the discharge, so that discharged debts do not continue to appear as current delinquencies.

Page 341

13.7.4 Utilities

Add to text after third sentence of subsection's fourth paragraph:

There is evidence of growing use of credit scores by utility companies as a means of determining whether to require deposits from customers.[383.1] In the absence of specific permission from the state utility commission, the use of credit scores or credit reports to deny or impose conditions on utility service may run afoul of the principle that a public utility provider has a common law duty to serve all members of the public within its service area.[383.2] The general rule is that utilities cannot deny service because of collateral matters.[383.3]

[383.1] See Ill. Admin. Code tit. 83, § 280.50(a) (allowing utility companies to require a deposit if applicant's credit score does not meet predetermined standard); Electric Utility Consultants, Inc., "Credit & Collections for Utilities" (brochure for conference May 5-6, 2003), *available at* www.euci.com/pdf/Credit.pdf. *See also* "Are Credit Scores Fair and Reliable When Assessing Risk for Utility Service Applicants?," published in "NCLC Energy & Utility Update." Vol. XX, No. 3 (Summer 2003).
[383.2] National Consumer Law Center, Access to Utility Service § 3.1 (2d ed. 2001 and Supp.).
[383.3] *Id.* § 3.2.

Page 345

Add new sections after § 13.7.9

13.7.10 Credit Counselors and Debt Consolidators

The credit counseling industry experienced tremendous growth during the 1990s. There were about two hundred agencies nationally in the early 1990s and more than 1000 by 2002.[397] Since 1994, 1215 credit counseling agencies have applied to the I.R.S. for §501(c)(3) tax-exempt status. Over 800 of these agencies applied between 2000 and 2003.[398] About nine million consumers in financial trouble have some contact with a credit counseling agency each year.[399] Based on the growing number of complaints about these agencies, many

114

consumers will not necessarily find desperately needed assistance, but may instead find themselves even deeper in debt or stuck with a secured consolidation loan.[400]

Initially, most credit counseling agencies were affiliated with the National Foundation for Credit Counseling (NFCC).[401] These agencies generally offered a variety of services. Their feature service, however, was debt management plans (DMPs). Through a DMP, a consumer sends the credit counseling agency a lump sum, which the agency then distributes to the consumer's creditors.

In contrast to credit counseling agencies that provide debt management services, most debt settlement and debt negotiation agencies are for-profit entities. The non-profit agencies that provide debt settlement services generally do not hold or escrow consumers' monthly payments. Instead, these agencies attempt to negotiate lump-sum pay-offs of a consumer's debts based on funds the consumer already has or can easily obtain.

A 2004 Federal Trade Commission action highlights many of the problems with debt settlement companies.[402] The FTC alleged that Briggs and Baker promised to negotiate reductions in unsecured debt by as much as 75 percent. Consumers who signed up were told to stop making payments to unsecured creditors because creditors would be more likely to settle if the consumer's account were sufficiently delinquent. The FTC raised violations of the federal FTC Act based on alleged misrepresentations and deceptive actions.[403]

There have been reports of problems with the NFCC agencies over the years. In particular, the agencies were accused of deceptive practices based on their failure to disclose that the vast majority of their funding came from creditors. Through this credit-based funding system, known as "Fair Share," creditors return back to the agencies a certain percentage of the funds disbursed to them.[404] In addition, there have been reports over the years that NFCC affiliates and other agencies have been reluctant to inform consumers of bankruptcy rights. Even prior to the huge growth in the industry, credit counseling agencies, both NFCC affiliates and others, have also been accused, among other problems, of failing to timely remit consumer payments to creditors and failing to disclose fees.[405]

These problems have increased in recent years, largely due to changes in the way the industry operates. Newcomers to the industry, including those agencies that are literally new to the field and older agencies that have begun to adopt the business strategies of the newer players, are more likely to offer services mainly by phone or Internet, to steer the vast majority of consumers into DMPs, to sell their services aggressively, and to charge high fees for service. Many are involved in a related industry, debt negotiation, which has also been the source of consumer complaints. Negotiation and settlement differ from DMPs mainly because the agencies do not send regular monthly payments to creditors. In fact, they encourage consumers to pay fees to the negotiation firm and not pay their creditors. These agencies generally maintain debtor funds in separate accounts, holding these funds until the agency believes it can settle the entire debt.

There are a number of possible remedies available to challenge problems with credit counseling. The closest statutory scheme at the federal level is the Credit Repair Organizations Act (CROA).[406] The CROA applies only to agencies that offer credit repair services. The definition is broad, encompassing any person who performs or offer to perform any service, for a fee or other valuable consideration, for the express or implied purpose of (i) improving any consumer's credit record, credit history, or credit rating or (ii) providing advice and assistance to any consumer with regard to any activity or service described above.[407] Many credit counseling agencies should fit this definition. However, a critical problem with the CROA and its state analogues[408] is that it does not apply to non-profit organizations.[409] Although the vast majority of agencies now charge at least some fees for service, nearly every organization in the industry operates as a non-profit. It may be possible to overcome this hurdle by arguing that a non-profit is a for-profit business in disguise either because it focuses entirely on selling DMPs or because of close connections to for-profit affiliates.[410] A key to improving regulation in this industry is for the I.R.S. and state regulators to aggressively enforce the standards for non-profit eligibility. There are promising signs that the I.R.S. is heading in this direction. First, in January 2003, the I.R.S. released a report signaling the agency's increased awareness of problems with credit counseling agencies.[411] Facing pressure throughout 2003, the I.R.S, along with the F.T.C. and state regulators, issued a rare joint announcement in October 2003 advising consumers to beware of problems with certain credit counseling organizations.[412] In the October advisory and subsequent statements, the I.R.S. discusses the standards it uses, or will use, to determine tax-exempt status for credit counseling agencies. Specifically, the agency stated that organizations that only offer debt management plans without significant education and counseling should not qualify for tax-exempt status.[413] The Federal Trade Commission and a number of state attorney general offices have begun pursuing credit counseling agencies more aggressively, often raising claims related to abuses of non-profit status.[414]

Many state laws specifically prohibit the business of debt pooling (also known as debt management plans, debt consolidation, budget planning, or debt prorating). With notable exceptions, these state laws are generally ineffective and/or under-enforced. The majority do not specifically provide for private enforcement. In fact, many of the laws are contained in the state criminal codes. Where no specific private remedy is provided, violations should be UDAP violations.[415] States have stepped up enforcement throughout 2003 and 2004. The state actions generally raise UDAP claims and in some cases claims based on violations of federal and state telemarketing laws or state debt management laws.[416] Some agencies have argued that they are subject to regulation only in the state in which they are incorporated. For example, in response to a request from a Kansas district attorney that it cease services in the state of Kansas, Cambridge Credit Counseling Corporation claimed that it is only subject to the laws in Massachusetts, its state of incorporation.[417] Although Cambridge Credit Counseling Corporation has customers throughout the country, including Kansas, it argued that prosecution under state laws deprives it of its rights under the Commerce Clause. The agency also argued that the Kansas debt management law is invalid because of the burden imposed on interstate business. Cambridge Credit Counseling Corporation filed a declaratory action in federal court arguing that Kansas' law was unconstitutional. The federal district court rejected these arguments, allowing the district attorney to proceed with her request that Cambridge cease doing business in the state.[418]

The state laws vary in scope. About half of the states require some type of licensing for agencies providing debt management services.[419] But nearly half of these states explicitly exempt most non-profits from the licensing requirements. A minority of states restrict debt management business in the state to non-profits and require these non-profits to be licensed.

The stronger state laws provide regulation beyond licensing and/or regulation. The most common substantive regulations include fee limits, requirements that consumers be given written contracts and that agencies maintain consumer payments in separate trust accounts. In addition, most of the states that require licenses also require agencies to post bonds.

With only a few exceptions, most of the states that have licensing requirements also limit the fees that licensed agencies are allowed to charge. Fee limits vary from state to state. Some states set very specific amounts for start-up and monthly fees. Arizona, for example, sets a ceiling of $39 for retainers and a monthly limit of three-quarters of 1 percent of the consumer's total indebtedness or $50, whichever is less.[420] Certain out-of-pocket expenses may also be charged with debtor approval.[421] California caps fees for enrollment (a one-time fee) at no more than $50 for education and counseling combined in connection with debt management or debt settlement services and a monthly sum not to exceed 6.5 percent of the money disbursed each month, or $20, whichever is less.[422] Other states use percentage limits for monthly fees, based on the level of the consumer's indebtedness (compared to income) or of the total amount of the monthly DMP payment. The percentages allowed are as high as 12 percent or 15 percent in some states. In other states, a maximum dollar cap is used.[423] At least a few states simply limit fees to bona fide and reasonable costs.[424] However, it is more common for states to use the more general standard when regulating fees for counseling and education and to set specific limits when regulating fees for debt management plans.

About twenty states take a different, generally less restrictive, approach. Most of these states generally prohibit debt adjusting, but allow a long list of exceptions. Most important, nearly all of the states exempt non-profit organizations from the general prohibition. Other states do not require licensing, but still limit fees agencies can charge and/or other practices.[425]

In addition to these specific debt management laws, advocates should also consider state credit repair laws and UDAP laws as discussed above. A Massachusetts court found that a debt consolidated service violated the state UDAP statute by promising to stop all bill collectors' calls, when actually some creditors would not agree to the plan but would continue to look to the debtor for money. Furthermore, the debt consolidation service promised to stop interest from accruing but the service charged such large fees that the debtor's payments were often increased. By leading the consumers to believe that creditors would agree to the plan, the debt consolidation service took unfair advantage of consumers and charged large up-front fees.[426] The court also held that it was a UDAP violation not to disclose: an initial 60-day delay in forwarding payments to creditors; the fact that certain creditors would not agree to debt pooling arrangements; the penalties for missed payments and termination; the total number of payments; and the total of fees. Unauthorized practice of law statutes and regulations[427] and state loan broker laws[428] may also apply.

13.8 Credit Issues for Immigrants

Immigrants have unique issues relating to credit and credit histories, which include a lack of credit history and insufficient documentation as to their identities, especially for undocumented immigrants. Many immigrants also are "unbanked," and tend not to have relationships with financial institutions like banks and other lenders, preferring instead to transact their business in cash rather than using credit cards or obtaining loans or lines of credit.

Lack of sufficient identification is a major impediment for immigrants to open up a deposit account and begin to have access to other services associated with banking, including loans. There are a few steps immigrants can take to address the problem of lack of identification. For undocumented immigrants, they can obtain an Individual Taxpayer Identification Number (ITIN).[429] An ITIN is number issued by the Internal Revenue Service for tax purposes for those who cannot obtain a Social Security Number. It consists of a 9-digit number, beginning with the number "9." At least one credit reporting agency (Experian) has stated that it accepts ITINs.[430] The IRS revised its application procedures for new ITINs. Applicants must use a revised Form W-7, Individual Taxpayer Identification Number Application. ITIN applicants also must provide proof that the ITIN will be used for tax administration purposes.[431] For applicants seeking an ITIN in order to file a tax return, the return must be filed along with the W-7. This change, effective December 17, 2003, was reportedly done because ITINs were not being used for tax purposes. The IRS issued letters to Governors and state motor vehicle departments advising them that ITINs were not to be used for identification purposes.[432] It is unclear what effect the IRS's change in procedures will have on immigrants and their ability to access financial services.

For immigrants from Mexico, the Mexican government has offered a form of identification called a *matriculas consulares*. Many banks, cities, counties and law local law enforcement agencies are accepting the *matriculas* for identification purposes. Under Treasury Department regulations recently promulgated pursuant to the USA PATRIOT Act, banks are permitted to accept *matriculas* for customer identification purposes.[433] This particular provision was controversial and the Treasury Department reopened comment on it in 2003.[434] However, the Treasury Department left the rule unchanged and banks may still use the *matriculas* for purposes of identification.

Immigrants can also rely on family members or friends who are legal residents or citizens and open joint accounts, using the joint account holder's Social Security Number. There are risks associated with this practice and immigrant consumers should be advised to choose a joint account holder they can trust.

Finally, some banks have offered secured credit cards to undocumented consumers to establish credit. Use of such cards comes with significant risks and costs, including

§ 13.8 *Fair Credit Reporting / 2004 Supplement*

application and processing fees, plus interest rates that often are higher than those associated with unsecured credit cards. This is not a recommended means of establishing credit, for immigrants or anyone else.

397   *See* Jennifer Barrett, *Debt Consolidation: Beware Big Fees and Big Promises*, Newsweek On-line, January 3, 2002; National Foundation for Credit Counseling, *Fact Sheet and Industry Background* (June 2003), *available on-line at* www.nfcc.org.

398   U.S. Senate Permanent Subcommittee on Investigations, Committee on Governmental Affairs, *Profiteering in a Non-Profit Industry: Abusive Practices in Credit Counseling* (Mar. 24, 2004), *available at* http://govt-aff.senate.gov/_files/032404psistaffreport_creditcounsel.pdf (last visited in March 2004).

399   Christopher H. Schmitt with Health Timmons and John Cady, *A Debt Trap for the Unwary*, Business Week, Oct. 29, 2001. In a 2002 Fact Sheet, the National Foundation for Credit Counseling stated that 1.5 million households contacted NFCC members in 2001 and that one million of those households received counseling.

400   *See generally* National Consumer Law Center and Consumer Federation of America, *Credit Counseling in Crisis*, April 2003. Available at www.nclc.org.

401   The Foundation (NFCC) was formerly known as the National Foundation for Consumer Credit.

402   FTC v. Innovative Sys. Tech., Inc., dba Briggs & Baker, CVO 4-0728 (C.D. Cal. complaint filed 2/4/04). On the same day the complaint was filed, a stipulated final judgment and order for permanent injunction was filed against defendant Jack Briggs. Both documents are available on the FTC web site, www.ftc.gov.

403   *Id.*

404   As a result of a settlement with the FTC in 1999, NFCC now includes in its best practices standards that member agencies must disclose this possible conflict. *See* Stephen Gardner, *Consumer Credit Counseling Services: The Need for Reform and Some Proposals for Change*, Advancing the Consumer Interest vol. 13 Fall 2001/Winter 2002. Fair Share issues are discussed in detail in the NCLC/CFA report, *Credit Counseling in Crisis*, supra note 399.

405   *See, e.g.*, FTC v. Credit-Care, Inc., 5 Trade Reg. Rep. (CCH). 23,296 (N.D. Ill. 1992) (consent decree) (alleging that Credi-Care kept a significant portion of consumer payments, assessed unfair fees, processed payments so slowly that most accounts became delinquent, and stopped payments on drafts sent to creditors when consumers tried to cancel the agreement); Commonwealth v. Legal Credit Counselors, Inc., Clearinghouse No. 41, 271 (Mass Super. Ct. 1983) (alleging that the agency took unfair advantage of persons in debt, enticing them into believing that creditors would agree to debt pooling arrangements, when many creditors would never agree, and then collecting large up-front fees as well as fees if the debtors was terminated from the services).

406   15 U.S.C. §§ 1679–1679j. *See* Ch. 15, *infra*.

407   15 U.S.C. § 1679a(3)(A).

408   *See* Ch. 15, *infra* (discussion of state credit repair organization laws).

409   15 U.S.C. § 1679a(3)(B)(i).

410   For example, a class action lawsuit against Cambridge Credit Counseling is based primarily on alleged violations of the federal CROA. *See* Zimmerman v. Cambridge Credit Counseling Corp. *et al*, Civ. Action 3:03-cv-30261-MAP, Clearinghouse # 55455 (D. Mass. filed Nov. 4, 2003). *See also* Plascek v. Debticated *et al*, Case No. 2:03cv 00730 (C.D. Cal. filed Jan. 31, 2003); Plattner v. Edge Solutions, Inc., 2003 WL 22859532 (N.D. Ill. Dec. 2, 2003) (in case challenging debt counseling and credit repair services, court found "who decides" clause in arbitration agreement to be unconscionable and stayed proceedings pending an action to compel arbitration in Illinois).

411   Debra Cowen and Debra Kawecki, *Credit Counseling Organizations*, CPE 2004-1 (Jan. 9, 2003), *available at* www.irs.gov/pub/irs-tege/eotopica04.pdf (last visited in March 2004).

412   FTC, IRS and State Regulators Urge Care When Seeking Help from Credit Counseling Organizations (Oct. 13, 2003), *available at* www.irs.gov/newsroom/article/0,,id=114574,00.html (last visited in March 2004).

413   *Id. See also IRS Takes Steps to Ensure Credit Counseling Organizations Comply with Requirements for Tax-Exempt Status* FS-2003-17 (Oct. 2003), *available at* www.irs.gov/newsroom/article/0,,id=114575,00.html (last visited in March 2004). Testifying in Congress in March 2004, I.R.S. Commissioner Mark Everson stated that his agency is examining the tax-exempt status of more than fifty credit counseling organizations. Senate Committee on Governmental Affairs, Profiteering in a Non-Profit Industry: Abusive Practices in Credit Counseling (Mar. 24, 2004) (statement of the Honorable Mark W. Everson), *available at* http://govt-aff.senate.gov/index.cfm?Fuseaction=Hearings.Testimony&HearingID=158&WitnessID=492.

414   *See* Fed. Trade Comm'n v. AmeriDebt Inc., DebtWorks, Inc., Andris Pukke and Pamela Pukke (D. Md. filed Nov. 19, 2003). The complaint is available at www.ftc.gov/os/caselist/0223171/031119compameridebt.pdf; Fed. Trade Comm'n v. Ballenger Group, L.L.C., and Ballenger Holdings, L.L.C. (D. Md. Filed Nov. 19, 2003). The complaint is available at www.ftc.gov/os/caselist/0223171/031119compballenger.pdf and the Stipulated Final Judgment at www.ftc.gov/os/caselist/0223171/031119stipballengerimage.pdf. A number of state Attorney General offices preceded the FTC in filing suit against AmeriDebt. The Illinois Attorney General's office was the first to sue AmeriDebt, in February 2003, followed by Missouri, Minnesota, and Texas. For a press release describing the Illinois suit filed on February 5, 2003, see www.ag.state.il.us/pressrelease/020503_b.htm; Mo. v. AmeriDebt Inc., Debticated Inc., *available at* http://ago.missouri.gov/lawsuits/2003/091103ameridebt.pdf (filed Sept. 11, 2003). The

Minnesota and Texas cases were filed on November 19, 2003. *See also* Commonwealth of Mass. v. Integrated Credit Solutions, Inc. and Flagship Capital Servs. Corp., Case No.: 1:02-cv-12431-JLT, Clearinghouse No. 55549 (D. Mass. filed Dec. 29, 2002).

415 As with the CROA and state credit repair laws, there may be issues in some states regarding whether the UDAP law applies to non-profit organizations. *See* National Consumer Law Center, Unfair and Deceptive Acts and Practices § 2.3.5 (5th ed. 2001 and Supp.).

416 A number of state Attorney General offices preceded the FTC in filing suit against AmeriDebt. The Illinois Attorney General's office was the first to sue AmeriDebt, in February 2003, followed by Missouri, Minnesota, and Texas. For a press release describing the Illinois suit filed on February 5, 2003, see www.ag.state.il.us/pressrelease/020503_b.htm; Mo. v. AmeriDebt Inc., Debticated Inc., *available at* http://ago.missouri.gov/lawsuits/2003/091103ameridebt.pdf (filed Sept. 11, 2003). The Minnesota and Texas cases were filed on November 19, 2003. *See also* Commonwealth of Mass. v. Integrated Credit Solutions, Inc. and Flagship Capital Services Corp., Case No.: 1:02-cv-12431-JLT, Clearinghouse No. 55549 (D. Mass. filed Dec. 29, 2002); Cambridge Credit Counseling Corp. v. Foulston, 2003 WL 23279978 (D. Kan. Sept. 25, 2003).

417 Cambridge Credit Counseling Corp. v. Foulston, 2003 WL 23279978 (D. Kan. Sept. 25, 2003).

418 *Id.* Cambridge Credit Counseling Corporation is appealing the district court decision. In addition, the Kansas legislature is considering more comprehensive regulation of debt management agencies. This legislation had not yet passed at the time this manual was written. See S.B. #509, introduced in the Kansas legislature on Feburary 11, 2004.

419 Some of the states listed below explicitly exempt non-profits from licensing or registration requirements. Others implicitly exempt at least some non-profit organizations by defining the practice or debt management to include only those organizations that charge fees or receive consideration for services. Thus, the minority of credit counseling agencies that do not charge fees for service are arguably not required to obtain licenses in these states:

Arizona: Ariz. Rev. Stat. §6-702-716. (exemption from licensing applies to non-profit agencies that do not collect any compensation directly or indirectly. Also requires bonding).

California: Cal. Fin. Code § 12100 *et seq.* (non-profit agencies exempted from licensing, but only if they abide by fee limits and other substantive provisions).

Connecticut: Conn. Gen. Stat. §36a-655-665 (only non-profits can engage in debt adjusting and must be licensed).

Idaho: Idaho Code §26-2223 (no exemptions for non-profits).

Illinois: 205 Ill. Comp. Stat. Ann. § 665/2 *et seq.* (non-profits that do not charge implicitly exempted from licensing).

Indiana: Ind. Code § 28-1-29-12 (non-profits explicitly exempted from licensing if they do not charge fees).

Iowa: Iowa Code § 533A.1 *et seq.* (certain non-profits offering free debt management services exempt from licensing, also implicitly exempted if they do not charge).

Louisiana: Louisiana has two laws governing debt adjusting that contradict each other. One law generally prohibits for-profit debt adjusting, but exempts non-profit organizations. La. Rev. Stat. Ann. § 14:331. A second law allows financial planning and management services, but requires the agencies to be licensed. Non-profits engaging in debt management services are exempted from the licensing requirement. La. Rev. Stat. Ann. § 37:2581.

Maine: Me. Rev. Stat. Ann. tit. 17 §701; Me. Rev. Stat. Ann. tit. 32, § 6172 *et seq.* (only non-profit agencies can operate in the state and must register with state, non-profits that do not charge implicitly exempted).

Maryland: Md. Fin. Inst. §12-901-12-931 (debt management service providers must be non-profit and must register with the state).

Michigan: Mich. Comp. Laws Ann. § 451.411 *et seq.* (certain non-profits may be exempt from licensing).

Minnesota: Minn. Stat. § 332.13 *et seq.* (non-profits that do not charge fees are explicitly exempt).

Mississippi: Miss. Code Ann. §81-22-1-81-22-29 (all debt management services providers must be licensed and only non-profits may apply for and receive licenses).

Nebraska: Neb. Rev. Stat. § 69-1201 *et seq.* (non-profits implicitly exempt).

Nevada: Nev. Rev. Stat. § 676.010 *et seq.* (exempts non-profits).

New Hampshire: N.H. Rev. Stat. Ann. § 399-D:15 (most non-profits exempt).

New Jersey: N.J. Stat. Ann. §§ 2C:21-19, 17:16G-1 (only non-profits can operate in the state and must be licensed).

New York: N.Y. Gen. Business Law. §455-457 (general prohibition of budget planning, but licensed non-profits and others including attorneys are exempted); N.Y. Banking Law §579-587 (budget planner licensing law).

Ohio: Ohio Rev. Code Ann. § 4710.01 *et seq.* (implicit exemption only).

Oregon: Or. Rev. Stat. § 697.602 *et seq.* (non-profits not exempted from registration).

Rhode Island: R.I. Gen. Law § 5-66-1 (only non-profits may operate in the state and must be licensed).

South Carolina: S.C. Code Ann. § 40-5-370 (only licensed attorneys may perform debt adjusting).

Vermont: Vt. Stat. Ann. tit. 8, § 4861 (certain non-profits exempted).

Virginia: Va. Code Ann. § 6.1-363.1 (only non-profits allowed and must have license). In 2004, the Virginia state assembly passed legislation that would significantly increase regulation of debt management service providers. *See* HB 471.

Wisconsin: Wis. Stat. § 218.02 (implicit exemption only).

Effective October 2003, Maryland has also passed a debt management law requiring, among other provisions, that credit counseling agencies must be licensed by the Commissioner of Financial Regulation. *See* Maryland S.B. 339, *amending* Md. Comm. Law § 14-1316.

420 Ariz. Rev. Stat. § 6-702 *et seq.*
421 *Id.*
422 Cal. Fin. Code §12104. The California legislature is likely to pass increases to these fee limits during the 2004 session. AB 403 was introduced in the California legislature on February 14, 2003.
423 For example, New Jersey sets a fee limit of no more than 1 percent of a consumer's monthly gross income but, in any case, no more than $15. Tennessee's limit is $20. N.J. Stat. Ann. §17:16G-5; Tenn. Code Ann. §39-14-142.
424 *See, e.g.*, Conn. Gen. Stat. § 36a-655 *et seq.;* Guam St. tit. 14 §7109; R.I. Gen. Laws §5-66-1 (limited to bona fide non-profits and costs must not exceed amounts required to defray bona fide expenses).
425 Ark. Code Ann. § 5-63-302; Colo. Rev. Stat. Ann. § 12-14-103 (debt collector law explicitly exempts non-profit credit counselors); Del. Code Ann. tit. 11, § 910; D.C. Code Ann. §22-1201; Fla. Stat. Ann. § 559.10; Ga. Code Ann. § 18-5-1; Guam St. tit. 14 §7101-7106; Haw. Rev. Stat. § 446-3; Kan. Stat. Ann. § 21-4402; Ky. Rev. Stat. § 380.010; Mass. Gen. Laws ch. 180, § 4A; Mo. Rev. Stat. § 425.010; Mont. Code Ann. § 31-3-201; N.M. Stat. Ann. § 56-2-1; N.C. Gen. Stat. § 14-423; N.D. Cent. Code §13-06-01 (definitions); 13-07-01-13-07-07; Okla. Stat. tit. 24, § 15; 18 Pa. Cons. Stat. § 7312; S.D. Codified Laws § 22-47-2; Tenn. Code Ann. § 39-14-142; Tex. Fin. Ann. Code § 394.101; Wash. Re. Code §18.28.010-18.28.9; W. Va. Code § 61-10-23; Wyo. Stat. Ann. § 33-14-101.
426 Commonwealth v. Legal Credit Counselors, Inc., Clearinghouse No. 41, 271 (Mass Super. Ct. 1983).
427 *See* National Consumer Law Center, Unfair and Deceptive Acts and Practices § 5.12.2.4 (5th ed. 2001 and Supp.).
428 See *Id.* § 5.1.11.1.
429 *See* National Consumer Law Center, *Guide to Consumer Rights For Immigrants* (2002). *See also* www.irs.gov/individuals/article/0,,id=96287,00.html.
430 *See* www.experian.com/ask_max/max031302b.html.
431 See www.irs.gov/newsroom/article/0,,id=112728,00.html.
432 *Id.*
433 68 Fed. Reg. 25,089 (May 9, 2003).
434 68 Fed. Reg. 39,039 (July 1, 2003).

Chapter 14 Credit Scoring

Page 347

14.1 Introduction

Replace last sentence in section's first paragraph with:

Despite their importance, until recently, the FCRA specifically exempted credit scores from disclosure. The Fair and Accurate Credit Transactions (FACT) Act of 2003 amended the FCRA to require disclosure of credit scores.[0.1]

0.1 See § 14.4.1, *infra*.

14.2 What Is Credit Scoring?

14.2.2 The Variations

Page 348

14.2.2.1 Credit Bureau Score

Replace sentences containing notes 13 and 14 with:

A borrower with a score of 660 or greater is generally considered to be less of a risk for the lender.[13] Many lenders are now differentiating by credit score within their prime categories, offering their best rates to consumers with scores over 720.[13.1] A score of 620 or lower is considered a poor risk.[13.2] According to Fair Isaac, the median score is 720, and about 80 percent of FICO scores are over 620.[14]

Fair Isaac has also developed a newer scoring model called "NextGen." NextGen scores range from 150–950.[14.1]

13   Freddie Mac, *Automated Underwriting: Making Mortgage Lending Simpler and Fairer for America's Families* 25 (Sept. 1996), *available at* www.freddiemac.com/corporate/reports/moseley/mosehome.htm.

13.1 For example, the Fair Isaac website lists sample mortgage rates, with the best rates requiring a credit score of 720 or higher. www.myfico.com. *See also* Cybele Weisser, Getting Behind the Numbers, Money Magazine, Nov. 1, 2003, at 157 (noting that a score of 620 is considered creditworthy, and a over 670 is excellent, but a score of 720 is required for the best rate). Lenders have shown a desire to more finely differentiate among consumers, and thus have created an increasing number of pricing points. Travis B. Plunkett, Consumer Federation of America, *Testimony Before the House Committee on Financial Services*, Subcommittee on Financial Institutions and Consumer Credit, June 12, 2003, at 4. For example, one advertisement for automobile financing required a FICO score of 775 for the best rate. Robert C. Mitchell, *Letter to FTC Chairman Timothy Muris and Federal Reserve Board Chair Alan Greenspan*, October 11, 2002, at 1.

13.2 Freddie Mac, *Automated Underwriting: Making Mortgage Lending Simpler and Fairer for America's Families* 25 (Sept. 1996), *available at* www.freddiemac.com/corporate/reports/moseley/mosehome.htm.

14   Fair Isaac, *How Do People Score*, available at www.myfico.com/MyFICO/CreditCentral/ScoringWorks/PeopleScore.htm; Eileen Ambrose, Getting Credit Nowadays Depends on Your Scorecard, Baltimore Sun, April 21, 2002 (quoting Fair Isaac spokesman that half of consumers score 720 or higher).

14.1 Nathalie Mainland and Julia Wooding, *NextGen FICO Risk Score Conversion FAQ*, Fair Isaac (Apr. 2002), at 2.

14.2.3 Definition of Credit Scoring in Regulation B

Replace section's first sentence with:

The Fair and Accurate Credit Transactions (FACT) Act of 2003 added a definition of "credit score" to the Fair Credit Reporting Act, which is different from the definition under Regulation B.[18.1] The FACTA defines a credit score as:

§ 14.3   *Fair Credit Reporting / 2004 Supplement*

> a numerical value or a categorization derived from a statistical tool or modeling system used by a person who makes or arranges a loan to predict the likelihood or certain credit behaviors, including default (and the numerical value or the categorization derived from such analysis may be referred to as a 'risk predictor' or 'risk score').[18.2]

The FACTA specifically excludes from the definition of "credit score" any score or rating from a mortgage automated underwriting system and any other elements of the underwriting process.[18.3]

18.1   FCRA, § 609(f)(1)(A), 15 U.S.C. 1681g(f)(1)(A), *added by* Pub. L. No. 108-159, § 212 (2003).
18.2   *Id.*
18.3   *Id.* See §§ 14.2.2.4, *supra,* and 14.5.3, *infra,* for a discussion of automated underwriting systems.

Page 349

Replace note 30 with:

30   *See* National Consumer Law Center, Credit Discrimination § 6.6.2 (3d ed. 2002 and Supp.).

Add text at end of subsection:

Furthermore, regulatory agencies may require a lender to meet Regulation B's requirements for credit scoring models.[30.1]

30.1   For example, the Office of the Comptroller of Currency has required the national banks that it regulates to ensure that the bank's scoring models meet the validation requirements of Regulation B's definition of credit scoring. Office of the Comptroller of the Currency, Credit Scoring Models (OCC Bull. 97-24, May 20, 1997).

14.3 Widespread Use of Credit Scores

Addition to note 33.

33   Kenneth Harney, A Clearer View Of Credit Scores, Washington Post, February 21, 2004, at F1. (Providian revealing that it obtains the credit scores of its customers on a monthly basis; National Credit Reporting Association stating that mortgage servicers regularly order credit scores on homeowners, often on a quarterly basis, for 30 to 40 cents per score).

Add note 34.1 to end of last sentence in section's second paragraph.

34.1   John Cook, *Credit Follows Us Everywhere,* Contra Costa Times, May 19, 2003, at 4.

Add to text at end of section's second paragraph:

Payday lenders use specialty scores to determine whether to grant a payday loan.[34.2] Scoring is also used to increase recovery rates from debt collection and to detect credit card fraud.[34.3]

The use of credit scores for non-credit related purposes has grown dramatically. In addition to insurance and employment, credit scores are being used to determine whether consumers must pay a deposit for utility service.[34.4] Probate judges are reviewing credit scores before allowing an individual to become an executor of a deceased's estate.[34.5] Credit scores are even being used by airlines to screen passengers and weed out potential terrorists.[34.6] Under the FCRA's standard of permissible use of credit reports for "a legitimate business need for the information in connection with a business transaction initiated by the consumer," there may be few limits on the use of credit scores for non-credit related consumer transactions.[34.7]

34.2   For example, Tele-Track offers an application scorecard for payday lenders that will analyze the likelihood of the borrower's check securing the loan becoming uncollectible. *See* Tele-Track, CheckScore, at www.teletrack.com/checkscore.html (viewed Oct. 2002). Interestingly, Tele-Track's website described scoring as "like one of those magazine surveys only instead of testing your luck with romance, it tests 'How Likely Are You to Write an Uncollectible Check?' " The use of specialty scores for payday lending is ironic, given that one of the selling points for these often abusive loans is the ability to obtain them despite a negative credit history.

34.3   Peter Lucas, *Why Recoveries Are on the Rise,* Credit Card Management, October 2000; Fair Isaac, *London Bridge Group and Fair Isaac Partnership Improves Debt Management and Recovery,* Press Release, May 5, 2003; Fair Isaac, *Fair Isaac Announces Next-Generation Fraud Management Solution,* Press Release, April 24, 2003. Debt collectors use credit scores to determine which borrowers to contact, how soon the borrower should be contacted in the month, what method of collection to use (phone versus letters) and how frequently to contact the borrower. Elizabeth Mays, *The Role of Credit Scores in Consumer Lending Today,* RMA Journal, October 1, 2003 (reprinting Chapter One of Elizabeth Mays, Credit Scoring for Risk Managers: The Handbook for Lenders (2004)).

34.4   Chris Pummer, *A Financial Strip-Search,* CBS Marketwatch, November 13, 2002. Fair, Isaac has

Credit Scoring / 2004 Supplement § 14.4.1

    developed a specialty credit score for telecommunication providers. Fair, Isaac, Scoring—Predictive Modeling—Telecom Scores, available at www.fairisaac.com/Fairisaac/Solutions/Product+Index/ Telecom+Models/ (last visited on March 2004).

34.5 Teresa Dixon Murray, *Knowing Score in the Credit Game*, Times-Picayune, June 1, 2002, at 1.

34.6 Donna Halvorsen, *For Some, Use of Credit Scores Doesn't Add Up*, Star Tribune (Minneapolis-St. Paul), March 13, 2003, at 1A.

34.7 15 U.S.C. § 1681(b)(a)(3)(F). *See generally* § 5.2.9, *supra*. The use of scoring, *i.e.*, using computer algorithms to evaluate data and produce a single number, has grown in general. In an ironic twist, institutional investors are using scores to rate corporations on their corporate governance. Monica Langley, *ISS Rates Firms—and Sells Roadmap to Boosting Score*, Wall Street Journal, June 6, 2003, at A1.

14.4 Disclosure to Consumers of Credit Score

14.4.1 Credit Scores Do Not Have to Be Disclosed Under the FCRA

Page 350

Add to text at end of subsection:

The Fair and Accurate Credit Transactions (FACT) Act of 2003,[37.1] amended the FCRA to require disclosure of credit scores, a provision that goes into effect on December 1, 2004.[37.2] Upon the request of a consumer, the FACTA requires credit bureaus to disclose the following:

- The current credit score of the consumer or most recent credit score that was previously calculated by the credit reporting agency related to the extension of credit.[37.3] The score must either (a) be generated using a scoring model that is widely distributed to users by the credit reporting agency or (b) assist the consumer in understanding the assessment by the credit scoring model of his or her credit behavior and predications about that behavior.[37.4]
- A statement indicating that the information and credit scoring model may be different than the credit score used by a lender.[37.5]
- The range of credit scores of the model used to generate the disclosed credit score.[37.6]
- The key factors that adversely affected the credit score of the consumer,[37.7] listed in order of impact.[37.8] The credit reporting agency cannot provide more than 4 key factors,[37.9] unless one of the factors is the number of "enquiries," in which case that factor must be included notwithstanding the 4 factor limit.[37.10]
- The date on which the credit score was created.[37.11]
- The name of the provider of the credit score or the credit file used to generate the score.[37.12]

The credit reporting agency may charge a fee for the credit score, to be determined by the Federal Trade Commission.[37.13] When consumers request their credit files, but not their credit scores, the FACTA also requires the CRA's to disclose the fact that the consumer has the right to obtain their credit score.[37.14]

Credit bureaus are not required to develop or disclose the score if the bureau does not distribute scores that are used in connection with residential real property loans or does not develop scores that assist credit providers in understanding the general credit behavior of a consumer and predicting the future behavior of the consumer.[37.15] These FACTA requirements are not to be construed to require credit bureaus to maintain credit scores in their files.[37.16]

In addition, the FACTA requires mortgage lenders who use credit scores in connection with an application for residential real-estate secured credit to provide, free of charge, the credit score and accompanying information that is either obtained from a credit bureau or was developed and used by the lender.[37.17] If the lender uses an automated underwriting system that does not provide a numerical score, the disclosure of the credit bureau score and associated key factors is sufficient.[37.18] However, if the automated underwriting system generates a numerical score, the lender may disclose that numerical score or a credit bureau

§ 14.4.2   *Fair Credit Reporting / 2004 Supplement*

score and associated key factors.[37.19] Mortgage lenders must also give a prescribed notice to the consumers.[37.20]

Finally, state laws regarding disclosure of credit scores are preempted, except for several existing state laws that are grandfathered in.[37.21]

37.1 Pub. L. No. 108-159 (2003).
37.2 16 C.F.R. § 602.1(c)(3)(x), *added by* 69 Fed. Reg. 6526–31 (Feb. 5, 2004).
37.3 FCRA, § 609(f)(1)(A), 15 U.S.C. 1681g(f)(1)(A), *added by* Pub. L. No. 108-159, § 212 (2003).
37.4 FCRA, § 609(f)(7)(A), 15 U.S.C. 1681g(f)(7)(A), *added by* Pub. L. No. 108-159, § 212 (2003).
37.5 FCRA, § 609(f)(1), 15 U.S.C. 1681g(f)(1), *added by* Pub. L. No. 108-159, § 212 (2003).
37.6 FCRA, § 609(f)(1)(B), 15 U.S.C. 1681g(f)(1)(B), *added by* Pub. L. No. 108-159, § 212 (2003).
37.7 FCRA, § 609(f)(1)(C), 15 U.S.C. 1681g(f)(1)(C), *added by* Pub. L. No. 108-159, § 212 (2003). For credit scores provided using Fair, Isaac scoring models, the key factors are probably the "reason codes" provided by FICO. *See* § 14.4.2, *infra*, for a discussion of reason codes.
37.8 FCRA, § 609(f)(2)(B), 15 U.S.C. 1681g(f)(2)(B), *added by* Pub. L. No. 108-159, § 212 (2003).
37.9 FCRA, § 609(f)(1)(C), 15 U.S.C. 1681g(f)(1)(C), *added by* Pub. L. No. 108-159, § 212 (2003).
37.10 FCRA, § 609(f)(9), 15 U.S.C. 1681g(f)(9), *added by* Pub. L. No. 108-159, § 212 (2003).
37.11 FCRA, § 609(f)(1)(D), 15 U.S.C. 1681g(f)(1)(D), *added by* Pub. L. No. 108-159, § 212 (2003).
37.12 FCRA, § 609(f)(1)(E), 15 U.S.C. 1681g(f)(1)(E), *added by* Pub. L. No. 108-159, § 212 (2003).
37.13 FCRA, § 609(f)(8), 15 U.S.C. 1681g(f)(8), *added by* Pub. L. No. 108-159, § 212 (2003).
37.14 FCRA, § 609(a)(6), 15 U.S.C. § 1681g(a)(6), *added by* Pub. L. No. 108-159, § 212 (2003). In addition, the Summary of Rights also must include a provision stating that the consumer has the right to obtain a credit score from a CRA and a description of how to obtain the score. FCRA, § 609 (c)(1)(B)(iv), 15 U.S.C. § 1681g(c)(1)(B)(iv), *added by* Pub. L. No. 108-159, § 211 (2003).
37.15 FCRA, § 609(f)(4), 15 U.S.C. 1681g(f)(4), *added by* Pub. L. No. 108-159, § 212 (2003).
37.16 FCRA, § 609(f)(6), 15 U.S.C. 1681g(f)(6), *added by* Pub. L. No. 108-159, § 212 (2003).
37.17 FCRA, § 609(g)(1)(A), 15 U.S.C. 1681g(g)(1)(A), *added by* Pub. L. No. 108-159, § 212 (2003) (requiring disclosure of the same information identified in FCRA, § 609(f), *i.e.*, the information described in the bullet list in this section).
37.18 FCRA, § 609(g)(1)(B)(i), 15 U.S.C. 1681g(g)(1)(B)(i), *added by* Pub. L. No. 108-159, § 212 (2003). See §§ 14.2.2.4, *supra*, and 14.5.3., *infra*, for a discussion of automated underwriting systems.
37.19 FCRA, § 609(g)(1)(B)(ii), 15 U.S.C. 1681g(g)(1)(B)(ii), *added by* Pub. L. No. 108-159, § 212 (2003).
37.20 FCRA, § 609(g)(1)(D), 15 U.S.C. 1681g(g)(1)(D), *added by* Pub. L. No. 108-159, § 212 (2003).
37.21 FCRA, § 625(b)(3), 15 U.S.C. 1681t(b)(3), *as amended by* Pub. L. No. 108-159, § 212 (2003).

14.4.2 Recent Availability of Credit Scores

Replace subsection's first bulleted item with:

- Fair, Isaac offers a number of different FICO score products to consumers. Consumers can purchase a copy of their FICO score based upon either their Equifax, Experian or Trans Union file.[40] Each FICO score currently costs $12.95 and includes a copy of the consumer's report from the repository upon which the score is based. Consumers can also get a three bureau consolidated credit report from the myfico.com website for $39.95, with a copy of their FICO score based upon their Trans Union file. As part of each product, consumers receive charts, details, and a list of the main reasons that determined their score.[41] Fair, Isaac also offers an array of other products, such as a product for homebuyers that provides an on-line "coach."

40 Fair Isaac states that it has sold over 2.5 million credit score products since it began providing them to consumers in March 2001. *In Brief: Prizes, Tips from Fair Isaac*, American Banker, April 22, 2003, at 9. It appears that FICO only accepts major credit or debit cards as a form of payment, which may present a practical barrier to consumers with low FICO scores who do not qualify for a credit or debit card. Fair Isaac, myFICO Questions, www.myfico.com/myFICO/FAQ/General.asp#Q62 (last viewed June 25, 2003). It also appears that consumers without Internet access will have difficulty obtaining their FICO scores.

41 Fair Isaac has a list of over 100 reasons and accompanying "reason codes" that are given to explain an applicant's credit scores. Fair Isaac, *Fair Isaac US Credit Bureau Risk Score Reason Codes*, May 2000. These reason codes may be used by lenders when preparing adverse action notices pursuant to § 615(a) of the FCRA, 15 U.S.C. § 1681m(a), as well as the Equal Credit Opportunity Act. Fair Isaac, *Understanding Your Credit Score* (July 2002), at 15. *See generally*, § 6.4, *supra*.

A recent study of 591 consumer credit files with credit scores around the cut-off for prime credit, or with scores that ranged over 50 points apart, found that a mere four reasons codes were used in 82 percent of the time as the primary contributing reason for the credit score. Three of these four codes involved either a serious delinquency, a derogatory public record, or collection action. These three reasons accounted for 67 percent of all primary reasons provided. Consumer Federation of America and National Credit

Credit Scoring / 2004 Supplement § 14.5.2.1

Reporting Association, *Credit Score Accuracy and Implications for Consumers*, December 17, 2002, at 22–23, *available at* www.consumerfed.org/121702CFA_NCRA_Credit_Score_Report_Final.pdf (last visited March 2003). The CFA/NCRA study noted that these reason codes might be too general to help a consumer seeking to improve a credit score. The codes do not provide information on which specific accounts are responsible for a low score, or sometimes even whether it was a delinquency versus a collection action that was responsible for the score. *Id.* at 40.

Add to text after sentence containing note 43:

An examination of over 500,000 consumer credit files found that 29 percent of consumers have credit scores that differ by at least 50 points between credit bureaus, while 4 percent have scores that differ by at least 100 points.[43.1] Furthermore, the median spread between the high score and low score for these consumer credit files was 35 points.[43.2]

    43.1   Consumer Federation of America and National Credit Reporting Association, *Credit Score Accuracy and Implications for Consumers*, December 17, 2002, at 24, *available at* www.consumerfed.org/121702CFA_NCRA_Credit_Score_Report_Final.pdf (last visited March 2003).

    43.2   *Id.*

Add to text at end of subsection's third paragraph:

To add even more variation, a consumer's credit score will also differ depending on whether a Classic FICO scoring model or a NextGen model is used.[43.3] In response to criticisms over variations in consumers' credit scores, Fair, Isaac had stated that its scoring models were developed to be predictive despite significant data variations at each credit bureau.[43.4]

    43.3   Nathalie Mainland and Julia Wooding, *NextGen FICO Risk Score Conversion FAQ*, Fair Isaac (April 2002), at 6.

    43.4   Cheri St. John, *Statement of Fair Isaac Before the U.S. House of Representatives, Committee on Financial Services*, June 4, 2003, at Attachment 5 (A Clarification of the Consumer Federation of America's Observations about Credit Score Accuracy).

14.5 How a Credit Score Is Calculated

Page 351

14.5.1 The Black Box

Add note 50.1 to end of subsection's last sentence.

    50.1   *See* § 14.9.1, *infra*.

14.5.2 How Fair, Isaac Scores Are Developed

14.5.2.1 Fair, Isaac's Scoring Factors

Replace last three sentences in subsection's first bulleted item with:

Some advocates have expressed concern that this factor hurts low- and moderate-income consumers more, because they have fewer credit accounts, so one late payment could have a disproportionate impact.[53.1] On the other hand, high-scoring consumers may also experience severe adverse effects from a single late payment, because it may lower a high FICO score by about 100 points.[54]

    53.1   One study has noted that an item of derogatory information has a greater impact on "thin" files. Consumer Federation of America and National Credit Reporting Association, *Credit Score Accuracy and Implications for Consumers*, December 17, 2002, at 27, *available at* www.consumerfed.org/121702CFA_NCRA_Credit_Score_Report_Final.pdf (last visited March 2003).

    54   Jay Romano, *Repairing Credit Problems*, New York Times, April 21, 2002, Section 11, at 5. Use of the FICO Score Simulator supports this theory. Supposedly, Fair Isaac's NextGen scoring systems is less drastic with this situation, giving higher scores to consumers who have just one or a few late payments. On the other hand, NextGen gives lower scores to consumers with more serious adverse events, such as collections, charge-offs, and bankruptcies. Nathalie Mainland and Julia Wooding, *NextGen FICO Risk Score Conversion FAQ*, Fair Isaac (April 2002), at 5.

Add to subsection's first bulleted item:

The larger the late or missed payment, the greater the adverse impact on a FICO score.[54.1] Another issue appears to be small dollar amount delinquencies that are sent to collections or appear in public records, such as parking tickets, video rental fees, and library fines, which depress a consumer's credit score. Fair, Isaac's latest version of NextGen supposedly reduces the impact of these items by ignoring any collections or public record items under $100.[54.2]

125

§ 14.5.4   *Fair Credit Reporting / 2004 Supplement*

    54.1   Cybele Weisser, *Getting Behind the Numbers*, Money Magazine, Nov. 1, 2003, at 157.
    54.2   Fair, Isaac, NextGen FICO Score Version 2.0, May 2003.

Add to subsection's second bulleted item:

According to Fair, Isaac, 54 percent of consumers carry less than $5000 of debt (excluding mortgage loans) and 48 percent of credit card holders have a balance of less than $1000.[55.1] The typical consumer has access to $12,190 in credit card available credit.[55.2] Revolving credit, *i.e.*, credit cards, appear to given more weight in the "amount owed" category than installment loans.[55.3] If consumers do not utilize their credit cards at all, they may score lower.[55.4] Interestingly, scoring models appear to treat a home equity line of credit differently depending on the amount withdrawn. A sizable withdrawal is treats as an installment loan, while a small withdrawal is treated as revolving credit.[55.5]

    55.1   Fair Isaac, *Average Credit Statistics*, available at www.myfico.com/myFICO/CreditCentral/AverageUse.asp (last viewed June 2003).
    55.2   *Id.*
    55.3   Cybele Weisser, *Getting Behind the Numbers*, Money Magazine, Nov. 1, 2003, at 157.
    55.4   Sandra Block, *Credit Report Worth A Look*, USA Today, August 29, 2003, at B3.
    55.5   Cybele Weisser, *Getting Behind the Numbers*, Money Magazine, Nov. 1, 2003, at 157.

Add to subsection's third bulleted item:

According to Fair, Isaac, the average consumer's oldest account is 13 years old.[56.1]

    56.1   Fair Isaac, *Average Credit Statistics*, available at www.myfico.com/myFICO/CreditCentral/AverageUse.asp (last viewed June 17, 2003).

Page 352

Add to subsection's fourth bulleted item:

According to Fair, Isaac, the average consumer has only about one inquiry within the past year.[58.1]

    58.1   Fair Isaac, *Average Credit Statistics*, available at www.myfico.com/myFICO/CreditCentral/AverageUse.asp (last viewed June 17, 2003).

Add to subsection's fifth bulleted item:

Given that a good mix of credit may be one that includes a mortgage loan, one question is whether FICO's scoring models explicitly give more points to mortgage holders.[58.2] This would mean that FICO's scoring models favor homeowners over renters.

    58.2   Cybele Weisser, *Getting Behind the Numbers*, Money Magazine, Nov. 1, 2003, at 157 (Noting that lenders prefer that a credit history include a mix of credit, such as student loans, a mortgage and credit cards; however, also quoting Fair, Isaac's spokesperson claiming that a "clean track record" on two credit cards is just as good as having several installment loans and a mortgage).

Add to text at end of subsection:

Fair, Isaac's latest version of NextGen supposedly has more liberal criteria for generating a credit score, permitting files with one tradeline to be scored if there is any activity within the past twelve months.[59.1]

    59.1   Fair, Isaac, NextGen FICO Score Version 2.0, May 2003.

Page 353

14.5.4 Ideas on How to Peek into the Black Box

Addition to note 66.

    66   *Replace NCLC citation with: See* National Consumer Law Center, Credit Discrimination § 6.4.2.4 (3d ed. 2002 and Supp.).

14.6 How Consumers Can Improve Their Credit Scores

14.6.1 Industry's Advice

Add note 67.1 to end of subsection's fourth bulleted item.

    67.1   There appears to be some question as to this advice. Contrary to Fair Isaac, both Trans Union and Equifax recommend closing unused accounts. *See* Kevin Beumel, *Trans Union Consumer Credit Overview*, May 23, 2003, at 17; Equifax, *Boosting Your Credit Score*, available at www.econsumer.equifax.com/consumer/forward.ehtml?forward=improving_yourcredit_boosting_score; Helen Huntley, *Making Your Credit Score Soar*, St. Petersburg Times, January 26, 2003, at 1 H.

Addition to note 68.   68   Replace NCLC citation with: National Consumer Law Center, Credit Discrimination § 9.4.2.1 (3d ed. 2002 and Supp.).

14.6.2 Additional Advice

Addition to note 69.   69   Also, during the pendency of a dispute, the credit scoring system supposedly will not take the disputed information into account in calculating the credit score. Anne Kadet, *How to Boost Credit Score*, Wall Street Journal, May 4, 2003, at 2.

Add note 69.1 to end of subsection's second bulleted item.   69.1   Anne Kadet, *FICO Frenzy*, SmartMoney, May 1, 2002, at 104.

Add to text at end of subsection:

- Do not pay off old collection accounts without reaching an agreement with the creditor or collection agency that addresses the credit reporting issues. Otherwise, payment may "re-age" the account, showing it as current collection activity.[69.2] In fact, Fair, Isaac in its advice on improving a credit score states that paying off a collection account does not remove it from the credit report, implying that it also does not help raise a credit score to pay it off.[69.3]
- Find out on what day a credit card issuer furnishes information to the credit bureaus. Pay the balance off before that day to create a zero ratio of credit used to credit limit, which will increase the "available credit" factor.
- Seek permission to be added as an authorized user to someone else's mature credit-card account with no delinquencies. The account will probably appear on the consumer's file[69.4] and increase her score.

An entire cottage industry has apparently grown around efforts to improve credit scores, and some consumers (ironically generally high-scoring ones) have become fixated on obtaining higher scores.[69.5]

69.2   Kathy Kristof, *Knowing the Score on Credit Can Help*, Los Angeles Times, May 25, 2003, at C3. If the consumer does want to pay off an old collection account, she should first condition that payment on the creditor agreeing to either to remove or modify the negative information, or not to verify the information if the consumer disputes it. Any such agreement must be in writing. *See* § 13.6.7, *supra*.

69.3   Fair Isaac, *Understanding Your Credit Score* (July 2002), at 9.

69.4   Official Staff Commentary to Regulation B, 12 C.F.R. § 202.10-2 (creditor may designate all authorized user accounts to reflect the participation of both parties, whether or not married). This tactic should be used with great caution, and only with account holders that the consumer trusts, because if account holder does subsequently become delinquent or default, this adverse information will end up on the consumer's credit report. In general, this section of the Commentary of Regulation B is not without controversy. *See* National Consumer Law Center, Credit Discrimination, § 9.4.2.1 (Supp. 2003).

69.5   Anne Kadet, *FICO Frenzy*, SmartMoney, May 1, 2002, at 104. These score-obsessed consumers go so far as to take out unnecessary loans just to have an installment account in order to maximize the number of points under the "types of credit mix" factor. *Id.*

14.7 Policy Concerns with Credit Scoring Systems

14.7.2 Lack of Flexibility

Add note 73.1 to end of first sentence in subsection's third paragraph.   73.1   Low-income consumers do have lower credit scores as a group. Thirty-three percent of households living in neighborhoods with low family incomes have low credit scores, whereas only 17 percent of households in high-income neighborhoods have low credit scores. Brent W. Ambrose, Thomas G. Thibodeau, and Kenneth Temkin, *An Analysis of the Effects of the GSE Affordable Goals on Low- and Moderate-Income Families*, U.S. Department of Housing and Urban Development, May 2002, at 13.

Add note 73.2 to end of sentence at the end of subsection's first paragraph.   73.2   There is some evidence that low-income and minority households are more prone to "application idiosyncrasies," *i.e.*, factors in their credit records that require a subjective interpretation. An example of such a factor would be a period of illness that caused past delinquencies from which the applicant has recovered. Stanley D. Longhofer, *Mortgage Scoring and the Myth of Overrides*, Perspectives on Credit

§ 14.7.3　　　　　　　　*Fair Credit Reporting / 2004 Supplement*

Scoring and Fair Mortgage Lending, Part 5: Communities & Bank, Federal Reserve Bank of Boston, Fall 2002, at 19. At least one study of insurance credit scores also indicated that scores were significantly worse for residents of low-income ZIP codes. Brent Kabler, Insurance-Based Credit Scores: Impact on Minority and Low Income Populations in Missouri, Missouri Department of Insurance—Statistics Section, January 2004. See § 14.10, *infra*, for a discussion of the insurance scoring studies.

Page 355

14.7.3 Credit Scores, Risk-Based Pricing, and Subprime Loans

Add to text at end of subsection:

There has also been a concern raised that credit scores do not predict risk all that well with respect to home mortgages. Credit scoring models are best at predicting early default within the first few months of a loan, while most mortgage defaults and foreclosures take place several years into the loan.[77.1] Credit scoring models can only predict early default because they do not incorporate many of the factors that cause defaults, such as job loss, divorce and medical problems.

The Fair and Accurate Credit Transactions Act (FACTA) of 2003 added a provision to the Fair Credit Reporting Act, effective December 1, 2004, requiring creditors to give consumers a notice relating to risk-based pricing.[77.2] Whenever a creditor extends credit on terms "materially less favorable than the most favorable terms available to a substantial proportion of consumers," the creditor must provide a notice.[77.3] The Federal Trade Commission and Federal Reserve Board must jointly prescribe rules that address the form and content of the notice, as well as the meaning of what credit terms are material and when credit terms are materially less favorable.[77.4]

77.1　Statement of Calvin Bradford, *Perspectives on Credit Scoring and Fair Mortgage Lending*, Federal Reserve Board Mortgage Credit Partnership Credit Scoring Committee, First Installment, Spring 2000, at 7. *Cf.* Bonnie Sinnock, *Changing Definitions Pose Challenge in Valuing Jumbo, Alt-A Loan Pools*, National Mortgage News, May 12, 2003, at 20 (noting that FICO scores are better at sizing up short-duration credit risks than long ones and scores are generally less important in the long term.).

77.2　FCRA, § 615(h)(1), 15 U.S.C. 1681m(h)(1), *added by* Pub. L. No. 108-159, § 311 (2003); 16 C.F.R. § 602.1(c)(3)(xiii), *added by* 69 Fed. Reg. 6526–31 (Feb. 5, 2004).

77.3　*Id.*

77.4　*Id.* at § 615(h)(6) 15 U.S.C. 1681m(h)(6).

14.8 Concerns over the Accuracy of Credit Scores

14.8.1 Garbage In, Garbage Out: The Effect of Credit Report Inaccuracies on Credit Scores

Add text after subsection's first paragraph:

One study has estimated that at least one in five borrowers is likely being penalized because of an inaccurate credit score due to credit reporting problems, but that one in five at risk borrowers is benefiting from scores that are inflated because of incomplete credit information.[78.1] This study also noted significant rates for specific types of errors, such as missing accounts[78.2] and inconsistent information regarding late payments.[78.3]

The study authors posited an interesting theory as to why credit scores are predictive despite substantial inaccuracies—that given the large number of borrowers most lenders have, lenders suffer little harm from inaccuracies so long as there is statistical equilibrium between the number of positive versus negative mistakes, that is, the mistakes cancel each other out.[78.4]

78.1　Consumer Federation of America and National Credit Reporting Association, *Credit Score Accuracy and Implications for Consumers*, December 17, 2002, at 23–24 available at www.consumerfed.org/121702CFA_NCRA_Credit_Score_Report Final.pdf (last visited March 2003).

78.2　See discussion at § 14.8.4, *infra*.

78.3　Consumer Federation of America and National Credit Reporting Association, *Credit Score Accuracy and Implications for Consumers*, December 17, 2002, at 30–35 *available at* www.consumerfed.org/121702CFA_NCRA_Credit_Score_Report_Final.pdf (last visited March 2003). For example, 43 percent of consumer files containing conflicting information between the three major bureaus on how often the consumer had been late by 30 days. *Id.* at 32. Consumers with credit blemishes who are already at most risk to have a subprime score may be those who are also most at risk for further damage due to incorrect or incomplete information. A study by the Federal Reserve found that among accounts with a major

Credit Scoring / 2004 Supplement § 14.8.3

derogatory piece of information as the most recent addition, almost three-fifths of the reports were not current. The study authors concluded that many of these accounts had been closed or transferred, and that it was likely that consumers who had paid off delinquent accounts since they were last reported were being penalized. Robert Avery, Paul Calem, Glenn Canner, and Raphael Bostic, *An Overview of Consumer Data and Credit Reporting*, Federal Reserve Bulletin, February 2003, at 71.

78.4 Consumer Federation of America and National Credit Reporting Association, *Credit Score Accuracy and Implications for Consumers*, December 17, 2002, at 24, available at www.consumerfed.org/121702CFA_NCRA_Credit_Score_Report_Final.pdf (last visited March 2003). *See also* Bruce Kellison and Patrick Brockett, *Check the Score; Credit Scoring and Insurance Losses: Is There a Connection?*, Texas Business Review, January 1, 2003 at 1 (noting that random and occasional errors will not significantly weaken the statistical correlation between credit scores and insurance loss history).

Page 356

14.8.2 Credit Scores Do Not Allow the FCRA's Dispute Mechanisms to Work as Intended

Add note 84.1 to end of last sentence in subsection's second paragraph.

84.1 Helen Huntley, *Making Your Credit Score Soar*, St. Petersburg Times, January 26, 2003, at 1H (noting that the consumer's submission of a written statement will not change a credit score).

Add text after subsection's second paragraph:

During the pendency of a dispute over inaccurate derogatory information, the credit scoring system supposedly will not take that information into account in calculating the credit score.[84.2] However, disputed information can affect a consumer's credit score in ways other than being treated as a delinquency, default, or collection. For example, if a consumer disputes a single charge on a credit card bill, the amount in dispute will not be considered delinquent but will be included in the balance of that credit card. If the amount in dispute is significant, that can result in a lower credit score because it appears that the consumer's ratio of amount owed to available credit is too high.

84.2 Anne Kadet, *How to Boost Credit Score*, Wall Street Journal (May 4, 2003), at 2.

Add to text at end of subsection:

There may also be a cause of action under the Equal Credit Opportunity Act, 15 U.S.C. § 1691(a)(3). The ECOA prohibits discrimination against a consumer for invoking any of her rights under the Consumer Credit Protection Act, which includes the FCRA.[85.1] The theory would be that credit scores, if they do not allow the FCRA's dispute mechanisms to work or if they ignore written protests, automatically penalize applicants who invoke their FCRA rights in violation of the ECOA.

85.1 *See* National Consumer Law Center, Credit Discrimination, § 3.4.4 (3d ed. 2002 and Supp.).

14.8.3 The Effect of Inaccurate, Non-Derogatory Information

Add text after subsection's second paragraph:

At least one credit card issuer (not a charge card issuer) has admitted that it deliberately omits information about consumers' credit limits when reporting to the credit bureaus for "competitive advantage."[86.1]

86.1 Michele Heller, *FCRA Hearing to Shine Spotlight on Credit Reports*, American Banker, June 12, 2003, at 10. *See* § 14.8.4, *infra*.

Add note 86.2 to end of the first sentence in subsection's fourth paragraph.

86.2 According to one study, an examination of over 1700 consumer files from the three major credit bureaus revealed that 29 percent of tradelines, 15 percent of inquiries, and 26 percent of public record entries were duplicates. Consumer Federation of America and National Credit Reporting Association, *Credit Score Accuracy and Implications for Consumers*, December 17, 2002, at 7 (describing 1994 study conducted by the National Association of Independent Credit Reporting Agencies), *available at* www.consumerfed.org/121702CFA_NCRA_Credit_Score_Report_Final.pdf (last visited March 2003).

Add note 86.3 to end of second sentence in subsection's fourth paragraph.

86.3 Consumer Federation of America and National Credit Reporting Association, *Credit Score Accuracy and Implications for Consumers*, December 17, 2002, at 34 (in 5.9 percent of all files examined, a collection action was reported more than once on a single credit report, artificially lowering the credit score), *available at* www.consumerfed.org/121702CFA_NCRA_Credit_Score_Report_Final.pdf (last visited March 2003). *See also* Robert Avery, Paul Calem, Glenn Canner, and Raphael Bostic, *An Overview of Consumer Data and Credit Reporting*, Federal Reserve Bulletin, February 2003, at 71 (40 percent of collection agency trades have multiple record items, many of which appeared to refer to the same episode).

§ 14.8.4 *Fair Credit Reporting / 2004 Supplement*

Addition to note 87.

87   One interesting issue is that some courts have held that the bankruptcy designation for a joint obligor does not violate the FCRA's requirements because it is "technically accurate." However, given that the bankruptcy designation results in a lowering of the credit score, one could argue it can never be considered "technically accurate" because of its significant impact on a credit score. *But see* Heupel v. Trans Union, 193 F. Supp. 2d 1234 (N.D. Ala. 2002) (court held that "included in bankruptcy" designation did not violate FCRA because it was "technically accurate" despite that fact that it had lowered the plaintiff's credit score enough to cause a rejection by a credit card issuer.). *See* § 7.8.3.2, *supra*.

Add note 87.1 to end of last sentence of subsection's fifth paragraph.

87.1   Several cases in which the "account included in bankruptcy" issue has been litigated indicate that this designation does affect the credit score of the consumer. Evantash v. G.E. Capital Mortgage Serv., 2003 WL 22844198 (E.D. Pa. Nov. 25, 2003); Clark v. Experian Information Solutions, 219 F.R.D. 375 (D.S.C. 2003), *later proceeding at* 2004 WL 256433 (D.S.C. Jan. 14, 2004); Heupel v. Trans Union, 193 F. Supp. 2d 1234 (N.D. Ala. 2002). The *Clark* class action resulted in a settlement with the three major credit bureaus requiring them to discontinue this practice. Clark v. Experian Information Solutions, 2004 WL 256433 (D.S.C. Jan. 14, 2004) *See* 7.8.3.2, *supra*.

Add note 87.2 to end of first sentence in subsection's last paragraph.

87.2   Consumer Federation of America and National Credit Reporting Association, *Credit Score Accuracy and Implications for Consumers*, December 17, 2002, at 34 (21.6 percent of all files contained errors regarding what type of account was involved in a tradeline), *available at* www.consumerfed.org/121702CFA_NCRA_Credit_Score_Report_Final.pdf (last visited March 2003).

Page 357

14.8.4 Unreported Information

Replace notes 91, 93 with:

91   Press Release, Office of the Comptroller of the Currency, *Comptroller Urges Industry to End Abusive Practices and Elevate Customer Service Standards* (No. 99-51, June 7, 1999), *available at* www.occ.treas.gov/ftp/release/99-51.txt (last viewed July 2003).

93   *See* National Consumer Law Center, Credit Discrimination § 8.2.2 (3d ed. 2002 and Supp.).

Add to text at end of subsection:

The practice of deliberately withholding information about borrowers to keep their credit scores low appears no longer limited to subprime customers. One issuer of credit cards (including prime credit cards) has admitted that it deliberately failed to report credit limits of its customers as a way to artificially depress credit scores, citing "competitive advantage."[93.1] This appears to be a common problem, given that research from the Federal Reserve Board indicates about 70 percent of consumers have at least one revolving account in their credit files that does not contain information about the credit limit.[93.2] One issue is whether the credit bureaus failure to require furnishers to report credit limits violates the FCRA's requirement to use reasonable procedures to ensure maximum possible accuracy.[93.3] Another example of a lender deliberately withholding credit information is student loan giant Sallie Mae, which has stopped reporting about its student loan customers to TransUnion and Experian.[93.4] Sallie Mae took this action to prevent other lenders from soliciting its customers (and thus preserve its advantage in cross-marketing to this lucrative young market). Sallie Mae's actions have artificially depressed the credit scores of its customers; in one case, a borrower's score dropped 40 points after his Sallie Mae loans were removed from his Experian and TransUnion files.[93.5] Sallie Mae's actions are especially problematic because the method by which many young consumers establish their credit histories is through repayment of student loans.

Another common occurrence is that information will be missing from files at one credit report agency, but be present in another agency's files, because of mistakes or the fact that creditors do not report to all three major credit bureaus. One study found, from a limited sample of 51 consumer files, that 78 percent of these consumers had a revolving account in good standing missing from their files at one of the three major credit bureaus.[93.6] One third of these files were missing a mortgage account that had never been late.[93.7] An earlier study examining over 1700 files from the three major credit bureaus revealed that 44 percent of these files had missing information in them.[93.8]

93.1   Michele Heller, *FCRA Hearing to Shine Spotlight on Credit Reports*, American Banker, June 12, 2003, at 10. *See* § 14.8.4, *infra*.

93.2   Robert Avery, Paul Calem, Glenn Canner, and Raphael Bostic, *An Overview of Consumer Data and Credit Reporting*, Federal Reserve Bulletin, February 2003, at 71. *See also* Federal Financial Institutions Examination Council, *Advisory Letter*, January 18, 2000 (stating that "certain large credit card issuers are

Credit Scoring / 2004 Supplement § 14.9.1

no longer reporting customer credit lines of high credit balances or both."), *available at* www.ffiec.gov/press/pr011800a.htm (last viewed July 2003).

93.3 See § 7.8.4.4, *supra*.

93.4 W.A. Lee, *Credit Data or Customer List? Sallie's Stance Drawing Heat*, American Banker, Oct. 7, 2003.

93.5 *Id.*

93.6 Consumer Federation of America and National Credit Reporting Association, *Credit Score Accuracy and Implications for Consumers*, December 17, 2002, at 30, *available at* www.consumerfed.org/121702CFA_NCRA_Credit_Score_Report_Final.pdf (last visited March 2003). While the sample size for this finding was limited, the study's authors noted that many of the findings are consistent with those reported in research by the Federal Reserve Board. Travis B. Plunkett, *Testimony Before the House Committee on Financial Services*, Subcommittee on Financial Institutions and Consumer Credit, June 12, 2003, at 5, n.8. A missing tradeline in good standing will most harm a consumer with thin file, which may tend to be a low-income or young consumer. Even for a thick file consumer, a missing account may result in a lower credit score because it might lower the amount of available credit, or it might be an older account that would have added more points under the "length of history" factor.

93.7 Consumer Federation of America and National Credit Reporting Association, *Credit Score Accuracy and Implications for Consumers*, December 17, 2002, at 30, *available at* www.consumerfed.org/121702CFA_NCRA_Credit_Score_Report_Final.pdf (last visited March 2003).

93.8 Consumer Federation of America and National Credit Reporting Association, *Credit Score Accuracy and Implications for Consumers*, December 17, 2002, at 7 (describing 1994 study conducted by the National Association of Independent Credit Reporting Agencies), *available at* www.consumerfed.org/121702CFA_NCRA_Credit_Score_Report_Final.pdf (last visited March 2003).

14.8.5 Lack of Validation and Re-Validation

Add to text at end of subsection:

There are signs that credit scoring models have underestimated the impact of the current economic slowdown on subprime credit card borrowers, resulting in significant losses to credit card issuers.[99.1] This is not surprising since many credit card issuers rely solely on the credit score in approving an account, and do not consider the borrower's income or other debt. Thus, these lenders may grant credit to borrowers who are extremely overextended.[99.2]

99.1 Heather Timmons, *The Cracks in Credit Scoring*, BusinessWeek, November 24, 2002, at 136 (noting that most credit scoring models only rely on two years of data). As early as 1997, the Office of Comptroller of Currency had warned banks to closely monitor the performance of their credit scoring models throughout economic cycles, advising them to retest models developed in prosperous times. Office of the Comptroller of the Currency, Credit Scoring Models (OCC Bull. 97-24, May 20, 1997).

99.2 *In re* Mercer, 246 F.3d 391 (5th Cir. 2001) (credit card issuer sent debtor a pre-approved card with a $3000 limit based on a FICO score of 735, despite the fact the debtor earned less than $25,000 annually and had recently acquired four other credit cards); *In re* Ellingsworth, 212 B.R. 326 (W.D. Mo. 1997) (debtor sent a pre-approved credit card with credit limit of $4000 based on her FICO score of 759 even though she had 16 other credit cards); *In re* Akins, 235 B.R. 866 (Bankr. W.E. Tex. 1999) (debtor obtained approval to use a convenience check up to her full $4000 credit limit based on acceptable FICO score even though she had two other credit cards totaling approximately $30,000 in debt, or 150 percent of her gross income).

14.8.6 Lender Misuse of Credit Scoring Models

Replace note 103 with:

103 *See generally* National Consumer Law Center, Credit Discrimination (3d ed. 2002 and Supp.).

14.9 Do Credit Scores Discriminate?

Page 358

14.9.1 Credit Scoring's Disparate Impact

Addition to note 105.

105 *Replace NCLC citation with*: *See* National Consumer Law Center, Credit Discrimination § 6.4 (3d ed. 2002 and Supp.).

Replace last sentence in subsection's first paragraph with:

A class action has been filed against Fannie Mae alleging that its use of credit scores in its Desktop Underwriter system discriminates against racial minorities.[106] The plaintiff's claims under the Fair Housing Act and Equal Opportunity Credit Act have survived a motion to dismiss.[106.1]

131

§ 14.9.1   *Fair Credit Reporting / 2004 Supplement*

> 106   Rahmaan v. Fed. Nat'l Mortg. Assoc., Clearinghouse No. 54573 (D.D.C. Sept. 13, 2002) (complaint). This case also alleged that Fannie Mae violated the FCRA and the Equal Opportunity Credit Act by failing to provide adverse action notices when consumers are denied mortgages as a result of rejection by Desktop Underwriter. *Id. See generally* § 6.4, *supra*.
>
> 106.1   Rahmaan v. Fed. Nat'l Mortgage Assoc., 2003 WL 21940044 (D.D.C. May 19, 2003). The court did express skepticism about the viability of the claims, noting the plaintiff had not made out a prima facie claim under a McDonnell-Douglas analysis. However, the plaintiff appeared to have brought both a disparate impact claim and a disparate treatment claim, and thus it was unclear why the court referred only to the McDonnell-Douglas analysis. *See* National Consumer Law Center, Credit Discrimination § 4.2.3.1 (3d. ed. 2002 and Supp.). The court did dismiss the claims based on the failure to provide an adverse action notice under the FCRA and the ECOA. *Id.*

Add to text after sentence containing note 107:

Fair, Isaac's own analysis showed that consumers living in minority neighborhoods had lower overall credit scores.[107.1]

> 107.1   Fair, Isaac & Co., *The Effectiveness of Scoring on Low-to-Moderate Income and High-Minority Area Populations*, Aug. 1997, at 22 (Figure 9).

Replace subsection's third paragraph with:

A later study by researchers at the University of North Carolina of borrowers who received community reinvestment mortgages showed that one-third of African Americans in this pool had credit scores under 620, as compared to only 15 percent of whites. Furthermore, this same study found that another one-third of African Americans had credit scores between 621 and 660 (as compared to 20 percent of whites), which means that two-thirds of African Americans in this pool had what is considered marginal or poor credit.[108] A recent analysis of two neighborhoods in San Antonio, Texas, indicated similar disparities in credit scores for Hispanics. The median credit score (using the Experian "Equivalency Score") for residents of a predominately white neighborhood in San Antonio was 86 points higher than the median score for a predominately Hispanic neighborhood.[108.1] In addition, there have been several studies examining the relationship between race and insurance credit scores, at least one of which showed a dramatic difference between the scores of whites and minorities. These studies are discussed in section 14.10, *infra*. The FACTA amendments require the Federal Trade Commission, Federal Reserve Board and Department of Housing and Urban Development to conduct a joint study on the potential disparate impact of credit scores.[108.2]

> 108   Roberto G. Quercia, Michael A. Stegman, Walter R. Davis and Eric Stein, *Performance of Community Reinvestment Loans: Implications for Secondary Market Purchases, in Low Income Homeownership: Examining the Unexamined Goal* (Nicolas P. Retsinas and Eric S. Belsky, eds. 2002), at 363: Table 12-7 (statistics derived from an analysis of 5549 community reinvestment loans.).
>
> 108.1   Dr. Robert Brischetto, Living on the Edge: The Problem of Credit on San Antonio's Westside (forthcoming 2004).
>
> 108.2   Fair and Accurate Credit Transactions Act of 2003, Pub. L. No. 108-159, § 215 (2003).

Addition to note 110.

> 110   In contrast, an examination of 500,000 consumer credit files found that for the general population, about 1 in 10 files did not have enough information to generate a score. Consumer Federation of America and National Credit Reporting Association, *Credit Score Accuracy and Implications for Consumers*, December 17, 2002, at 38, *available at* www.consumerfed.org/121702CFA_NCRA_Credit_Score_Report_Final.pdf (last visited March 2003).

Add to text after sentence containing note 113:

Federal regulatory examiners have focused on racial disparities in the use of credit scoring.[113.1]

> 113.1   *See* Federal Trade Commission, *Public Forum on the Consumer and Credit Scoring*, Matter No. P994810, July 22, 1999, at 175 (statement of Bob Cook, Senior Fair Lending Specialist, Federal Reserve Board), available at www.ftc.gov/bcp/creditscoring.

Add to text at end of subsection's sixth paragraph:

To address these concerns, there have been several initiatives to establish "alternative" credit profiles for populations without a credit history, such as immigrants and young consumers. One company has established a credit reporting agency that compiles credit histories using rent, utility, insurance, and other monthly payments.[113.2] Fair, Isaac has undertaken efforts to create credit scores using nontraditional credit information.[113.3] First American has announced plans to create credit assessment products using files from its consumer reporting agency subsidiaries that include tenant screening, subprime and finance company lending databases, utility payment files, and rent-to-own records.[113.4]

Credit Scoring / 2004 Supplement § 14.9.1

113.2 Kenneth R. Harney, *Renters Soon Get a Chance to Boost Credit Records*, Washington Post, January 10, 2004, at F1.
113.3 Kenneth R. Harney, *Grading Buyers Who Lack Credit Scores*, Washington Post, October 25, 2003 10, 2004, at F1.
113.4 *Id.*

Addition to notes 114–117.

114 *See* Federal Trade Commission, *Public Forum on the Consumer and Credit Scoring*, Matter No. P994810, July 22, 1999, at 234 (statement of Peter McCorkell, General Counsel, Fair Isaac), *available at* www.ftc.gov/bcp/creditscoring.
115 Mortgage lenders claim they have not adopted NextGen because Fannie Mae and Freddie Mac have not yet agreed to accept NextGen scores. Kenneth Harney, *Lenders Slow to Adopt New FICO Scoring Model*, Wash. Post, Nov. 30, 2002, at H1.
116 Nathalie Mainland and Julia Wooding, *NextGen FICO Risk Score Conversion FAQ*, Fair Isaac (April 2002), at 3.

Page 359

117 Nathalie Mainland and Julia Wooding, *NextGen FICO Risk Score Conversion FAQ*, Fair Isaac (April 2002), at 5 ("NextGen does tend to push thicker files upward in the score distribution, while pushing thinner files downward.") In general, NextGen benefits higher-scoring consumers and thus may exacerbate, not improve, racial disparities in credit scoring. *Id.*

Add to text after sentence containing note 118:

Another potential issue is whether credit scoring systems give more points to homeowners. For example, according to Fair, Isaac, one of the categories of factors used to derive FICO scores is the types of credit in use. A good mix may be one that includes a mortgage loan.[118.1] One question is whether FICO's scoring models explicitly give more points to mortgage holders, which would mean homeowners are favored over renters. Racial minorities have lower rates of homeownership than whites.[118.2]

Finally, there is a question as to whether credit scoring discriminates against other groups protected by credit discrimination laws.[118.3] For example, commentators have noted that the "length of credit history" factor may have a disparate impact on women, who on average have shorter credit histories than men.[118.4]

118.1 *See* § 14.5.2.1, *supra*.
118.2 *See* U.S. Department of Housing and Urban Development, *HUD Statement on Record Homeownership Rates in 2002*, January 27, 2003 (minorities have homeownership rate of 49.9 percent compared to the overall homeownership rate of 68 percent).
118.3 *See* National Consumer Law Center, Credit Discrimination Ch. 3 (3d ed. 2002 and Supp.) for discussions on which groups are protected under federal and state credit discrimination laws.
118.4 Cynthia Glassman and Howard Wilkins, *Credit Scoring: Probabilities and Pitfalls*, Journal of Retail Banking Serv., Volume XIX, No. 2, Summer 1997, at 56.

Addition to note 119.

119 Fair, Isaac has maintained that its scoring models do not include prohibited factors, such as race, national origin, or gender. Fair, Isaac, *Understanding Your Credit Score* (November 2003), at 6.

Add to text at end of subsection:

If a credit scoring model contains a factor that had a disparate impact on minorities or another protected group, it does not necessarily mean the model violates the Equal Credit Opportunity Act or other fair lending laws. Under the disparate impact analysis, a creditor can show a business necessity for using a policy or factor that has a disparate impact.[120.1] An example in the Commentary to Regulation B indicates that creditors can show business necessity by showing a "demonstrable relationship" between a policy and creditworthiness.[120.2] In the case of credit scoring, the Office of Comptroller of Currency has stated that the business necessity for including a variable in a credit scoring model would be shown if "the variable is statistically related to loan performance, and has an understandable relationship" to creditworthiness.[120.3] Thus, if a variable or factor in a credit scoring model causes a disparate impact, but is "demonstrably" or "understandably" related to creditworthiness, it may be permissible under fair lending laws, unless the plaintiff can show that there is a factor that serves the same purpose and creates a less discriminatory impact.[120.4]

Note that the business necessity analysis may differ for scoring models used for credit versus insurance. Because credit scores are based on credit histories, there is a logical connection to their use to measure creditworthiness. While there might be some correlation between insurance credit scores and loss history, there has been no definitive reason as to why credit scores are a good measure of "insurance worthiness." Furthermore, at least one study

§ 14.9.2   Fair Credit Reporting / 2004 Supplement

has found that models using attributes other than credit score yield almost the same correlations with loss ratios as models that use credit scores.[120.5] Thus, it may be easier to show the existence of a "less discriminatory alternative" for insurance scoring.

120.1   See National Consumer Law Center, Credit Discrimination § 4.3.2.5 (3d ed. 2002 and Supp.).
120.2   Official Staff Commentary to Regulation B, 12 C.F.R. § 202.6(a)-2.
120.3   Office of the Comptroller of the Currency, Credit Scoring Models (OCC Bull. 97-24, May 20, 1997), Appendix at 11. While the OCC's pronouncement is only authoritative as to national banks, it may be indicative of how other federal regulators will view this issue.
120.4   See National Consumer Law Center, Credit Discrimination § 4.3.2.6 (3d ed. 2002 and Supp.).
120.5   Wayne D. Holdredge and Katharine Barnes, *Good News, Bad News or Both?*, Tillinghast-Towers Perrin, February 2003.

14.9.2 Discriminatory Credit Score Thresholds or Overrides

Replace notes 121, 124 with:

121   United States v. Associates Nat'l Bank, Civ. No. 99-196 (D. Del. Mar. 29, 1999). For more about the DOJ's action against ANB, see National Consumer Law Center, Credit Discrimination § 12.4.3.5 (3d ed. 2002 and Supp.).

124   See United States v. Deposit Guar. Nat'l Bank, Civ. Action No. 3:99CV67OLN (S.D. Miss. 1999). For more about the DOJ's action against DGNB, see National Consumer Law Center, Credit Discrimination § 12.4.3.5 (3d ed. 2002 and Supp.).

Page 360

14.10 Credit Scores and Insurance

Replace last sentence of subsection's first paragraph with:

Consumers can obtain one version of their insurance scores from ChoicePoint for $12.95.[128.1]

128.1   See ChoicePoint's consumer website at www.choicetrust.com.

Addition to note 133.

133   Several states have passed laws based on model legislation written by the National Conference of Insurance Legislators and supported by the insurance industry. *See, e.g.*, 2003 Ark. Acts 1452; 2003 Ind. Leis. Serv. P.L. 201-2003; 2003 Ga. Laws 79. A summary of some of the state insurance laws governing use of credit information is included in Appx. B.3, *infra*.

Replace sentence containing note 135.

A number of class actions have been filed challenging the practice.[135]

135   DeHoyos v. Allstate Corp, 345 F.3d 290 (5th Cir. 2003) (holding that a challenge to credit scoring under the Fair Housing Act and federal Civil Rights Acts was not preempted by the McCarran-Ferguson Act); Owens v. Nationwide Mutual Insurance Co., 2003 WL 22364319 (N.D. Tex. Oct. 1, 2003) (class action alleging that use of credit scores for homeowners insurance violates section 3604 of the Fair Housing Act and the federal Civil Rights Acts); Ashby v. Farmers Group, Inc., 261 F. Supp. 2d 1213 (D. Or. 2003) (dismissal of FCRA claim against insurance management services company that used credit scores in ratesetting); National Fair Housing Alliance v. Prudential Insurance Co., 208 F. Supp. 2d 46 (D.D.C. 2002) (class action alleging that the use of credit scores to determine eligibility for homeowners insurance has a disparate impact on minorities in violation of the Fair Housing Act); Wells v. Shelter General Insurance Co., 217 F. Supp. 2d 744 (S.D. Miss. 2002) (class action challenging use of credit scores under Mississippi insurance law).

Replace sentence containing note 136.

Insurance regulators in both Texas and California have taken enforcement actions against insurance companies over this practice.[136]

136   Press Release, Texas Department of Insurance, State of Texas, Farmers Insurance Reach Agreement (Nov. 30, 2003) (resulting in a $100 million settlement, including $30 million in refunds for improper use of credit scores. Settlement does not prohibit use of credit scoring in insurance, and requires only disclosures acceptable to the Attorney General); R.J. Lehman, *Allstate Settles California Insurance-Scoring Dispute for $3 Million*, Bestwire, March 5, 2004 (Allstate allegedly violated California law prohibiting use of credit information in underwriting or ratesetting for auto insurance; settlement prohibits use of credit scores and imposes a $3 million fine).

Add to text at end of section:

A number of state insurance commissions have conducted studies on the relationship between insurance scores and certain demographic characteristics, including race, gender, age, and income. A study by the Virginia Bureau of Insurance concluded that credit scoring is an ineffective tool for an insurer to engage in redlining, that is, disparate treatment, because income and race alone are not reliable predictors of credit score; however, this study did not report findings on disparate impact.[137] A study commissioned by the Washington State Insurance Commissioner showed a correlation between insurance scores and income; however, its findings regarding the racial impact of insurance scoring were inconclusive, primarily because of the small number of minorities sampled from Washington State's relatively homogeneous population.[138] A Maryland study showed a correlation between race, income and insurance score, finding that in Baltimore City, the percentage of residents with high credit scores decreased as the percentage of minorities and lower-income households increased in a neighborhood.[139] However, because the study used data prior to the passage of Maryland's statute regulating insurance scoring, the Maryland Insurance Administration declined to conclude that there was sufficient data to determine whether the use of credit scoring had an adverse impact on low-income or minority populations.[140]

The most dramatic results were from a study conducted by the Missouri Department of Insurance, which found a stunning correlation between insurance scores and race, as well as income, age, marital status, and educational attainment.[141] Using credit score data aggregated at the ZIP code level collected from the highest volume insurers in Missouri, the study found:[142]

- Insurance scores were significantly worse for residents of high-minority ZIP codes. The average consumer in an "all minority" neighborhood had a credit score that fell into the 18.4th percentile, while the average consumer in a "no minority" neighborhood had a credit score that fell into the 57.3rd percentile—a difference of 38.9 percentage points.
- Insurance scores were significantly worse for residents of low-income ZIP codes. The average consumer in the poorest neighborhood had a credit score 12.8 percentage points lower than residents in the wealthiest communities.
- The correlation between race (high minority neighborhoods) and credit scores remained even after eliminating other variables, such as income, education, marital status, and unemployment. Residency in a minority concentration neighborhood provided to be the single most reliable predictor of credit scores.
- The gap in credit scores translated into the individual level. The average gap between the percentage of minorities with poor scores and non-minorities with poor scores was 28.9 points. The gap between lower-income and higher-income households was 29.2 percentage points.

The author and researcher of the Missouri study concluded that "the evidence appears to be credible, substantial, and compelling that credit scores have a significant disproportionate impact on minorities and on the poor."[143]

137 Virginia Bureau of Insurance, Report on the Use of Credit Reports in Underwriting to the State Commerce and Labor Committee of the General Assembly, December 1999.
138 Dave Pavelchek and Bruce Brown, Effect of Credit Scoring on Auto Insurance Underwriting and Pricing, Office of Washington State Insurance Commissioner, January 2003.
139 Maryland Insurance Administration, Report on the Credit Scoring Data of Insurers in Maryland, February 2004.
140 Id.
141 Brent Kabler, Insurance-Based Credit Scores: Impact on Minority and Low Income Populations in Missouri, Missouri Department of Insurance—Statistics Section, January 2004.
142 Id.
143 Id

Chapter 15 Credit Repair Agencies

Page 361

15.1 General

Addition to note 4.

4   FTC v. ICR Servs., Civ. No. 03-C-5532 (N.D. Ill. Aug. 11, 2003), *available at* www.ftc.gov/opa/2003/08/nationwide.htm (consent order requiring $1.15 million consumer redress); FTC v. Clifton W. Cross, Civ. Action No. M0-99CA018, 5 Trade Reg. Rptr. (CCH) ¶ 15,124 (W.D. Tex. June 21, 2001) (consent decree against credit repair website operator who sold instructions about how to build new credit profile with fake SSN). *See also* FTC v. Gill, 265 F.3d 944 (9th Cir. 2001) (suit under Credit Repair Organizations Act).

Add to text after paragraph containing note 4:

Other credit repair agencies do not promise to make the actual improvements to the consumer's credit report, but sell credit repair books, CD-Roms, or other materials, often accompanied by a promise to provide personal credit repair advice to the consumer. There have been reports of creditors selling these services, or even requiring consumers to buy them, as a condition of an extension of credit.

Page 362

Add to text after subsection's third paragraph:

The FCRA allows credit reporting agencies to disregard disputes of items on consumers' credit reports that are generated by credit repair organizations.[6.1] The credit reporting agency must notify the consumer that it has deemed the request frivolous.[6.2] Creditors who furnish information to credit reporting agencies may also disregard disputes sent by credit repair organizations.[6.3]

6.1   15 U.S.C. § 1681i(a)(3); FTC Official Staff Commentary § 611 item 11 (reprinted at Appx. C, *infra*). See § 7.3.3, *supra*.
6.2   15 U.S.C. § 1681i(a)(3)(B).
6.3   15 U.S.C. § 623(a)(8)(G), *added by* Pub. L. No. 108-159, § 312 (2003). See Ch. 3, *supra*.

15.2 Federal Credit Repair Organizations Act

15.2.1 Introduction

Addition to notes 11, 14.

11   *See also* Shulman v. CRS Fin. Servs., Inc., 2003 WL 22400211 (N.D. Ill. Oct. 21, 2003) (refusing to apply CROA to contract entered into before effective date).
14   *Add at end of note*: and in Parker v. 1-800 Bar None, 2002 WL 215530 (N.D. Ill. Feb. 12, 2002).

15.2.2 Scope: Who Is a Credit Repair Organization?

Page 363

15.2.2.1 General Definition

Add to text after sentence containing note 27:

An organization that merely advises or assists a consumer in credit repair is covered even if all actual credit repair steps are undertaken by the consumer.[27.1]

27.1   15 U.S.C. § 1679a(3)(A)(ii).

15.2.2.2 Exceptions

Replace "the Act does not apply" in subsection's third sentence with:

the provisions of the Act that apply only to credit repair organizations do not apply

Add to text after sentence following sentence containing note 33:

If a credit repair organization claims to be a non-profit but appears to be operating as a for-profit entity, it may be worthwhile to review its annual tax return forms (Form 990). IRS regulations require section 501(c)(3) organizations to post their tax return forms on the Internet, or provide copies of their three most recent annual returns within thirty days of a written request at no charge other than a reasonable fee to cover photocopying and mailing.[33.1]

  33.1   26 C.F.R. §§ 301.6104(d)-1, 301.6104(d)-2.

Add to text at end of sentence containing note 34:

without complying with the requirements of the Act that apply only to credit repair organizations.

Add to text after sentence containing note 35:

There is no exemption for other financial institutions, lenders, and creditors, however. A non-exempt lender or loan broker who sells credit repair services along with the extension of credit is covered by the Act. Some courts have, however, held that the Act does not cover organizations that provide credit repair services that are ancillary to another activity.[35.1]

  35.1   See § 15.2.2.3, infra.

Page 364

15.2.2.3 Credit Repair Services That Are Ancillary to Another Activity

Replace "are covered by the Act" in subsection's first sentence with:

make an organization a credit repair organization as defined by the Act

15.2.2.4 Attorneys

Replace "the Act should not apply" in first sentence of subsection's second paragraph with:

the provisions of the Act that apply only to credit repair organizations should not apply

Addition to note 40.

  40   See also Iosello v. Lexington Law Firm, 2003 WL 21920237 (N.D. Ill. Aug. 7, 2003) (attorneys who act in the manner of a credit repair organization are covered).

Add to text at end of subsection:

Nonetheless, in order to avoid any issue regarding the Act's applicability, some attorneys who correspond with credit reporting agencies as a preliminary step before filing suit under the FCRA provide that service free of charge.

Page 365

15.2.2.5 Assignees, Purchasers of Debt, and Debt Collectors

Addition to note 46.

  46   But see Oslan v. Collection Bureau, 206 F.R.D. 109 (E.D. Pa. 2001) (debt collector is covered only if receives or solicits payment beyond repayment of debt).

Replace "should also be covered by the Act" in sentence containing note 46 with:

should also be considered credit repair organizations as defined by the Act

15.2.2.6 Creditors

Add to text at end of subsection:

Outside the context of restructuring of debts, the only exemption for creditors is limited to depository institutions, credit unions, and their subsidiaries and affiliates.[51.1] Non-exempt creditors who sell credit repair programs in connection with the initial extension of credit are covered by the Act, although there is some issue about whether credit repair services that are ancillary to another activity are covered.[51.2]

51.1 15 U.S.C. § 1679a(3)(B)(iii).
51.2 See § 15.2.2.3, supra.

15.2.2.7 Sellers Who Advertise Credit Repair

Addition to notes 52, 54.

52 But cf. Wojcik v. Courtesy Auto Sales, Inc., 2002 WL 31663298 (D. Neb. Nov. 25, 2002) (auto dealer not credit repair organization where plaintiffs were not lured in by any credit repair advertising).

54 See also Wojcik v. Courtesy Auto Sales, Inc., 2002 WL 31663298 (D. Neb. Nov. 25, 2002) (must be additional fee for credit repair service).

Page 366

Replace sentence containing note 55 with:

Courts have tended to agree when interpreting similar language in state credit repair statutes, although there have been some lower court opinions finding no such requirement.[55]

55 See § 15.3.4, infra. But see Midstate Siding & Window Co. v. Rogers, 789 N.E.2d 1248 (Ill. 2003) (goods and services must be related to an extension of credit for consumer or improvement of consumer's credit record, history or rating and supported by additional consideration for such assistance).

Addition to note 57.

57 But cf. Wojcik v. Courtesy Auto Sales, Inc., 2002 WL 31663298, at *8 (D. Neb. Nov. 25, 2002) (noting that a dealership "could obviously fit into the credit repair organization category," but finding this dealership not covered for other reasons).

15.2.5 Prohibited Practices

Page 368

15.2.5.2 Misstatements to Consumer Reporting Agencies or Creditors

Addition to note 79.

79 See FTC v. IRC Servs. (N.D. Ill. Aug. 11, 2003) (consent order against credit repair organization that made untrue and misleading statements to credit reporting agencies), available at www.ftc.gov/opa/2003/08/nationwide.htm.

Add to text after sentence containing note 80:

This prohibition might apply to a loan broker or retailer who falsifies a consumer's credit application and submits it to a potential creditor. Significantly, this prohibition is not confined to entities that meet the definition of "credit repair organization," so the consumer need not show that the defendant provided services in return for money or other valuable consideration. The consumer may be able to show actual damages if the falsified credit application was the means by which the defendant bound the consumer to an unaffordable, disadvantageous transaction. A claim along these lines will raise difficult issues if the consumer was complicit in the falsification, so the attorney should investigate the facts carefully.

15.2.5.3 Concealment of the Consumer's Identity

Add to text at end of subsection:

This prohibition may apply to a car dealer who sets up a sale with a "straw purchaser" to conceal the real buyer's identity from the entity financing the sale. Such a claim will raise difficult issues, however, if the consumer was complicit in the falsification, so the attorney should investigate the facts carefully.

15.2.6 Private Remedies

Page 370

15.2.6.1 Noncomplying Contract Is Void

Add to text after sentence containing note 98:

In addition, since consumers seek the services of a credit repair organization only when they are in dire financial straits, an arbitration clause that imposes high up-front costs on the consumer is particularly vulnerable to an unconscionability challenge.[98.1]

15.3 State Credit Repair Laws

98.1   See Plattner v. Edge Solutions Inc., 2003 WL 22859532 (N.D. Ill. Dec. 2, 2003) (finding arbitration clause in credit repair contract unconscionable). See generally National Consumer Law Center, Consumer Arbitration Agreements Ch. 4 (3d ed. 2003).

15.3.1 Introduction

Page 372

Replace note 128 with:

128   Mitchell v. Am. Fair Credit Ass'n, 99 Cal. App. 4th 1345, 122 Cal. Rptr. 2d 193 (2002) (statute explicitly requires liberal construction).

15.3.2 Coverage

Addition to note 131:

131   See also Lewis v. Delta Funding Corp. (In re Lewis), 290 B.R. 541 (Bankr. E.D. Pa. 2003) (mortgage loan broker met Pa. definition of credit services organization).

Add to text after sentence containing note 133:

In addition, others involved in the credit repair organization's activities may be liable. One decision finds that a lender who prepared the broker agreement for the mortgage broker, and then funded the loan, violated the state credit repair law even though only the broker met the statutory definition of credit services organization.[133.1] But another decision from the same district holds that others who participate in the scheme with a credit repair organization but do not themselves meet the statutory definition are not subject to the statute.[133.2]

133.1   Lewis v. Delta Funding Corp. (In re Lewis), 290 B.R. 541 (Bankr. E.D. Pa. 2003).
133.2   Allen v. Advanta Fin. Corp., 2002 U.S. Dist. LEXIS 11650 (E.D. Pa. Jan. 3, 2002).

15.3.4 Do State Credit Repair Laws Apply to Retailers Who Arrange Credit for Customers?

15.3.4.2 Requirement of Payment of Fee for the Credit Services

Addition to note 141:

141   Replace Strohmaier citation with: 211 F. Supp. 2d 1036 (N.D. Ill. 2001). Replace Midstate Siding review granted citation with: 204 Ill. 2d 314, 789 N.E.2d 1248, 273 Ill. Dec. 816 (2003)

Replace last sentence of paragraph containing note 141 with:

However, the Illinois Supreme Court reversed this decision, holding that there had to be a specific payment for the credit services; a payment for other goods or services is insufficient.[141.1]

141.1   Midstate Siding & Window Co. v. Rogers, 204 Ill. 2d 314, 789 N.E.2d 1248, 273 Ill. Dec. 816 (2003). See also Oslan v. Collection Bureau, 206 F.R.D. 109 (E.D. Pa. 2001) (debt collector is covered by federal CROA only if receives or solicits payment beyond repayment of debt).

Page 374

Add note 142.1 at end of sentence following sentence containing note 142.

142.1   But see Cannon v. William Chevrolet/Geo, Inc., 341 Ill. App. 3d 674, 794 N.E.2d 843, 276 Ill. Dec. 593 (2003) (finding car dealership not to be a credit repair organization even though it required consumer to pay a 4.5 percent higher interest rate than bank required).

Add to text at end of subsection:

Another possibility is that the dealership may have charged the consumer a document preparation fee.[142.2] The consumer can probably show through discovery that the primary purpose of such a fee was to compensate the retailer for preparing the credit contract, the credit application, and other credit documents.

142.2   But see Cannon v. William Chevrolet/Geo, Inc., 341 Ill. App. 3d 674, 794 N.E.2d 843, 276 Ill. Dec. 593 (2003) (finding car dealership not to be a credit repair organization even though it required consumer to pay documentary fee of $46.88).

Credit Repair Agencies / 2004 Supplement § 15.4.1

Page 375

15.3.4.4 Legislative Intent

Addition to note 146.

146 · *Replace Midstate Siding review granted citation with*: 204 Ill. 2d 314, 789 N.E.2d 1248, 273 Ill. Dec. 816 (2003).

Add to text at end of sentence following sentence containing note 146:

In reversing, the Illinois Supreme Court construed the statutory language to require a specific payment for the credit services.[146.1] The high court did not reach the question of whether the retail seller would have been exempt if such a payment had been shown.

146.1 Midstate Siding & Window Co. v. Rogers, 204 Ill. 2d 314, 789 N.E.2d 1248, 273 Ill. Dec. 816 (2003).

Replace first three words of second sentence of subsection's second paragraph with:

The Illinois Court of Appeals

Add to text after sentence containing note 147:

When the Illinois Supreme Court reversed the Court of Appeals decision, it rejected this view, stating that the legislature had not intended to regulate retailers primarily engaged in the business of selling goods and services to their customers.[147.1] Nonetheless, the argument may be persuasive in other states.

147.1 Midstate Siding & Window Co. v. Rogers, 204 Ill. 2d 314, 789 N.E.2d 1248, 273 Ill. Dec. 816 (2003). *See also* Cannon v. William Chevrolet/Geo, Inc., 341 Ill. App. 3d 674, 794 N.E.2d 843, 276 Ill. Dec. 593 (2003) (state credit repair law does not apply to car dealerships primarily in the business of selling and leasing cars).

Page 376

15.3.6 Private Causes of Action

Add to text after second sentence of subsection's last paragraph:

Even if the state credit repair law does not explicitly state that a violation is a UDAP violation, in many states any violation of a consumer protection law is a *per se* UDAP violation.[152.1] In addition, the credit repair organization is likely to have made many misstatements that will be actionable under a state UDAP statute.

152.1 *See* National Consumer Law Center, Unfair and Deceptive Acts and Practices § 3.2.7 (5th ed. 2001 and Supp.).

15.4 Federal Telemarketing Statutes and Regulations

Page 377

15.4.1 Federal Telemarketing and Consumer Fraud and Abuse Prevention Act

Addition to note 166.

166 *Delete last sentence and final citation.*

Add to text after sentence containing note 167:

The Rule was extensively amended effective March 31, 2003,[167.1] but the amendments do not have a significant impact on the restrictions that apply to credit repair organizations.

167.1 68 Fed. Reg. 4530 (Jan. 29, 2003).

Replace note 168 with:

168 16 C.F.R. §§ 310.2(cc) (definition of telemarketing), 310.6(b)(3), *as amended by* 68 Fed. Reg. 4530 (Jan. 29, 2003) [former §§ 310.2(u), 310.6(c)].

Replace sentence containing note 169 with:

It specifically covers cases where the consumer makes the first call to the credit repair organization in response to an advertisement or direct mail solicitation, including those transmitted by fax, e-mail, or similar methods.[169]

169 16 C.F.R. § 310.6(b)(5), (6), *as amended by* 68 Fed. Reg. 4530 (Jan. 29, 2003). The former version of these sections of the rule, 16 C.F.R. § 310.6(e), (f), did not specifically mention fax and e-mail transmission.

Addition to note 170.

170 *Replace first citation in note with*: 16 C.F.R. § 310.6(b)(1), *as amended by* 68 Fed. Reg. 4530 (Jan. 29, 2003) [formerly § 310.6(a)].

§ 15.4.3 *Fair Credit Reporting / 2004 Supplement*

Add to text after sentence containing note 170:

The Rule does not cover charitable organizations, but covers for-profit organizations that solicit contributions or sell goods or services on behalf of non-profit organizations.[170.1]

170.1   *See* 68 Fed. Reg. 4530, 4589–90 (Jan. 29, 2003).

Addition to note 172.

172   *Add at end of note*: This subsection was not changed by the FTC's 2003 amendments to the Rule.

Replace notes 173–175 with:

173   16 C.F.R. § 310.4(a)(4). This section was not changed by the FTC's 2003 amendments to the Rule, but when proposing the amended rule the FTC commented that advance fee credit card offers violate the Rule. 67 Fed. Reg. 4492, 4512 (Jan. 30, 2002).

174   16 C.F.R. § 310.3, *as amended by* 68 Fed. Reg. 4530 (Jan. 29, 2003).

175   16 C.F.R. § 310.3(a)(1), *as amended by* 68 Fed. Reg. 4530 (Jan. 29, 2003).

Add to text after subsection's second-to-last paragraph:

The 2003 amendments to the Rule establish a nationwide do-not-call list.[175.1] **Consumers who have received telephone solicitations from credit repair organizations should consider adding their names to the do-not-call list.**[175.2]

175.1   16 C.F.R. § 310.4(b)(iii)(B), *as amended by* 68 Fed. Reg. 4530 (Jan. 29, 2003).

175.2   Consumers may add their names to the do-not-call list by calling 1-888-382-1222 (TTY 1-866-290-4236) or on-line at www.ftc.gov/donotcall.

Page 378

15.4.3 Telephone Consumer Protection Act

Replace note 183 with:

183   47 C.F.R. § 64.1200(a)(1).

Add to text after "automatic dialing system" in sentence containing note 183:

or using an artificial or pre-recorded voice

Replace note 184 with:

184   47 U.S.C. § 227(b)(1)(B); 47 C.F.R. § 64.1200(a)(2), (c).

Chapter 16   Privacy Protection

Page 379

16.1 Overview

Add to text at end of second paragraph of subsection:

Web bugs, tiny graphics that are put into web pages and e-mails, can monitor who views the information. Clickstream data can tell website owners which pages of the site were viewed and for how long.[2.1] "Cookies" dropped into a computer may not identify the user by name but do identify the particular computer, which allows an interested party to assemble a great deal of information about that computer's user.

    2.1   *See also* Gavin Skok, *Establishing a Legitimate Expectation of Privacy in Clickstream Data*, 6 Mich. Telecomm. Tech. L. Rev. 61 (2000), *available at* www.mttlr.org/volsix/skok.html.

Page 380

Addition to note 9.

    9   Note that the USA PATROT Act expanded the list of disclosures permitted by the Cable Communications Policy Act by adding certain disclosures made to specified government authorities. Pub. L. No. 107-56, § 211 (Oct. 26, 2001), *amending* 47 U.S.C. § 551(c).

Add to text immediately following note 9:

, medical records,[9.1]

    9.1   As of April 14, 2003, most health plans and providers had to begin complying with the Standards for Privacy of Individually Identifiable Health Information promulgated by the Secretary of Health and Human Services. 67 Fed. Reg. 53226–53272 (Aug. 14, 2002), *codified at* 45 C.F.R. §§ 160.101–160.312, 164.102–164.534. Regulations issued by HHS generally prohibit covered entities from using or disclosing protected health information except as specifically allowed. Among the permitted disclosures are those to consumer reporting agencies for purposes of payment, so long as the disclosure is limited to: name and address; date of birth, social security number, payment history, account number, and name and address of the health care provider. 45 C.F.R. §§ 164.501, 164.506(c)(1).

Add to text at end of paragraph containing note 13:

The FACTA of 2003 federalized the means through which consumers can protect their files from the work of identity thieves and purge from those files debts arising from theft.[13.1] The Act also sets the table for more thorough protection of financial information—at least of information acquired from consumer reporting agencies—by requiring designated federal agencies to create regulations that will require those who have information from consumer reports to properly dispose of it.[13.2]

    13.1   Pub. L. No. 108-159 (2003).
    13.2   15 U.S.C. § 1681w, *added by* Pub. L. No. 108-159, § 216 (2003).

16.2 Privacy from Governmental Intrusion

Addition to note 19.

    19   Katz v. U.S., 389 U.S. 347 (1967).

Add to text at end of subsection:

The ability of the federal government to obtain information, including financial information, about an individual from third parties expanded significantly with the USA PATRIOT Act.[25.1] Among other provisions that diminish privacy, the Act allows the FBI to seek a judicial order that requires a third party to produce all tangible things that party holds with respect to a specified person.[25.2] The FBI is entitled to the order upon merely asserting that the items are sought for an authorized investigation to protect against international terrorism or clandestine intelligence activities.[25.3] Furthermore, the Act prohibits the third party from

§ 16.3   *Fair Credit Reporting / 2004 Supplement*

disclosing that the FBI has sought or obtained the records and immunizes it from liability for its disclosures.[25.4]

- 25.1   Pub. L. No. 107-56, 115 Stat. 272 (2001).
- 25.2   *Id.* at § 215.
- 25.3   *Id.* The power is qualified by the provision that the investigation of a U.S. person may not be conducted solely on the basis of activities protected by the first amendment. *Id.*
- 25.4   *Id.*

Page 381

16.3 Tort of Invasion of Privacy

Addition to notes 26, 28, 29, 37, 39.

- 26   A nineteenth-century law review article advanced the idea of privacy in American tort law considerably. Samuel D. Warren & Louis D. Brandeis, *The Right to Privacy*, 4 Harvard L. Rev. 193 (1890). The authors, who deplored the "overstepping" of the press and the "numerous mechanical devices" that were breaching privacy cited the "general right of the individual to be let alone" as the basis of the tort.
- 28   *See also* Sloan v. S.C. Dept. of Pub. Safety, 586 S.E.2d 108, 110 (S.C. 2003) (because state law authorized sale of images on drivers' licenses, no liability for misappropriation).
- 29   Blakey v. Victory Equip. Sales, Inc., 576 S.E.2d 288, 292 (Ga. Ct. App. 2002) (no false light claim where defendant disclosed information only to credit reporting agency, not to "public").
- 37   *See, e.g.*, Phillips v. Grendahl, 312 F.3d 357, 371–72 (8th Cir. 2002); Robins v. Conseco Fin. Loan Co., 656 N.W.2d 241 (Minn. Ct. App. 2003).
- 39   *See, e.g.*, Phillips v. Grendahl, 312 F.3d 357, 372 (8th Cir. 2002) (disclosure of credit report to just one person failed publicity element); Olwell v. Med. Info. Bureau, 2003 WL 79035 (D. Minn. Jan. 7, 2003) (granting summary judgment to defendant on publication of private facts claim that alleged the defendant improperly disclosed the results of plaintiff's drug test to three insurance company); Blakey v. Victory Equip. Sales, Inc., 576 S.E.2d 288, 292 (Ga. Ct. App. 2002) (publication of information to single credit reporting agency failed to meet publicity element of public disclosure of private facts claim); Robins v. Conseco Fin. Loan Co., 656 N.W.2d 241 (Minn. Ct. App. 2003) (plaintiff failed to establish publicity element of public disclosure of private facts claim based on lender's disclosure of plaintiff's poor credit history to a co-worker, from whom plaintiff sought to purchase a mobile home); Bodah v. Lakeville Motor Express, Inc., 663 N.W.2d 550 (Minn. 2003) (employer's disclosure of 204 employee names and social security numbers to sixteen trucking terminals in six states did not meet publicity element of public disclosure of private facts claim; specifically evaluating the publicity element).

Add to text after sentence containing note 40:

However, a Wisconsin case upheld an invasion of privacy verdict based on a single disclosure to a single person, stating that the jury may consider the type and character of the person to whom the defendant disclosed the information in determining whether the plaintiff satisfied the publicity element of the tort.[40.1] If the persons to whom the defendant discloses the private matter have a special relationship with the plaintiff, disclosure to just a couple of people may satisfy the element.[40.2]

- 40.1   Pachowitz v. Ledoux, 666 N.W.2d 88 (Wis. Ct. App. 2003).
- 40.2   Chisholm v. Foothill Capital Corp., 3 F. Supp. 2d 925, 941 (N.D. Ill. 1998) (disclosure of plaintiff's affair with a married man to two of her potential business clients could satisfy publicity element; however, plaintiff failed to show that the information was private and that its disclosure would be highly offensive to a reasonable person, therefore action dismissed).

Page 382

Addition to notes 42, 43.

- 42   Phillips v. Grendahl, 312 F.3d 357, 372 (8th Cir. 2002); Olwell v. Med. Info. Bureau, 2003 WL 79035 (D. Minn. Jan. 7, 2003); Joseph v. J.J. Mac Intyre Cos., L.L.C., 238 F. Supp. 2d 1158, 1169 (N.D. Cal. 2002); Irvine v. Akron Beacon Journal, 770 N.E.2d 1105 (Ohio Ct. App. 2002) (affirming jury's award of $100,000 in punitive damages for defendant's repeated computer-dialed sales calls to plaintiff's home).
  Replace Remsburg citation with: 816 A.2d 1001 (N.H. 2003).
- 43   *See, e.g.*, Lowe v. Surpas Resource Corp., 253 F. Supp. 2d 1209 (D. Kan. 2003) (for jury to decide whether debt collector's actions intruded upon borrower's seclusion); Pulla v. Amoco Oil Co., 882 F. Supp. 836 (S.D. Iowa 1994) (affirming verdict that defendant had intruded upon the seclusion of plaintiff, who was defendant's employee, by accessing his credit card records to check his activities on days he had called in sick; rejecting defense that defendant had a legitimate objective in reviewing the records), *aff'd in part, rev'd in part on other grounds*, 72 F.3d 648 (8th Cir. 1995); Remsburg v. Docusearch, Inc., 816 A.2d 1001, 1008–09 (N.H. 2001) (people have a reasonable expectation that someone to whom they disclose their social security numbers will keep the numbers private, and therefore the wrongful disclosure of the number may be considered sufficiently offensive to support an action based on intrusion upon seclusion; however, people do not have a similar expectation of privacy as to their work addresses, and therefore no intrusion

Privacy Protection / 2004 Supplement § 16.4.1.1

upon seclusion action can be based on the release of that information). *But see* Phillips v. Grendahl, 312 F.3d 357, 372 (8th Cir. 2002) (future mother-in-law's improper purpose to obtain credit report on plaintiff did not render acquisition "highly offensive" for purposes of intrusion upon seclusion invasion of privacy tort); *In re* Trans Union Corp. Privacy Litig., 211 F.R.D. 328, 343–42 (N.D. Ill. 2002) (consumer reporting agency's disclosure of plaintiffs' credit reports to target marketing firms did not meet highly offensive element of intrusion upon seclusion invasion of privacy claim); Fabio v. Credit Bureau of Hutchison, Inc., 210 F.R.D. 688 (D. Minn. 2002) (debt collector's use of curse words in telephone demands for payment did not render intrusion highly offensive).

Add at end of sentence containing note 43:

, or access to a credit report.[43.1]

    43.1 Smith v. Bob Smith Chevrolet, Inc., 275 F. Supp. 2d 808, 822 (W.D. Ky. 2003) (denying defendant's motion for summary judgment).

Add to text after sentence containing note 44:

While social security numbers are private, courts differ as to whether transmission of social security numbers can constitute an intrusion upon seclusion.[44.1]

    44.1 Phillips v. Grendahl, 312 F.3d 357 (8th Cir. 2002) (no); Remsburg v. Docusearch, 816 A.2d 1001 (N.H. 2003) (yes); Bodah v. Lakeville Motor Express, Inc., 649 N.W.2d 859, 863 (Minn. Ct. App. 2002) (recognizing privacy of social security numbers), *rev'd on other grounds*, 663 N.W.2d 550 (Minn. 2003).

Addition to notes 47, 48, 50.

    47 *Replace citation to Blanche v. First Nationwide Mortg. Corp. with*: 74 S.W.3d 444 (Tex. Ct. App. 2002).
    48 *Add to end of footnote*: *See* Remsburg v. Docusearch, Inc., 816 A.2d 1001 (N.H. 2003).
    50 *See also* Lowe v. Surpas Resource Corp., 253 F. Supp. 2d 1209 (D. Kan. 2003) (debt collector's repeated calls to identity theft victim could be basis of intrusion upon seclusion claim).

Add to text after sentence containing note 50:

The tort of appropriation at first glance appears to be apropos to identity theft. After all, the essence of identity theft is the thief's appropriation the victim's name or likeness for the thief's own benefit.[50.1] Traditionally, the elements of the tort have been: (i) an appropriation of the plaintiff's name or likeness for the value associated with it, and not in an incidental manner or for a newsworthy purpose; (ii) a publication with which the plaintiff can be identified; and (iii) an advantage or benefit to the defendant.[50.2] The traditional use of the tort has been read to intend to protect the value of an individual's celebrity or image, such as when an advertiser pastes a picture of a star athlete onto an ad to market a product or service without actually obtaining the athlete's endorsement. Arguably, an identity thief seizes a plaintiff' name (and social security number) for the benefit of the credit reputation associated with it, uses that information in a way with which not only is the plaintiff identified, but only the plaintiff is identified, and does so for the thief's benefit—to obtain goods and services without the burden of paying for them. Nonetheless, as yet appropriation has not been recognized as a viable claim in ordinary identity theft cases.[50.3]

    50.1 Restatement (Second) of Torts § 652C ("[o]ne who appropriates to his own use or benefit the name or likeness of another is subject to liability to the other for invasion of his privacy").
    50.2 Matthews v. Wozencraft, 15 F.3d 432, 437 (5th Cir. 1994).
    50.3 *Cf.* Remsburg v. Docusearch, Inc., 816 A.2d 1001 (N.H. 2001) (investigator who sells personal information cannot be liable for appropriation because the benefit to the investigator does not derive from the social or commercial standing of the persona whose information is sold, but from the client's willingness to pay for the information).

16.4 Statutory Protection of Financial Information

16.4.1 The Gramm-Leach-Bliley Act

Page 383

16.4.1.1 Overview

Replace first thirteen words of sentence containing note 60 with:

The FTC has issued its Safeguard Rules, which became effective May 23, 2003;

145

§ 16.4.1.2   *Fair Credit Reporting / 2004 Supplement*

Page 384

Addition to note 60.

60   Replace first two citations to Code of Federal Regulations with: 16 C.F.R. pt. 314. *Replace last citation to Code of Federal Regulations with*: 16 C.F.R. § 314.5.

Add to text at end of subsection:

As yet, not many cases have tested the contours of Gramm-Leach-Bliley. Preliminary uses of Gramm-Leach-Bliley have been to defend against a litigation opponent's discovery request for customer information.[60.1]

60.1   *See, e.g., In re* Boston Herald, Inc., 321 F.3d 174, 190 (1st Cir. 2003) (citing Gramm-Leach-Bliley in support of its ruling that newspaper could not have access to sealed financial documents submitted by a criminal defendant who sought government funding for his legal bills; stating that "[p]ersonal financial information, such as one's income or bank account balance, is universally presumed to be private, not public, for disclosure purposes"); Landry v. Union Planters Corp., 2003 WL 21355462 (E.D. La. June 6, 2003) (party's discovery of customer information would not violate Gramm-Leach-Bliley Act so long as all nonpublic personal information was redacted from the materials); Union Planters Bank, N.A. v. Gavel, 2003 WL 1193671 (E.D. La. Mar. 12, 2003) (granting bank a permanent injunction against party who had been issued a subpoena for the disclosure of information that related to plaintiff bank's customers, on grounds that the Gramm-Leach-Bliley Act prohibited the defendant from revealing that information without the customers' consent); ArborPlace, LP v. Encore Opportunity Fund, L.L.C., 2002 WL 205681 (Del. Ch. Jan. 29, 2002) (Gramm-Leach-Bliley regulations did not require limited liability company to shield its membership lists from limited partner, information was exempt from notice and opt-out requirements by 17 C.F.R. § 248.15, the SEC's equivalent to the FTC's regulation at 16 C.F.R. § 313.15).

16.4.1.2 "Financial Institutions"—Entities That Must Comply with Gramm-Leach-Bliley

Addition to note 61.

61   *See also* Lacerte Software Corp. v. Prof'l Tax Servs., L.L.C., 2004 WL 180321 at *1-2 (N.D. Tex. Jan. 6, 2004) (finding software company not a financial institution, denying defendant's motion to dismiss based on argument that plaintiff included defendant's personal credit card number and signature in exhibit to complaint); N.Y. State Bar Ass'n v. F.T.C., 276 F. Supp. 2d 110, 146 (D.D.C. 2003) (holding that Gramm-Leach-Bliley's privacy provisions did not apply to attorneys and suggesting that, even if it were, the FTC should consider whether attorneys are entitled to a *de minimis* exemption under the Act).

16.4.1.4 "Nonpublic Personal Information"—The Information Covered by Gramm-Leach-Bliley

Addition to note 73.

73   *See also* Landry v. Union Planters Corp., 2003 WL 21355462 at *6–*7 (E.D. La. June 6, 2003) (Gramm-Leach-Bliley Act's privacy provisions do not apply to redacted or aggregated financial data; such data is not "nonpublic information"; party's discovery of customer information would not violate Gramm-Leach-Bliley Act so long as all nonpublic personal information was redacted from the materials); Union Planters Bank, N.A. v. Gavel, 2003 WL 1193671 (E.D. La. Mar. 12, 2003) (granting bank a permanent injunction against party who had been issued a subpoena for the disclosure of information that related to plaintiff bank's customers, on grounds that the Gramm-Leach-Bliley Act prohibited the defendant from revealing that information without the customers' consent; it is unclear whether the defendant sought to employ the Act's exception for subpoenas, found at 16 C.F.R. § 313.15).

Page 386

16.4.1.5 Exempt Disclosures

Add note 84.1 to end of seventeenth bulleted item.

84.1   Cash Today of Texas, Inc. v. Greenberg, 2002 WL 31414138 (D. Del. Oct. 23, 2002) (ruling against bank that objected to a subpoena for the production of documents relating to transactions between bank and plaintiff on the grounds that the Gramm-Leach-Bliley Act prohibited such disclosure; court applied subpoena exception in Act, found at 16 C.F.R. § 313.15); ArborPlace, LP v. Encore Opportunity Fund, L.L.C., 2002 WL 205681 (Del. Ch. Jan. 29, 2002) (Gramm-Leach-Bliley regulations did not require limited liability company to shield its membership lists from limited partner, information was exempt from notice and opt-out requirements by 17 C.F.R. § 248.15, the SEC's equivalent to the FTC's regulation at 16 C.F.R. § 313.15).

Add note 84.2 to end of subsection's bulleted list.

84.2   16 C.F.R. § 313.15. *See also* Marks v. Global Mortgage Group, Inc., 218 F.R.D. 492, 496 (S.D. W. Va. 2003) (judicial process exception permitted defendant to disclose its customers' nonpublic personal information in response to plaintiffs' discovery request); Martino v. Barnett, 2003 WL 23327487 (W. Va. Mar. 15, 2004) (Gramm-Leach-Bliley Act allows use of judicial process to obtain information relevant to

16.4.1.11 Weaknesses of Gramm-Leach-Bliley

Add note 143.1 to end of first sentence of subsection's fourth paragraph.

143.1 See Borinski v. Williamson, 2004 WL 433746 at *3 (N.D. Tex. Mar. 1, 2004) (no private cause of action under Gramm-Leach-Bliley); Lacerte Software Corp. v. Prof'l Tax Servs., L.L.C., 2004 WL 180321 at *2 (N.D. Tex. Jan. 6, 2004) (same); Menton v. Experian Corp., 2003 WL 21692820 at *3 (S.D.N.Y. July 21, 2003) (same).

Addition to note 147.

147 *Replace Individual Reference citation with*: Trans Union L.L.C. v. FTC, 295 F.3d 42 (D.C. Cir. 2002).

16.4.2 Other State and Federal Protections

16.4.2.1 General

Add to text after sentence containing note 149:

Furthermore, a federal district court has held that the Act did not bar the use of cookies or other data mining activities.[149.1]

149.1 *In re* DoubleClick Inc. Privacy Litig., 154 F. Supp. 2d 497, 519 (S.D.N.Y. 2001).

Add to text at end of subsection:

The federal Electronic Communications Privacy Act of 1986 outlaws the interception of certain wire, oral and electronic communications, and provides a cause of action to those whose privacy has been breached in that manner.[151.1] However, that act does not restrict surreptitious Internet data collection. The Children's Online Privacy Protection Act (COPPA) restricts website operators and on-line services from collecting identifying information from children, but does not provide private parties with enforcement power.[151.2] The Telecommunications Act of 1996 contains a customer privacy provision that imposes on telecommunications carriers a duty to protect the confidentiality of customers' proprietary information, prohibits them from using information acquired from another carrier for marketing efforts, and requires customer approval to disclose customer proprietary network information.[151.3]

151.1 18 U.S.C. §§ 2510–2522. However, if the subject of the intercepted communication involves a matter of public interest, the First Amendment may prohibit a private action based on its disclosure. Bartnicki v. Vopper, 532 U.S. 514 (2001).

151.2 13 U.S.C. §§ 1301–1308.

151.3 47 U.S.C. § 222. *See also* 47 C.F.R. § 2005 (corresponding privacy regulation issued by the FCC). The FCC's regulation was struck down by the Tenth Circuit on First Amendment grounds, the court holding that the FCC had failed to show that the dissemination of the information would inflict "specific or significant harm on individuals," rejecting the government's assertion that a broad privacy interest justified the restriction on the carriers' commercial speech. U.S. West, Inc. v. FCC, 182 F.3d 1224 (10th Cir. 1999), *cert. denied sub nom.* Competition Policy Inst. v. U.S. West, Inc., 530 U.S. 1213 (2000).

Add new subsection after § 16.4.2.3.

16.4.2.3a The FCRA as Amended by the FACTA

The FCRA as amended by the FACTA provides addition protection of medical information that is connected with credit reports.[160.1] Consumers now also have extended rights to prevent themselves from being used for marketing purposes. As of December 1, 2004, the FACTA will extend the opt-out period for prescreening lists from two years to five.[160.2] Consumers may now opt out of marketing solicitations by users who acquired their information through an affiliate or pursuant to first-hand knowledge.[160.3]

The FCRA exempts from the definition of "consumer report" the information relating to transactions or experiences between the consumer and a person, the communication of such information between affiliates, and the communication of other information among affiliates, though consumers have the right to opt out of the last.[160.4] The FCRA now not only allows a consumer to opt out of the use by an affiliate of this exempt information to market its products or services but requires affiliates to notify the consumer both of the possibility that an affiliate may use the consumer's information for marketing and of the consumer's right to opt out of such use.[160.5] As with the opt-out right consumers can use to escape "firm offers,"[160.6] the opt-out lasts for five years and consumers may extend it for an additional five years.[160.7]

160.1 See § 6.5.3, *supra*.
160.2 15 U.S.C. § 1681b(e)(4)(B)(i); 16 C.F.R. § 602.1(c)(3)(xi), *added by* 69 Fed. Reg. 6526–31 (Feb. 5, 2004). See also §§ 5.3.8.4.4, 10.2.2.7, *supra*.
160.3 15 U.S.C. § 1681s-3, *added by* Pub. L. No. 108-159, § 214(a). *See also* § 2.4.2, *supra*.
160.4 15 U.S.C. § 1681a(d)(2)(A).
160.5 15 U.S.C. § 1681s-3, *added by* Pub. L. No. 108-159, § 214 (2003). Certain exemptions apply. 15 U.S.C. § 1681s-3(a)(4).
160.6 See § 5.3.8.4, *supra*.
160.7 15 U.S.C. § 1681s-3 (a)(3), *added by* Pub. L. No. 108-159, § 214 (2003).

16.4.2.4 State Statutes

Addition to note 163.

163 See, e.g., Fla. Stat. § 655.059 (financial institution's books and records are confidential); Haw. Rev. Stat. § 412:2-603 (misdemeanor for institution to disclose any information derived from a financial institution's records except in the regular course of business); Mo. Rev. Stat. § 326.105 (prohibiting disclosures by a financial institution that violate Gramm-Leach-Bliley); N.H. Rev. Stat. Ann. § 406-C:9 (prohibiting disclosures that do not comply with Gramm-Leach-Bliley Act). *See also* McCarty v. McCarty, 2003 WL 721681 (Conn. Super. Jan. 22, 2003) (though bank failed to fully comply with state statute's requirements regarding a bank's duties upon receiving a subpoena for customer records, sanctions were not appropriate because evidence did not show that bank willfully subverted the plaintiff's rights); Burford v. First Nat'l Bank in Mansfield, 557 So. 2d 1147 (La. App. 1990) (state privacy statute imposed on bank a duty to maintain the confidentiality of plaintiff's financial statement); Walker v. White, 89 S.W.3d 573 (Tenn. Ct. App. 2002) (customers had no cause of action against bank under Tennessee Financial Records Privacy Act because Act did not apply to subpoena issued by a federal agency).
Replace citation to Alaska Statutes with: Alaska Stat. § 06.01.028.

Add to text at end of subsection:

Finally, some state constitutions contain privacy provisions that may be a source of policy, if not actual precedent, to support a privacy claim.[164.1]

164.1 Alaska Const. art. I, § 22; Ariz. Const. art. II, § 8; Cal. Const. art. I, § 1; Mont. Const. art. II, § 10; Wash. Const. art. I, § 7. Some other state constitutions have privacy provisions that mirror the Fourth Amendment to the U.S. Constitution, targeted toward people's right to privacy from governmental, as opposed to general, intrusion. *See, e.g.*, Fla. Const. art. I, § 23; Ill. Const. art. I, § 6; La. Const. art. I, § 5; N.Y. Const. art. I, § 12; S.C. Const. art. I, § 10.

16.5 Common Law Protection of Financial Information

Addition to notes 165, 168, 169, 171.

165 See, e.g., Jordan v. Shattuck Nat'l Bank, 868 F.2d 383 (10th Cir. 1989) (plaintiff stated a cause of action against his bank for its wrongful disclosure of confidential loan application information). *See also* Roth v. First Natl. State Bank of N.J., 404 A.2d 1182 (N.J. Super. App. Div. 1979) (bank was not liable for teller's disclosure to accomplice that bank customer's custom of withdrawing large amounts of cash at particular times, on the agency grounds that teller's behavior was outside the scope of her employment).
Replace O'Halloran citation with: 205 F. Supp. 2d 1296, 1301 (M.D. Fla. 2002), *vacated and remanded on other grounds*, 350 F.3d 1197 (11th Cir. 2003). *Replace Heritage Surveyors citation with*: 801 A.2d 1248, 1252–53 (Pa. Super. 2002).

Page 393

168 Roth v. First Natl. State Bank of N.J., 404 A.2d 1182 (N.J. Super. App. Div. 1979) (bank was not liable for teller's disclosure to accomplice that bank customer's custom of withdrawing large amounts of cash at particular times, on the agency grounds that teller's behavior was outside the scope of her employment).
169 Boccardo v. Citibank, N.A., 579 N.Y.S.2d 836 (N.Y.Sup. Ct. 1991) (bank did not owe customer with line of credit a duty of confidentiality notwithstanding that customer had not yet drawn on line of credit).
171 Jordan v. Shattuck Natl Bank, 868 F.2d 383 (10th Cir. 1989) (reversing lower court's directed verdict in favor of the bank).

Add to text following sentence containing note 171:

Representations made by the bank in its contract with the customer or in its published privacy policy or other promotional materials should be a basis for a cause of action when the bank discloses information in violation of those representations. However, a New York court dismissed a class action brought by credit card holders and mortgagors against a bank based

Privacy Protection / 2004 Supplement § 16.6.1a.1

on its release of their information to marketers, on the grounds that the customers had failed to fulfill the damage element required by either a UDAP claim or a breach of contract claim.[171.1] In the court's view, the only consequences to the bank's customers were that they were "offered products and services which they were free to decline. This does not qualify as actual harm."[171.2] The case illustrates the trivial value many courts put on personal privacy.

171.1 Smith v. Chase Manhattan Bank, USA, 741 N.Y.S.2d 100 (N.Y. App. Div. 2002). The court also rejected an unjust enrichment claim by framing the alleged enrichment as the payments made by the customers for products and services marketed to them, finding that since the purchasers received the benefit of the products and services, no unjust enrichment arose. *Id.* at 102–03. However, the court framed the enrichment as arising from the profits the bank earned as commissions on the purchases made as a result of the marketing. The framing overlooks that the bank received the commission as a result not just of the sale of products to the customers who wished to purchase from marketers, but also from the disclosure of the financial information of all the members of the class, including the (probably majority) group who did not buy anything from the marketers to whom their confidential information was disclosed, and who thus received absolutely no benefit from the disclosure.

171.2 *Id.* at 102.

Addition to note 172.

172 *See also* Commercial Cotton Co. v. United Cal. Bank, 163 Cal. App. 3d 511, 516 (1985) (upholding verdict against bank in case claiming that it breached its covenant of good faith and fair dealing with a depositor, describing a bank's relationship with its depositor as "at least quasi-fiduciary").

16.6 Identity Theft

Page 394

16.6.1 General

Replace sentence containing note 174 with:

In 2002 the Federal Trade Commission received reports from 161,819 victims of identity theft; calls to its hotline increased by nearly 24 percent over the course of the year.[174]

174 Federal Trade Commission, Information on Identity Theft for Consumers & Victims From January, 2002 Through December, 2002, www.consumer.gov/idtheft/reports/CY2002ReportFinal.pdf, at 1.

Add to text after subsection's first paragraph:

The impact of identity theft on consumers led to the passage of the FACTA of 2003, which amended the FCRA to provide identity theft victims with tools to halt a thief's use of the victim's identity and to repair the damage done by a thief to the victim's credit record.[174.1] Until the passing of the FACTA, consumers had to seek relief through the FCRA's mechanisms for ordinary inaccuracies in a report[174.2] or through state identity theft laws.[174.3]

174.1 Pub. L. No. 108-159 (2003).
174.2 *See* Ch. 7, *supra.*
174.3 *See* § 16.6.3, Appx. B.3, *infra.* Although Congress enacted the Identity Theft and Assumption Deterrence Act to formally criminalize identity theft, the Act does not provide consumers with the ability to enforce it. *See* § 16.6.2, *infra.*

Replace sentence containing note 177 with:

Practical advice for coping with identity theft is found elsewhere in the manual.[177]

177 Retain as in main edition.

Add new subsection after § 16.6.1.

16.6.1a The FCRA's Identity Theft Prevention, Credit Restoration, and Financial Information Integrity & Privacy Provisions

16.6.1a.1 Overview

The FACTA adds to the FCRA significant provisions designed to prevent identity theft, limits the consequences of identity theft to victims' credit records, and help victims clear their credit records of identity-theft related information. The FCRA, as amended, sets up a web of communication among consumers, agencies, and furnishers that—if properly implemented and employed—could allow them, once they learn that a consumer's identity has been stolen, to synchronize consumer reports and purge theft-related information from agencies' and furnishers' files.

As described in more detail below, as of December 1, 2004, a consumer who is the victim of identity theft can

§ 16.6.1a.1

require a nationwide consumer reporting agency[177.1] to put a fraud alert in the victim's file; the agency must then notify the other nationwide agencies of the alert, which will require them to also place the alert in their files. The alert must notify all prospective users that the consumer does not authorize any user to establish any new credit plan or extension of credit[177.2] and users of a report containing such an alert must take steps to verify the consumer's identity before extending credit.[177.3] Beginning December 1, 2004, agencies must refer consumer complaints of identity theft to one another, and notified agencies must include the alert in their files as well.[177.4]

The victim can also identify fraudulent information in the consumer's report for the agency; the agency must block the fraudulent information and notify the furnisher of that information. Once notified, the furnisher must both reinvestigate the information and take steps to prevent it from being refurnished to any agency.

By December 1, 2004, furnishers must have reasonable procedures to respond to notices of information blocked due to identity theft[177.5] and, if furnished with an identity theft report, the furnisher must stop furnishing that information.[177.6] As revised, the Act now envisions a process through which a consumer can dispute information directly with a furnisher.[177.7] However, this provision will not become effective until the FTC issues regulations that identify the circumstances under which a furnisher must follow up on such a notice of dispute by reinvestigating the underlying information.[177.8] The agency will also have to provide the victim with a summary of identity theft victim's rights under the Act, once the FTC prepares it.[177.9]

Additional fraud prevention measures are forthcoming. The FACTA proposes adding regulations that will establish "red flag guidelines" for the use of institutions to identify identity fraud risks to account holders or customers.[177.10]

The revisions extend responsibility beyond agencies and furnishers. As of December 1, 2004, creditors will be prohibited from transferring a debt that a consumer has identified as resulting from identity theft.[177.11] Also, as of that date, if a debt collector learns that any information relating to a debt sought to be collected may either be fraudulent or may be the result of identity theft, the debt collector must notify the creditor and, upon the consumer's request, provide the consumer with the same information about the debt that the consumer would have been entitled to had the consumer actually incurred the debt.[177.12]

The FACTA adds a potentially powerful tool that allows an identity theft victim to obtain information from any business that transacted with the thief in the victim's name. This which may allow a victim to more quickly find and stop the thief.[177.13] Fraud victims now have a new right to a free credit report, over and above the free annual report that all consumers are now entitled to.[177.14] These reports should help fraud victims track and block false debts accrued in their names. The FTC is to prepare a summary of the new rights of victims of identity theft and fraud under the FCRA. Agencies must provide the summary to any victim who contacts an agency about such theft or fraud.[177.15] Furthermore, each nationwide consumer reporting agency must prepare and submit to the FTC an annual report summarizing consumer complaints received on identity theft or fraud alerts, which should lead to a nationwide picture of the effect of identity theft on the accuracy and integrity of consumers' credit files.[177.16]

The FACTA goes beyond addressing the surface problem of identity theft by addressing its underlying cause: The failure of businesses to properly verify, protect, and dispose of consumer financial information. Eventually, furnishers will have to comply with accuracy and integrity guidelines,[177.17] and those that collect consumers' information will eventually have to protect it from misuse pursuant to forthcoming regulations that will require persons who maintain information derived from a consumer report to "properly dispose" of such information.[177.18]

177.1 15 U.S.C. § 1681c-1; *added by* Pub. L. No. 108-159, § 112 (2003);16 C.F.R. § 602.1(c)(3)(xi), *added by* 69 Fed. Reg. 6526–31 (Feb. 5, 2004). An agency "that regularly engages in the practice of assembling or evaluating, and maintaining, for the purpose of furnishing consumer reports to third parties bearing on a consumer's credit worthiness, credit standing, or credit capacity . . . [p]ublic record information [and] [c]redit account information from persons who furnish that information regularly and in the ordinary course of business" about consumers "residing nationwide." 15 U.S.C. § 1681a(p).

177.2 15 U.S.C. § 1681c-1(h)(1)(A).

177.3 15 U.S.C. § 1681c-1(h)(1)(B).

177.4 Pub. L. No. 108-159, § 153, adding § 1681s(f); 16 C.F.R. § 602.1(c)(3)(vi), *added by* 69 Fed. Reg. 6526–31 (Feb. 5, 2004).

177.5 Pub. L. No. 108-159, § 154, adding 15 U.S.C. § 1681s–2(a)(6); 16 C.F.R. § 602.1(c)(3)(vii), *added by* 69 Fed. Reg. 6526–31 (Feb. 5, 2004).

177.6 *Id.*

177.7 Pub. L. No. 108-159, § 312(c) adding 15 U.S.C. § 1681s–2 (a)(8).

177.8 *Id.*

177.9 15 U.S.C. § 1681g(d), *added by* Pub. L. No. 108-159, § 151 (2003). Note that "credit," "creditor," and "electronic funds transaction" are all defined terms. 15 U.S.C. §§ 1681a(r), (s), *added by* Pub. L. No. 108-159, § 111 (2003). *See also* § 6.3, *supra*

177.10 Pub. L. No. 108-159, § 114, adding 15 U.S.C. § 1681m(e).

177.11 Pub. L. No. 108-159, § 154(b), adding 15 U.S.C. § 1681m(f); 16 C.F.R. § 602.1(c)(3)(vii), *added by* 69 Fed. Reg. 6526–31 (Feb. 5, 2004).

177.12 Pub. L. No. 108-159, § 115, adding 15 U.S.C. § 1681m(g); 16 C.F.R. § 602.1(c)(3)(viii), *added by* 69 Fed. Reg. 6526–31 (Feb. 5, 2004). *See* 3.3.4.2a, *supra*.

177.13 Pub. L. No. 108-159, § 151, adding 15 U.S.C. § 1681c(e).

177.14 Pub. L. No. 108-159, §211(a)(4), adding 15 U.S.C. § 1681j(d).

177.15 15 U.S.C. § 1681g(d), *added by* Pub. L. No. 108-159, § 151 (2003).

177.16 15 U.S.C. § 1681i(e), *added by* Pub. L. No. 108-159, § 313(a).

177.17 Pub. L. No. 108-159, § 312(a).

177.18 Pub. L. No. 108-159, § 216, adding § 1681w.

However, consumers may not realize the full value of these new anti-fraud provisions. While at first glance these amendments appear to give identity theft victims significant rights, what the amendments give with one hand they take away with another. The FACTA preempts certain state laws that address identity theft.[177.19] Furthermore, the FACTA specifically prohibits consumers from enforcing many of the new rights, stating that the liability provisions of the Act[177.20] do not apply to most of the new obligations of furnishers or to any violations of the forthcoming accuracy and integrity regulations or red-flag guidelines.[177.21] Furthermore, identity theft victims may not enforce the new obligation of businesses to provide them with the thief's transaction information.[177.22] Consumers will have to rely on the FTC and state agencies to enforce these provisions.

16.6.1a.2 Fraud Alerts and Active Military Duty Alerts

16.6.1a.2.1 General

The FACTA adds a new section to the FCRA that provides for three varieties of alerts that consumers may add to their files with nationwide consumer reporting agencies; they differ in their initiation requirements, time periods, and limits on users. However, all three require the agency receiving the alert to refer it to the other nationwide agencies; in theory, this process will allow consumers to issue the alert to all the agencies with "one call."

The form of these alerts and their effects on users should lead them to be significantly more effective than a simple dispute notice allowed by another preexisting provision of the Act.[177.23] Furthermore, since the new section does not limit liability, consumers can enforce it against agencies and users pursuant to the willful and negligent noncompliance provisions of the FCRA.[177.24] States, however, are preempted from imposing any "requirement or prohibition" with respect to the "conduct required" by the fraud alerts provision.[177.25]

16.6.1a.2.2 Initial fraud alerts

With respect to a first type of alert, the FCRA as revised allows consumers who believe that they are or might be victimized by identity theft fraud or any other sort of fraud to require all nationwide consumer reporting agencies to add a fraud alert to their files simply by calling one such agency.[177.26] It is called a "one-call" alert because the agency must refer the alert to other nationwide agencies and all the agencies must not only include the alert in the consumer's file but provide the alert each time they generate that consumer's credit score.

To provide the alert, the agencies must present to any user a "clear and conspicuous" view of the alert, which must notify users of the consumer's report that the consumer may be a victim of fraud—including, but not limited to, identity theft.[177.27] In addition to placing the alert, the agency must provide the consumer with a summary of the consumer's rights under the identity theft provisions of the Act,[177.28] must notify the consumer of the consumer's right to a free credit report, and must provide a requested report within three business days of the consumer's request.[177.29]

A fraud alert need stay active for only ninety days (though a consumer may request the agency to lift the alert earlier);[177.30] for a sustained alert, the consumer may obtain an extended fraud alert, described below. However, only consumers who file an identity theft report may seek an extended fraud alert.[177.31] Accordingly, the initial fraud alert is appropriate for consumers who are unsure whether they have actually been defrauded or who believe they may be the victim of a fraud other than identity theft.

16.6.1a.2.3 Extended fraud alerts

An identity theft victim can seek a second type of alert, an extended fraud alert, once the victim has filed a qualifying identity theft report with a law enforcement agency. The FTC must define an "identity theft report" in regulations but, at a minimum, such a report must include allegations of

---

177.19 15 U.S.C. § 1681t, *as amended by* Pub. L. No. 108-159.

177.20 15 U.S.C. §§ 1681n, 1681o (2003). *See* Ch. 11, *supra*.

177.21 Pub. L. No. 108-159, § 312(e), *amending* 15 U.S.C. § 1681s–2(c).

177.22 15 U.S.C. § 1681m(e), *added by* Pub. L. No. 108-159, § 114 (2003).

177.23 15 U.S.C. § 1681i(b). *See* § 7.6.1, *supra*.

177.24 15 U.S.C. §§ 1681n, 1681o.

177.25 15 U.S.C. § 1681t(b)(5)(B), *added by* Pub. L. No. 108-159, § 711 (2003).

177.26 FCRA § 15 U.S.C. § 1681c-1(a), *added by* Pub. L. No. 108-159, § 112 (2003). This provision will become effective on December 1, 2004. 16 C.F.R. § 602.1(c)(3)(i), *added by* 69 Fed. Reg. 6526–31 (Feb. 5, 2004). Nationwide consumer reporting agencies are those "that regularly engage[] in the practice of assembling or evaluating, and maintaining, for the purpose of furnishing consumer reports to third parties bearing on a consumer's credit worthiness, credit standing, or credit capacity . . . [p]ublic record information [and] [c]redit account information from persons who furnish that information regularly and in the ordinary course of business" about consumers "residing nationwide." 15 U.S.C. § 1681a(p), *added by* Pub. L. No. 108-159, § 111 (2003).

177.27 "Identity theft" is "a fraud committed using the identifying information of another person." 15 U.S.C. § 1681a(q)(4) *added by* Pub. L. No. 108-159 § 111 (2003).

177.28 15 U.S.C. § 1681g(d), *added by* Pub. L. No. 108-159, § 151 (2003). *See also* § 6.3a, *supra*.

177.29 15 U.S.C. § 1681j(d), *added by* Pub. L. No. 108-159, § 211(a)(4) (2003).

177.30 15 U.S.C. § 1681c-1(1)(A). The agency may choose to provide the alert for a longer period. *Id.*

177.31 15 U.S.C. § 1681c-1(b)(1), *added by* Pub. L. No. 108-159, § 112 (a)(1) (2003).

identity theft, must be an official valid report filed by a consumer with federal, state, or local law enforcement agency, and must subject the consumer to criminal penalties for false information.[177.32]

By submitting the identity theft report to a nationwide consumer reporting agency, the consumer may add to his or her credit file an extended fraud alert that can last for seven years.[177.33] As with the initial fraud alert, the agency must refer the alert to the other nationwide agencies, all of whom must provide a "clear and conspicuous view" of the alert each time they generate the consumer's credit score.[177.34]

The extended fraud alert provides additional protection to identity theft victims by requiring the agencies to exclude, for five years, the consumer from any lists generated to sell to users for transactions not initiated by the consumer (prescreening lists),[177.35] a provision that should curtail access by new thieves to the consumer's identity.[177.36] This feature, along with the extended term of the alert—which lasts as long as a negative item of credit information may be included in a consumer's file[177.37]—are what distinguish the extended fraud alert from the initial alert. The agencies must also notify the consumer of the consumer's right to two free credit reports over the subsequent twelve months.[177.38] As with the fraud alert, an agency must provide the consumer's file to the consumer within three business days of the consumer's request.[177.39]

16.6.1a.2.4 Active military duty alerts

Consumers on active military duty can alert report users of their status by adding an alert to their files.[177.40] Once a military consumer requests the active duty alert, it will become part of the consumer's credit report for twelve months.[177.41] Similar to an extended fraud alert, an active military duty alert gives the consumer relief from prescreening lists, though for only two years as opposed to five.[177.42]

The active duty alert should also be used by creditors to comply with the Soldier and Sailors Relief Act[177.43] when engaged in collection activity. It can also help to prevent identity theft from victimizing military personnel who are stationed away from old addresses. However, unlike the fraud alert and extended alert, an active duty alert does not entitle a consumer to a free credit report.

16.6.1a.2.5 Effects of alerts

All three varieties of alerts must state that the consumer does not authorize new credit, an additional card on an existing account, or any increase in the credit limit of any existing account.[177.44] In addition, once the FTC prescribes a model summary of identity theft victim's rights, an agency that is contacted by a consumer who expresses a belief that the consumer is a victim of fraud or identity theft involving credit, an electronic funds transaction, or an account or transfer at or with another financial institution or other creditor, must provide the consumer with the summary of rights.[177.45]

The alerts also impose new responsibilities on users to verify the identity of credit applicants, provisions that should interrupt a thief's abuse of a consumer's identity. A user of a report containing an initial fraud alert or active military duty alert may not proceed with a credit transaction unless the user "utilizes reasonable policies and procedures to form a reasonable belief that the user knows the identity of the person making the request."[177.46] If the alert is an extended fraud alert, the prohibition extends to users of credit scores as well.[177.47]

Consumers may provide a telephone number in the alert; in the case of an extended fraud alert the user *must* use the number to verify the requester's identity.[177.48] However, if the alert is an initial fraud alert or an active duty alert, the user can "take reasonable steps" to verify the consumer's

---

177.32 15 U.S.C. § 1681a(q)(4), *added by* Pub. L. No. 108-159, § 111 (2003).

177.33 15 U.S.C. § 1681c-1(b), *added by* Pub. L. No. 108-159, § 112 (2003). This provision will become effective on December 1, 2004. 16 C.F.R. § 602.1(c)(3)(i), *added by* 69 Fed. Reg. 6526-31 (Feb. 5, 2004).

177.34 15 U.S.C. § 1681a(q)(2)(B), *added by* Pub. L. No. 108-159, § 111 (2003).

177.35 *See* § 5.3.8.4, *supra*.

177.36 Note that the term of this exclusion is even with the newly extended five-year effective term of a consumer's opt-out of prescreening lists pursuant to 15 U.S.C. § 1681b(e). *See* § 5.3.8.4.4, *supra*.

177.37 15 U.S.C. § 1681c(a)(5). *See also* Ch. 8, *supra*.

177.38 15 U.S.C. § 1681g(d).

177.39 *Id.*

177.40 § 15 U.S.C. § 1681c-1(c), *added by* Pub. L. No. 108-159, § 112 (2003). This provision will become effective on December 1, 2004. 16 C.F.R. § 602.1(c)(3)(i), *added by* 69 Fed. Reg. 6526-31 (Feb. 5, 2004). The Act defines an "active duty military consumer" to mean "a consumer in military service who . . . is on active duty or a reservist called to active duty . . . and who is assigned to service away from the usual duty station of the consumer." 15 U.S.C. § 1681a(q)(1) (*citing* 10 U.S.C. §§ 101(d)(1) and (a)(13)).

177.41 § 15 U.S.C. § 1681c-1(c)(1), *added by* Pub. L. No. 108-159, § 111 (2003).

177.42 § 15 U.S.C. § 1681c-1(c)(2).

177.43 50 U.S.C. App. §§ 501-591. *See* § 13.2.8.3, *supra*.

177.44 Other than an extension under an existing open-end credit account, that is, a credit card. 15 U.S.C. §§ 1681c-1(h)(1)(A)(initial fraud and active military duty alerts), 1681c-1(h)(2)(A) (active military duty alerts).

177.45 15 U.S.C. § 1681g(d), *added by* Pub. L. No. 108-159, § 151 (2003). Note that "credit," "creditor," and "electronic funds transaction" are all defined terms. 15 U.S.C. §§ 1681a(r), (s), *added by* Pub. L. No. 108-159, § 111 (2003).

177.46 § 15 U.S.C. § 1681c-1(h)(1)(B)(i), *added by* Pub. L. No. 108-159, § 112 (2003).

177.47 § 15 U.S.C. § 1681c-1(h)(2)(b).

177.48 § 15 U.S.C. § 1681c-1(h)(2)(B), *added by* Pub. L. No. 108-159, § 112 (2003). The consumer may provide another "reasonable contact method." *Id.* at 1681c-1(h)(2)(A)(ii).

identity instead of calling the consumer.[177.49] The FTC will prescribe regulations that will define the appropriate proof of identity.[177.50]

16.6.1a.3 Identity Theft Victim's Access to Information About the Theft

16.6.1a.3.1 Access to thief's transaction information

The Act as revised requires businesses that have dealt with an identity thief to provide information about the transactions to the thief's victim and to law enforcement agencies, a requirement may help a consumer to document fraud transactions and find the thief.[177.51] Finding the thief is necessary to the prosecution and conviction of the thief; some states' identity theft laws allow a judge to order a thief to compensate a victim and to order record rehabilitation only upon actual conviction.[177.52]

In theory, the provision could allow identity theft victims access to the thief's application for credit and any business records—information that could reveal the source of the theft.[177.53] The consumer must make a written request for the information, mailed to the address specified by the business entity, and include any relevant information about the transaction requested by the business.[177.54] The victim must further provide proof of positive identification, consisting, at the business' election, of one of the following: a government-issued identification card; personally identifying information of the same type as the thief provided to the business; or personally identifying information of the type that the business usually requests from new applicants.[177.55] The victim must also provide proof of the identity theft claim, which the business can designate from a choice of a copy of a police report evidencing the claim,[177.56] a properly completed FTC Identity Theft Affidavit, or another affidavit acceptable to the business.[177.57] Upon receiving this information, the business should provide the victim with copies of the application and business transaction records.[177.58]

Nonetheless, a business can thwart a victim's access to such records. Even if a victim complies with all the prerequisites to obtain the transaction information, a business may still decline to provide the information if the business determines "in the exercise of good faith" that any of the following exceptions exists:

- the business does not have a "high degree of confidence in knowing the true identity of the individual" requesting the information, notwithstanding the victim's satisfaction of the identity verification requirements,
- the request is based on a misrepresentation of fact, or
- the information requested is "Internet navigational data or similar information."[177.59]

Since consumers have no right to enforce the business transaction provision[177.60] and states are preempted from regulating not just the conduct required by the new provision but the subject matter itself,[177.61] the effectiveness of this provision will depend upon the willingness of businesses to comply with it.

177.49 § 15 U.S.C. § 1681c-1(h)1)(B)(ii), *added by* Pub. L. No. 108-159, § 112 (2003).

177.50 15 U.S.C. § 1681c-1, note.

177.51 15 U.S.C. § 1681g(e), *as amended by* Pub. L. No. 108-159, § 151 (2003). The main directive provides as follows:

> For the purpose of documenting fraudulent transactions resulting from identity theft, not later than 30 days after the date of receipt of a request from a victim in accordance with paragraph (3), and subject to verification of the identity of the victim and the claim of identity theft in accordance with paragraph (2), a business entity that has provided credit to, provided for consideration products, goods, or services to, accepted payment from, or otherwise entered into a commercial transaction for consideration with, a person who has allegedly made unauthorized use of the means of identification of the victim, shall provide a copy of application and business transaction records in the control of the business entity, whether maintained by the business entity or by another person on behalf of the business entity, evidencing any transaction alleged to be a result of identity theft to—
> (A) the victim;
> (B) any Federal, State, or local government law enforcement agency or officer specified by the victim in such a request; or
> (C) any law enforcement agency investigating the identity theft and authorized by the victim to take receipt of records provided under this subsection.
>
> 15 U.S.C. § 1681g(e)(1).

177.52 *See, e.g.,* Md. Code Ann. Crim. Law § 8-301. *See also* Appx. B.3, *infra.*

177.53 15 U.S.C. § 1681g(e)(1) Pub. L. No. 108-159, § 151 (2003).

177.54 15 U.S.C. § 1681g(e)(3).

177.55 15 U.S.C. § 1681g(e)(2). The amendments do not clarify the distinction between the proof of identification required from the consumer here and the "proper identification" required under § 1681g(a)(1). Ironically enough, an identity theft victim may have to provide more identifying information to see the records of the thief's transactions than the thief had to provide to create those transactions.

177.56 A document meeting the Act's definition of "identity theft report" should qualify. 15 U.S.C. § 1681a(q)(4).

177.57 15 U.S.C. § 1681g(e)(2)(B). Note that Congress could have designated the Commission's affidavit as acceptable, which would have furthered the goal of standardizing identity theft prevention.

177.58 15 U.S.C. § 1681g(e)(1).

177.59 *Id.* One concern is that businesses may use this last exception to shield a thief's on-line applications and transactions from the victim without providing an adequate substitute for the information.

177.60 15 U.S.C. § 1681g(e)(6).

177.61 15 U.S.C. § 1681t(b)(1)(G), *added by* Pub. L. No. 108-159, § 151 (2003).

16.6.1a.3.2 Debt collectors must provide information to victims

The FACTA imposes new notification responsibilities on debt collectors that should lead to victims being able to identify the original entities that provided credit to a thief in the victim's name. Once a consumer notifies a debt collector that a debt may be fraudulent or may have resulted from identity theft, the debt collector must notify the creditor of that allegation and must provide the consumer with all information about the debt to which the consumer would be entitled if the consumer were in fact the liable party.[177.62]

This provision appears to demand that the collector comply with the debt validation provisions of the Fair Debt Collection Practices Act, which require a debt collector to provide a written notice containing the amount of the debt, the name of the creditor to whom the debt is owed, a statement that unless the consumer disputes the validity of the debt within thirty days the debt collector will assume the debt to be valid, and a statement that, if the consumer disputes the debt in writing within that period, the collector will provide verification of the debt and the name and address of the original creditor.[177.63]

16.6.1a.4 Blocking of Fraudulent Information

16.6.1a.4.1 Agency responsibilities

As of December 1, 2004, victimized consumers will be able to require nationwide consumer reporting agencies[177.64] to block theft-related debts from their files.[177.65] To activate a block, a consumer must provide the agency with the following information: proof of the consumer's identity, a copy of an identity theft report, the consumer's identification of the fraudulent information, and the consumer's statement that the information does not relate to any transaction by the consumer.[177.66] Once the agency has received this information, the agency must block the identified items from the consumer's file within four business days.[177.67] Blocking the information should restore the consumer's file with that agency; the consumer can request the same block from the other nationwide agencies. Another credit history restoration feature, described above § 16.6.1a.2, *supra*, requires a nationwide consumer reporting agency that receives a consumer's complaint of identity theft or request for a fraud alert to notify the other nationwide agencies of the complaint.[177.68]

An agency can rescind a block if the agency "reasonably determines" that one of the following circumstances exists: the consumer erroneously requested the information; the consumer made a material misrepresentation of fact relevant to the block request; or the consumer acquired goods, services, or money as a result of the blocked transaction.[177.69] Apparently this right to rescind seeks to prevent consumers from abusing the blocking provision by requesting that genuine debts be blocked.

If the agency decides to unblock the information, the agency must both notify the consumer of the rescission and the specific reason for the rescission within five business days, just as an agency must notify a consumer that it is reinserting formerly deleted information.[177.70] Thus, when an agency has improperly determined that it should rescind a block, the consumer will learn of the rescission and can then reassert the fraud claim.

Resellers[177.71] also have blocking responsibilities. If the consumer notifies a reseller that a report contains identity-theft-caused information, the reseller must block the report.[177.72] Upon blocking the file, the reseller must notify the consumer of the block and provide the name, address, and telephone number of the consumer reporting agency from which the reseller acquired the consumer's file.[177.73] Although a reseller need not notify the original furnisher of the information, it must identify the consumer agency from which the reseller obtained the fraudulent information,[177.74] which will allow the consumer to enforce the right to block the information with that agency, who will then be required to notify the original furnisher. Check services companies are exempted from the blocking requirements, although the provision requires them to cease furnishing the identity theft-caused information to a nationwide consumer reporting agency for four business days.[177.75]

177.62   15 U.S.C § 1681m(g), *added by* Pub. L. No. 108-159, § 155 (2003).

177.63   15 U.S.C. § 1692g. *See* National Consumer Law Center, *Fair Debt Collection* § 5.7 (4th ed. 2000 and Supp.).

177.64   Those described in 15 U.S.C. § 1681a(p).

177.65   15 U.S.C. § 1681c-2(a), *added by* Pub. L. No. 108-159, § 152 (2003); 16 C.F.R. § 602.1(c)(3)(v), *added by* 69 Fed. Reg. 6526–31 (Feb. 5, 2004).

177.66   15 U.S.C. § 1681c-2(a).

177.67   15 U.S.C. § 1681c-2(a).

177.68   15 U.S.C. § 1681s(f), *as amended by* Pub. L. No. 108-159, § 153 (2003). This provision will become effective on December 1, 2004. 16 C.F.R. § 602.1(c)(3)(vi), *added by* 69 Fed. Reg. 6526–31 (Feb. 5, 2004). Here, too, states are preempted from regulating the required conduct. 15 U.S.C. § 1681t(b)(5)(G). An argument exists that, since the new provisions only directly impose requirements on the identified agencies and not on furnishers, actions against the furnishers are not preempted.

177.69   15 U.S.C. § 1681c-2(c), Pub. L. No. 108-159, § 152 (2003).

177.70   15 U.S.C. § 1681c-2(c) (*citing* 15 U.S.C. § 1681i(a)(5)), *added by* Pub. L. No. 108-159, § 152 (2003).

177.71   The term "reseller" is defined in 15 U.S.C. § 1681a(u), *added by* Pub. L. No. 108-159, § 111 (2003).

177.72   15 U.S.C. § 1681c-2(d), *added by* Pub. L. No. 108-159, § 152 (2003).

177.73   *Id.*

177.74   *Id.*

177.75   15 U.S.C. § 1681c-2(e), *added by* Pub. L. No. 108-159, § 152 (2003). Although states are preempted from regulating the conduct required of agencies and resellers under the new block-

16.6.1a.4.2 Furnisher responsibilities

Requesting a block also pulls the furnisher of the fraudulent information into the credit restoration process by triggering a duty on the agency's part to notify the furnisher that the blocked information may be the result of identity theft, that the consumer has filed an identity theft report, and that the consumer has requested that the agency block the information that the furnisher furnished, along with the effective date of the block.[177.76] Once notified, furnishers must implement procedures to prevent them from re-furnishing such information (to anyone, apparently, not just the notifying agency).[177.77] Similar to the provision that requires furnishers to cease furnishing information that a consumer has disputed,[177.78] this provision should help the agency maintain the purged version of the victim's file. The consumer can also trigger that responsibility by submitting an identity theft report to the furnisher directly at the address specified for such reports.[177.79]

Beginning December 1, 2004, once the consumer submits the report and states that the information resulted from identity theft, the furnisher must cease furnishing the fraudulent information unless the furnisher subsequently "knows" that the information is correct.[177.80] This appears to be a very high standard.

However, consumers have no right to enforce these provisions against furnishers,[177.81] and states are preempted from regulating the subject matter of the provisions.[177.82] Accordingly, they may provoke little change in furnishers' behavior. But notice of a block should also trigger a separate responsibility, that a furnisher not furnish information it "knows or has reason to believe" is inaccurate.[177.83] States are not preempted from regulating this conduct.

An agency's notice to a furnisher that it has blocked information has another effect. As of December 1, 2004, once a furnisher has been notified that an agency has blocked a consumer's information as having resulted from identity theft, the furnisher may not sell or transfer the debt or place it for collection.[177.84] This provision should help victims by pinning the debt to one furnisher so that the victim does not have to chase down a moving target. However, states are preempted from regulating this conduct.[177.85]

16.6.1a.5 Preventing Theft of Consumer's Identification Information

The FACTA adds several provisions that seek to protect sensitive consumer information, thus decreasing the chance of identity theft. Merchants that accept credit cards or debit cards[177.86] will have to truncate credit and debit card numbers on electronically printed receipts.[177.87] As of December 1, 2004, consumers requesting a report to be issued to someone else may now order the agency to withhold the last five digits of the consumer's social security number on the report.[177.88] How much real protection that will provide, given that every user-requested report contains that number, remains to be seen. In addition, as of December 1, 2004, an

---

ing section, consumers may use the FCRA's liability provisions to enforce it. 15 U.S.C. § 1681t(b)(5)(C), *as amended by* Pub. L. No. 108-159, § 711 (2003).

177.76 §15 U.S.C. § 1681c-2(b)(1)-(4).

177.77 15 U.S.C. § 1681s–2(a)(6), *added by* Pub. L. No. 108-159, § 154 (2003). This provision will become effective on December 1, 2004. 16 C.F.R. § 602.1(c)(3)(vii), *added by* 69 Fed. Reg. 6526-31 (Feb. 5, 2004).

177.78 See § 13.5.3, *supra*.

177.79 15 U.S.C. § 1681s–2(a)(6)(B), *as amended by* Pub. L. No. 108-159, § 154 (2003).

177.80 15 U.S.C. § 1681s–2(a)(6)(B); 16 C.F.R. § 602.1(c)(3)(vii), *added by* 69 Fed. Reg. 6526-31 (Feb. 5, 2004). The furnisher can also commence re-furnishing of the information if the consumer informs the furnisher that the information is correct.

177.81 15 U.S.C. § 1681s–2(c), *as amended by* Pub. L. No. 108-159, § 312 (2003).

177.82 15 U.S.C. § 1681t(b)(5)(H), *added by* Pub. L. No. 108-159, § 711 (2003).

177.83 15 U.S.C. § 1681s–2(a)(1)(A), *amended by* Pub. L. No. 108-159, § 312(b) (2003).

177.84 15 U.S.C. § 1681m, *added by* Pub. L. No. 108-159, § 154 (2003); 16 C.F.R. § 602.1(c)(3)(vii), *added by* 69 Fed. Reg. 6526-31 (Feb. 5, 2004). However, the prohibition does not extend to the following:

   (A) the repurchase of a debt in any case in which the assignee of the debt requires such repurchase because the debt has resulted from identity theft;
   (B) the securitization of a debt or the pledging of a portfolio of debt as collateral in connection with a borrowing; or
   (C) the transfer of a debt as a result of a merger, acquisition, purchase and assumption transaction, or transfer of substantially all of the assets of an entity.

   15 U.S.C. § 1681m(f)(3).

177.85 15 U.S.C. § 1681s–2(b)(5)(G), *added by* Pub. L. No. 108-159, § 711 (2003).

177.86 These terms are defined in 15 U.S.C. §§ 1681a(2) and (3).

177.87 Pub. L. No. 108-159, § 113 (2003). The truncation provision will become effective on December 4, 2006, for receipt-printing machines in use before January 1, 2005, and will become effective December 4, 2004, with respect to machines first put into use on or after January 1, 2005. 15 U.S.C. §§ 1681c(g)(3)(A), (B). The Act preempts states from regulating conduct required by this section. Some states have enacted provisions requiring similar, and possibly identical, conduct, but, arguably, even if they were subject to the preemption, they would remain in effect until the Act's provision becomes effective, under the reasoning that the Act does not "require" the truncation conduct until that time. *See, e.g.*, Ariz. Rev. Stat. § 44-1367; Cal. Civ. Code § 1747.9; 815 Ill. Comp. Stat. 616/50 (violation is a deceptive trade practice); Me. Rev. Stat. § 1149. Note that the FCRA's provision may not fully substitute for such state statutes because to state a claim under the FCRA a consumer must show negligence or willfulness, whereas a state may impose liability under a lesser standard. *See* 15 U.S.C. §§ 1681n, 1681o.

177.88 15 U.S.C. § 1681g(a)(1), *as amended by* Pub. L. No. 108-159, § 115 (2003); 16 C.F.R. § 602.1(c)(3)(iii), *added by* 69 Fed. Reg. 6526-31 (Feb. 5, 2004). *See* § 4.4.3.2, *supra*.

agency that receives a request for a consumer's report that includes an address for the consumer that substantially differs from the addresses in the file of the consumer, must notify the requester of the discrepancy if the agency provides a consumer report in response to the request.[177.89] Forthcoming regulations are to require users to properly dispose of the consumer information they acquire through consumer reports,[177.90] which should help prevent the illicit disclosure and use of consumer financial information.

16.6.1a.6 Creditor Implementation of Red Flag Guidelines

The FACTA calls for the FTC, the NCUA, and specified banking agencies to issue regulations that will require each financial institution[177.91] and creditor[177.92] to "establish reasonable policies and procedures" for issuing and implementing "red flag" guidelines regarding identity theft.[177.93] The beneficiaries of these guidelines will be the institution's guidelines that account holders and customers.[177.94]

The guidelines must prevent "account-takeover" identity theft by imposing special verification procedures on a card issuer[177.95] that receives a request for an additional or a replacement card on an existing account within thirty days of receiving a change of address notice. Before issuing the card the issuer must do one of the following:

- Notify the cardholder of the request at the former address,
- Notify the cardholder of the request by such other agreed means, or
- Validate the change of address in accordance with the regulation.[177.96]

16.6.1a.6.1 Furnisher obligations regarding information accuracy and integrity

Furnishers have new responsibilities to ensure that the information they report on a consumer is accurate. These responsibilities include an obligation to cease furnishing blocked identity-theft related information, to follow forthcoming accuracy and integrity guidelines, to notify customers (in the case of financial institutions, that the institution is furnishing negative information about the customer to a consumer reporting agency), and to respond to disputes by consumers of furnished information. In addition, the FACTA raised the accuracy standard that furnishers must meet when furnishing consumer information.

Under the prior version of the FCRA, once an agency notified a furnisher that a consumer had disputed information which the furnisher had reported to the agency, the furnisher had to reinvestigate that item and report the results of the investigation back to the agency.[177.97] As discussed above,[177.98] now the furnisher must also take steps to modify, delete or block that information to prevent it from re-reporting the inaccurate information.[177.99]

The agencies that enforce the FCRA will establish guidelines for furnishers regarding the accuracy and integrity of furnished information and will issue regulations requiring furnishers to establish reasonable policies and procedures for implementing those guidelines.[177.100] However, consumers may not enforce these new responsibilities,[177.101] and states are preempted from regulating the subject matter of the provision.[177.102] Thus, such provisions may not ultimately lead to furnishers' improving the accuracy and integrity of consumer information.

As of December 1, 2004, the FCRA will require a financial institution[177.103] to notify a customer that it is furnishing negative information about that customer.[177.104] This provision should alert consumers to inaccurate information in the institution's records; once alerted, the consumer can use a new provision, discussed below, allowing consumers to dispute information directly with a furnisher to try to repair the institution's records. Once notified about an account, the consumer is not entitled to further notices when additional negative information is reported about that account.[177.105] The institution must give the notice within thirty days of reporting negative information.[177.106] How-

---

177.89 15 U.S.C. § 1681c(h), added by Pub. L. No. 108-159, § 315 (2003); 16 C.F.R. § 602.1(c)(3)(xi), added by 69 Fed. Reg. 6526-31 (Feb. 5, 2004).
177.90 15 U.S.C. § 1681v, added by Pub. L. No. 108-159, § 216 (2003).
177.91 Defined in 15 U.S.C. § 1681a(t).
177.92 Defined in 15 U.S.C. § 1681a (r).
177.93 Pub. L. No. 108-159, § 114 (2003), amending 15 U.S.C. § 1681m.
177.94 15 U.S.C. § 1681m(e)(1)(A).
177.95 Defined in 15 U.S.C. § 1681a(r)(1).
177.96 15 U.S.C. § 1681m (e)(1)(C). States are preempted from regulating the conduct required by the new red flag provision. 15 U.S.C. § 1681t(b)(5)(F), as amended by Pub. L. No. 108-159, § 711 (2003).

177.97 15 U.S.C. § 1681s–2(b).
177.98 See § 16.6.1a.2.1, supra.
177.99 15 U.S.C. § 1681s–2(b), as amended by Pub. L. No. 108-159, § 314 (2003).
177.100 15 U.S.C. § 1681s–2(e), added by Pub. L. No. 108-159, § 312 (2003). This provision will become effective on December 1, 2004. 16 C.F.R. § 602.1(c)(3)(xiv), added by 69 Fed. Reg. 6526-31 (Feb. 5, 2004).
177.101 15 U.S.C. § 1681s–2(c)(2), added by Pub. L. No. 108-159, § 312 (2003). However, consumers may bring an action against furnishers for behavior that independently violates § 1681s–2(b). Id.
177.102 15 U.S.C. § 1681t(b)(1)(F).
177.103 Defined in 15 U.S.C. § 1681a(t).
177.104 15 U.S.C. § 1681s–2(a)(7), added by Pub. L. No. 108-159, § 217 (2003); 16 C.F.R. § 602.1(c)(3)(xii), added by 69 Fed. Reg. 6526-31 (Feb. 5, 2004). See § 3.8a, supra. Consumers may not enforce this provision through the FCRA. 15 U.S.C. § 1681s–2(c)(1), as amended by Pub. L. No. 108-159, § 312 (2003).
177.105 15 U.S.C. § 1681s–2(a)(7)(A)(ii).
177.106 15 U.S.C. § 1681s–2 (a)(7)(B)(i).

ever, financial institutions may take advantage of a safe-harbor provision.[177.107] The Federal Reserve Board is to provide a model notice not to exceed thirty words,[177.108] and a financial institution may provide the notice without submitting the negative information.[177.109] The notice may not be included with disclosures under § 127 of the Truth In Lending Act.[177.110]

The prior version of the FCRA had no provision by which a consumer could dispute an inaccurate item of information directly with the furnisher; rather, the consumer had to dispute the item with the agency, which was then required by the Act to notify the furnisher.[177.111] The FCRA required the furnisher to reinvestigate the item only upon receiving the agency's notice. Notice from the consumer was irrelevant and ineffective.[177.112]

Beginning December 1, 2004, a consumer may trigger a furnisher's responsibility to reinvestigate by disputing the item directly with the furnisher when the circumstances of the dispute meet the conditions of to-be-prescribed regulations.[177.113] The new provision specifically provides, however, that such a reinvestigation responsibility will not be initiated by a notice from or prepared by a credit repair organization,[177.114] and furnishers need not respond to "frivolous" disputes (though the furnisher must notify the consumer within five business days that it considers the dispute frivolous, the reason it considers the dispute frivolous, and what information the consumer must provide to convert the dispute into one that will start a reinvestigation).[177.115]

The furnisher must investigate the dispute and report the results back to the consumer in the same time frame allowed agencies for reinvestigation.[177.116] If the furnisher finds the information to be inaccurate the furnisher must correct the information with each agency to which the furnisher furnished the information.[177.117] As with the pre-existing reinvestigation responsibilities that arise upon notice from an agency, states are preempted from regulating the subject matter of the provision;[177.118] however, unlike those responsibilities, consumers may not enforce this provision against furnishers.[177.119]

The prior version of the FCRA prohibited a furnisher from reporting to agencies information that it "[knew] or consciously avoid[ed] knowing" was inaccurate.[177.120] Now a furnisher may not report information that it "*knows or has reasonable cause to believe*" is inaccurate.[177.121] While this stricter standard appears at first likely to enhance the accuracy of consumer information, since the FCRA defines the standard such that a consumer's allegations that the information is inaccurate alone will not serve as reasonable cause, it may only prevent the furnishing of information that the furnisher's own records or another source's notification has put in question.[177.122] Nonetheless, both old and new provisions of the revised Act require notices of inaccuracy to furnishers that may be sufficient to satisfy the reasonable cause standard, for example, an agency's notice to a furnisher that a consumer has disputed an item of information;[177.123] an agency's notice to a furnisher that furnished information has been modified or deleted as unverifiable;[177.124] an agency's notice that it has blocked furnished information as being the result of identity theft;[177.125] or a debt collector's notice that a consumer has claimed that a debt was incurred by an identity thief.[177.126]

177.107 The safe harbor protects the institution from liability if it maintained reasonable compliance policies and procedures or reasonably believed that it was prohibited by law from contacting the consumer. 15 U.S.C. § 1681s–2(a)(7)(F).
177.108 15 U.S.C. § 1681s–2(a)(7)(D)(i).
177.109 *Id.*
177.110 15 U.S.C. § 1681s–2 (a)(7)(B)(ii).
177.111 15 U.S.C. § 1681i(a)(2).
177.112 15 U.S.C. § 1681s–2(b). *See* § 3.5.2, *supra*.
177.113 15 U.S.C. § 1681s–2(a)(8), *added by* Pub. L. No. 108-159, § 312 (2003); 16 C.F.R. § 602.1(c)(3)(xiv), *added by* 69 Fed. Reg. 6526-31 (Feb. 5, 2004).
177.114 15 U.S.C. § 1681s–2(a)(8)(G). Even notices from or prepared by organizations that are not defined to be credit repair organizations under the Credit Repair Organizations Act (16 U.S.C. § 1679a) because of their non-profit status will not trigger a reinvestigation. *Id.*
177.115 15 U.S.C. § 1681t(a)(8)(F).

177.116 15 U.S.C. § 1681t(a)(8)(E), *added by* Pub. L. No. 108-159, § 312 (2003).
177.117 *Id.*
177.118 15 U.S.C. § 1681t(b)(1)(F).
177.119 15 U.S.C. § 1681s–2(c)(1), *added by* Pub. L. No. 108-159, § 312 (2003).
177.120 15 U.S.C. § 1681s–2(a)(1)(A) (2000).
177.121 15 U.S.C. § 1681s–2(a)(1)(A), *as amended by* Pub. L. No. 108-159, § 312 (2003) (emphasis added).
177.122 15 U.S.C. § 1681s–2(a)(1)(D), *as amended by* Pub. L. No. 108-159, § 312 (2003).
177.123 15 U.S.C. § 1681i(a)(2).
177.124 15 U.S.C. § 1681i(a)(5), *added by* Pub. L. No. 108-159, § 314 (2003).
177.125 15 U.S.C. § 1681c–2(b), *added by* Pub. L. No. 108-159, § 152 (2003).
177.126 15 U.S.C. § 1681m(g).

16.6.2 Identity Theft and Assumption Deterrence Act

Replace note 178 with: 178   Pub. L. No. 105-318, 112 Stat. 3007 (Oct. 28, 1998), *codified at* 18 U.S.C. § 1028, 28 U.S.C. § 994.

§ 16.6.3 — Fair Credit Reporting / 2004 Supplement

Add note 183.1 at end of second sentence of subsection's last paragraph.

183.1 The FACTA of 2003 amended the FCRA to ease such cleanup. *See* § 16.6.1a, *infra*.

Addition to note 184.

184 Huggins v. Citibank, N.A., 585 S.E.2d 275 (S.C. 2003) (state does not recognize tort of negligent enablement of imposter fraud).

Page 396

16.6.3 State Identity Theft Statutes

Addition to note 205.

205 Cal. Civ. Code Ann. § 1785.16(k) (requiring consumer reporting agencies to "promptly and permanently" block information that a consumer alleges to be present due to identity theft, substantiated by a police report; information may only be unblocked if furnisher meets the statute's criteria for showing that item was legitimate). *See also* Cal. Civ. Code Ann. § 1785.11.2 (allowing consumers to put a security freeze on the consumer's report so that the consumer reporting agency is prohibited from releasing the report without the consumer's express authorization; exceptions provided).

Add to text at end of subsection:

Note, however, that these statutes may now be preempted by the FACTA's preemption provisions, which generally bar states from regulating any "conduct required by" the new identity theft provisions.[206.1]

206.1 *See* 15 U.S.C. § 1681t(b)(5), *added by* Pub. L. No. 108-159, § 711(2) (2003). *See also* § 10.4.4, *supra*. With respect to the new right to transaction information, provided in 15 U.S.C. § 1681g(e), the FACTA preempts not just the conduct required by the provision but the entire subject matter. 15 U.S.C. § 1681t(b)(1)(g), *added by* Pub. L. No. 108-159, § 151(2) (2003). *See also* § 16.6.1a, *supra*.

16.7 Interests Impeding Legislative Protection of Financial Information

Replace section's last paragraph with:

Consumer information furnishers arguably received a good deal more than they lost in the FACTA. In return for reasonably mild requirements on agencies to issue fraud alerts and block information and to comply with eventual accuracy and integrity guidelines,[214] they won freedom from any new state laws regulating furnishers through the revocation of the sunset provision that would have allowed states to regulate furnishers as of January 1, 2004.[215] They were also freed from most state identity theft laws that applied to their conduct.[216] Accordingly, they were able to significantly narrow their responsibilities to comply with state laws, past and future, protecting consumers from identity theft. Furthermore, the FCRA, as amended, shields most of the duties demanded from furnishers from private enforcement and from meaningful state enforcement In short, the FCRA's new privacy protections may be mere paper privileges.

214 *See* § 16.6.1a, *supra*.
215 15 U.S.C. § 1681t(d) (2002).
216 15 U.S.C. § 1681t(b), *as amended by* Pub. L. No. 108-159 (2004).
217 Reserved.
218 Reserved.
219 Reserved.

Appendix A   Fair Credit Reporting Act, Other Federal Statutes and Regulations

Page 399

Add to text prior to A.1: This appendix contains several important laws, regulations and agency interpretations on fair credit reporting. Included in this appendix is a cross-reference Table of 15 U.S.C. section numbers with the Fair Credit Reporting Act section numbers. Also in this appendix is the Fair Credit Reporting Act (FCRA) prior to the 2003 amendments (A.2.1); a red-lined version of the FCRA based on the 2003 amendments (A.2.2); the Fair and Accurate Credit Transactions Act of 2003 (FACTA) (A.2.3); The Federal Trade Commission and Federal Reserve Board regulations on effective dates of the FACTA amendments (A.2.4). Appendix A also includes a version of the Fair Credit Reporting Act prior to the 1996 amendments (A.3); the Credit Repair Organizations Act (A.4); selected provisions of the Gram-Leach-Bliley Act (A.5.1) with related rules (A.5.2) and federal standards as to the FCRA's applicability to affiliate information sharing by the Federal Trade Commission (A.6.1) and the Office of Comptroller of the Currency and other agencies (A.6.2).

Page 400 **A.2 The Fair Credit Reporting Act**

Add new subheading: **A.2.1 Fair Credit Reporting Act Prior to FACTA**

Page 422

Add new subsections after A.2: **A.2.2 Redline Version of FCRA Including FACTA**

Sec.
§ 1681. Congressional findings and statement of purpose
§ 1681a. Definitions; rules of construction
§ 1681b. Permissible purposes of consumer reports
§ 1681c. Requirements relating to information contained in consumer reports
§ 1681c-1. Identity theft prevention; fraud alerts and active duty alerts
§ 1681c-2. Block of information resulting from identity theft
§ 1681d. Disclosure of investigative consumer reports
§ 1681e. Compliance procedures
§ 1681f. Disclosures to governmental agencies
§ 1681g. Disclosures to consumers
§ 1681h. Conditions and form of disclosure to consumers
§ 1681i. Procedure in case of disputed accuracy
§ 1681j. Charges for certain disclosures
§ 1681k. Public record information for employment purposes
§ 1681*l*. Restrictions on investigative consumer reports
§ 1681m. Requirements on users of consumer reports
§ 1681n. Civil liability for willful noncompliance
§ 1681o. Civil liability for negligent noncompliance
§ 1681p. Jurisdiction of courts; limitation of actions
§ 1681q. Obtaining information under false pretenses
§ 1681r. Unauthorized disclosures by officers or employees
§ 1681s. Administrative enforcement
§ 1681s-1. Information on overdue child support obligations
§ 1681s-2. Responsibilities of furnishers of information to consumer reporting agencies
§ 1681s-3. Affiliate sharing
§ 1681t. Relation to State laws
§ 1681u. Disclosures to FBI for counterintelligence purposes
§ 1681v. Disclosures to governmental agencies for counterterrorism purposes
§ 1681w. Disposal of records
§ 1681x. Corporate and technological circumvention prohibited

159

§ 1681. Congressional findings and statement of purpose [FCRA § 602]

(a) Accuracy and fairness of credit reporting

The Congress makes the following findings:

(1) The banking system is dependent upon fair and accurate credit reporting. Inaccurate credit reports directly impair the efficiency of the banking system, and unfair credit reporting methods undermine the public confidence which is essential to the continued functioning of the banking system.

(2) An elaborate mechanism has been developed for investigating and evaluating the creditworthiness, credit standing, credit capacity, character, and general reputation of consumers.

(3) Consumer reporting agencies have assumed a vital role in assembling and evaluating consumer credit and other information on consumers.

(4) There is a need to insure that consumer reporting agencies exercise their grave responsibilities with fairness, impartiality, and a respect for the consumer's right to privacy.

(b) Reasonable procedures

It is the purpose of this subchapter to require that consumer reporting agencies adopt reasonable procedures for meeting the needs of commerce for consumer credit, personnel, insurance, and other information in a manner which is fair and equitable to the consumer, with regard to the confidentiality, accuracy, relevancy, and proper utilization of such information in accordance with the requirements of this subchapter.

§ 1681a. Definitions; rules of construction [FCRA § 603]

(a) Definitions and rules of construction set forth in this section are applicable for the purposes of this subchapter.

(b) The term "person" means any individual, partnership, corporation, trust, estate, cooperative, association, government or governmental subdivision or agency, or other entity.

(c) The term "consumer" means an individual.

(d) **Consumer report.—**

(1) **In general.—**The term "consumer report" means any written, oral, or other communication of any information by a consumer reporting agency bearing on a consumer's credit worthiness, credit standing, credit capacity, character, general reputation, personal characteristics, or mode of living which is used or expected to be used or collected in whole or in part for the purpose of serving as a factor in establishing the consumer's eligibility for—

(A) credit or insurance to be used primarily for personal, family, or household purposes;

(B) employment purposes; or

(C) any other purpose authorized under section 1681b of this title.

(2) **Exclusions.—**Except as provided in paragraph (3), the term The term "consumer report" does not include—

(A) subject to section 1681s-3, any—

(i) report containing information solely as to transactions or experiences between the consumer and the person making the report;

(ii) communication of that information among persons related by common ownership or affiliated by corporate control; or

(iii) communication of other information among persons related by common ownership or affiliated by corporate control, if it is clearly and conspicuously disclosed to the consumer that the information may be communicated among such persons and the consumer is given the opportunity, before the time that the information is initially communicated, to direct that such information not be communicated among such persons;

(B) any authorization or approval of a specific extension of credit directly or indirectly by the issuer of a credit card or similar device;

(C) any report in which a person who has been requested by a third party to make a specific extension of credit directly or indirectly to a consumer conveys his or her decision with respect to such request, if the third party advises the consumer of the name and address of the person to whom the request was made, and such person makes the disclosures to the consumer required under section 1681m of this title; or

(D) a communication described in subsection (*o*) or (x) of this section.

(3) **Restriction on sharing of medical information.—**Except for information or any communication of information disclosed as provided in section 1681b(g)(3), the exclusions in paragraph (2) shall not apply with respect to information disclosed to any person related by common ownership or affiliated by corporate control, if the information is—

(A) medical information;

(B) an individualized list or description based on the payment transactions of the consumer for medical products or services; or

(C) an aggregate list of identified consumers based on payment transactions for medical products or services.

(e) The term "investigative consumer report" means a consumer report or portion thereof in which information on a consumer's character, general reputation, personal characteristics, or mode of living is obtained through personal interviews with neighbors, friends, or associates of the consumer reported on or with others with whom he is acquainted or who may have knowledge concerning any such items of information. However, such information shall not include specific factual information on a consumer's credit record obtained directly from a creditor of the consumer or from a consumer reporting agency when such information was obtained directly from a creditor of the consumer or from the consumer.

(f) The term "consumer reporting agency" means any person which, for monetary fees, dues, or on a cooperative nonprofit basis, regularly engages in whole or in part in the practice of assembling or evaluating consumer credit information or other information on consumers for the purpose of furnishing consumer reports to third parties, and which uses any means or facility of interstate commerce for the purpose of preparing or furnishing consumer reports.

(g) The term "file," when used in connection with information on any consumer, means all of the information on that consumer recorded and retained by a consumer reporting agency regardless of how the information is stored.

(h) The term "employment purposes" when used in connection with a consumer report means a report used for the purpose of evaluating a consumer for employment, promotion, reassignment or retention as an employee.

(i) Medical information.—The term 'medical information'—

(1) means information or data, whether oral or recorded, in any form or medium, created by or derived from a health care provider or the consumer, that relates to—

(A) the past, present, or future physical, mental, or behavioral health or condition of an individual;

(B) the provision of health care to an individual; or

(C) the payment for the provision of health care to an individual.

(2) does not include the age or gender of a consumer, demographic information about the consumer, including a consumer's residence address or e-mail address, or any other information about a consumer that does not relate to the physical, mental, or behavioral health or condition of a consumer, including the existence or value of any insurance policy.

~~(i) The term "medical information" means information or records obtained, with the consent of the individual to whom it relates, from licensed physicians or medical practitioners, hospitals, clinics, or other medical or medically related facilities.~~

(j) Definitions relating to child support obligations

(1) Overdue support

The term "overdue support" has the meaning given to such term in section 666(e) of Title 42.

(2) State or local child support enforcement agency

The term "State or local child support enforcement agency" means a State or local agency which administers a State or local program for establishing and enforcing child support obligations.

(k) Adverse action.—

(1) Actions included.—The term "adverse action"—

(A) has the same meaning as in section 1691(d)(6) of this title; and

(B) means—

(i) a denial or cancellation of, an increase in any charge for, or a reduction or other adverse or unfavorable change in the terms of coverage or amount of, any insurance, existing or applied for, in connection with the underwriting of insurance;

(ii) a denial of employment or any other decision for employment purposes that adversely affects any current or prospective employee;

(iii) a denial or cancellation of, an increase in any charge for, or any other adverse or unfavorable change in the terms of, any license or benefit described in section 1681b(a)(3)(D) of this title; and

(iv) an action taken or determination that is—

(I) made in connection with an application that was made by, or a transaction that was initiated by, any consumer, or in connection with a review of an account under section 1681b(a)(3)(F)(ii) of this title; and

(II) adverse to the interests of the consumer.

(2) Applicable findings, decisions, commentary, and orders.—For purposes of any determination of whether an action is an adverse action under paragraph (1)(A), all appropriate final findings, decisions, commentary, and orders issued under section 1691(d)(6) of this title by the Board of Governors of the Federal Reserve System or any court shall apply.

(*l*) Firm offer of credit or insurance.—The term "firm offer of credit or insurance" means any offer of credit or insurance to a consumer that will be honored if the consumer is determined, based on information in a consumer report on the consumer, to meet the specific criteria used to select the consumer for the offer, except that the offer may be further conditioned on one or more of the following:

(1) The consumer being determined, based on information in the consumer's application for the credit or insurance, to meet specific criteria bearing on credit worthiness or insurability, as applicable, that are established—

(A) before selection of the consumer for the offer; and

(B) for the purpose of determining whether to extend credit or insurance pursuant to the offer.

(2) Verification—

(A) that the consumer continues to meet the specific criteria used to select the consumer for the offer, by using information in a consumer report on the consumer, information in the consumer's application for the credit or insurance, or other information bearing on the credit worthiness or insurability of the consumer; or

(B) of the information in the consumer's application for the credit or insurance, to determine that the consumer meets the specific criteria bearing on credit worthiness or insurability.

(3) The consumer furnishing any collateral that is a requirement for the extension of the credit or insurance that was—

(A) established before selection of the consumer for the offer of credit or insurance; and

(B) disclosed to the consumer in the offer of credit or insurance.

(m) **Credit or insurance transaction that is not initiated by the consumer.**—The term "credit or insurance transaction that is not initiated by the consumer" does not include the use of a consumer report by a person with which the consumer has an account or insurance policy, for purposes of—

(1) reviewing the account or insurance policy; or

(2) collecting the account.

(n) **State.**—The term "State" means any State, the Commonwealth of Puerto Rico, the District of Columbia, and any territory or possession of the United States.

(o) **Excluded communications.**—A communication is described in this subsection if it is a communication—

(1) that, but for subsection (d)(2)(D) of this section, would be an investigative consumer report;

(2) that is made to a prospective employer for the purpose of—

(A) procuring an employee for the employer; or

(B) procuring an opportunity for a natural person to work for the employer;

(3) that is made by a person who regularly performs such procurement;

(4) that is not used by any person for any purpose other than a purpose described in subparagraph (A) or (B) of paragraph (2); and

(5) with respect to which—

(A) the consumer who is the subject of the communication—

(i) consents orally or in writing to the nature and scope of the communication, before the collection of any information for the purpose of making the communication;

(ii) consents orally or in writing to the making of the communication to a prospective employer, before the making of the communication; and

(iii) in the case of consent under clause (i) or (ii) given orally, is provided written confirmation of that consent by the person making the communication, not later than 3 business days after the receipt of the consent by that person;

(B) the person who makes the communication does not, for the purpose of making the communication, make any inquiry that if made by a prospective employer of the consumer who is the subject of the communication would violate any applicable Federal or State equal employment opportunity law or regulation; and

(C) the person who makes the communication—

(i) discloses in writing to the consumer who is the subject of the communication, not later than 5 business days after receiving any request from the consumer for such disclosure, the nature and substance of all information in the consumer's file at the time of the request, except that the sources of any information that is acquired solely for use in making the communication and is actually used for no other purpose, need not be disclosed other than under appropriate discovery procedures in any court of competent jurisdiction in which an action is brought; and

(ii) notifies the consumer who is the subject of the communication, in writing, of the consumer's right to request the information described in clause (i).

(p) **Consumer reporting agency that compiles and maintains files on consumers on a nationwide basis.**—The term "consumer reporting agency that compiles and maintains files on consumers on a nationwide basis" means a consumer reporting agency that regularly engages in the practice of assembling or evaluating, and maintaining, for the purpose of furnishing consumer reports to third parties bearing on a consumer's credit worthiness, credit standing, or credit capacity, each of the following regarding consumers residing nationwide:

(1) Public record information.

(2) Credit account information from persons who furnish that information regularly and in the ordinary course of business.

(q) **Definitions relating to fraud alerts.**—

(1) **Active duty military consumer.**—The term 'active duty military consumer' means a consumer in military service who—

(A) is on active duty (as defined in section 101(d)(1) of title 10, United States Code) or is a reservist performing duty under a call or order to active duty under a provision of law referred to in section 101(a)(13) of title 10, United States Code; and

(B) is assigned to service away from the usual duty station of the consumer.

(2) **Fraud alert; active duty alert.**—The terms 'fraud alert' and 'active duty alert' mean a statement in the file of a consumer that—

(A) notifies all prospective users of a consumer report relating to the consumer that the consumer may be a victim of fraud, including identity theft, or is an active duty military consumer, as applicable; and

(B) is presented in a manner that facilitates a clear and conspicuous view of the statement described in subparagraph (A) by any person requesting such consumer report.

(3) **Identity theft.**—The term 'identity theft' means a fraud committed using the identifying information of another person, subject to such further definition as the Commission may prescribe, by regulation.

(4) **Identity theft report.**—The term 'identity theft report' has the meaning given that term by rule of the Commission, and means, at a minimum, a report—

(A) that alleges an identity theft;

(B) that is a copy of an official, valid report filed by a consumer with an appropriate Federal, State, or local law enforcement agency, including the United States Postal Inspection Service, or such other government agency deemed appropriate by the Commission; and

(C) the filing of which subjects the person filing the report to criminal penalties relating to the filing of false information if, in fact, the information in the report is false.

(5) New credit plan.—The term 'new credit plan' means a new account under an open end credit plan (as defined in section 103(i) of the Truth in Lending Act) or a new credit transaction not under an open end credit plan.

(r) Credit and debit related terms.—

(1) Card issuer.—The term 'card issuer' means—

(A) a credit card issuer, in the case of a credit card; and

(B) a debit card issuer, in the case of a debit card.

(2) Credit card.—The term 'credit card' has the same meaning as in section 103 of the Truth in Lending Act.

(3) Debit card.—The term 'debit card' means any card issued by a financial institution to a consumer for use in initiating an electronic fund transfer from the account of the consumer at such financial institution, for the purpose of transferring money between accounts or obtaining money, property, labor, or services.

(4) Account and electronic fund transfer.—The terms 'account' and 'electronic fund transfer' have the same meanings as in section 903 of the Electronic Fund Transfer Act.

(5) Credit and creditor.—The terms 'credit' and 'creditor' have the same meanings as in section 702 of the Equal Credit Opportunity Act.

(s) Federal banking agency.—The term 'Federal banking agency' has the same meaning as in section 3 of the Federal Deposit Insurance Act.

(t) Financial institution.—The term 'financial institution' means a State or National bank, a State or Federal savings and loan association, a mutual savings bank, a State or Federal credit union, or any other person that, directly or indirectly, holds a transaction account (as defined in section 19(b) of the Federal Reserve Act) belonging to a consumer.

(u) Reseller.—The term 'reseller' means a consumer reporting agency that—

(1) assembles and merges information contained in the database of another consumer reporting agency or multiple consumer reporting agencies concerning any consumer for purposes of furnishing such information to any third party, to the extent of such activities; and

(2) does not maintain a database of the assembled or merged information from which new consumer reports are produced.

(v) Commission.—The term 'Commission' means the Federal Trade Commission.

(w) Nationwide specialty consumer reporting agency.—The term 'nationwide specialty consumer reporting agency' means a consumer reporting agency that compiles and maintains files on consumers on a nationwide basis relating to—

(1) medical records or payments;

(2) residential or tenant history;

(3) check writing history;

(4) employment history; or

(5) insurance claims.

(x) Exclusion of certain communications for employee investigations.—

(1) Communications described in this subsection.—A communication is described in this subsection if—

(A) but for subsection (d)(2)(D), the communication would be a consumer report;

(B) the communication is made to an employer in connection with an investigation of—

(i) suspected misconduct relating to employment; or

(ii) compliance with Federal, State, or local laws and regulations, the rules of a self-regulatory organization, or any preexisting written policies of the employer;

(C) the communication is not made for the purpose of investigating a consumer's credit worthiness, credit standing, or credit capacity; and

(D) the communication is not provided to any person except—

(i) to the employer or an agent of the employer;

(ii) to any Federal or State officer, agency, or department, or any officer, agency, or department of a unit of general local government;

(iii) to any self-regulatory organization with regulatory authority over the activities of the employer or employee;

(iv) as otherwise required by law; or

(v) pursuant to section 1681f.

(2) Subsequent disclosure.—After taking any adverse action based in whole or in part on a communication described in paragraph (1), the employer shall disclose to the consumer a summary containing the nature and substance of the communication upon which the adverse action is based, except that the sources of information acquired solely for use in preparing what would be but for subsection (d)(2)(D) an investigative consumer report need not be disclosed.

(3) Self-regulatory organization defined.—For purposes of this subsection, the term 'self-regulatory organization' includes any self-regulatory organization (as defined in section 3(a)(26) of the Securities Exchange Act of 1934), any entity established under title I of the Sarbanes-Oxley Act of 2002, any board of trade designated by the Commodity Futures Trading Commission, and any futures association registered with such Commission.

§ 1681b. Permissible purposes of consumer reports [FCRA § 604]

(a) **In general.**—Subject to subsection (c) of this section, any consumer reporting agency may furnish a consumer report under the following circumstances and no other:

(1) In response to the order of a court having jurisdiction to issue such an order, or a subpoena issued in connection with proceedings before a Federal grand jury.

(2) In accordance with the written instructions of the consumer to whom it relates.

(3) To a person which it has reason to believe—

(A) intends to use the information in connection with a credit transaction involving the consumer on whom the information is to be furnished and involving the extension of credit to, or review or collection of an account of, the consumer; or

(B) intends to use the information for employment purposes; or

(C) intends to use the information in connection with the underwriting of insurance involving the consumer; or

(D) intends to use the information in connection with a determination of the consumer's eligibility for a license or other benefit granted by a governmental instrumentality required by law to consider an applicant's financial responsibility or status; or

(E) intends to use the information, as a potential investor or servicer, or current insurer, in connection with a valuation of, or an assessment of the credit or prepayment risks associated with, an existing credit obligation; or

(F) otherwise has a legitimate business need for the information—

(i) in connection with a business transaction that is initiated by the consumer; or

(ii) to review an account to determine whether the consumer continues to meet the terms of the account.

(4) In response to a request by the head of a State or local child support enforcement agency (or a State or local government official authorized by the head of such an agency), if the person making the request certifies to the consumer reporting agency that—

(A) the consumer report is needed for the purpose of establishing an individual's capacity to make child support payments or determining the appropriate level of such payments;

(B) the paternity of the consumer for the child to which the obligation relates has been established or acknowledged by the consumer in accordance with State laws under which the obligation arises (if required by those laws);

(C) the person has provided at least 10 days' prior notice to the consumer whose report is requested, by certified or registered mail to the last known address of the consumer, that the report will be requested; and

(D) the consumer report will be kept confidential, will be used solely for a purpose described in subparagraph (A), and will not be used in connection with any other civil, administrative, or criminal proceeding, or for any other purpose.

(5) To an agency administering a State plan under section 654 of Title 42 for use to set an initial or modified child support award.

(b) **Conditions for furnishing and using consumer reports for employment purposes.**—

(1) **Certification from user.**—A consumer reporting agency may furnish a consumer report for employment purposes only if—

(A) the person who obtains such report from the agency certifies to the agency that—

(i) the person has complied with paragraph (2) with respect to the consumer report, and the person will comply with paragraph (3) with respect to the consumer report if paragraph (3) becomes applicable; and

(ii) information from the consumer report will not be used in violation of any applicable Federal or State equal employment opportunity law or regulation; and

(B) the consumer reporting agency provides with the report, or has previously provided, of the consumer's rights under this subchapter, as prescribed by the Federal Trade Commission under section 1681g(c)(3) of this title.

(2) **Disclosure to consumer.**—

(A) **In general.**—Except as provided in subparagraph (B), a person may not procure a consumer report, or cause a consumer report to be procured, for employment purposes with respect to any consumer, unless—

(i) a clear and conspicuous disclosure has been made in writing to the consumer at any time before the report is procured or caused to be procured, in a document that consists solely of the disclosure, that a consumer report may be obtained for employment purposes; and

(ii) the consumer has authorized in writing (which authorization may be made on the document referred to in clause (i)) the procurement of the report by that person.

(B) **Application by mail, telephone, computer, or other similar means.**—If a consumer described in subparagraph (C) applies for employment by mail, telephone, computer, or other similar means, at any time before a consumer report is procured or caused to be procured in connection with that application—

(i) the person who procures the consumer report on the consumer for employment purposes shall provide to the consumer, by oral, written, or electronic means, notice that a consumer report may be obtained for employment purposes, and a summary of the consumer's rights under section 1681m(a)(3); and

(ii) the consumer shall have consented, orally, in writing, or electronically to the procurement of the report by that person.

(C) Scope.—Subparagraph (B) shall apply to a person procuring a consumer report on a consumer in connection with the consumer's application for employment only if—

(i) the consumer is applying for a position over which the Secretary of Transportation has the power to establish qualifications and maximum hours of service pursuant to the provisions of section 31502 of title 49, or a position subject to safety regulation by a State transportation agency; and

(ii) as of the time at which the person procures the report or causes the report to be procured the only interaction between the consumer and the person in connection with that employment application has been by mail, telephone, computer, or other similar means.

(3) Conditions on use for adverse actions.—

(A) In general.—Except as provided in subparagraph (B), in using a consumer report for employment purposes, before taking any adverse action based in whole or in part on the report, the person intending to take such adverse action shall provide to the consumer to whom the report relates—

(i) a copy of the report; and

(ii) a description in writing of the rights of the consumer under this title, as prescribed by the Federal Trade Commission under section 1681g(c)(3) of this title.

(B) Application by mail, telephone, computer, or other similar means.—

(i) If a consumer described in subparagraph (C) applies for employment by mail, telephone, computer, or other similar means, and if a person who has procured a consumer report on the consumer for employment purposes takes adverse action on the employment application based in whole or in part on the report, then the person must provide to the consumer to whom the report relates, in lieu of the notices required under subparagraph (A) of this section and under section 1681m(a) of this title, within 3 business days of taking such action, an oral, written or electronic notification—

(I) that adverse action has been taken based in whole or in part on a consumer report received from a consumer reporting agency;

(II) of the name, address and telephone number of the consumer reporting agency that furnished the consumer report (including a toll-free telephone number established by the agency if the agency compiles and maintains files on consumers on a nationwide basis);

(III) that the consumer reporting agency did not make the decision to take the adverse action and is unable to provide to the consumer the specific reasons why the adverse action was taken; and

(IV) that the consumer may, upon providing proper identification, request a free copy of a report and may dispute with the consumer reporting agency the accuracy or completeness of any information in a report.

(ii) If, under clause (B)(i)(IV), the consumer requests a copy of a consumer report from the person who procured the report, then, within 3 business days of receiving the consumer's request, together with proper identification, the person must send or provide to the consumer a copy of a report and a copy of the consumer's rights as prescribed by the Federal Trade Commission under section 1681g(c)(3) of this title.

(C) Scope.—Subparagraph (B) shall apply to a person procuring a consumer report on a consumer in connection with the consumer's application for employment only if—

(i) the consumer is applying for a position over which the Secretary of Transportation has the power to establish qualifications and maximum hours of service pursuant to the provisions of section 31502 of title 49, or a position subject to safety regulation by a State transportation agency; and

(ii) as of the time at which the person procures the report or causes the report to be procured the only interaction between the consumer and the person in connection with that employment application has been by mail, telephone, computer, or other similar means.

(4) Exception for national security investigations.—

(A) In general.—In the case of an agency or department of the United States Government which seeks to obtain and use a consumer report for employment purposes, paragraph (3) shall not apply to any adverse action by such agency or department which is based in part on such consumer report, if the head of such agency or department makes a written finding that—

(i) the consumer report is relevant to a national security investigation of such agency or department;

(ii) the investigation is within the jurisdiction of such agency or department;

(iii) there is reason to believe that compliance with paragraph (3) will—

(I) endanger the life or physical safety of any person;

(II) result in flight from prosecution;

(III) result in the destruction of, or tampering with, evidence relevant to the investigation;

(IV) result in the intimidation of a potential witness relevant to the investigation;

(V) result in the compromise of classified information; or

(VI) otherwise seriously jeopardize or unduly delay the investigation or another official proceeding.

(B) Notification of consumer upon conclusion of investigation.—Upon the conclusion of a national security investigation described in subparagraph (A), or upon the determination that the exception under subparagraph (A) is no longer required for the reasons set forth in such subparagraph, the official exercising the authority in such subparagraph shall provide to the consumer who is the subject of the consumer report with regard to which such finding was made—

(i) a copy of such consumer report with any classified information redacted as necessary;

(ii) notice of any adverse action which is based, in part, on the consumer report; and

(iii) the identification with reasonable specificity of the nature of the investigation for which the consumer report was sought.

(C) Delegation by head of agency or department.—For purposes of subparagraphs (A) and (B), the head of any agency or department of the United States Government may delegate his or her authorities under this paragraph to an official of such agency or department who has personnel security responsibilities and is a member of the Senior Executive Service or equivalent civilian or military rank.

(D) Report to the congress.—Not later than January 31 of each year, the head of each agency and department of the United States Government that exercised authority under this paragraph during the preceding year shall submit a report to the Congress on the number of times the department or agency exercised such authority during the year.

(E) Definitions.—For purposes of this paragraph, the following definitions shall apply:

(i) **Classified information.**—The term "classified information" means information that is protected from unauthorized disclosure under Executive Order No. 12958 or successor orders.

(ii) **National security investigation.**—The term "national security investigation" means any official inquiry by an agency or department of the United States Government to determine the eligibility of a consumer to receive access or continued access to classified information or to determine whether classified information has been lost or compromised.

(c) Furnishing reports in connection with credit or insurance transactions that are not initiated by the consumer.—

(1) In general.—A consumer reporting agency may furnish a consumer report relating to any consumer pursuant to subparagraph (A) or (C) of subsection (a)(3) of this section in connection with any credit or insurance transaction that is not initiated by the consumer only if—

(A) the consumer authorizes the agency to provide such report to such person; or

(B)(i) the transaction consists of a firm offer of credit or insurance;

(ii) the consumer reporting agency has complied with subsection (e) of this section; and

(iii) there is not in effect an election by the consumer, made in accordance with subsection (e), to have the consumer's name and address excluded from lists of names provided by the agency pursuant to this paragraph.

(2) Limits on information received under paragraph (1)(B).—A person may receive pursuant to paragraph (1)(B) only—

(A) the name and address of a consumer;

(B) an identifier that is not unique to the consumer and that is used by the person solely for the purpose of verifying the identity of the consumer; and

(C) other information pertaining to a consumer that does not identify the relationship or experience of the consumer with respect to a particular creditor or other entity.

(3) Information regarding inquiries.—Except as provided in section 1681g(a)(5) of this title, a consumer reporting agency shall not furnish to any person a record of inquiries in connection with a credit or insurance transaction that is not initiated by a consumer.

(d) Reserved

(e) Election of consumer to be excluded from lists.—

(1) In general.—A consumer may elect to have the consumer's name and address excluded from any list provided by a consumer reporting agency under subsection (c)(1)(B) of this section in connection with a credit or insurance transaction that is not initiated by the consumer, by notifying the agency in accordance with paragraph (2) that the consumer does not consent to any use of a consumer report relating to the consumer in connection with any credit or insurance transaction that is not initiated by the consumer.

(2) Manner of notification.—A consumer shall notify a consumer reporting agency under paragraph (1)—

(A) through the notification system maintained by the agency under paragraph (5); or

(B) by submitting to the agency a signed notice of election form issued by the agency for purposes of this subparagraph.

(3) Response of agency after notification through system.—Upon receipt of notification of the election of a consumer under paragraph (1) through the notification system maintained by the agency under paragraph (5), a consumer reporting agency shall—

(A) inform the consumer that the election is effective only for the ~~2-year period~~ 5-year period following the election if the consumer does not submit to the agency a signed notice of election form issued by the agency for purposes of paragraph (2)(B); and

(B) provide to the consumer a notice of election form, if requested by the consumer, not later than 5 business days after receipt of the notification of the election through the system established under paragraph (5), in the case of a request made at the time the consumer provides notification through the system.

(4) **Effectiveness of election.**—An election of a consumer under paragraph (1)—

(A) shall be effective with respect to a consumer reporting agency beginning 5 business days after the date on which the consumer notifies the agency in accordance with paragraph (2);

(B) shall be effective with respect to a consumer reporting agency—

(i) subject to subparagraph (C), during the ~~2-year period~~ 5-year period beginning 5 business days after the date on which the consumer notifies the agency of the election, in the case of an election for which a consumer notifies the agency only in accordance with paragraph (2)(A); or

(ii) until the consumer notifies the agency under subparagraph (C), in the case of an election for which a consumer notifies the agency in accordance with paragraph (2)(B);

(C) shall not be effective after the date on which the consumer notifies the agency, through the notification system established by the agency under paragraph (5), that the election is no longer effective; and

(D) shall be effective with respect to each affiliate of the agency.

(5) **Notification system.**—

(A) **In general.**—Each consumer reporting agency that, under subsection (c)(1)(B) of this section, furnishes a consumer report in connection with a credit or insurance transaction that is not initiated by a consumer, shall—

(i) establish and maintain a notification system, including a toll-free telephone number, which permits any consumer whose consumer report is maintained by the agency to notify the agency, with appropriate identification, of the consumer's election to have the consumer's name and address excluded from any such list of names and addresses provided by the agency for such a transaction; and

(ii) publish by not later than 365 days after September 30, 1996, and not less than annually thereafter, in a publication of general circulation in the area served by the agency—

(I) a notification that information in consumer files maintained by the agency may be used in connection with such transactions; and

(II) the address and toll-free telephone number for consumers to use to notify the agency of the consumer's election under clause(i).

(B) **Establishment and maintenance as compliance.**—Establishment and maintenance of a notification system (including a toll-free telephone number) and publication by a consumer reporting agency on the agency's own behalf and on behalf of any of its affiliates in accordance with this paragraph is deemed to be compliance with this paragraph by each of those affiliates.

(6) **Notification system by agencies that operate nationwide.**—Each consumer reporting agency that compiles and maintains files on consumers on a nationwide basis shall establish and maintain a notification system for purposes of paragraph (5) jointly with other such consumer reporting agencies.

(f) **Certain use or obtaining of information prohibited.**—A person shall not use or obtain a consumer report for any purpose unless—

(1) the consumer report is obtained for a purpose for which the consumer report is authorized to be furnished under this section; and

(2) the purpose is certified in accordance with section 1681e of this title by a prospective user of the report through a general or specific certification.

~~(g) Furnishing reports containing medical information.—A consumer reporting agency shall not furnish for employment purposes, or in connection with a credit or insurance transaction, a consumer report that contains medical information about a consumer, unless the consumer consents to the furnishing of the report.~~

(g) **Protection of medical information.**—

(1) **Limitation on consumer reporting agencies.**—A consumer reporting agency shall not furnish for employment purposes, or in connection with a credit or insurance transaction, a consumer report that contains medical information (other than medical contact information treated in the manner required under section 1681c(a)(6)) about a consumer, unless—

(A) if furnished in connection with an insurance transaction, the consumer affirmatively consents to the furnishing of the report;

(B) if furnished for employment purposes or in connection with a credit transaction—

(i) the information to be furnished is relevant to process or effect the employment or credit transaction; and

(ii) the consumer provides specific written consent for the furnishing of the report that describes in clear and conspicuous language the use for which the information will be furnished; or

(C) the information to be furnished pertains solely to transactions, accounts, or balances relating to debts arising from the receipt of medical services, products, or devises, where such information, other than account status or amounts, is restricted or reported using codes that do not identify, or do not provide information sufficient to infer, the specific provider or the nature of such services, products, or devices, as provided in section 1681c(a)(6).

(2) Limitation on creditors.—Except as permitted pursuant to paragraph (3)(C) or regulations prescribed under paragraph (5)(A), a creditor shall not obtain or use medical information (other than medical information treated in the manner required under section 1681c(a)(6)) pertaining to a consumer in connection with any determination of the consumer's eligibility, or continued eligibility, for credit.

(3) Actions authorized by federal law, insurance activities and regulatory determinations.—Section 1681a(d)(3) shall not be construed so as to treat information or any communication of information as a consumer report if the information or communication is disclosed—

(A) in connection with the business of insurance or annuities, including the activities described in section 18B of the model Privacy of Consumer Financial and Health Information Regulation issued by the National Association of Insurance Commissioners (as in effect on January 1, 2003);

(B) for any purpose permitted without authorization under the Standards for Individually Identifiable Health Information promulgated by the Department of Health and Human Services pursuant to the Health Insurance Portability and Accountability Act of 1996, or referred to under section 1179 of such Act, or described in section 502(e) of Public Law 106-102; or

(C) as otherwise determined to be necessary and appropriate, by regulation or order and subject to paragraph (6), by the Commission, any Federal banking agency or the National Credit Union Administration (with respect to any financial institution subject to the jurisdiction of such agency or Administration under paragraph (1), (2), or (3) of section 1681s(b), or the applicable State insurance authority (with respect to any person engaged in providing insurance or annuities).

(4) Limitation on redisclosure of medical information.—Any person that receives medical information pursuant to paragraph (1) or (3) shall not disclose such information to any other person, except as necessary to carry out the purpose for which the information was initially disclosed, or as otherwise permitted by statute, regulation, or order.

(5) Regulations and effective date for paragraph (2).—

(A) **Regulations required.**—Each Federal banking agency and the National Credit Union Administration shall, subject to paragraph (6) and after notice and opportunity for comment, prescribe regulations that permit transactions under paragraph (2) that are determined to be necessary and appropriate to protect legitimate operational, transactional, risk, consumer, and other needs (and which shall include permitting actions necessary for administrative verification purposes), consistent with the intent of paragraph (2) to restrict the use of medical information for inappropriate purposes.

(B) **Final regulations required.**—The Federal banking agencies and the National Credit Union Administration shall issue the regulations required under subparagraph (A) in final form before the end of the 6-month period beginning on the date of enactment of the Fair and Accurate Credit Transactions Act of 2003.

(6) Coordination with other laws.—No provision of this subsection shall be construed as altering, affecting, or superseding the applicability of any other provision of Federal law relating to medical confidentiality.

§ 1681c. Requirements relating to information contained in consumer reports [FCRA § 605]

(a) Information excluded from consumer reports—Prohibited items

Except as authorized under subsection (b) of this section, no consumer reporting agency may make any consumer report containing any of the following items of information:

(1) Cases under Title 11 or under the Bankruptcy Act that, from the date of entry of the order for relief or the date of adjudication, as the case may be, antedate the report by more than 10 years.

(2) Civil suits, civil judgments, and records of arrest that, from date of entry, antedate the report by more than seven years or until the governing statute of limitations has expired, whichever is the longer period.

(3) Paid tax liens which, from date of payment, antedate the report by more than seven years.

(4) Accounts placed for collection or charged to profit and loss which antedate the report by more than seven years.

(5) Any other adverse item of information, other than records of convictions of crimes, which antedates the report by more than seven years.

(6) [Redesignated as paragraph (5).]

(6) The name, address, and telephone number of any medical information furnisher that has notified the agency of its status, unless—

(A) such name, address, and telephone number are restricted or reported using codes that do not identify, or provide information sufficient to infer, the specific provider or the nature of such services, products, or devices to a person other than the consumer; or

(B) the report is being provided to an insurance company for a purpose relating to engaging in the business of insurance other than property and casualty insurance.

(b) Exempted cases

The provisions of paragraphs (1) through (5) of subsection (a)The provisions of subsection (a) of this section are not applicable in the case of any consumer credit report to be used in connection with—

(1) a credit transaction involving, or which may reasonably be expected to involve, a principal amount of $150,000 or more;

(2) the underwriting of life insurance involving, or which may reasonably be expected to involve, a face amount of $150,000 or more; or

(3) the employment of any individual at an annual salary which equals, or which may reasonably be expected to equal $75,000, or more.

(c) Running of reporting period

(1) In general.—The 7-year period referred to in paragraphs (4) and (6) of subsection (a) of this section shall begin, with respect to any delinquent account that is placed for collection (internally or by referral to a third party, whichever is earlier), charged to profit and loss, or subjected to any similar action, upon the expiration of the 180-day period beginning on the date of the commencement of the delinquency which immediately preceded the collection activity, charge to profit and loss, or similar action.

(2) Effective date.—Paragraph (1) shall apply only to items of information added to the file of a consumer on or after the date that is 455 days after Sept. 30, 1996.

(d) Information required to be disclosed Disclosed

Any consumer reporting agency **(1) Title 11 information.**—Any consumer reporting agency that furnishes a consumer report that contains information regarding any case involving the consumer that arises under Title 11, shall include in the report an identification of the chapter of such Title 11 under which such case arises if provided by the source of the information. If any case arising or filed under Title 11, is withdrawn by the consumer before a final judgment, the consumer reporting agency shall include in the report that such case or filing was withdrawn upon receipt of documentation certifying such withdrawal.

(2) Key factor in credit score information.—Any consumer reporting agency that furnishes a consumer report that contains any credit score or any other risk score or predictor on any consumer shall include in the report a clear and conspicuous statement that a key factor (as defined in section 1681g(f)(2)(B)) that adversely affected such score or predictor was the number of enquiries, if such a predictor was in fact a key factor that adversely affected such score. This paragraph shall not apply to a check services company, acting as such, which issues authorizations for the purpose of approving or processing negotiable instruments, electronic fund transfers, or similar methods of payments, but only to the extent that such company is engaged in such activities.

(e) Indication of closure of account by consumer

If a consumer reporting agency is notified pursuant to section 1681s-2(a)(4) of this title that a credit account of a consumer was voluntarily closed by the consumer, the agency shall indicate that fact in any consumer report that includes information related to the account.

(f) Indication of dispute by consumer

If a consumer reporting agency is notified pursuant to section 1681s-2(a)(3) of this title that information regarding a consumer who was furnished to the agency is disputed by the consumer, the agency shall indicate that fact in each consumer report that includes the disputed information.

(g) Truncation of credit card and debit card numbers.—

(1) In general.—Except as otherwise provided in this subsection, no person that accepts credit cards or debit cards for the transaction of business shall print more than the last 5 digits of the card number or the expiration date upon any receipt provided to the cardholder at the point of the sale or transaction.

(2) Limitation.—This subsection shall apply only to receipts that are electronically printed, and shall not apply to transactions in which the sole means of recording a credit card or debit card account number is by handwriting or by an imprint or copy of the card.

(3) Effective date.—This subsection shall become effective—

(A) 3 years after the date of enactment of this subsection, with respect to any cash register or other machine or device that electronically prints receipts for credit card or debit card transactions that is in use before January 1, 2005; and

(B) 1 year after the date of enactment of this subsection, with respect to any cash register or other machine or device that electronically prints receipts for credit card or debit card transactions that is first put into use on or after January 1, 2005.

(h) Notice of discrepancy in address.—

(1) In general.—If a person has requested a consumer report relating to a consumer from a consumer reporting agency described in section 1681a(p), the request includes an address for the consumer that substantially differs from the addresses in the file of the consumer, and the agency provides a consumer report in response to the request, the consumer reporting agency shall notify the requester of the existence of the discrepancy.

(2) Regulations.—

(A) Regulations required.—The Federal banking agencies, the National Credit Union Administration, and the Commission shall jointly, with respect to the entities that are subject to their respective enforcement authority under section 1681s, prescribe regulations providing guidance regarding reasonable policies and procedures that a user of a consumer report should employ when such user has received a notice of discrepancy under paragraph (1).

(B) Policies and procedures to be included.—The regulations prescribed under subparagraph (A) shall describe reasonable policies and procedures for use by a user of a consumer report—

(i) to form a reasonable belief that the user knows the identity of the person to whom the consumer report pertains; and

(ii) if the user establishes a continuing relationship with the consumer, and the user regularly and in the ordinary course of business furnishes information to the consumer reporting agency from which the notice of discrepancy pertaining to the consumer was obtained, to reconcile the address of the consumer with the consumer reporting agency by furnishing such address to such consumer reporting agency as part of information regularly furnished by the user for the period in which the relationship is established.

§ 1681c-1. Identity theft prevention; fraud alerts and active duty alerts [FCRA § 605A]

(a) One-call fraud alerts.—

(1) Initial alerts.—Upon the direct request of a consumer, or an individual acting on behalf of or as a personal representative of a consumer, who asserts in good faith a suspicion that the consumer has been or is about to become a victim of fraud or related crime, including identity theft, a consumer reporting agency described in section 1681a(p) that maintains a file on the consumer and has received appropriate proof of the identity of the requester shall—

(A) include a fraud alert in the file of that consumer, and also provide that alert along with any credit score generated in using that file, for a period of not less than 90 days, beginning on the date of such request, unless the consumer or such representative requests that such fraud alert be removed before the end of such period, and the agency has received appropriate proof of the identity of the requester for such purpose; and

(B) refer the information regarding the fraud alert under this paragraph to each of the other consumer reporting agencies described in section 1681a(p), in accordance with procedures developed under section 1681s(f).

(2) Access to free reports.—In any case in which a consumer reporting agency includes a fraud alert in the file of a consumer pursuant to this subsection, the consumer reporting agency shall—

(A) disclose to the consumer that the consumer may request a free copy of the file of the consumer pursuant to section 1681j(d); and

(B) provide to the consumer all disclosures required to be made under section 1681g, without charge to the consumer, not later than 3 business days after any request described in subparagraph (A).

(b) Extended alerts.—

(1) In general.—Upon the direct request of a consumer, or an individual acting on behalf of or as a personal representative of a consumer, who submits an identity theft report to a consumer reporting agency described in section 1681a(p) that maintains a file on the consumer, if the agency has received appropriate proof of the identity of the requester, the agency shall—

(A) include a fraud alert in the file of that consumer, and also provide that alert along with any credit score generated in using that file, during the 7-year period beginning on the date of such request, unless the consumer or such representative requests that such fraud alert be removed before the end of such period and the agency has received appropriate proof of the identity of the requester for such purpose;

(B) during the 5-year period beginning on the date of such request, exclude the consumer from any list of consumers prepared by the consumer reporting agency and provided to any third party to offer credit or insurance to the consumer as part of a transaction that was not initiated by the consumer, unless the consumer or such representative requests that such exclusion be rescinded before the end of such period; and

(C) refer the information regarding the extended fraud alert under this paragraph to each of the other consumer reporting agencies described in section 1681a(p), in accordance with procedures developed under section 1681s(f).

(2) Access to free reports.—In any case in which a consumer reporting agency includes a fraud alert in the file of a consumer pursuant to this subsection, the consumer reporting agency shall—

(A) disclose to the consumer that the consumer may request 2 free copies of the file of the consumer pursuant to section 1681j(d) during the 12-month period beginning on the date on which the fraud alert was included in the file; and

(B) provide to the consumer all disclosures required to be made under section 1681g, without charge to the consumer, not later than 3 business days after any request described in subparagraph (A).

(c) Active duty alerts.—Upon the direct request of an active duty military consumer, or an individual acting on behalf of or as a personal representative of an active duty military consumer, a consumer reporting agency described in section 1681a(p) that maintains a file on the active duty military consumer and has received appropriate proof of the identity of the requester shall—

(1) include an active duty alert in the file of that active duty military consumer, and also provide that alert along with any credit score generated in using that file, during a period of not less than 12 months, or such longer period as the Commission shall determine, by regulation, beginning on the date of the request, unless the active duty military consumer or such representative requests that such fraud alert be removed before the end of such period, and the agency has received appropriate proof of the identity of the requester for such purpose;

(2) during the 2-year period beginning on the date of such request, exclude the active duty military consumer from any list of consumers prepared by the consumer reporting agency and provided to any third party to offer credit or insurance to the consumer as part of a transaction that was not initiated by the consumer, unless the consumer requests that such exclusion be rescinded before the end of such period; and

(3) refer the information regarding the active duty alert to each of the other consumer reporting agencies described in section 1681a(p), in accordance with procedures developed under section 1681s(f).

(d) Procedures.—Each consumer reporting agency described in section 1681a(p) shall establish policies and procedures to comply with this section, including procedures that inform consumers of the availability of initial, extended, and active duty alerts and procedures that allow consumers and active duty military consumers to request initial, extended, or active duty alerts (as applicable) in a simple and easy manner, including by telephone.

(e) Referrals of alerts.—Each consumer reporting agency described in section 1681a(p) that receives a referral of a fraud alert or active duty alert from another consumer reporting agency pursuant to this section shall, as though the agency received the request from the consumer directly, follow the procedures required under—

(1) paragraphs (1)(A) and (2) of subsection (a), in the case of a referral under subsection (a)(1)(B);

(2) paragraphs (1)(A), (1)(B), and (2) of subsection (b), in the case of a referral under subsection (b)(1)(C); and

(3) paragraphs (1) and (2) of subsection (c), in the case of a referral under subsection (c)(3).

(f) Duty of reseller to reconvey alert.—A reseller shall include in its report any fraud alert or active duty alert placed in the file of a consumer pursuant to this section by another consumer reporting agency.

(g) Duty of other consumer reporting agencies to provide contact information.—If a consumer contacts any consumer reporting agency that is not described in section 1681a(p) to communicate a suspicion that the consumer has been or is about to become a victim of fraud or related crime, including identity theft, the agency shall provide information to the consumer on how to contact the Commission and the consumer reporting agencies described in section 1681a(p) to obtain more detailed information and request alerts under this section.

(h) Limitations on use of information for credit extensions.—

(1) Requirements for initial and active duty alerts.—

(A) Notification.—Each initial fraud alert and active duty alert under this section shall include information that notifies all prospective users of a consumer report on the consumer to which the alert relates that the consumer does not authorize the establishment of any new credit plan or extension of credit, other than under an open-end credit plan (as defined in section 103(i)), in the name of the consumer, or issuance of an additional card on an existing credit account requested by a consumer, or any increase in credit limit on an existing credit account requested by a consumer, except in accordance with subparagraph (B).

(B) Limitation on users.—

(i) In general.—No prospective user of a consumer report that includes an initial fraud alert or an active duty alert in accordance with this section may establish a new credit plan or extension of credit, other than under an open-end credit plan (as defined in section 103(i)), in the name of the consumer, or issue an additional card on an existing credit account requested by a consumer, or grant any increase in credit limit on an existing credit account requested by a consumer, unless the user utilizes reasonable policies and procedures to form a reasonable belief that the user knows the identity of the person making the request.

(ii) Verification.—If a consumer requesting the alert has specified a telephone number to be used for identity verification purposes, before authorizing any new credit plan or extension described in clause (i) in the name of such consumer, a user of such consumer report shall contact the consumer using that telephone number or take reasonable steps to verify the consumer's identity and confirm that the application for a new credit plan is not the result of identity theft.

(2) Requirements for extended alerts.—

(A) Notification.—Each extended alert under this section shall include information that provides all prospective users of a consumer report relating to a consumer with—

(i) notification that the consumer does not authorize the establishment of any new credit plan or extension of credit described in clause (i), other than under an open-end credit plan (as defined in section 103(i)), in the name of the consumer, or issuance of an additional card on an existing credit account requested by a consumer, or any increase in credit limit on an existing credit account requested by a consumer, except in accordance with subparagraph (B); and

(ii) a telephone number or other reasonable contact method designated by the consumer.

(B) Limitation on users.—No prospective user of a consumer report or of a credit score generated using the information in the file of a consumer that includes an extended fraud alert in accordance with this section may establish a new credit plan or extension of credit, other than under an open-end credit plan (as defined in section 103(i)), in the name of the consumer, or issue an additional card on an existing credit account requested by a consumer, or any increase in credit limit on an existing credit account requested by a consumer, unless the user contacts the consumer in person or using the contact method described in subparagraph (A)(ii) to confirm that the application for a new credit plan or increase in credit limit, or request for an additional card is not the result of identity theft.

§ 1681c-2. Block of information resulting from identity theft [FCRA § 605B]

(a) Block.—Except as otherwise provided in this section, a consumer reporting agency shall block the reporting of any information in the file of a consumer that the consumer identifies as information that resulted from an alleged identity theft, not later than 4 business days after the date of receipt by such agency of—

(1) appropriate proof of the identity of the consumer;

(2) a copy of an identity theft report;

(3) the identification of such information by the consumer; and

(4) a statement by the consumer that the information is not information relating to any transaction by the consumer.

(b) Notification.—A consumer reporting agency shall promptly notify the furnisher of information identified by the consumer under subsection (a)—

(1) that the information may be a result of identity theft;

(2) that an identity theft report has been filed;

(3) that a block has been requested under this section; and

(4) of the effective dates of the block.

(c) Authority to decline or rescind.—

(1) In general.—A consumer reporting agency may decline to block, or may rescind any block, of information relating to a consumer under this section, if the consumer reporting agency reasonably determines that—

(A) the information was blocked in error or a block was requested by the consumer in error;

(B) the information was blocked, or a block was requested by the consumer, on the basis of a material misrepresentation of fact by the consumer relevant to the request to block; or

(C) the consumer obtained possession of goods, services, or money as a result of the blocked transaction or transactions.

(2) Notification to consumer.—If a block of information is declined or rescinded under this subsection, the affected consumer shall be notified promptly, in the same manner as consumers are notified of the reinsertion of information under section 1681i(a)(5)(B).

(3) Significance of block.—For purposes of this subsection, if a consumer reporting agency rescinds a block, the presence of information in the file of a consumer prior to the blocking of such information is not evidence of whether the consumer knew or should have known that the consumer obtained possession of any goods, services, or money as a result of the block.

(d) Exception for resellers.—

(1) No reseller file.—This section shall not apply to a consumer reporting agency, if the consumer reporting agency—

(A) is a reseller;

(B) is not, at the time of the request of the consumer under subsection (a), otherwise furnishing or reselling a consumer report concerning the information identified by the consumer; and

(C) informs the consumer, by any means, that the consumer may report the identity theft to the Commission to obtain consumer information regarding identity theft.

(2) Reseller with file.—The sole obligation of the consumer reporting agency under this section, with regard to any request of a consumer under this section, shall be to block the consumer report maintained by the consumer reporting agency from any subsequent use, if—

(A) the consumer, in accordance with the provisions of subsection (a), identifies, to a consumer reporting agency, information in the file of the consumer that resulted from identity theft; and

(B) the consumer reporting agency is a reseller of the identified information.

(3) Notice.—In carrying out its obligation under paragraph (2), the reseller shall promptly provide a notice to the consumer of the decision to block the file. Such notice shall contain the name, address, and telephone number of each consumer reporting agency from which the consumer information was obtained for resale.

(e) Exception for verification companies.—The provisions of this section do not apply to a check services company, acting as such, which issues authorizations for the purpose of approving or processing negotiable instruments, electronic fund transfers, or similar methods of payments, except that, beginning 4 business days after receipt of information described in paragraphs (1) through (3) of subsection (a), a check services company shall not report to a national consumer reporting agency described in section 1681a(p), any information identified in the subject identity theft report as resulting from identity theft.

(f) Access to blocked information by law enforcement agencies.—No provision of this section shall be construed as requiring a consumer reporting agency to prevent a Federal, State, or local law enforcement agency from accessing blocked information in a consumer file to which the agency could otherwise obtain access under this title.

§ 1681d. Disclosure of investigative consumer reports [FCRA § 606]

(a) Disclosure of fact of preparation

A person may not procure or cause to be prepared an investigative consumer report on any consumer unless—

(1) it is clearly and accurately disclosed to the consumer that an investigative consumer report including information as to his character, general reputation, personal characteristics, and mode of living, whichever are applicable, may be made, and such disclosure **(A)** is made in a writing mailed, or otherwise delivered, to the consumer, not later than three days after the date on which the report was first requested, and **(B)** includes a statement informing the consumer of his right to request the additional disclosures provided for under subsection (b) of this section and the written summary of the rights of the consumer prepared pursuant to section 1681g(c) of this title; and

(2) the person certifies or has certified to the consumer reporting agency that—

(A) the person has made the disclosures to the consumer required by paragraph (1); and

(B) the person will comply with subsection (b) of this section.

(b) Disclosure on request of nature and scope of investigation

Any person who procures or causes to be prepared an investigative consumer report on any consumer shall, upon written request made by the consumer within a reasonable period of time after the receipt by him of the disclosure required by subsection (a)(1) of this section, shall make a complete and accurate disclosure of the nature and scope of the investigation requested. This disclosure shall be made in a writing mailed, or otherwise delivered, to the consumer not later than five days after the date on which the request for such disclosure was received from the consumer or such report was first requested, whichever is the later.

(c) Limitation on liability upon showing of reasonable procedures for compliance with provisions

No person may be held liable for any violation of subsection (a) or (b) of this section if he shows by a preponderance of the evidence that at the time of the violation he maintained reasonable procedures to assure compliance with subsection (a) or (b) of this section.

(d) Prohibitions

(1) **Certification.**—A consumer reporting agency shall not prepare or furnish investigative consumer report unless the agency has received a certification under subsection (a)(2) from the person who requested the report.

(2) **Inquiries.**—A consumer reporting agency shall not make an inquiry for the purpose of preparing an investigative consumer report on a consumer for employment purposes if the making of the inquiry by an employer or prospective employer of the consumer would violate any applicable Federal or State equal employment opportunity law or regulation.

(3) **Certain public record information.**—Except as otherwise provided in section 1681k of this title, a consumer reporting agency shall not furnish an investigative consumer report that includes information that is a matter of public record and that relates to an arrest, indictment, conviction, civil judicial action, tax lien, or outstanding judgment, unless the agency has verified the accuracy of the information during the 30-day period ending on the date on which the report is furnished.

(4) **Certain adverse information.**—A consumer reporting agency shall not prepare or furnish an investigative consumer report on a consumer that contains information that is adverse to the interest of the consumer and that is obtained through a personal interview with a neighbor, friend, or associate of the consumer or with another person with whom the consumer is acquainted or who has knowledge of such item of information, unless—

(A) the agency has followed reasonable procedures to obtain confirmation of the information, from an additional source that has independent and direct knowledge of the information; or

(B) the person interviewed is the best possible source of the information.

§ 1681e. Compliance procedures [FCRA § 607]

(a) Identity and purposes of credit users

Every consumer reporting agency shall maintain reasonable procedures designed to avoid violations of section 1681c of this title and to limit the furnishing of consumer reports to the purposes listed under section 1681b of this title. These procedures shall require that prospective users of the information identify themselves, certify the purposes for which the information is sought, and certify that the information will be used for no other purpose. Every consumer reporting agency shall make a reasonable effort to verify the identity of a new prospective user and the uses certified by such prospective user prior to furnishing such user a consumer report. No consumer reporting agency may furnish a consumer report to any person if it has reasonable grounds for believing that the consumer report will not be used for a purpose listed in section 1681b of this title.

(b) Accuracy of report

Whenever a consumer reporting agency prepares a consumer report it shall follow reasonable procedures to assure maximum possible accuracy of the information concerning the individual about whom the report relates.

(c) Disclosure of consumer reports by users allowed

A consumer reporting agency may not prohibit a user of a consumer report furnished by the agency on a consumer from disclosing the contents of the report to the consumer, if adverse action against the consumer has been taken by the user based in whole or in part on the report.

(d) Notice to users and furnishers of information

(1) **Notice requirement.**—A consumer reporting agency shall provide to any person—

(A) who regularly and in the ordinary course of business furnishes information to the agency with respect to any consumer; or

(B) to whom a consumer report is provided by the agency;

a notice of such person's responsibilities under this subchapter.

(2) **Content of notice.**—The Federal Trade Commission shall prescribe the content of notices under paragraph (1), and a consumer reporting agency shall be in compliance with this subsection if it provides a notice under paragraph (1) that is substantially similar to the Federal Trade Commission prescription under this paragraph.

(e) Procurement of consumer report for resale

(1) **Disclosure.**—A person may not procure a consumer report for purposes of reselling the report (or any information in the report) unless the person discloses to the consumer reporting agency that originally furnishes the report—

(A) the identity of the end-user of the report (or information); and

(B) each permissible purpose under section 1681b of this title for which the report is furnished to the end-user of the report (or information).

(2) Responsibilities of procurers for resale.—A person who procures a consumer report for purposes of reselling the report (or any information in the report) shall—

(A) establish and comply with reasonable procedures designed to ensure that the report (or information) is resold by the person only for a purpose for which the report may be furnished under section 1681b of this title, including by requiring that each person to which the report (or information) is resold and that resells or provides the report (or information) to any other person—

(i) identifies each end user of the resold report (or information);

(ii) certifies each purpose for which the report (or information) will be used; and

(iii) certifies that the report (or information) will be used for no other purpose; and

(B) before reselling the report, make reasonable efforts to verify the identifications and certifications made under subparagraph (A).

(3) Resale of consumer report to a federal agency or department.—Notwithstanding paragraph (1) or (2), a person who procures a consumer report for purposes of reselling the report (or any information in the report) shall not disclose the identity of the end-user of the report under paragraph (1) or (2) if—

(A) the end user is an agency or department of the United States Government which procures the report from the person for purposes of determining the eligibility of the consumer concerned to receive access or continued access to classified information (as defined in section 604(b)(4)(E)(i)); and

(B) the agency or department certifies in writing to the person reselling the report that nondisclosure is necessary to protect classified information or the safety of persons employed by or contracting with, or undergoing investigation for work or contracting with the agency or department.

§ 1681f. Disclosures to governmental agencies [FCRA § 608]

Notwithstanding the provisions of section 1681b of this title, a consumer reporting agency may furnish identifying information respecting any consumer, limited to his name, address, former addresses, places of employment, or former places of employment, to a governmental agency.

§ 1681g. Disclosures to consumers [FCRA § 609]

(a) Information on file; sources; report recipients

Every consumer reporting agency shall, upon request, and subject to section 1681h(a)(1) of this title, clearly and accurately disclose to the consumer:

(1) All information in the consumer's file at the time of the request, ~~except that nothing~~ except that—

(A) if the consumer to whom the file relates requests that the first 5 digits of the social security number (or similar identification number) of the consumer not be included in the disclosure and the consumer reporting agency has received appropriate proof of the identity of the requester, the consumer reporting agency shall so truncate such number in such disclosure; and

(B) nothing in this paragraph shall be construed to require a consumer reporting agency to disclose to a consumer any information concerning credit scores or any other risk scores or predictors relating to the consumer.

(2) The sources of the information; except that the sources of information acquired solely for use in preparing an investigative consumer report and actually used for no other purpose need not be disclosed: *Provided*, That in the event an action is brought under this subchapter, such sources shall be available to the plaintiff under appropriate discovery procedures in the court in which the action is brought.

(3)(A) Identification of each person (including each end-user identified under section 1681e(e)(1)) that procured a consumer report—

(i) for employment purposes, during the 2-year period preceding the date on which the request is made; or

(ii) for any other purpose, during the 1-year period preceding the date on which the request is made.

(B) An identification of a person under subparagraph (A) shall include—

(i) the name of the person or, if applicable, the trade name (written in full) under which such person conducts business; and

(ii) upon request of the consumer, the address and telephone number of the person.

(C) Subparagraph (A) does not apply if—

(i) the end user is an agency or department of the United States Government that procures the report from the person for purposes of determining the eligibility of the consumer to whom the report relates to receive access or continued access to classified information (as defined in section 1681b(b)(4)(E)(i) of this title); and

(ii) the head of the agency or department makes a written finding as prescribed under section 1681b(b)(4)(A) of this title.

(4) The dates, original payees, and amounts of any checks upon which is based any adverse characterization of the consumer, included in the file at the time of the disclosure.

(5) A record of all inquiries received by the agency during the 1-year period preceding the request that identified the consumer in connection with a credit or insurance transaction that was not initiated by the consumer.

(6) If the consumer requests the credit file and not the credit score, a statement that the consumer may request and obtain a credit score.

(b) Exempt information

The requirements of subsection (a) of this section respecting the disclosure of sources of information and the recipients of consumer reports do not apply to information received or consumer reports furnished prior to the effective date of this subchapter except to the extent that the matter involved is contained in the files of the consumer reporting agency on that date.

~~**(c) Summary of rights required to be included with disclosure**~~

~~**(1) Summary of rights.**—A consumer reporting agency shall provide to a consumer, with each written disclosure by the agency to the consumer under this section—~~

~~**(A)** a written summary of all of the rights that the consumer has under this subchapter; and~~

~~**(B)** in the case of a consumer reporting agency that compiles and maintains files on consumers on a nationwide basis, a toll-free telephone number established by the agency, at which personnel are accessible to consumers during normal business hours.~~

~~**(2) Specific items required to be included.**—The summary of rights required under paragraph (1) shall include—~~

~~**(A)** a brief description of this subchapter and all rights of consumers under this subchapter;~~

~~**(B)** an explanation of how the consumer may exercise the rights of the consumer under this subchapter;~~

~~**(C)** a list of all Federal agencies responsible for enforcing any provision of this subchapter and the address and any appropriate phone number of each such agency, in a form that will assist the consumer in selecting the appropriate agency;~~

~~**(D)** a statement that the consumer may have additional rights under State law and that the consumer may wish to contact a State or local consumer protection agency or a State attorney general to learn of those rights; and~~

~~**(E)** a statement that a consumer reporting agency is not required to remove accurate derogatory information from a consumer's file, unless the information is outdated under section 1681c of this title or cannot be verified.~~

~~**(3) Form of summary of rights.**—For purposes of this subsection and any disclosure by a consumer reporting agency required under this subchapter with respect to consumers' rights, the Federal Trade Commission (after consultation with each Federal agency referred to in section 1681s(b) of this title) shall prescribe the form and content of any such disclosure of the rights of consumers required under this subchapter. A consumer reporting agency shall be in compliance with this subsection if it provides disclosures under paragraph (1) that are substantially similar to the Federal Trade Commission prescription under this paragraph.~~

~~**(4) Effectiveness.**—No disclosures shall be required under this subsection until the date on which the Federal Trade Commission prescribes the form and content of such disclosures under paragraph (3).~~

(c) Summary of rights to obtain and dispute information in consumer reports and to obtain credit scores.—

(1) Commission summary of rights required.—

(A) In general.—The Commission shall prepare a model summary of the rights of consumers under this title.

(B) Content of summary.—The summary of rights prepared under subparagraph (A) shall include a description of—

(i) the right of a consumer to obtain a copy of a consumer report under subsection (a) from each consumer reporting agency;

(ii) the frequency and circumstances under which a consumer is entitled to receive a consumer report without charge under section 1681j;

(iii) the right of a consumer to dispute information in the file of the consumer under section 1681i;

(iv) the right of a consumer to obtain a credit score from a consumer reporting agency, and a description of how to obtain a credit score;

(v) the method by which a consumer can contact, and obtain a consumer report from, a consumer reporting agency without charge, as provided in the regulations of the Commission prescribed under section 211(c) of the Fair and Accurate Credit Transactions Act of 2003; and

(vi) the method by which a consumer can contact, and obtain a consumer report from, a consumer reporting agency described in section 1681a(w), as provided in the regulations of the Commission prescribed under section 1681j(a)(1)(C).

(C) Availability of summary of rights.—The Commission shall—

(i) actively publicize the availability of the summary of rights prepared under this paragraph;

(ii) conspicuously post on its Internet website the availability of such summary of rights; and

(iii) promptly make such summary of rights available to consumers, on request.

(2) Summary of rights required to be included with agency disclosures.—A consumer reporting agency shall provide to a consumer, with each written disclosure by the agency to the consumer under this section—

(A) the summary of rights prepared by the Commission under paragraph (1);

(B) in the case of a consumer reporting agency described in section 1681a(p), a toll-free telephone number established by the agency, at which personnel are accessible to consumers during normal business hours;

(C) a list of all Federal agencies responsible for enforcing any provision of this title, and the address and any appropriate phone number of each such agency, in a form that will assist the consumer in selecting the appropriate agency;

(D) a statement that the consumer may have additional rights under State law, and that the consumer may wish to contact a State or local consumer protection agency or a State attorney general (or the equivalent thereof) to learn of those rights; and

(E) a statement that a consumer reporting agency is not required to remove accurate derogatory information from the file of a consumer, unless the information is outdated under section 1681c or cannot be verified.

(d) Summary of rights of identity theft victims.—

(1) In general.—The Commission, in consultation with the Federal banking agencies and the National Credit Union Administration, shall prepare a model summary of the rights of consumers under this title with respect to the procedures for remedying the effects of fraud or identity theft involving credit, an electronic fund transfer, or an account or transaction at or with a financial institution or other creditor.

(2) Summary of rights and contact information.—Beginning 60 days after the date on which the model summary of rights is prescribed in final form by the Commission pursuant to paragraph (1), if any consumer contacts a consumer reporting agency and expresses a belief that the consumer is a victim of fraud or identity theft involving credit, an electronic fund transfer, or an account or transaction at or with a financial institution or other creditor, the consumer reporting agency shall, in addition to any other action that the agency may take, provide the consumer with a summary of rights that contains all of the information required by the Commission under paragraph (1), and information on how to contact the Commission to obtain more detailed information.

(e) Information available to victims.—

(1) In general.—For the purpose of documenting fraudulent transactions resulting from identity theft, not later than 30 days after the date of receipt of a request from a victim in accordance with paragraph (3), and subject to verification of the identity of the victim and the claim of identity theft in accordance with paragraph (2), a business entity that has provided credit to, provided for consideration products, goods, or services to, accepted payment from, or otherwise entered into a commercial transaction for consideration with, a person who has allegedly made unauthorized use of the means of identification of the victim, shall provide a copy of application and business transaction records in the control of the business entity, whether maintained by the business entity or by another person on behalf of the business entity, evidencing any transaction alleged to be a result of identity theft to—

(A) the victim;

(B) any Federal, State, or local government law enforcement agency or officer specified by the victim in such a request; or

(C) any law enforcement agency investigating the identity theft and authorized by the victim to take receipt of records provided under this subsection.

(2) Verification of identity and claim.—Before a business entity provides any information under paragraph (1), unless the business entity, at its discretion, otherwise has a high degree of confidence that it knows the identity of the victim making a request under paragraph (1), the victim shall provide to the business entity—

(A) as proof of positive identification of the victim, at the election of the business entity—

(i) the presentation of a government-issued identification card;

(ii) personally identifying information of the same type as was provided to the business entity by the unauthorized person; or

(iii) personally identifying information that the business entity typically requests from new applicants or for new transactions, at the time of the victim's request for information, including any documentation described in clauses (i) and (ii); and

(B) as proof of a claim of identity theft, at the election of the business entity—

(i) a copy of a police report evidencing the claim of the victim of identity theft; and

(ii) a properly completed—

(I) copy of a standardized affidavit of identity theft developed and made available by the Commission; or

(II) an affidavit of fact that is acceptable to the business entity for that purpose.

(3) Procedures.—The request of a victim under paragraph (1) shall—

(A) be in writing;

(B) be mailed to an address specified by the business entity, if any; and

(C) if asked by the business entity, include relevant information about any transaction alleged to be a result of identity theft to facilitate compliance with this section including—

(i) if known by the victim (or if readily obtainable by the victim), the date of the application or transaction; and

(ii) if known by the victim (or if readily obtainable by the victim), any other identifying information such as an account or transaction number.

(4) No charge to victim.—Information required to be provided under paragraph (1) shall be so provided without charge.

(5) Authority to decline to provide information.—A business entity may decline to provide information under paragraph (1) if, in the exercise of good faith, the business entity determines that—

(A) this subsection does not require disclosure of the information;

(B) after reviewing the information provided pursuant to paragraph (2), the business entity does not have a high degree of confidence in knowing the true identity of the individual requesting the information;

(C) the request for the information is based on a misrepresentation of fact by the individual requesting the information relevant to the request for information; or

(D) the information requested is Internet navigational data or similar information about a person's visit to a website or online service.

(6) Limitation on liability.—Except as provided in section 1681s, sections 1681n and 1681o do not apply to any violation of this subsection.

(7) Limitation on civil liability.—No business entity may be held civilly liable under any provision of Federal, State, or other law for disclosure, made in good faith pursuant to this subsection.

(8) No new recordkeeping obligation.—Nothing in this subsection creates an obligation on the part of a business entity to obtain, retain, or maintain information or records that are not otherwise required to be obtained, retained, or maintained in the ordinary course of its business or under other applicable law.

(9) Rule of construction.—

(A) **In general.**—No provision of subtitle A of title V of Public Law 106-102, prohibiting the disclosure of financial information by a business entity to third parties shall be used to deny disclosure of information to the victim under this subsection.

(B) **Limitation.**—Except as provided in subparagraph (A), nothing in this subsection permits a business entity to disclose information, including information to law enforcement under subparagraphs (B) and (C) of paragraph (1), that the business entity is otherwise prohibited from disclosing under any other applicable provision of Federal or State law.

(10) Affirmative defense.—In any civil action brought to enforce this subsection, it is an affirmative defense (which the defendant must establish by a preponderance of the evidence) for a business entity to file an affidavit or answer stating that—

(A) the business entity has made a reasonably diligent search of its available business records; and

(B) the records requested under this subsection do not exist or are not reasonably available.

(11) Definition of victim.—For purposes of this subsection, the term 'victim' means a consumer whose means of identification or financial information has been used or transferred (or has been alleged to have been used or transferred) without the authority of that consumer, with the intent to commit, or to aid or abet, an identity theft or a similar crime.

(12) Effective date.—This subsection shall become effective 180 days after the date of enactment of this subsection.

(13) Effectiveness study.—Not later than 18 months after the date of enactment of this subsection, the Comptroller General of the United States shall submit a report to Congress assessing the effectiveness of this provision.

(f) Disclosure of credit scores.—

(1) In general.—Upon the request of a consumer for a credit score, a consumer reporting agency shall supply to the consumer a statement indicating that the information and credit scoring model may be different than the credit score that may be used by the lender, and a notice which shall include—

(A) the current credit score of the consumer or the most recent credit score of the consumer that was previously calculated by the credit reporting agency for a purpose related to the extension of credit;

(B) the range of possible credit scores under the model used;

(C) all of the key factors that adversely affected the credit score of the consumer in the model used, the total number of which shall not exceed 4, subject to paragraph (9);

(D) the date on which the credit score was created; and

(E) the name of the person or entity that provided the credit score or credit file upon which the credit score was created.

(2) Definitions.—For purposes of this subsection, the following definitions shall apply:

(A) **Credit score.**—The term 'credit score'—

(i) means a numerical value or a categorization derived from a statistical tool or modeling system used by a person who makes or arranges a loan to predict the likelihood of certain credit behaviors, including default (and the numerical value or the categorization derived from such analysis may also be referred to as a 'risk predictor' or 'risk score'); and

(ii) does not include—

(I) any mortgage score or rating of an automated underwriting system that considers one or more factors in addition to credit information, including the loan to value ratio, the amount of down payment, or the financial assets of a consumer; or

(II) any other elements of the underwriting process or underwriting decision.

(B) **Key factors.**—The term 'key factors' means all relevant elements or reasons adversely affecting the credit score for the particular individual, listed in the order of their importance based on their effect on the credit score.

(3) Timeframe and manner of disclosure.—The information required by this subsection shall be provided in the same timeframe and manner as the information described in subsection (a).

(4) Applicability to certain uses.—This subsection shall not be construed so as to compel a consumer reporting agency to develop or disclose a score if the agency does not—

(A) distribute scores that are used in connection with residential real property loans; or

(B) develop scores that assist credit providers in understanding the general credit behavior of a consumer and predicting the future credit behavior of the consumer.

(5) Applicability to credit scores developed by another person.—

(A) In general.—This subsection shall not be construed to require a consumer reporting agency that distributes credit scores developed by another person or entity to provide a further explanation of them, or to process a dispute arising pursuant to section 1681i, except that the consumer reporting agency shall provide the consumer with the name and address and website for contacting the person or entity who developed the score or developed the methodology of the score.

(B) Exception.—This paragraph shall not apply to a consumer reporting agency that develops or modifies scores that are developed by another person or entity.

(6) Maintenance of credit scores not required.—This subsection shall not be construed to require a consumer reporting agency to maintain credit scores in its files.

(7) Compliance in certain cases.—In complying with this subsection, a consumer reporting agency shall—

(A) supply the consumer with a credit score that is derived from a credit scoring model that is widely distributed to users by that consumer reporting agency in connection with residential real property loans or with a credit score that assists the consumer in understanding the credit scoring assessment of the credit behavior of the consumer and predictions about the future credit behavior of the consumer; and

(B) a statement indicating that the information and credit scoring model may be different than that used by the lender.

(8) Fair and reasonable fee.—A consumer reporting agency may charge a fair and reasonable fee, as determined by the Commission, for providing the information required under this subsection.

(9) Use of enquiries as a key factor.—If a key factor that adversely affects the credit score of a consumer consists of the number of enquiries made with respect to a consumer report, that factor shall be included in the disclosure pursuant to paragraph (1)(C) without regard to the numerical limitation in such paragraph.

(g) Disclosure of credit scores by certain mortgage lenders.—

(1) In general.—Any person who makes or arranges loans and who uses a consumer credit score, as defined in subsection (f), in connection with an application initiated or sought by a consumer for a closed end loan or the establishment of an open end loan for a consumer purpose that is secured by 1 to 4 units of residential real property (hereafter in this subsection referred to as the 'lender') shall provide the following to the consumer as soon as reasonably practicable:

(A) Information required under subsection (f).—

(i) In general.—A copy of the information identified in subsection (f) that was obtained from a consumer reporting agency or was developed and used by the user of the information.

(ii) Notice under subparagraph (d).—In addition to the information provided to it by a third party that provided the credit score or scores, a lender is only required to provide the notice contained in subparagraph (D).

(B) Disclosures in case of automated underwriting system.—

(i) In general.—If a person that is subject to this subsection uses an automated underwriting system to underwrite a loan, that person may satisfy the obligation to provide a credit score by disclosing a credit score and associated key factors supplied by a consumer reporting agency.

(ii) Numerical credit score.—However, if a numerical credit score is generated by an automated underwriting system used by an enterprise, and that score is disclosed to the person, the score shall be disclosed to the consumer consistent with subparagraph (C).

(iii) Enterprise defined.—For purposes of this subparagraph, the term 'enterprise' has the same meaning as in paragraph (6) of section 1303 of the Federal Housing Enterprises Financial Safety and Soundness Act of 1992.

(C) Disclosures of credit scores not obtained from a consumer reporting agency.—A person that is subject to the provisions of this subsection and that uses a credit score, other than a credit score provided by a consumer reporting agency, may satisfy the obligation to provide a credit score by disclosing a credit score and associated key factors supplied by a consumer reporting agency.

(D) Notice to home loan applicants.—A copy of the following notice, which shall include the name, address, and telephone number of each consumer reporting agency providing a credit score that was used:

Notice to the Home Loan Applicant

In connection with your application for a home loan, the lender must disclose to you the score that a consumer reporting agency distributed to users and the lender used in connection with your home loan, and the key factors affecting your credit scores.

The credit score is a computer generated summary calculated at the time of the request and based on information that a consumer reporting agency or lender has on file. The scores are based on data about your credit history and payment patterns. Credit scores are important because they are used to assist the lender in determining whether you will obtain a loan. They may also be used to determine what interest rate you may be offered on the mortgage. Credit scores can change over time, depending on your conduct, how your credit history and payment patterns change, and how credit scoring technologies change.

Because the score is based on information in your credit history, it is very important that you review the credit-related information that is being furnished to make sure it is accurate. Credit records may vary from one company to another.

If you have questions about your credit score or the credit information that is furnished to you, contact the consumer reporting agency at the address and telephone number provided with this notice, or contact the lender, if the lender developed or generated the credit score. The consumer reporting agency plays no part in the decision to take any action on the loan application and is unable to provide you with specific reasons for the decision on a loan application.

If you have questions concerning the terms of the loan, contact the lender.

(E) Actions not required under this subsection.—This subsection shall not require any person to—

(i) explain the information provided pursuant to subsection (f);

(ii) disclose any information other than a credit score or key factors, as defined in subsection (f);

(iii) disclose any credit score or related information obtained by the user after a loan has closed;

(iv) provide more than 1 disclosure per loan transaction; or

(v) provide the disclosure required by this subsection when another person has made the disclosure to the consumer for that loan transaction.

(F) No obligation for content.—

(i) **In general.**—The obligation of any person pursuant to this subsection shall be limited solely to providing a copy of the information that was received from the consumer reporting agency.

(ii) **Limit on liability.**—No person has liability under this subsection for the content of that information or for the omission of any information within the report provided by the consumer reporting agency.

(G) Person defined as excluding enterprise.—As used in this subsection, the term 'person' does not include an enterprise (as defined in paragraph (6) of section 1303 of the Federal Housing Enterprises Financial Safety and Soundness Act of 1992).

(2) Prohibition on disclosure clauses null and void.—

(A) In general.—Any provision in a contract that prohibits the disclosure of a credit score by a person who makes or arranges loans or a consumer reporting agency is void.

(B) No liability for disclosure under this subsection.—A lender shall not have liability under any contractual provision for disclosure of a credit score pursuant to this subsection.

§ 1681h. Conditions and form of disclosure to consumers [FCRA § 610]

(a) In general

(1) Proper identification.—A consumer reporting agency shall require, as a condition of making the disclosures required under section 1681g of this title, that the consumer furnish proper identification.

(2) Disclosure in writing.—Except as provided in subsection (b) of this section, the disclosures required to be made under section 1681g of this title shall be provided under that section in writing.

(b) Other forms of disclosure

(1) In general.—If authorized by a consumer, a consumer reporting agency may make the disclosures required under 1681g of this title—

(A) other than in writing; and

(B) in such form as may be—

(i) specified by the consumer in accordance with paragraph (2); and

(ii) available from the agency.

(2) Form.—A consumer may specify pursuant to paragraph (1) that disclosures under section 1681g of this title shall be made—

(A) in person, upon the appearance of the consumer at the place of business of the consumer reporting agency where disclosures are regularly provided, during normal business hours, and on reasonable notice;

(B) by telephone, if the consumer has made a written request for disclosure by telephone;

(C) by electronic means, if available from the agency; or

(D) by any other reasonable means that is available from the agency.

(c) Trained personnel

Any consumer reporting agency shall provide trained personnel to explain to the consumer any information furnished to him pursuant to section 1681g of this title.

(d) Persons accompanying consumer

The consumer shall be permitted to be accompanied by one other person of his choosing, who shall furnish reasonable identification. A consumer reporting agency may require the consumer to furnish a written statement granting permission to the consumer reporting agency to discuss the consumer's file in such person's presence.

(e) Limitation of liability

Except as provided in sections 1681n and 1681o of this title, no consumer may bring any action or proceeding in the nature of defamation, invasion of privacy, or negligence with respect to the reporting of information against any consumer reporting agency, any user of information, or any person who furnishes information to a consumer reporting agency, based on information disclosed pursuant to section 1681g, 1681h, or 1681m of this title, or based on information disclosed by a user of a consumer report to or for a consumer against whom the user has taken adverse action, based in whole or in part on the report except as to false information furnished with malice or willful intent to injure such consumer.

§ 1681i. Procedure in case of disputed accuracy [FCRA § 611]

(a) Reinvestigations of disputed information

(1) Reinvestigation required.—

(A) In general.—If the completeness Subject to subsection (f), if the completeness or accuracy of any item of information contained in a consumer's file at a consumer reporting agency is disputed by the consumer and the consumer notifies the agency directly, or indirectly through a reseller, of such dispute, the agency shall reinvestigate free of charge shall, free of charge, conduct a reasonable reinvestigation to determine whether the disputed information is inaccurate and record the current status of the disputed information, or delete the item from the file in accordance with paragraph (5), before the end of the 30-day period beginning on the date on which the agency receives the notice of the dispute from the consumer or reseller.

(B) Extension of period to reinvestigate.—Except as provided in subparagraph (C), the 30-day period described in subparagraph (A) may be extended for not more than 15 additional days if the consumer reporting agency receives information from the consumer during that 30-day period that is relevant to the reinvestigation.

(C) Limitations on extension of period to reinvestigate.—Subparagraph (B) shall not apply to any reinvestigation in which, during the 30-day period described in subparagraph (A), the information that is the subject of the reinvestigation is found to be inaccurate or incomplete or the consumer reporting agency determines that the information cannot be verified.

(2) Prompt notice of dispute to furnisher of information.—

(A) In general.—Before the expiration of the 5-business-day period beginning on the date on which a consumer reporting agency receives notice of a dispute from any consumer or a reseller in accordance with paragraph (1), the agency shall provide notification of the dispute to any person who provided any item of information in dispute, at the address and in the manner established with the person. The notice shall include all relevant information regarding the dispute that the agency has received from the consumer or reseller.

(B) Provision of other information from consumer.—The consumer reporting agency shall promptly provide to the person who provided the information in dispute all relevant information regarding the dispute that is received by the agency from the consumer or the reseller after the period referred to in subparagraph (A) and before the end of the period referred to in paragraph (1)(A).

(3) Determination that dispute is frivolous or irrelevant.—

(A) In general.—Notwithstanding paragraph (1), a consumer reporting agency may terminate a reinvestigation of information disputed by a consumer under that paragraph if the agency reasonably determines that the dispute by the consumer is frivolous or irrelevant, including by reason of a failure by a consumer to provide sufficient information to investigate the disputed information.

(B) Notice of determination.—Upon making any determination in accordance with subparagraph (A) that a dispute is frivolous or irrelevant, a consumer reporting agency shall notify the consumer of such determination not later than 5 business days after making such determination, by mail or, if authorized by the consumer for that purpose, by any other means available to the agency.

(C) Contents of notice.—A notice under subparagraph (B) shall include—

(i) the reasons for the determination under subparagraph (A); and

(ii) identification of any information required to investigate the disputed information, which may consist of a standardized form describing the general nature of such information.

(4) Consideration of consumer information.—In conducting any reinvestigation under paragraph (1) with respect to disputed information in the file of any consumer, the consumer reporting agency shall review and consider all relevant information submitted by the consumer in the period described in paragraph (1)(A) with respect to such disputed information.

(5) Treatment of inaccurate or unverifiable information.—

(A) In general.—If, after any reinvestigation under paragraph (1) of any information disputed by a consumer, an item of the information is found to be inaccurate or incomplete or cannot be verified, the consumer reporting agency shall—promptly delete that item of information from the consumer's file or modify that item of information, as appropriate, based on the results of the reinvestigation.

(i) promptly delete that item of information from the file of the consumer, or modify that item of information, as appropriate, based on the results of the reinvestigation; and

(ii) promptly notify the furnisher of that information that the information has been modified or deleted from the file of the consumer.

(B) Requirements relating to reinsertion of previously deleted material.—

(i) Certification of accuracy of information.—If any information is deleted from a consumer's file pursuant to subparagraph (A), the information may not be reinserted in the file by the consumer reporting agency unless the person who furnishes the information certifies that the information is complete and accurate.

(ii) Notice to consumer.—If any information that has been deleted from a consumer's file pursuant to subparagraph (A) is reinserted in the file, the consumer reporting agency shall notify the consumer of the reinsertion in writing not later than 5 business days after the reinsertion or, if authorized by the consumer for that purpose, by any other means available to the agency.

(iii) Additional information.—As part of, or in addition to, the notice under clause (ii), a consumer reporting agency shall provide to a consumer in writing not later than 5 business days after the date of the reinsertion—

(I) a statement that the disputed information has been reinserted;

(II) the business name and address of any furnisher of information contacted and the telephone number of such furnisher, if reasonably available, or of any furnisher of information that contacted the consumer reporting agency, in connection with the reinsertion of such information; and

(III) a notice that the consumer has the right to add a statement to the consumer's file disputing the accuracy or completeness of the disputed information.

(C) Procedures to prevent reappearance.—A consumer reporting agency shall maintain reasonable procedures designed to prevent the reappearance in a consumer's file, and in consumer reports on the consumer, of information that is deleted pursuant to this paragraph (other than information that is reinserted in accordance with subparagraph (B)(i)).

(D) Automated reinvestigation system.—Any consumer reporting agency that compiles and maintains files on consumers on a nationwide basis shall implement an automated system through which furnishers of information to that consumer reporting agency may report the results of a reinvestigation that finds incomplete or inaccurate information in a consumer's file to other such consumer reporting agencies.

(6) Notice of results of reinvestigation.—

(A) In general.—A consumer reporting agency shall provide written notice to a consumer of the results of a reinvestigation under this subsection not later than 5 business days after the completion of the reinvestigation, by mail or, if authorized by the consumer for that purpose, by other means available to the agency.

(B) Contents.—As part of, or in addition to, the notice under subparagraph (A), a consumer reporting agency shall provide to a consumer in writing before the expiration of the 5-day period referred to in subparagraph (A)—

(i) a statement that the reinvestigation is completed;

(ii) a consumer report that is based upon the consumer's file as that file is revised as a result of the reinvestigation;

(iii) a notice that, if requested by the consumer, a description of the procedure used to determine the accuracy and completeness of the information shall be provided to the consumer by the agency, including the business name and address of any furnisher of information contacted in connection with such information and the telephone number of such furnisher, if reasonably available;

(iv) a notice that the consumer has the right to add a statement to the consumer's file disputing the accuracy or completeness of the information; and

(v) a notice that the consumer has the right to request under subsection (d) that the consumer reporting agency furnish notifications under that subsection.

(7) Description of reinvestigation procedure.—A consumer reporting agency shall provide to a consumer a description referred to in paragraph (6)(B)(iii) by not later than 15 days after receiving a request from the consumer for that description.

(8) Expedited dispute resolution.—If a dispute regarding an item of information in a consumer's file at a consumer reporting agency is resolved in accordance with paragraph (5)(A) by the deletion of the disputed information by not later than 3 business days after the date on which the agency receives notice of the dispute from the consumer in accordance with paragraph (1)(A), then the agency shall not be required to comply with paragraphs (2), (6), and (7) with respect to that dispute if the agency—

(A) provides prompt notice of the deletion to the consumer by telephone;

(B) includes in that notice, or in a written notice that accompanies a confirmation and consumer report provided in accordance with subparagraph (C), a statement of the consumer's right to request under subsection (d) of this section that the agency furnish notifications under that subsection; and

(C) provides written confirmation of the deletion and a copy of a consumer report on the consumer that is based on the consumer's file after the deletion, not later than 5 business days after making the deletion.

(b) Statement of dispute

If the reinvestigation does not resolve the dispute, the consumer may file a brief statement setting forth the nature of the dispute. The consumer reporting agency may limit such statements to not more than one hundred words if it provides the consumer with assistance in writing a clear summary of the dispute.

(c) Notification of consumer dispute in subsequent consumer reports

Whenever a statement of a dispute is filed, unless there is reasonable grounds to believe that it is frivolous or irrelevant, the consumer reporting agency shall, in any subsequent consumer report containing the information in question, clearly note that it is disputed by the consumer and provide either the consumer's statement or a clear and accurate codification or summary thereof.

(d) Notification of deletion of disputed information

Following any deletion of information which is found to be inaccurate or whose accuracy can no longer be verified or any notation as to disputed information, the consumer reporting agency shall, at the request of the consumer, furnish notification that the item has been deleted or the statement, codification or summary pursuant to subsection (b) or (c) of this section to any person specifically designated by the consumer who has within two years prior thereto received a consumer report for employment purposes, or within six months prior thereto received a consumer report for any other purpose, which contained the deleted or disputed information.

(e) Treatment of complaints and report to Congress.—

(1) **In general.**—The Commission shall—

(A) compile all complaints that it receives that a file of a consumer that is maintained by a consumer reporting agency described in section 1681a(p) contains incomplete or inaccurate information, with respect to which, the consumer appears to have disputed the completeness or accuracy with the consumer reporting agency or otherwise utilized the procedures provided by subsection (a); and

(B) transmit each such complaint to each consumer reporting agency involved.

(2) **Exclusion.**—Complaints received or obtained by the Commission pursuant to its investigative authority under the Federal Trade Commission Act shall not be subject to paragraph (1).

(3) **Agency responsibilities.**—Each consumer reporting agency described in section 1681a(p) that receives a complaint transmitted by the Commission pursuant to paragraph (1) shall—

(A) review each such complaint to determine whether all legal obligations imposed on the consumer reporting agency under this title (including any obligation imposed by an applicable court or administrative order) have been met with respect to the subject matter of the complaint;

(B) provide reports on a regular basis to the Commission regarding the determinations of and actions taken by the consumer reporting agency, if any, in connection with its review of such complaints; and

(C) maintain, for a reasonable time period, records regarding the disposition of each such complaint that is sufficient to demonstrate compliance with this subsection.

(4) **Rulemaking authority.**—The Commission may prescribe regulations, as appropriate to implement this subsection.

(5) **Annual report.**—The Commission shall submit to the Committee on Banking, Housing, and Urban Affairs of the Senate and the Committee on Financial Services of the House of Representatives an annual report regarding information gathered by the Commission under this subsection.

(f) Reinvestigation requirement applicable to resellers.—

(1) **Exemption from general reinvestigation requirement.**—Except as provided in paragraph (2), a reseller shall be exempt from the requirements of this section.

(2) **Action required upon receiving notice of a dispute.**—If a reseller receives a notice from a consumer of a dispute concerning the completeness or accuracy of any item of information contained in a consumer report on such consumer produced by the reseller, the reseller shall, within 5 business days of receiving the notice, and free of charge—

(A) determine whether the item of information is incomplete or inaccurate as a result of an act or omission of the reseller; and

(B) if—

(i) the reseller determines that the item of information is incomplete or inaccurate as a result of an act or omission of the reseller, not later than 20 days after receiving the notice, correct the information in the consumer report or delete it; or

(ii) if the reseller determines that the item of information is not incomplete or inaccurate as a result of an act or omission of the reseller, convey the notice of the dispute, together with all relevant information provided by the consumer, to each consumer reporting agency that provided the reseller with the information that is the subject of the dispute, using an address or a notification mechanism specified by the consumer reporting agency for such notices.

(3) **Responsibility of consumer reporting agency to notify consumer through reseller.**—Upon the completion of a reinvestigation under this section of a dispute concerning the completeness or accuracy of any information in the file of a consumer by a consumer reporting agency that received notice of the dispute from a reseller under paragraph (2)—

(A) the notice by the consumer reporting agency under paragraph (6), (7), or (8) of subsection (a) shall be provided to the reseller in lieu of the consumer; and

(B) the reseller shall immediately reconvey such notice to the consumer, including any notice of a deletion by telephone in the manner required under paragraph (8)(A).

(4) **Reseller reinvestigations.**—No provision of this subsection shall be construed as prohibiting a reseller from conducting a reinvestigation of a consumer dispute directly.

§ 1681j. Charges for certain disclosures [FCRA § 612]

(a) Free annual disclosure.—

(1) **Nationwide consumer reporting agencies.—**

(A) In general.—All consumer reporting agencies described in subsections (p) and (w) of section 1681a shall make all disclosures pursuant to section 1681g once during any 12-month period upon request of the consumer and without charge to the consumer.

(B) Centralized source.—Subparagraph (A) shall apply with respect to a consumer reporting agency described in section 1681a(p) only if the request from the consumer is made using the centralized source established for such purpose in accordance with section 211(c) of the Fair and Accurate Credit Transactions Act of 2003.

(C) Nationwide specialty consumer reporting agency.—

   (i) In general.—The Commission shall prescribe regulations applicable to each consumer reporting agency described in section 1681a(w) to require the establishment of a streamlined process for consumers to request consumer reports under subparagraph (A), which shall include, at a minimum, the establishment by each such agency of a toll-free telephone number for such requests.

   (ii) Considerations.—In prescribing regulations under clause (i), the Commission shall consider—

   (I) the significant demands that may be placed on consumer reporting agencies in providing such consumer reports;

   (II) appropriate means to ensure that consumer reporting agencies can satisfactorily meet those demands, including the efficacy of a system of staggering the availability to consumers of such consumer reports; and

   (III) the ease by which consumers should be able to contact consumer reporting agencies with respect to access to such consumer reports.

   (iii) Date of issuance.—The Commission shall issue the regulations required by this subparagraph in final form not later than 6 months after the date of enactment of the Fair and Accurate Credit Transactions Act of 2003.

   (iv) Consideration of ability to comply.—The regulations of the Commission under this subparagraph shall establish an effective date by which each nationwide specialty consumer reporting agency (as defined in section 1681a(w)) shall be required to comply with subsection (a), which effective date—

   (I) shall be established after consideration of the ability of each nationwide specialty consumer reporting agency to comply with subsection (a); and

   (II) shall be not later than 6 months after the date on which such regulations are issued in final form (or such additional period not to exceed 3 months, as the Commission determines appropriate).

(2) Timing.—A consumer reporting agency shall provide a consumer report under paragraph (1) not later than 15 days after the date on which the request is received under paragraph (1).

(3) Reinvestigations.—Notwithstanding the time periods specified in section 1681i(a)(1), a reinvestigation under that section by a consumer reporting agency upon a request of a consumer that is made after receiving a consumer report under this subsection shall be completed not later than 45 days after the date on which the request is received.

(4) Exception for first 12 months of operation.—This subsection shall not apply to a consumer reporting agency that has not been furnishing consumer reports to third parties on a continuing basis during the 12-month period preceding a request under paragraph (1), with respect to consumers residing nationwide.

(a) Reasonable charges allowed for certain disclosures.

(1) In general.—Except as provided in subsections (b), (c), and (d) of this section, a consumer reporting agency may impose a reasonable charge on a consumer—

   (A) for making a disclosure to the consumer pursuant to section 1681g of this title, which charge—

   (i) shall not exceed $8; and

   (ii) shall be indicated to the consumer before making the disclosure; and

   (B) for furnishing, pursuant to section 1681i(d) of this title, following a reinvestigation under section 1681i(a) of this title, a statement, codification, or summary to a person designated by the consumer under that section after the 30-day period beginning on the date of notification of the consumer under paragraph (6) or (8) of section 1681i(a) of this title with respect to the reinvestigation, which charge—

   (i) shall not exceed the charge that the agency would impose on each designated recipient for a consumer report; and

   (ii) shall be indicated to the consumer before furnishing such information.

(2) Modification of amount.—The Federal Trade Commission shall increase the amount referred to in paragraph (1)(A)(i) on January 1 of each year, based proportionally on changes in the Consumer Price Index, with fractional changes rounded to the nearest fifty cents.

(b) Free disclosure after adverse notice to consumer

Each consumer reporting agency that maintains a file on a consumer shall make all disclosures pursuant to section 1681g of this title without charge to the consumer if, not later than 60 days after receipt by such consumer of a notification pursuant to section 1681m of this title, or of a notification from a debt collection agency affiliated with that consumer reporting agency stating that the consumer's credit rating may be or has been adversely affected, the consumer makes a request under section 1681g of this title.

(c) Free disclosure under certain other circumstances

Upon the request of the consumer, a consumer reporting agency shall make all disclosures pursuant to section 1681g of this title once during any 12-month period without charge to that consumer if the consumer certifies in writing that the consumer—

(1) is unemployed and intends to apply for employment in the 60-day period beginning on the date on which the certification is made;

(2) is a recipient of public welfare assistance; or

(3) has reason to believe that the file on the consumer at the agency contains inaccurate information due to fraud.

(d) Free disclosures in connection with fraud alerts.—Upon the request of a consumer, a consumer reporting agency described in section 1681a(p) shall make all disclosures pursuant to section 1681g without charge to the consumer, as provided in subsections (a)(2) and (b)(2) of section 1681c-1, as applicable.

(d)(e) Other charges prohibited

A consumer reporting agency shall not impose any charge on a consumer for providing any notification required by this subchapter or making any disclosure required by this subchapter, except as authorized by subsection (f)subsection (a) of this section.

(a)(f) Reasonable charges allowed for certain disclosures.

(1) In general.—Except as provided in subsections (b), (c), and (d) of this section, In the case of a request from a consumer other than a request that is covered by any of subsections (a) through (d), a consumer reporting agency may impose a reasonable charge on a consumer—

(A) for making a disclosure to the consumer pursuant to section 1681g of this title, which charge—

(i) shall not exceed $8; and

(ii) shall be indicated to the consumer before making the disclosure; and

(B) for furnishing, pursuant to section 1681i(d) of this title, following a reinvestigation under section 1681i(a) of this title, a statement, codification, or summary to a person designated by the consumer under that section after the 30-day period beginning on the date of notification of the consumer under paragraph (6) or (8) of section 1681i(a) of this title with respect to the reinvestigation, which charge—

(i) shall not exceed the charge that the agency would impose on each designated recipient for a consumer report; and

(ii) shall be indicated to the consumer before furnishing such information.

(2) Modification of amount.—The Federal Trade Commission shall increase the amount referred to in paragraph (1)(A)(i) on January 1 of each year, based proportionally on changes in the Consumer Price Index, with fractional changes rounded to the nearest fifty cents.

§ 1681k. Public record information for employment purposes [FCRA § 613]

(a) In General.—

A consumer reporting agency which furnishes a consumer report for employment purposes and which for that purpose compiles and reports items of information on consumers which are matters of public record and are likely to have an adverse effect upon a consumer's ability to obtain employment shall—

(1) at the time such public record information is reported to the user of such consumer report, notify the consumer of the fact that public record information is being reported by the consumer reporting agency, together with the name and address of the person to whom such information is being reported; or

(2) maintain strict procedures designed to insure that whenever public record information which is likely to have an adverse effect on a consumer's ability to obtain employment is reported it is complete and up to date. For purposes of this paragraph, items of public record relating to arrests, indictments, convictions, suits, tax liens, and outstanding judgments shall be considered up to date if the current public record status of the item at the time of the report is reported.

(b) Exemption for National Security Investigations.—Subsection (a) does not apply in the case of an agency or department of the United States Government that seeks to obtain and use a consumer report for employment purposes, if the head of the agency or department makes a written finding as prescribed under section 1681b(b)(4)(A) of this title.

§ 1681*l*. Restrictions on investigative consumer reports [FCRA § 614]

Whenever a consumer reporting agency prepares an investigative consumer report, no adverse information in the consumer report (other than information which is a matter of public record) may be included in a subsequent consumer report unless such adverse information has been verified in the process of making such subsequent consumer report, or the adverse information was received within the three-month period preceding the date the subsequent report is furnished.

§ 1681m. Requirements on users of consumer reports [FCRA § 615]

(a) Duties of users taking adverse actions on the basis of information contained in consumer reports

If any person takes any adverse action with respect to any consumer that is based in whole or in part on any information contained in a consumer report, the person shall—

(1) provide oral, written, or electronic notice of the adverse action to the consumer;

(2) provide to the consumer orally, in writing, or electronically—

(A) the name, address, and telephone number of the consumer reporting agency (including a toll-free telephone number established by the agency if the agency compiles and maintains files on consumers on a nationwide basis) that furnished the report to the person; and

(B) a statement that the consumer reporting agency did not make the decision to take the adverse action and is unable to provide the consumer the specific reasons why the adverse action was taken; and

(3) provide to the consumer an oral, written, or electronic notice of the consumer's right—

(A) to obtain, under section 1681j of this title, a free copy of a consumer report on the consumer from the consumer reporting agency referred to in paragraph (2), which notice shall include an indication of the 60-day period under that section for obtaining such a copy; and

(B) to dispute, under section 1681i of this title, with a consumer reporting agency the accuracy or completeness of any information in a consumer report furnished by the agency.

(b) Adverse action based on information obtained from third parties other than consumer reporting agencies.

(1) In general.—Whenever credit for personal, family, or household purposes involving a consumer is denied or the charge for such credit is increased either wholly or partly because of information obtained from a person other than a consumer reporting agency bearing upon the consumer's credit worthiness, credit standing, credit capacity, character, general reputation, personal characteristics, or mode of living, the user of such information shall, within a reasonable period of time, upon the consumer's written request for the reasons for such adverse action received within sixty days after learning of such adverse action, disclose the nature of the information to the consumer. The user of such information shall clearly and accurately disclose to the consumer his right to make such written request at the time such adverse action is communicated to the consumer.

(2) Duties of person taking certain actions based on information provided by affiliate.—

(A) **Duties, generally.**—If a person takes an action described in subparagraph (B) with respect to a consumer, based in whole or in part on information described in subparagraph (C), the person shall—

(i) notify the consumer of the action, including a statement that the consumer may obtain the information in accordance with clause (ii); and

(ii) upon a written request from the consumer received within 60 days after transmittal of the notice required by clause (i), disclose to the consumer the nature of the information upon which the action is based by not later than 30 days after receipt of the request.

(B) **Action described.**—An action referred to in subparagraph (A) is an adverse action described in section 1681a(k)(1)(A) of this title, taken in connection with a transaction initiated by the consumer, or any adverse action described in clause (i) or (ii) of section 1681a(k)(1)(B) of this title.

(C) **Information described.**—Information referred to in subparagraph (A)—

(i) except as provided in clause (ii), is information that—

(I) is furnished to the person taking the action by a person related by common ownership or affiliated by common corporate control to the person taking the action; and

(II) bears on the credit worthiness, credit standing, credit capacity, character, general reputation, personal characteristics, or mode of living of the consumer; and

(ii) does not include—

(I) information solely as to transactions or experiences between the consumer and the person furnishing the information; or

(II) information in a consumer report.

(c) Reasonable procedures to assure compliance

No person shall be held liable for any violation of this section if he shows by a preponderance of the evidence that at the time of the alleged violation he maintained reasonable procedures to assure compliance with the provisions of this section.

(d) Duties of users making written credit or insurance solicitations on the basis of information contained in consumer files

(1) In general.—Any person who uses a consumer report on any consumer in connection with any credit or insurance transaction that is not initiated by the consumer, that is provided to that person under section 1681b(c)(1)(B) of this title, shall provide with each written solicitation made to the consumer regarding the transaction a clear and conspicuous statement that—

(A) information contained in the consumer's consumer report was used in connection with the transaction;

(B) the consumer received the offer of credit or insurance because the consumer satisfied the criteria for credit worthiness or insurability under which the consumer was selected for the offer;

(C) if applicable, the credit or insurance may not be extended if, after the consumer responds to the offer, the consumer does not meet the criteria used to select the consumer for the offer or any applicable criteria bearing on credit worthiness or insurability or does not furnish any required collateral;

(D) the consumer has a right to prohibit information contained in the consumer's file with any consumer reporting agency from being used in connection with any credit or insurance transaction that is not initiated by the consumer; and

(E) the consumer may exercise the right referred to in subparagraph (D) by notifying a notification system established under section 1681b(e) of this title.

~~(2) Disclosure of address and telephone number.—A statement under paragraph (1) shall include the address and toll-free telephone number of the appropriate notification system established under section 1681b(e) of this title.~~

(2) Disclosure of address and telephone number; format.—A statement under paragraph (1) shall—

(A) include the address and toll-free telephone number of the appropriate notification system established under section 1681b(e); and

(B) be presented in such format and in such type size and manner as to be simple and easy to understand, as established by the Commission, by rule, in consultation with the Federal banking agencies and the National Credit Union Administration.

(3) Maintaining criteria on file.—A person who makes an offer of credit or insurance to a consumer under a credit or insurance transaction described in paragraph (1) shall maintain on file the criteria used to select the consumer to receive the offer, all criteria bearing on credit worthiness or insurability, as applicable, that are the basis for determining whether or not to extend credit or insurance pursuant to the offer, and any requirement for the furnishing of collateral as a condition of the extension of credit or insurance, until the expiration of the 3-year period beginning on the date on which the offer is made to the consumer.

(4) Authority of federal agencies regarding unfair or deceptive acts or practices not affected.—This section is not intended to affect the authority of any Federal or State agency to enforce a prohibition against unfair or deceptive acts or practices, including the making of false or misleading statements in connection with a credit or insurance transaction that is not initiated by the consumer.

(e) Red Flag Guidelines and Regulations Required.—

(1) Guidelines.—The Federal banking agencies, the National Credit Union Administration, and the Commission shall jointly, with respect to the entities that are subject to their respective enforcement authority under section 1681s—

(A) establish and maintain guidelines for use by each financial institution and each creditor regarding identity theft with respect to account holders at, or customers of, such entities, and update such guidelines as often as necessary;

(B) prescribe regulations requiring each financial institution and each creditor to establish reasonable policies and procedures for implementing the guidelines established pursuant to subparagraph (A), to identify possible risks to account holders or customers or to the safety and soundness of the institution or customers; and

(C) prescribe regulations applicable to card issuers to ensure that, if a card issuer receives notification of a change of address for an existing account, and within a short period of time (during at least the first 30 days after such notification is received) receives a request for an additional or replacement card for the same account, the card issuer may not issue the additional or replacement card, unless the card issuer, in accordance with reasonable policies and procedures—

(i) notifies the cardholder of the request at the former address of the cardholder and provides to the cardholder a means of promptly reporting incorrect address changes;

(ii) notifies the cardholder of the request by such other means of communication as the cardholder and the card issuer previously agreed to; or

(iii) uses other means of assessing the validity of the change of address, in accordance with reasonable policies and procedures established by the card issuer in accordance with the regulations prescribed under subparagraph (B).

(2) Criteria.—

(A) In general.—In developing the guidelines required by paragraph (1)(A), the agencies described in paragraph (1) shall identify patterns, practices, and specific forms of activity that indicate the possible existence of identity theft.

(B) Inactive accounts.—In developing the guidelines required by paragraph (1)(A), the agencies described in paragraph (1) shall consider including reasonable guidelines providing that when a transaction occurs with respect to a credit or deposit account that has been inactive for more than 2 years, the creditor or financial institution shall follow reasonable policies and procedures that provide for notice to be given to a consumer in a manner reasonably designed to reduce the likelihood of identity theft with respect to such account.

(3) Consistency with verification requirements.—Guidelines established pursuant to paragraph (1) shall not be inconsistent with the policies and procedures required under section 5318(l) of title 31, United States Code.

(f) Prohibition on Sale or Transfer of Debt Caused by Identity Theft.—

(1) In general.—No person shall sell, transfer for consideration, or place for collection a debt that such person has been notified under section 1681c-2 has resulted from identity theft.

(2) Applicability. The prohibitions of this subsection shall apply to all persons collecting a debt described in paragraph (1) after the date of a notification under paragraph (1).

(3) Rule of construction.—Nothing in this subsection shall be construed to prohibit—

(A) the repurchase of a debt in any case in which the assignee of the debt requires such repurchase because the debt has resulted from identity theft;

(B) the securitization of a debt or the pledging of a portfolio of debt as collateral in connection with a borrowing; or

(C) the transfer of debt as a result of a merger, acquisition, purchase and assumption transaction, or transfer of substantially all of the assets of an entity.

(g) Debt Collector Communications Concerning Identity Theft.—If a person acting as a debt collector (as that term is defined in title VIII) on behalf of a third party that is a creditor or other user of a consumer report is notified that any information relating to a debt that the person is attempting to collect may be fraudulent or may be the result of identity theft, that person shall—

(1) notify the third party that the information may be fraudulent or may be the result of identity theft; and

(2) upon request of the consumer to whom the debt purportedly relates, provide to the consumer all information to which the consumer would otherwise be entitled if the consumer were not a victim of identity theft, but wished to dispute the debt under provisions of law applicable to that person.

(h) Duties of users in certain credit transactions.—

(1) In general.—Subject to rules prescribed as provided in paragraph (6), if any person uses a consumer report in connection with an application for, or a grant, extension, or other provision of, credit on material terms that are materially less favorable than the most favorable terms available to a substantial proportion of consumers from or through that person, based in whole or in part on a consumer report, the person shall provide an oral, written, or electronic notice to the consumer in the form and manner required by regulations prescribed in accordance with this subsection.

(2) Timing.—The notice required under paragraph (1) may be provided at the time of an application for, or a grant, extension, or other provision of, credit or the time of communication of an approval of an application for, or grant, extension, or other provision of, credit, except as provided in the regulations prescribed under paragraph (6).

(3) Exceptions.—No notice shall be required from a person under this subsection if—

(A) the consumer applied for specific material terms and was granted those terms, unless those terms were initially specified by the person after the transaction was initiated by the consumer and after the person obtained a consumer report; or

(B) the person has provided or will provide a notice to the consumer under subsection (a) in connection with the transaction.

(4) Other notice not sufficient.—A person that is required to provide a notice under subsection (a) cannot meet that requirement by providing a notice under this subsection.

(5) Content and delivery of notice.—A notice under this subsection shall, at a minimum—

(A) include a statement informing the consumer that the terms offered to the consumer are set based on information from a consumer report;

(B) identify the consumer reporting agency furnishing the report;

(C) include a statement informing the consumer that the consumer may obtain a copy of a consumer report from that consumer reporting agency without charge; and

(D) include the contact information specified by that consumer reporting agency for obtaining such consumer reports (including a toll-free telephone number established by the agency in the case of a consumer reporting agency described in section 1681a(p)).

(6) Rulemaking.—

(A) Rules required.—The Commission and the Board shall jointly prescribe rules.

(B) Content.—Rules required by subparagraph (A) shall address, but are not limited to—

(i) the form, content, time, and manner of delivery of any notice under this subsection;

(ii) clarification of the meaning of terms used in this subsection, including what credit terms are material, and when credit terms are materially less favorable;

(iii) exceptions to the notice requirement under this subsection for classes of persons or transactions regarding which the agencies determine that notice would not significantly benefit consumers;

(iv) a model notice that may be used to comply with this subsection; and

(v) the timing of the notice required under paragraph (1), including the circumstances under which the notice must be provided after the terms offered to the consumer were set based on information from a consumer report.

(7) Compliance.—A person shall not be liable for failure to perform the duties required by this section if, at the time of the failure, the person maintained reasonable policies and procedures to comply with this section.

(8) Enforcement.—

(A) No civil actions.—Sections 1681n and 1681*o* shall not apply to any failure by any person to comply with this section.

(B) Administrative enforcement.—This section shall be enforced exclusively under section 1681s by the Federal agencies and officials identified in that section.

§ 1681n. Civil liability for willful noncompliance [FCRA § 616]

(a) In general

Any person who willfully fails to comply with any requirement imposed under this subchapter with respect to any consumer is liable to that consumer in an amount equal to the sum of—

(1)(A) any actual damages sustained by the consumer as a result of the failure or damages of not less than $100 and not more than $1,000; or

(B) in the case of liability of a natural person for obtaining a consumer report under false pretenses or knowingly without a permissible purpose, actual damages sustained by the consumer as a result of the failure or $1,000, whichever is greater;

(2) such amount of punitive damages as the court may allow; and

(3) in the case of any successful action to enforce any liability under this section, the costs of the action together with reasonable attorney's fees as determined by the court.

(b) Civil liability for knowing noncompliance

Any person who obtains a consumer report from a consumer reporting agency under false pretenses or knowingly without a permissible purpose shall be liable to the consumer reporting agency for actual damages sustained by the consumer reporting agency or $1,000, whichever is greater.

(c) Attorney's fees

Upon a finding by the court that an unsuccessful pleading, motion, or other paper filed in connection with an action under this section was filed in bad faith or for purposes of harassment, the court shall award to the prevailing party attorney's fees reasonable in relation to the work expended in responding to the pleading, motion, or other paper.

§ 1681o. Civil liability for negligent noncompliance [FCRA § 617]

(a) In general

Any person who is negligent in failing to comply with any requirement imposed under this subchapter with respect to any consumer is liable to that consumer in an amount equal to the sum of—

(1) any actual damages sustained by the consumer as a result of the failure; and

(2) in the case of any successful action to enforce any liability under this section, the costs of the action together with reasonable attorney's fees as determined by the court.

(b) Attorney's fees

On a finding by the court that an unsuccessful pleading, motion, or other paper filed in connection with an action under this section was filed in bad faith or for purposes of harassment, the court shall award to the prevailing party attorney's fees reasonable in relation to the work expended in responding to the pleading, motion, or other paper.

§ 1681p. Jurisdiction of courts; limitation of actions [FCRA § 618]

An action to enforce any liability created under this subchapter may be brought in any appropriate United States district court without regard to the amount in controversy, or in any other court of competent jurisdiction, within two years from the date on which the liability arises, except that where a defendant has materially and willfully misrepresented any information required under this subchapter to be disclosed to an individual and the information so misrepresented is material to the establishment of the defendant's liability to that individual under this subchapter, the action may be brought at any time within two years after discovery by the individual of the misrepresentation.

An action to enforce any liability created under this title may be brought in any appropriate United States district court, without regard to the amount in controversy, or in any other court of competent jurisdiction, not later than the earlier of—

(1) 2 years after the date of discovery by the plaintiff of the violation that is the basis for such liability; or

(2) 5 years after the date on which the violation that is the basis for such liability occurs.

§ 1681q. Obtaining information under false pretenses [FCRA § 619]

Any person who knowingly and willfully obtains information on a consumer from a consumer reporting agency under false pretenses shall be fined under Title 18, imprisoned for not more than 2 years, or both.

§ 1681r. Unauthorized disclosures by officers or employees [FCRA § 620]

Any officer or employee of a consumer reporting agency who knowingly and willfully provides information concerning an individual from the agency's files to a person not authorized to receive that information shall be fined under Title 18, imprisoned for not more than 2 years, or both.

§ 1681s. Administrative enforcement [FCRA § 621]

(a) Federal Trade Commission; powers

(1) Enforcement by Federal Trade Commission. Compliance with the requirements imposed under this subchapter shall be enforced under the Federal Trade Commission Act [15 U.S.C. 41 et seq.] by the Federal Trade Commission with respect to consumer reporting agencies and all other persons subject thereto, except to the extent that enforcement of the requirements imposed under this subchapter is specifically committed to some other government agency under subsection (b) hereof. For the purpose of the exercise by the Federal Trade Commission of its functions and powers under the Federal Trade Commission Act, a violation of any requirement or prohibition imposed under this subchapter shall constitute an unfair or deceptive act or practice in commerce in violation of section 5(a) of the Federal Trade Commission Act [15 U.S.C. 45(a)] and shall be subject to enforcement by the Federal Trade Commission under section 5(b) thereof [15 U.S.C. 45(b)] with respect to any consumer reporting agency or person subject to enforcement by the Federal Trade Commission pursuant to this subsection, irrespective of whether that person is engaged in commerce or meets any other jurisdictional tests in the Federal Trade Commission Act. The Federal Trade Commission shall have such procedural, investigative, and enforcement powers, including the power to issue procedural rules in enforcing compliance with the requirements imposed under this subchapter and to require the filing of reports, the production of documents, and the appearance of witnesses as though the applicable terms and conditions of the Federal Trade Commission Act were part of this subchapter. Any person violating any of the provisions of this subchapter shall be subject to the penalties and entitled to the privileges and immunities provided in the Federal Trade Commission Act as though the applicable terms and provisions thereof were part of this subchapter.

(2)(A) In the event of a knowing violation, which constitutes a pattern or practice of violations of this subchapter, the Commission may commence a civil action to recover a civil penalty in a district court of the United States against any person that violates this subchapter. In such action, such person shall be liable for a civil penalty of not more than $2,500 per violation.

(B) In determining the amount of a civil penalty under subparagraph (A), the court shall take into account the degree of culpability, any history of prior such conduct, ability to pay, effect on ability to continue to do business, and such other matters as justice may require.

(3) Notwithstanding paragraph (2), a court may not impose any civil penalty on a person for a violation of section 1681s-2(a)(1) of this title unless the person has been enjoined from committing the violation, or ordered not to commit the violation, in an action or proceeding brought by or on behalf of the Federal Trade Commission, and has violated the injunction or order, and the court may not impose any civil penalty for any violation occurring before the date of the violation of the injunction or order.

(4) Neither the Commission nor any other agency referred to in subsection (b) may prescribe trade regulation rules or other regulations with respect to this subchapter.

(b) Enforcement by other agencies

Compliance with the requirements imposed under this subchapter with respect to consumer reporting agencies, persons who use consumer reports from such agencies, persons who furnish information to such agencies, and users of information that are subject to subsection (d) of section 1681m of this title shall be enforced under—

(1) section 8 of the Federal Deposit Insurance Act [12 U.S.C. § 1818], in the case of—

(A) national banks, and Federal branches and Federal agencies of foreign banks, by the Office of the Comptroller of the Currency;

(B) member banks of the Federal Reserve System (other than national banks), branches and agencies of foreign banks (other than Federal branches, Federal agencies, and insured State branches of foreign banks), commercial lending companies owned or controlled by foreign banks, and organizations operating under section 25 or 25A of the Federal Reserve Act [12 U.S.C. §§ 601 et seq., 611 et seq.], by the Board of Governors of the Federal Reserve System; and

(C) banks insured by the Federal Deposit Insurance Corporation (other than members of the Federal Reserve System) and insured State branches of foreign banks, by the Board of Directors of the Federal Deposit Insurance Corporation;

(2) Section 8 of the Federal Deposit Insurance Act [12 U.S.C. § 1818], by the Director of the Office of Thrift Supervision, in the case of a savings association the deposits of which are insured by the Federal Deposit Insurance Corporation.

(3) the Federal Credit Union Act [12 U.S.C. 1751 et seq.], by the Administrator of the National Credit Union Administration with respect to any Federal credit union;

(4) subtitle IV of Title 49, by the Secretary of Transportation, with respect to all carriers subject to the jurisdiction of the Surface Transportation Board;

(5) part A of subtitle VII of title 49, by the Secretary of Transportation with respect to any air carrier or foreign air carrier subject to that part; and

(6) the Packers and Stockyards Act, 1921 [7 U.S.C. 181 et seq.] (except as provided in section 406 of that Act [7 U.S.C. 226, 227]), by the Secretary of Agriculture with respect to any activities subject to that Act.

The terms used in paragraph (1) that are not defined in this subchapter or otherwise defined in section 3(s) of the Federal Deposit Insurance Act (12 U.S.C. 1813(s)) shall have the meaning given to them in section 1(b) of the International Banking Act of 1978 (12 U.S.C. 3101).

(c) State action for violations

(1) Authority of States.—In addition to such other remedies as are provided under State law, if the chief law enforcement officer of a State, or an official or agency designated by a State, has reason to believe that any person has violated or is violating this subchapter, the State—

(A) may bring an action to enjoin such violation in any appropriate United States district court or in any other court of competent jurisdiction;

(B) subject to paragraph (5), may bring an action on behalf of the residents of the State to recover—

(i) damages for which the person is liable to such residents under sections 1681n and 1681*o* of this title as a result of the violation;

(ii) in the case of a violation ~~of section 1681s-2(a)~~described in any of paragraphs (1) through (3) of section 1681s-2(c) of this title, damages for which the person would, but for section 1681s-2(c) of this title, be liable to such residents as a result of the violation; or

(iii) damages of not more than $1,000 for each willful or negligent violation; and

(C) in the case of any successful action under subparagraph (A) or (B), shall be awarded the costs of the action and reasonable attorney fees as determined by the court.

(2) Rights of Federal regulators.—The State shall serve prior written notice of any action under paragraph (1) upon the Federal Trade Commission or the appropriate Federal regulator determined under subsection (b) of this section and provide the Commission or appropriate Federal regulator with a copy of its complaint, except in any case in which such prior notice is not feasible, in which case the State shall serve such notice immediately upon instituting such action. The Federal Trade Commission or appropriate Federal regulator shall have the right—

(A) to intervene in the action;

(B) upon so intervening, to be heard on all matters arising therein;

(C) to remove the action to the appropriate United States district court; and

(D) to file petitions for appeal.

(3) Investigatory powers.—For purposes of bringing any action under this subsection, nothing in this subsection shall prevent the chief law enforcement officer, or an official or agency designated by a State, from exercising the powers conferred on the chief law enforcement officer or such official by the laws of such State to conduct investigations or to administer oaths or affirmations or to compel the attendance of witnesses or the production of documentary and other evidence.

(4) Limitation on State action while Federal action pending.—If the Federal Trade Commission or the appropriate Federal regulator has instituted a civil action or an administrative action under section 1818 of Title 12 for a violation of this subchapter, no State may, during the pendency of such action, bring an action under this section against any defendant named in the complaint of the Commission or the appropriate Federal regulator for any violation of this subchapter that is alleged in that complaint.

~~(5) Limitations on State actions for violation of section 1681s-2(a)(1) of this title.—~~

(5) Limitations on state actions for certain violations.—

(A) **Violation of injunction required.**—A State may not bring an action against a person under paragraph (1)(B) for a violation ~~of section 1681s-2(a)(1) of this title,~~ described in any of paragraphs (1) through (3) of section 1681s-2(c) of this title, unless—

(i) the person has been enjoined from committing the violation, in an action brought by the State under paragraph (1)(A); and

(ii) the person has violated the injunction.

(B) **Limitation on damages recoverable.**—In an action against a person under paragraph (1)(B) for a violation ~~of section 1681s-2(a)(1)~~ described in any of paragraphs (1) through (3) of section 1681s-2(c) of this title, a State may not recover any damages incurred before the date of the violation of an injunction on which the action is based.

(d) Enforcement under other authority

For the purpose of the exercise by any agency referred to in subsection (b) of this section of its powers under any Act referred to in that subsection, a violation of any requirement imposed under this subchapter shall be deemed to be a violation of a requirement imposed under that Act. In addition to its powers under any provision of law specifically referred to in subsection (b) of this section, each of the agencies referred to in that subsection may exercise, for the purpose of enforcing compliance with any requirement imposed under this subchapter any other authority conferred on it by law.

(e) Regulatory Authority.—

(1) The Federal banking agencies referred to in paragraphs (1) and (2) of subsection (b) shall jointly prescribe such regulations as necessary to carry out the purposes of this Act with respect to any persons identified under paragraphs (1) and (2) of subsection (b), and the Board of Governors of the Federal Reserve System shall have authority to prescribe regulations consistent with such joint regulations with respect to bank holding companies and affiliates (other than depository institutions and consumer reporting agencies) of such holding companies.

(2) The Board of the National Credit Union Administration shall prescribe such regulations as necessary to carry out the purposes of this Act with respect to any persons identified under paragraph (3) of subsection (b).

(f) Coordination of Consumer Complaint Investigations.—

(1) In general.—Each consumer reporting agency described in section 1681a(p) shall develop and maintain procedures for the referral to each other such agency of any consumer complaint received by the agency alleging identity theft, or requesting a fraud alert under section 1681c-1 or a block under section 1681c-2.

(2) Model form and procedure for reporting identity theft.—The Commission, in consultation with the Federal banking agencies and the National Credit Union Administration, shall develop a model form and model procedures to be used by consumers who are victims of identity theft for contacting and informing creditors and consumer reporting agencies of the fraud.

(3) Annual summary reports.—Each consumer reporting agency described in section 1681a(p) shall submit an annual summary report to the Commission on consumer complaints received by the agency on identity theft or fraud alerts.

(g) FTC regulation of coding of trade names.—If the Commission determines that a person described in paragraph (9) of section 1681s-2(a) has not met the requirements of such paragraph, the Commission shall take action to ensure the person's compliance with such paragraph, which may include issuing model guidance or prescribing reasonable policies and procedures, as necessary to ensure that such person complies with such paragraph.

§ 1681s-1. Information on overdue child support obligations [FCRA § 622]

Notwithstanding any other provision of this subchapter, a consumer reporting agency shall include in any consumer report furnished by the agency in accordance with section 1681b of this title, any information on the failure of the consumer to pay overdue support which—

(1) is provided—

(A) to the consumer reporting agency by a State or local child support enforcement agency; or

(B) to the consumer reporting agency and verified by any local, State, or Federal government agency; and

(2) antedates the report by 7 years or less.

§ 1681s-2. Responsibilities of furnishers of information to consumer reporting agencies [FCRA § 623]

(a) Duty of furnishers of information to provide accurate information.—

(1) Prohibition

(A) Reporting information with actual knowledge of errors

A person shall not furnish any information relating to a consumer to any consumer reporting agency if the person ~~knows or consciously avoids knowing that the information is inaccurate~~ knows or has reasonable cause to believe that the information is inaccurate.

(B) Reporting information after notice and confirmation of errors

A person shall not furnish information relating to a consumer to any consumer reporting agency if—

(i) the person has been notified by the consumer, at the address specified by the person for such notices, that specific information is inaccurate; and

(ii) the information is, in fact, inaccurate.

(C) No address requirement

A person who clearly and conspicuously specifies to the consumer an address for notices referred to in subparagraph (B) shall not be subject to subparagraph (A); however, nothing in subparagraph (B) shall require a person to specify such an address.

(D) Definition.—For purposes of subparagraph (A), the term 'reasonable cause to believe that the information is inaccurate' means having specific knowledge, other than solely allegations by the consumer, that would cause a reasonable person to have substantial doubts about the accuracy of the information.

(2) Duty to correct and update information

A person who—

(A) regularly and in the ordinary course of business furnishes information to one or more consumer reporting agencies about the person's transactions or experiences with any consumer; and

(B) has furnished to a consumer reporting agency information that the person determines is not complete or accurate,

shall promptly notify the consumer reporting agency of that determination and provide to the agency any corrections to that information, or any additional information, that is necessary to make the information provided by the person to the agency complete and accurate, and shall not thereafter furnish to the agency any of the information that remains not complete or accurate.

(3) Duty to provide notice of dispute

If the completeness or accuracy of any information furnished by any person to any consumer reporting agency is disputed to such person by a consumer, the person may not furnish the information to any consumer reporting agency without notice that such information is disputed by the consumer.

(4) Duty to provide notice of closed accounts

A person who regularly and in the ordinary course of business furnishes information to a consumer reporting agency regarding a consumer who has a credit account with that person shall notify the agency of the voluntary closure of the account by the consumer, in information regularly furnished for the period in which the account is closed.

(5) Duty to provide notice of delinquency of accounts

(A) In general.—A person who furnishes information to a consumer reporting agency regarding a delinquent account being placed for collection, charged to profit or loss, or subjected to any similar action shall, not later than 90 days after furnishing the information, notify the agency of the date of delinquency on the account, which shall be the month and year of the commencement of the delinquency on the account that immediately preceded the action.

(B) Rule of construction.—For purposes of this paragraph only, and provided that the consumer does not dispute the information, a person that furnishes information on a delinquent account that is placed for collection, charged for profit or loss, or subjected to any similar action, complies with this paragraph, if—

(i) the person reports the same date of delinquency as that provided by the creditor to which the account was owed at the time at which the commencement of the delinquency occurred, if the creditor previously reported that date of delinquency to a consumer reporting agency;

(ii) the creditor did not previously report the date of delinquency to a consumer reporting agency, and the person establishes and follows reasonable procedures to obtain the date of delinquency from the creditor or another reliable source and reports that date to a consumer reporting agency as the date of delinquency; or

(iii) the creditor did not previously report the date of delinquency to a consumer reporting agency and the date of delinquency cannot be reasonably obtained as provided in clause (ii), the person establishes and follows reasonable procedures to ensure the date reported as the date of delinquency precedes the date on which the account is placed for collection, charged to profit or loss, or subjected to any similar action, and reports such date to the credit reporting agency.

(6) Duties of furnishers upon notice of identity theft-related information.—

(A) **Reasonable procedures.**—A person that furnishes information to any consumer reporting agency shall have in place reasonable procedures to respond to any notification that it receives from a consumer reporting agency under section 1681c-2 relating to information resulting from identity theft, to prevent that person from refurnishing such blocked information.

(B) **Information alleged to result from identity theft.**—If a consumer submits an identity theft report to a person who furnishes information to a consumer reporting agency at the address specified by that person for receiving such reports stating that information maintained by such person that purports to relate to the consumer resulted from identity theft, the person may not furnish such information that purports to relate to the consumer to any consumer reporting agency, unless the person subsequently knows or is informed by the consumer that the information is correct.

(7) Negative information.—

(A) **Notice to consumer required.—**

(i) **In general.**—If any financial institution that extends credit and regularly and in the ordinary course of business furnishes information to a consumer reporting agency described in section 1681a(p) furnishes negative information to such an agency regarding credit extended to a customer, the financial institution shall provide a notice of such furnishing of negative information, in writing, to the customer.

(ii) **Notice effective for subsequent submissions.**—After providing such notice, the financial institution may submit additional negative information to a consumer reporting agency described in section 1681a(p) with respect to the same transaction, extension of credit, account, or customer without providing additional notice to the customer.

(B) **Time of notice.—**

(i) **In general.**—The notice required under subparagraph (A) shall be provided to the customer prior to, or no later than 30 days after, furnishing the negative information to a consumer reporting agency described in section 1681a(p).

(ii) **Coordination with new account disclosures.**—If the notice is provided to the customer prior to furnishing the negative information to a consumer reporting agency, the notice may not be included in the initial disclosures provided under section 127(a) of the Truth in Lending Act.

(C) **Coordination with other disclosures.**—The notice required under subparagraph (A)—

(i) may be included on or with any notice of default, any billing statement, or any other materials provided to the customer; and

(ii) must be clear and conspicuous.

(D) **Model disclosure.—**

(i) **Duty of board to prepare.**—The Board shall prescribe a brief model disclosure a financial institution may use to comply with subparagraph (A), which shall not exceed 30 words.

(ii) **Use of model not required.**—No provision of this paragraph shall be construed as requiring a financial institution to use any such model form prescribed by the Board.

(iii) **Compliance using model.**—A financial institution shall be deemed to be in compliance with subparagraph (A) if the financial institution uses any such model form prescribed by the Board, or the financial institution uses any such model form and rearranges its format.

(E) **Use of notice without submitting negative information.**—No provision of this paragraph shall be construed as requiring a financial institution that has provided a customer with a notice described in subparagraph (A) to furnish negative information about the customer to a consumer reporting agency.

(F) **Safe harbor.**—A financial institution shall not be liable for failure to perform the duties required by this paragraph if, at the time of the failure, the financial institution maintained reasonable policies and procedures to comply with this paragraph or the financial institution reasonably believed that the institution is prohibited, by law, from contacting the consumer.

(G) **Definitions.**—For purposes of this paragraph, the following definitions shall apply:

(i) **Negative information.**—The term 'negative information' means information concerning a customer's delinquencies, late payments, insolvency, or any form of default.

The Consumer Credit and Sales Legal Practice Series

Precise, easy-to-follow practice manuals for lawyers in *all 50 states*.

"A monumental undertaking ... should become a standard reference set."
— American Bar Association Journal

NCLC Consumer Law Manuals with Companion CD-Roms

Written by the Nation's Experts
The National Consumer Law Center, a nonprofit corporation, has offered technical assistance, publications, and training for lawyers since 1969. NCLC is widely consulted as the nation's consumer law authority.

The Consumer Law "Bibles"
Consumer and industry lawyers tell us they view the NCLC manuals as their indispensable bibles for consumer law.

Designed for Use in All 50 States
The manuals detail state legislation and case law in all 50 states, in addition to comprehensive analysis of federal laws, regulations, cases, agency interpretations, and even informal letters. Available individually, by subject library discount, or as a complete 16-volume set discount.

Highly Practical
Sample pleadings, checklists, forms, and practice pointers make each manual a powerful tool for the practitioner. Each manual provides guidance to spot multiple claims in a case, maximizing client recovery and attorney fees.

The Series is Continuously Updated

NCLC Manuals Are as Current as Possible
NCLC manuals reliably predict trends and advise on novel legal strategies, so that our readers are always at least one step ahead.

We Keep Our Manuals Current in Three Ways
- Annual cumulative supplements with cumulative CD-Roms
- Periodic revised editions
- The NCLC REPORTS newsletter is issued 24 times a year.

Order securely online at www.consumerlaw.org

We Make Upkeep Affordable
- Four months FREE supplements, CD-Roms, and revised editions
- Companion CD-Roms come FREE with all supplements and revised editions and include all manual appendices and many extra features
- FREE shipping
- Our supplement prices are among the lowest in legal publishing today
- 20% discounts off our already low prices for revised editions
- Set subscribers receive 30% discount on all future supplements and revised editions
- New manual purchasers automatically receive a FREE four month, 8-issue NCLC REPORTS newsletter trial subscription, your hotline to new ideas, trends and tactics in the practice of consumer law.

Keyword Search All NCLC Manuals at Our Website
NCLC's CD-Roms and our website do not include the text of the book chapters, but you can pinpoint in seconds the number of times on every page in every manual where a particular term appears. Search by case name, party name, statutory or regulatory citation, or any other terms. Just type in the search term or terms at:

www.consumerlaw.org/keyword

The tables of contents, CD-Rom contents, and indexes for all our manuals are also found at www.consumerlaw.org.

National Consumer Law Center
77 Summer Street • 10th Floor • Boston MA 02110 • (617) 542-9595 • Fax (617) 542-8028 • www.consumerlaw.org

---

FOLLOW THE EXPERTS

The Consumer Credit and Sales Legal Practice Series of manuals with companion CD-Roms are designed to be the primary — and often only — resource an attorney or advocate needs to understand the rights of consumers under federal and state law:

DEBTOR RIGHTS LIBRARY
- ☐ Consumer Bankruptcy Law and Practice
- ☐ Fair Debt Collection
- ☐ Repossessions and Foreclosures
- ☐ Student Loan Law
- ☐ Access to Utility Service

CONSUMER LITIGATION LIBRARY
- ☐ Consumer Arbitration Agreements
- ☐ Consumer Class Actions
- ☐ Consumer Law Pleadings

CREDIT AND BANKING LIBRARY
- ☐ Truth in Lending
- ☐ Fair Credit Reporting
- ☐ Consumer Banking and Payments Law
- ☐ The Cost of Credit
- ☐ Credit Discrimination

DECEPTION AND WARRANTIES LIBRARY
- ☐ Unfair and Deceptive Acts and Practices
- ☐ Automobile Fraud
- ☐ Consumer Warranty Law

OTHER NCLC PUBLICATIONS
- ☐ The Practice of Consumer Law with CD-Rom
- ☐ Stop Predatory Lending with CD-Rom
- ☐ Consumer Law in A Box CD-Rom
- ☐ NCLC Reports Newsletter
- ☐ Return to Sender: Getting a Refund or Replacement for Your Lemon Car
- ☐ NCLC Guide to Surviving Debt
- ☐ NCLC Guide to Mobile Homes
- ☐ NCLC Guide to Consumer Rights for Immigrants

ORDER TODAY! For Faster Service, Call (617) 542-9595

FREE SHIPPING

04S

☐ Please send me more information on the titles checked above.

Name/Organization _____
Address _____ City _____ State _____ Zip _____
Fax (___) _____ E-mail _____

Order securely online at www.consumerlaw.org

National Consumer Law Center
77 Summer Street • 10th Floor • Boston MA 02110 • (617) 542-9595 • Fax (617) 542-8028 • www.consumerlaw.org

THE PRACTICE OF CONSUMER LAW
Seeking Economic Justice
2003 First Edition with CD-Rom (328 pages)

A practical volume to get you started or help you stay on track in a consumer law practice:

- Opening a private consumer law practice: choosing a specialty, fee agreements, networking with others, how to market yourself
- Making even small consumer claims cost-effective
- Sample consumer law pleadings, client retainer forms, co-counseling agreements, checklists and interview questionnaires, discovery, and trial documents
- Consumer law remedies in individual suits and defense tactics
- How to take an out-of-state deposition
- Challenging 13 types of abusive businesses and
- Biographies of over 100 consumer law attorneys, describing the nature of their practice and more.

The National Consumer Law Center Guide to
SURVIVING DEBT
2002 Fourth Edition (422 pages)

NCLC's popular handbook, *Surviving Debt* provides precise, practical, and hard-hitting advice on how to deal with an overwhelming debt load. Contains contributions from more than a dozen consumer law experts.

"A gold mine on topics like how to handle collectors, which debts to pay first, and how collection lawsuits work."
— U.S. News and World Report

Surviving Debt tells consumers, counselors, and lawyers what they need to know about:

- Dealing with debt collectors
- What you need to know about your credit rating
- Which debts to pay first
- Refinancing do's and don'ts
- Saving your home from foreclosure
- Automobile repossessions
- Evictions and utility shutoffs
- Credit card debt
- Student loans
- Collection lawsuits
- Your bankruptcy rights and much much more.

STOP PREDATORY LENDING
A Guide for Legal Advocates
2002 First Edition with CD-Rom (240 pages)

The exponential growth of predatory lending has left financial havoc in its wake. This handbook explains the nature of the problem and provides a roadmap to practical legal strategies to remedy and prevent predatory lending relating to home mortgages, payday loans, rent-to-own, auto title pawns, tax refund anticipation loans and more:

- Careful explanation of the nature and scope of predatory lending
- Analyzing loan documents: a step-by-step approach
- Overview of legal claims and defense to predatory loans
- Home Ownership and Equity Protection Act (HOEPA)
- The Truth In Lending Act simplified
- Collecting the relevant loan documents
- Spotting the issues in a case
- Selecting, defending, and resisting a litigation forum
- Holding the players liable
- Crafting a community response to predatory lending.

A Great Introduction That is Easy to Read:
- Graphs, charts, and illustrations
- Factual examples
- Checklists and quotes
- Glossary and index.

The Companion CD-Rom is a Key Resource:
- Consumer law math programs
- HOEPA regulatory changes
- Relevant sample pleadings, motions, and briefs re TIL, HOEPA, home improvement fraud, loan flipping, RESPA, land contracts, mobile homes, and fringe lending
- HOEPA fees and points worksheet
- Model Home Loan Protection Act and commentary
- Model Payday Loan Act and commentary
- Fannie Mae, Freddie Mac, and Chicago underwriting guidelines for alternative loan products that allow homeowners to refinance out of predatory loans.

Order securely online at www.consumerlaw.org

National Consumer Law Center
77 Summer Street • 10th Floor • Boston MA 02110 • (617) 542-9595 • Fax (617) 542-8028 • www.consumerlaw.org

BUSINESS REPLY MAIL
FIRST-CLASS MAIL   PERMIT NO. 1639   BOSTON, MA

POSTAGE WILL BE PAID BY ADDRESSEE

National Consumer Law Center
Publications Department
77 Summer Street, 10th Floor
Boston, MA 02110-9828

NO POSTAGE NECESSARY IF MAILED IN THE UNITED STATES

04S

(ii) **Customer; financial institution.**—The terms 'customer' and 'financial institution' have the same meanings as in section 509 Public Law 106-102.

(8) **Ability of consumer to dispute information directly with furnisher.**—

(A) **In general.**—The Federal banking agencies, the National Credit Union Administration, and the Commission shall jointly prescribe regulations that shall identify the circumstances under which a furnisher shall be required to reinvestigate a dispute concerning the accuracy of information contained in a consumer report on the consumer, based on a direct request of a consumer.

(B) **Considerations.**—In prescribing regulations under subparagraph (A), the agencies shall weigh—

(i) the benefits to consumers with the costs on furnishers and the credit reporting system;

(ii) the impact on the overall accuracy and integrity of consumer reports of any such requirements;

(iii) whether direct contact by the consumer with the furnisher would likely result in the most expeditious resolution of any such dispute; and

(iv) the potential impact on the credit reporting process if credit repair organizations, as defined in section 403(3), including entities that would be a credit repair organization, but for section 403(3)(B)(i), are able to circumvent the prohibition in subparagraph (G).

(C) **Applicability.**—Subparagraphs (D) through (G) shall apply in any circumstance identified under the regulations promulgated under subparagraph (A).

(D) **Submitting a notice of dispute.**—A consumer who seeks to dispute the accuracy of information shall provide a dispute notice directly to such person at the address specified by the person for such notices that—

(i) identifies the specific information that is being disputed;

(ii) explains the basis for the dispute; and

(iii) includes all supporting documentation required by the furnisher to substantiate the basis of the dispute.

(E) **Duty of person after receiving notice of dispute.**—After receiving a notice of dispute from a consumer pursuant to subparagraph (D), the person that provided the information in dispute to a consumer reporting agency shall—

(i) conduct an investigation with respect to the disputed information;

(ii) review all relevant information provided by the consumer with the notice;

(iii) complete such person's investigation of the dispute and report the results of the investigation to the consumer before the expiration of the period under section 1681i(a)(1) within which a consumer reporting agency would be required to complete its action if the consumer had elected to dispute the information under that section; and

(iv) if the investigation finds that the information reported was inaccurate, promptly notify each consumer reporting agency to which the person furnished the inaccurate information of that determination and provide to the agency any correction to that information that is necessary to make the information provided by the person accurate.

(F) **Frivolous or irrelevant dispute.**—

(i) **In general.**—This paragraph shall not apply if the person receiving a notice of a dispute from a consumer reasonably determines that the dispute is frivolous or irrelevant, including—

(I) by reason of the failure of a consumer to provide sufficient information to investigate the disputed information; or

(II) the submission by a consumer of a dispute that is substantially the same as a dispute previously submitted by or for the consumer, either directly to the person or through a consumer reporting agency under subsection (b), with respect to which the person has already performed the person's duties under this paragraph or subsection (b), as applicable.

(ii) **Notice of determination.**—Upon making any determination under clause (i) that a dispute is frivolous or irrelevant, the person shall notify the consumer of such determination not later than 5 business days after making such determination, by mail or, if authorized by the consumer for that purpose, by any other means available to the person.

(iii) **Contents of notice.**—A notice under clause (ii) shall include—

(I) the reasons for the determination under clause (i); and

(II) identification of any information required to investigate the disputed information, which may consist of a standardized form describing the general nature of such information.

(G) **Exclusion of credit repair organizations.**—This paragraph shall not apply if the notice of the dispute is submitted by, is prepared on behalf of the consumer by, or is submitted on a form supplied to the consumer by, a credit repair organization, as defined in section 403(3), or an entity that would be a credit repair organization, but for section 403(3)(B)(i).

(9) **Duty to provide notice of status as medical information furnisher.**—A person whose primary business is providing medical services, products, or devices, or the person's agent or assignee, who furnishes information to a consumer reporting

agency on a consumer shall be considered a medical information furnisher for purposes of this title, and shall notify the agency of such status.

(b) Duties of furnishers of information upon notice of dispute

(1) In general

After receiving notice pursuant to section 1681i(a)(2) of this title of a dispute with regard to the completeness or accuracy of any information provided by a person to a consumer reporting agency, the person shall—

(A) conduct an investigation with respect to the disputed information;

(B) review all relevant information provided by the consumer reporting agency pursuant to section 1681i(a)(2) of this title;

(C) report the results of the investigation to the consumer reporting agency; ~~and~~

(D) if the investigation finds that the information is incomplete or inaccurate, report those results to all other consumer reporting agencies to which the person furnished the information and that compile and maintain files on consumers on a nationwide basis~~.~~; and

(E) if an item of information disputed by a consumer is found to be inaccurate or incomplete or cannot be verified after any reinvestigation under paragraph (1), for purposes of reporting to a consumer reporting agency only, as appropriate, based on the results of the reinvestigation promptly—

(i) modify that item of information;

(ii) delete that item of information; or

(iii) permanently block the reporting of that item of information.

(2) Deadline

A person shall complete all investigations, reviews, and reports required under paragraph (1) regarding information provided by the person to a consumer reporting agency, before the expiration of the period under section 1681i(a)(1) of this title within which the consumer reporting agency is required to complete actions required by that section regarding that information.

~~**(c) Limitation on liability**~~

~~Sections 1681n and 1681o do not apply to any failure to comply with subsection (a) of this section, except as provided in section 1681s(c)(1)(B) of this title.~~

~~**(d) Limitation on enforcement**~~

~~Subsection (a) of this section shall be enforced exclusively under section 1681s of this title by the Federal agencies and officials and the State officials identified in that section.~~

(c) Limitation on liability.—Except as provided in section 1681s(c)(1)(B), sections 1681n and 1681o do not apply to any violation of—

(1) subsection (a) of this section, including any regulations issued thereunder;

(2) subsection (e) of this section, except that nothing in this paragraph shall limit, expand, or otherwise affect liability under section 1681n or 1681o, as applicable, for violations of subsection (b) of this section; or

(3) subsection (e) of section 1681m.

(d) Limitation on enforcement.—The provisions of law described in paragraphs (1) through (3) of subsection (c) (other than with respect to the exception described in paragraph (2) of subsection (c)) shall be enforced exclusively as provided under section 1681s by the Federal agencies and officials and the State officials identified in section 1681s.

(e) Accuracy guidelines and regulations required.—

(1) Guidelines.—The Federal banking agencies, the National Credit Union Administration, and the Commission shall, with respect to the entities that are subject to their respective enforcement authority under section 1681s, and in coordination as described in paragraph (2)—

(A) establish and maintain guidelines for use by each person that furnishes information to a consumer reporting agency regarding the accuracy and integrity of the information relating to consumers that such entities furnish to consumer reporting agencies, and update such guidelines as often as necessary; and

(B) prescribe regulations requiring each person that furnishes information to a consumer reporting agency to establish reasonable policies and procedures for implementing the guidelines established pursuant to subparagraph (A).

(2) Coordination.—Each agency required to prescribe regulations under paragraph (1) shall consult and coordinate with each other such agency so that, to the extent possible, the regulations prescribed by each such entity are consistent and comparable with the regulations prescribed by each other such agency.

(3) Criteria.—In developing the guidelines required by paragraph (1)(A), the agencies described in paragraph (1) shall—

(A) identify patterns, practices, and specific forms of activity that can compromise the accuracy and integrity of information furnished to consumer reporting agencies;

(B) review the methods (including technological means) used to furnish information relating to consumers to consumer reporting agencies;

(C) determine whether persons that furnish information to consumer reporting agencies maintain and enforce policies to assure the accuracy and integrity of information furnished to consumer reporting agencies; and

(D) examine the policies and processes that persons that furnish information to consumer reporting agencies employ to conduct reinvestigations and correct inaccurate information relating to consumers that has been furnished to consumer reporting agencies.

§ 1681s-3. Affiliate sharing [FCRA § 624]

(a) Special rule for solicitation for purposes of marketing.—

(1) Notice.—Any person that receives from another person related to it by common ownership or affiliated by corporate control a communication of information that would be a consumer report, but for clauses (i), (ii), and (iii) of section 1681a(d)(2)(A), may not use the information to make a solicitation for marketing purposes to a consumer about its products or services, unless—

(A) it is clearly and conspicuously disclosed to the consumer that the information may be communicated among such persons for purposes of making such solicitations to the consumer; and

(B) the consumer is provided an opportunity and a simple method to prohibit the making of such solicitations to the consumer by such person.

(2) Consumer choice.—

(A) **In general.—**The notice required under paragraph (1) shall allow the consumer the opportunity to prohibit all solicitations referred to in such paragraph, and may allow the consumer to choose from different options when electing to prohibit the sending of such solicitations, including options regarding the types of entities and information covered, and which methods of delivering solicitations the consumer elects to prohibit.

(B) **Format.—**Notwithstanding subparagraph (A), the notice required under paragraph (1) shall be clear, conspicuous, and concise, and any method provided under paragraph (1)(B) shall be simple. The regulations prescribed to implement this section shall provide specific guidance regarding how to comply with such standards.

(3) Duration.—

(A) **In general.—**The election of a consumer pursuant to paragraph (1)(B) to prohibit the making of solicitations shall be effective for at least 5 years, beginning on the date on which the person receives the election of the consumer, unless the consumer requests that such election be revoked.

(B) **Notice upon expiration of effective period.—**At such time as the election of a consumer pursuant to paragraph (1)(B) is no longer effective, a person may not use information that the person receives in the manner described in paragraph (1) to make any solicitation for marketing purposes to the consumer, unless the consumer receives a notice and an opportunity, using a simple method, to extend the opt-out for another period of at least 5 years, pursuant to the procedures described in paragraph (1).

(4) Scope.—This section shall not apply to a person—

(A) using information to make a solicitation for marketing purposes to a consumer with whom the person has a pre-existing business relationship;

(B) using information to facilitate communications to an individual for whose benefit the person provides employee benefit or other services pursuant to a contract with an employer related to and arising out of the current employment relationship or status of the individual as a participant or beneficiary of an employee benefit plan;

(C) using information to perform services on behalf of another person related by common ownership or affiliated by corporate control, except that this subparagraph shall not be construed as permitting a person to send solicitations on behalf of another person, if such other person would not be permitted to send the solicitation on its own behalf as a result of the election of the consumer to prohibit solicitations under paragraph (1)(B);

(D) using information in response to a communication initiated by the consumer;

(E) using information in response to solicitations authorized or requested by the consumer; or

(F) if compliance with this section by that person would prevent compliance by that person with any provision of State insurance laws pertaining to unfair discrimination in any State in which the person is lawfully doing business.

(5) No retroactivity.—This subsection shall not prohibit the use of information to send a solicitation to a consumer if such information was received prior to the date on which persons are required to comply with regulations implementing this subsection.

(b) Notice for other purposes permissible.—A notice or other disclosure under this section may be coordinated and consolidated with any other notice required to be issued under any other provision of law by a person that is subject to this section, and a notice or other disclosure that is equivalent to the notice required by subsection (a), and that is provided by a person described in subsection (a) to a consumer together with disclosures required by any other provision of law, shall satisfy the requirements of subsection (a).

(c) User requirements.—Requirements with respect to the use by a person of information received from another person related to it by common ownership or affiliated by corporate control, such as the requirements of this section, constitute requirements with respect to the exchange of information among persons affiliated by common ownership or common corporate control, within the meaning of section 1681t(b)(2).

(d) Definitions.—For purposes of this section, the following definitions shall apply:

(1) Pre-existing business relationship.—The term 'pre-existing business relationship' means a relationship between a person, or a person's licensed agent, and a consumer, based on—

(A) a financial contract between a person and a consumer which is in force;

(B) the purchase, rental, or lease by the consumer of that person's goods or services, or a financial transaction (including holding an active account or a policy in force or having another continuing relationship) between the consumer and that person during the 18-month period immediately preceding the date on which the consumer is sent a solicitation covered by this section;

(C) an inquiry or application by the consumer regarding a product or service offered by that person, during the 3-month period immediately preceding the date on which the consumer is sent a solicitation covered by this section; or

(D) any other pre-existing customer relationship defined in the regulations implementing this section.

(2) **Solicitation.**—The term 'solicitation' means the marketing of a product or service initiated by a person to a particular consumer that is based on an exchange of information described in subsection (a), and is intended to encourage the consumer to purchase such product or service, but does not include communications that are directed at the general public or determined not to be a solicitation by the regulations prescribed under this section.

§ 1681t. Relation to State laws [FCRA § 6245]

(a) In general

Except as provided in subsections (b) and (c) of this section, this subchapter does not annul, alter, affect, or exempt any person subject to the provisions of this subchapter from complying with the laws of any State with respect to the collection, distribution, or use of any information on consumers, or for the prevention or mitigation of identity theft, except to the extent that those laws are inconsistent with any provision of this subchapter, and then only to the extent of the inconsistency.

(b) General exceptions

No requirement or prohibition may be imposed under the laws of any State—

(1) with respect to any subject matter regulated under—

(A) subsection (c) or (e) of section 1681b of this title, relating to the prescreening of consumer reports;

(B) section 1681i of this title, relating to the time by which a consumer reporting agency must take any action, including the provision of notification to a consumer or other person, in any procedure related to the disputed accuracy of information in a consumer's file, except that this subparagraph shall not apply to any State law in effect on September 30, 1996;

(C) subsections (a) and (b) of section 1681m of this title, relating to the duties of a person who takes any adverse action with respect to a consumer;

(D) section 1681m(d) of this title, relating to the duties of persons who use a consumer report of a consumer in connection with any credit or insurance transaction that is not initiated by the consumer and that consists of a firm offer of credit or insurance;

(E) section 1681c of this title, relating to information contained in consumer reports, except that this subparagraph shall not apply to any State law in effect on September 30, 1996; or

(F) section 1681s-2 of this title, relating to the responsibilities of persons who furnish information to consumer reporting agencies, except that this paragraph shall not apply—

(i) with respect to section 54A(a) of chapter 93 of the Massachusetts Annotated Laws (as in effect on September 30, 1996); or

(ii) with respect to section 1785.25(a) of the California Civil Code (as in effect on September 30, 1996);

(G) section 1681g(e), relating to information available to victims under section 1681g (e);

(H) section 1681s-3, relating to the exchange and use of information to make a solicitation for marketing purposes; or

(I) section 1681m(h), relating to the duties of users of consumer reports to provide notice with respect to terms in certain credit transactions;

(2) with respect to the exchange of information among persons affiliated by common ownership or common corporate control, except that this paragraph shall not apply with respect to subsection (a) or (c)(1) of section 2480e of title 9, Vermont Statutes Annotated (as in effect on September 30, 1996); or

(3) with respect to the form and content of any disclosure required to be made under section 1681g(c) of this title.

(3) with respect to the disclosures required to be made under subsection (c), (d), (e), or (g) of section 1681g, or subsection (f) of section 1681g relating to the disclosure of credit scores for credit granting purposes, except that this paragraph—

(A) shall not apply with respect to sections 1785.10, 1785.16, and 1785.20.2 of the California Civil Code (as in effect on the date of enactment of the Fair and Accurate Credit Transactions Act of 2003) and section 1785.15 through section 1785.15.2 of such Code (as in effect on such date);

(B) shall not apply with respect to sections 5-3-106(2) and 212-14.3-104.3 of the Colorado Revised Statutes (as in effect on the date of enactment of the Fair and Accurate Credit Transactions Act of 2003); and

(C) shall not be construed as limiting, annulling, affecting, or superseding any provision of the laws of any State regulating the use in an insurance activity, or regulating disclosures concerning such use, of a credit-based insurance score of a consumer by any person engaged in the business of insurance;

(4) with respect to the frequency of any disclosure under section 1681j(a), except that this paragraph shall not apply—

(A) with respect to section 12-14.3-105(1)(d) of the Colorado Revised Statutes (as in effect on the date of enactment of the Fair and Accurate Credit Transactions Act of 2003);

(B) with respect to section 10-1-393(29)(C) of the Georgia Code (as in effect on the date of enactment of the Fair and Accurate Credit Transactions Act of 2003);

(C) with respect to section 1316.2 of title 10 of the Maine Revised Statutes (as in effect on the date of enactment of the Fair and Accurate Credit Transactions Act of 2003);

(D) with respect to sections 14-1209(a)(1) and 14-1209(b)(1)(i) of the Commercial Law Article of the Code of Maryland (as in effect on the date of enactment of the Fair and Accurate Credit Transactions Act of 2003);

(E) with respect to section 59(d) and section 59(e) of chapter 93 of the General Laws of Massachusetts (as in effect on the date of enactment of the Fair and Accurate Credit Transactions Act of 2003);

(F) with respect to section 56:11-37.10(a)(1) of the New Jersey Revised Statutes (as in effect on the date of enactment of the Fair and Accurate Credit Transactions Act of 2003); or

(G) with respect to section 2480c(a)(1) of title 9 of the Vermont Statutes Annotated (as in effect on the date of enactment of the Fair and Accurate Credit Transactions Act of 2003); or

(5) with respect to the conduct required by the specific provisions of—

(A) section 1681c(g);

(B) section 1681c-1;

(C) section 1681c-2;

(D) section 1681g(a)(1)(A);

(E) section 1681j(a);

(F) subsections (e), (f), and (g) of section 1681m;

(G) section 1681s(f);

(H) section 1681s-2(a)(6); or

(I) section 1681w.

(c) Definition of firm offer of credit or insurance

Notwithstanding any definition of the term "firm offer of credit or insurance" (or any equivalent term) under the laws of any State, the definition of that term contained in section 1681a(*l*) of this title shall be construed to apply in the enforcement and interpretation of the laws of any State governing consumer reports.

(d) Limitations

Subsections (b) and (c) of this section—

(1) do not affect and (c) do not affect any settlement, agreement, or consent judgment between any State Attorney General and any consumer reporting agency in effect on September 30, 1996.; and

(2) do not apply to any provision of State law (including any provision of a State constitution) that—

(A) is enacted after January 1, 2004;

(B) states explicitly that the provision is intended to supplement this subchapter; and

(C) gives greater protection to consumers than is provided under this subchapter.

§ 1681u. Disclosures to FBI for counterintelligence purposes [FCRA § 6256]

(a) Identity of financial institutions

Notwithstanding section 1681b of this title or any other provision of this subchapter, a consumer reporting agency shall furnish to the Federal Bureau of Investigation the names and addresses of all financial institutions (as that term is defined in section 3401 of Title 12) at which a consumer maintains or has maintained an account, to the extent that information is in the files of the agency, when presented with a written request for that information, signed by the Director of the Federal Bureau of Investigation, or the Director's designee in a position not lower than Deputy Assistant Director at Bureau headquarters or a Special Agent in Charge of a Bureau field office designated by the Director, which certifies compliance with this section. The Director or the Director's designee may make such a certification only if the Director or the Director's designee has determined in writing, that such information is sought for the conduct of an authorized investigation to protect against international terrorism or clandestine intelligence activities, provided that such an investigation of a United States person is not conducted solely upon the basis of activities protected by the first amendment to the Constitution of the United States.

(b) Identifying information

Notwithstanding the provisions of section 1681b of this title or any other provision of this subchapter, a consumer reporting agency shall furnish identifying information respecting a consumer, limited to name, address, former addresses, places of employment, or former places of employment, to the Federal Bureau of Investigation when presented with a written request, signed by the Director or the Director's designee in a position not lower than Deputy Assistant Director at Bureau headquarters or a Special Agent in Charge of a Bureau field office designated by the Director, which certifies compliance with this subsection. The Director or the Director's designee may make such a certification only if the Director or the Director's designee has determined in writing that such information is sought for the conduct of an authorized investigation to protect against international terrorism or clandestine intelligence activities, provided that such an investigation of a United States person is not conducted solely upon the basis of activities protected by the first amendment to the Constitution of the United States.

(c) Court order for disclosure of consumer reports

Notwithstanding section 1681b of this title or any other provision of this subchapter, if requested in writing by the Director of the Federal Bureau of Investigation, or a designee of the Director in a position not lower than Deputy Assistant Director at Bureau headquarters or a Special Agent in Charge in a Bureau field office designated by the Director, a court may issue an order ex parte directing a consumer reporting agency to furnish a consumer report to the Federal Bureau of Investigation, upon a showing in camera that the consumer report is sought for the conduct of an authorized investigation to protect against international terrorism or clandestine intelligence activities, provided that such an investigation of a United States person is not conducted solely upon the basis of activities protected by the first amendment to the Constitution of the United States.

The terms of an order issued under this subsection shall not disclose that the order is issued for purposes of a counterintelligence investigation.

(d) Confidentiality

No consumer reporting agency or officer, employee, or agent of a consumer reporting agency shall disclose to any person, other than those officers, employees, or agents of a consumer reporting agency necessary to fulfill the requirement to disclose information to the Federal Bureau of Investigation under this section, that the Federal Bureau of Investigation has sought or obtained the identity of financial institutions or a consumer report respecting any consumer under subsection (a), (b), or (c) of this section, and no consumer reporting agency or officer, employee, or agent of a consumer reporting agency shall include in any consumer report any information that would indicate that the Federal Bureau of Investigation has sought or obtained such information or a consumer report.

(e) Payment of fees

The Federal Bureau of Investigation shall, subject to the availability of appropriations, pay to the consumer reporting agency assembling or providing report or information in accordance with procedures established under this section a fee for reimbursement for such costs as are reasonably necessary and which have been directly incurred in searching, reproducing, or transporting books, papers, records, or other data required or requested to be produced under this section.

(f) Limit on dissemination

The Federal Bureau of Investigation may not disseminate information obtained pursuant to this section outside of the Federal Bureau of Investigation, except to other Federal agencies as may be necessary for the approval or conduct of a foreign counterintelligence investigation, or, where the information concerns a person subject to the Uniform Code of Military Justice, to appropriate investigative authorities within the military department concerned as may be necessary for the conduct of a joint foreign counterintelligence investigation.

(g) Rules of construction

Nothing in this section shall be construed to prohibit information from being furnished by the Federal Bureau of Investigation pursuant to a subpoena or court order, in connection with a judicial or administrative proceeding to enforce the provisions of this subchapter. Nothing in this section shall be construed to authorize or permit the withholding of information from the Congress.

(h) Reports to Congress

On a semiannual basis, the Attorney General shall fully inform the Permanent Select Committee on Intelligence and the Committee on Banking, Finance and Urban Affairs of the House of Representatives, and the Select Committee on Intelligence and the Committee on Banking, Housing, and Urban Affairs of the Senate concerning all requests made pursuant to subsections (a), (b), and (c) of this section.

(i) Damages

Any agency or department of the United States obtaining or disclosing any consumer reports, records, or information contained therein in violation of this section is liable to the consumer to whom such consumer reports, records, or information relate in an amount equal to the sum of—

(1) $100, without regard to the volume of consumer reports, records, or information involved;

(2) any actual damages sustained by the consumer as a result of the disclosure;

(3) if the violation is found to have been willful or intentional, such punitive damages as a court may allow; and

(4) in the case of any successful action to enforce liability under this subsection, the costs of the action, together with reasonable attorney fees, as determined by the court.

(j) Disciplinary actions for violations

If a court determines that any agency or department of the United States has violated any provision of this section and the court finds that the circumstances surrounding the violation raise questions of whether or not an officer or employee of the agency or department acted willfully or intentionally with respect to the violation, the agency or department shall promptly initiate a proceeding to determine whether or not disciplinary action is warranted against the officer or employee who was responsible for the violation.

(k) Good-faith exception

Notwithstanding any other provision of this subchapter, any consumer reporting agency or agent or employee thereof making disclosure of consumer reports or identifying information pursuant to this subsection in good-faith reliance upon a certification of the Federal Bureau of Investigation pursuant to provisions of this section shall not be liable to any person for such disclosure under this subchapter, the constitution of any State, or any law or regulation of any State or any political subdivision of any State.

(*l*) Limitation of remedies

Notwithstanding any other provision of this subchapter, the remedies and sanctions set forth in this section shall be the only judicial remedies and sanctions for violation of this section.

(m) Injunctive relief

In addition to any other remedy contained in this section, injunctive relief shall be available to require compliance with the procedures of this section. In the event of any successful action under this subsection, costs together with reasonable attorney fees, as determined by the court, may be recovered.

§ 1681v Disclosures to governmental agencies for counterterrorism purposes [FCRA § 6267]

(a) Disclosure

Notwithstanding ~~section 604~~section 1681b or any other provision of this title, a consumer reporting agency shall furnish a consumer report of a consumer and all other information in a consumer's file to a government agency authorized to conduct investigations of, or intelligence or counterintelligence activities or analysis related to, international terrorism when presented with a written certification by such government agency that such information is necessary for the agency's conduct or such investigation, activity or analysis.

(b) Form of Certification

The certification described in subsection (a) shall be signed by a supervisory official designated by the head of a Federal agency or an officer of a Federal agency whose appointment to office is required to be made by the President, by and with the advice and consent of the Senate.

(c) Confidentiality

No consumer reporting agency, or officer, employee, or agent of such consumer reporting agency, shall disclose to any person, or specify in any consumer report, that a government agency has sought or obtained access to information under subsection (a).

(d) Rule of Construction

Nothing in ~~section 625~~section 1681u shall be construed to limit the authority of the Director of the Federal Bureau of Investigation under this section.

(e) Safe Harbor

Notwithstanding any other provision of this title, any consumer reporting agency or agent or employee thereof making disclosure of consumer reports or other information pursuant to this section in good-faith reliance upon a certification of a governmental agency pursuant to the provisions of this section shall not be liable to any person for such disclosure under this subchapter, the constitution of any State, or any law or regulation of any State or any political subdivision of any State.

§ 1681w. Disposal of records [FCRA § 628]

(a) Regulations.—

(1) In general.—Not later than 1 year after the date of enactment of this section, the Federal banking agencies, the National Credit Union Administration, and the Commission with respect to the entities that are subject to their respective enforcement authority under section 1681s, and the Securities and Exchange Commission, and in coordination as described in paragraph (2), shall issue final regulations requiring any person that maintains or otherwise possesses consumer information, or any compilation of consumer information, derived from consumer reports for a business purpose to properly dispose of any such information or compilation.

(2) **Coordination.**—Each agency required to prescribe regulations under paragraph (1) shall—

(A) consult and coordinate with each other such agency so that, to the extent possible, the regulations prescribed by each such agency are consistent and comparable with the regulations by each such other agency; and

(B) ensure that such regulations are consistent with the requirements and regulations issued pursuant to Public Law 106-102 and other provisions of Federal law.

(3) Exemption authority.—In issuing regulations under this section, the Federal banking agencies, the National Credit Union Administration, the Commission, and the Securities and Exchange Commission may exempt any person or class of persons from application of those regulations, as such agency deems appropriate to carry out the purpose of this section.

(b) Rule of construction.—Nothing in this section shall be construed—

(1) to require a person to maintain or destroy any record pertaining to a consumer that is not imposed under other law; or

(2) to alter or affect any requirement imposed under any other provision of law to maintain or destroy such a record.

§ 1681x. Corporate and technological circumvention prohibited [FCRA § 629]

The Commission shall prescribe regulations, to become effective not later than 90 days after the date of enactment of this section, to prevent a consumer reporting agency from circumventing or evading treatment as a consumer reporting agency described in section 1681a(p) for purposes of this title, including—

(1) by means of a corporate reorganization or restructuring, including a merger, acquisition, dissolution, divestiture, or asset sale of a consumer reporting agency; or

(2) by maintaining or merging public record and credit account information in a manner that is substantially equivalent to that described in paragraphs (1) and (2) of section 1681a(p), in the manner described in section 1681a(p).

A.2.3 Fair and Accurate Credit Transactions Act of 2003

FACTA, Public Law Number 108-159 (Dec. 4, 2003)

FAIR AND ACCURATE CREDIT TRANSACTIONS ACT OF 2003

Public Law 108-159

108th Congress

Dec. 4, 2003

An Act

To amend the Fair Credit Reporting Act, to prevent identity theft, improve resolution of consumer disputes, improve the accuracy of consumer records, make improvements in the use of, and consumer access to, credit information, and for other purposes.

Be it enacted by the Senate and House of Representatives of the United States of America in Congress assembled,

SECTION 1. SHORT TITLE; TABLE OF CONTENTS.

(a) SHORT TITLE.—This Act may be cited as the "Fair and Accurate Credit Transactions Act of 2003".

(b) TABLE OF CONTENTS.—The table of contents for this Act is as follows:

Sec. 1. Short title; table of contents.
Sec. 2. Definitions.
Sec. 3. Effective dates.

TITLE I—IDENTITY THEFT PREVENTION AND CREDIT HISTORY RESTORATION

Subtitle A—Identity Theft Prevention

Sec. 111. Amendment to definitions.
Sec. 112. Fraud alerts and active duty alerts.
Sec. 113. Truncation of credit card and debit card account numbers.
Sec. 114. Establishment of procedures for the identification of possible instances of identity theft.
Sec. 115. Authority to truncate social security numbers.

Subtitle B—Protection and Restoration of Identity Theft Victim Credit History

Sec. 151. Summary of rights of identity theft victims.
Sec. 152. Blocking of information resulting from identity theft.
Sec. 153. Coordination of identity theft complaint investigations.
Sec. 154. Prevention of repollution of consumer reports.
Sec. 155. Notice by debt collectors with respect to fraudulent information.
Sec. 156. Statute of limitations.
Sec. 157. Study on the use of technology to combat identity theft.

TITLE II—IMPROVEMENTS IN USE OF AND CONSUMER ACCESS TO CREDIT INFORMATION

Sec. 211. Free consumer reports.
Sec. 212. Disclosure of credit scores.

Sec. 213. Enhanced disclosure of the means available to opt out of prescreened lists.
Sec. 214. Affiliate sharing.
Sec. 215. Study of effects of credit scores and credit-based insurance scores on availability and affordability of financial products.
Sec. 216. Disposal of consumer report information and records.
Sec. 217. Requirement to disclose communications to a consumer reporting agency.

TITLE III—ENHANCING THE ACCURACY OF CONSUMER REPORT INFORMATION

Sec. 311. Risk-based pricing notice.
Sec. 312. Procedures to enhance the accuracy and integrity of information furnished to consumer reporting agencies.
Sec. 313. FTC and consumer reporting agency action concerning complaints.
Sec. 314. Improved disclosure of the results of reinvestigation.
Sec. 315. Reconciling addresses.
Sec. 316. Notice of dispute through reseller.
Sec. 317. Reasonable reinvestigation required.
Sec. 318. FTC study of issues relating to the Fair Credit Reporting Act.
Sec. 319. FTC study of the accuracy of consumer reports.

TITLE IV—LIMITING THE USE AND SHARING OF MEDICAL INFORMATION IN THE FINANCIAL SYSTEM

Sec. 411. Protection of medical information in the financial system.
Sec. 412. Confidentiality of medical contact information in consumer reports.

TITLE V—FINANCIAL LITERACY AND EDUCATION IMPROVEMENT

Sec. 511. Short title.
Sec. 512. Definitions.
Sec. 513. Establishment of Financial Literacy and Education Commission.
Sec. 514. Duties of the Commission.
Sec. 515. Powers of the Commission.
Sec. 516. Commission personnel matters.
Sec. 517. Studies by the Comptroller General.
Sec. 518. The national public service multimedia campaign to enhance the state of financial literacy.
Sec. 519. Authorization of appropriations.

TITLE VI—PROTECTING EMPLOYEE MISCONDUCT INVESTIGATIONS

Sec. 611. Certain employee investigation communications excluded from definition of consumer report.

TITLE VII—RELATION TO STATE LAWS

Sec. 711. Relation to State laws.

TITLE VIII—MISCELLANEOUS

Sec. 811. Clerical amendments.

SEC. 2. DEFINITIONS.

As used in this Act—

(1) the term "Board" means the Board of Governors of the Federal Reserve System;

(2) the term "Commission", other than as used in title V, means the Federal Trade Commission;

(3) the terms "consumer", "consumer report", "consumer reporting agency", "creditor", "Federal banking agencies", and "financial institution" have the same meanings as in section 603 of the Fair Credit Reporting Act, as amended by this Act; and

(4) the term "affiliates" means persons that are related by common ownership or affiliated by corporate control.

SEC. 3. EFFECTIVE DATES.

Except as otherwise specifically provided in this Act and the amendments made by this Act—

(1) before the end of the 2-month period beginning on the date of enactment of this Act, the Board and the Commission shall jointly prescribe regulations in final form establishing effective dates for each provision of this Act; and

(2) the regulations prescribed under paragraph (1) shall establish effective dates that are as early as possible, while allowing a reasonable time for the implementation of the provisions of this Act, but in no case shall any such effective date be later than 10 months after the date of issuance of such regulations in final form.

TITLE I—IDENTITY THEFT PREVENTION AND CREDIT HISTORY RESTORATION

Subtitle A—Identity Theft Prevention

SEC. 111. AMENDMENT TO DEFINITIONS.

Section 603 of the Fair Credit Reporting Act (15 U.S.C. 1681a) is amended by adding at the end the following:

"(q) DEFINITIONS RELATING TO FRAUD ALERTS.—

"(1) ACTIVE DUTY MILITARY CONSUMER.—The term 'active duty military consumer' means a consumer in military service who—

"(A) is on active duty (as defined in section 101(d)(1) of title 10, United States Code) or is a reservist performing duty under a call or order to active duty under a provision of law referred to in section 101(a)(13) of title 10, United States Code; and

"(B) is assigned to service away from the usual duty station of the consumer.

"(2) FRAUD ALERT; ACTIVE DUTY ALERT.—The terms 'fraud alert' and 'active duty alert' mean a statement in the file of a consumer that—

"(A) notifies all prospective users of a consumer report relating to the consumer that the consumer may be a victim of fraud, including identity theft, or is an active duty military consumer, as applicable; and

"(B) is presented in a manner that facilitates a clear and conspicuous view of the statement described in subparagraph (A) by any person requesting such consumer report.

"(3) IDENTITY THEFT.—The term 'identity theft' means a fraud committed using the identifying information of another person, subject to such further definition as the Commission may prescribe, by regulation.

"(4) IDENTITY THEFT REPORT.—The term 'identity theft report' has the meaning given that term by rule of the Commission, and means, at a minimum, a report—

"(A) that alleges an identity theft;

"(B) that is a copy of an official, valid report filed by a consumer with an appropriate Federal, State, or local law enforcement agency, including the United States Postal

Inspection Service, or such other government agency deemed appropriate by the Commission; and

"(C) the filing of which subjects the person filing the report to criminal penalties relating to the filing of false information if, in fact, the information in the report is false.

"(5) NEW CREDIT PLAN.—The term 'new credit plan' means a new account under an open end credit plan (as defined in section 103(i) of the Truth in Lending Act) or a new credit transaction not under an open end credit plan.

"(r) Credit and Debit Related Terms—

"(1) CARD ISSUER.—The term 'card issuer' means—

"(A) a credit card issuer, in the case of a credit card; and

"(B) a debit card issuer, in the case of a debit card.

"(2) CREDIT CARD.—The term 'credit card' has the same meaning as in section 103 of the Truth in Lending Act.

"(3) DEBIT CARD.—The term 'debit card' means any card issued by a financial institution to a consumer for use in initiating an electronic fund transfer from the account of the consumer at such financial institution, for the purpose of transferring money between accounts or obtaining money, property, labor, or services.

"(4) ACCOUNT AND ELECTRONIC FUND TRANSFER.—The terms 'account' and 'electronic fund transfer' have the same meanings as in section 903 of the Electronic Fund Transfer Act.

"(5) CREDIT AND CREDITOR.—The terms 'credit' and 'creditor' have the same meanings as in section 702 of the Equal Credit Opportunity Act.

"(s) FEDERAL BANKING AGENCY.—The term 'Federal banking agency' has the same meaning as in section 3 of the Federal Deposit Insurance Act.

"(t) FINANCIAL INSTITUTION.—The term 'financial institution' means a State or National bank, a State or Federal savings and loan association, a mutual savings bank, a State or Federal credit union, or any other person that, directly or indirectly, holds a transaction account (as defined in section 19(b) of the Federal Reserve Act) belonging to a consumer.

"(u) RESELLER.—The term 'reseller' means a consumer reporting agency that—

"(1) assembles and merges information contained in the database of another consumer reporting agency or multiple consumer reporting agencies concerning any consumer for purposes of furnishing such information to any third party, to the extent of such activities; and

"(2) does not maintain a database of the assembled or merged information from which new consumer reports are produced.

"(v) COMMISSION.—The term 'Commission' means the Federal Trade Commission.

"(w) NATIONWIDE SPECIALTY CONSUMER REPORTING AGENCY.—The term 'nationwide specialty consumer reporting agency' means a consumer reporting agency that compiles and maintains files on consumers on a nationwide basis relating to—

"(1) medical records or payments;

"(2) residential or tenant history;

"(3) check writing history;

"(4) employment history; or

"(5) insurance claims.".

SEC. 112. FRAUD ALERTS AND ACTIVE DUTY ALERTS.

(a) FRAUD ALERTS.—The Fair Credit Reporting Act (15 U.S.C. 1681 et seq.) is amended by inserting after section 605 the following:

"§ 605A. Identity theft prevention; fraud alerts and active duty alerts

"(a) ONE-CALL FRAUD ALERTS.—

"(1) INITIAL ALERTS.—Upon the direct request of a consumer, or an individual acting on behalf of or as a personal representative of a consumer, who asserts in good faith a suspicion that the consumer has been or is about to become a victim of fraud or related crime, including identity theft, a consumer reporting agency described in section 603(p) that maintains a file on the consumer and has received appropriate proof of the identity of the requester shall—

"(A) include a fraud alert in the file of that consumer, and also provide that alert along with any credit score generated in using that file, for a period of not less than 90 days, beginning on the date of such request, unless the consumer or such representative requests that such fraud alert be removed before the end of such period, and the agency has received appropriate proof of the identity of the requester for such purpose; and

"(B) refer the information regarding the fraud alert under this paragraph to each of the other consumer reporting agencies described in section 603(p), in accordance with procedures developed under section 621(f).

"(2) ACCESS TO FREE REPORTS.—In any case in which a consumer reporting agency includes a fraud alert in the file of a consumer pursuant to this subsection, the consumer reporting agency shall—

"(A) disclose to the consumer that the consumer may request a free copy of the file of the consumer pursuant to section 612(d); and

"(B) provide to the consumer all disclosures required to be made under section 609, without charge to the consumer, not later than 3 business days after any request described in subparagraph (A).

"(b) EXTENDED ALERTS.—

"(1) IN GENERAL.—Upon the direct request of a consumer, or an individual acting on behalf of or as a personal representative of a consumer, who submits an identity theft report to a consumer reporting agency described in section 603(p) that maintains a file on the consumer, if the agency has received appropriate proof of the identity of the requester, the agency shall—

"(A) include a fraud alert in the file of that consumer, and also provide that alert along with any credit score generated in using that file, during the 7-year period beginning on the date of such request, unless the consumer or such representative requests that such fraud alert be removed before the end of such period and the agency has received appropriate proof of the identity of the requester for such purpose;

"(B) during the 5-year period beginning on the date of such request, exclude the consumer from any list of consumers prepared by the consumer reporting agency and provided to any third party to offer credit or insurance to the consumer as part of a transaction that was not initiated by the consumer, unless the consumer or such representative requests that such exclusion be rescinded before the end of such period; and

"(C) refer the information regarding the extended fraud alert under this paragraph to each of the other consumer reporting agencies described in section 603(p), in accordance with procedures developed under section 621(f).

"(2) ACCESS TO FREE REPORTS.—In any case in which a consumer reporting agency includes a fraud alert in the file of a consumer pursuant to this subsection, the consumer reporting agency shall—

"(A) disclose to the consumer that the consumer may request 2 free copies of the file of the consumer pursuant to section 612(d) during the 12-month period beginning on the date on which the fraud alert was included in the file; and

"(B) provide to the consumer all disclosures required to be made under section 609, without charge to the consumer, not later than 3 business days after any request described in subparagraph (A).

"(c) ACTIVE DUTY ALERTS.—Upon the direct request of an active duty military consumer, or an individual acting on behalf of or as a personal representative of an active duty military consumer, a consumer reporting agency described in section 603(p) that maintains a file on the active duty military consumer and has received appropriate proof of the identity of the requester shall—

"(1) include an active duty alert in the file of that active duty military consumer, and also provide that alert along with any credit score generated in using that file, during a period of not less than 12 months, or such longer period as the Commission shall determine, by regulation, beginning on the date of the request, unless the active duty military consumer or such representative requests that such fraud alert be removed before the end of such period, and the agency has received appropriate proof of the identity of the requester for such purpose;

"(2) during the 2-year period beginning on the date of such request, exclude the active duty military consumer from any list of consumers prepared by the consumer reporting agency and provided to any third party to offer credit or insurance to the consumer as part of a transaction that was not initiated by the consumer, unless the consumer requests that such exclusion be rescinded before the end of such period; and

"(3) refer the information regarding the active duty alert to each of the other consumer reporting agencies described in section 603(p), in accordance with procedures developed under section 621(f).

"(d) PROCEDURES.—Each consumer reporting agency described in section 603(p) shall establish policies and procedures to comply with this section, including procedures that inform consumers of the availability of initial, extended, and active duty alerts and procedures that allow consumers and active duty military consumers to request initial, extended, or active duty alerts (as applicable) in a simple and easy manner, including by telephone.

"(e) REFERRALS OF ALERTS.—Each consumer reporting agency described in section 603(p) that receives a referral of a fraud alert or active duty alert from another consumer reporting agency pursuant to this section shall, as though the agency received the request from the consumer directly, follow the procedures required under—

"(1) paragraphs (1)(A) and (2) of subsection (a), in the case of a referral under subsection (a)(1)(B);

"(2) paragraphs (1)(A), (1)(B), and (2) of subsection (b), in the case of a referral under subsection (b)(1)(C); and

"(3) paragraphs (1) and (2) of subsection (c), in the case of a referral under subsection (c)(3).

"(f) DUTY OF RESELLER TO RECONVEY ALERT.—A reseller shall include in its report any fraud alert or active duty alert placed in the file of a consumer pursuant to this section by another consumer reporting agency.

"(g) DUTY OF OTHER CONSUMER REPORTING AGENCIES TO PROVIDE CONTACT INFORMATION.—If a consumer contacts any consumer reporting agency that is not described in section 603(p) to communicate a suspicion that the consumer has been or is about to become a victim of fraud or related crime, including identity theft, the agency shall provide information to the consumer on how to contact the Commission and the consumer reporting agencies described in section 603(p) to obtain more detailed information and request alerts under this section.

"(h) LIMITATIONS ON USE OF INFORMATION FOR CREDIT EXTENSIONS.—

"(1) REQUIREMENTS FOR INITIAL AND ACTIVE DUTY ALERTS.—

"(A) NOTIFICATION.—Each initial fraud alert and active duty alert under this section shall include information that notifies all prospective users of a consumer report on the consumer to which the alert relates that the consumer does not authorize the establishment of any new credit plan or extension of credit, other than under an open-end credit plan (as defined in section 103(i)), in the name of the consumer, or issuance of an additional card on an existing credit account requested by a consumer, or any increase in credit limit on an existing credit account requested by a consumer, except in accordance with subparagraph (B).

"(B) LIMITATION ON USERS.—

"(i) IN GENERAL.—No prospective user of a consumer report that includes an initial fraud alert or an active duty alert in accordance with this section may establish a new credit plan or extension of credit, other than under an open-end credit plan (as defined in section 103(i)), in the name of the consumer, or issue an additional card on an existing credit account requested by a consumer, or grant any increase in credit limit on an existing credit account requested by a consumer, unless the user utilizes reasonable policies and procedures to form a reasonable belief that the user knows the identity of the person making the request.

"(ii) VERIFICATION.—If a consumer requesting the alert has specified a telephone number to be used for identity verification purposes, before authorizing any new credit plan or extension described in clause (i) in the name of such consumer, a user of such consumer report shall contact the consumer using that telephone number or take reasonable steps to verify the consumer's identity and confirm that the application for a new credit plan is not the result of identity theft.

"(2) REQUIREMENTS FOR EXTENDED ALERTS.—

"(A) NOTIFICATION.—Each extended alert under this section shall include information that provides all prospective users of a consumer report relating to a consumer with—

"(i) notification that the consumer does not authorize the establishment of any new credit plan or extension of credit described in clause (i), other than under an open-end credit plan (as defined in section 103(i)), in the name of the consumer, or issuance of an additional card on an existing credit account requested by a consumer, or any increase in credit limit on an existing credit account requested by a consumer, except in accordance with subparagraph (B); and

"(ii) a telephone number or other reasonable contact method designated by the consumer.

"(B) LIMITATION ON USERS.—No prospective user of a consumer report or of a credit score generated using the information in the file of a consumer that includes an extended fraud alert in accordance with this section may establish a new credit plan or extension of credit, other than under an open- end credit plan (as defined in section 103(i)), in the name of the consumer, or issue an additional card on an existing credit account requested by a consumer, or any increase in credit limit on an existing credit account requested by a consumer, unless the user contacts the consumer in person or using the contact method described in subparagraph (A)(ii) to confirm that the application for a new credit plan or increase in credit limit, or request for an additional card is not the result of identity theft.".

(b) RULEMAKING.—The Commission shall prescribe regulations to define what constitutes appropriate proof of identity for purposes of sections 605A, 605B, and 609(a)(1) of the Fair Credit Reporting Act, as amended by this Act.

SEC. 113. TRUNCATION OF CREDIT CARD AND DEBIT CARD ACCOUNT NUMBERS.

Section 605 of the Fair Credit Reporting Act (15 U.S.C. 1681c) is amended by adding at the end the following:

"(g) TRUNCATION OF CREDIT CARD AND DEBIT CARD NUMBERS.—

"(1) IN GENERAL.—Except as otherwise provided in this subsection, no person that accepts credit cards or debit cards for the transaction of business shall print more than the last 5 digits of the card number or the expiration date upon any receipt provided to the cardholder at the point of the sale or transaction.

"(2) LIMITATION.—This subsection shall apply only to receipts that are electronically printed, and shall not apply to transactions in which the sole means of recording a credit card or debit card account number is by handwriting or by an imprint or copy of the card.

"(3) EFFECTIVE DATE.—This subsection shall become effective—

"(A) 3 years after the date of enactment of this subsection, with respect to any cash register or other machine or device that electronically prints receipts for credit card or debit card transactions that is in use before January 1, 2005; and

"(B) 1 year after the date of enactment of this subsection, with respect to any cash register or other machine or device that electronically prints receipts for credit card or debit card transactions that is first put into use on or after January 1, 2005.".

SEC. 114. ESTABLISHMENT OF PROCEDURES FOR THE IDENTIFICATION OF POSSIBLE INSTANCES OF IDENTITY THEFT.

Section 615 of the Fair Credit Reporting Act (15 U.S.C. 1681m) is amended—

(1) by striking "(e)" at the end; and
(2) by adding at the end the following:
"(e) RED FLAG GUIDELINES AND REGULATIONS REQUIRED.—
"(1) GUIDELINES.—The Federal banking agencies, the National Credit Union Administration, and the Commission shall jointly, with respect to the entities that are subject to their respective enforcement authority under section 621—
"(A) establish and maintain guidelines for use by each financial institution and each creditor regarding identity theft with respect to account holders at, or customers of, such entities, and update such guidelines as often as necessary;
"(B) prescribe regulations requiring each financial institution and each creditor to establish reasonable policies and procedures for implementing the guidelines established pursuant to subparagraph (A), to identify possible risks to account holders or customers or to the safety and soundness of the institution or customers; and
"(C) prescribe regulations applicable to card issuers to ensure that, if a card issuer receives notification of a change of address for an existing account, and within a short period of time (during at least the first 30 days after such notification is received) receives a request for an additional or replacement card for the same account, the card issuer may not issue the additional or replacement card, unless the card issuer, in accordance with reasonable policies and procedures—
"(i) notifies the cardholder of the request at the former address of the cardholder and provides to the cardholder a means of promptly reporting incorrect address changes;
"(ii) notifies the cardholder of the request by such other means of communication as the cardholder and the card issuer previously agreed to; or
"(iii) uses other means of assessing the validity of the change of address, in accordance with reasonable policies and procedures established by the card issuer in accordance with the regulations prescribed under subparagraph (B).
"(2) CRITERIA.—
"(A) IN GENERAL.—In developing the guidelines required by paragraph (1)(A), the agencies described in paragraph (1) shall identify patterns, practices, and specific forms of activity that indicate the possible existence of identity theft.
"(B) INACTIVE ACCOUNTS.—In developing the guidelines required by paragraph (1)(A), the agencies described in paragraph (1) shall consider including reasonable guidelines providing that when a transaction occurs with respect to a credit or deposit account that has been inactive for more than 2 years, the creditor or financial institution shall follow reasonable policies and procedures that provide for notice to be given to a consumer in a manner reasonably designed to reduce the likelihood of identity theft with respect to such account.
"(3) CONSISTENCY WITH VERIFICATION REQUIREMENTS.—Guidelines established pursuant to paragraph (1) shall not be inconsistent with the policies and procedures required under section 5318(l) of title 31, United States Code.".

SEC. 115. AUTHORITY TO TRUNCATE SOCIAL SECURITY NUMBERS.

Section 609(a)(1) of the Fair Credit Reporting Act (15 U.S.C. 1681g(a)(1)) is amended by striking "except that nothing" and inserting the following: "except that—

"(A) if the consumer to whom the file relates requests that the first 5 digits of the social security number (or similar identification number) of the consumer not be included in the disclosure and the consumer reporting agency has received appropriate proof of the identity of the requester, the consumer reporting agency shall so truncate such number in such disclosure; and

"(B) nothing".

Subtitle B—Protection and Restoration of Identity Theft Victim Credit History

SEC. 151. SUMMARY OF RIGHTS OF IDENTITY THEFT VICTIMS.

(a) IN GENERAL.—

(1) SUMMARY.—Section 609 of the Fair Credit Reporting Act (15 U.S.C. 1681g) is amended by adding at the end the following:

"(d) SUMMARY OF RIGHTS OF IDENTITY THEFT VICTIMS.—

"(1) IN GENERAL.—The Commission, in consultation with the Federal banking agencies and the National Credit Union Administration, shall prepare a model summary of the rights of consumers under this title with respect to the procedures for remedying the effects of fraud or identity theft involving credit, an electronic fund transfer, or an account or transaction at or with a financial institution or other creditor.

"(2) SUMMARY OF RIGHTS AND CONTACT INFORMATION.—Beginning 60 days after the date on which the model summary of rights is prescribed in final form by the Commission pursuant to paragraph (1), if any consumer contacts a consumer reporting agency and expresses a belief that the consumer is a victim of fraud or identity theft involving credit, an electronic fund transfer, or an account or transaction at or with a financial institution or other creditor, the consumer reporting agency shall, in addition to any other action that the agency may take, provide the consumer with a summary of rights that contains all of the information required by the Commission under paragraph (1), and information on how to contact the Commission to obtain more detailed information.

"(e) INFORMATION AVAILABLE TO VICTIMS.—

"(1) IN GENERAL.—For the purpose of documenting fraudulent transactions resulting from identity theft, not later than 30 days after the date of receipt of a request from a victim in accordance with paragraph (3), and subject to verification of the identity of the victim and the claim of identity theft in accordance with paragraph (2), a business entity that has provided credit to, provided for consideration products, goods, or services to, accepted payment from, or otherwise entered into a commercial transaction for consideration with, a person who has allegedly made unauthorized use of the means of identification of the victim, shall provide a copy of application and business transaction records in the control of the business entity, whether maintained by the business entity or by another person on behalf of the business entity, evidencing any transaction alleged to be a result of identity theft to—

"(A) the victim;

"(B) any Federal, State, or local government law enforcement agency or officer specified by the victim in such a request; or

"(C) any law enforcement agency investigating the identity theft and authorized by the victim to take receipt of records provided under this subsection.

"(2) VERIFICATION OF IDENTITY AND CLAIM.—Before a business entity provides any information under paragraph (1), unless the business entity, at its discretion, otherwise has a high degree of confidence that it knows the identity of the victim making a request under paragraph (1), the victim shall provide to the business entity—

"(A) as proof of positive identification of the victim, at the election of the business entity—

"(i) the presentation of a government-issued identification card;

"(ii) personally identifying information of the same type as was provided to the business entity by the unauthorized person; or "(iii) personally identifying information that the business entity typically requests from new applicants or for new transactions, at the time of the victim's request for information, including any documentation described in clauses (i) and (ii); and

"(B) as proof of a claim of identity theft, at the election of the business entity—

"(i) a copy of a police report evidencing the claim of the victim of identity theft; and

"(ii) a properly completed—

"(I) copy of a standardized affidavit of identity theft developed and made available by the Commission; or

"(II) an affidavit of fact that is acceptable to the business entity for that purpose.

"(3) PROCEDURES.—The request of a victim under paragraph (1) shall—

"(A) be in writing;

"(B) be mailed to an address specified by the business entity, if any; and

"(C) if asked by the business entity, include relevant information about any transaction alleged to be a result of identity theft to facilitate compliance with this section including—

"(i) if known by the victim (or if readily obtainable by the victim), the date of the application or transaction; and

"(ii) if known by the victim (or if readily obtainable by the victim), any other identifying information such as an account or transaction number.

"(4) NO CHARGE TO VICTIM.—Information required to be provided under paragraph (1) shall be so provided without charge.

"(5) AUTHORITY TO DECLINE TO PROVIDE INFORMATION.—A business entity may decline to provide information under paragraph (1) if, in the exercise of good faith, the business entity determines that—

"(A) this subsection does not require disclosure of the information;

"(B) after reviewing the information provided pursuant to paragraph (2), the business entity does not have a high degree of confidence in knowing the true identity of the individual requesting the information;

"(C) the request for the information is based on a misrepresentation of fact by the individual requesting the information relevant to the request for information; or

"(D) the information requested is Internet navigational data or similar information about a person's visit to a website or online service.

"(6) LIMITATION ON LIABILITY.—Except as provided in section 621, sections 616 and 617 do not apply to any violation of this subsection.

"(7) LIMITATION ON CIVIL LIABILITY.—No business entity may be held civilly liable under any provision of Federal, State, or other law for disclosure, made in good faith pursuant to this subsection.

"(8) NO NEW RECORDKEEPING OBLIGATION.—Nothing in this subsection creates an obligation on the part of a business entity to obtain, retain, or maintain information or records that are not otherwise required to be obtained, retained, or maintained in the ordinary course of its business or under other applicable law.

"(9) RULE OF CONSTRUCTION.—

"(A) IN GENERAL.—No provision of subtitle A of title V of Public Law 106-102, prohibiting the disclosure of financial information by a business entity to third parties shall be used to deny disclosure of information to the victim under this subsection.

"(B) LIMITATION.—Except as provided in subparagraph (A), nothing in this subsection permits a business entity to disclose information, including information to law enforcement under subparagraphs (B) and (C) of paragraph (1), that the business entity is otherwise prohibited from disclosing under any other applicable provision of Federal or State law.

"(10) AFFIRMATIVE DEFENSE.—In any civil action brought to enforce this subsection, it is an affirmative defense (which the defendant must establish by a preponderance of the evidence) for a business entity to file an affidavit or answer stating that—

"(A) the business entity has made a reasonably diligent search of its available business records; and

"(B) the records requested under this subsection do not exist or are not reasonably available.

"(11) DEFINITION OF VICTIM.—For purposes of this subsection, the term 'victim' means a consumer whose means of identification or financial information has been used or transferred (or has been alleged to have been used or transferred) without the authority of that consumer, with the intent to commit, or to aid or abet, an identity theft or a similar crime.

"(12) EFFECTIVE DATE.—This subsection shall become effective 180 days after the date of enactment of this subsection.

"(13) EFFECTIVENESS STUDY.—Not later than 18 months after the date of enactment of this subsection, the Comptroller General of the United States shall submit a report to Congress assessing the effectiveness of this provision.".

(2) RELATION TO STATE LAWS.—Section 625(b)(1) of the Fair Credit Reporting Act (15 U.S.C. 1681t(b)(1), as so redesignated) is amended by adding at the end the following new subparagraph:

"(G) section 609(e), relating to information available to victims under section 609(e);".

(b) PUBLIC CAMPAIGN TO PREVENT IDENTITY THEFT.—Not later than 2 years after the date of enactment of this Act, the Commission shall establish and implement a media and distribution campaign to teach the public how to prevent identity theft. Such campaign shall include existing Commission education materials, as well as radio, television, and print public service announcements, video cassettes, interactive digital video discs (DVD's) or compact audio discs (CD's), and Internet resources.

SEC. 152. BLOCKING OF INFORMATION RESULTING FROM IDENTITY THEFT.

(a) IN GENERAL.—The Fair Credit Reporting Act (15 U.S.C. 1681 et seq.) is amended by inserting after section 605A, as added by this Act, the following:

"§ 605B. Block of information resulting from identity theft

"(a) BLOCK.—Except as otherwise provided in this section, a consumer reporting agency shall block the reporting of any information in the file of a consumer that the consumer identifies as information that resulted from an alleged identity theft, not later than 4 business days after the date of receipt by such agency of—

"(1) appropriate proof of the identity of the consumer;

"(2) a copy of an identity theft report;

"(3) the identification of such information by the consumer; and

"(4) a statement by the consumer that the information is not information relating to any transaction by the consumer.

"(b) NOTIFICATION.—A consumer reporting agency shall promptly notify the furnisher of information identified by the consumer under subsection (a)—

"(1) that the information may be a result of identity theft;

"(2) that an identity theft report has been filed;

"(3) that a block has been requested under this section; and

"(4) of the effective dates of the block.

"(c) AUTHORITY TO DECLINE OR RESCIND.—

"(1) IN GENERAL.—A consumer reporting agency may decline to block, or may rescind any block, of information relating to a consumer under this section, if the consumer reporting agency reasonably determines that—

"(A) the information was blocked in error or a block was requested by the consumer in error;

"(B) the information was blocked, or a block was requested by the consumer, on the basis of a material misrepresentation of fact by the consumer relevant to the request to block; or

"(C) the consumer obtained possession of goods, services, or money as a result of the blocked transaction or transactions.

"(2) NOTIFICATION TO CONSUMER.—If a block of information is declined or rescinded under this subsection, the affected consumer shall be notified promptly, in the same manner as consumers are notified of the reinsertion of information under section 611(a)(5)(B).

"(3) SIGNIFICANCE OF BLOCK.—For purposes of this subsection, if a consumer reporting agency rescinds a block, the presence of information in the file of a consumer prior to the blocking of such information is not evidence of whether the consumer knew or should have known that the consumer obtained possession of any goods, services, or money as a result of the block.

"(d) EXCEPTION FOR RESELLERS.—

"(1) NO RESELLER FILE.—This section shall not apply to a consumer reporting agency, if the consumer reporting agency—

"(A) is a reseller;

"(B) is not, at the time of the request of the consumer under subsection (a), otherwise furnishing or reselling a consumer report concerning the information identified by the consumer; and

"(C) informs the consumer, by any means, that the consumer may report the identity theft to the Commission to obtain consumer information regarding identity theft.

"(2) RESELLER WITH FILE.—The sole obligation of the consumer reporting agency under this section, with regard to any request of a consumer under this section, shall be to block the consumer report maintained by the consumer reporting agency from any subsequent use, if—

"(A) the consumer, in accordance with the provisions of subsection (a), identifies, to a consumer reporting agency, information in the file of the consumer that resulted from identity theft; and

"(B) the consumer reporting agency is a reseller of the identified information.

"(3) NOTICE.—In carrying out its obligation under paragraph (2), the reseller shall promptly provide a notice to the consumer of the decision to block the file. Such notice shall contain the name, address, and telephone number of each consumer reporting agency from which the consumer information was obtained for resale.

"(e) EXCEPTION FOR VERIFICATION COMPANIES.—The provisions of this section do not apply to a check services company, acting as such, which issues authorizations for the purpose of approving or processing negotiable instruments, electronic fund transfers, or similar methods of payments, except that, beginning 4 business days after receipt of information described in paragraphs (1) through (3) of subsection (a), a check services company shall not report to a national consumer reporting agency described in section 603(p), any information identified in the subject identity theft report as resulting from identity theft.

"(f) ACCESS TO BLOCKED INFORMATION BY LAW ENFORCEMENT AGENCIES.—No provision of this section shall be construed as requiring a consumer reporting agency to prevent a Federal, State, or local law enforcement agency from accessing blocked information in a consumer file to which the agency could otherwise obtain access under this title.".

(b) CLERICAL AMENDMENT.—The table of sections for the Fair Credit Reporting Act (15 U.S.C. 1681 et seq.) is amended by inserting after the item relating to section 605 the following new items:

"605A. Identity theft prevention; fraud alerts and active duty alerts.
"605B. Block of information resulting from identity theft.".

SEC. 153. COORDINATION OF IDENTITY THEFT COMPLAINT INVESTIGATIONS.

Section 621 of the Fair Credit Reporting Act (15 U.S.C. 1681s) is amended by adding at the end the following:

"(f) COORDINATION OF CONSUMER COMPLAINT INVESTIGATIONS.—

"(1) IN GENERAL.—Each consumer reporting agency described in section 603(p) shall develop and maintain procedures for the referral to each other such agency of any consumer complaint received by the agency alleging identity theft, or requesting a fraud alert under section 605A or a block under section 605B.

"(2) MODEL FORM AND PROCEDURE FOR REPORTING IDENTITY THEFT.—The Commission, in consultation with the Federal banking agencies and the National Credit Union Administration, shall develop a model form and model procedures to be used by consumers who are victims of identity theft for contacting and informing creditors and consumer reporting agencies of the fraud.

"(3) ANNUAL SUMMARY REPORTS.—Each consumer reporting agency described in section 603(p) shall submit an annual summary report to the Commission on consumer complaints received by the agency on identity theft or fraud alerts.".

SEC. 154. PREVENTION OF REPOLLUTION OF CONSUMER REPORTS.

(a) PREVENTION OF REINSERTION OF ERRONEOUS INFORMATION.—Section 623(a) of the Fair Credit Reporting Act (15 U.S.C. 1681s-2(a)) is amended by adding at the end the following:

"(6) DUTIES OF FURNISHERS UPON NOTICE OF IDENTITY THEFT-RELATED INFORMATION.—

"(A) REASONABLE PROCEDURES.—A person that furnishes information to any consumer reporting agency shall have in place reasonable procedures to respond to any notification that it receives from a consumer reporting agency under section 605B relating to information resulting from identity theft, to prevent that person from refurnishing such blocked information.

"(B) INFORMATION ALLEGED TO RESULT FROM IDENTITY THEFT.—If a consumer submits an identity theft report to a person who furnishes information to a consumer reporting agency at the address specified by that person for receiving such reports stating that information maintained by such person that purports to relate to the consumer resulted from identity theft, the person may not furnish such information that purports to relate to the consumer to any consumer reporting agency, unless the person subsequently knows or is informed by the consumer that the information is correct.".

(b) PROHIBITION ON SALE OR TRANSFER OF DEBT CAUSED BY IDENTITY THEFT.—Section 615 of the Fair Credit Reporting Act (15 U.S.C. 1681m), as amended by this Act, is amended by adding at the end the following:

"(f) PROHIBITION ON SALE OR TRANSFER OF DEBT CAUSED BY IDENTITY THEFT.—

"(1) IN GENERAL.—No person shall sell, transfer for consideration, or place for collection a debt that such person has been notified under section 605B has resulted from identity theft.

"(2) APPLICABILITY.—The prohibitions of this subsection shall apply to all persons collecting a debt described in paragraph (1) after the date of a notification under paragraph (1).

"(3) RULE OF CONSTRUCTION.—Nothing in this subsection shall be construed to prohibit—

"(A) the repurchase of a debt in any case in which the assignee of the debt requires such repurchase because the debt has resulted from identity theft;

"(B) the securitization of a debt or the pledging of a portfolio of debt as collateral in connection with a borrowing; or

"(C) the transfer of debt as a result of a merger, acquisition, purchase and assumption transaction, or transfer of substantially all of the assets of an entity.".

SEC. 155. NOTICE BY DEBT COLLECTORS WITH RESPECT TO FRAUDULENT INFORMATION.

Section 615 of the Fair Credit Reporting Act (15 U.S.C. 1681m), as amended by this Act, is amended by adding at the end the following:

"(g) DEBT COLLECTOR COMMUNICATIONS CONCERNING IDENTITY THEFT.—If a person acting as a debt collector (as that term is defined in title VIII) on behalf of a third party that is a creditor or other user of a consumer report is notified that any information relating to a debt that the person is attempting to collect may be fraudulent or may be the result of identity theft, that person shall—

"(1) notify the third party that the information may be fraudulent or may be the result of identity theft; and

"(2) upon request of the consumer to whom the debt purportedly relates, provide to the consumer all information to which the consumer would otherwise be entitled if the consumer were not a victim of identity theft, but wished to dispute the debt under provisions of law applicable to that person.".

SEC. 156. STATUTE OF LIMITATIONS.

Section 618 of the Fair Credit Reporting Act (15 U.S.C. 1681p) is amended to read as follows:

"§ 618. Jurisdiction of courts; limitation of actions

"An action to enforce any liability created under this title may be brought in any appropriate United States district court, without regard to the amount in controversy, or in any other court of competent jurisdiction, not later than the earlier of—

"(1) 2 years after the date of discovery by the plaintiff of the violation that is the basis for such liability; or

"(2) 5 years after the date on which the violation that is the basis for such liability occurs.".

SEC. 157. STUDY ON THE USE OF TECHNOLOGY TO COMBAT IDENTITY THEFT.

(a) STUDY REQUIRED.—The Secretary of the Treasury shall conduct a study of the use of biometrics and other similar technologies to reduce the incidence and costs to society of identity theft by providing convincing evidence of who actually performed a given financial transaction.

(b) CONSULTATION.—The Secretary of the Treasury shall consult with Federal banking agencies, the Commission, and representatives of financial institutions, consumer reporting agencies, Federal, State, and local government agencies that issue official forms or means of identification, State prosecutors, law enforcement agencies, the biometric industry, and the general public in formulating and conducting the study required by subsection (a).

(c) AUTHORIZATION OF APPROPRIATIONS.—There are authorized to be appropriated to the Secretary of the Treasury for fiscal year 2004, such sums as may be necessary to carry out the provisions of this section.

(d) REPORT REQUIRED.—Before the end of the 180-day period beginning on the date of enactment of this Act, the Secretary shall submit a report to Congress containing the findings and conclusions of the study required under subsection (a), together with such recommendations for legislative or administrative actions as may be appropriate.

TITLE II—IMPROVEMENTS IN USE OF AND CONSUMER ACCESS TO CREDIT INFORMATION

SEC. 211. FREE CONSUMER REPORTS.

(a) IN GENERAL.—Section 612 of the Fair Credit Reporting Act (15 U.S.C. 1681j) is amended—

(1) by redesignating subsection (a) as subsection (f), and transferring it to the end of the section;

(2) by inserting before subsection (b) the following:

"(a) FREE ANNUAL DISCLOSURE.—

"(1) NATIONWIDE CONSUMER REPORTING AGENCIES.—

"(A) IN GENERAL.—All consumer reporting agencies described in subsections (p) and (w) of section 603 shall make all disclosures pursuant to section 609 once during any 12-month period upon request of the consumer and without charge to the consumer.

"(B) CENTRALIZED SOURCE.—Subparagraph (A) shall apply with respect to a consumer reporting agency described in section 603(p) only if the request from the consumer is made using the centralized source established for such purpose in accordance with section 211(c) of the Fair and Accurate Credit Transactions Act of 2003.

"(C) NATIONWIDE SPECIALTY CONSUMER REPORTING AGENCY.—

"(i) IN GENERAL.—The Commission shall prescribe regulations applicable to each consumer reporting agency described in section 603(w) to require the establishment of a streamlined process for consumers to request consumer reports under subparagraph (A), which shall include, at a minimum, the establishment by each such agency of a toll-free telephone number for such requests.

"(ii) CONSIDERATIONS.—In prescribing regulations under clause (i), the Commission shall consider—

"(I) the significant demands that may be placed on consumer reporting agencies in providing such consumer reports;

"(II) appropriate means to ensure that consumer reporting agencies can satisfactorily meet those demands, including the efficacy of a system of staggering the availability to consumers of such consumer reports; and

"(III) the ease by which consumers should be able to contact consumer reporting agencies with respect to access to such consumer reports.

"(iii) DATE OF ISSUANCE.—The Commission shall issue the regulations required by this subparagraph in final form not later than 6 months after the date of enactment of the Fair and Accurate Credit Transactions Act of 2003.

"(iv) CONSIDERATION OF ABILITY TO COMPLY.—The regulations of the Commission under this subparagraph shall establish an effective date by which each nationwide specialty consumer reporting agency (as defined in section 603(w)) shall be required to comply with subsection (a), which effective date—

"(I) shall be established after consideration of the ability of each nationwide specialty consumer reporting agency to comply with subsection (a); and

"(II) shall be not later than 6 months after the date on which such regulations are issued in final form (or such additional period not to exceed 3 months, as the Commission determines appropriate).

"(2) TIMING.—A consumer reporting agency shall provide a consumer report under paragraph (1) not later than 15 days after the date on which the request is received under paragraph (1).

"(3) REINVESTIGATIONS.—Notwithstanding the time periods specified in section 611(a)(1), a reinvestigation under that section by a consumer reporting agency upon a request of a consumer that is made after receiving a consumer report under this subsection shall be completed not later than 45 days after the date on which the request is received.

"(4) EXCEPTION FOR FIRST 12 MONTHS OF OPERATION.—This subsection shall not apply to a consumer reporting agency that has not been furnishing consumer reports to third parties on a continuing basis during the 12-month period preceding a request under paragraph (1), with respect to consumers residing nationwide.";

(3) by redesignating subsection (d) as subsection (e);

(4) by inserting before subsection (e), as redesignated, the following:

"(d) FREE DISCLOSURES IN CONNECTION WITH FRAUD ALERTS.—Upon the request of a consumer, a consumer reporting agency described in section 603(p) shall make all disclosures pursuant to section 609 without charge to the consumer, as provided in subsections (a)(2) and (b)(2) of section 605A, as applicable.";

(5) in subsection (e), as redesignated, by striking "subsection (a)" and inserting "subsection (f)"; and

(6) in subsection (f), as redesignated, by striking "Except as provided in subsections (b), (c), and (d), a" and inserting "In the case of a request from a consumer other than a request that is covered by any of subsections (a) through (d), a".

(b) CIRCUMVENTION PROHIBITED.—The Fair Credit Reporting Act (15 U.S.C. 1681 et seq.) is amended by adding after section 628, as added by section 216 of this Act, the following new section:

"§ 629. Corporate and technological circumvention prohibited

"The Commission shall prescribe regulations, to become effective not later than 90 days after the date of enactment of this section, to prevent a consumer reporting agency from circumventing or evading treatment as a consumer reporting agency described in section 603(p) for purposes of this title, including—

"(1) by means of a corporate reorganization or restructuring, including a merger, acquisition, dissolution, divestiture, or asset sale of a consumer reporting agency; or

"(2) by maintaining or merging public record and credit account information in a manner that is substantially equivalent to that described in paragraphs (1) and (2) of section 603(p), in the manner described in section 603(p).".

(c) SUMMARY OF RIGHTS TO OBTAIN AND DISPUTE INFORMATION IN CONSUMER REPORTS AND TO OBTAIN CREDIT SCORES.—Section 609(c) of the Fair Credit Reporting Act (15 U.S.C. 1681g) is amended to read as follows:

"(c) SUMMARY OF RIGHTS TO OBTAIN AND DISPUTE INFORMATION IN CONSUMER REPORTS AND TO OBTAIN CREDIT SCORES.—

"(1) COMMISSION SUMMARY OF RIGHTS REQUIRED.—

"(A) IN GENERAL.—The Commission shall prepare a model summary of the rights of consumers under this title.

"(B) CONTENT OF SUMMARY.—The summary of rights prepared under subparagraph (A) shall include a description of—

"(i) the right of a consumer to obtain a copy of a consumer report under subsection (a) from each consumer reporting agency;

"(ii) the frequency and circumstances under which a consumer is entitled to receive a consumer report without charge under section 612;

"(iii) the right of a consumer to dispute information in the file of the consumer under section 611;

"(iv) the right of a consumer to obtain a credit score from a consumer reporting agency, and a description of how to obtain a credit score;

"(v) the method by which a consumer can contact, and obtain a consumer report from, a consumer reporting agency without charge, as provided in the regulations of the Commission prescribed under section 211(c) of the Fair and Accurate Credit Transactions Act of 2003; and

"(vi) the method by which a consumer can contact, and obtain a consumer report from, a consumer reporting agency described in section 603(w), as provided in the regulations of the Commission prescribed under section 612(a)(1)(C).

"(C) AVAILABILITY OF SUMMARY OF RIGHTS.—The Commission shall—

"(i) actively publicize the availability of the summary of rights prepared under this paragraph;

"(ii) conspicuously post on its Internet website the availability of such summary of rights; and

"(iii) promptly make such summary of rights available to consumers, on request.

"(2) SUMMARY OF RIGHTS REQUIRED TO BE INCLUDED WITH AGENCY DISCLOSURES.—A consumer reporting agency shall provide to a consumer, with each written disclosure by the agency to the consumer under this section—

"(A) the summary of rights prepared by the Commission under paragraph (1);

"(B) in the case of a consumer reporting agency described in section 603(p), a toll-free telephone number established by the agency, at which personnel are accessible to consumers during normal business hours;

"(C) a list of all Federal agencies responsible for enforcing any provision of this title, and the address and any appropriate phone number of each such agency, in a form that will assist the consumer in selecting the appropriate agency;

"(D) a statement that the consumer may have additional rights under State law, and that the consumer may wish to contact a State or local consumer protection agency or a State attorney general (or the equivalent thereof) to learn of those rights; and

"(E) a statement that a consumer reporting agency is not required to remove accurate derogatory information from the file of a consumer, unless the information is outdated under section 605 or cannot be verified.".

(d) RULEMAKING REQUIRED.—

(1) IN GENERAL.—The Commission shall prescribe regulations applicable to consumer reporting agencies described in section 603(p) of the Fair Credit Reporting Act, to require the establishment of—

(A) a centralized source through which consumers may obtain a consumer report from each such consumer reporting agency, using a single request, and without charge to the consumer, as provided in section 612(a) of the Fair Credit Reporting Act (as amended by this section); and

(B) a standardized form for a consumer to make such a request for a consumer report by mail or through an Internet website.

(2) CONSIDERATIONS.—In prescribing regulations under paragraph (1), the Commission shall consider—

(A) the significant demands that may be placed on consumer reporting agencies in providing such consumer reports;

(B) appropriate means to ensure that consumer reporting agencies can satisfactorily meet those demands, including the efficacy of a system of staggering the availability to consumers of such consumer reports; and

(C) the ease by which consumers should be able to contact consumer reporting agencies with respect to access to such consumer reports.

(3) CENTRALIZED SOURCE.—The centralized source for a request for a consumer report from a consumer required by this subsection shall provide for—

(A) a toll-free telephone number for such purpose;

(B) use of an Internet website for such purpose; and

(C) a process for requests by mail for such purpose.

(4) TRANSITION.—The regulations of the Commission under paragraph (1) shall provide

for an orderly transition by consumer reporting agencies described in section 603(p) of the Fair Credit Reporting Act to the centralized source for consumer report distribution required by section 612(a)(1)(B), as amended by this section, in a manner that—

(A) does not temporarily overwhelm such consumer reporting agencies with requests for disclosures of consumer reports beyond their capacity to deliver; and

(B) does not deny creditors, other users, and consumers access to consumer reports on a time-sensitive basis for specific purposes, such as home purchases or suspicions of identity theft, during the transition period.

(5) TIMING.—Regulations required by this subsection shall—

(A) be issued in final form not later than 6 months after the date of enactment of this Act; and

(B) become effective not later than 6 months after the date on which they are issued in final form.

(6) SCOPE OF REGULATIONS.—

(A) IN GENERAL.—The Commission shall, by rule, determine whether to require a consumer reporting agency that compiles and maintains files on consumers on substantially a nationwide basis, other than one described in section 603(p) of the Fair Credit Reporting Act, to make free consumer reports available upon consumer request, and if so, whether such consumer reporting agencies should make such free reports available through the centralized source described in paragraph (1)(A).

(B) CONSIDERATIONS.—Before making any determination under subparagraph (A), the Commission shall consider—

(i) the number of requests for consumer reports to, and the number of consumer reports generated by, the consumer reporting agency, in comparison with consumer reporting agencies described in subsections (p) and (w) of section 603 of the Fair Credit Reporting Act;

(ii) the overall scope of the operations of the consumer reporting agency;

(iii) the needs of consumers for access to consumer reports provided by consumer reporting agencies free of charge;

(iv) the costs of providing access to consumer reports by consumer reporting agencies free of charge; and

(v) the effects on the ongoing competitive viability of such consumer reporting agencies if such free access is required.

SEC. 212. DISCLOSURE OF CREDIT SCORES.

(a) STATEMENT ON AVAILABILITY OF CREDIT SCORES.—Section 609(a) of the Fair Credit Reporting Act (15 U.S.C. 1681g(a)) is amended by adding at the end the following new paragraph:

"(6) If the consumer requests the credit file and not the credit score, a statement that the consumer may request and obtain a credit score.".

(b) DISCLOSURE OF CREDIT SCORES.—Section 609 of the Fair Credit Reporting Act (15 U.S.C. 1681g), as amended by this Act, is amended by adding at the end the following:

"(f) DISCLOSURE OF CREDIT SCORES.—

"(1) IN GENERAL.—Upon the request of a consumer for a credit score, a consumer reporting agency shall supply to the consumer a statement indicating that the information and credit scoring model may be different than the credit score that may be used by the lender, and a notice which shall include—

"(A) the current credit score of the consumer or the most recent credit score of the consumer that was previously calculated by the credit reporting agency for a purpose related to the extension of credit;

"(B) the range of possible credit scores under the model used;

"(C) all of the key factors that adversely affected the credit score of the consumer in the model used, the total number of which shall not exceed 4, subject to paragraph (9);

"(D) the date on which the credit score was created; and

"(E) the name of the person or entity that provided the credit score or credit file upon which the credit score was created.

"(2) DEFINITIONS.—For purposes of this subsection, the following definitions shall apply:

"(A) CREDIT SCORE.—The term 'credit score'—

"(i) means a numerical value or a categorization derived from a statistical tool or modeling system used by a person who makes or arranges a loan to predict the likelihood of certain credit behaviors, including default (and the numerical value or the categorization derived from such analysis may also be referred to as a 'risk predictor' or 'risk score'); and

"(ii) does not include—

"(I) any mortgage score or rating of an automated underwriting system that considers one or more factors in addition to credit information, including the loan to value ratio, the amount of down payment, or the financial assets of a consumer; or

"(II) any other elements of the underwriting process or underwriting decision.

"(B) KEY FACTORS.—The term 'key factors' means all relevant elements or reasons adversely affecting the credit score for the particular individual, listed in the order of their importance based on their effect on the credit score.

"(3) TIMEFRAME AND MANNER OF DISCLOSURE.—The information required by this subsection shall be provided in the same timeframe and manner as the information described in subsection (a).

"(4) APPLICABILITY TO CERTAIN USES.—This subsection shall not be construed so as to compel a consumer reporting agency to develop or disclose a score if the agency does not—

"(A) distribute scores that are used in connection with residential real property loans; or

"(B) develop scores that assist credit providers in understanding the general credit behavior of a consumer and predicting the future credit behavior of the consumer.

"(5) APPLICABILITY TO CREDIT SCORES DEVELOPED BY ANOTHER PERSON.—

"(A) IN GENERAL.—This subsection shall not be construed to require a consumer reporting agency that distributes credit scores developed by another person or entity to provide a further explanation of them, or to process a dispute arising pursuant to section 611, except that the consumer reporting agency shall provide the consumer with the name and address and website for contacting the person or entity who developed the score or developed the methodology of the score.

"(B) EXCEPTION.—This paragraph shall not apply to a consumer reporting agency that develops or modifies scores that are developed by another person or entity.

"(6) MAINTENANCE OF CREDIT SCORES NOT REQUIRED.—This subsection shall not be construed to require a consumer reporting agency to maintain credit scores in its files.

"(7) COMPLIANCE IN CERTAIN CASES.—In complying with this subsection, a consumer reporting agency shall—

"(A) supply the consumer with a credit score that is derived from a credit scoring model that is widely distributed to users by that consumer reporting agency in connection with residential real property loans or with a credit score that assists the consumer in understanding the credit scoring assessment of the credit behavior of the consumer and predictions about the future credit behavior of the consumer; and

"(B) a statement indicating that the information and credit scoring model may be different than that used by the lender.

"(8) FAIR AND REASONABLE FEE.—A consumer reporting agency may charge a fair and reasonable fee, as determined by the Commission, for providing the information required under this subsection.

"(9) USE OF ENQUIRIES AS A KEY FACTOR.—If a key factor that adversely affects the credit score of a consumer consists of the number of enquiries made with respect to a consumer report, that factor shall be included in the disclosure pursuant to paragraph (1)(C) without regard to the numerical limitation in such paragraph.".

(c) DISCLOSURE OF CREDIT SCORES BY CERTAIN MORTGAGE LENDERS.— Section 609 of the Fair Credit Reporting Act (15 U.S.C. 1681g), as amended by this Act, is amended by adding at the end the following:

"(g) DISCLOSURE OF CREDIT SCORES BY CERTAIN MORTGAGE LENDERS.—

"(1) IN GENERAL.—Any person who makes or arranges loans and who uses a consumer credit score, as defined in subsection (f), in connection with an application initiated or sought by a consumer for a closed end loan or the establishment of an open end loan for a consumer purpose that is secured by 1 to 4 units of residential real property (hereafter in this subsection referred to as the 'lender') shall provide the following to the consumer as soon as reasonably practicable:

"(A) INFORMATION REQUIRED UNDER SUBSECTION (f).—

"(i) IN GENERAL.—A copy of the information identified in subsection (f) that was obtained from a consumer reporting agency or was developed and used by the user of the information.

"(ii) NOTICE UNDER SUBPARAGRAPH (D).—In addition to the information provided to it by a third party that provided the credit score or scores, a lender is only required to provide the notice contained in subparagraph (D).

"(B) DISCLOSURES IN CASE OF AUTOMATED UNDERWRITING SYSTEM.—

"(i) IN GENERAL.—If a person that is subject to this subsection uses an automated underwriting system to underwrite a loan, that person may satisfy the obligation to provide a credit score by disclosing a credit score and associated key factors supplied by a consumer reporting agency.

"(ii) NUMERICAL CREDIT SCORE.—However, if a numerical credit score is generated by an automated underwriting system used by an enterprise, and that score is disclosed to the person, the score shall be disclosed to the consumer consistent with subparagraph (C).

"(iii) ENTERPRISE DEFINED.—For purposes of this subparagraph, the term 'enterprise' has the same meaning as in paragraph (6) of section 1303 of the Federal Housing Enterprises Financial Safety and Soundness Act of 1992.

"(C) DISCLOSURES OF CREDIT SCORES NOT OBTAINED FROM A CONSUMER REPORTING AGENCY.—A person that is subject to the provisions of this subsection and that uses a credit score, other than a credit score provided by a consumer reporting agency, may satisfy the obligation to provide a credit score by disclosing a credit score and associated key factors supplied by a consumer reporting agency.

"(D) NOTICE TO HOME LOAN APPLICANTS.—A copy of the following notice, which shall include the name, address, and telephone number of each consumer reporting agency providing a credit score that was used:

'NOTICE TO THE HOME LOAN APPLICANT

'In connection with your application for a home loan, the lender must disclose to you the score that a consumer reporting agency distributed to users and the lender used in connection with your home loan, and the key factors affecting your credit scores.

'The credit score is a computer generated summary calculated at the time of the request and based on information that a consumer reporting agency or lender has on file. The scores are based on data about your credit history and payment patterns. Credit scores are important because they are used to assist the lender in determining whether you will obtain a loan. They may also be used to determine what interest rate you may be offered on the mortgage. Credit scores can change over time, depending on your conduct, how your credit history and payment patterns change, and how credit scoring technologies change.

'Because the score is based on information in your credit history, it is very important that you review the credit-related information that is being furnished to make sure it is accurate. Credit records may vary from one company to another.

'If you have questions about your credit score or the credit information that is furnished to you, contact the consumer reporting agency at the address and telephone number provided with this notice, or contact the lender, if the lender developed or generated the credit score. The consumer reporting agency plays no part in the decision to take any action on the loan application and is unable to provide you with specific reasons for the decision on a loan application.

'If you have questions concerning the terms of the loan, contact the lender.'.

"(E) ACTIONS NOT REQUIRED UNDER THIS SUBSECTION.—This subsection shall not require any person to—

"(i) explain the information provided pursuant to subsection (f);

"(ii) disclose any information other than a credit score or key factors, as defined in subsection (f);

"(iii) disclose any credit score or related information obtained by the user after a loan has closed;

"(iv) provide more than 1 disclosure per loan transaction; or

"(v) provide the disclosure required by this subsection when another person has made the disclosure to the consumer for that loan transaction.

"(F) NO OBLIGATION FOR CONTENT.—

"(i) IN GENERAL.—The obligation of any person pursuant to this subsection shall be limited solely to providing a copy of the information that was received from the consumer reporting agency.

"(ii) LIMIT ON LIABILITY.—No person has liability under this subsection for the content of that information or for the omission of any information within the report provided by the consumer reporting agency.

"(G) PERSON DEFINED AS EXCLUDING ENTERPRISE.—As used in this subsection, the term 'person' does not include an enterprise (as defined in paragraph (6) of section 1303 of the Federal Housing Enterprises Financial Safety and Soundness Act of 1992).

"(2) PROHIBITION ON DISCLOSURE CLAUSES NULL AND VOID.—

"(A) IN GENERAL.—Any provision in a contract that prohibits the disclosure of a credit score by a person who makes or arranges loans or a consumer reporting agency is void.

"(B) NO LIABILITY FOR DISCLOSURE UNDER THIS SUBSECTION.—A lender shall not have liability under any contractual provision for disclosure of a credit score pursuant to this subsection.".

(d) INCLUSION OF KEY FACTOR IN CREDIT SCORE INFORMATION IN CONSUMER REPORT.—Section 605(d) of the Fair Credit Reporting Act (15 U.S.C. 1681c(d)) is amended—

(1) by striking "DISCLOSED.—Any consumer reporting agency" and inserting "DISCLOSED.—

"(1) TITLE 11 INFORMATION.—Any consumer reporting agency"; and

(2) by adding at the end the following new paragraph:

"(2) KEY FACTOR IN CREDIT SCORE INFORMATION.—Any consumer reporting agency that furnishes a consumer report that contains any credit score or any other risk score or predictor on any consumer shall include in the report a clear and conspicuous statement that a key factor (as defined in section 609(f)(2)(B)) that adversely affected such score or predictor was the number of enquiries, if such a predictor was in fact a key factor that adversely affected such score. This paragraph shall not apply to a check services company, acting as such, which issues authorizations for the purpose of approving or processing negotiable instruments, electronic fund transfers, or similar methods of payments, but only to the extent that such company is engaged in such activities.''.

(e) TECHNICAL AND CONFORMING AMENDMENTS.—Section 625(b) of the Fair Credit Reporting Act (15 U.S.C. 1681t(b)), as so designated by section 214 of this Act, is amended—

(1) by striking ''or'' at the end of paragraph (2); and
(2) by striking paragraph (3) and inserting the following:
''(3) with respect to the disclosures required to be made under subsection (c), (d), (e), or (g) of section 609, or subsection (f) of section 609 relating to the disclosure of credit scores for credit granting purposes, except that this paragraph—
''(A) shall not apply with respect to sections 1785.10, 1785.16, and 1785.20.2 of the California Civil Code (as in effect on the date of enactment of the Fair and Accurate Credit Transactions Act of 2003) and section 1785.15 through section 1785.15.2 of such Code (as in effect on such date);
''(B) shall not apply with respect to sections 5-3-106(2) and 212-14.3-104.3 of the Colorado Revised Statutes (as in effect on the date of enactment of the Fair and Accurate Credit Transactions Act of 2003); and
''(C) shall not be construed as limiting, annulling, affecting, or superseding any provision of the laws of any State regulating the use in an insurance activity, or regulating disclosures concerning such use, of a credit-based insurance score of a consumer by any person engaged in the business of insurance;
''(4) with respect to the frequency of any disclosure under section 612(a), except that this paragraph shall not apply—
''(A) with respect to section 12-14.3-105(1)(d) of the Colorado Revised Statutes (as in effect on the date of enactment of the Fair and Accurate Credit Transactions Act of 2003);
''(B) with respect to section 10-1-393(29)(C) of the Georgia Code (as in effect on the date of enactment of the Fair and Accurate Credit Transactions Act of 2003);
''(C) with respect to section 1316.2 of title 10 of the Maine Revised Statutes (as in effect on the date of enactment of the Fair and Accurate Credit Transactions Act of 2003);
''(D) with respect to sections 14-1209(a)(1) and 14-1209(b)(1)(i) of the Commercial Law Article of the Code of Maryland (as in effect on the date of enactment of the Fair and Accurate Credit Transactions Act of 2003);
''(E) with respect to section 59(d) and section 59(e) of chapter 93 of the General Laws of Massachusetts (as in effect on the date of enactment of the Fair and Accurate Credit Transactions Act of 2003);
''(F) with respect to section 56:11-37.10(a)(1) of the New Jersey Revised Statutes (as in effect on the date of enactment of the Fair and Accurate Credit Transactions Act of 2003); or
''(G) with respect to section 2480c(a)(1) of title 9 of the Vermont Statutes Annotated (as in effect on the date of enactment of the Fair and Accurate Credit Transactions Act of 2003); or''.

SEC. 213. ENHANCED DISCLOSURE OF THE MEANS AVAILABLE TO OPT OUT OF PRESCREENED LISTS.

(a) NOTICE AND RESPONSE FORMAT FOR USERS OF REPORTS.—Section 615(d)(2) of the Fair Credit Reporting Act (15 U.S.C. 1681m(d)(2)) is amended to read as follows:

''(2) DISCLOSURE OF ADDRESS AND TELEPHONE NUMBER; FORMAT.—A statement under paragraph (1) shall—
(A) include the address and toll-free telephone number of the appropriate notification

system established under section 604(e); and

"(B) be presented in such format and in such type size and manner as to be simple and easy to understand, as established by the Commission, by rule, in consultation with the Federal banking agencies and the National Credit Union Administration.".

(b) RULEMAKING SCHEDULE.—Regulations required by section 615(d)(2) of the Fair Credit Reporting Act, as amended by this section, shall be issued in final form not later than 1 year after the date of enactment of this Act.

(c) DURATION OF ELECTIONS.—Section 604(e) of the Fair Credit Reporting Act (15 U.S.C. 1681b(e)) is amended in each of paragraphs (3)(A) and (4)(B)(i), by striking "2-year period" each place that term appears and inserting "5-year period".

(d) PUBLIC AWARENESS CAMPAIGN.—The Commission shall actively publicize and conspicuously post on its website any address and the toll-free telephone number established as part of a notification system for opting out of prescreening under section 604(e) of the Fair Credit Reporting Act (15 U.S.C. 1681b(e)), and otherwise take measures to increase public awareness regarding the availability of the right to opt out of prescreening.

(e) ANALYSIS OF FURTHER RESTRICTIONS ON OFFERS OF CREDIT OR INSURANCE.—

(1) IN GENERAL.—The Board shall conduct a study of—

(A) the ability of consumers to avoid receiving written offers of credit or insurance in connection with transactions not initiated by the consumer; and

(B) the potential impact that any further restrictions on providing consumers with such written offers of credit or insurance would have on consumers.

(2) REPORT.—The Board shall submit a report summarizing the results of the study required under paragraph (1) to the Congress not later than 12 months after the date of enactment of this Act, together with such recommendations for legislative or administrative action as the Board may determine to be appropriate.

(3) CONTENT OF REPORT.—The report described in paragraph (2) shall address the following issues:

(A) The current statutory or voluntary mechanisms that are available to a consumer to notify lenders and insurance providers that the consumer does not wish to receive written offers of credit or insurance.

(B) The extent to which consumers are currently utilizing existing statutory and voluntary mechanisms to avoid receiving offers of credit or insurance.

(C) The benefits provided to consumers as a result of receiving written offers of credit or insurance.

(D) Whether consumers incur significant costs or are otherwise adversely affected by the receipt of written offers of credit or insurance.

(E) Whether further restricting the ability of lenders and insurers to provide written offers of credit or insurance to consumers would affect—

(i) the cost consumers pay to obtain credit or insurance;

(ii) the availability of credit or insurance;

(iii) consumers' knowledge about new or alternative products and services;

(iv) the ability of lenders or insurers to compete with one another; and

(v) the ability to offer credit or insurance products to consumers who have been traditionally underserved.

SEC. 214. AFFILIATE SHARING.

(a) LIMITATION.—The Fair Credit Reporting Act (15 U.S.C. 1601 et seq.) is amended—

(1) by redesignating sections 624 (15 U.S.C. 1681t), 625 (15 U.S.C. 1681u), and 626 (15 U.S.C. 6181v) as sections 625, 626, and 627, respectively; and

(2) by inserting after section 623 the following:

"§ 624. Affiliate sharing

"(a) SPECIAL RULE FOR SOLICITATION FOR PURPOSES OF MARKETING.—

"(1) NOTICE.—Any person that receives from another person related to it by common ownership or affiliated by corporate control a communication of information that would be a consumer report, but for clauses (i), (ii), and (iii) of section 603(d)(2)(A), may not use the information to make a solicitation for marketing purposes to a consumer about its products or services, unless—

"(A) it is clearly and conspicuously disclosed to the consumer that the information may be communicated among such persons for purposes of making such solicitations to the consumer; and

"(B) the consumer is provided an opportunity and a simple method to prohibit the making of such solicitations to the consumer by such person.

"(2) CONSUMER CHOICE.—

"(A) IN GENERAL.—The notice required under paragraph (1) shall allow the consumer the opportunity to prohibit all solicitations referred to in such paragraph, and may allow the consumer to choose from different options when electing to prohibit the sending of such solicitations, including options regarding the types of entities and information covered, and which methods of delivering solicitations the consumer elects to prohibit.

"(B) FORMAT.—Notwithstanding subparagraph (A), the notice required under paragraph (1) shall be clear, conspicuous, and concise, and any method provided under paragraph (1)(B) shall be simple. The regulations prescribed to implement this section shall provide specific guidance regarding how to comply with such standards.

"(3) DURATION.—

"(A) IN GENERAL.—The election of a consumer pursuant to paragraph (1)(B) to prohibit the making of solicitations shall be effective for at least 5 years, beginning on the date on which the person receives the election of the consumer, unless the consumer requests that such election be revoked.

"(B) NOTICE UPON EXPIRATION OF EFFECTIVE PERIOD.—At such time as the election of a consumer pursuant to paragraph (1)(B) is no longer effective, a person may not use information that the person receives in the manner described in paragraph (1) to make any solicitation for marketing purposes to the consumer, unless the consumer receives a notice and an opportunity, using a simple method, to extend the opt-out for another period of at least 5 years, pursuant to the procedures described in paragraph (1).

"(4) SCOPE.—This section shall not apply to a person—

"(A) using information to make a solicitation for marketing purposes to a consumer with whom the person has a pre-existing business relationship;

"(B) using information to facilitate communications to an individual for whose benefit the person provides employee benefit or other services pursuant to a contract with an employer related to and arising out of the current employment relationship or status of the individual as a participant or beneficiary of an employee benefit plan;

"(C) using information to perform services on behalf of another person related by common ownership or affiliated by corporate control, except that this subparagraph shall not be construed as permitting a person to send solicitations on behalf of another person, if such other person would not be permitted to send the solicitation on its own behalf as a result of the election of the consumer to prohibit solicitations under paragraph (1)(B);

"(D) using information in response to a communication initiated by the consumer;

"(E) using information in response to solicitations authorized or requested by the consumer; or

"(F) if compliance with this section by that person would prevent compliance by that person with any provision of State insurance laws pertaining to unfair discrimination in any State in which the person is lawfully doing business.

"(5) NO RETROACTIVITY.—This subsection shall not prohibit the use of information to send a solicitation to a consumer if such information was received prior to the date on which persons are required to comply with regulations implementing this subsection.

"(b) NOTICE FOR OTHER PURPOSES PERMISSIBLE.—A notice or other disclosure under this section may be coordinated and consolidated with any other notice required to be issued under any other provision of law by a person that is subject to this section, and a notice or other disclosure that is equivalent to the notice required by subsection (a), and that is provided by a person described in subsection (a) to a consumer together with disclosures required by any other provision of law, shall satisfy the requirements of subsection (a).

"(c) USER REQUIREMENTS.—Requirements with respect to the use by a person of information received from another person related to it by common ownership or affiliated by corporate control, such as the requirements of this section, constitute requirements with respect to the exchange of information among persons affiliated by common ownership or common corporate control, within the meaning of section 625(b)(2).

"(d) DEFINITIONS.—For purposes of this section, the following definitions shall apply:

"(1) PRE-EXISTING BUSINESS RELATIONSHIP.—The term 'pre-existing business relationship' means a relationship between a person, or a person's licensed agent, and a consumer, based on—

"(A) a financial contract between a person and a consumer which is in force;

"(B) the purchase, rental, or lease by the consumer of that person's goods or services, or a financial transaction (including holding an active account or a policy in force or having another continuing relationship) between the consumer and that person during the 18-month period immediately preceding the date on which the consumer is sent a solicitation covered by this section;

"(C) an inquiry or application by the consumer regarding a product or service offered by that person, during the 3-month period immediately preceding the date on which the consumer is sent a solicitation covered by this section; or

"(D) any other pre-existing customer relationship defined in the regulations implementing this section.

"(2) SOLICITATION.—The term 'solicitation' means the marketing of a product or service initiated by a person to a particular consumer that is based on an exchange of information described in subsection (a), and is intended to encourage the consumer to purchase such product or service, but does not include communications that are directed at the general public or determined not to be a solicitation by the regulations prescribed under this section.".

(b) RULEMAKING REQUIRED.—

(1) IN GENERAL.—The Federal banking agencies, the National Credit Union Administration, and the Commission, with respect to the entities that are subject to their respective enforcement authority under section 621 of the Fair Credit Reporting Act and the Securities and Exchange Commission, and in coordination as described in paragraph (2), shall prescribe regulations to implement section 624 of the Fair Credit Reporting Act, as added by this section.

(2) COORDINATION.—Each agency required to prescribe regulations under paragraph (1) shall consult and coordinate with each other such agency so that, to the extent possible, the regulations prescribed by each such entity are consistent and comparable with the regulations prescribed by each other such agency.

(3) CONSIDERATIONS.—In promulgating regulations under this subsection, each agency referred to in paragraph (1) shall—

(A) ensure that affiliate sharing notification methods provide a simple means for consumers to make determinations and choices under section 624 of the Fair Credit Reporting Act, as added by this section;

(B) consider the affiliate sharing notification practices employed on the date of enactment of this Act by persons that will be subject to that section 624; and

(C) ensure that notices and disclosures may be coordinated and consolidated, as provided in subsection (b) of that section 624.

(4) TIMING.—Regulations required by this subsection shall—

(A) be issued in final form not later than 9 months after the date of enactment of this Act; and

(B) become effective not later than 6 months after the date on which they are issued in final form.

(c) TECHNICAL AND CONFORMING AMENDMENTS.—

(1) DEFINITIONS.—Section 603(d)(2)(A) of the Fair Credit Reporting Act (15 U.S.C. 1681(d)(2)(A)) is amended by inserting "subject to section 624," after "(A)".

(2) RELATION TO STATE LAWS.—Section 625(b)(1) of the Fair Credit Reporting Act (15 U.S.C. 1681t(b)(1)), as so designated by subsection (a) of this section, is amended—

(A) by striking "or" after the semicolon at the end of subparagraph (E); and

(B) by adding at the end the following new subparagraph:

"(H) section 624, relating to the exchange and use of information to make a solicitation for marketing purposes; or".

(3) CROSS REFERENCE CORRECTION.—Section 627(d) of the Fair Credit Reporting Act (15 U.S.C. 1681v(d)), as so designated by subsection (a) of this section, is amended by striking "section 625" and inserting "section 626".

(4) TABLE OF SECTIONS.—The table of sections for title VI of the Consumer Credit Protection Act (15 U.S.C. 1601 et seq.) is amended by striking the items relating to sections 624 through 626 and inserting the following:

"624. Affiliate sharing.

"625. Relation to State laws.

"626. Disclosures to FBI for counterintelligence purposes.

"627. Disclosures to governmental agencies for counterintelligence purposes.".

(e) STUDIES OF INFORMATION SHARING PRACTICES.—

(1) IN GENERAL.—The Federal banking agencies, the National Credit Union Administration, and the Commission shall jointly conduct regular studies of the consumer information sharing practices by financial institutions and other persons that are creditors or users of consumer reports with their affiliates.

(2) MATTERS FOR STUDY.—In conducting the studies required by paragraph (1), the agencies described in paragraph (1) shall—

(A) identify—

(i) the purposes for which financial institutions and other creditors and users of consumer reports share consumer information;

(ii) the types of information shared by such entities with their affiliates;

(iii) the number of choices provided to consumers with respect to the control of such sharing, and the degree to and manner in which consumers exercise such choices, if at all; and

(iv) whether such entities share or may share personally identifiable transaction or experience information with affiliates for purposes—

(I) that are related to employment or hiring, including whether the person that is the subject of such information is given notice of such sharing, and the specific uses of such shared information; or

(II) of general publication of such information; and

(B) specifically examine the information sharing practices that financial institutions and other creditors and users of consumer reports and their affiliates employ for the purpose of making underwriting decisions or credit evaluations of consumers.

(3) REPORTS.—

(A) INITIAL REPORT.—Not later than 3 years after the date of enactment of this Act, the Federal banking agencies, the National Credit Union Administration, and the Commission shall jointly submit a report to the Congress on the results of the initial study conducted in accordance with this subsection, together with any recommendations for legislative or regulatory action.

(B) FOLLOWUP REPORTS.—The Federal banking agencies, the National Credit Union Administration, and the Commission shall, not less frequently than once every 3 years following the date of submission of the initial report under subparagraph (A), jointly submit a report to the Congress that, together with any recommendations for legislative or regulatory action—

(i) documents any changes in the areas of study referred to in paragraph (2)(A) occurring since the date of submission of the previous report;

(ii) identifies any changes in the practices of financial institutions and other creditors and users of consumer reports in sharing consumer information with their affiliates for the purpose of making underwriting decisions or credit evaluations of consumers occurring since the date of submission of the previous report; and

(iii) examines the effects that changes described in clause (ii) have had, if any, on the degree to which such affiliate sharing practices reduce the need for financial institutions, creditors, and other users of consumer reports to rely on consumer reports for such decisions.

SEC. 215. STUDY OF EFFECTS OF CREDIT SCORES AND CREDIT-BASED INSURANCE SCORES ON AVAILABILITY AND AFFORDABILITY OF FINANCIAL PRODUCTS.

(a) STUDY REQUIRED.—The Commission and the Board, in consultation with the Office of Fair Housing and Equal Opportunity of the Department of Housing and Urban Development, shall conduct a study of—

(1) the effects of the use of credit scores and credit-based insurance scores on the availability and affordability of financial products and services, including credit cards, mortgages, auto loans, and property and casualty insurance;

(2) the statistical relationship, utilizing a multivariate analysis that controls for prohibited factors under the Equal Credit Opportunity Act and other known risk factors, between credit scores and credit-based insurance scores and the quantifiable risks and actual losses experienced by businesses;

(3) the extent to which, if any, the use of credit scoring models, credit scores, and credit-based insurance scores impact on the availability and affordability of credit and insurance to the extent information is currently available or is available through proxies, by geography, income, ethnicity, race, color, religion, national origin, age, sex, marital status, and creed, including the extent to which the consideration or lack of consideration of certain factors by credit scoring systems could result in negative or differential treatment of protected classes under the Equal Credit Opportunity Act, and the extent to which, if any, the use of underwriting systems relying on these models could achieve comparable results through the use of factors with less negative impact; and

(4) the extent to which credit scoring systems are used by businesses, the factors considered by such systems, and the effects of variables which are not considered by such systems.

(b) PUBLIC PARTICIPATION.—The Commission shall seek public input about the prescribed methodology and research design of the study described in subsection (a), including from relevant Federal regulators, State insurance regulators, community, civil rights, consumer, and housing groups.

(c) REPORT REQUIRED.—

(1) IN GENERAL.—Before the end of the 24-month period beginning on the date of enactment of this Act, the Commission shall submit a detailed report on the study conducted pursuant to subsection (a) to the Committee on Financial Services of the House

of Representatives and the Committee on Banking, Housing, and Urban Affairs of the Senate.

(2) CONTENTS OF REPORT.—The report submitted under paragraph (1) shall include the findings and conclusions of the Commission, recommendations to address specific areas of concerns addressed in the study, and recommendations for legislative or administrative action that the Commission may determine to be necessary to ensure that credit and credit-based insurance scores are used appropriately and fairly to avoid negative effects.

SEC. 216. DISPOSAL OF CONSUMER REPORT INFORMATION AND RECORDS.

(a) IN GENERAL.—The Fair Credit Reporting Act (15 U.S.C. 1681 et seq.), as amended by this Act, is amended by adding at the end the following:

"**§ 628. Disposal of records**

"(a) REGULATIONS.—

"(1) IN GENERAL.—Not later than 1 year after the date of enactment of this section, the Federal banking agencies, the National Credit Union Administration, and the Commission with respect to the entities that are subject to their respective enforcement authority under section 621, and the Securities and Exchange Commission, and in coordination as described in paragraph (2), shall issue final regulations requiring any person that maintains or otherwise possesses consumer information, or any compilation of consumer information, derived from consumer reports for a business purpose to properly dispose of any such information or compilation.

"(2) COORDINATION.—Each agency required to prescribe regulations under paragraph (1) shall—

"(A) consult and coordinate with each other such agency so that, to the extent possible, the regulations prescribed by each such agency are consistent and comparable with the regulations by each such other agency; and

"(B) ensure that such regulations are consistent with the requirements and regulations issued pursuant to Public Law 106-102 and other provisions of Federal law.

"(3) EXEMPTION AUTHORITY.—In issuing regulations under this section, the Federal banking agencies, the National Credit Union Administration, the Commission, and the Securities and Exchange Commission may exempt any person or class of persons from application of those regulations, as such agency deems appropriate to carry out the purpose of this section.

"(b) RULE OF CONSTRUCTION.—Nothing in this section shall be construed—

"(1) to require a person to maintain or destroy any record pertaining to a consumer that is not imposed under other law; or

"(2) to alter or affect any requirement imposed under any other provision of law to maintain or destroy such a record.".

(b) CLERICAL AMENDMENT.—The table of sections for title VI of the Consumer Credit Protection Act (15 U.S.C. 1601 et seq.) is amended by inserting after the item relating to section 627, as added by section 214 of this Act, the following:

"628. Disposal of records.
"629. Corporate and technological circumvention prohibited.".

SEC. 217. REQUIREMENT TO DISCLOSE COMMUNICATIONS TO A CONSUMER REPORTING AGENCY.

(a) IN GENERAL.—Section 623(a) of the Fair Credit Reporting Act (15 U.S.C. 1681s-2(a)) as amended by this Act, is amended by inserting after paragraph (6), the following new paragraph:

"(7) NEGATIVE INFORMATION.—
"(A) NOTICE TO CONSUMER REQUIRED.—
"(i) IN GENERAL.—If any financial institution that extends credit and regularly and in the ordinary course of business furnishes information to a consumer reporting agency described in section 603(p) furnishes negative information to such an agency regarding credit extended to a customer, the financial institution shall provide a notice of such furnishing of negative information, in writing, to the customer.
"(ii) NOTICE EFFECTIVE FOR SUBSEQUENT SUBMISSIONS.—After providing such notice, the financial institution may submit additional negative information to a consumer reporting agency described in section 603(p) with respect to the same transaction, extension of credit, account, or customer without providing additional notice to the customer.
"(B) TIME OF NOTICE.—
"(i) IN GENERAL.—The notice required under subparagraph (A) shall be provided to the customer prior to, or no later than 30 days after, furnishing the negative information to a consumer reporting agency described in section 603(p).
"(ii) COORDINATION WITH NEW ACCOUNT DISCLOSURES.—If the notice is provided to the customer prior to furnishing the negative information to a consumer reporting agency, the notice may not be included in the initial disclosures provided under section 127(a) of the Truth in Lending Act.
"(C) COORDINATION WITH OTHER DISCLOSURES.—The notice required under subparagraph (A)—
"(i) may be included on or with any notice of default, any billing statement, or any other materials provided to the customer; and
"(ii) must be clear and conspicuous.
"(D) MODEL DISCLOSURE.—
"(i) DUTY OF BOARD TO PREPARE.—The Board shall prescribe a brief model disclosure a financial institution may use to comply with subparagraph (A), which shall not exceed 30 words.
"(ii) USE OF MODEL NOT REQUIRED.—No provision of this paragraph shall be construed as requiring a financial institution to use any such model form prescribed by the Board.
"(iii) COMPLIANCE USING MODEL.—A financial institution shall be deemed to be in compliance with subparagraph (A) if the financial institution uses any such model form prescribed by the Board, or the financial institution uses any such model form and rearranges its format.
"(E) USE OF NOTICE WITHOUT SUBMITTING NEGATIVE INFORMATION.—No provision of this paragraph shall be construed as requiring a financial institution that has provided a customer with a notice described in subparagraph (A) to furnish negative information about the customer to a consumer reporting agency.
"(F) SAFE HARBOR.—A financial institution shall not be liable for failure to perform the duties required by this paragraph if, at the time of the failure, the financial institution maintained reasonable policies and procedures to comply with this paragraph or the financial institution reasonably believed that the institution is prohibited, by law, from contacting the consumer.
"(G) DEFINITIONS.—For purposes of this paragraph, the following definitions shall apply:
"(i) NEGATIVE INFORMATION.—The term 'negative information' means information concerning a customer's delinquencies, late payments, insolvency, or any form of default.
"(ii) CUSTOMER; FINANCIAL INSTITUTION.—The terms 'customer' and 'financial institution' have the same meanings as in section 509 Public Law 106-102.".
(b) MODEL DISCLOSURE FORM.—Before the end of the 6-month period beginning on the date of enactment of this Act, the Board shall adopt the model disclosure required under the amendment made by subsection (a) after notice duly given in the Federal Register and an opportunity for public comment in accordance with section 553 of title 5, United States Code.

TITLE III—ENHANCING THE ACCURACY OF CONSUMER REPORT INFORMATION

311. RISK-BASED PRICING NOTICE.

DUTIES OF USERS.—Section 615 of the Fair Credit Reporting Act (15 U.S.C. 1681m), as amended by this Act, is amended by adding at the end the following:

(h) DUTIES OF USERS IN CERTAIN CREDIT TRANSACTIONS.—

"(1) IN GENERAL.—Subject to rules prescribed as provided in paragraph (6), if any person uses a consumer report in connection with an application for, or a grant, extension, or other provision of, credit on material terms that are materially less favorable than the most favorable terms available to a substantial proportion of consumers from or through that person, based in whole or in part on a consumer report, the person shall provide an oral, written, or electronic notice to the consumer in the form and manner required by regulations prescribed in accordance with this subsection.

"(2) TIMING.—The notice required under paragraph (1) may be provided at the time of an application for, or a grant, extension, or other provision of, credit or the time of communication of an approval of an application for, or grant, extension, or other provision of, credit, except as provided in the regulations prescribed under paragraph (6).

"(3) EXCEPTIONS.—No notice shall be required from a person under this subsection if—

(A) the consumer applied for specific material terms and was granted those terms, unless those terms were initially specified by the person after the transaction was initiated by the consumer and after the person obtained a consumer report; or

"(B) the person has provided or will provide a notice to the consumer under subsection (a) in connection with the transaction.

"(4) OTHER NOTICE NOT SUFFICIENT.—A person that is required to provide a notice under subsection (a) cannot meet that requirement by providing a notice under this subsection.

"(5) CONTENT AND DELIVERY OF NOTICE.—A notice under this subsection shall, at a minimum—

"(A) include a statement informing the consumer that the terms offered to the consumer are set based on information from a consumer report;

"(B) identify the consumer reporting agency furnishing the report;

"(C) include a statement informing the consumer that the consumer may obtain a copy of a consumer report from that consumer reporting agency without charge; and

"(D) include the contact information specified by that consumer reporting agency for obtaining such consumer reports (including a toll-free telephone number established by the agency in the case of a consumer reporting agency described in section 603(p)).

"(6) RULEMAKING.—

"(A) RULES REQUIRED.—The Commission and the Board shall jointly prescribe rules.

"(B) CONTENT.—Rules required by subparagraph (A) shall address, but are not limited to—

"(i) the form, content, time, and manner of delivery of any notice under this subsection;

"(ii) clarification of the meaning of terms used in this subsection, including what credit terms are material, and when credit terms are materially less favorable;

"(iii) exceptions to the notice requirement under this subsection for classes of persons or transactions regarding which the agencies determine that notice would not significantly benefit consumers;

"(iv) a model notice that may be used to comply with this subsection; and

"(v) the timing of the notice required under paragraph (1), including the circumstances under which the notice must be provided after the terms offered to the consumer were set based on information from a consumer report.

"(7) COMPLIANCE.—A person shall not be liable for failure to perform the duties required by this section if, at the time of the failure, the person maintained reasonable policies and procedures to comply with this section.

"(8) ENFORCEMENT.—

"(A) NO CIVIL ACTIONS.—Sections 616 and 617 shall not apply to any failure by any person to comply with this section.

"(B) ADMINISTRATIVE ENFORCEMENT.—This section shall be enforced exclusively under section 621 by the Federal agencies and officials identified in that section.".

(b) RELATION TO STATE LAWS.—Section 625(b)(1) of the Fair Credit Reporting Act (15 U.S.C. 1681t(b)(1)), as so designated by section 214 of this Act, is amended by adding at the end the following:

"(I) section 615(h), relating to the duties of users of consumer reports to provide notice with respect to terms in certain credit transactions;".

SEC. 312. PROCEDURES TO ENHANCE THE ACCURACY AND INTEGRITY OF INFORMATION FURNISHED TO CONSUMER REPORTING AGENCIES.

(a) ACCURACY GUIDELINES AND REGULATIONS.—Section 623 of the Fair Credit Reporting Act (15 U.S.C. 1681s-2) is amended by adding at the end the following:

"(e) ACCURACY GUIDELINES AND REGULATIONS REQUIRED.—

"(1) GUIDELINES.—The Federal banking agencies, the National Credit Union Administration, and the Commission shall, with respect to the entities that are subject to their respective enforcement authority under section 621, and in coordination as described in paragraph (2)—

"(A) establish and maintain guidelines for use by each person that furnishes information to a consumer reporting agency regarding the accuracy and integrity of the information relating to consumers that such entities furnish to consumer reporting agencies, and update such guidelines as often as necessary; and

"(B) prescribe regulations requiring each person that furnishes information to a consumer reporting agency to establish reasonable policies and procedures for implementing the guidelines established pursuant to subparagraph (A).

"(2) COORDINATION.—Each agency required to prescribe regulations under paragraph (1) shall consult and coordinate with each other such agency so that, to the extent possible, the regulations prescribed by each such entity are consistent and comparable with the regulations prescribed by each other such agency.

"(3) CRITERIA.—In developing the guidelines required by paragraph (1)(A), the agencies described in paragraph (1) shall—

"(A) identify patterns, practices, and specific forms of activity that can compromise the accuracy and integrity of information furnished to consumer reporting agencies;

"(B) review the methods (including technological means) used to furnish information relating to consumers to consumer reporting agencies;

"(C) determine whether persons that furnish information to consumer reporting agencies maintain and enforce policies to assure the accuracy and integrity of information furnished to consumer reporting agencies; and

"(D) examine the policies and processes that persons that furnish information to consumer reporting agencies employ to conduct reinvestigations and correct inaccurate information relating to consumers that has been furnished to consumer reporting agencies.".

(b) DUTY OF FURNISHERS TO PROVIDE ACCURATE INFORMATION.—Section 623(a)(1) of the Fair Credit Reporting Act (15 U.S.C. 1681s-2(a)(1)) is amended—

(1) in subparagraph (A), by striking "knows or consciously avoids knowing that the information is inaccurate" and inserting "knows or has reasonable cause to believe that the information is inaccurate"; and

(2) by adding at the end the following:

"(D) DEFINITION.—For purposes of subparagraph (A), the term 'reasonable cause to believe that the information is inaccurate' means having specific knowledge, other than solely allegations by the consumer, that would cause a reasonable person to have substantial doubts about the accuracy of the information.".

(c) ABILITY OF CONSUMER TO DISPUTE INFORMATION DIRECTLY WITH FURNISHER.—Section 623(a) of the Fair Credit Reporting Act (15 U.S.C. 1681s-2(a)), as amended by this Act, is amended by adding at the end the following:

"(8) ABILITY OF CONSUMER TO DISPUTE INFORMATION DIRECTLY WITH FURNISHER.—

"(A) IN GENERAL.—The Federal banking agencies, the National Credit Union Administration, and the Commission shall jointly prescribe regulations that shall identify the circumstances under which a furnisher shall be required to reinvestigate a dispute concerning the accuracy of information contained in a consumer report on the consumer, based on a direct request of a consumer.

"(B) CONSIDERATIONS.—In prescribing regulations under subparagraph (A), the agencies shall weigh—

"(i) the benefits to consumers with the costs on furnishers and the credit reporting system;

"(ii) the impact on the overall accuracy and integrity of consumer reports of any such requirements;

"(iii) whether direct contact by the consumer with the furnisher would likely result in the most expeditious resolution of any such dispute; and

"(iv) the potential impact on the credit reporting process if credit repair organizations, as defined in section 403(3), including entities that would be a credit repair organization, but for section 403(3)(B)(i), are able to circumvent the prohibition in subparagraph (G).

"(C) APPLICABILITY.—Subparagraphs (D) through (G) shall apply in any circumstance identified under the regulations promulgated under subparagraph (A).

"(D) SUBMITTING A NOTICE OF DISPUTE.—A consumer who seeks to dispute the accuracy of information shall provide a dispute notice directly to such person at the address specified by the person for such notices that—

"(i) identifies the specific information that is being disputed;

"(ii) explains the basis for the dispute; and

"(iii) includes all supporting documentation required by the furnisher to substantiate the basis of the dispute.

"(E) DUTY OF PERSON AFTER RECEIVING NOTICE OF DISPUTE.—After receiving a notice of dispute from a consumer pursuant to subparagraph (D), the person that provided the information in dispute to a consumer reporting agency shall—

"(i) conduct an investigation with respect to the disputed information;

"(ii) review all relevant information provided by the consumer with the notice;

"(iii) complete such person's investigation of the dispute and report the results of the investigation to the consumer before the expiration of the period under section 611(a)(1) within which a consumer reporting agency would be required to complete its action if the consumer had elected to dispute the information under that section; and

"(iv) if the investigation finds that the information reported was inaccurate, promptly notify each consumer reporting agency to which the person furnished the inaccurate information of that determination and provide to the agency any correction to that information that is necessary to make the information provided by the person accurate.

"(F) FRIVOLOUS OR IRRELEVANT DISPUTE.—

"(i) IN GENERAL.—This paragraph shall not apply if the person receiving a notice of a dispute from a consumer reasonably determines that the dispute is frivolous or irrelevant, including—

"(I) by reason of the failure of a consumer to provide sufficient information to investigate the disputed information; or

"(II) the submission by a consumer of a dispute that is substantially the same as a dispute previously submitted by or for the consumer, either directly to the person or through a consumer reporting agency under subsection (b), with respect to which the person has already performed the person's duties under this paragraph or subsection (b), as applicable.

"(ii) NOTICE OF DETERMINATION.—Upon making any determination under clause (i) that a dispute is frivolous or irrelevant, the person shall notify the consumer of such determination not later than 5 business days after making such determination, by mail or, if authorized by the consumer for that purpose, by any other means available to the person.

"(iii) CONTENTS OF NOTICE.—A notice under clause (ii) shall include—

"(I) the reasons for the determination under clause (i); and

"(II) identification of any information required to investigate the disputed information, which may consist of a standardized form describing the general nature of such information.

"(G) EXCLUSION OF CREDIT REPAIR ORGANIZATIONS.—This paragraph shall not apply if the notice of the dispute is submitted by, is prepared on behalf of the consumer by, or is submitted on a form supplied to the consumer by, a credit repair organization, as defined in section 403(3), or an entity that would be a credit repair organization, but for section 403(3)(B)(i).".

(d) FURNISHER LIABILITY EXCEPTION.—Section 623(a)(5) of the Fair Credit Reporting Act (15 U.S.C. 1681s-2(a)(5)) is amended—

(1) by striking "A person" and inserting the following:

"(A) IN GENERAL.—A person";

(2) by inserting "date of delinquency on the account, which shall be the" before "month";

(3) by inserting "on the account" before "that immediately preceded"; and

(4) by adding at the end the following:

"(B) RULE OF CONSTRUCTION.—For purposes of this paragraph only, and provided that the consumer does not dispute the information, a person that furnishes information on a delinquent account that is placed for collection, charged for profit or loss, or subjected to any similar action, complies with this paragraph, if—

"(i) the person reports the same date of delinquency as that provided by the creditor to which the account was owed at the time at which the commencement of the delinquency occurred, if the creditor previously reported that date of delinquency to a consumer reporting agency;

"(ii) the creditor did not previously report the date of delinquency to a consumer reporting agency, and the person establishes and follows reasonable procedures to obtain the date of delinquency from the creditor or another reliable source and reports that date to a consumer reporting agency as the date of delinquency; or

"(iii) the creditor did not previously report the date of delinquency to a consumer reporting agency and the date of delinquency cannot be reasonably obtained as provided in clause (ii), the person establishes and follows reasonable procedures to ensure the date reported as the date of delinquency precedes the date on which the account is placed for collection, charged to profit or loss, or subjected to any similar action, and reports such date to the credit reporting agency.".

(e) LIABILITY AND ENFORCEMENT.—

(1) CIVIL LIABILITY.—Section 623 of the Fair Credit Reporting Act (15 U.S.C. 1681s-2) is amended by striking subsections (c) and (d) and inserting the following:

"(c) LIMITATION ON LIABILITY.—Except as provided in section 621(c)(1)(B), sections 616 and 617 do not apply to any violation of—
   "(1) subsection (a) of this section, including any regulations issued thereunder;
   "(2) subsection (e) of this section, except that nothing in this paragraph shall limit, expand, or otherwise affect liability under section 616 or 617, as applicable, for violations of subsection (b) of this section; or
   "(3) subsection (e) of section 615.
"(d) LIMITATION ON ENFORCEMENT.—The provisions of law described in paragraphs (1) through (3) of subsection (c) (other than with respect to the exception described in paragraph (2) of subsection (c)) shall be enforced exclusively as provided under section 621 by the Federal agencies and officials and the State officials identified in section 621.".
(2) STATE ACTIONS.—Section 621(c) of the Fair Credit Reporting Act (15 U.S.C. 1681s(c)) is amended—
   (A) in paragraph (1)(B)(ii), by striking "of section 623(a)" and inserting "described in any of paragraphs (1) through (3) of section 623(c)"; and
   (B) in paragraph (5)—
      (i) in each of subparagraphs (A) and (B), by striking "of section 623(a)(1)" each place that term appears and inserting "described in any of paragraphs (1) through (3) of section 623(c)"; and
      (ii) by amending the paragraph heading to read as follows:
"(5) LIMITATIONS ON STATE ACTIONS FOR CERTAIN VIOLATIONS.—".

(f) RULE OF CONSTRUCTION.—Nothing in this section, the amendments made by this section, or any other provision of this Act shall be construed to affect any liability under section 616 or 617 of the Fair Credit Reporting Act (15 U.S.C. 1681n, 1681o) that existed on the day before the date of enactment of this Act.

SEC. 313. FTC AND CONSUMER REPORTING AGENCY ACTION CONCERNING COMPLAINTS.

(a) IN GENERAL.—Section 611 of the Fair Credit Reporting Act (15 U.S.C. 1681i) is amended by adding at the end the following:

"(e) TREATMENT OF COMPLAINTS AND REPORT TO CONGRESS.—
   "(1) IN GENERAL.—The Commission shall—
      "(A) compile all complaints that it receives that a file of a consumer that is maintained by a consumer reporting agency described in section 603(p) contains incomplete or inaccurate information, with respect to which, the consumer appears to have disputed the completeness or accuracy with the consumer reporting agency or otherwise utilized the procedures provided by subsection (a); and
      "(B) transmit each such complaint to each consumer reporting agency involved.
   "(2) EXCLUSION.—Complaints received or obtained by the Commission pursuant to its investigative authority under the Federal Trade Commission Act shall not be subject to paragraph (1).
   "(3) AGENCY RESPONSIBILITIES.—Each consumer reporting agency described in section 603(p) that receives a complaint transmitted by the Commission pursuant to paragraph (1) shall—
      "(A) review each such complaint to determine whether all legal obligations imposed on the consumer reporting agency under this title (including any obligation imposed by an applicable court or administrative order) have been met with respect to the subject matter of the complaint;
      "(B) provide reports on a regular basis to the Commission regarding the determinations of and actions taken by the consumer reporting agency, if any, in connection with its review of such complaints; and
      "(C) maintain, for a reasonable time period, records regarding the disposition of each such complaint that is sufficient to demonstrate compliance with this subsection.

"(4) RULEMAKING AUTHORITY.—The Commission may prescribe regulations, as appropriate to implement this subsection.

"(5) ANNUAL REPORT.—The Commission shall submit to the Committee on Banking, Housing, and Urban Affairs of the Senate and the Committee on Financial Services of the House of Representatives an annual report regarding information gathered by the Commission under this subsection.".

(b) PROMPT INVESTIGATION OF DISPUTED CONSUMER INFORMATION.—

(1) STUDY REQUIRED.—The Board and the Commission shall jointly study the extent to which, and the manner in which, consumer reporting agencies and furnishers of consumer information to consumer reporting agencies are complying with the procedures, time lines, and requirements under the Fair Credit Reporting Act for the prompt investigation of the disputed accuracy of any consumer information, the completeness of the information provided to consumer reporting agencies, and the prompt correction or deletion, in accordance with such Act, of any inaccurate or incomplete information or information that cannot be verified.

(2) REPORT REQUIRED.—Before the end of the 12-month period beginning on the date of enactment of this Act, the Board and the Commission shall jointly submit a progress report to the Congress on the results of the study required under paragraph (1).

(3) CONSIDERATIONS.—In preparing the report required under paragraph (2), the Board and the Commission shall consider information relating to complaints compiled by the Commission under section 611(e) of the Fair Credit Reporting Act, as added by this section.

(4) RECOMMENDATIONS.—The report required under paragraph (2) shall include such recommendations as the Board and the Commission jointly determine to be appropriate for legislative or administrative action, to ensure that—

(A) consumer disputes with consumer reporting agencies over the accuracy or completeness of information in a consumer's file are promptly and fully investigated and any incorrect, incomplete, or unverifiable information is corrected or deleted immediately thereafter;

(B) furnishers of information to consumer reporting agencies maintain full and prompt compliance with the duties and responsibilities established under section 623 of the Fair Credit Reporting Act; and

(C) consumer reporting agencies establish and maintain appropriate internal controls and management review procedures for maintaining full and continuous compliance with the procedures, time lines, and requirements under the Fair Credit Reporting Act for the prompt investigation of the disputed accuracy of any consumer information and the prompt correction or deletion, in accordance with such Act, of any inaccurate or incomplete information or information that cannot be verified.

SEC. 314. IMPROVED DISCLOSURE OF THE RESULTS OF REINVESTIGATION.

(a) IN GENERAL.—Section 611(a)(5)(A) of the Fair Credit Reporting Act (15 U.S.C. 1681i(a)(5)(A)) is amended by striking "shall" and all that follows through the end of the subparagraph, and inserting the following: "shall—

"(i) promptly delete that item of information from the file of the consumer, or modify that item of information, as appropriate, based on the results of the reinvestigation; and

"(ii) promptly notify the furnisher of that information that the information has been modified or deleted from the file of the consumer.".

(b) FURNISHER REQUIREMENTS RELATING TO INACCURATE, INCOMPLETE, OR UNVERIFIABLE INFORMATION.—Section 623(b)(1) of the Fair Credit Reporting Act (15 U.S.C. 1681s–2(b)(1)) is amended—

(1) in subparagraph (C), by striking "and" at the end; and

(2) in subparagraph (D), by striking the period at the end and inserting the following: "; and

"(E) if an item of information disputed by a consumer is found to be inaccurate or incomplete or cannot be verified after any reinvestigation under paragraph (1), for purposes of reporting to a consumer reporting agency only, as appropriate, based on the results of the reinvestigation promptly—

"(i) modify that item of information;

"(ii) delete that item of information; or

"(iii) permanently block the reporting of that item of information.".

SEC. 315. RECONCILING ADDRESSES.

Section 605 of the Fair Credit Reporting Act (15 U.S.C. 1681c), as amended by this Act, is amended by adding at the end the following:

"(h) NOTICE OF DISCREPANCY IN ADDRESS.—

"(1) IN GENERAL.—If a person has requested a consumer report relating to a consumer from a consumer reporting agency described in section 603(p), the request includes an address for the consumer that substantially differs from the addresses in the file of the consumer, and the agency provides a consumer report in response to the request, the consumer reporting agency shall notify the requester of the existence of the discrepancy.

"(2) REGULATIONS.—

"(A) REGULATIONS REQUIRED.—The Federal banking agencies, the National Credit Union Administration, and the Commission shall jointly, with respect to the entities that are subject to their respective enforcement authority under section 621, prescribe regulations providing guidance regarding reasonable policies and procedures that a user of a consumer report should employ when such user has received a notice of discrepancy under paragraph (1).

"(B) POLICIES AND PROCEDURES TO BE INCLUDED.—The regulations prescribed under subparagraph (A) shall describe reasonable policies and procedures for use by a user of a consumer report—

"(i) to form a reasonable belief that the user knows the identity of the person to whom the consumer report pertains; and

"(ii) if the user establishes a continuing relationship with the consumer, and the user regularly and in the ordinary course of business furnishes information to the consumer reporting agency from which the notice of discrepancy pertaining to the consumer was obtained, to reconcile the address of the consumer with the consumer reporting agency by furnishing such address to such consumer reporting agency as part of information regularly furnished by the user for the period in which the relationship is established.".

SEC. 316. NOTICE OF DISPUTE THROUGH RESELLER.

(a) REQUIREMENT FOR REINVESTIGATION OF DISPUTED INFORMATION UPON NOTICE FROM A RESELLER.—Section 611(a) of the Fair Credit Reporting Act (15 U.S.C. 1681i(a)(1)(A)) is amended—

(1) in paragraph (1)(A)—

(A) by striking "If the completeness" and inserting "Subject to subsection (f), if the completeness";

(B) by inserting ", or indirectly through a reseller," after "notifies the agency directly"; and

(C) by inserting "or reseller" before the period at the end;

(2) in paragraph (2)(A)—

(A) by inserting "or a reseller" after "dispute from any consumer"; and

(B) by inserting "or reseller" before the period at the end; and

(3) in paragraph (2)(B), by inserting "or the reseller" after "from the consumer".

(b) REINVESTIGATION REQUIREMENT APPLICABLE TO RESELLERS.—Section 611 of the Fair Credit Reporting Act (15 U.S.C. 1681i), as amended by this Act, is amended by adding at the end the following:

"(f) REINVESTIGATION REQUIREMENT APPLICABLE TO RESELLERS.—

"(1) EXEMPTION FROM GENERAL REINVESTIGATION REQUIREMENT.—Except as provided in paragraph (2), a reseller shall be exempt from the requirements of this section.

"(2) ACTION REQUIRED UPON RECEIVING NOTICE OF A DISPUTE.—If a reseller receives a notice from a consumer of a dispute concerning the completeness or accuracy of any item of information contained in a consumer report on such consumer produced by the reseller, the reseller shall, within 5 business days of receiving the notice, and free of charge—

"(A) determine whether the item of information is incomplete or inaccurate as a result of an act or omission of the reseller; and

"(B) if—

"(i) the reseller determines that the item of information is incomplete or inaccurate as a result of an act or omission of the reseller, not later than 20 days after receiving the notice, correct the information in the consumer report or delete it; or

"(ii) if the reseller determines that the item of information is not incomplete or inaccurate as a result of an act or omission of the reseller, convey the notice of the dispute, together with all relevant information provided by the consumer, to each consumer reporting agency that provided the reseller with the information that is the subject of the dispute, using an address or a notification mechanism specified by the consumer reporting agency for such notices.

"(3) RESPONSIBILITY OF CONSUMER REPORTING AGENCY TO NOTIFY CONSUMER THROUGH RESELLER.—Upon the completion of a reinvestigation under this section of a dispute concerning the completeness or accuracy of any information in the file of a consumer by a consumer reporting agency that received notice of the dispute from a reseller under paragraph (2)—

"(A) the notice by the consumer reporting agency under paragraph (6), (7), or (8) of subsection (a) shall be provided to the reseller in lieu of the consumer; and

"(B) the reseller shall immediately reconvey such notice to the consumer, including any notice of a deletion by telephone in the manner required under paragraph (8)(A).

"(4) RESELLER REINVESTIGATIONS.—No provision of this subsection shall be construed as prohibiting a reseller from conducting a reinvestigation of a consumer dispute directly.".

(c) TECHNICAL AND CONFORMING AMENDMENT.—Section 611(a)(2)(B) of the Fair Credit Reporting Act (15 U.S.C. 1681i(a)(2)(B)) is amended in the subparagraph heading, by striking "FROM CONSUMER".

SEC. 317. REASONABLE REINVESTIGATION REQUIRED.

Section 611(a)(1)(A) of the Fair Credit Reporting Act (15 U.S.C. 1681i(a)(1)(A)) is amended by striking "shall reinvestigate free of charge" and inserting "shall, free of charge, conduct a reasonable reinvestigation to determine whether the disputed information is inaccurate".

SEC. 318. FTC STUDY OF ISSUES RELATING TO THE FAIR CREDIT REPORTING ACT.

(a) STUDY REQUIRED.—

(1) IN GENERAL.—The Commission shall conduct a study on ways to improve the operation of the Fair Credit Reporting Act.

(2) AREAS FOR STUDY.—In conducting the study under paragraph (1), the Commission shall review—

(A) the efficacy of increasing the number of points of identifying information that a credit reporting agency is required to match to ensure that a consumer is the correct individual to whom a consumer report relates before releasing a consumer report to a user, including—

(i) the extent to which requiring additional points of such identifying information to match would—

(I) enhance the accuracy of credit reports; and

(II) combat the provision of incorrect consumer reports to users;

(ii) the extent to which requiring an exact match of the first and last name, social security number, and address and ZIP Code of the consumer would enhance the likelihood of increasing credit report accuracy; and

(iii) the effects of allowing consumer reporting agencies to use partial matches of social security numbers and name recognition software on the accuracy of credit reports;

(B) requiring notification to consumers when negative information has been added to their credit reports, including—

(i) the potential impact of such notification on the ability of consumers to identify errors on their credit reports; and

(ii) the potential impact of such notification on the ability of consumers to remove fraudulent information from their credit reports;

(C) the effects of requiring that a consumer who has experienced an adverse action based on a credit report receives a copy of the same credit report that the creditor relied on in taking the adverse action, including—

(i) the extent to which providing such reports to consumers would increase the ability of consumers to identify errors in their credit reports; and

(ii) the extent to which providing such reports to consumers would increase the ability of consumers to remove fraudulent information from their credit reports;

(D) any common financial transactions that are not generally reported to the consumer reporting agencies, but would provide useful information in determining the credit worthiness of consumers; and

(E) any actions that might be taken within a voluntary reporting system to encourage the reporting of the types of transactions described in subparagraph (D).

(3) COSTS AND BENEFITS.—With respect to each area of study described in paragraph (2), the Commission shall consider the extent to which such requirements would benefit consumers, balanced against the cost of implementing such provisions.

(b) REPORT REQUIRED.—Not later than 1 year after the date of enactment of this Act, the chairman of the Commission shall submit a report to the Committee on Banking, Housing, and Urban Affairs of the Senate and the Committee on Financial Services of the House of Representatives containing a detailed summary of the findings and conclusions of the study under this section, together with such recommendations for legislative or administrative actions as may be appropriate.

SEC. 319. FTC STUDY OF THE ACCURACY OF CONSUMER REPORTS.

(a) STUDY REQUIRED.—Until the final report is submitted under subsection (b)(2), the Commission shall conduct an ongoing study of the accuracy and completeness of information contained in consumer reports prepared or maintained by consumer reporting agencies and methods for improving the accuracy and completeness of such information.

(b) BIENNIAL REPORTS REQUIRED.—

(1) INTERIM REPORTS.—The Commission shall submit an interim report to the Congress on the study conducted under subsection (a) at the end of the 1-year period beginning on the date of enactment of this Act and biennially thereafter for 8 years.

(2) FINAL REPORT.—The Commission shall submit a final report to the Congress on the study conducted under subsection (a) at the end of the 2-year period beginning on the date on which the final interim report is submitted to the Congress under paragraph (1).

(3) CONTENTS.—Each report submitted under this subsection shall contain a detailed summary of the findings and conclusions of the Commission with respect to the study required under subsection (a) and such recommendations for legislative and administrative action as the Commission may determine to be appropriate.

TITLE IV—LIMITING THE USE AND SHARING OF MEDICAL INFORMATION IN THE FINANCIAL SYSTEM

SEC. 411. PROTECTION OF MEDICAL INFORMATION IN THE FINANCIAL SYSTEM.

(a) IN GENERAL.—Section 604(g) of the Fair Credit Reporting Act (15 U.S.C. 1681b(g)) is amended to read as follows:

"(g) PROTECTION OF MEDICAL INFORMATION.—

"(1) LIMITATION ON CONSUMER REPORTING AGENCIES.—A consumer reporting agency shall not furnish for employment purposes, or in connection with a credit or insurance transaction, a consumer report that contains medical information about a consumer, unless—

"(A) if furnished in connection with an insurance transaction, the consumer affirmatively consents to the furnishing of the report;

"(B) if furnished for employment purposes or in connection with a credit transaction—

"(i) the information to be furnished is relevant to process or effect the employment or credit transaction; and

"(ii) the consumer provides specific written consent for the furnishing of the report that describes in clear and conspicuous language the use for which the information will be furnished; or

"(C) the information to be furnished pertains solely to transactions, accounts, or balances relating to debts arising from the receipt of medical services, products, or devises, where such information, other than account status or amounts, is restricted or reported using codes that do not identify, or do not provide information sufficient to infer, the specific provider or the nature of such services, products, or devices, as provided in section 605(a)(6).

"(2) LIMITATION ON CREDITORS.—Except as permitted pursuant to paragraph (3)(C) or regulations prescribed under paragraph (5)(A), a creditor shall not obtain or use medical information pertaining to a consumer in connection with any determination of the consumer's eligibility, or continued eligibility, for credit.

"(3) ACTIONS AUTHORIZED BY FEDERAL LAW, INSURANCE ACTIVITIES AND REGULATORY DETERMINATIONS.—Section 603(d)(3) shall not be construed so as to treat information or any communication of information as a consumer report if the information or communication is disclosed—

"(A) in connection with the business of insurance or annuities, including the activities described in section 18B of the model Privacy of Consumer Financial and Health Information Regulation issued by the National Association of Insurance Commissioners (as in effect on January 1, 2003);

"(B) for any purpose permitted without authorization under the Standards for Individually Identifiable Health Information promulgated by the Department of Health and Human Services pursuant to the Health Insurance Portability and Accountability

Act of 1996, or referred to under section 1179 of such Act, or described in section 502(e) of Public Law 106-102; or

"(C) as otherwise determined to be necessary and appropriate, by regulation or order and subject to paragraph (6), by the Commission, any Federal banking agency or the National Credit Union Administration (with respect to any financial institution subject to the jurisdiction of such agency or Administration under paragraph (1), (2), or (3) of section 621(b), or the applicable State insurance authority (with respect to any person engaged in providing insurance or annuities).

"(4) LIMITATION ON REDISCLOSURE OF MEDICAL INFORMATION.—Any person that receives medical information pursuant to paragraph (1) or (3) shall not disclose such information to any other person, except as necessary to carry out the purpose for which the information was initially disclosed, or as otherwise permitted by statute, regulation, or order.

"(5) REGULATIONS AND EFFECTIVE DATE FOR PARAGRAPH (2).—

"(A) REGULATIONS REQUIRED.—Each Federal banking agency and the National Credit Union Administration shall, subject to paragraph (6) and after notice and opportunity for comment, prescribe regulations that permit transactions under paragraph (2) that are determined to be necessary and appropriate to protect legitimate operational, transactional, risk, consumer, and other needs (and which shall include permitting actions necessary for administrative verification purposes), consistent with the intent of paragraph (2) to restrict the use of medical information for inappropriate purposes.

"(B) FINAL REGULATIONS REQUIRED.—The Federal banking agencies and the National Credit Union Administration shall issue the regulations required under subparagraph (A) in final form before the end of the 6-month period beginning on the date of enactment of the Fair and Accurate Credit Transactions Act of 2003.

"(6) COORDINATION WITH OTHER LAWS.—No provision of this subsection shall be construed as altering, affecting, or superseding the applicability of any other provision of Federal law relating to medical confidentiality.".

(b) RESTRICTION ON SHARING OF MEDICAL INFORMATION.—Section 603(d) of the Fair Credit Reporting Act (15 U.S.C. 1681a(d)) is amended—

(1) in paragraph (2), by striking "The term" and inserting "Except as provided in paragraph (3), the term"; and

(2) by adding at the end the following new paragraph:

"(3) RESTRICTION ON SHARING OF MEDICAL INFORMATION.—Except for information or any communication of information disclosed as provided in section 604(g)(3), the exclusions in paragraph (2) shall not apply with respect to information disclosed to any person related by common ownership or affiliated by corporate control, if the information is—

"(A) medical information;

"(B) an individualized list or description based on the payment transactions of the consumer for medical products or services; or

"(C) an aggregate list of identified consumers based on payment transactions for medical products or services.".

(c) DEFINITION.—Section 603(i) of the Fair Credit Reporting Act (15 U.S.C. 1681a(i)) is amended to read as follows:

"(i) MEDICAL INFORMATION.—The term 'medical information'—

"(1) means information or data, whether oral or recorded, in any form or medium, created by or derived from a health care provider or the consumer, that relates to—

"(A) the past, present, or future physical, mental, or behavioral health or condition of an individual;

"(B) the provision of health care to an individual; or

"(C) the payment for the provision of health care to an individual.

"(2) does not include the age or gender of a consumer, demographic information about the consumer, including a consumer's residence address or e- mail address, or any other information about a consumer that does not relate to the physical, mental, or behavioral health or condition of a consumer, including the existence or value of any insurance policy.".

(d) EFFECTIVE DATES.—This section shall take effect at the end of the 180-day period beginning on the date of enactment of this Act, except that paragraph (2) of section 604(g) of the Fair Credit Reporting Act (as amended by subsection (a) of this section) shall take effect on the later of—

(1) the end of the 90-day period beginning on the date on which the regulations required under paragraph (5)(B) of such section 604(g) are issued in final form; or

(2) the date specified in the regulations referred to in paragraph (1).

SEC. 412. CONFIDENTIALITY OF MEDICAL CONTACT INFORMATION IN CONSUMER REPORTS.

(a) DUTIES OF MEDICAL INFORMATION FURNISHERS.—Section 623(a) of the Fair Credit Reporting Act (15 U.S.C. 1681s-2(a)), as amended by this Act, is amended by adding at the end the following:

"(9) DUTY TO PROVIDE NOTICE OF STATUS AS MEDICAL INFORMATION FURNISHER.—A person whose primary business is providing medical services, products, or devices, or the person's agent or assignee, who furnishes information to a consumer reporting agency on a consumer shall be considered a medical information furnisher for purposes of this title, and shall notify the agency of such status.".

(b) RESTRICTION OF DISSEMINATION OF MEDICAL CONTACT INFORMATION.—Section 605(a) of the Fair Credit Reporting Act (15 U.S.C. 1681c(a)) is amended by adding at the end the following:

"(6) The name, address, and telephone number of any medical information furnisher that has notified the agency of its status, unless—

"(A) such name, address, and telephone number are restricted or reported using codes that do not identify, or provide information sufficient to infer, the specific provider or the nature of such services, products, or devices to a person other than the consumer; or

"(B) the report is being provided to an insurance company for a purpose relating to engaging in the business of insurance other than property and casualty insurance.".

(c) NO EXCEPTIONS ALLOWED FOR DOLLAR AMOUNTS.—Section 605(b) of the Fair Credit Reporting Act (15 U.S.C. 1681c(b)) is amended by striking "The provisions of subsection (a)" and inserting "The provisions of paragraphs (1) through (5) of subsection (a)".

(d) COORDINATION WITH OTHER LAWS.—No provision of any amendment made by this section shall be construed as altering, affecting, or superseding the applicability of any other provision of Federal law relating to medical confidentiality.

(e) FTC REGULATION OF CODING OF TRADE NAMES.—Section 621 of the Fair Credit Reporting Act (15 U.S.C. 1681s), as amended by this Act, is amended by adding at the end the following:

"(g) FTC REGULATION OF CODING OF TRADE NAMES.—If the Commission determines that a person described in paragraph (9) of section 623(a) has not met the requirements of such paragraph, the Commission shall take action to ensure the person's compliance with such paragraph, which may include issuing model guidance or prescribing reasonable policies and procedures, as necessary to ensure that such person complies with such paragraph.".

(f) TECHNICAL AND CONFORMING AMENDMENTS.—Section 604(g) of the Fair Credit Reporting Act (15 U.S.C. 1681b(g)), as amended by section 411 of this Act, is amended—

(1) in paragraph (1), by inserting "(other than medical contact information treated in the manner required under section 605(a)(6))" after "a consumer report that contains medical information"; and

(2) in paragraph (2), by inserting "(other than medical information treated in the manner required under section 605(a)(6))" after "a creditor shall not obtain or use medical information".

(g) EFFECTIVE DATE.—The amendments made by this section shall take effect at the end of the 15-month period beginning on the date of enactment of this Act.

[*ED. NOTE: Title V-Financial Literacy and Education Improvement OMITTED*]

TITLE VI—PROTECTING EMPLOYEE MISCONDUCT INVESTIGATIONS

SEC. 611. CERTAIN EMPLOYEE INVESTIGATION COMMUNICATIONS EXCLUDED FROM DEFINITION OF CONSUMER REPORT.

(a) IN GENERAL.—Section 603 of the Fair Credit Reporting Act (15 U.S.C. 1681a), as amended by this Act is amended by adding at the end the following:

"(x) EXCLUSION OF CERTAIN COMMUNICATIONS FOR EMPLOYEE INVESTIGATIONS.—

"(1) COMMUNICATIONS DESCRIBED IN THIS SUBSECTION.—A communication is described in this subsection if—

"(A) but for subsection (d)(2)(D), the communication would be a consumer report;

"(B) the communication is made to an employer in connection with an investigation of—

"(i) suspected misconduct relating to employment; or

"(ii) compliance with Federal, State, or local laws and regulations, the rules of a self-regulatory organization, or any preexisting written policies of the employer;

"(C) the communication is not made for the purpose of investigating a consumer's credit worthiness, credit standing, or credit capacity; and

"(D) the communication is not provided to any person except—

"(i) to the employer or an agent of the employer;

"(ii) to any Federal or State officer, agency, or department, or any officer, agency, or department of a unit of general local government;

"(iii) to any self-regulatory organization with regulatory authority over the activities of the employer or employee;

"(iv) as otherwise required by law; or

"(v) pursuant to section 608.

"(2) SUBSEQUENT DISCLOSURE.—After taking any adverse action based in whole or in part on a communication described in paragraph (1), the employer shall disclose to the consumer a summary containing the nature and substance of the communication upon which the adverse action is based, except that the sources of information acquired solely for use in preparing what would be but for subsection (d)(2)(D) an investigative consumer report need not be disclosed.

"(3) SELF-REGULATORY ORGANIZATION DEFINED.—For purposes of this subsection, the term 'self-regulatory organization' includes any self-regulatory organization (as defined in section 3(a)(26) of the Securities Exchange Act of 1934), any entity established under title I of the Sarbanes-Oxley Act of 2002, any board of trade designated by the Commodity Futures Trading Commission, and any futures association registered with such Commission.".

(b) TECHNICAL AND CONFORMING AMENDMENT.—Section 603(d)(2)(D) of the Fair Credit Reporting Act (15 U.S.C. 1681a(d)(2)(D)) is amended by inserting "or (x)" after "subsection (o)".

TITLE VII—RELATION TO STATE LAWS

SEC. 711. RELATION TO STATE LAWS.

Section 625 of the Fair Credit Reporting Act (15 U.S.C. 1681t), as so designated by section 214 of this Act, is amended—

(1) in subsection (a), by inserting "or for the prevention or mitigation of identity theft," after "information on consumers,";
(2) in subsection (b), by adding at the end the following:
"(5) with respect to the conduct required by the specific provisions of—
"(A) section 605(g);
"(B) section 605A;
"(C) section 605B;
"(D) section 609(a)(1)(A);
"(E) section 612(a);
"(F) subsections (e), (f), and (g) of section 615;
"(G) section 621(f);
"(H) section 623(a)(6); or
"(I) section 628.'; and
(3) in subsection (d)—
(A) by striking paragraph (2);
(B) by striking "(c)—" and all that follows through "do not affect" and inserting "(c) do not affect"; and
(C) by striking "1996; and" and inserting "1996.".

TITLE VIII—MISCELLANEOUS

SEC. 811. CLERICAL AMENDMENTS.

(a) SHORT TITLE.—Section 601 of the Fair Credit Reporting Act (15 U.S.C. 1601 note) is amended by striking "the Fair Credit Reporting Act." and inserting "the 'Fair Credit Reporting Act'.".

(b) Section 604—Section 604(a) of the Fair Credit Reporting Act (15 U.S.C. 1681b(a)) is amended in paragraphs (1) through (5), other than subparagraphs (E) and (F) of paragraph (3), by moving each margin 2 ems to the right.

(c) Section 605—
(1) Section 605(a)(1) of the Fair Credit Reporting Act (15 U.S.C. 1681c(a)(1)) is amended by striking "(1) cases" and inserting "(1) Cases".
(2)(A) Section 5(1) of Public Law 105-347 (112 Stat. 3211) is amended by striking "Judgments which" and inserting "judgments which".
(B) The amendment made by subparagraph (A) shall be deemed to have the same effective date as section 5(1) of Public Law 105-347 (112 Stat. 3211).

(d) Section 609—Section 609(a) of the Fair Credit Reporting Act (15 U.S.C. 1681g(a)) is amended—

(1) in paragraph (2), by moving the margin 2 ems to the right; and

(2) in paragraph (3)(C), by moving the margins 2 ems to the left.

(e) Section 617—Section 617(a)(1) of the Fair Credit Reporting Act (15 U.S.C. 1681o(a)(1)) is amended by adding "and" at the end.

(f) Section 621—Section 621(b)(1)(B) of the Fair Credit Reporting Act (15 U.S.C. 1681s(b)(1)(B)) is amended by striking "25(a)" and inserting "25A".

(g) Title 31—Section 5318 of title 31, United States Code, is amended by redesignating the second item designated as subsection (l) (relating to applicability of rules) as subsection (m).

(h) CONFORMING AMENDMENT.—Section 2411(c) of Public Law 104-208 (110 Stat. 3009-445) is repealed.

A.2.4 Regulation on Effective Date of FACTA Amendments

A.2.4.1 Joint Interim Final Rules

68 Fed. Reg. 74467 (Dec. 24, 2003)

FEDERAL RESERVE SYSTEM

12 CFR Part 222

FEDERAL TRADE COMMISSION

16 CFR Part 602

[Regulation V; Docket No. R–1172]

RIN 3084–AA94 Project No. P044804

Effective Dates for the Fair and Accurate Credit Transactions Act of 2003

AGENCIES: Board of Governors of the Federal Reserve System (Board) and Federal Trade Commission (FTC).

ACTION: Joint interim final rules.

SUMMARY: The recently enacted Fair and Accurate Credit Transactions Act of 2003 (FACT Act or the Act) requires the Board and the FTC (the Agencies) jointly to adopt rules establishing the effective dates for provisions of the Act that do not contain specific effective dates. The Agencies are taking two related actions to comply with this requirement. In this action, the Agencies are jointly adopting interim final rules that establish December 31, 2003, as the effective date for provisions of the Act that determine the relationship between the Fair Credit Reporting Act (FCRA) and state laws and provisions that authorize rulemakings or other implementing action by various agencies. In the second action, published elsewhere in today's **Federal Register**, the Agencies jointly propose rules establishing a schedule of effective dates for other provisions of the FACT Act.

DATES: Comments must be submitted on or before January 12, 2004. The Agencies' interim final rules are effective on December 31, 2003.

ADDRESSES: Because the Agencies will jointly review all of the comments submitted, interested parties may send comments to either of the Agencies and need not send comments (or copies) to both of the Agencies. Because paper mail in the Washington area and at the Agencies is subject to delay, please consider submitting your comments by e-mail. Commenters are encouraged to use the title "Interim Final Rules for the FACT Act" to facilitate the organization and distribution of comments among the Agencies. Interested parties are invited to submit written comments to:

Board of Governors of the Federal Reserve System: Comments should refer to Docket No. R–1172 and may be mailed to Ms. Jennifer J. Johnson, Secretary, Board of Governors of the Federal Reserve System, 20th Street and Constitution Avenue, NW., Washington, DC 20551. Please consider submitting your comments by e-mail to *regs.comments@federalreserve.gov,* or faxing them to the Office of the Secretary at (202) 452–3819 or (202) 452–3102. Members of the public may inspect comments in Room MP–500 between 9 a.m. and 5 p.m. on weekdays pursuant to section 261.12, except as provided in section 261.14, of the Board's Rules Regarding Availability of Information, 12 CFR 261.12 and 261.14.

Federal Trade Commission: Comments should refer to "Interim Final Rules for the FACT Act, Project No. P044804." Comments filed in paper form should be mailed or delivered to: Federal Trade Commission/Office of the Secretary, Room 159–H, 600 Pennsylvania Avenue, NW., Washington, DC 20580. Comments filed in electronic form (in ASCII format, WordPerfect, or Microsoft Word) should be sent to: *FACTAdates@ftc.gov.* If the comment contains any material for which confidential treatment is requested, it must be filed in paper (rather than electronic) form, and the first page of the document must be clearly labeled "Confidential."[1] Regardless of the form in which they are filed, the Commission will consider all timely comments, and will make the comments available (with confidential material redacted) for public inspection and copying at the Commission's principal office and on the Commission Web site at *http://www.ftc.gov.* As a matter of discretion, the Commission makes every effort to remove home contact information for individuals from the public comments it receives before placing those comments on the FTC Web site.

FOR FURTHER INFORMATION CONTACT:

---
[1] Commission Rule 4.2(d), 16 CFR 4.2(d). The comment must also be accompanied by an explicit request for confidential treatment, including the factual and legal basis for the request, and must identify the specific portions of the comment to be withheld from the public record. The request will be granted or denied by the Commission's General Counsel, consistent with applicable law and the public interest. *See* Commission Rule 4.9(c), 16 CFR 4.9(c).

Board: Thomas E. Scanlon, Counsel, Legal Division, (202) 452–3594; David A. Stein, Counsel, Minh-Duc T. Le, Ky Tran-Trong, Senior Attorneys, Krista P. DeLargy, Attorney, Division of Consumer and Community Affairs, (202) 452–3667 or (202) 452–2412; for users of Telecommunications Device for the Deaf ("TDD") only, contact (202) 263–4869.

FTC: Christopher Keller or Katherine Armstrong, Attorneys, Division of Financial Practices, (202) 326–3224.

SUPPLEMENTARY INFORMATION: Congress enacted the FACT Act, which the President signed into law on December 4, 2003. Pub. L. 108–159, 117 Stat. 1952. In general, the Act amends the FCRA to enhance the ability of consumers to combat identity theft, to increase the accuracy of consumer reports, and to allow consumers to exercise greater control regarding the type and amount of marketing solicitations they receive. The FACT Act also restricts the use and disclosure of sensitive medical information that is contained in a consumer report. To bolster efforts to improve financial literacy among consumers, title V of the Act (entitled the "Financial Literacy and Education Improvement Act") creates a new Financial Literacy and Education Commission empowered to take appropriate actions to improve the financial literacy and education programs, grants, and materials of the Federal government. Lastly, to promote increasingly efficient national credit markets, the FACT Act establishes uniform national standards in key areas of regulation regarding consumer report information.

The Act includes effective dates for many of its sections that vary to take account of the need for rulemaking, implementation efforts by industry, and other policy concerns. Section 3 of the FACT Act requires the Agencies to prescribe joint regulations establishing an effective date for each provision of the Act for which the Act itself does not specifically provide an effective date. The FACT Act requires that the Agencies jointly adopt final rules establishing the effective dates within two months of the date of enactment of the Act. The Act also provides that each of these effective dates must be "as early as possible, while allowing a reasonable time for the implementation" of that provision, but in no case later than ten months after the date of issuance of the Agencies' joint final rules establishing the effective dates for the Act (117 Stat. 1953).

The Agencies are jointly adopting these interim final rules that establish December 31, 2003, as the effective date for section 711 and certain other provisions of the Act that establish the relationship between the FCRA and state laws, as well as for the provisions that authorize rulemaking and other agency action under the FACT Act. In a separate notice published in conjunction with this action, the Agencies are jointly proposing regulations that establish effective dates for the other applicable provisions of the FACT Act. As noted above, the Agencies must complete these effective date rules by February 4, 2004.

The Administrative Procedure Act (APA) (5 U.S.C. 551 *et seq.*) generally requires an agency to publish a notice of a proposed rule and afford interested persons an opportunity to participate in the rulemaking by providing comments prior to promulgation of the rule. The requirement for providing notice of the proposed rule and an opportunity for public comment do not apply "when the agency for good cause finds (and incorporates the finding and a brief statement of reasons therefore in the rules issued) that notice and public procedure thereon are impracticable, unnecessary, or contrary to the public interest." Correspondingly, a rule may not be made effective less than thirty days after publication, unless as otherwise provided by the agency for good cause found and published with the rule.[2]

The current FCRA contains provisions that preempt state laws in seven areas governed by the FCRA. Under section 624(d)(2) of the FCRA, these provisions expire on January 1, 2004.[3] One of the central aims of the FACT Act is to eliminate this so-called sunset provision and make permanent the current preemption provisions and add others.[4] In these interim final rules, the Agencies are establishing December 31, 2003, as the effective date for section 711 of the FACT Act, which amends section 624(d)(2) of the FCRA, as well as for sections 151(a)(2), 212(e), 214(c), and 311(b) of the FACT Act, each of which similarly determines the relationship of state laws to areas governed by the FCRA.

The Agencies believe that there is good cause for adopting these rules as interim final rules effective without advance public comment or delay. As noted above, the current preemption provisions in the FCRA expire on January 1, 2004. Delaying final action on these provisions of the FACT Act would undermine the purpose of these provisions and is likely to provoke substantial confusion about the applicability of some state laws in areas that Congress has determined should be governed by uniform nationwide standards. Adopting these rules in final form on an interim basis also will have the effect of preserving the current state of the law while comment is received. Implementing these interim final rules is consistent with the statutory directive to act quickly and to "establish effective dates that are as early as possible."

Certain provisions of the Act require one or more agencies to undertake an action or rulemaking within a specified period of time after enactment of the Act. For example, section 213(b) states that the Commission's regulations implementing that section "shall be issued in final form not later than 1 year after the date of enactment of this Act." The Agencies have determined that no joint regulations under section 3 of the FACT Act are required to make these provisions effective. The Agencies believe that, in these cases, Congress has specified the date of enactment as the lawful effective date because that is the predicate for mandating that an agency action be performed within a specified period of time after the date of enactment.

There are, however, several sections of the Act that do not specify the period for rulemaking or other action. To address this, the Agencies' interim final rules establish December 31, 2003, as the effective date for each provision of the FACT Act that authorizes an agency, without establishing an implementation date, to issue a regulation or to take other action to implement the Act or the applicable provision of the FCRA, as amended by the FACT Act. The Agencies believe that there is good cause for adopting these rules in final form on an interim basis without advance public comment or delay. Establishing an early effective date for these regulatory provisions would allow the agencies to begin immediately to perform their responsibilities under the FACT Act. The Agencies note that this section of the interim final rules applies only to the provisions of the FACT Act without effective dates that relate to an agency's authority to issue a regulation or to take other action to implement the Act. These interim final rules do not affect the substantive provisions of the FACT Act implemented by an agency rule. The substantive provisions of the Act become effective as provided in the Act, as provided in the Agencies joint effective date rules, or as provided by the substantive rules promulgated by the agencies, as appropriate.

---

[2] 5 U.S.C. 553(b)(3)(B) and (d)(3).
[3] 15 U.S.C. 1681t(d)(2).
[4] See, *e.g.*, S. Rep. No. 108–166 (2003) at 10–11, 25.

Accordingly, the Agencies find good cause for adopting these rules as interim final rules effective on December 31, 2003.

To allow for public participation and assure that these interim rules are appropriate, the Agencies invite comment on the interim final rules and on the Agencies' findings. Based on comments received, the Agencies may adjust the effective date of a section governed by the interim final rules as necessary.

Regulatory Analysis

Paperwork Reduction Act

In accordance with the Paperwork Reduction Act of 1995 (44 U.S.C. 3506; 5 CFR 1320 Appendix A.1), the Agencies have reviewed the interim final rules. (The Board has done so under authority delegated to the Board by the Office of Management and Budget.) The rules contain no collections of information pursuant to the Paperwork Reduction Act.

Communications by Outside Parties to Commissioners and Their Advisors

Written communications and summaries or transcripts of oral communications respecting the merits of this proceeding from any outside party to any Commissioner or Commissioner's advisor will be placed on the public record. 16 CFR 1.26(b)(5)

Solicitation of Comments on Use of Plain Language

Section 722(a) of the Gramm-Leach-Bliley Act requires the Federal banking agencies to use plain language in all proposed and final rules published after January 1, 2000.[5] In light of this requirement, the Board has sought to present the provisions of the joint interim final rule in a simple and straightforward manner. The Board invites your comments on how to make the rule easier to understand. For example:

• Have we organized the material to suit your needs? If not, how could this material be better organized?

• Do the regulations contain technical language or jargon that is not clear? If so, which language requires clarification?

• Would a different format (grouping and order of sections, use of headings, paragraphing) make the regulation easier to understand? If so, what changes to the format would make the regulation easier to understand?

• What else could we do to make the regulation easier to understand?

[5] Pub. L. 106–102, 113 Stat. 1338 (1999), codified at 12 U.S.C. 4809.

List of Subjects

12 CFR Part 222

Banks, banking, Holding companies, state member banks.

16 CFR Part 602

Consumer reports, Consumer reporting agencies, Credit, Trade practices.

12 CFR Chapter II—Federal Reserve System

Authority and Issuance

For the reasons set forth in the preamble, the Board adds a new 12 CFR part 222 to read as follows:

PART 222—FAIR CREDIT REPORTING (REGULATION V)

Authority: 15 U.S.C. 1681s; Sec 3, Pub. L. 108–159, 117 Stat. 1953.

Subpart A—General Provisions

§ 222.1 Purpose, scope, and effective dates.

(a)–(b) [Reserved]

(c) *Effective dates.* The applicable provisions of the Fair and Accurate Credit Transactions Act of 2003 (FACT Act), Pub. L. 108–159, 117 Stat. 1952, shall be effective in accordance with the following schedule:

(1) *Provisions effective December 31, 2003.*

(i) Sections 151(a)(2), 212(e), 214(c), 311(b), and 711, concerning the relation to state laws; and

(ii) Each of the provisions of the FACT Act that authorizes an agency to issue a regulation or to take other action to implement the applicable provision of the FACT Act or the applicable provision of the Fair Credit Reporting Act, as amended by the FACT Act, but only with respect to that agency's authority to propose and adopt the implementing regulation or to take such other action.

(2) [Reserved]

16 CFR Chapter I—Federal Trade Commission

Authority and Issuance

For the reasons set forth in the preamble, the FTC adds a new 16 CFR part 602 to read as follows:

PART 602—FAIR CREDIT REPORTING

Authority: 15 U.S.C. 1681s; Sec. 3, Pub. L. 108–159, 117 Stat. 1953.

Subpart A—General Provisions

§ 602.1 Purpose, scope, and effective dates.

(a)–(b) [Reserved]

(c) *Effective dates.* The applicable provisions of the Fair and Accurate Credit Transactions Act of 2003 (FACT Act), Pub. L. 108–159, 117 Stat. 1952, shall be effective in accordance with the following schedule:

(1) *Provisions effective December 31, 2003.*

(i) Sections 151(a)(2), 212(e), 214(c), 311(b), and 711, concerning the relation to state laws; and

(ii) Each of the provisions of the FACT Act that authorizes an agency to issue a regulation or to take other action to implement the applicable provision of the FACT Act or the applicable provision of the Fair Credit Reporting Act, as amended by the FACT Act, but only with respect to that agency's authority to propose and adopt the implementing regulation or to take such other action.

(2) [Reserved]

A.2.4.2 Joint Final Rules

69 Fed. Reg. 6526 (Feb. 11, 2004)

FEDERAL RESERVE SYSTEM

12 CFR Part 222

FEDERAL TRADE COMMISSION

16 CFR Part 602

[Regulation V; Docket Nos. R–1172 and R–1175; and Project No. P044804]

RIN 3084–AA94

Effective Dates for the Fair and Accurate Credit Transactions Act of 2003

AGENCIES: Board of Governors of the Federal Reserve System (Board) and Federal Trade Commission (FTC).

ACTION: Joint final rules.

SUMMARY: The recently enacted Fair and Accurate Credit Transactions Act of 2003 (FACT Act or the Act) requires the Board and the FTC (the Agencies) jointly to adopt rules establishing the effective dates for provisions of the Act that do not contain specific effective dates. The Agencies are adopting joint final rules that establish a schedule of effective dates for many of the provisions of the FACT Act for which the Act itself does not specifically provide an effective date. The Agencies also are jointly making final rules that previously were adopted on an interim basis. Those rules establish December 31, 2003, as the effective date for provisions of the Act that determine the relationship between the Fair Credit Reporting Act (FCRA) and state laws and provisions that authorize rulemakings and other implementing action by various agencies.

EFFECTIVE DATE: Effective on March 12, 2004.

FOR FURTHER INFORMATION CONTACT:

Board: Thomas E. Scanlon, Counsel, Legal Division, (202) 452–3594; David A. Stein, Counsel, Minh-Duc T. Le, Ky Tran-Trong, Senior Attorneys, Krista P. DeLargy, Attorney, Division of Consumer and Community Affairs, (202) 452–3667 or (202) 452–2412; for users of Telecommunications Device for the Deaf ("TDD") only, contact (202) 263–4869.

FTC: Christopher Keller or Katherine Armstrong, Attorneys, Division of Financial Practices, (202) 326–3224.

SUPPLEMENTARY INFORMATION:

I. Background

The FACT Act became law on December 4, 2003. Pub. L. 108–159, 117 Stat. 1952. In general, the Act amends the FCRA to enhance the ability of consumers to combat identity theft, to increase the accuracy of consumer reports, and to allow consumers to exercise greater control regarding the type and amount of marketing solicitations they receive. The FACT Act also restricts the use and disclosure of sensitive medical information. To bolster efforts to improve financial literacy among consumers, title V of the Act (entitled the "Financial Literacy and Education Improvement Act") creates a new Financial Literacy and Education Commission empowered to take appropriate actions to improve the financial literacy and education programs, grants, and materials of the Federal government. Lastly, to promote increasingly efficient national credit markets, the FACT Act establishes uniform national standards in key areas of regulation.

The Act includes effective dates for many of its sections that vary to take account of the need for rulemaking, implementation efforts by industry, and other policy concerns. Section 3 of the FACT Act requires the Agencies to prescribe joint regulations establishing an effective date for each provision of the Act "[e]xcept as otherwise specifically provided in this Act and the amendments made by this Act." The FACT Act requires that the Agencies jointly adopt final rules establishing the effective dates within two months of the date of the enactment of the Act. Thus, by law, the Agencies must complete these rulemaking efforts by February 4, 2004. The Act also provides that each of the effective dates set by the Agencies must be "as early as possible, while allowing a reasonable time for the implementation" of that provision, but in no case later than ten months after the date of issuance of the Agencies' joint final rules establishing the effective dates for the Act. 117 Stat. 1953.

In mid-December of 2003, the Agencies took two related actions to comply with the requirement to establish effective dates for the Act. In the first action, the Agencies implemented joint interim final rules that establish December 31, 2003, as the effective date for sections 151(a)(2), 212(e), 214(c), 311(b), and 711 of the FACT Act, each of which determines the relationship of State laws to areas governed by the FCRA. *See* 68 FR 74467 (Dec. 24, 2003). In the second action, the Agencies proposed joint rules that would establish a schedule of effective dates for certain other provisions of the FACT Act for which the Act itself does not specifically provide an effective date. *See* 68 FR 74529 (Dec. 24, 2003). The Agencies sought comment on both of these related actions.

II. Overview of the Comments Received

The Agencies collectively received more than 50 comments in response to the joint interim final and proposed rules; many commenters sent copies of the same letter to each of the Agencies and submitted separate comments on both the joint interim final and proposed rules.[1] Most of the comments were submitted by financial institutions and associations that represent financial institutions. Other comments were submitted by the National Association of Attorneys General and by groups that represent consumers, including the Consumer Federation of America. Three members of Congress also submitted comments in response to the Agencies' joint interim and proposed rules.

Overall, commenters supported the Agencies' approach to establish effective dates in a bifurcated structure that distinguished the provisions that require immediate effective dates (primarily those that relate to state laws) from the other provisions of the FACT Act. The comments also expressed support for the Agencies' joint proposal to establish a schedule of effective dates that would make certain provisions effective as early as March 31, 2004, and others effective December 1, 2004. Commenters focused on two main issues: first, with respect to the Agencies' joint interim final rules, commenters raised concerns about establishing December 31, 2003, as the effective date for the preemption provisions of the FCRA, as amended by the FACT Act; and second, commenters raised concerns about establishing December 1, 2004, as the effective date for section 214(a) of the FACT Act, which relates to using information for making solicitations to a consumer. After reviewing the comments received, the Agencies have determined to make final the joint interim rules and have modified the joint proposed rules in certain respects, as discussed below.[2]

III. Section-by-Section Analysis

In the supplementary information to the joint interim final rules, the Agencies addressed the effective dates for certain provisions of the FACT Act that require one or more agencies to undertake an action or rulemaking within a specified period of time after enactment of the Act. 68 FR 74468. The Agencies determined that no joint regulations under section 3 of the FACT Act are required to make these provisions effective. The Agencies found that, in these cases, the date of enactment of the statute is specified as the lawful effective date because that is the predicate for mandating that an agency action be performed within a period of time after the date of enactment. The commenters addressing this determination supported the Agencies' finding and interpretation under section 3 with respect to these provisions of the Act. The Agencies have not established in these joint final rules the effective dates that apply to these provisions of the Act.

Section__.1(c)(1)(i): Provisions that relate to State laws

The Agencies received several comments on the joint interim final rules that establish December 31, 2003, as the effective date for the provisions of the FACT Act that make permanent the existing preemption provisions of the FCRA and add others.

Overall, commenters supported the Agencies' determination that a final rule should be prescribed immediately to implement December 31, 2003, as the effective date for paragraph (3) of section 711 of the FACT Act. That section eliminates the so-called sunset provision and thus makes permanent the current provisions preempting State laws in seven areas regulated under the FCRA.

Commenters presented several different views on the Agencies' joint interim final rule that also establishes December 31, 2003, as the effective date for paragraph (2) of section 711 of the Act. This sub-provision amends the FCRA by providing that no requirement or prohibition may be imposed by the laws of any State "with respect to the conduct required by the specific provisions of" nine sections of the FCRA, as amended by the FACT Act. Several commenters argued that the effective dates for the new preemption provisions added in paragraph (2) should be linked with the effective dates of the substantive provisions of the Act.[3] These commenters argued that, if the FACT Act provisions are read to preempt existing State laws prior to the time that the FACT Act provisions are actually implemented, then consumers who reside in several States may be deprived of the protections under State laws before the Federal protections become effective.

Other commenters argued in contrast that the Agencies should clarify that the FACT Act provisions preempt State laws immediately and without regard to when the underlying Federal provision becomes effective.[4] These commenters contended that it would be costly and confusing to delay the preemptive effect of the FACT Act provisions and thereby subject financial institutions, consumer reporting agencies, and others to State law requirements for the brief period of time until rules implementing the Federal provisions become effective.

The Agencies are required by section 3 of the FACT Act to establish effective dates for various provisions of the FACT Act, and to set those dates not later than 10 months after the issuance of the final joint rules. When and whether State laws are preempted by these provisions of the FACT Act is determined by each specific provision of the FACT Act and the provisions of the FCRA that the FACT Act amends. In establishing December 31, 2003, as the effective date for the provisions of the FACT Act that address the relation to State laws, the Agencies did not determine when or whether any particular State law was or would be preempted.

After review of the comments, the Agencies adopt section __.1(c)(1)(i) as set forth in the interim rules.

The Agencies note that section 711(2) of the FACT Act adds a new provision to the FCRA that bars any requirement or prohibition under any State laws *"with respect to the conduct required by the specific provisions"* of the FCRA, as amended by the FACT Act. The joint final rules are based on the Agencies' view that the specific protections afforded under the FCRA override State laws only when the referenced Federal provisions that require conduct by the affected persons are in effect because that is the time when conduct is required by those provisions of the FCRA. Similarly, section 151(a)(2) of the FACT Act adds a new provision to section 625(b)(1) of the FCRA that preempts any State law *"with respect to any subject matter regulated under"* that provision. Only when a Federal provision is in effect does the subject matter become regulated under that section and, consequently, State law preempted.[5] In both of these situations,

---

[1] Comments submitted to the Commission can be found at http://www.ftc.gov/os/comments/factactcomments/index.html; for the Board, http://federalreserve.gov/generalinfo/foia/index.cfm?doc_id=R%2D1175&ShowAll=Yes and http://federalreserve.gov/generalinfo/foia/index.cfm?doc_id=R%2D1728&ShowAll=Yes

[2] The Agencies note that the citations used in the discussion below refer to the subsections of their respective regulations, leaving citations to the part number used by each agency blank.

[3] *See* Nat'l Assoc. of Attorneys General, Consumer Federation of America, *et al.*, Privacy Rights Clearinghouse, Senators Paul S. Sarbanes and Dianne Feinstein, and Representative Barney Frank.

[4] *See, e.g.*, Bank of America, FleetBoston Financial Corp., Financial Services Roundtable, Visa USA, Inc., and Wells Fargo & Co.

[5] Identical language in the FCRA prefaces the preemption provisions established in sections 214(c) and 311(b) of the FACT Act, and similar

Continued

the Agencies believe that a requirement that applies under an existing State law will remain in effect until the applicable specific provision of the FCRA, as amended by the FACT Act, becomes effective. Consequently, because the substantive Federal provisions actually will become effective at different times, from six months to three years after the FACT Act was enacted, establishing December 31, 2003, as the effective date for the preemption provisions would allow the State law to continue in effect until the respective Federal protections underlying each of the Federal preemption provisions comes into effect.

Section ____.1(c)(1)(ii): Provisions relating to agency action

In the joint interim final rules, the Agencies determined that December 31, 2003, is the effective date for each of the provisions of the FACT Act that authorizes an agency to issue a regulation or to take other action to implement the applicable provision of the FACT Act or of the FCRA. This subsection of the joint interim final rules limited the immediate effective date only to an agency's authority to propose and adopt the implementing regulation or to take such other action. In reaching that determination, the Agencies explained that joint interim final rules would not affect the substantive provisions of the FACT Act implemented by an agency rule.

Commenters supported the Agencies' finding and determination to establish an immediate effective date for the provisions of the Act that relate to an agency's authority to issue a regulation or take other action. After review of the comments received and for the reasons set forth in the joint interim final rules, the Agencies adopt section __.1(c)(1)(ii) as set forth in the interim rules. The Agencies reassert the position that the substantive provisions of the Act become effective as provided in the Act, as provided in the Agencies' joint effective date rules, or as provided by the substantive rules promulgated by the agencies, as appropriate.

Section ____.1(c)(2): Provisions effective March 31, 2004

As the Agencies observed in the joint proposal, the FACT Act contains a number of provisions that clarify or address rights and requirements under the FCRA that are self-effectuating but that do not contain a specific effective date. These provisions are: Section 156 (statute of limitations); sections 312(d)

language prefaces the preemption provision established in section 212(e).

(furnisher liability exception), (e) (liability and enforcement), and (f) (rule of construction); section 313(a) (action concerning complaints); section 611 (communications for certain employee investigations); and section 811 (clerical amendments). Section 111 (amendment to definitions) contains definitions that are self-effectuating but that do not contain specific effective dates. The Agencies proposed to establish March 31, 2004, as the effective date for each of the provisions of the Act listed above.

Overall, commenters supported the Agencies' proposal to establish March 31, 2004, as the effective date for these provisions. Many of the commenters specifically stated that the proposed effective date is appropriate for each of these provisions and would allow a reasonable period of time for affected entities to adjust or develop their systems to comply with the applicable requirements. For example, one financial institution observed that these provisions should not require significant changes to existing business practices conducted by financial institutions.[6]

One commenter argued that the Agencies should establish a later effective date for section 111 of the Act, which relates to certain definitions for the FCRA.[7] This commenter argued that section 111 designates a new type of consumer reporting agency, defined as a "reseller," that is specifically exempted from certain requirements that generally apply to all consumer reporting agencies. Under the Agencies' proposed rule, the definition of "reseller" would be effective earlier than the provisions that exempt a "reseller" from certain obligations, which would be effective on December 1, 2004. The commenter believed that, during that intervening period a "reseller" may be subject to certain requirements under the FCRA, but unable to avail itself of an exemption until the applicable statutory provision added by the FACT Act later becomes effective.

The Agencies have established March 31, 2004, as the effective date for section 111 as proposed. Establishing the effective date for section 111, which includes only definitions of terms used throughout the new provisions of the FCRA added by the FACT Act, does not impose any substantive obligation on a "reseller" or others referenced in that section. All the obligations, if any, are imposed by the substantive provisions of the FACT Act and FCRA, which become effective according to the terms of the applicable statutory provision, the

[6] Capital One Financial Corp.
[7] Countrywide Financial Corp.

Agencies' joint rules, or as provided by the substantive implementing regulation by an agency, as appropriate. The Agencies also believe that establishing a relatively early effective date for all of the definitions set forth in section 111 is appropriate because the new terms apply to a variety of statutory provisions and implementing regulations that become effective at various times.

One commenter urged the Agencies to adopt a later effective date for section 156 of the Act, which pertains to the statute of limitations.[8] Relative to the time periods that currently apply to actions involving violations of the FCRA, section 156 extends the statute of limitations to permit a plaintiff to bring an action in an appropriate court not later than the earlier of (1) two years after the date of discovery by the plaintiff of the violation or (2) five years after the date on which the violation that is the basis for such liability occurs. This commenter argued that the "extended statute of limitations for many causes of action will require users of consumer reports and others to reevaluate and alter their recordkeeping systems in order to retain the appropriate documents and other information that may be necessary for use in future causes of action."

The Agencies recognize that financial institutions and others undoubtedly will be affected by the amendment to the statute of limitations. Nevertheless, the Agencies find, upon review of all of the comments received on the proposal, that the potentially adverse effects that may arise due to a three-month implementation period (following the date of the Agencies' proposal) are minimal. In light of the mandate in section 3 of the Act to "establish effective dates that are as early as possible, while allowing a reasonable time for the implementation of the provisions of this Act," the Agencies have determined that March 31, 2004, is a reasonable effective date for section 156.

Upon review of the comments received on the other provisions of the Act subject to this part of the joint proposal, the Agencies believe that the "reasonable time to implement" standard of section 3 of the Act permits an early effective date because, in general, these provisions do not require significant changes to business procedures. Furthermore, the Agencies note that the commenters did not disagree with the Agencies' preliminary view that each of these provisions furnishes important benefits to consumers and affected businesses. The

[8] MasterCard Int'l.

Agencies find that March 31, 2004, is an appropriate date that balances the statutory mandate to effectuate provisions of the Act "as early as possible" while allowing a reasonable time for the implementation of the provisions described in this part of the joint proposal.

Section ____.1(c)(3): Provisions effective December 1, 2004

In general, commenters supported the Agencies' proposal to establish December 1, 2004, as the effective date for provisions that require changes in systems, disclosure forms or practices, or implementing regulations to be administered effectively. With a few exceptions discussed below, the commenters stated that allowing the maximum time permitted under section 3 of the Act for these provisions to become effective is appropriate and would allow a reasonable period of time for affected entities to adjust or develop their systems to comply with the applicable requirements.

Many commenters expressed concerns about the Agencies' proposal to establish December 1, 2004, as the effective date for section 214(a) of the Act, which creates a new section 624 of the FCRA.[9] This new section sets forth a special rule that applies to the use of information by an affiliate for making solicitations to a consumer. Commenters argued, in general, that the Agencies' proposed effective date would be inconsistent with the time frame contemplated by the statute itself for implementing this provision. Commenters observed that section 214(b) of the FACT Act provides that regulations "*to implement* section 624 of the [FCRA]" must be prescribed no later than September 4, 2004, and those implementing regulations must become effective not later than six months thereafter. Commenters noted that aligning the effective date of the statutory provision with the time frame for prescribing the applicable regulations for that provision would, as a practical matter, assist companies to coordinate the notices to consumers required by this new law with their other notices, such as their privacy notices required by the Gramm-Leach-Bliley Act.[10]

Based on the comments received on the joint proposal, the Agencies have reconsidered whether it is necessary for the Agencies to establish an effective date for section 214(a) under section 3 of the FACT Act. Section 624(a)(5) of the FCRA, as added by section 214(a) of the FACT Act, restricts the use of customer information shared by a financial institution with its affiliate. That section also specifically provides that "[t]his subsection shall not prohibit the use of information to send a solicitation to a consumer if such information was received prior to the date on which persons are required to comply with regulations implementing this subsection." As noted above, subsection 214(b) establishes specific dates for the issuance and effectiveness of the implementing regulations for section 214(a). The Agencies believe that this "no-retroactivity" paragraph, which specifically references the date of the rules adopted under section 214(b), inextricably connects the underlying obligations imposed by section 214(a) with the effective date(s) specifically set by Congress in section 214(b). Read together, these provisions establish a specific effective date for the obligations in section 214(a).

Section 3 of the FACT Act mandates that the Agencies jointly establish effective dates for the provisions of the Act "[e]xcept as otherwise specifically provided in this Act and the amendments made by this Act." Because the obligations in section 214(a) are specifically referenced and directly connected to the rulemaking schedule specified in section 214(b), the Agencies believe Congress has established the effective date for section 214(a), which is the effective date of the rules implementing that section. Accordingly, the Agencies have determined that the Agencies are not required by section 3 of the FACT Act to establish an effective date for section 214(a) and that section becomes effective according to the schedule established by section 214(b).

The Agencies believe that the same analysis applies to sections 211(a) (concerning free consumer reports) and 216 (concerning the disposal of consumer report information and records). Each of these sections specifically references and depends upon the implementation of regulations that Congress has required be issued by specific dates.[11] Consequently, Congress has specified the effective dates of these sections to be the effective dates of the implementing rules, which must be completed by specific dates. For this reason, the Agencies believe that the Agencies are not required by section 3 of the FACT Act to set effective dates for section 211(a) or section 216. These sections will become effective on the dates that the implementing rules become effective. The FACT Act contains a number of other provisions without effective dates that would require changes in systems, disclosure forms or practices, or implementing regulations to be administered effectively. The Agencies have determined that December 1, 2004, is an appropriate effective date for all of the provisions included in subsection __.1(c)(3) of the joint proposed rules, except for sections 211(a), 214(a), and 216, as discussed above. Providing the full 10-month period permitted by the Act will allow industry and the various agencies a reasonable time to establish systems and rules to implement these sections effectively. Each of these sections is listed in the final joint rules.[12]

One commenter suggested that the Agencies should establish December 4, 2004, instead of December 1, 2004, as proposed, as the effective date for these provisions of the Act.[13] This commenter noted that December 1, 2004, falls on a Wednesday and contended that an effective date that falls during the middle of the week "could work a hardship on many companies." The commenter indicated that establishing December 4, 2004, as the effective date for these provisions may help to ensure that implementation processes proceed smoothly because companies would be provided with more time to implement and test new systems in place over that weekend. By contrast, other commenters stated that December 1, 2004, is consistent with the maximum 10-month period permitted under the statute and did not note any adverse consequences that could be posed by that particular day.

Section 3 of the FACT Act permits the Agencies to establish an effective date as late as 10 months following the effective date of the Agencies' joint final rules. This date was uncertain at the time the rules were proposed. The Agencies believed that adopting a date certain would reduce burden on all affected by the joint rules by removing uncertainty about the effective date. The Agencies proposed December 1, 2004, as a date that would both be within the 10-month statutory period and allow affected entities to begin implementation efforts

---

[9] *See, e.g.*, America's Community Bankers, Bank of America, MBNA America, FleetBoston Financial Corp., Capital One Financial Corp., Financial Services Roundtable, Household Automative Finance Corp., Household Bank, Visa USA, Inc., and Bank One Corp.

[10] 15 U.S.C. 6802–03.

[11] *See* sections 612(a)(1)(B), (C)(iii), and (C)(iv) of the FCRA, as added by section 211 of the FACT Act, and section 211(d) of the Act; section 628(a)(1) of the FCRA as added by section 216 of the FACT Act.

[12] The Agencies note that a portion of the amendment made by section 151(a)(1) (which adds section 609(e) to the FCRA) becomes effective 180 days after enactment of the Act.

[13] American Council of Life Insurers.

at the start of a new month. Based on all of the comments, the Agencies continue to believe that, on balance, December 1, 2004, is an appropriate effective date for the provisions of the statute described in section __.1(c)(3) of the joint rules because the first day of the month sharply demarcates the start date for these provisions of the new law and reduces burden on entities that use a monthly cycle.

Regulatory Analysis

Paperwork Reduction Act

In accordance with the Paperwork Reduction Act of 1995 (44 U.S.C. 3506; 5 CFR 1320 Appendix A.1), the Agencies have reviewed the joint final rules. (The Board has done so under authority delegated to the Board by the Office of Management and Budget.) The joint final rules contain no collections of information pursuant to the Paperwork Reduction Act.

Regulatory Flexibility Act

In accordance with section 3(a) of the Regulatory Flexibility Act (5 U.S.C. 603(a)), the Agencies must publish a final regulatory flexibility analysis with these joint rules. The joint rules establish effective dates for several provisions of the FACT Act. Prior to the enactment of the FACT Act, the FCRA imposed various duties on parties that furnish information to consumer reporting agencies, on parties that use consumer reports, and on consumer reporting agencies themselves. The FACT Act modifies and extends some of these existing duties and imposes new duties on these respective parties. The schedule of effective dates established by the Agencies would make the newly-enacted statutory provisions applicable with respect to these parties.

Because the rules merely establish effective dates, the rules themselves impose no reporting, recordkeeping or other requirements, which would arise either from obligations imposed by the statute itself or as a result of rulemaking or other implementing actions that may be taken by agencies under the statute.

List of Subjects

12 CFR Part 222

Banks, banking, Holding companies, state member banks.

16 CFR Part 602

Consumer reports, Consumer reporting agencies, Credit, Trade practices.

Federal Reserve System

12 CFR Chapter II

Authority and Issuance

■ For the reasons set forth in the preamble, the Board amends 12 CFR part 222 as follows:

PART 222—FAIR CREDIT REPORTING (REGULATION V)

■ 1. The authority citation for 12 CFR part 222 continues to read as follows:

Authority: 15 U.S.C. 1681j; Sec. 3, Pub. L. 108–159; 117 Stat. 1953.

■ 2. In § 222.1, paragraphs (c)(2) and (c)(3) are added to read as follows:

Subpart A—General Provisions

§ 222.1 Purpose, scope, and effective dates.

* * * * *

(c) *Effective dates.* * * *

(2) *Provisions effective March 31, 2004.*

(i) Section 111, concerning the definitions;

(ii) Section 156, concerning the statute of limitations;

(iii) Sections 312(d), (e), and (f), concerning the furnisher liability exception, liability and enforcement, and rule of construction, respectively;

(iv) Section 313(a), concerning action regarding complaints;

(v) Section 611, concerning communications for certain employee investigations; and

(vi) Section 811, concerning clerical amendments.

(3) *Provisions effective December 1, 2004.*

(i) Section 112, concerning fraud alerts and active duty alerts;

(ii) Section 114, concerning procedures for the identification of possible instances of identity theft;

(iii) Section 115, concerning truncation of the social security number in a consumer report;

(iv) Section 151(a)(1), concerning the summary of rights of identity theft victims;

(v) Section 152, concerning blocking of information resulting from identity theft;

(vi) Section 153, concerning the coordination of identity theft complaint investigations;

(vii) Section 154, concerning the prevention of repollution of consumer reports;

(viii) Section 155, concerning notice by debt collectors with respect to fraudulent information;

(ix) Section 211(c), concerning a summary of rights of consumers;

(x) Section 212(a)–(d), concerning the disclosure of credit scores;

(xi) Section 213(c), concerning enhanced disclosure of the means available to opt out of prescreened lists;

(xii) Section 217(a), concerning the duty to provide notice to a consumer;

(xiii) Section 311(a), concerning the risk-based pricing notice;

(xiv) Section 312(a)–(c), concerning procedures to enhance the accuracy and integrity of information furnished to consumer reporting agencies;

(xv) Section 314, concerning improved disclosure of the results of reinvestigation;

(xvi) Section 315, concerning reconciling addresses;

(xvii) Section 316, concerning notice of dispute through reseller; and

(xviii) Section 317, concerning the duty to conduct a reasonable reinvestigation.

Federal Trade Commission

16 CFR Chapter 1

Authority and Issuance

■ For the reasons set forth in the preamble, the FTC amends 16 CFR part 602 as follows:

PART 602—FAIR CREDIT REPORTING

■ 1. The authority citation for 16 CFR part 602 continues to read as follows:

Authority: 15 U.S.C. 1681a; Sec. 3, Pub. L. 108–159; 117 Stat. 1953.

■ 2. In § 602.1, paragraphs (c)(2) and (c)(3) are added to read as follows:

Subpart A—General Provisions

§ 602.1 Purpose, scope, and effective dates.

* * * * *

(c) *Effective dates.* * * *

(2) *Provisions effective March 31, 2004.*

(i) Section 111, concerning the definitions;

(ii) Section 156, concerning the statute of limitations;

(iii) Sections 312(d), (e), and (f), concerning the furnisher liability exception, liability and enforcement, and rule of construction, respectively;

(iv) Section 313(a), concerning action regarding complaints;

(v) Section 611, concerning communications for certain employee investigations; and

(vi) Section 811, concerning clerical amendments.

(3) *Provisions effective December 1, 2004.*

(i) Section 112, concerning fraud alerts and active duty alerts;

(ii) Section 114, concerning procedures for the identification of possible instances of identity theft;

(iii) Section 115, concerning truncation of the social security number in a consumer report;

(iv) Section 151(a)(1), concerning the summary of rights of identity theft victims;

(v) Section 152, concerning blocking of information resulting from identity theft;

(vi) Section 153, concerning the coordination of identity theft complaint investigations;

(vii) Section 154, concerning the prevention of repollution of consumer reports;

(viii) Section 155, concerning notice by debt collectors with respect to fraudulent information;

(ix) Section 211(c), concerning a summary of rights of consumers;

(x) Section 212(a)–(d), concerning the disclosure of credit scores;

(xi) Section 213(c), concerning enhanced disclosure of the means available to opt out of prescreened lists;

(xii) Section 217(a), concerning the duty to provide notice to a consumer;

(xiii) Section 311(a), concerning the risk-based pricing notice;

(xiv) Section 312(a)–(c), concerning procedures to enhance the accuracy and integrity of information furnished to consumer reporting agencies;

(xv) Section 314, concerning improved disclosure of the results of reinvestigation;

(xvi) Section 315, concerning reconciling addresses;

(xvii) Section 316, concerning notice of dispute through reseller; and

(xviii) Section 317, concerning the duty to conduct a reasonable reinvestigation.

By order of the Board of Governors of the Federal Reserve System, February 5, 2004.

Jennifer J. Johnson,
Secretary of the Board.

Dated: February 5, 2004.

By Direction of the Commission.

Donald S. Clark,
Secretary.

[FR Doc. 04–2913 Filed 2–10–04; 8:45 am]
BILLING CODES 6210–01; 6750–01–P

A.5 Gramm-Leach-Bliley

Page 438

Add to text at end of list of subsections:

A.5.2 FTC Rules—Selected Provisions

PART 314 – STANDARDS FOR SAFEGUARDING CUSTOMER INFORMATION

314.1 Purpose and scope.
314.2 Definitions.
314.3 Standards for safeguarding customer information.
314.4 Elements.
314.5 Effective Date

Page 452

Add at end of subsection:

PART 314 – STANDARDS FOR SAFEGUARDING CUSTOMER INFORMATION

16 C.F.R. sec.

314.1 Purpose and scope.
314.2 Definitions.
314.3 Standards for safeguarding customer information.
314.4 Elements.
314.5 Effective Date

§ 314.1 Purpose and scope.

(a) *Purpose.* This part, which implements sections 501 and 505(b)(2) of the Gramm-Leach-Bliley Act, sets forth standards for developing, implementing, and maintaining reasonable administrative, technical, and physical safeguards to protect the security, confidentiality, and integrity of customer information.

(b) *Scope.* This part applies to the handling of customer information by all financial institutions over which the Federal Trade Commission ("FTC" or "Commission") has jurisdiction. This part refers to such entities as "you." This part applies to all customer information in your possession, regardless of whether such information pertains to individuals with whom you have a customer relationship, or pertains to the customers of other financial institutions that have provided such information to you.

§ 314.2 Definitions.

(a) *In general.* Except as modified by this part or unless the context otherwise requires, the terms used in this part have the same meaning as set forth in the Commission's rule governing the Privacy of Consumer Financial Information, 16 CFR part 313.

(b) Customer information means any record containing nonpublic personal information as defined in 16 CFR 313.3(n), about a customer of a financial institution, whether in paper, electronic, or other form, that is handled or maintained by or on behalf of you or your affiliates.

(c) Information security program means the administrative, technical, or physical safeguards you use to access, collect, distribute, process, protect, store, use, transmit, dispose of, or otherwise handle customer information.

(d) Service provider means any person or entity that receives, maintains, processes, or otherwise is permitted access to customer information through its provision of services directly to a financial institution that is subject to this part.

§ 314.3 Standards for safeguarding customer information.

(a) *Information security program.* You shall develop, implement, and maintain a comprehensive information security program that is written in one or more readily accessible parts and contains administrative, technical, and physical safeguards that are appropriate to your size and complexity, the nature and scope of your activities, and the sensitivity of any customer information at issue. Such safeguards shall include the elements set forth in § 314.4 and shall be reasonably designed to achieve the objectives of this part, as set forth in paragraph (b) of this section.

(b) *Objectives.* The objectives of section 501(b) of the Act, and of this part, are to:

(1) Insure the security and confidentiality of customer information;

(2) Protect against any anticipated threats or hazards to the security or integrity of such information; and

(3) Protect against unauthorized access to or use of such information that could result in substantial harm or inconvenience to any customer.

§ 314.4 Elements.

In order to develop, implement, and maintain your information security program, you shall:

(a) Designate an employee or employees to coordinate your information security program.

(b) Identify reasonably foreseeable internal and external risks to the security, confidentiality, and integrity of customer information that could result in the unauthorized disclosure, misuse, alteration, destruction or other compromise of such information, and assess the sufficiency of any safeguards in place to control these risks. At a minimum, such a risk assessment should include consideration of risks in each relevant area of your operations, including:

(1) Employee training and management;

(2) Information systems, including network and software design, as well as information processing, storage, transmission and disposal; and

(3) Detecting, preventing and responding to attacks, intrusions, or other systems failures.

(c) Design and implement information safeguards to control the risks you identify through risk assessment, and regularly test or otherwise monitor the effectiveness of the safeguards' key controls, systems, and procedures.

(d) Oversee service providers, by:

(1) Taking reasonable steps to select and retain service providers that are capable of maintaining appropriate safeguards for the customer information at issue; and

(2) Requiring your service providers by contract to implement and maintain such safeguards.

(e) Evaluate and adjust your information security program in light of the results of the testing and monitoring required by paragraph (c) of this section; any material changes to your operations or business arrangements; or any other circumstances that you know or have reason to know may have a material impact on your information security program.

§ 314.5 Effective date.

(a) Each financial institution subject to the Commission's jurisdiction must implement an information security program pursuant to this part no later than May 23, 2003.

(b) Two-year grandfathering of service contracts. Until May 24, 2004, a contract you have entered into with a nonaffiliated third party to perform services for you or functions on your behalf satisfies the provisions of § 314.4(d), even if the contract does not include a

A.6 Federal Standards as to FCRA's Applicability to Affiliate Information Sharing

Page 452

A.6.1 Proposed FTC Interpretations

Add to text at end of subsection's second paragraph:

The Fair and Accurate Credit Transactions Act of 2003,[38.1] added an additional opt-out right to consumers that will allow them to direct that affiliates not use information that would be a consumer report but for the exclusion for solicitations to the consumer for marketing purposes.[38.2] However, this opt out right will not become effective until a date to be set by the Federal Trade Commission in regulations that implement the new opt-out provision.[38.3]

 38.1 15 U.S.C. § 1681s-3, *added by* Pub. L. No. 108-159, § 214(a) (2003).
 38.2 *Id.. See also* § 4.4.1.5, *supra.*
 38.3 15 U.S.C. § 1681s.3(a)(5), *added by* Pub. L. No. 108-159, § 214(a)(2003).

Replace Appendix B with:

Appendix B Summary of Federal and State Laws on Consumer Reporting and Theft of Identity

B.1 Introduction

This appendix provides a state-by-state analysis of state laws which affect a consumer's credit report. Most states have a state fair credit reporting statute. Over the past several years, a number of states have enacted statutes governing "credit service organizations" or "credit repair organizations," which offer to improve a consumer's credit rating or history for a fee. A few states have other provisions dealing with credit reports, the most common involving the reporting of child support debts. Increasingly, states are enacting laws intended to address the problem of identity theft. Summaries of these identity theft statutes are included in Appendix B.3, *infra*.

The appendix also provides a summary of two federal laws: the Fair Credit Reporting Act and the Credit Repair Organizations Act. Since state fair credit reporting legislation generally follows the federal statute, the summary is intended to provide a frame of reference for analysis of state statutes. The Federal Fair Credit Reporting Act was extensively amended by FACTA of 2003 (Pub. L. No. 108-159 (2003); it is the statute, as amended, which is summarized in B.2.1, *infra*.

The 1996 amendments also enacted, for the first time, a Federal Credit Repair Organizations Act which is summarized in B.2.2, *infra*.

While this appendix is intended to be useful as a general guide, readers are cautioned to refer to the statutory language for detail and context. Note also that this appendix only analyzes the statutory language itself, and does not include judicial interpretations of that language. Such interpretations are found at the applicable sections of the manual's text. Furthermore some state provisions have been preempted by the 1996 amendments; we have noted many of these in footnotes, but readers must carefully consider the full effect of federal preemption on each particular application of state law being considered. Many provisions of state credit repair statutes are preempted by the comprehensive Federal Credit Repair Organization Act, and are not detailed in this appendix. *See also* § 10.4.4, *supra*.

B.2 Summary of Federal Credit Reporting Laws

B.2.1 Fair Credit Reporting Act

Federal Fair Credit Reporting Act, 15 U.S.C. §§ 1681 to 1681u (as amended)

Scope: Reports on consumers when used for insurance, credit, or employment, or other authorized uses under the statute. DOES NOT cover business credit reports or business insurance reports. Beginning January 1, 2001, all of these specific preemptions may be overridden by state legislative action which gives consumer greater protection. Information shared by affiliated companies is not a consumer report, although some disclosure is still required, and consumers may opt-out of certain uses of their information by affiliates for marketing purposes.

Purposes for Which Reports May Be Issued: 1) To determine the eligibility for credit or insurance issued primarily for personal, household, or family purpose. 2) In response to a court order or subpoena issued in connection with proceedings before a federal grand jury. 3) According to written instructions from the consumer. 4) In connection with a credit transaction, or review or collection of a consumer account. 5) Employment purposes. 6) Underwriting of insurance involving the consumer. 7) Determining eligibility for a license or government benefit. 8) In connection with valuation or assessment of the credit or prepayment risks associated with existing credit obligations by a potential investor or servicer, or current insurer. 9) Any legitimate business need in connection with a business transaction initiated by the consumer or to review an account to determine whether the consumer still meets the terms of account. 10) In response to a request by state or local child support enforcement agency for the purposes of establishing individual's capacity to pay child support. 11) For certain counterintelligence purposes by the FBI. An investigative report cannot be used without disclosure to the consumer. An employer needs permission of the employee before obtaining a consumer report. Reports in connection with certain employer investigations are exempt from most requirements imposed on other consumer reports.

Consumer Access and Disclosure: Upon request by consumer: 1) All information in consumer's file including credit scores and a limited number of risk predictors. Nationwide agencies must provide one free annual report to consumers. 2) The sources of the information except those used solely for an investigative report. 3) The recipients of any consumer report furnished for employment purposes within preceding two years, and for any other purposes within preceding one year, except reports furnished to the federal government for national security purposes. 4) Summary of rights of consumer under FCRA. 5) Nationwide consumer reporting agency must provide a toll-free number for consumers to call during normal business hours. 6) Notice that information previously deleted as a result of a consumer's dispute is being reinstated into consumer's file.

Disclosures to Consumers By Users: User must notify consumer that adverse action was based on consumer report; consumer has right to dispute accuracy of report; a full copy of report is available at no charge upon request made within sixty days; and toll-free number of nationwide reporting agency. Employers must disclose that a report may be requested and provide copy of report if adverse action taken. Less disclosure is required if adverse action based on information received from an affiliated company. No one can procure an investigative report without written disclosure to the consumer of the nature and scope of the investigation. If an adverse credit action is based on information from other than the consumer reporting agency, the consumer must be notified of the right to request the nature of the information used. A creditor who offers credit to a consumer on less advantageous terms than offered to other consumers with better credit records must disclose that fact to the consumer through a risk-based pricing notice.

Restrictions on Content of Reports: Paid tax liens or bad debts if over seven years old. Bankruptcies over ten years old. Civil suits and judgments or arrest records antedating a report by over seven years or the statute of limitations, whichever is longer. All other information over seven years old, except records of criminal convictions.

Consumer Disputes: When the accuracy or completeness of information is disputed by the consumer, the agency must conduct a reinvestigation free of charge to be completed within thirty days. A fifteen-day extension is available to the agency if the consumer supplies additional information during the reinvestigation. Within five days of receipt of a consumer complaint, the agency must notify the creditor (or other person) who originally supplied the disputed information. The agency and furnisher must review and consider all relevant information provided by the consumer. Once information is deleted, an agency must notify the consumer if the information is later reinserted into its reports. If the reinvestigation does not solve the dispute, the consumer may file a brief statement of contentions. A subsequent report must note the dispute and include the consumer statement and the agency must inform the consumer of the right to request that a corrected notification be sent at no charge within 30 days to all users within six months and employers within two years.

Duties of Furnishers: Furnishers must provide reporting agencies generally accurate information; note if information it reports to agencies is disputed; provide notice when accounts were closed voluntarily by consumer; provide agency notice of date delinquencies commenced; participate in reinvestigations of accuracy or completeness conducted by consumer reporting agency and consider all relevant information provided by consumer.

Consumer Remedies: Any person is liable for negligent and willful violations, except liability of furnishers limited to failures to participate as required in reinvestigations conducted by consumer reporting agencies. Furthermore, identity theft victims may not bring a private cause of action for a business' failure to provide an identity thief's transaction information to the victim. Similarly, consumers may not enforce the new obligations of users to issue risk-based pricing notices. Willful violations: actual damages or statutory damages of $100 to $1,000; punitive damages; attorney fees and court costs. Negligent violations: actual damages, attorney fees and court costs. Liability and $1,000 statutory damages for knowingly obtaining reports without permissible purpose or under false pretense. Consumer reporting agency defense for inaccurate information if maintained reasonable procedures. Attorney fees may also be awarded if opposing attorney files pleadings in bad faith.

Statute of Limitations: A consumer must bring suit within two years of the discovery of the violation, but no later than five years from the date of the violation.

Miscellaneous: Every agency must maintain reasonable procedures to avoid misuse of reports. Agencies must require prospective user to identify itself and certify the purposes for which the information is sought. Reasonable efforts to verify the identity of new user are required. Public record information which is likely to have an adverse effect upon employment prospects must be kept up-to-date and complete. Consumers may opt out of pre-screened mailing lists compiled by consumer reporting agencies.

Identity Theft Prevention and Remediation Provisions: A victim of identity theft can demand that agency put a fraud alert in his or her file that alerts users of the theft and that requires users to take steps to verify the identity of those applying for credit in the victim's name. Agencies will have to notify each other of such alerts and provide victims with free credit reports and a summary of their rights. Those consumers on active military duty can also have an alert put in their files. A victim can also require agencies to block fraudulent information; the agencies must then notify the furnishers of such fraudulent information that the information has bee blocked; those furnishers must then cease their furnishing of the information. Creditors may not sell or transfer debts that result from identity theft and debt collectors must notify creditors of a consumer's claim that a debt resulted from identity theft. Merchants who have done business with an identity thief must disclose transaction information to the thief's victim. Eventually financial institutions will have to implement red flag guidelines to spot identity theft of consumers' accounts.

B.2.2 Credit Repair Organizations Act

Federal Credit Repair Organizations Act, 15 U.S.C. §§ 1679 to 1679j

Scope: Any person who performs or offers to perform, for a fee, any service for the purpose of improving a consumer's credit record, history or rating. Section 501(c)(3) organizations, creditors restructuring a consumer's debt, and depository institutions are excluded. State laws are preempted to the extent of any inconsistency with the federal act.

Consumer Access and Disclosure: Before entering into any service contract with consumer, must provide consumer separate written notice of self-help rights under the Federal FCRA and CROA. Credit repair organization must retain copy of disclosure, signed by consumer, for two years.

Contract Requirements: A written contract, including the terms and conditions of payment, the total amount due, a detailed description of the services to be performed, the estimated date by which performance will be completed, and a conspicuous boldface disclosure of the three-day right to cancel placed "in immediate proximity" to the consumer's signature, is required. No services may be provided before the end of the three-day cooling off period. Consumers must receive a copy of the contract and any other document they sign.

Right to Cancel: Consumer given right to cancel until midnight of the third business day following 1) execution of the contract, or 2) when the contract becomes enforceable.

Prohibited Practices: False or misleading statements or advice. Statements which upon the exercise of reasonable care should be known to be false or misleading. Engaging or attempting to engage in any other form of deception directed at a consumer, a credit reporting agency, a creditor or any person to whom a consumer has applied or is applying to for credit. Encouraging consumers to alter their identification.

Violations/Penalties: Noncomplying contracts are void and unenforceable. Damages available include the greater of actual damages or the amount paid by the consumer to the credit repair organization, punitive damages, costs and reasonable attorney fees. Class actions contemplated. Actions by state officials on consumers' behalf explicitly authorized.

Statute of Limitations: Within five years of violation or discovery of a credit repair organization's willful and material failure to disclose.

Miscellaneous: The Federal Trade Commission is given enforcement powers. Any waiver of rights by consumer void. Credit repair organization may not receive payment for any service until service fully performed.

B.3 State-by-State Summaries of Laws on Credit Reports and Identity Theft

Alabama

State Identity Theft Statute: **Ala. Code §§ 13A-8-190 to -201**.

Definition of Offense: Identity theft: Obtains, records or accesses identifying information that would aid in accessing financial resources, or obtaining benefits or identifying documents of victim; obtains goods or services by use of victim's identifying information; obtains identifying documents in victim's name. Trafficking in Stolen Identities: Manufactures, sells, purchases, transfers, or possesses with intent to manufacture, sell, etc., for the purpose of committing identity theft, identifying documents or identifying information of another; unauthorized possession of five identifying documents of one person, or identifying documents of five people creates an inference of intent to commit identify theft.

Victim Remedies in Criminal Case: Mandatory restitution. May include any costs incurred by the victim in correcting credit history or credit rating or costs incurred in connection with any civil or administrative proceeding to satisfy any debt, lien, or other obligations resulting from the theft, including lost wages and attorney fees. The court may order restitution for financial loss to any other person or entity that suffers a loss from the violation. Court records must be corrected if there was a conviction under a stolen name, to indicate that victim did not commit the crime. Court should make detailed order for correction of public and private records, which may then be used by victim in a civil proceeding to set aside a judgment, or submitted it to governmental entity or private business to show that accounts, etc. were not those of victim.

Special Record-Clearing Provisions: No specific provisions.

Duties of Private Entities: If consumer presents court order (see above) agency must within thirty days block all information resulting from the ID theft.

Private Right of Action: Civil action against thief for greater of $5000 or treble damages, reasonable attorney fees and costs. Intentional or reckless violation by agency gives consumer cause of action for actual damages, and attorney fees, and for an injunction (reasonable procedures are a defense).

Alaska

Child Support Debts: **Alaska Stat. § 25.27.273 (Michie)**. Child support enforcement agency may report delinquencies but must immediately report payments if delinquency was reported. May only report the payment history of the obligor.

***State Credit Information in Personal Insurance Statute:* Alaska Stat. § 21.36.460**

Scope: Credit information used in underwriting or rating consumer for personal insurance: coverage of residence or personal property, including private vehicles.

Disclosures: Insurer must disclose in writing (or in same medium as application) at time of application that credit information will be obtained and used. If third party used to develop insurance score, must advise consumer that third party will be used. Insurer must notify consumer if it bases adverse action on credit report or insurance score, and advise consumer of procedure for correcting errors in credit report.

Dispute Resolution: Insurer who bases adverse action on credit report or insurance score, must provide consumer with opportunity to request reconsideration. If dispute resolution pursuant to Federal FCRA results in corrected credit report, insurer must re-underwrite, using correct information. If refund is due, it should be for lesser of policy period or 12 months. If insurance is denied, and credit history is being disputed, pursuant to FCRA, and consumer notifies insurer, it must re-underwrite without using credit information.

Prohibited Practices: May not use an insurance score based on income, age, sex, address, zip code, census block, ethnic group, religion, marital status or nationality. May use credit information to cancel, deny, underwrite or rate personal insurance only "in combination with other substantive underwriting factors." May not use credit history to determine insurance score, if information obtained more than 90 days before policy issued. May not refuse to renew, or again underwrite or rate at renewal, based in whole or in part on credit report or insurance score. May not take adverse action based on lack of credit history, certain types of credit inquiries, collection accounts with a medical industry code, lack of a credit card or use of particular kind of credit card, credit history that has been adversely affected by former spouse (or current spouse who is party to divorce action).

Other: No relevant provisions.

Arizona

***State FCRA Statute*: Ariz. Rev. Stat. Ann. §§ 44-1691 to 44-1697 (West).**

Scope: Definitions similar to the federal law.

Purposes for Which Reports May Be Issued: Similar to federal law, except no authorization for provision to potential investors or servicers, or current insurers, in connection with the evaluation of credit or prepayment risks associated with existing credit obligations. Limited information to government agencies.

Consumer Access and Disclosure: Upon consumer request;

all information and sources in addition to all persons receiving information within the last six months.

Disclosures to Consumers By User: Name of the consumer reporting agency, without consumer request.

Restriction on Content of Reports: The number of days an account has been delinquent may not be rounded up by more than four days.[1]

Consumer Disputes: Written notice to the consumer reporting agency. Thirty days to respond.[2] If disputed information inaccurate, must notify consumer and users within past six months, if requested by consumer; if agency denies information is inaccurate, must notify consumer in writing of the basis for its denial, the name and address and telephone number (if reasonably available) of any furnisher contacted; and notice that the consumer may request description of the procedures used in the reinvestigation.

Duties of Furnishers: A furnisher may not round up by more than four days the number of days an account has been delinquent.[3]

Consumer Remedies: No liability if information is correct. Refusal to correct: court costs, damages, and attorney fees. Willful or gross negligence: actual damages, attorney fees, court costs, and punitive damages.

Statute of Limitations: No relevant provisions.

Miscellaneous: A consumer may file a written statement regarding the contents of the consumer's file, and provided the statement is not frivolous or irrelevant, the agency must include the statement in future reports without charge to the consumer. The agency may limit such statements to 100 words if the agency assists the consumer in writing the statement. Intentional violations, obtaining information under false pretenses or knowingly furnishing false information, are misdemeanors.

***Child Support Debts*: Ariz. Rev. Stat. Ann. § 25-512 (West).** Child support delinquencies shall be reported to consumer reporting agencies after fifteen days advance notice and opportunity for administrative review.

***State Credit Repair Statute*: Ariz. Rev. Stat. Ann. §§ 44-1701 to -1712**

Covered Activities: Improving credit record or obtaining extension of credit, in return for money or other consideration.

Exemptions: Lenders licensed or authorized under federal or Arizona's law; banks and savings associations eligible for FDIC insurance; nonprofit organizations; licensed real estate brokers acting within scope of license; Arizona lawyers

---

1. Note that for preemption purposes, this provision was not in effect on Sept. 30, 1996, and as it regulates the contents of consumer reports, it may be preempted. See § 10.4.4, *supra*.
2. This provision was in effect on September 30, 1996, so although it regulates the time allowed for an agency to reinvestigate a dispute, it is not preempted. See § 10.4.4, *supra*.
3. Most state laws concerning the duties of furnishers are now preempted. See § 10.4.4, *supra*.

acting within scope of law practice; registered securities broker-dealers.
Right to Cancel? Yes (3 days).
Prohibitions: Charging before complete performance, unless organization has posted bond; charging for referring buyer to retail seller for credit on same terms as generally available to public; making or advising false statements to creditors or credit reporting agencies; making false statements about services offered; requiring buyer to waive rights.
Other Substantive Requirements: Disclosures.
Bond: Five percent of the amount of fees charged during the prior 12 months; not less than $5000 or more than $25,000; to be adjusted yearly.
Private Cause of Action: Actual damages, not less than the amount paid by buyer; attorney fees and costs; punitive damages allowed.

State Identity Theft Statute: Ariz. Rev. Stat. Ann. § 13-2008 (West).

Definition of Offense: Takes, uses, sells or transfers any personal identifying information of another, without authority, with the intent to obtain, use, sell or transfer the other person's identity for any unlawful purpose or to cause loss to a person.
Victim Remedies in Criminal Case: No specific provisions.
Special Record-Clearing Provisions: No specific provisions.
Duties of Private Entities: No specific provisions.
Private Right of Action: No specific provisions.

Other State Provisions: Ariz. Rev. Stat. §§ 20-1652 (Reasons for Cancellation) and 20-2102 through 20-2122 (Insurance Information Practices). Arizona's insurance information practices statute, which covers all kinds of personal insurance (life, health and disability, as well as residential and vehicle), requires that if an insurer plans to use an investigative consumer report, it must advise the consumer of the right to be interviewed and to receive a copy of the report. If an adverse action is based on credit-related information, insurer must disclose that the decision was based on a credit report or lack of credit history; source of consumer report, and how to get a copy; a description of up to four factors that were the primary cause for the adverse action. If insurer uses information from consumer reporting agency or insurance support organization, insurer must obtain information as soon as possible; must be before issuing binder or insurance coverage. After 30 days from application, insurer may not deny or terminate based on information in consumer report. Insurer may not use the following kinds of credit history, or knowingly use an insurance score based on them: absence of credit history; collection accounts with a medical industry code; bankruptcy or lien satisfaction more than 7 years old; use of particular kind of credit card.

Arkansas

State FCRA Statute: Ark. Code Ann. §§ 4-93-101 to 4-93-104.

Scope: Consumer credit (employment, insurance, etc. not mentioned).
Purposes for Which Reports May Be Issued: Granting, denying or limiting of consumer credit.
Consumer Access and Disclosures: No relevant provisions.
Disclosures to Consumer by User: If user denies credit, the further extension of existing credit, or an increase in credit limit for personal, family or household purposes, wholly or partly because of information in a credit report, it shall so advise the consumer. Must disclose action taken, name and address of creditor and of consumer reporting agency, and consumer's social security number.
Restrictions on Content of Reports: No relevant provisions.
Consumer Disputes: No relevant provisions.
Duties of Furnishers: No relevant provisions.
Consumer Remedies: Any person who fails to provide notification required by this chapter shall be liable to the injured party for actual damages.
Statute of Limitations: No relevant provisions.

Child Support Debts: Ark. Code Ann. § 9-14-209. Child support delinquencies shall be reported to consumer reporting agencies after seven days advance notice to obligor and an opportunity to contest accuracy of the information.

State Credit Repair Statute: Ark. Stat. Ann. §§ 4-91-101 to -109

Covered Activities: Improving credit record or obtaining extension of credit, in return for money or other consideration.
Exemptions: Regulated and supervised lenders; mortgage lenders approved by HUD; banks and savings associations eligible for FDIC insurance; credit unions; nonprofit organizations; licensed real estate brokers acting within scope of license; Arkansas lawyers acting within scope of law practice; registered securities broker-dealers; collection agencies acting within scope of license; consumer reporting agencies.
Right to Cancel? Yes (5 days).
Prohibitions: Charging before complete performance, unless organization has posted bond; charging for referring buyer to retail seller for credit on same terms as generally available to public; making or advising false statements to creditors or credit reporting agencies; making false statements about services offered; requiring buyer to waive rights.
Other Substantive Requirements: Disclosures.
Bond: $10,000.
Private Cause of Action: Actual damages, not less than amount paid by buyer; attorney fees and costs; punitive damages allowed.

State Identity Theft Statute: Ark. Code Ann. § 5-37-227.

Definition of Offense: With intent to unlawfully appropriate financial resources of another to his or her own use or to the use of third party, obtains or records without authority identifying information [defined] that would assist in accessing the financial resources of the other, or accesses or attempts to access the financial resources of the other through the use of the identifying information.
Victim Remedies in Criminal Case: No specific provisions.
Special Record-Clearing Provisions: No specific provisions.
Duties of Private Entities: No specific provisions.
Private Right of Action: Violation is a deceptive trade practice, within the meaning of Ark. Code Ann. § 4-88-101.

State Credit Information in Personal Insurance Statute: Ark. Code Ann. §§ 23-67-401 to 415

Scope: Use of credit information in personal (i.e., non-commercial) insurance. (private vehicle, boat, or recreational vehicle, homeowners, including mobile home, non-commercial fire).
Disclosures: Must disclose to consumer in writing (or same medium as application) at time of application if credit information will be used. In case of adverse action, must explain reasons and provide notification in accordance with Federal FCRA (including source of credit report, and dispute resolution procedure).
Dispute Resolution: On consumer's written request, insurer must re-rate or re-underwrite based on corrected consumer report or recalculated credit score. (Not more than once in 12 months).
Prohibited Practices: May not base adverse action solely on credit information, without "other applicable underwriting factor" independent of credit information and not expressly prohibited; take adverse action against consumer solely because he or she does not have a credit card. Absence of credit information or inability to calculate credit score must be treated as neutral, unless insurer can show that the absence or inability relates to the risk for insurer. May not use credit score that was calculated using income, gender, address, zip code, ethnic group, religion, marital status or nationality. May not base adverse action on credit report or credit score issued or calculated more than 90 days before date policy issued or renewed. If credit information used, insurer must recalculate score or obtain new report every 36 months. May not count as negative factor medical collection accounts, and certain kinds of credit inquiries.
Other: Insurers who use credit scores must file their scoring models with state Insurance Department.

California

State FCRA Statute: Cal. Civ. Code §§ 1785.1 to 1787.3.

Scope: Detective agencies may be excluded. (*See* § 1785.4)
Purposes for Which Reports May Be Issued: Similar to the federal law, and may be issued for rental of a dwelling and insurance claims settlements. No express authorization, however, for provision to potential investors or servicers, or current insurers, in connection with the evaluation of the credit or repayment risks associated with existing credit obligations. Agencies must match at least three pieces of identifying information in a consumer's file with information provided by proposed retail seller users before providing a report, and retail sellers must certify that they require photo identification from all who apply for credit in person. Agencies must keep a record of the purposes of the report as stated by the user. Consumers must be given the opportunity to opt out of prescreened lists.[4]
Consumer Access and Disclosure: Similar to the federal law, except all information in file must be disclosed. The agency may charge up to an $8 preparation fee. Notice or disclosure is required only to those consumers who have mailing addresses in California. Upon request, agency must disclose all recipients of the report within a twelve month period (or two years, if for employment purposes) § 1785.10(d). For an investigative consumer report, agency must disclose all recipients within three years § 1786.10(c). If a credit score is used the agency must, upon request, disclose the score, the key factors used to determine it, and related information as defined by § 1785.15.1. The agency may charge a reasonable fee to provide this information. If security alert is placed, agency must supply consumer, upon request, with free copy of report at expiration of 90 day alert period. (§ 1785.11.3). If a consumer provides a copy of a police report dealing with identity theft, the agency must provide monthly credit reports (up to 12) free.
Disclosures to Consumers By User: Similar to the federal law. The user, if requested, may ask the agency to investigate inaccuracies. Insurers, landlords, and employers must inform a consumer of a request for an investigative report no later than three days after the report request. A user for employment purposes must disclose to the consumer before requesting a report, and offer the consumer a free copy of the report. A lender who uses credit scores must disclose the score and the key factors used to determine it to the consumer. The statute prescribes a form of notice to home loan applicants if credit scores are used. A contractual provision that forbids a lender to disclose the credit scores furnished by an agency is void.
Restrictions on Content of Reports:[5] Similar to federal law, and criminal records more than seven years old or where offense pardoned or no conviction obtained. Inquiries re

---

[4] State laws regarding the use of prescreened reports are preempted. *See* § 10.4.4, *supra*.

[5] Most of these various stricter definitions of information which may not under California law be contained in a consumer report, were in effect on Sept. 30, 1996, and therefore, although they regulate the contents of consumer reports and might otherwise be, they are not preempted. *See* § 10.4.4, *supra*.

sulting from credit transactions not initiated by a consumer. Unlawful detainer (eviction) actions where the defendant is the prevailing party or the action is settled. Medical information reported to creditors or employers without a consumer's consent. Liens or encumbrances, including lis pendens, which have a court order with them striking the lien or encumbrance because against the property of a public officer or employee.[6] Must delete from the file any inquiries for credit reports based on applications for credit initiated as a result of identity theft. Cal. Civ. Code § 1785.16.1. Requires certain precautions by users of consumer reports to prevent identity theft (*i.e.*, further checking if applicant's address doesn't agree with address in credit report, or if some information in credit report is blocked because of reported identity theft). Cal. Civ. Code § 1785.20.3.

Consumer Disputes: Similar to the federal law except 30 business days to reinvestigate. In addition, an agency must notify a consumer if information reinserted or the agency refuses to (re)investigate. If a consumer files a police report alleging that consumer's personal identification information is being used without consumer's consent, agency must block any information in consumer's file which consumer alleges appears on report due to illegal usage and must notify furnishers. A creditor may not sell a consumer's debt if the information regarding that debt is blocked pursuant to this section, or if consumer has provided sufficient information to creditor concerning the identity theft. A consumer may place a "security alert" on his or her account, by notifying the reporting agency that the consumer's identity may have been used without consent to fraudulently obtain goods or services. The agency must have a toll-free number, available 24 hours per day, to receive requests for security alerts, and must place an alert in a consumers account within five business days of the request. The agency must notify all who request credit information on a consumer that a security alert is in place. The alert remains in place for 90 days, and may be renewed at the consumer's request. (Cal. Civ. Code § 1785.11.1) A consumer may also place a "security freeze" on his or account, which forbids the agency from releasing credit information without the consumer's specific consent, including the use of a "unique identification number" that the agency must assign when it implements the freeze. (certain exceptions, mainly for tax and law enforcement). Cal. Civ. Code § 1785.11.2.

Duties of Furnishers: A furnisher of information must investigate disputed information upon notice of dispute by a consumer reporting agency. If a dispute remains after reinvestigation by the consumer reporting agency, the consumer may demand that the furnisher of the information correct the disputed information. A creditor must notify the consumer when first furnishing negative credit information to a consumer reporting agency.[7]

Consumer Remedies: Similar to the federal law; in addition, prevailing plaintiffs get court costs and reasonable attorney fees, and debt collector defendants get reasonable attorney fees for actions brought in bad faith by consumers. Negligence can result in damages for loss of wages and for pain and suffering. A willful violation results in punitive damages of $100 to $5000 per violation. Injunctions and class actions can result in punitive damages. Civil fines of $2500 for willfully obtaining or using a report without a legitimate purpose. A credit card issuer knowingly communicating false information about a cardholder may be liable for three times actual damages, court costs, and attorney fees. Cal. Civ. Code § 1747.70. For statutory violations by reporting agency, with regard to investigative reports: greater of actual damages or (except in case of class action) $10,000, costs and attorney fees. Punitive damages for grossly negligent or willful violations. Cal. Civ. Code § 1786.50. Non-government creditor who fails to comply with provisions regarding disclosure of reasons for credit denial, liable for actual damages, costs and attorney fees, with possible punitive damages up to $10,000 (or in a class action, lesser of $500,000 or 1% of creditor's net worth). Cal. Civ. Code § 1787.3. No liability if creditor acts in accordance with Federal Reserve Board rules, interpretations or approvals.

Statute of Limitations: Two years from violation or time of discovery but, effective July 1, 1998, not more than seven years.

Miscellaneous: The seven year limit for reporting delinquent accounts begins 180 days after delinquency. Reports of bankruptcies under Title 11 must refer to Title 11 of the Bankruptcy Code if that can be ascertained from the agency's source. Adverse information must be reported to a cosigner at the same time as to the consumer reporting agency. Prospective users who intend to extend credit through solicitation by mail must mail the extension of credit to same address as on the solicitation unless user verifies address change by such method as contacting the person solicited. This statute does not affect a consumer's ability to sue agencies, furnishers or users for defamation or invasion of privacy. A federal FCRA action will bar action under this statue for the same act or omission. Cal. Civ. Code § 1786.52.

Child Support Debts: Cal. Civ. Code § 1785.13(g) (West). A consumer reporting agency shall include in its credit reports information about overdue child or spousal support, if the information has been reported or verified by a federal, state or local governmental agency. **Cal. Fam. Code § 4701.** Department of Child Support Services administers a statewide program for monthly reporting of court-ordered child

---

[6] Note that for preemption purposes, this provision was not in effect on Sept. 30, 1996, and therefore may be preempted by 15 U.S.C. § 1681c. *See* § 10.4.4, *supra*.

[7] California law regarding the responsibilities of furnishers of information is explicitly not preempted by federal law. 15 U.S.C. § 1681t(b)(1)(F). *See* § 10.4.4, *supra*.

support obligations to credit reporting agencies. Before initial reporting of obligation or delinquency, department must attempt to contact obligor, and give 30 days to pay or contest the accuracy of the obligation.

State Credit Repair Statute: Cal. Civ. Code §§ 1789.10 to .26

Covered Activities: Improving credit record or obtaining extension of credit, in return for money or other consideration.

Exemptions: Regulated and supervised lenders; banks and savings associations eligible for FDIC insurance; nonprofit organizations; licensed real estate brokers and proraters acting within scope of license; California lawyers acting within scope of law practice, unless an employee or direct affiliate of credit services organization; registered securities broker-dealers; consumer reporting agencies.

Right to Cancel? Yes (5 days).

Prohibitions: Charging before complete performance; failing to perform services contracted for within 6 months; charging for referring buyer to retail seller for credit on same terms as generally available to public; making or advising false statements to creditors or credit reporting agencies; advising or creating false identity for buyer to obtain new credit record; submitting a buyer's dispute to credit reporting agency without buyer's knowledge; any fraudulent or deceptive practices; making false statements about services offered; requiring buyer to waive rights.

Other Substantive Requirements: Disclosures.

Bond: $100,000.

Private Cause of Action: Injunctive relief; actual damages, not less than amount paid by buyer; attorney fees and costs; punitive damages allowed. Actions available to consumers, consumer credit agencies, or furnishers of credit information.

State Identity Theft Statute: Cal. Penal Code §§ 530.5 to 530.8; Cal. Civ. Code §§ 1798.92 to .97, 1785.11.1 and 11.2, 1785.16(k), 1785.16.1 and .2 and 1785.20.3.

Definition of Offense: Willfully obtains personal identifying information, [defined] of another person, and uses that information for any unlawful purpose, including to obtain, or attempt to obtain, credit, goods, services, or medical information in the name of the other person without the consent.

Victim Remedies in Criminal Case: If person convicted under false name, court record must show that identity theft victim did not commit crime. Person who suspects he or she is victim of identity theft may initiate law enforcement investigation, receive copy of police report, and petition court for expedited determination and certification of factual innocence if identity thief has been charged with crime under victim's name. California Department of Justice must maintain a data base of identity theft victims, accessible to law enforcement, to victims, and to persons authorized by victims. Victim who wishes to be included must submit fingerprints and copy of police report.

Special Record-Clearing Provisions: If a victim of identity theft (defined in Civil Code as unauthorized use of another person's personal identifying information [defined] to obtain credit, goods, services, money, or property) is sued on an obligation resulting from the theft, victim may bring a cross claim alleging identity theft. If victim prevails, he or she is entitled to a judgment stating that the victim is not obligated on the claim, any security interest in the victim's property resulting from the claim is void and unenforceable, and an injunction restraining any collection efforts. Victim may join other claimants, and court may keep continuing jurisdiction for up to ten years, so as to deal with all claims resulting from the identity theft.

Duties of Private Entities: If victim submits copy of police report or DMV report, credit reporting agency must block all information resulting from identity theft, and must notify furnishers of that information; victim has right upon request to free report each month for up to 12 consecutive months. May unblock only if block resulted from fraud by consumer, or if consumer agrees block was erroneous, or if consumer knowingly received goods or services as a result of blocked transaction. Credit reporting agency must maintain 24-hour toll-free number, to allow consumers to report identity thefts, and seek a security alert or security freeze on account and must inform victim of rights under § 1785.16(k). Alert requires agency to inform all users who request information that a security alert is in place. Freeze requires agency to release information only in response to request by the consumer. Agency must delete from file records of any inquiries based on applications for credit initiated as a result of identity theft. Creditor may not sell debt if information about debt is blocked pursuant to this section, or if consumer provides sufficient information to show identity theft. Users of reports must take certain precautions against identity theft, i.e. check further if consumer's address does not agree with that in report, or if some information in credit report is blocked because of reported identity theft. If a security alert is in place, users must take specific precautions before selling goods or extending credit. Consumer may provide a telephone number, and request that he or she be called to confirm identity before any sale or extension of credit. Any person who learns that an application has been made or an account opened in his or her name without authority may provide the person or entity that received the application or opened the account with a copy of a police report and a request for information. The entity must provide the victim or designated law enforcement agency with all relevant records, i.e. type of personal information used, etc. Must be supplied within ten days of report.

Private Right of Action: Against user of credit report who omits required precautions, for actual damages, costs and attorney fees, and, if appropriate, punitive damages up to $30,000. Victim who brings cross-claim against one attempting to collect a debt that resulted from identity theft (see above) is entitled to actual damages, attorney fees and costs, if victim proves that notice was given—including a copy of a police report—to the claimant thirty days before filing the cross-claim. A civil penalty of up to $30,000 if claimant, after being notified of possible identity theft, pursued the claim without diligently investigating the possibility of identity theft. The provisions for cross-claim, etc. do not bar any other cause of action against the thief or anyone who used or possessed the goods, services or property obtained by the theft. Remedies under this section are cumulative to rights and remedies under other laws. Penalty of $100 per day, plus reasonable attorney fees, for entity that fails to provide records to victim or law enforcement within ten days, as required by Penal Code § 530.8. Statute of limitations, 4 years from date when consumer knew, or in the exercise of reasonable diligence should have known, of facts giving rise to cause of action.

Other State Provisions: **Cal. Civ. Code § 1785.13(c), (e) (West)**. If a bankruptcy is reported, the report must specify the chapter of the Bankruptcy Act. If an open-end credit account was closed by the consumer, the report must say so. **Cal. Ins. Code §§ 791.02, .04, .07**. The insurance information practices statute, which regulates all use of personal information in insurance, requires an insurer who seeks to use an investigative consumer report to advise the consumer of the right to be interviewed and to receive a copy of the report.

Colorado

State FCRA Statute: **Colo. Rev. Stat. §§ 12-14.3-101 to 12.14.3-109**.

Scope: Same as the federal law.
Purposes for Which Reports May Be Issued: Same as the federal law, except that use for insurance underwriting requires prior notice to consumer.
Consumer Access and Disclosure: Upon request by consumer: 1) All information in its files; 2) Names of persons requesting reports within previous twelve months; 3) A toll-free number for use in resolving disputes submitted in writing to a consumer reporting agency which operates nationwide. No fee for first report requested by consumer each year; 4) Information as to credit scoring § 12-14.3-104.3. Agency must notify consumer once per year of right to free report, if agency has either 1) received eight credit inquiries on consumer or 2) received a report that would add negative information to consumer's file. The disclosures may be given in a form letter if it advises the consumer of the number and type of events, and includes a notice or separate form by which the consumer may request a free copy of her credit report.
Disclosures to Consumer by User: A person who intends to use credit-scoring information in connection with the underwriting or rating of the insurance must notify the consumer in writing or in the same medium used in the application of insurance.
Restrictions on Content of Reports: Similar to federal law, and criminal records more than seven years old.[8] *See* § 12-.14.3-105.3
Consumer Disputes: Same as the federal law, but consumer reporting agency must reinvestigate within thirty days and must correct reports within five days after it receives corrections from furnisher.
Duties of Furnishers: No relevant provisions.
Consumer Remedies: Disputes may be submitted to court or binding arbitration after attempt made to resolve with consumer reporting agency under Act's procedures. Willful violations: three times actual damages or $1000 per inaccurate entry disputed by consumer, whichever is greater, reasonable attorney fees and costs. Negligent violations: actual damages or $1000 per inaccurate entry disputed by consumer which affects consumer's creditworthiness, whichever is greater, reasonable attorney fees and costs. If negligent violation does not affect consumer's creditworthiness, minimum damages are limited to $1000 for all inaccurate entries. No liability for negligent violations if corrected within thirty days of notice from consumer. If consumer's file remains uncorrected ten days after entry of any judgment for damages, additional penalty of $1000 per day per inaccurate entry available, until inaccurate entry corrected.
Miscellaneous: Agency shall not provide users with names of others who have requested consumer's file or with the number of other inquiries.[9]

Child Support Debts: **Colo. Rev. Stat. § 26-13-116**. Child support enforcement agencies may report information on child support debts to consumer reporting agencies. Prior to furnishing such information, an agency must provide to the obligor parent advance notice containing an explanation of the obligor parent's right to contest the accuracy of the information.

State Credit Repair Statute: **Colo. Rev. Stat. §§ 12-14.5-101 to -113**

Covered Activities: Improving credit record in return for money or other consideration.
Exemptions: Nonprofit organizations; Colorado lawyers acting within scope of law practice.
Right to Cancel? Yes (5 days).
Prohibitions: Charging before complete performance; making or advising false statements to creditors or credit reporting agencies; making false statements about services offered; advising buyer to request credit agency to verify

---

[8] This obsolescence standard was not in effect on Sept. 30, 1996, and therefore it is probably not preempted. *See* § 10.4.4, *supra*.
[9] Note that for preemption purposes, this provision was not in effect on Sept. 30, 1996. *See* § 10.4.4, *supra*.

credit report information, unless buyer states in writing belief and specific basis for belief that such information is inaccurate; requiring buyer to waive rights.
Other Substantive Requirements: Disclosures.
Bond: No relevant provisions.
Private Cause of Action: Actual damages, not less than amount paid by consumer; attorney fees and costs; twice actual damages if finding of willfulness.

State Identity Theft Statute: **Colo. Rev. Stat. §§ 12-14.3-106.5 to 108.**

Definition of Offense: Obtains by fraud, theft, or other criminal act personal identifying information in order to obtain credit, goods, services, or moneys in consumer's name.
Victim's Remedies in Criminal Case: No specific provision.
Special Record Clearing Provisions: See *Consumer Disputes* under state FCRA Statute.
Duties of Private Entities: Permanently block reporting of any information included in police report or court order regarding identity theft and inform consumer of block.
Private Right of Action: Right to court action as provided by federal FCRA or right to submit to binding arbitration, § 12-14.3-107. For remedies for failure to block information, see *Consumer Remedies* under state FCRA Statute.

Other State Provisions: **Colo. Rev. Stat. § 5-5-111(3)** Creditor may not report cosigner's liability to consumer reporting agency without providing notice of right to cure as specified in statute. **Colo. Rev. Stat. Ann. § 10-4-616** regulates the use of credit reports in personal automobile insurance. Applicants and policy holders must be notified if credit information is to be used in underwriting or rating. Upon consumer's request, insurer must explain the "significant characteristics" of the credit information that will impact the insurance score. If adverse action is based on credit information, the insurer must provide notice as required by Federal FCRA (i.e., source of report, dispute resolution procedure, etc.).

Connecticut

State FCRA Statute: **Conn. Gen. Stat. §§ 36a-695 to 36a-699e.**

Scope: Credit for personal, family, or household purposes. Does not apply to disclosure made to federal, state, or local government officers or upon court order.
Purposes for Which Reports May Be Issued: Same as federal law, except credit transactions not initiated by the consumer, if the consumer gives agency written notice withholding consent.[10]
Consumer Access and Disclosure: Within five business days of receipt of request by consumer: 1) Nature and substance of all information in its files, including any credit score; and 2) Written summary of consumer's rights under state and federal law in form substantially similar to Conn. Gen. Stat. § 36a-ag.[11] No charge if requested within 60 days after the consumer is notified of adverse action taken by a creditor; otherwise $5 maximum charge for first report each year, $7.50 for subsequent reports.
Disclosures to Consumer by User: No relevant provisions. Before taking adverse action against consumer based on credit report, user must disclose to consumer the name and address of the agency that issued the report.
Restrictions on Content of Reports: No relevant provisions.
Consumer Disputes: An agency must correct an inaccuracy upon proof of error. Procedures are the same as under FCRA, but consumer reporting agency must provide consumer with its toll-free number to use in resolving dispute. If consumer reporting agency fails to meet relevant thirty or forty-five day deadline, disputed information must be deleted.
Duties of Furnishers: No relevant provisions.
Consumer Remedies: Criminal fine; cease and desist order.
Statute of Limitations: No relevant provisions.
Miscellaneous: No relevant provisions.

Child Support Debts: **Conn. Gen. Stat. § 52-362d.** The Department of Social Services shall report to any participating consumer reporting agency any overdue support in the amount of $1000 or more. Prior to a report, the Department must give the obligor notice and opportunity for a hearing.

State Credit Repair Statute: **Conn. Gen. Stat. § 36a-700**

Covered Activities: "Credit clinics" advising or offering to modify adverse entries in credit record or rating in return for fee.
Exemptions: Credit rating agencies; nonprofit organizations; Connecticut lawyers acting within scope of law practice.
Right to Cancel? No.
Prohibitions: Charging before complete performance.
Other Substantive Requirements: Disclosures.
Bond: N/A
Private Cause of Action: A violation is a UDAP violation. Contract voidable.

State Identity Theft Statute: **Conn. Gen. Stat. § 53a-129a; Conn. Gen. Stat. § 52-571h.**

Definition of Offense: Intentionally, and without authority, obtains personal identifying information of another and uses that information for any unlawful purpose including, but not limited to, obtaining, or attempting to obtain, credit, goods, services or medical information in the name of that person.
Victim Remedies in Criminal Case: No specific provisions.

---

10 State provisions concerning prescreened lists are preempted. See § 10.4.4, *supra*.

11 State laws regarding the contents of the summary of federal rights which must be disclosed to consumers are preempted. See § 10.4.4, *supra*.

Special Record-Clearing Provisions: No specific provisions.
Duties of Private Entities: No specific provisions.
Private Right of Action: Person aggrieved by violation of 53a-129a may bring civil action for greater of treble damages or $1000, plus costs and attorney fees.

Other State Provisions: **Conn. Gen. Stat. Ann. §§ 38a-976, -982.** The Insurance Information and Privacy Act requires an insurer that seeks to use an investigative consumer report to notify the consumer of the right to be interviewed and to receive a copy of the report.

Delaware

Child Support Debts: **Del. Code Ann. tit. 13, § 2217.** Information regarding child support delinquencies shall be reported to consumer reporting agencies, provided that the amount of the delinquency is not less than $500 and the obligor is given notice and a period of twenty days to contest the accuracy of the information.

State Credit Repair Statute: **Del. Code Ann. tit. 6, §§ 2401 to 2414**

Covered Activities: Improving credit record or obtaining extension of credit, in return for money or other consideration.
Exemptions: Regulated and supervised lenders; mortgage lenders approved by HUD; banks and savings associations eligible for FDIC insurance; credit unions; nonprofit organizations; licensed lenders, public accountants, and real estate brokers acting within scope of license; mortgage brokers not engaged in covered activities; Delaware lawyers acting within scope of law practice; registered securities broker-dealers; consumer reporting agencies.
Right to Cancel? Yes (3 days).
Prohibitions: Charging before complete performance, unless organization has posted bond; charging for referring buyer to retail seller for credit on same terms as generally available to public; making or advising false statements to creditors or credit reporting agencies; making false statements about services offered; fraudulent and deceptive practices; requiring buyer to waive rights.
Other Substantive Requirements: Disclosures.
Bond: $15,000.
Private Cause of Action: Damages, not less than amount paid by buyer; attorney fees and costs; punitive damages allowed; 4-year statute of limitations.

State Identity Theft Statute: **Del. Code Ann. tit. 11, § 854.**

Definition of Offense: Knowingly or recklessly obtains, produces, possesses, uses, sells, gives or transfers personal identifying information belonging or pertaining to another person without authority and with intent to use the information to commit or facilitate any crime set forth in this title [theft and related offenses], or recklessly obtains, etc. thereby knowingly or recklessly facilitating the use of the information by a third person to commit or facilitate any crime set forth in this title. (Enhanced penalties if victim is age 62 or over.)
Victim Remedies in Criminal Case: Upon conviction, court must order full restitution for monetary loss, including documented loss of wages and reasonable attorney fees, suffered by the victim.
Special Record-Clearing Provisions: No specific provisions.
Duties of Private Entities: No specific provisions.
Private Right of Action: No specific provisions.

District of Columbia

Child Support Debts: **D.C. Code § 46-225.** Support obligations, of $1000 or more, over thirty days past due shall be reported to consumer reporting agencies, provided that the obligor are given thirty days advance notice and an opportunity to contest in writing the accuracy of the information.

State Credit Repair Statute: **D.C. Code §§ 28-4601 to -4608**

Covered Activities: Improving credit record or obtaining extension of credit, in return for money or other consideration.
Exemptions: Regulated and supervised lenders; mortgage lenders approved by HUD; banks and savings associations eligible for FDIC insurance; credit unions; nonprofit organizations; collection agency operators acting within scope of license; D.C. lawyers acting within scope of law practice; registered securities broker-dealers; consumer reporting agencies.
Right to Cancel? Yes (5 days).
Prohibitions: Charging before complete performance, unless organization has posted bond; charging for referring buyer to retail seller for credit on same terms as generally available to public; making or advising false statements to creditors or credit reporting agencies; making false statements about services offered; misuse of word "repair" to suggest ability to immediately correct credit problems; requiring buyer to waive rights.
Other Substantive Requirements: Disclosures.
Bond: $25,000.
Private Cause of Action: Actual damages, not less than amount paid by consumer; attorney fees and costs; punitive damages allowed; 3-year statute of limitations.

Florida

Child Support Debts: **Fla. Stat. Ann. § 61.1354.** Information regarding child support delinquencies shall be reported to consumer reporting agencies. Written notice to be given obligor fifteen days in advance, including notice of right to request a hearing to dispute the accuracy of the information. Notice and hearing required only for initial reporting, not for periodic release of updated information.

State Credit Repair Statute: **Fla. Stat. Ann. §§ 817.7001 to .706**

Covered Activities: Improving credit record or obtaining extension of credit, in return for money or other consideration.

Exemptions: Lenders authorized under Florida or federal law; mortgage lenders approved by HUD; banks and savings associations eligible for FDIC insurance; credit unions; nonprofit organizations; licensed collection agencies and real estate brokers acting within scope of license; Florida lawyers acting within scope of law practice; registered securities broker-dealers; consumer reporting agencies.

Right to Cancel? Yes (5 days).

Prohibitions: Charging before complete performance, unless organization has posted bond; charging for referring buyer to retail seller for credit on same terms as generally available to public; making or advising false statements to creditors or credit reporting agencies; making false statements about services offered; requiring buyer to waive rights.

Other Substantive Requirements: Disclosures.

Bond: $10,000.

Private Cause of Action: Actual damages, not less than amount paid by consumer; attorney fees and costs; punitive damages allowed.

State Identity Theft Statute: Fla. Stat. Ann. § 817.568.

Definition of Offense: Willfully and without authorization fraudulently uses or possesses with intent to use, personal identification information of another.

Victim Remedies in Criminal Case: Restitution of out-of-pocket costs, including attorney fees incurred in clearing victim's credit history or credit rating, and costs in any civil or administrative proceeding to satisfy debts, liens or obligations of victim arising from the defendant's actions. Court may issue orders necessary to clear any public record that contains false information given in violation of this section.

Special Record-Clearing Provisions: No specific provisions.

Duties of Private Entities: No specific provisions.

Private Right of Action: No specific provisions.

State Credit Information in Personal Insurance Statute: Fla. Stat. § 626.9741.

Scope: Use of credit reports or credit scores for underwriting and rating personal lines motor vehicle and residential insurance.

Disclosure: Insurer must disclose at time of application, in same medium as application, if a credit report or credit score will be requested. If adverse decision based on credit report, insurer must explain reasons, and provide either a free copy of the credit report, or the name, address and toll-free number of the consumer reporting agency.

Dispute Resolution: Insurer must provide means of appeal for applicant whose credit report or credit score was "unduly influenced" by dissolution of marriage, death of a spouse, or temporary loss of employment. Must complete review within ten days, and if it finds that credit information was "unduly influenced" it must exclude credit information or treat it as neutral, whichever is more favorable. Must establish policies to review the credit history of individual who was adversely affected by credit history at time of application or renewal. (Must do this every 2 years, or at request of insured.) May not cancel, non-renew, or require a change in payment plan as a result of this review.

Prohibited Practices: Insurer may not: request credit score based on race, color, religion, marital status, age, gender, income, national origin or place of residence; base an adverse decision solely on credit information, without considering other rating or underwriting factor; treat lack of credit history as negative factor, unless it can show that this relates to risk; base negative decision on collection account with medical industry code, or on certain types of credit inquiries.

Other: Insurer must comply with restrictions of Federal FCRA and rules. Insurers must report to Office of Insurance Regulation regarding their use of credit information.

Georgia

State FCRA Statute: **Ga. Code Ann. §§ 10-1-392 and 10-1-393(b)(29)**.

Scope: Covers consumer reporting agencies.

Purposes for Which Reports May Be Issued: No relevant provisions.

Consumer Access and Disclosure: Two free reports per year upon consumer request.

Disclosures to Consumer by User: No relevant provisions.

Restrictions on Content of Reports: No relevant provisions.

Consumer Disputes: No relevant provisions.

Duties of Furnishers: No relevant provisions.

Consumer Remedies: No relevant provisions.

Statute of Limitations: No relevant provisions.

Miscellaneous: No relevant provisions.

Child Support Debts: **Ga. Code Ann. § 19-11-25**. The Department of Human Resources shall make available information regarding the amount of overdue support by an absent parent to any consumer reporting agency upon request, if amount of overdue support exceeds $1000, and may do so when the amount is less than $1000. Information will be made available only after notice is sent to the absent parent and the absent parent has been given reasonable opportunity to contest.

State Credit Repair Statute: Ga. Code Ann. § 16-9-59.

Covered Activities: Improving credit record or obtaining extension of credit, in return for money or other consideration.

Exemptions: Lenders authorized under Georgia or federal law; banks and savings associations eligible for FDIC in-

surance; nonprofit organizations; licensed real estate brokers acting within scope of license; Georgia lawyers acting within scope of law practice; registered securities broker-dealers; consumer reporting agencies.
Right to Cancel? No.
Prohibitions: Owning or operating a credit repair organization.
Other Substantive Requirements: None.
Bond: N/A
Private Cause of Action: None.

State Identity Theft Statute: Ga. Code §§ 16-9-121 to -132.

Definition of Offense: Without authorization, and with intent to appropriate financial resources of or cause physical harm to another, obtains or records identifying information, or access or attempts to access financial resources through use of identifying information.
Victim Remedies in Criminal Case: Court may order restitution and may issue any order necessary to correct any public record that contains false information resulting from the actions that resulted in the conviction.
Special Record-Clearing Provisions: No specific provisions.
Duties of Private Entities: No specific provisions.
Private Right of Action: Right to court action for business or consumer victim. Individual or class consumer action for general or punitive damages, including treble damages, attorney fees, costs, injunctive relief.
Other: Administrator of Fair Business Practices Act may investigate complaints, with all the powers granted by that Act.

State Credit Information in Personal Insurance statute: Ga. Code Ann. §§ 33-24-90 to –98.

Scope: Credit information used in underwriting personal insurance (private vehicle, homeowners, including mobile home, and recreational vehicle).
Disclosures: Must disclose at time of application, in writing or same medium as application, if credit report or credit score will be used. If adverse action is based on credit information, insurer must explain reasons and provide notification as required by Federal FCRA (source of information, dispute resolution procedure, etc.).
Dispute Resolution: At time of renewal, consumer may request reunderwriting or rerating based on current credit report or credit score—company must warn consumer that this might result in higher or lower rate, or termination or non-renewal. If an item in a credit report is being disputed pursuant to Federal FCRA, then during the 45 days after item was placed in dispute, insurer must either not use credit information, or treat credit information as neutral with respect to the disputed item(s).
Prohibited Practices: Insurer may not use insurance score calculated using income, gender, race, address, zip code, ethnic group, religion, marital status or nationality; take adverse action, or base renewal rates solely on credit information without consideration of other underwriting factors; take adverse action because consumer does not have credit card; treat absence of credit information as negative, unless it can show that this relates to risk; take adverse action based on credit report issued or insurance score calculated more than 180 days before date of issuance or renewal of policy; use credit information if it does not obtain updated credit information at least every 36 months. May not consider as negative factor collection accounts with medical industry code, or certain credit inquiries.
Other: Insurer must file scoring models with commissioner of insurance.

Guam

Child Support Debts: **5 Guam Code Ann. § 34130**. Child Support Enforcement Office shall report child support arrears to consumer reporting agencies where delinquency is $1000 or more; may report arrears if less. Obligors must be notified prior to release of information and informed that they have ten days to request a meeting with the head of the Child Support Enforcement Office to contest accuracy of information.

Hawaii

Child Support Debts: **Haw. Rev. Stat. § 576D-6(6)**. Information regarding child support delinquencies shall be made available to consumer reporting agencies. Delinquent parents must be given notice and the opportunity to contest accuracy of the information prior to reporting.

State Credit Repair Statute: Haw. Rev. Stat. § 481B-12

Covered Activities: Modifying credit record in return for money or other consideration.
Exemptions: None.
Right to Cancel? No.
Prohibitions: Charging for referring buyer to retail seller for credit on same terms as generally available to public; making or advising false statements to creditors or credit reporting agencies; making false statements about services offered. The Telemarketing Fraud Prevention Act, Haw. Stat. § 481P-3(2) forbids telemarketers to request a fee to remove derogatory information from or improve a consumer's credit record or credit history, unless the telemarketer provides the consumer with a credit report, from a credit reporting agency, showing that the promised results have been achieved. The report must have been issued at least six months after the results were achieved.
Other Substantive Requirements: None.
Bond: N/A
Private Cause of Action: Violation is UDAP violation.

Identity Theft: Haw. Stat. §§ 708-839.6 to -839.8.

Definition of Offense: 1st degree: makes or causes to be made a transmission of any personal information of another

with the intent to facilitate the commission of certain felonies (including murder, kidnapping, extortion) or to commit first degree theft from the person whose information was used, or from another. 2d degree: makes or causes to be made, etc. with intent to commit 2d degree theft. 3d degree: same, with intent to commit third degree theft.
Victim Remedies in Criminal Case: No relevant provisions.
Special Record Clearing Provisions: No relevant provisions.
Duties of Private Entities: No relevant provisions.
Private Right of action: No relevant provisions.

Idaho

State Credit Repair Statute: Idaho Code §§ 26-2221 to -2251 ("Collection Agencies" statute)

Covered Activities: Credit or debt "counselors," engaging in applying, paying, or prorating creditors or credit counseling for compensation. § 26-2223(6), (7).
Exemptions: Mortgage lenders approved by HUD; banks and savings associations eligible for FDIC insurance; licensed mortgage companies and real estate brokers acting within scope of license; any governmental body; abstract and title companies doing an escrow business; Idaho lawyers acting within scope of law practice.
Right to Cancel? No.
Prohibitions: Deceptive dealings. Only a non-profit organization may be licensed as a credit counselor. § 26-2222(11).
Other Substantive Requirements: N/A
Bond: $15,000.
Private Cause of Action: None.

State Identity Theft Statute: Idaho Code §§ 18-3126 and –3128; §§ 28-51-101 and -102.

Definition of Offense: Obtain or record personal identifying information of another without authorization, with intent to obtain credit, money, goods or services in the name of that person.
Victim Remedies in Criminal Case: No specific provisions.
Special Record-Clearing Provisions: No specific provisions.
Duties of Private Entities: Credit reporting agency must block information resulting from violation of Idaho Code § 18-3126, and notify furnisher that a block is in place. Agency and furnisher may refuse to block, or rescind, if block is result of misrepresentation by consumer, if consumer agrees block was in error, or if consumer knowingly received goods or services as a result of the blocked transaction.
Private Right of Action: For violation of § 28-51-102 (duties of agency and furnisher) consumer has private right of action for damages, attorney fees, injunction and "other appropriate relief."

Other State Provisions: Idaho Code § 41-1843 (effective January 1, 2003). Forbids property or casualty insurers to charge a higher premium, or to cancel, nonrenew or refuse to issue a policy "based primarily upon an individual's credit rating or credit history." The statute applies only to property or casualty insurance (as defined in Idaho Code Ch. 5, title 41) issued primarily for personal, family or household purposes.

Illinois

Child Support Debts: 305 Ill. Comp. Stat. Ann. § 5/10-16.4; 750 Ill. Comp. Stat. Ann. § 5/706.3. Courts finding obligers owing more than $10,000 or an amount equal to at least three months support obligation shall direct the clerk of the court to make the information available to consumer reporting agencies.

State Credit Repair Statute: 815 Ill. Comp. Stat. Ann. §§ 605/1 to 605/16

Covered Activities: Improving credit record or obtaining extension of credit, in return for money or other consideration.
Exemptions: Persons authorized to make loans or extend credit under Illinois or federal law; HUD-approved lenders; banks, savings and loan associations, and subsidiaries eligible for FDIC or FSLIC insurance; credit unions; nonprofit organizations that do not charge consumer prior to or upon execution of contract; licensed real estate brokers and attorneys; securities broker-dealers; consumer reporting agencies; licensed residential mortgage loan brokers and bankers.
Right to Cancel? Yes (3 days).
Prohibitions: Charging before complete performance, unless organization has posted bond; charging for referring buyer to retail seller for credit on same terms as generally available to public; making or advising consumer to make untrue or misleading statements to credit reporting agencies or creditors; making false statements about services offered; inducing consumers to waive rights.
Other Substantive Requirements: Disclosures.
Bond: $100,000.
Private Cause of Action: Actual damages, punitive damages, attorney fees, and court costs; injunction; violation is also a UDAP violation.

State Identity Theft Statute: 720 Ill. Comp. Stat. Ann. § 5/16G-1 to -30.

Definition of Offense: Knowingly uses personal identifying document or information of another to fraudulently obtain credit, money, goods, services or other property uses personal information or personal identification document of another with intent to commit felony theft, or any other felony; obtains, records, possesses, transfers, sells or manufactures personal identification information or document with intent to commit, or aid and abet the commission of, a felony; uses, transfers or possesses document making implements to produce false identification or false documents, with knowledge that they will be used to commit a felony. Enhanced penalty if victim age 60 or over, or disabled.

Victim Remedies in Criminal Case: If a crime has been committed under a stolen name, an identity theft victim may petition the court for, or a court may issue of its own motion, a declaration of factual innocence, and may order the relevant records sealed, corrected, or labeled to indicate that the data do not indicate the defendant's true identity. Person who suspects he or she is victim of ID theft may initiate an investigation and cause a police report to be filed.

Special Record-Clearing Provisions: No specific provisions.

Duties of Private Entities: UDAP statute, 815 Ill. Comp. Stat. Ann. § 505/2MM, provides that any person who uses a credit report in connection with an extension of credit, and who receives notice that a police report of identity theft has been filed with a consumer reporting agency, may not extend credit or lend money without taking reasonable steps to confirm consumer's identity and confirm that the application is not the result of identity theft. Credit card issuer who mails a solicitation, and receives a response with a different address, may not issue a card until it takes reasonable steps to confirm consumer's change of address.

Private Right of Action: Thief liable for damages, attorney fees, and costs.

Other State Provisions: Solicitations or applications to sell consumer access to reports or government records must disclose that such records and reports are otherwise available free or for nominal cost. 815 Ill. Comp. Stat. Ann. § 505/2B.2. No person may report adverse information to a credit reporting agency unless the cosigner is notified first that the primary obligor has become delinquent or defaulted, that the cosigner is responsible for payment, and that the cosigner has fifteen days to pay or make arrangements for payment. Violation is an unlawful act and may result in up to $250 in actual damages in addition to attorney fees.[12] 815 Ill. Comp. Stat. Ann. § 505/2S.

State Credit Information in Personal Insurance statute: 215 Ill. Comp. Stat. Ann. §§ 157/1 through 157/99.

Scope: Use of credit information in underwriting personal insurance: private passenger vehicle or recreational vehicle, homeowners (including mobile home), noncommercial fire insurance, individually underwritten for personal, family, or household use.

Disclosures: Insurer must disclose at time of application, in writing or in same medium as application, if it will use credit information. If insurer takes adverse action based on credit report, it must explain reasons to consumer, and provide notice as required by FCRA (source of report, dispute resolution procedure, etc.).

Dispute Resolution: At time of renewal consumer may request company to re-underwrite or re-rate based on current credit report. If information in credit report is disputed, pursuant to the Federal FCRA and found incorrect, insurer must re-underwrite or re-rate within 30 days after notice. If refund is required it should be for the lesser of policy period or 12 months.

Prohibited Practices: Insurer may not use credit score based on income, gender, address, ethnic group, religion, marital status or nationality; deny, cancel, or non-renew based wholly on credit information without, another applicable underwriting factor independent of credit information; base renewal rates solely on credit information; take adverse action based on lack of credit card; count lack of credit history as a negative factor, unless insurer can show relationship to risk; take adverse action based on credit report issued or credit score calculated more than 90 days before policy was written or renewed; use credit information if it does not recalculate every 36 months based on current credit report; treat as a negative factor collection accounts with a medical industry code, or certain credit inquiries.

Other: Insurer who uses insurance scores must file scoring model with Department of Insurance.

Indiana

State Credit Repair Statute: Ind. Code §§ 24-5-15-1 to 24-5-15-11

Covered Activities: Improving credit record or obtaining extension of credit, in return for money or other consideration.

Exemptions: Regulated and supervised lenders; mortgage lenders approved by HUD; banks and savings associations eligible for FDIC insurance; credit unions; nonprofit organizations; licensed real estate brokers acting within scope of license; Indiana lawyers acting within scope of law practice; registered securities broker-dealers; consumer reporting agencies.

Right to Cancel? Yes (3 days).

Prohibitions: Charging before complete performance, unless organization has posted bond; charging for referring buyer to retail seller for credit on same terms as generally available to public; making or advising false statements to creditors or credit reporting agencies; making false statements about services offered; requiring buyer to waive rights.

Other Substantive Requirements: Disclosures.

Bond: $10,000.

Private Cause of Action: Twice actual damages or $1000, whichever is greater, plus attorney fees.

State Identity Theft Statute: Ind. Code §§ 35-38-1-2.5, 35-43-5-1 and -3.5.

Definition of Offense: Knowingly uses or intentionally obtains, possesses, transfers or uses the identifying information of another without authorization, and with intent to harm or defraud another.

Victim Remedies in Criminal Case: During or after sentenc-

---

12 Most state laws concerning the duties of furnishers are now preempted. *See* § 10.4.4, *supra*.

ing of thief, the court may issue an order describing the person whose credit history may be affected by the crime of deception, with sufficient identifying information to assist another person in correcting the credit history, and stating that the person was the victim of a crime of deception that may have affected the person's credit history. This order may be used to correct the credit history of any person described in the order.

Special Record-Clearing Provisions: No specific provisions.
Duties of Private Entities: No specific provisions.
Private Right of Action: No specific provisions.

State Credit Information in Personal Insurance Statute: Ind. Code §§ 27-2-21-1 through 23.

Scope: Use of credit information in personal insurance, i.e. for personal, family or household use, including accident, theft, liability, including homeowners and vehicle.

Disclosures: Insurer must disclose at time of application, in writing or in same medium as application, if it will use credit information. If insurer takes adverse action based on credit report, it must explain reasons to consumer, and provide notice as required by FCRA (source of report, dispute resolution procedure, etc.).

Dispute Resolution: If information in credit report is disputed, pursuant to the Federal FCRA, and found incorrect, insurer must re-underwrite or re-rate within 30 days after notice. If refund is required it should be for the lesser of policy period or 12 months.

Prohibited Practices: Insurer may not use credit score based on income, gender, address, ethnic group, religion, marital status or nationality; deny, cancel, or non-renew based wholly on credit information without, another applicable underwriting factor independent of credit information; base renewal rates solely on credit information; treat consumer's lack of a credit card as a negative factor, treat lack of credit information as a negative factor, unless insurer can show relationship to risk; take adverse action based on credit report issued or credit score calculated more than 90 days before policy was written or renewed; use credit information if it does not recalculate every 36 months based on current credit report; treat as a negative factor collection accounts with a medical industry code, or certain credit inquiries.

Other: Insurer who uses insurance score must file scoring model with department of insurance. Violation is a UDAP.

Iowa

State Credit Repair Statute: Iowa Code §§ 538A.1 to .14.

Covered Activities: Improving credit record in return for money or other consideration.

Exemptions: Regulated and supervised lenders; mortgage lenders approved by HUD; banks and savings associations eligible for FDIC insurance; credit unions; nonprofit organizations; licensed real estate brokers acting within scope of license; Iowa lawyers acting within scope of law practice; registered securities broker-dealers; consumer reporting agencies.

Right to Cancel? Yes (3 days).

Prohibitions: Charging before complete performance, unless organization has posted bond; charging for referring buyer to retail seller for credit on same terms as generally available to public; making or advising false statements to creditors or credit reporting agencies; making false statements about services offered; requiring buyer to waive rights.

Other Substantive Requirements: Disclosures.

Bond: $10,000.

Private Cause of Action: Injunctive relief (10-year statute of limitations). Actual damages, not less than amount paid by buyer; attorney fees and costs; punitive damages allowed (4-year statute of limitations).

State Identity Theft Statute: Iowa Code §§ 714.16B and 715A.8 and .9.

Definition of Offense: With intent to obtain a benefit, fraudulently obtains identifying information of another, and uses or attempts to use it without authorization to obtain credit, property, or services.

Victim Remedies in Criminal Case: No specific provisions.
Special Record-Clearing Provisions: No specific provisions.
Duties of Private Entities: No specific provisions.
Private Right of Action: In addition to other remedies provided by law, person who suffers pecuniary loss from identity theft has civil action for the greater of treble damages or $1000, plus reasonable costs and attorney fees. Violation of this section is also an unlawful practice under § 714.16 (UDAP).

Other State Provisions: **Iowa Code § 654.18(4)**. A mortgagee shall not report that a mortgagor is delinquent on the mortgage if the mortgagor agrees to an alternative non-judicial voluntary foreclosure procedure. The mortgagee may report that an alternative non-judicial voluntary foreclosure procedure was used.[13]

Kansas

State FCRA Statute: Kan. Stat. Ann. §§ 50-701 to 50-722.

Scope: Same as the federal law.

Purposes for Which Reports May Be Issued: Similar to federal law, except no authorization for provision to potential investors or servicers, or current insurers, in connection with evaluation of the credit or repayment risks associated with existing credit obligations.

Consumer Access and Disclosure: Similar to federal law, except agency only required to disclose non-employment report recipients within previous six months.

Disclosures to Consumers By Users: Similar to federal law.
Restrictions on Content of Reports: Similar to federal law

---

13 Most state laws concerning the duties of furnishers are now preempted. *See* § 10.4.4, *supra*.

except criminal records more than seven years old or bankruptcies more than fourteen years old.[14] Adverse information (except public record information) from investigative consumer reports may not be used in subsequent reports unless it has been verified while preparing the new report or was received within three months.

Consumer Disputes: Agency must investigate within a reasonable time if informed by consumer of dispute. Must delete if information is inaccurate or no longer verifiable. If dispute not resolved, consumer may file statement, up to 100 words, describing the dispute. If information is deleted, consumer may request agency to inform users who obtained reports within two years for employment purposes or six months for other purposes. Agency must inform consumer of this right.

Duties of Furnishers: No relevant provisions.

Consumer Remedies: Civil liability for agencies and users: actual damages plus costs and reasonable attorney fees; punitive damages for willful violations. Criminal penalties also available.

Statute of Limitations: Two years from violation or time of discovery.

Miscellaneous: No relevant provisions.

Child Support Debts: **Kan. Stat. Ann. § 23-4145**. The Secretary of Social and Rehabilitation Services must make available information concerning support arrearages in excess of $1000 owed or assigned to the Secretary or owed to any person who has applied for services, upon the request of a consumer reporting agency. The Secretary may make information concerning smaller arrearages available. Before making this information available, the Secretary must provide advance notice to the obligor.

State Credit Repair Statute: **Kan. Stat. Ann. §§ 50-1101 to -1115**

Covered Activities: Improving credit record or obtaining extension of credit, in return for money or other consideration.

Exemptions: Regulated and supervised lenders; mortgage lenders approved by HUD; banks and savings associations eligible for FDIC insurance; credit unions; person whose primary business is loans secured by liens on realty; loan brokers registered with Kansas commissioner; nonprofit organizations; licensed real estate brokers acting within scope of license; Kansas lawyers acting within scope of law practice; registered securities broker-dealers; consumer reporting agencies.

Right to Cancel? Yes (3 days).

Prohibitions: Charging before complete performance, unless organization has posted bond; charging for referring buyer to retail seller for credit on same terms as generally available to public; making or advising false statements to creditors or credit reporting agencies; making false statements about services offered; fraudulent and deceptive practices; requiring buyer to waive rights.

Other Substantive Requirements: Disclosures.

Bond: $25,000.

Private Cause of Action: Actual damages, not less than amount paid by buyer; attorney fees and costs; punitive damages allowed; a violation is a UDAP violation; 2-year statute of limitations. Injunctive relief.

State Identity Theft Statute: **Kan. Stat. Ann. § 21-4018**.

Definition of Offense: Knowingly and with intent to defraud for economic benefit, obtains, transfers, possesses or uses, or attempts to obtain, transfer, possess or use, an identification document or PIN number of another.

Victim Remedies in Criminal Case: No specific provisions.

Special Record-Clearing Provisions: No specific provisions.

Duties of Private Entities: No specific provisions.

Private Right of Action: No specific provisions.

Kentucky

State FCRA Statute: **Ky. Rev. Stat. Ann. §§ 367.310 and 367.990(16)**.

Scope: No relevant provisions.

Purposes for Which Reports May Be Issued: No relevant provisions.

Consumer Access and Disclosures: No relevant provisions.

Disclosures to Consumer by User: No relevant provisions.

Restrictions on Content of Reports: Criminal charge in Kentucky court which did not result in conviction.[15]

Consumer Disputes: No relevant provisions.

Duties of Furnishers: No relevant provisions.

Consumer Remedies: Civil liability: each violation may result in a fine of up to $200.

Statute of Limitations: No relevant provisions.

Miscellaneous: No relevant provisions.

Child Support Debts: **Ky. Rev. Stat. Ann. § 205.768**. Child support arrearages shall be reported to consumer reporting agencies, provided that advance notice is given to the obligor explaining the methods available to contest the accuracy of the information.

State Identity Theft Statute: **Ky. Rev. Stat. Ann. §§ 411.210, 514.160 and .170, and 532.034**.

Definition of Offense: Theft of identity: Without consent, knowingly possesses or uses identifying information of another to deprive that person of property, obtain benefits to

---

14 These two definitions of information which may not be contained under Kansas law in a consumer report were in effect on Sept. 30, 1996, and therefore are not preempted, although they regulate the contents of consumer reports and might otherwise be preempted. *See* § 10.4.4, *supra*.

15 This provision was in effect on Sept. 30, 1996, so even if it could be said to be otherwise preempted by 15 U.S.C. § 1681c, it is not preempted. *See* § 10.4.4, *supra*.

which not entitled, make financial or credit transactions using identity of another, avoid detection, or obtain commercial or political benefit. Trafficking in stolen identities: Manufactures, possesses, transfers, sells or possesses with intent to manufacture, transfer or sell, the personal identity of another for purposes forbidden by theft of identity section. Possession of 5 or more identities is prima facie evidence of possession for trafficking.

Victim Remedies in Criminal Case: Upon conviction, shall pay restitution for financial loss by victim, which may include any costs incurred in correcting credit history, or in any civil or administrative proceeding to satisfy debt or obligation, including lost wages and attorney fees. Victim includes financial institution, insurance company or bonding company that suffers financial loss.

Special Record-Clearing Provisions: No specific provisions.

Duties of Private Entities: No specific provisions.

Private Right of Action: Victim of identity theft or trafficking in stolen identities has cause of action for compensatory and punitive damages. Theft is violation of Consumer Protection Act. Statute of limitations, 5 years.

Other: Attorney General (Financial Integrity Enforcement Division) shall coordinate with the Department of Financial Institutions, the U.S. Secret Service, and the Kentucky Bankers' Association to prepare and disseminate information to prevent identity theft.

Louisiana

State FCRA Statute: La. Rev. Stat. Ann. §§ 9:3571.1 and 9:3571.2.

Scope: Consumer's credit-worthiness, credit standing or credit capacity.

Purposes for Which Reports May Be Issued: A motor vehicle dealer may not request or review a report without consumer's written permission in connection with a test drive, a request to test drive, a request for pricing or financing, or negotiations with a consumer, unless consumer has already applied to lease or finance a vehicle.

Consumer Access and Disclosure: Similar to federal law, but must be made within five days of written request and agency only required to disclose non-employment report recipients within previous six months. Agency may charge $8 fee (unless request made within sixty days of adverse action based on consumer report). Amount of fee may increase annually with increases in consumer price index.

Disclosures to Consumer by User: Name and address of credit reporting agency, if adverse action based wholly or partially on report; notice of right to free report.

Restrictions on Content of Reports: No relevant provisions.

Consumer Disputes: Must investigate and correct or update within 45 days of a consumer's written notification of dispute.

Duties of Furnishers: No relevant provisions.

Consumer Remedies: Intentional or negligent violation: actual damages plus reasonable attorney fees, court costs, and other reasonable costs of prosecution.

If denied credit, insurance, or employment on the basis of erroneous or inaccurate information furnished by a credit reporting agency, and the erroneous or inaccurate information was the significant material cause of the denial, and if the credit reporting agency failed to use ordinary care or failed to exercise due diligence in discovering such error (i.e., by not complying with the FCRA, CCPA, or other provision of this section), the credit reporting agency is liable. The consumer is entitled to actual damages in addition to reasonable attorney fees and court costs.

If a person is required to have erroneous or inaccurate information removed from a credit report as a condition to having a credit, insurance, or employment application approved and the erroneous or inaccurate information was a significant material cause of the request for removal, and if the credit reporting agency failed to use ordinary care or failed to exercise due diligence in discovering such error, the credit reporting agency is liable. The consumer is entitled to actual damages in addition to reasonable attorney fees and court costs.

Violations of § 9:3571.2 (requests by motor vehicle dealers before test drive, pricing inquiry or negotiations): civil penalty of up to $2500 per violation.

Statute of Limitations: No relevant provisions.

Miscellaneous: No relevant provisions.

State Credit Repair Statute: La. Rev. Stat. Ann. §§ 9:3573.1 to .16

Covered Activities: Improving credit record in return for money or other consideration.

Exemptions: Regulated and supervised lenders; mortgage lenders, provided the credit repair service is in connection with the loan, and no additional fee is charged approved by HUD; banks and savings associations eligible for FDIC insurance; credit unions; nonprofit organizations; licensed certified public accountants acting within scope of license; Louisiana lawyers acting within scope of law practice; consumer reporting agencies.

Right to Cancel? Yes (5 days).

Prohibitions: Charging before complete performance, unless organization has posted bond; making or advising false statements to creditors or credit reporting agencies; making false statements about services offered; making nonessential requests for credit information from any source where no cost for such information; engaging in fraudulent or deceptive practices; requiring buyer to waive rights. Structure a transaction so as to circumvent the provisions of this act, or violate any provision of the Federal Credit Repair Organizations Act.

Other Substantive Requirements: Disclosures.

Bond: $25,000.

Private Cause of Action: Actual damages, no less than amount paid by buyer; costs; attorney fees based on time expended, not on amount of recovery where willful violation, an additional amount twice actual damages. Injunctive relief. 4-year statute of limitations.

State Identity Theft Statute: La. Rev. Stat. Ann. §§ 9:3568, 14:67.16.

Definition of Offense: Intentional use or attempted use of identifying information of another, without authorization, to obtain credit, money, goods, services or anything else of value.

Victim Remedies in Criminal Case: Court may order full restitution to the victim, or any other who suffered financial loss. If defendant is indigent, a payment plan may be ordered. Victim may file police report in victim's place of domicile, or with state department of justice. Investigating officer should make detailed written report: name of victim, type of information misused, etc. and provide a copy to the victim

Special Record-Clearing Provisions: Consumer may place security alert in file, indicating that identity may have been used without consent to fraudulently obtain goods or services in consumer's name. If consumer provides proper identification, alert must be placed within 5 days of request, and will remain in effect for 90 days. Agency must send alert to any person who requests a consumer report on the consumer. Agency that compiles and maintains files on a nationwide basis must have 24-hour toll free telephone number for receiving security alert requests.

Duties of Private Entities: Creditor that grants credit as result of ID theft must provide victim with information (i.e., billing statements, etc.) needed by victim to undo the effects of the crime. Creditor may require from victim a written statement, copy of the police report, proper identification, and request for information. No creditor may be held liable for good faith release of information to provide information about actual or potential violations to other financial institutions, law enforcement, or victims who provide required written materials, or who assist a victim in recovery of funds or rehabilitation of credit. A person who receives information about a security alert, pursuant to § 9:3571.1 shall not extend credit, lend money, etc. until it takes reasonable steps to verify the identity of the consumer. IF consumer has included a phone number in the security alert, creditor should contact the consumer using that number.

Private Right of Action: A creditor, potential creditor, credit reporting agency or other entity that violates the provisions governing security alerts, and assistance to victims of identity theft, will be liable to the victim of ID theft for all documented expenses suffered as a result, plus reasonable attorney fees.

State Credit Information in Personal Insurance statute: La. Rev. Stat. Ann. §§ 1481 to 1494.

Scope: Use of credit information for personal insurance, i.e. for personal, family or household use: homeowners (including mobile home), noncommercial fire, motor vehicle and recreational vehicle.

Disclosures: Insurer must disclose at time of application, in writing or same medium as application, that credit information will be used. If adverse action is based on credit information, insurer must explain the reasons, and give notification as required by Federal FCRA (source of report, dispute resolution procedure, etc.).

Dispute Resolution: If information in credit report is disputed, pursuant to the Federal FCRA and found incorrect, insurer must re-underwrite or re-rate within 30 days after notice. If refund is required it should be for the lesser of policy period or 12 months. Insurer who uses credit information must provide process for consumer to appeal "the underwriting or rating of risks for which credit scoring may be an inappropriate factor."

Prohibited Practices: Insurer may not use credit score based on income, gender, address, ethnic group, religion, marital status or nationality; deny, cancel, or non-renew based wholly on credit information without, another applicable underwriting factor independent of credit information; base renewal rates solely on credit information; treat consumer's lack of a credit card as a negative factor, treat lack of credit information as a negative factor, unless insurer can show relationship to risk; take adverse action based on credit report issued or credit score calculated more than 180 days before policy was written or renewed; use credit information if it does not recalculate every 36 months based on current credit report; treat as a negative factor collection accounts with a medical industry code, or certain credit inquiries.

Other: Insurer must provide reasonable exemptions from the use of credit information for consumer who can show that credit history was "unduly influenced" by medical crisis, death of a spouse, identity theft, the personal guarantee of a business loan, or other catastrophic event as deemed by the commissioner of insurance. Insurers who use insurance scores must file scoring models with department of insurance.

Maine

State FCRA Statute: Me. Rev. Stat. Ann. tit. 10, §§ 1311 to 1329 (*See also* Advisory Rulings of Bureau of Consumer Protection).

Scope: Investigative consumer report includes telephone information. Adverse information is deemed to be any information likely to have a negative effect on the ability of the consumer to obtain credit, credit insurance, employment, benefits, goods or services.

Purposes for Which Reports May Be Issued: Same as the federal law, but reports listing a consumer as having been denied credit where the sole reason for denial was insufficient information for the granting of credit may not be issued, unless report states denial was for that reason.[16]

Consumer Access and Disclosure: The consumer has the right to have medical information given to the licensed physician of his or her choice. Only requires agency to disclose users for non-employment purposes within previous six months. Right to receive copy of file. Maximum charge: Actual costs for second or subsequent report within 12 months, $5, unless a copy is requested within 60 days after an adverse consumer determination, in which case it is free. Public record information is the same as federal law. Must disclose to consumer the substance of public record information provided for employment purposes. Must advise consumer of the procedures adopted by the agency to enable a consumer to correct any inaccurate information.

Disclosures to Consumers By User: Notice of requests for investigative reports must be delivered three business days prior to the investigation.

Restrictions on Content of Reports: Reporting information which cannot be verified unless the report also contains attempts to verify. Adverse information in investigative reports which is not reverified or received within previous three months. Reporting that a consumer was denied credit if the sole reason for denial is lack of credit information, unless the report states that denial was for that reason.[17] A debt collector may not disclose an overdue debt for medical expenses of a minor child, unless the debtor is the responsible party according to a court or administrative order (provided that the collector has been informed of the existence of the order), and the responsible party has been notified and given an opportunity to pay.

Consumer Disputes: Agency must reinvestigate within twenty-one days; otherwise similar to federal law.[18] In addition, an agency must retain inaccurate information in a separate folder which can only be used as defenses in a civil action. Immediate notice to a consumer if a dispute is considered "frivolous."[19] If information is found to be inaccurate or unverifiable, agency must notify users who obtained reports for employment purposes within 2 years or other purposes within six months.

Duties of Furnishers: May not furnish information it knows or should know is inaccurate. May not furnish information if it is informed by consumer that information is inaccurate, and information is, in fact, inaccurate. One who regularly furnishes information to consumer reporting agency must notify agency of corrections, if any information supplied is later found to be inaccurate. Must notify agency if consumer disputes the information. Regular furnisher must investigate dispute reported by consumer. (No private right of action for violations of these requirements; enforcement only by administrator).

Consumer Remedies: Similar to the federal law for willful noncompliance, but treble damages rather than punitive damages. For negligent violations, in addition to actual damages, minimum damages of at least $100 per violation and each report containing inaccurate or irrelevant information which contributed to an adverse consumer decision. Criminal penalties for obtaining information from a consumer reporting agency on false pretenses, or for unauthorized disclosures by agency officers or employees.

Statute of Limitations: Same as the federal law.

Miscellaneous: Investigative reports must be updated every three months. Reports must be in writing and retained in a file for two years for employment purposes, six months for other purposes. (*See Equifax Services, Inc. v. Cohen*, 420 A.2d 189 (Me. 1980)). If a bankruptcy is reported, must indicate which chapter, if known. If bankruptcy withdrawn by consumer before final judgment, agency must report this. If a credit account is voluntarily closed by consumer, agency must report this along when it reports information about the account.

Child Support Debts: Me. Rev. Stat. Ann. tit. 10, § 1329. The Department of Human Services, upon the request of a consumer reporting agency, shall make available information regarding the amount of overdue child support owed by any parent. Prior to making the information available to the requesting agency, the Department shall provide the obligor parent with notice of the proposed action. The parent shall be given twenty days prior notice to contest the accuracy of the information. The Department may voluntarily provide this information as well.

State Credit Repair Statute: Me. Rev. Stat. Ann. tit. 9-A, §§ 10-101 to -401

Covered Activities: Improving credit record or obtaining extension of credit, in return for money or other consideration.

Exemptions: Regulated and supervised lenders; nonprofit organizations; licensed real estate brokers acting within scope of license; Maine lawyers acting within scope of law practice; consumer reporting agencies; certain affiliates or employees of supervised lenders; person who performs marketing services for lender, if person not compensated by consumer for credit services; seller of consumer goods, or seller's employee, who performs services in connection with sale or proposed sale, and is not compensated by the consumer for the services.

Right to Cancel? No.

---

16 This provision was in effect on Sept. 30, 1996, so even if it could be said to be otherwise preempted by 15 U.S.C. § 1681c, it is not preempted. *See* § 10.4.4, *supra*.

17 These provisions were in effect on Sept. 30, 1996, so although they may regulate the time allowed for an agency to reinvestigate a dispute, or the contents of reports, they are not preempted. *See* § 10.4.4, *supra*.

18 Provision was in effect on Sept. 30, 1996, so although it regulates the time allowed for an agency to reinvestigate a dispute, it is not preempted. *See* § 10.4.4, *supra*.

19 This provision was in effect on Sept. 30, 1996, so although it regulates the time allowed for part of the reinvestigation process, it is not preempted. *See* § 10.4.4, *supra*.

Prohibitions: False and misleading advertising regarding terms and conditions of services offered.
Other Substantive Requirements: Disclosures. Consumer fees to placed in escrow account pending completion of services contracted for; comply with Federal statute and rules governing the privacy of consumer financial information.
Bond: $10,000.
Private Cause of Action: Actual damages; attorney fees and costs. Restitution after administrative hearing.

State Identity Theft Statute: Maine Rev. Stat. Ann. title 17-A, § 905-A. See also Maine Rev. Stat. Ann. title 17-A, § 354.

Definition of Offense: Misuse of Identification: presents or uses a credit or debit card . . . obtained as a result of fraud or deception; presents or uses an account, credit or billing number that the person is not authorized to use or that was obtained as a result of fraud or deception; presents or uses a form of legal identification that the person is not authorized to use. Definition of theft by deception includes deception as to identity.
Victim Remedies in Criminal Case: No specific provisions.
Special Record-clearing Provisions: No specific provisions.
Duties of Private Entities: No specific provisions.
Private Right of Action: No specific provisions.
Other: No specific provisions.

State Credit Information in Personal Insurance statute: Me. Rev. Stat. Ann. tit. 24-A, §§ 2169-B and 2201, et. seq.

Scope: Use of consumer reports in personal insurance, i.e. individually underwritten for personal, family or household use: private passenger vehicle or recreational vehicle, homeowners, noncommercial fire. (§ 2169-B). Use of personal information about Maine residents in most insurance transactions (exceptions for workers' comp., medical malpractice, fidelity, suretyship, boiler and machinery, and certain public record information collected for title insurance purposes) (§§ 2201 et. seq.).
Disclosure: Insurer must disclose at time of application, in writing or in same medium as application, if it will use credit information. If insurer takes adverse action based on credit report, it must explain reasons to consumer, and provide notice as required by state and Federal FCRA (source of report, dispute resolution procedure, etc.). (§ 2169-B) Consumers must be provided with notice of insurer's information practices. (§ 2206) Insurer that plans to use investigative consumer report must comply with state FCRA, and inform consumer in writing of right to be interviewed. (§ 2209).
Dispute Resolution: If information in credit report is disputed, pursuant to the Federal FCRA and found incorrect, insurer must re-underwrite or re-rate within 30 days after notice. If refund is required it should be for the lesser of policy period or 12 months. (§ 2169-B) If an insurer receives a written request to amend or correct personal information, based on a consumer report, it must advise consumer of name and address of reporting agency, and of procedure under state FCRA for challenging the information. (§ 2211).
Prohibited Practices: Insurer may not use credit score based on income, gender, address, ethnic group, religion, marital status or nationality; deny, cancel, or non-renew based wholly on credit information without, another applicable underwriting factor independent of credit information; base renewal rates solely on credit information; take adverse action based on consumer's lack of a credit card, consider the absence of credit information, the inability to calculate a credit score, or the number of credit inquiries, unless insurer can show relationship to risk; take adverse action based on credit report issued or credit score calculated more than 90 days before policy was written or renewed; use credit information if it does not recalculate every 36 months based on current credit report. (§ 2169-B)
Other: Insurer who uses scores must file scoring model with superintendent. (§ 2169-B)

Maryland

State FCRA Statute: Md. Code Ann. Com. Law §§ 14-1201 to 14-1218; *see also* Md. Regs. Code tit. 9, §§ 09.03.07.01 to 09.03.07.04.

Scope: Similar to Federal.
Purposes for Which Reports May Be Issued: Similar to federal law, except no authorization for provision to potential investors or servicers, or current insurers, in connection with evaluation of credit or prepayment risks associated with existing credit obligations.
Consumer Access and Disclosure: Upon customer request all information in file except medical information; in addition, an explanation of code or trade language is required. Must provide one free copy per year, may charge up to a $5.00 fee for additional copies. Substance of any public record information reported for employment purposes.
Disclosures to Consumers By User: Same as the federal law. Must inform consumer if an investigative report is being requested. Must disclose to consumer, upon request, the scope of the proposed investigative report.
Restrictions on Content of Reports: Obsolete information: same as federal law except criminal records more than seven years after disposition, release or parole.[20] Adverse information in investigative reports which is not reverified or received within previous three months.[21]
Consumer Disputes: Disputed information must be investigated within thirty days of written notification by a con-

---

20 These two definitions of information which may not be contained under Maryland law in a consumer report were in effect on Sept. 30, 1996, and therefore are not preempted, although they regulate the contents of consumer reports and might otherwise be preempted. See § 10.4.4, *supra*.
21 *Id.*

sumer.[22] If found to be inaccurate, the consumer and users must be notified within seven days; if found to be accurate, the consumer must be notified within seven days. Consumer must be notified within seven days if agency considers dispute to be frivolous.

Duties of Furnishers: No relevant provisions.

Consumer Remedies: Actual damages, reasonable attorney fees and costs are available for negligent violations, plus punitive damages for willful violations. Violations made unintentionally and in good faith are not actionable. Criminal penalties for obtaining information from agency under false pretenses, or for unauthorized disclosure by officers or employees of agency.

Statute of Limitations: Same as the federal law.

Miscellaneous: Cannot provide prescreened information if the consumer precludes it in writing.[23]

Child Support Debts: Md. Code Fam. Law § 10-108.1. Upon request, the Child Support Enforcement Administration shall report child support arrearages of sixty days for longer duration. Written notice and a reasonable opportunity to contest the accuracy of the information must be given to the obligor before the information is reported.

State Credit Repair Statute: Md. Com. Law Code Ann. §§ 14-1901 to -1916

Covered Activities: Improving credit record or obtaining extension of credit, in return for money or other consideration.

Exemptions: Lenders authorized under Maryland or federal law; licensed mortgage lenders, banks and savings associations eligible for FDIC insurance; nonprofit organizations; licensed real estate brokers acting within scope of license; public accountants and Maryland lawyers acting within scope of practice; registered securities broker-dealers; consumer reporting agencies.

Right to Cancel? Yes (3 days).

Prohibitions: Charging before complete performance; charging for referring buyer to retail seller for credit on same terms as generally available to public; making or advising false statements to creditors or credit reporting agencies; making false statements about services offered; assisting in or creating new identity for buyer for credit purposes; unfair and deceptive practices; requiring buyer to waive rights; assists consumer to obtain credit at a rate of interest that, but for federal preemption of state law would be forbidden by title 12.

Other Substantive Requirements: Disclosures.

Bond: Bond required pursuant to title 11, subtitle 3 of Financial Institutions Code. *See* Md. Fin. Instit. Code § 11-206.

Private Cause of Action: Contract voidable. Where willful non-compliance, thrice amount collected from consumer; attorney fees and costs; punitive damages allowed; 2-year statute of limitations, from date of discovery of misrepresentation; for willful violations, statute of limitations is 2 years from discovery of violation. Where negligent non-compliance, actual damages; attorney fees and costs; 2-year statute of limitations, from date of violation. A violation is a UDAP violation.

State Identity Theft Statute: Md. Code Ann., Crim. § 8-301, Md. Regs. Code tit. 9, § 09.03.07.04; *see also* Md. Govt. Code § 6-202.

Definition of Offense: Knowingly, willfully, without authority, with fraudulent intent obtain or help another to obtain personal identifying information of another, with intent to obtain any benefit, credit, goods, services or other thing of value in the name of another; or knowingly or willfully assume the identity of another to fraudulently obtain any benefit, etc., or evade payment of debt or legal obligation.

Victim Remedies in Criminal Case: In addition to restitution required by other provisions of criminal code, court may order restitution to victim for reasonable costs incurred including attorney fees, in clearing victims credit history or credit rating, and in connection with any civil or administrative proceeding to satisfy a debt, lien, judgment or other obligation arising form the identity fraud.

Special Record-Clearing Provisions: No specific provisions.

Duties of Private Entities: If a consumer alleges that errors in the credit report result from identity theft, or mixing of the consumer's information with that of another, the complaint is presumed to be accurate and must receive expedited handling. The agency must make an investigation using the consumer's social security number. If the presumption of accuracy is rebutted, the consumer must be notified, and advised of the appeal procedures provided by the state fair credit law. If the presumption of accuracy is not rebutted, the agency must delete the information from its files, send written notice to every person designated by the consumer, and advise the consumer of the rights of action provided by the state fair credit reporting law.

Private Right of Action: No specific provisions.

Other: Electronic Transaction Education, Advocacy and Mediation Unit, in the Office of the Attorney General is empowered to investigate and assist in the prosecution of identity fraud, and to provide public education regarding the prevention of identity fraud.

Other State Provisions: Md. Ins. Code § 27-605. If an insurer takes adverse action on motor vehicle liability policy based in whole or in part on credit report or credit score, it must disclose the name, address, and toll-free number of the credit reporting agency, and consumer's rights under the Federal FCRA to a copy of the report, and dispute resolution procedure.

---

22 These provisions were in effect on Sept. 30, 1996, so although they regulate the time allowed an agency to reinvestigate the contents of reports, they are not preempted. *See* § 10.4.4, *supra*.

23 State law provisions concerning prescreening lists are now preempted. *See* § 10.4.4, *supra*.

Massachusetts

State FCRA Statute: Mass. Gen. Laws Ann. ch. 93, §§ 50–68.

Scope: Same as the federal definitions except the consumer report does not include information communicated by the consumer reporting agency on reputation, character, personal characteristics, or mode of living. Issuance of investigative consumer reports requires the prior written permission of the consumer.

Purposes for Which Reports May Be Issued: Similar to federal law, however business transaction use restricted to transactions where a party transfers interest in real or personal property, pays money or renders services, or becomes obligated to do so; and no authorization for provision to potential investors or servicers, or current insurers, in connection with evaluation of credit or prepayment rules associated with existing credit obligations. Consumers must be given the opportunity, via a toll-free telephone number, to opt-out of prescreened lists.[24]

Consumer Access and Disclosure: Similar to the federal law; in addition, upon customer request, contents of all nonmedical information in files must be disclosed. Nationwide agencies must provide one free copy per year, $5 from local agencies; subsequent reports $8.

Disclosures to Consumers By User: Same as the federal law.

Restrictions on Content of Reports: Same as federal law except criminal records more than seven years after disposition, release or parole and bankruptcies over fourteen year old.[25]

Consumer Disputes: Similar to federal law, except that the consumer reporting agency must reinvestigate within thirty days and notify the consumer of the results within a further ten days. If agency determines dispute frivolous, it must notify consumer of specific reasons for decision within five days. Agency must delete information found to be inaccurate within three days and must issue corrected reports within fifteen days of request by consumer.[26] In addition, a consumer reporting agency does not have the right to limit the length of the statement filed by the consumer on the dispute.

Duties of Furnishers: Furnishers of information liable from first for failing to establish reasonable procedures to ensure accuracy of information reported, or for reporting information they know or should know is inaccurate. In addition, furnishers must report voluntary account closures and must include consumer disputes and commencement dates of any delinquencies, when reporting delinquencies.[27]

Consumer Remedies: Fine and/or imprisonment for willful introduction of false information into a file for the purpose of either damaging or enhancing a consumer's credit information or for obtaining information from agency under false pretenses, or unauthorized disclosure by agency personnel. Agencies, users and furnishers are liable for actual damages, reasonable attorney fees and costs, plus punitive damages for willful violations. In addition, remedies in relation to negligent noncompliance are specifically nonexclusive. Failure to comply with any provision is a violation of the state deceptive practices statute.

Statute of Limitations: Two years from date of violation or discovery for willful misrepresentation.

Miscellaneous: Adverse information in an investigative report must be reverified or less than three months old to be included on a subsequent report.[28]

Child Support Debts: Mass. Gen. Laws Ann. ch. 93, § 52A. Child support arrearages in excess of $500 must be reported upon request of consumer reporting agency. Fifteen-day advance notice must be given to obligor parent, who has right to contest accuracy of information before it is reported to agency.

State Credit Repair Statute: Mass. Gen. Laws Ann. ch. 93, § 68A-68E

Covered Activities: Improving credit record or obtaining extension of credit, in return for money or other consideration.

Exemptions: Regulated and supervised lenders; mortgage lenders approved by HUD; banks eligible for FDIC insurance; credit unions; nonprofit organizations; licensed real estate brokers acting within scope of license; Massachusetts lawyers acting within scope of law practice; registered securities broker-dealers; consumer reporting agencies.

Right to Cancel? Yes (3 days).

Prohibitions: Charging before complete performance, unless organization has posted bond; charging for referring buyer to retail seller for credit on same terms as generally available to public; making or advising false statements to creditors or credit reporting agencies; making false statements about services offered; any act intended to defraud or deceive buyer.

Other Substantive Requirements: Disclosures.

Bond: $10,000.

Private Cause of Action: A violation is a UDAP violation.

---

[24] State law provisions concerning prescreening lists are now preempted. See § 10.4.4, *supra*.

[25] These two definitions of information which may not be contained under Massachusetts law in a consumer report were in effect on Sept. 30, 1996, and therefore are not preempted, although they regulate the contents of consumer reports and might otherwise be preempted. See § 10.4.4, *supra*.

[26] These provisions were in effect on Sept. 30, 1996, so although they regulate the time allowed an agency to reinvestigate a dispute, they are not preempted. See § 10.4.4, *supra*.

[27] Massachusetts law regarding the responsibilities of furnishers of information is explicitly not preempted by federal law. See § 10.4.4, *supra*.

[28] This provision was in effect on Sept. 30, 1996, so even if it could be said to be otherwise preempted by 15 U.S.C. § 1681c, it is not preempted. See § 10.4.4, *supra*.

State Identity Theft Statute: Mass. Gen. Laws Ann. ch. 266, § 37E.

Definition of Offense: Poses as another person and uses that persons identifying information without authority to obtain money, credit, goods, or other thing of value, or identifying documents of that person; or obtains identifying information for purpose of posing as that person or enabling another to pose as that person, for purposes listed above.

Victim Remedies in Criminal Case: In addition to any other punishment, court must order restitution for financial loss, which may include costs of correcting credit history and credit rating, civil or administrative proceeding to satisfy debt or other obligation, including lost wages and attorney fees.

Special Record-Clearing Provisions: No specific provisions.
Duties of Private Entities: No specific provisions.
Private Right of Action: No specific provisions.

Other State Provisions: **Mass. Gen. L. Ann. Ch. 175I, §§ 2 and 7.** The Insurance Information and Privacy Protection statute requires that insurer who wishes to use investigative consumer report must advise consumer of right to be interviewed, and to receive a copy of report. The report may not include information about the sexual orientation of any person, or about counseling related to AIDS.

Michigan

Child Support Debts: **Mich. Comp. Laws § 552.512**. The office of friend of the court shall report to a consumer reporting agency support information concerning all child support payers with an arrearage of two months or more. Prior to making such information available, the office of friend of the court shall provide twenty-one days advance notice to the payer and a review enabling the payer to object. Any incorrect information reported must be corrected within fourteen days.

State Credit Repair Statute: **Mich. Comp. Laws §§ 445.1821 to 445.1826**

Covered Activities: Improving credit record, obtaining extension of credit, advising or assisting regarding foreclosure of real estate mortgage, or serving as intermediary for debtor with creditor with respect to prior debt, in return for money or other consideration.

Exemptions: Lenders licensed or authorized under state law; federal or state chartered banks, credit unions, savings bank, savings and loans, farm credit entities, and subsidiaries; anyone with a state occupational license when engaged in regular course of business; Michigan attorneys acting within scope of law practice who do not engage in business of credit services organization on regular and continuing basis; judicial officer; persons acting under court agency; consumer reporting agencies; licensed debt management businesses; registered investment advisors and securities broker-dealers; nonprofit organizations; and finance subsidiaries of manufacturers.

Right to Cancel? No.

Prohibitions: Charging for obtaining extension of credit before closing the loan; charging for services before completing them; charging for referring buyer to retail seller for credit on same terms as generally available to public; making false statements in offer or sale of services; engaging in fraudulent or deceptive act in connection with offer or sale of services; failing to perform agreed services within 90 days; advise buyer to make false statement to creditor or credit reporting agency; remove or assist removal of accurate non-obsolete information; create or assist creation of new identity; submit dispute without buyer's knowledge; provide service without written contract.

Other Substantive Requirements: None.
Bond: N/A

Private Cause of Action: Buyer may sue for injunction, declaratory judgment, actual damages, attorney fees, costs, and punitive damages (4-year statute of limitations). Credit services organization that violates the act is also barred from recovering fees or other charges from buyer.

State Identity Theft Statute: **Mich. Comp. Laws § 750.285**.

Definition of Offense: Obtaining or attempting to obtain personal identity information of another without authority, with the intent to use it to: obtain credit, buy or lease property, obtain employment, access medical records, or commit any illegal act.

Victim Remedies in Criminal Case: No specific provisions.
Special Record-Clearing Provisions: No specific provisions.
Duties of Private Entities: No specific provisions.
Private Right of Action: No specific provisions.

Other State Provisions: **Mich. Comp. Laws §§ 445.271 to 445.273.** No creditor may report adverse information about a cosigner without thirty days notice, or if the cosigner makes satisfactory arrangements in response to a notice.[29]

Minnesota

State FCRA Statute: **Minn. Stat. §§ 13C.001 to 13C.04; 72A.496 to 72A.505 (insurance investigative reports)**.

Scope: Similar to Federal.

Purposes for Which Reports May Be Issued: Same as federal law.

Consumer Access and Disclosures: Detailed requirements for medical information in insurance reports: may be disclosed to named health care provider instead of directly to consumer; if disclosure could create risk of harm to patient or others, must be disclosed only to treating physician. Insurance company must disclose reasons for adverse underwriting decision, including credit scores. Before seeking

---

[29] Most state laws concerning duties of furnishers of information are now preempted. See § 10.4.4, *supra*.

information, insurer must obtain consumer's written authorization; form must be in plain language, disclose what information is being sought, and authorization must be for a limited time. Agencies must provide one report per year for a charge of not more than three dollars.

Disclosures to Consumer By User: Similar to federal law, however, no one can procure a consumer report for employment purposes without written disclosure to the consumer prior to the preparation of the report; and the disclosure must include a box for the consumer to check to obtain a free copy of the report. This copy must be sent by the agency to the consumer within twenty-four hours of the time it delivers report to the user. If the report requested is an investigative consumer report, must disclose that the report may include information obtained through personal interviews regarding the consumer's character, general reputation, personal characteristics, or mode of living. Disclosure is not required if the report is to be used for employment purposes for which the consumer has not specifically applied, used for an investigation of a current violation of a criminal or civil statute by a current employer, or used for an investigation of employee conduct for which the employer may be liable. Users who request an investigative report for insurance purposes must notify consumer of right to be interviewed during the investigation and the right to request a copy of the report.

Restrictions on Content of Reports: No relevant provisions.
Consumer Disputes: Adverse decisions regarding insurance reports may be appealed to insurance commissioner.
Duties of Furnishers: No relevant provisions.
Consumer Remedies: Actual damages, equitable relief, and costs and disbursements (including costs of investigation and reasonable attorney fees). Violations of insurance information statute treated like violations of government data practices law: actual damages, costs and attorney fees; exemplary damages for willful violation of $100 to $10,000 per violation; injunction also available. Criminal penalties for obtaining data in violation of the insurance statute.
Statute of Limitations: No relevant provisions.
Miscellaneous: No relevant provisions.

State Credit Repair Statute: Minn. Stat. Ann. §§ 332.52 to .60

Covered Activities: Improving credit record or obtaining extension of credit, in return for money or other consideration.
Exemptions: Regulated and supervised lenders; banks and savings associations eligible for FDIC insurance; credit unions; nonprofit organizations; prorating agencies, collections agencies, and licensed real estate brokers acting within scope of license; Minnesota lawyers acting within scope of law practice; registered securities broker-dealers; consumer reporting agencies.
Right to Cancel? Yes (5 days).
Prohibitions: Charging before complete performance; charging for referring buyer to retail seller for credit on same terms as generally available to public; making or advising false statements to creditors or credit reporting agencies; making false statements about services offered; requiring buyer to waive rights.
Other Substantive Requirements: Disclosures.
Bond: $10,000.
Private Cause of Action: Actual damages, not less than amount paid by buyer; attorney fees and costs; punitive damages allowed. A violation is a UDAP violation.

State Identity Theft Statute: Minn. Stat. § 609.527.

Definition of Offense: Transfers, possesses or uses an identity not one's own, with the intent to commit, aid or abet any unlawful activity.
Victim Remedies in Criminal Case: Court-ordered restitution available, also eligible for crime victims' compensation under Ch. 611A.
Special Record-Clearing Provisions: No specific provisions.
Duties of Private Entities: No specific provisions.
Private Right of Action: No specific provisions.

State Credit Information in Personal Insurance statute: Minn. Stat. § 72A.20, subd. 36. and 72A.49, et. seq.

Scope: Use of credit information for homeowners' or private passenger motor vehicle insurance. (§ 72A.20) personal (i.e., not business or professional) insurance transactions involving Minnesota residents. (§ 72A.49 et seq.)
Disclosures: Insurer must disclose if credit information will be obtained and used.(§ 72A.20). Insurer must disclose its information practices to consumer. (§ 72A.494). Insurer that plans to use investigative consumer report must inform consumer of right to be interviewed and receive copy of report. (§ 72A.496). If consumer seeks disclosure of credit information that Federal law prohibits insurer from disclosing, must advise consumer of name, address and phone number of credit reporting agency that issued report. (§ 72A.497.) If adverse decision is based on credit report, insurer must disclose reasons in writing. (§ 72A.499).
Prohibited Practices: May not use insurance inquiries or inquiries not instituted by consumer as factor in calculating credit score; use credit information if credit score is adversely impacted or cannot be generated because of absence of credit history; use credit score that incorporates gender, race, nationality, or religion. (§ 72A.20)
Other: Insurer must provide reasonable underwriting exemptions for consumer whose credit history has been adversely impacted by catastrophic illness or injury, temporary loss of employment, or death of an immediate family member (may require documentation). (§ 72A.20) Insurers who use credit scores must file scoring methodology, and information that supports its use, with commissioner. (§ 72A.20) Aggrieved person entitled to civil remedies provided by § 13.08 (data practices statute). (§ 72A.49 et seq.)

Mississippi

Child Support Debts: Miss. Code Ann. § 93-11-69. The Department of Human Services shall make information about child support debts, thirty days or more overdue, available to consumer reporting agencies; fifteen days advance notice and an opportunity to contest the information must be provided to obligers.

State Identity Theft Statute: Miss. Code Ann. § 97-19-85.

Definition of Offense: False statement as to identity, Social Security, credit or debit card number, or other identifying information, with intent to fraudulently obtain goods, services or other thing of value.
Victim Remedies in Criminal Case: Court must order restitution, as provided by § 99-37-1. (General criminal restitution statute).
Special Record-Clearing Provisions: No specific provisions.
Duties of Private Entities: No specific provisions.
Private Right of Action: No specific provisions.

Missouri

Child Support Debts: Mo. Ann. Stat. § 454.512 (West). State division of child support enforcement shall periodically report all child support arrearages, the noncustodial parent shall be provided notice and a reasonable opportunity to contest such information before it is reported.

State Credit Repair Statute: Mo. Rev. Stat. §§ 407.635 to .644

Covered Activities: Improving credit record or obtaining extension of credit, in return for money or other consideration.
Exemptions: Regulated and supervised lenders; lenders making loans secured by liens on realty; banks and savings associations eligible for FDIC insurance; credit unions; nonprofit organizations; licensed real estate brokers acting within scope of license; Missouri lawyers acting within scope of law practice; registered securities broker-dealers; consumer reporting agencies.
Right to Cancel? Yes (3 days).
Prohibitions: Charging before complete performance, unless organization has posted bond; charging for referring buyer to retail seller for credit on same terms as generally available to public; making or advising false statements to creditors or credit reporting agencies; making false statements about services offered; requiring buyer to waive rights.
Other Substantive Requirements: Disclosures.
Bond: $10,000.
Private Cause of Action: Damages not less than amount paid by consumer; attorney fees and costs; punitive damages allowed; 4-year statute of limitations. A violation is a UDAP violation.

State Identity Theft Statute: Mo. Ann. Stat. § 570.223 (West).

Definition of Offense: Knowingly and with intent to deceive or defraud, obtains, transfers, possesses or uses, or attempts to obtain, transfer or use, one or more means of identification not lawfully issued for his use.
Victim Remedies in Criminal Case: Court may order restitution to victim, including costs and attorney fees incurred in clearing credit history or credit rating, and in any civil or administrative proceeding to satisfy a debt, lien or other obligation resulting from the identity theft.
Special Record-Clearing Provisions: No specific provisions.
Duties of Private Entities: No specific provisions.
Private Right of Action: No specific provisions.

State Credit Information in Personal Insurance: Mo. Rev. Stat. §§ 375.918

Scope: Use of credit reports or credit scores in underwriting new or renewal private automobile or homeowners (including mobile home and renters) insurance.
Disclosures: Insurer must disclose at time of application that if it will use credit information. If adverse action taken, must notify consumer of name of credit agency furnishing report, and rights to copy of report, and dispute procedure.
Dispute Resolution: If consumer requests in writing within 30 days after notice of adverse action, insurer must provide explanation (i.e., what "significant characteristics" or credit history impacted the insurance credit score). Applicant or insured may request reconsideration, based on corrections made to credit report or credit score.
Prohibited Practices: Insurer who uses credit report or insurance credit score in underwriting may not take adverse action based on this, without consideration of other non-credit-related factor. May not take adverse action based on credit information that is subject to dispute, not yet resolved in accordance with FCRA. Insurer may use credit report or score for new or renewal contracts, but may not use it to take adverse action on renewals until the third anniversary of the contract.

Montana

State FCRA Statute: Mont. Code Ann. §§ 31-3-101 to 31-3-153. *See also* Mont. Admin. R. 2.61.301.

Scope: Same as the federal law.
Purposes for Which Reports May Be Issued: Similar to the federal law except no authorization for provision to potential investors or servicers, or current insurers, in connection with evaluation of the credit or prepayment risks associated with existing credit obligations.
Consumer Access and Disclosure: Upon consumer request, the nature and substance of all information, except medical, in its files, and the sources of the information must be disclosed. The request must be written. Response may be

over the phone; the consumer pays the toll charge. The agency must notify the consumer if information of public record with an adverse effect on employment has been reported.

Disclosures to Consumers By User: Notice that an investigative report may be requested is required within three days of request, but is not required pursuant to an employment application. If credit is denied or its cost is increased due to information obtained from a person other than an agency, the user must notify the consumer and must disclose the nature of the adverse information if a request is made within sixty days.

Restrictions on Content of Reports: Similar to federal law, except criminal records more than seven years after disposition, release or parole, and bankruptcies over fourteen years old.[30] No adverse information from a prior investigative report unless it is reverified.[31]

Consumer Disputes: False information must be deleted and users must be notified. The consumer must be notified as to which users have the disputed information.

Consumer Remedies: Actual damages, costs and attorney fees, plus punitive damages for willful violations. Civil action for defamation, invasion or privacy or negligence is available against agencies which do not comply with this statute, or wrongfully judge a dispute frivolous or refuse to delete inaccurate information, and against furnishers (except the Department of Public Health and Human Services) who provide misinformation maliciously or with intent to injure. Administrative procedure available for complaints against the Department. Violation of this statute violates the unfair and deceptive practices statute.

Miscellaneous: A credit rating is a property right with full Montana constitutional protection. An agency must maintain a record of all furnishers and users. Credit reporting agencies must warn all furnishers that they are liable to suit if the information they furnish is false, or is furnished with malice or willful intent to injure the consumer. Adverse information in investigative report may not be reused in later report unless it is verified while preparing the new report.

Child Support Debts: Mont. Code Ann. §§ 40-5-261 & 40-5-262. The Department of Public Health may make information about child support debts available to consumer reporting agencies; advance notice and an opportunity to contest the information's accuracy must be provided to obligors.

State Identity Theft Statute: Mont. Code Ann. 45-6-332.

Definition of Offense: Purposely or knowingly obtains personal identifying information of another, and uses it without authority for any unlawful purpose, including to obtain credit, goods, services, financial or medical information, in name of another.

Victim Remedies in Criminal Case: May include costs incurred by the victim, including attorney fees, for clearing credit record or credit report, or in any civil or administrative proceeding to satisfy any debt, lien or obligation resulting from defendant's actions.

Special Record-Clearing Provisions: No specific provisions.
Duties of Private Entities: No specific provisions.
Private Right of Action: No specific provisions.

Other State Provisions: Mont. Code Ann. § 33-18-210(11). Use of credit history in homeowners' or private automobile insurance. Credit history includes only debt payment history or lack of history—not public information such as bankruptcies, lawsuits, and criminal convictions. May not take adverse action unless: can provide documentation that credit history is correlated with risk; insurer informs consumer of reasons for action, and, if requested provides either copy of report, or name, address and phone number of reporting agency, within ten days of request. **Mont. Code Ann. §§ 33-19-101, et. seq.** (insurance information and privacy protections – individual property, casualty, life, health and disability) Insurer that wishes to use investigative consumer report must advise consumer of right to be interviewed and to receive copy of report. (§ 33-19-205).

Nebraska

State FCRA Statute: Neb. Rev. Stat. § 20-149.

Scope: Similar to Federal.
Purposes for Which Reports May Be Issued: No relevant provisions.
Consumer Access and Disclosure: A photocopy or typewritten copy of a report or file information is available for a reasonable fee, if disclosure is required by terms of federal FCRA as it existed on August 26, 1983; otherwise, as required by the federal law.
Disclosures to Consumer by User: No relevant provisions.
Restrictions on Content of Reports: No relevant provisions.
Consumer Disputes: No relevant provisions.
Duties of Furnishers: No relevant provisions.
Consumer Remedies: Misdemeanor.
Statute of Limitations: No relevant provisions.
Miscellaneous: No relevant provisions.

State Credit Repair Statute: Neb. Rev. Stat. §§ 45-801 to -814 (Credit Services Organizations)

Covered Activities: Improving credit record or obtaining extension of credit, in return for money or other consideration.
Exemptions: Regulated and supervised lenders; mortgage lenders approved by HUD; banks and savings associations

---

30 These two definitions of information which may not be contained under Montana law in a consumer report were in effect on Sept. 30, 1996, and therefore are not preempted, although they regulate the contents of consumer reports and might otherwise be preempted. *See* § 10.4.4, *supra*.

31 This provision was in effect on Sept. 30, 1996, so even if it could be said to be otherwise preempted by 15 U.S.C. § 1681c, it is not preempted. *See* § 10.4.4, *supra*.

eligible for FDIC insurance; persons whose primary business is loans secured by liens on realty; credit unions; nonprofit organizations; licensed real estate brokers and collection agencies acting within scope of license; Nebraska lawyers acting within scope of law practice; registered securities broker-dealers; consumer reporting agencies; licensed debt management organizations (see below).
Right to Cancel? Yes (3 days).
Prohibitions: Charging before complete performance of obtaining an extension of credit, or, before performance of any other service, unless organization has posted bond; charging for referring buyer to retail seller for credit on same terms as generally available to public; making or advising false statements to creditors or credit reporting agencies; making false statements about services offered; engaging in unfair and deceptive practices; requiring buyer to waive rights.
Other Substantive Requirements: Disclosures.
Bond: $100,000.
Private Cause of Action: Injunctive relief. Actual damages; attorney fees and costs; a violation is a UDAP violation; 4-year statute of limitations.

State Credit Repair Statute: Neb. Rev. Stat. §§ 69-1201 to 1207 ("Debt Management" organizations)

Covered Activities: Planning and managing debtor's financial affairs for a fee; receiving money or evidences for distribution to creditors for a fee.
Exemptions: Attorneys; banks and lending institutions duly authorized to do business in Nebraska; title insurers and abstract companies doing an escrow business in Nebraska; judicial officers.
Right to Cancel? No.
Prohibitions: Unlicensed practice; contracting for services to extend beyond 36 months; charging fees for more than 15% of amount to be paid creditor, or, collecting fees prior to debtor's approval of debt management program; purchasing debtor obligations from creditor; acting as collections agent while managing client's debt; accepting promissory note or mortgage as payment; paying bonus for referrals; misleading advertising.
Other Substantive Requirements: Special bank accounts for debtor funds.
Bond: $10,000.
Private Cause of Action: None.

State Identity Theft Statute: Neb. Rev. Stat. § 28-608 (1)(d).

Definition of Offense: Without authorization, and with intent to deceive or harm another, obtains or records personal identification documents [defined] or personal identifying information [defined] and accesses or attempts to access the financial resources of another for the purpose of obtaining credit, money, goods, or any other thing of value.
Victim Remedies in Criminal Case: Restitution.
Special Record-clearing Provisions: No specific provisions.
Duties of Private Entities: No specific provisions.

Private Right of Action: No specific provisions.

Credit Insurance in Personal Insurance Statute: Neb. Rev. Stat. §§ 44-7701 to -12.

Scope: Use of credit information in personal insurance, individually underwritten for personal, family or household purposes: private passenger vehicle, recreational vehicle, homeowners (including mobile home), and non-commercial fire.
Disclosures: Insurer must notify consumer at time of application, in writing or in same medium as application, if it intends to use credit information. IF adverse action based on credit report, insurer must disclose reasons to consumer, and provide notification as required by Federal FCRA (source of report, dispute resolution procedure, etc.).
Dispute Resolution: If, after dispute resolution procedure pursuant to Federal FCRA information in credit report is found to be incorrect, insurer must, within 30 days after notice, re-underwrite or re-rate based on corrected report. If refund is required, it must be for lesser of policy period or 12 months.
Prohibited Practices: Insurer may not use credit score based on income, gender, address, ethnic group, religion, marital status or nationality; deny, cancel, or non-renew based wholly on credit information without, another applicable underwriting factor independent of credit information; base renewal rates solely on credit information; take adverse action based on lack of credit card; count lack of credit history as a negative factor, unless insurer can show relationship to risk; take adverse action based on credit report issued or credit score calculated more than 90 days before policy was written or renewed; use credit information if it does not recalculate every 36 months based on current credit report; treat as a negative factor collection accounts with a medical industry code, or certain credit inquiries.
Other: Insurer who uses scores must file scoring model with department of insurance.

Nevada

State FCRA Statute: Nev. Rev. Stat. §§ 598C.010 to 598C.200.

Scope: Similar to Federal.
Purposes for Which Reports May Be Issued: Same as the federal law. Consumers must be given the opportunity to opt out of prescreened lists.[32]
Consumer Access and Disclosure: Rights under state FCRA. The nature and substance of a report in the files at the time of the request and disclosure of the name of the institutional sources of information. On request, shall provide a readable copy and the name of each person who has received a report within the preceding two years, if for employment purposes,

---

32 State laws concerning prescreened lists are now preempted. *See* § 10.4.4, *supra*.

or the preceding six months if for any other purpose.

Disclosures to Consumers By User: A consumer must be notified if adverse action is taken on the basis of a credit report, and the consumer must be given notice of the name and address of the reporting agency and of the right to obtain a copy of the report from the agency.

Restrictions on Content of Reports: Same as federal law except agencies are forbidden to report criminal proceedings over seven years old and medical information.[33]

Consumer Disputes: Within five days after a consumer disputes the accuracy of any information, agency must notify any institutional sources of the information, and must complete reinvestigation within thirty days.[34] If the information is found to be incorrect, the files must be corrected and the consumer notified. No information that was deleted because of an inaccuracy may be reinserted unless reasonable procedures are used to maximize accuracy, and the consumer is notified within five business days after the reinsertion and offered the opportunity to add a brief statement disputing or adding to the information.

Duties of Furnishers: No relevant provisions.

Consumer Remedies: Willful noncompliance: actual damages, punitive damages, costs, and reasonable attorney fees. Negligent noncompliance: actual damages, costs, and reasonable attorney fees.

Statute of Limitations: No relevant provisions.

Miscellaneous: No relevant provisions.

Child Support Debts: **Nev. Rev. Stat. § 598C.110.** Reports shall include information concerning delinquent child support payments if they are presented in an acceptable format by the welfare division or district attorney.

State Credit Repair Statute: Nev. Rev. Stat. §§ 598.741 to .787.

Covered Activities: Improving credit record or obtaining extension of credit, in return for money or other consideration, unauthorized debt adjustment counseling.

Exemptions: Regulated and supervised lenders; banks and savings associations eligible for FDIC insurance; credit unions; licensed debt adjusters; licensed real estate brokers acting within scope of license; Nevada lawyers acting within scope of law practice; registered securities broker-dealers; consumer reporting agencies.

Right to Cancel? Yes (5 days).

Prohibitions: Charging before complete performance; charging for referring buyer to retail seller for credit on same terms as generally available to public; making or advising false statements to creditors or credit reporting agencies; making false statements about services offered; creating new credit record by use of new identification for buyer; submitting buyer dispute to reporting agency without buyer's knowledge; calling reporting agency by a person falsely identified as the buyer; requiring buyer to waive rights.

Other Substantive Requirements: Disclosures.

Bond: None, but $100,000 security deposit required with regulatory agency.

Private Cause of Action: Actual damages, not less than amount paid by buyer; attorney fees and costs; punitive damages allowed. A violation is a UDAP violation.

State Identity Theft Statute: Nev. Rev. Stat. §§ 41.1345, 205.463 and .465.

Definition of Offense: Obtains personal identifying information [very broadly defined] of another, and uses it to harm that person, or for unlawful purpose, including but not limited to obtaining goods, credit, services or other thing of value in that person's name, or to delay or avoid being prosecuted for any unlawful act. Possesses, sells or transfers any document or personal identifying information, for the purpose of establishing a false identity for self or another.

Victim Remedies in Criminal Case: Court must order restitution, including costs and attorney fees incurred in clearing credit record or credit rating, and in any civil or administrative proceeding to satisfy debt or obligation incurred as a result of the identity theft.

Special Record-Clearing Provisions: No specific provisions.

Duties of Private Entities: No specific provisions.

Private Right of Action: Person injured as proximate result of violation of § 205.463 has private right of action for actual damages, reasonable costs and attorney fees, and such punitive damages as the facts may warrant.

State Credit Information in Personal Insurance statute: Nev. Rev. Stat. §§ 686A.600 to .730.

Scope: Use of credit information in personal insurance, i.e. not commercial, business or surety.

Disclosures: Insurer must notify consumer at time of application, in writing or in same medium as application, if it intends to use credit information. IF adverse action based on credit report, insurer must disclose reasons to consumer, and provide notification as required by Federal FCRA (source of report, dispute resolution procedure, etc.)

Dispute Resolution: If, after dispute resolution procedure pursuant to Federal FCRA information in credit report is found to be incorrect, insurer must, within 30 days after notice, re-underwrite or re-rate based on corrected report. If refund is required, it must be for lesser of policy period or 12 months. At annual renewal, consumer may request re-underwriting or re-rating based on current credit report.

Prohibited Practices: Insurer may not use credit score based on income, gender, address, ethnic group, religion, marital status or nationality; deny, cancel, or non-renew based wholly on credit information without, another applicable

---

33 These provisions were in effect on Sept. 30, 1996, so even if they could be said to be otherwise preempted by 15 U.S.C. § 1681c, they are not preempted. See § 10.4.4, *supra*.

34 This provision was in effect on Sept. 30, 1996, so although it regulates the time allowed an agency for reinvestigation, it is not preempted. See § 10.4.4, *supra*.

underwriting factor independent of credit information; base renewal rates solely on credit information; take adverse action based on lack of credit card; count lack of credit history as a negative factor, unless insurer can show relationship to risk; take adverse action based on credit report issued or credit score calculated more than 90 days before policy was written or renewed; use credit information if it does not recalculate every 36 months based on current credit report; treat as a negative factor collection accounts with a medical industry code, or certain credit inquiries.
Other: No relevant provisions.

New Hampshire

State FCRA Statute: **N.H. Rev. Stat. Ann. §§ 359-B:1 to 359-B:21**.

Scope: Same as the federal law.
Purposes for Which Reports May Be Issued: Similar to federal law except no authorization for provision to potential investors or servicers, or current insurers, in connection with the evaluation of the credit or prepayment risks associated with existing credit obligations. Consumers must be given the opportunity via a toll-free telephone number to opt out of prescreened lists.[35]
Consumer Access and Disclosure: Upon consumer request, an agency must disclose the nature and substance of all information, except medical information, in its files. Consumers must pay a reasonable copy fee.
Disclosures to Consumers By User: Similar to federal law.
Restrictions on Content of Reports: Similar to federal law except bankruptcies over fourteen years old and criminal records more than seven years after date of disposition, release or parole.[36]
Consumer Disputes: Similar to federal law, except that the consumer reporting agency must reinvestigate within thirty days and notify the consumer of the results within a further ten days.[37] Agency must inform consumer of right to request description of procedures used to reinvestigate, including name, address and telephone number of person(s) contacted.
Duties of Furnishers: No relevant provisions.
Consumer Remedies: Actual damages, costs and reasonable attorney fees, plus punitive damages for willful violations. Criminal penalties for obtaining information from agency by false pretenses, or for unauthorized disclosures by agency personnel.
Statute of Limitations: Two years from accrual (or from discovery, if delay resulted from willful and material mis-representations by defendant).
Miscellaneous: Adverse information in investigative reports must be reverified or less than three months old to be included in a subsequent report.[38]

State Credit Repair Statute: **N.H. Rev. Stat. Ann. §§ 359-D:1 to D:11**

Covered Activities: Improving credit record or obtaining extension of credit, in return for money or other consideration.
Exemptions: Lenders authorized by N.H. and federal law; banks and savings associations eligible for FDIC insurance; nonprofit organizations; licensed real estate brokers acting within scope of license; N.H. lawyers acting within scope of law practice; registered securities broker-dealers; consumer reporting agencies.
Right to Cancel? Yes (5 days).
Prohibitions: Charging before complete performance, unless organization has posted bond; charging for referring buyer to retail seller for credit on same terms as generally available to public; making or advising false statements to creditors or credit reporting agencies; making false statements about services offered; requiring buyer to waive rights.
Other Substantive Requirements: Disclosures.
Bond: 5% of amount of fees charged during prior 12 months, not less than $5000 or more than $25,000, to be adjusted annually.
Private Cause of Action: Actual damages, not less than amount paid by buyer; attorney fees and costs; punitive damages allowed.

State Identity Theft Statute: **N.H. Rev. Stat. Ann. §§ 638:25 to :27**.

Definition of Offense: Poses as another with intent to defraud to obtain money, credit, goods, services or other thing of value, or confidential information about that person not available to the general public; obtains records or personal identifying information of another with intent to pose as that person or enable another to do so.
Victim Remedies in Criminal Case: Court shall order restitution for victim's economic loss.
Special Record-Clearing Provisions: No specific provisions.
Duties of Private Entities: No specific provisions.
Private Right of Action: No specific provisions.

Other State Provisions: **N.H. Rev. Stat. Ann. §§ 412:15.** Use of credit reports, credit histories, and credit scoring models in homeowners and personal motor vehicle insurance must be "based on objective, documented and measurable standards" and used in a manner that "affords appropriate consumer protections, including consumer no-

---

[35] State laws concerning prescreened lists are now preempted. *See* § 10.4.4, *supra*.

[36] This provision was in effect on Sept. 30, 1996, so even if it could be said to be otherwise preempted by 15 U.S.C. § 1681c, it is not preempted. *See* § 10.4.4, *supra*.

[37] This provision was in effect on Sept. 30, 1996, so although it regulates the time allowed an agency for reinvestigation, it is not preempted. *See* § 10.4.4, *supra*.

[38] This provision was in effect on Sept. 30, 1996, so even if it could be said to be otherwise preempted by 15 U.S.C. § 1681c, it is not preempted. *See* § 10.4.4, *supra*.

tice provisions and confidentiality protections." Commissioner shall make rules. Scoring models must be approved by department.

New Jersey

State FCRA Statute: N.J. Stat. Ann. §§ 56:11-28 to 56:11-41.

Scope: Similar to Federal.
Purposes for Which Reports May Be Issued: Generally same as federal law, but consumers must give prior written consent for the inclusion of medical information in reports used for employment, credit, insurance or direct marketing purposes, and for the preparation of investigative consumer reports.
Consumer Access and Disclosure: Similar to federal law, but must disclose all information in file. Must provide one free report per twelve month period; subsequent reports $8. Must disclose the dates, original payees and amounts of any checks that are the basis for any adverse characterization. Must disclose requests (for purposes other than a credit transaction initiated by the consumer) within one year.
Disclosures to Consumers By User: Prior to requesting an investigative report must disclose precise nature and scope of investigation and consumer's right to a free copy of the report, and must obtain consumer's prior written consent.
Restrictions on Content of Reports: No relevant provisions.
Consumer Disputes: Similar to federal law, except agency must notify consumer written five business days of determination that dispute is frivolous, including the reasons for its decision.
Duties of Furnishers: No relevant provisions.
Consumer Remedies: Negligent violations: actual damages, costs and reasonable attorney fees. Willful violations: actual damages or minimum damages of at least $100 but not more than $1000, punitive damages, costs and reasonable attorney fees. Those who file pleadings in bad faith or to harass liable for prevailing party's attorney fees for responding to that pleading. Criminal penalties for obtaining information from agency under false pretenses.
Statute of Limitations: No relevant provisions.
Miscellaneous: No relevant provisions.

Child Support Debts: N.J. Stat. Ann. § 2A:17-56.21. The state Department of Human Services shall report child support arrearages to consumer reporting agencies. The Department must give obligor prior notice and an opportunity to contest the accuracy of the information.

State Identity Theft Statute: N.J. Stat. Ann. §§ 2C:21-17 to 2C:21-17.5.

Definition of Offense: Impersonates another or assumes a false identity for purpose of obtaining a pecuniary benefit, or injuring or defrauding another; obtains personal identifying information of another and uses it without authority to fraudulently obtain a pecuniary benefit or services, or avoid the payment of a debt, or avoid criminal prosecution; or assists another person in using the information for these purposes. Possesses, manufactures or distributes items containing personal identification information of another, without authority, with knowledge that one is facilitating a fraud or injury to another.
Victim Remedies in Criminal Case: Restitution. Restitution includes costs incurred in clearing credit history or credit rating, and in any civil or administrative proceeding to satisfy any lien or debt or other obligation resulting from the actions of the thief. Sentencing court shall issue orders necessary to correct any public record that contains false information as a result of the identity theft.
Special Record-Clearing Provisions: At victim's request, or on court's own motion, court may grant an order requiring all consumer reporting agencies doing business in New Jersey to delete any false information resulting from the theft, and give consumer a free copy of the corrected credit report.
Duties of Private Entities: At victim's request, agency must provided corrected report to any person specified by the victim who has received a report within two years for employment purposes, or one year for any other purpose, if the report contained the false information.
Private Right of Action: Anyone who suffers ascertainable loss of money or property may bring action for treble damages, plus costs and attorney fees. (Damages may be awarded to businesses, financial institutions, etc, but any damages to natural persons must be fully satisfied before any payment to businesses, etc.). Standard of proof is preponderance of evidence; civil action may be brought even if criminal case ends in acquittal. (Conviction in criminal case will estop defendant from denying the conduct in a civil action.)

New Mexico

State FCRA Statute: N.M. Stat. Ann. §§ 56-3-1 to 56-3-8.

Scope: A consumer is any natural person seeking credit for personal, family, or household purposes.
Purposes for Which Reports May Be Issued: Credit reports for the granting of credit. Other bona fide business transactions. Employment purposes. No financial information to non-credit granting government agencies except by court order.
Consumer Access and Disclosure: Upon consumer request, an agency must disclose all information in a credit report or rating.
Disclosures to Consumer by User: No relevant provisions.
Restrictions on Content of Reports: A credit bureau must delete any derogatory data as soon as practical after ascertaining it can no longer be verified. A credit bureau cannot merge specialized information which is applicable only to

personnel investigations.[39] Criminal records over seven years old, convictions if a full pardon is granted, and arrests and indictments if learned no conviction resulted.[40] Bankruptcies over 14 years.

Consumer Disputes: A credit bureau must give a consumer who is examining credit reports forms on which to designate errors. If disputed, an agency must reinvestigate at no cost to the consumer if the consumer is denied credit. If the consumer is not denied credit, the consumer can be charged up to $5 for the reinvestigation.

Duties of Furnishers: No relevant provisions.

Consumer Remedies: After a credit bureau is given notice of an error, it is liable for any subsequent report which fails to correct the error. It is not liable for damages for an unintentional error prior to receiving notice of its existence. Damages for negligence include actual damages, costs and attorney fees, plus punitive damages for willful violations. Criminal penalties for obtaining information from agency under false pretenses, and for unauthorized disclosures by agency personnel.

Statute of Limitations: No relevant provisions.

Miscellaneous: A credit bureau must require service contracts in which the user certifies that inquiries will be made only for proper purposes; a credit bureau must refuse services to one who will not certify.

Child Support Debts: N.M. Stat. Ann. § 56-3-3. Child Support Enforcement Division may obtain credit reports for use in locating obligors and enforcing obligations. Division must furnish to credit bureau, on request, the judgment or case number for the obligation for which a report is requested.

State Identity Theft Statute: N.M. Stat. Ann. § 30-16-24.1.

Definition of Offense: Willfully obtaining, recording or transferring personal identifying information of another, without authority, and with intent to defraud that person or another.

Victim Remedies in Criminal Case: Out-of-pocket costs, plus expenses incurred, including attorney fees, in clearing credit record or credit report, and in civil or administrative proceeding to satisfy any debt, lien or obligation resulting from the theft. Sentencing court shall issue written findings of fact, and make such orders as are necessary to correct a public record that contains misinformation as a result of the theft.

Special Record-Clearing Provisions: No specific provisions.

Duties of Private Entities: No specific provisions.

Private Right of Action: No specific provisions.

New York

State FCRA Statute: N.Y. Gen. Bus. Law §§ 380 to 380-t.

Scope: Adverse information is any information that is likely to have a negative effect upon the ability or eligibility of a consumer to obtain credit insurance, employment or other benefits, goods or services, or information responsible for increases in charges for credit or insurance.

Purposes for Which Reports May Be Issued: Similar to the federal law, but explicitly authorize use for residential rentals and does not authorize provision to potential investors or servicers, or current insurers, in connection with evaluation of the credit or prepayment risks associated with existing credit obligations. May not issue reports listing credit denial if the denial is only due to insufficient information.[41]

Consumer Access and Disclosure: Similar to federal law, except that all information in files must be disclosed. Medical information only to be disclosed to physician designated by consumer. An agency must inform a consumer upon any contact of the right to receive a credit report. All consumers denied credit must be notified of the right to receive a report within thirty days at no charge. All requests for reports for employment purposes for two years, for other purposes for six months. If medical information, or reasons for an adverse action based on medical information must be disclosed, it should be disclosed to a physician designated by the consumer.

Disclosures to Consumers By User: Similar to the federal law, except that a consumer must be informed in writing that a credit report may be requested.[42] Upon consumer request, a user must tell a consumer if a credit report is actually used, and the source of the report. For an investigative consumer report, the user must obtain authorization in all situations. An authorization must state that the consumer can request a credit report, and that the user may request a report from the agency and, upon request, will inform a consumer whether it has done so. A consumer must be furnished with the reason for the denial of credit (statute refers to Federal Equal Credit Opportunity Act); cannot furnish the report to others without a legitimate business need.

Restrictions on Content of Reports: Similar to the federal law. Judgments over five years old which have been paid. Bankruptcies over fourteen years old. Information known to be incorrect. In addition:[43] information relative to an arrest or criminal charge unless it is still pending or resulted in conviction. Criminal convictions seven years after disposition, release or parole. Information on race, religion, color, or ethnic origin. Drug/alcohol addiction or mental institution

---

39 This provision was in effect on Sept. 30, 1996, so even if it could be said to be otherwise preempted by 15 U.S.C. § 1681c, it is not preempted. See § 10.4.4, *supra*.

40 These provisions were in effect on Sept. 30, 1996, so even if they could be said to be otherwise preempted by 15 U.S.C. § 1681c, the are not preempted. See § 10.4.4, *supra*.

41 This provision was in effect on Sept. 30, 1996, so even if it could be said to be otherwise preempted by 15 U.S.C. § 1681c, it is not preempted. See § 10.4.4, *supra*.

42 Scott v. Real Estate Finance Group, 183 F.3d 97 (2d Cir. 1999).

43 Even if these provisions could be said to be otherwise preempted by 15 U.S.C. § 1681c, they were in effect on September 30, 1996 and therefore not preempted.

confinement information over seven years old. Agencies may not collect or maintain in its files any information related to or derived from a polygraph examination or similar device. For employment purposes only, an agency may report information related to the detention of an individual by a retail establishment if an uncoerced admission of wrongdoing was executed, and the retail establishment notified the individual that it is furnishing information to a reporting agency, and that the individual may dispute the information's completeness or accuracy.
Consumer Disputes: Similar to the federal law. If an item is corrected or can no longer be verified, an agency must mail a corrected copy to the consumer at no charge.
Duties of Furnishers: No relevant provisions.
Consumer Remedies: Actual damages, costs and reasonable attorney fees, plus punitive damages for willful violations. Criminal penalties for obtaining information from agency under false pretenses; for willfully introducing or attempting to introduce false information into file to damage or enhance credit rating; and for unauthorized disclosures by agency personnel.
Statute of Limitations: Two years from accrual (or from discovery, if delay results from willful material misrepresentation by defendant).
Miscellaneous: No adverse information may be included within a subsequent investigative consumer report unless it is reverified or less than three months old.[44]

State Credit Repair Statute: N.Y. Gen. Bus. Law §§ 458-a to -k

Covered Activities: Improving credit record in return for money or other consideration.
Exemptions: Nonprofit organizations. N.Y. licensed lawyers, rendering services within the scope of their law practice.
Right to Cancel? Yes (3 days).
Prohibitions: Charging before complete performance; charging for referring buyer to retail seller for credit on same terms as generally available to public; making or advising false statements to creditors or credit reporting agencies; making false statements about services offered; misrepresenting ability to obtain credit card for buyer; requiring buyer to waive rights.
Other Substantive Requirements: Disclosures.
Bond: N/A
Private Cause of Action: No more than thrice actual damages and no less than amount paid by buyer; attorney fees. Contract voidable. A violation is UDAP violation.

State Identity Theft Statute: N.Y. Penal Law §§ 190.77 to 190.84. See also N.Y. Gen. Bus. Law § 380-s.

Definition of Offense: Identity theft: Knowingly with intent to defraud assumes identity of another, by presenting self as another, or using personal identifying information of that person, with intent to obtain goods, money, services or credit, or cause financial loss to that person or another, or commit a crime. Degree of offense depends on amount of financial loss caused, or seriousness of crime committed. Unlawful possession of personal identification information: Knowingly possesses certain identifying information of another, knowing it is to be used in furtherance of a crime defined by this chapter [larceny]. Degree of crime depends on number of items possessed or accomplices supervised. *See also* Gen. Bus. Law § 380-s, a civil statute which forbids knowingly and with intent to defraud obtaining, transferring, processing using, or attempting to obtain, etc., credit, goods services or anything of value in the name of another person without that person's consent.
Victim Remedies in Criminal Case: No specific provisions.
Special Record-clearing Provisions: No specific provisions.
Duties of Private Entities: No specific provisions.
Private Right of Action: Any person, firm, partnership, or corporation whose knowing and willful violation of § 380-s resulted in the transmission or provision to a credit reporting agency of information that would not otherwise have been transmitted or provided is liable for actual and punitive damages, costs and attorney fees.

North Carolina

State Credit Repair Statute: N.C. Gen Stat. §§ 66-220 to -226

Covered Activities: Improving credit record or obtaining extension of credit, in return for money or other consideration.
Exemptions: Banks and savings associations authorized by N.C. or federal law; licensed consumer finance lenders; credit unions; nonprofit organizations; licensed real estate brokers acting within scope of license; N.C. lawyers acting within scope of law practice; registered securities broker-dealers; consumer reporting agencies.
Right to Cancel? Yes (3 days).
Prohibitions: Charging before complete performance; charging for referring buyer to retail seller for credit on same terms as generally available to public; making or advising false statements to creditors or credit reporting agencies; making false statements about services offered; requiring buyer to waive rights.
Other Substantive Requirements: Disclosures.
Bond: $10,000.
Private Cause of Action: Contract voidable with complete refund; attorney fees and any other additional damages. A violation is a UDAP violation.

State Identity Theft Statute: N.C. Gen. Stat. § 14-113.20 to .23.

Definition of Offense: Financial identity fraud: Knowingly

---

44 This provision was in effect on September 30, 1996, so even if it could be said to be otherwise preempted by 15 U.S.C. § 1681c, it is not preempted. *See* § 10.4.4, *supra*.

obtains, possesses or uses personal identifying information of another, without authority, with intent to fraudulently represent self to be that person for purposes of making financial or credit transactions, or avoiding legal consequences. Punishment is enhanced if victim suffers arrest, detention or conviction as a proximate result of the fraud. Trafficking in stolen identities: Sells, transfers or purchases identifying information of another, with intent to commit financial identity fraud, or assist another in doing so.

Victim Remedies in Criminal Case: If person commits a crime under a stolen name, court records shall reflect that ID theft victim did not commit the crime. Restitution. Restitution includes lost wages, attorney fees or other costs incurred in correcting credit record or in connection with any civil, criminal or administrative proceeding brought against the victim as a result of the theft.

Special Record-Clearing Provisions: No specific provisions.

Duties of Private Entities: No specific provisions.

Private Right of Action: Victim also has a cause of action under § 1-539.2C, the civil theft statute, for greater of treble damages or $5000. This civil action available whether or not criminal prosecution is brought. Thief is liable for damages; injunctive relief; attorney fees.

Other State Provisions: **N.C. Gen. Stat. § 25B-2**. Agency, upon written request by married person, must report both separate credit history of each spouse and history of joint accounts, if any.

State Credit Insurance in Private Insurance statute: N.C. Gen. Stat. Ann. § 58-36-90. See also N.C. Gen. Stat. §§ 58-39-1 to -76.

Scope: Credit reports or credit scores used in non-commercial insurance underwriting (i.e., residential or non-commercial vehicle).

Disclosures: If credit score or credit report is used as basis for adverse action, must notify consumer of factors used in determining credit score; name, address and toll-free phone number of credit bureau that issued report, and notice that consumer has right to challenge information in report. The insurance information and privacy protection statute, N.C. Gen. Stat. §§ 58-39-1 to –76, requires insurer to disclose their information practices. An insurer who wishes to use investigative consumer report must notify consumer of right to be interviewed and to receive copy of report. (§ 58-39-40).

Dispute Resolution: If, after dispute procedure provided by Federal FCRA, information is found to be inaccurate or incomplete, insurer must, within 30 days of being notified, re-underwrite or re-rate. If a refund is required, it should be for the shorter of 12 months or the actual policy period.

Prohibited Practices: Insurers may not use credit scores as sole reason for terminating existing policy of noncommercial vehicle or residential insurance.

North Dakota

Child Support Debts: **N.D. Cent. Code § 50-09-08.4**. Enforcement agencies may report past due support amounts provided obligors given notice and a reasonable opportunity to contest the accuracy of the report first.

State Identity Theft Statute: **N.D. Cent. Code § 12.1-23–11**.

Definition of Offense: Uses personal identifying information of another without authority to obtain credit, money, goods, services or anything of value, while representing self to be another or to be acting under that person's authority

Victim Remedies in Criminal Case: No specific provisions.

Special Record-Clearing Provisions: No specific provisions.

Duties of Private Entities: No specific provisions.

Private Right of Action: No specific provisions.

State Credit Information in Private Insurance statute: N.D. Cent. Code §§ 26.1–25.1-01 to -11

Scope: Credit information used in underwriting personal insurance, i.e. policies individually underwritten for personal, family or household purposes.

Disclosures: Insurer must notify consumer at time of application that credit information will be used. Insurer must notify consumer of reasons for adverse action, if based on credit information.

Dispute Resolution: If, after dispute procedure provided by Federal FCRA, information is found to be inaccurate or incomplete, insurer must, within 30 days of being notified, re-underwrite or re-rate. If a refund is required, it should be for the shorter of 12 months or the actual policy period.

Prohibited Practices: Insurer may not use an insurance score that is based on income, gender, address, zip code, ethnic group, marital status or nationality; deny, cancel or nonrenew based solely on credit information; take adverse action solely because consumer does not have credit card; take adverse action based on credit report unless report is issued or score calculated within one hundred twenty days of date when policy is issued or renewed; use credit information; use credit information if it does not recalculate or obtain updated report at least every 36 months; consider the following as negative factors: inquiries not initiated nor requested by consumer, inquiries relating to insurance coverage, collection accounts with medical industry code, certain multiple lender inquiries (i.e. relating to home mortgage or auto loan).

Other: No relevant provisions.

Ohio

State FCRA Statute: Ohio Rev. Code Ann. §§ 3904.01 to 3904.22.

Scope: Consumer reports used in connection with a life, health or disability insurance transaction.

Purposes for Which Reports May Be Issued: Life, health or disability insurance transactions.

Consumer Access and Disclosures: Authorization to obtain information must be in plain language, in writing, signed by consumer, indicate what information is sought, be dated, and limited to a specific time. Medical information may be provided to a medical professional designated by the consumer. Disclosure requirements do not apply to certain information gathered in connection with or reasonable anticipation of, civil or criminal proceeding involving the consumer.

Disclosures to Consumer By User: Insurance institutions or agents must disclose that a report may be requested and provide a notice of information practices summarizing consumers' rights under Ohio law. No insurance institution, agent or insurance support organization may procure an investigative consumer report in connection with an insurance transaction without informing consumer of their right to be interviewed for the report and to receive a copy of the report. Upon written request, insurance institutions, agents or insurance support organizations must disclose all recorded personal information to consumer and the sources of such information, and must provide a summary of procedures available to request correction, amendment or deletion of such information. Insurance institutions or agents must notify consumer of reasons for adverse underwriting decision and, if requested within ninety business days, the specific items and sources of information that support those reasons.

Restrictions on Content of Reports: No relevant provisions.

Consumer Disputes: Within thirty days of being informed of dispute, must either correct or delete the information or inform the consumer of its refusal, the reasons, and the right to file a statement describing the dispute. If information is changed or deleted, must notify (at request of consumer) users who have received reports within two years. Must notify insurance support organizations which use the information, or which supplied the information.

Duties of Furnishers: Imposes disputed accuracy procedures similar to those imposed upon consumer reporting agencies by federal law upon insurance institutions, agents and insurance support organizations. Also imposes duties similar to federal law upon insurance institutions, agents and insurance support organizations when furnishing information to others.

Consumer Remedies: Actual damages only available for unauthorized disclosure of information to others, equitable relief available to remedy violations of some other provisions. Costs and reasonable attorney fees available to prevailing party. Criminal penalties for obtaining information from agency under false pretenses. Administrative enforcement by commissioner of insurance, who may issue cease and desist orders, suspend or revoke licenses, and impose civil penalties: up to $10,000 or for violations frequent enough to be a general business practice, up to $50,000.

Statute of Limitations: Two years from date violation is or should have been discovered.

Miscellaneous: No relevant provisions.

Child Support Debts: Ohio Rev. Code Ann. §§ 3123.91 to 3123.932 (West). If the court or agency makes a final determination that an obligor is delinquent, it must report this information to at least one consumer reporting agency. If the entire arrearage is paid, the reporting agency may not record the payment until it is confirmed by the child support agency. Any credit reporting agency may request information regarding child support from the child support agency, which may report whether the consumer is obliged to pay child support, the court or agency that issued the order, and whether the order is being administered by the child support agency.

State Credit Repair Statute: Ohio Rev. Code Ann. §§ 4712.01 to .99

Covered Activities: Improving credit record or obtaining extension of credit, in return for money or other consideration.

Exemptions: Regulated and supervised lenders; mortgage lenders approved by HUD; banks and savings associations eligible for FDIC insurance; credit unions; nonprofit organizations; licensed motor vehicle dealers acting within scope of license; public agencies; colleges or universities; registered mortgage brokers; consumer reporting agencies.

Right to Cancel? Yes (3 days).

Prohibitions: Charging before complete performance; charging for referring buyer to retail seller for credit on same terms as generally available to public; making or advising false statements to creditors or credit reporting agencies; making false statements about services offered; submitting disputes to reporting agency without buyer's consent; any fraudulent or deceptive practices; requiring buyer to waive rights.

Other Substantive Requirements: Disclosures.

Bond: $50,000.

Private Cause of Action: Actual damages, not less than amount paid by buyer; attorney fees and costs; punitive damages allowed. A violation is a UDAP violation. Injunctive relief. Statute of limitations, four years.

State Identity Theft Statute: Ohio Rev. Code Ann. § 2913.49.

Definition of Offense: Without authority uses, obtains, or possesses personal identifying information of another with intent to hold self out as the other person, or represent that person's identifying information as their own; creates, obtains, possesses or uses the personal identifying information of another with intent to aid another in violating this section; possesses personal identifying information with another's permission, but uses it with intent to defraud; allows another to use one's personal identifying information with intent to

defraud. Degree of crime depends upon value of credit, property, services, or debt involved.
Victim Remedies in Criminal Case: No specific provisions.
Special Record-Clearing Provisions: No specific provisions.
Duties of Private Entities: No specific provisions.
Private Right of Action: No specific provisions.

Oklahoma

State FCRA Statute: **Okla. Stat. tit. 24, §§ 81–86, 147–148**.

Scope: Credit rating book or list published to retail or wholesale businesses.
Purposes for Which Reports May Be Issued: Oklahoma law regulates the business of credit rating.
Consumer Access and Disclosure: Similar to federal statute. Before giving an opinion upon any consumer's credit standing to a retail merchant, an agency must mail a copy of the opinion to the consumer.
Disclosures to Consumers By User: Anyone having a rating book or list must show a consumer his/her rating upon request. Similar to Federal statute; when a report is requested for employment purposes, consumers must be given the option to receive a copy.
Restrictions on Content of Reports: Tax liens may not be disclosed unless the information is obtained directly from the state tax commission, and the reporting agency uses due diligence in updating the status of the liens.
Consumer Disputes: No relevant provisions.
Duties of Furnishers: No relevant provisions.
Consumer Remedies: Anyone who knowingly publishes a false opinion in a book or list and circulates it to retail or wholesale business concerns is liable for the amount of injuries in addition to exemplary damages, as determined by a jury. Fine for failure to show a consumer rating upon request. Criminal penalties for introducing false information to damage or enhance credit rating, or for willfully circulating false report.
Statute of Limitations: No relevant provisions.
Miscellaneous: No relevant provisions.

State Credit Repair Statute: **Okla. Stat. tit. 24, §§ 131 to 148**

Covered Activities: Improving credit record or obtaining extension of credit, in return for money or other consideration.
Exemptions: Regulated and supervised lenders; mortgage lenders approved by HUD; banks and savings associations eligible for FDIC insurance; credit unions; nonprofit organizations; licensed real estate brokers acting within scope of license; Oklahoma lawyers acting within scope of law practice; registered securities broker-dealers; consumer reporting agencies; residential mortgage brokers; insurance companies; persons authorized to file electronic tax returns, who do not receive any compensation for refund anticipation loans.
Right to Cancel? Yes (5 days).
Prohibitions: Charging before complete performance, unless organization has posted bond; charging for referring buyer to retail seller for credit on same terms as generally available to public; making or advising false statements to creditors or credit reporting agencies; making false statements about services offered; requiring buyer to waive rights.
Other Substantive Requirements: Disclosures.
Bond: $10,000.
Private Cause of Action: Actual damages, not less than amount paid by buyer; attorney fees and costs; punitive damages allowed.

State Identity Theft Statute: **Okla. Stat. tit. 21, § 1533.1**.

Definition of Offense: Willfully and with fraudulent intent obtain the personal identifying information of another with intent to use, sell, or allow another to use or sell it, to obtain or attempt to obtain credit, goods, property or services in the name of another; or offer another the use of one's own personal identifying information for the purpose of obtaining a false identifying document.
Victim Remedies in Criminal Case: No specific provisions.
Special Record-Clearing Provisions: No specific provisions.
Duties of Private Entities: No specific provisions.
Private Right of Action: No specific provisions.

Other State Provisions: **Okla. Stat. tit. 24, § 81.** Before rating, a consumer agency must attempt to obtain from the person to be rated a statement of assets and liabilities.

Child Support Debts: **Okla. Stat. tit. 56, § 240.7.** Department of Human Services shall report child support arrearages to consumer reporting agencies. Obligers must be notified prior to the release of the information and be given a reasonable opportunity to contest the accuracy of the information.

State Credit Information in Private Insurance statute: **Okla. Stat. tit. 36, §§ 950 to 959.**

Scope: Use of credit information in personal insurance, individually underwritten for personal, family or household use: personal vehicle, recreational vehicle, homeowners (including mobile home), and non-commercial fire.
Disclosures: Insurer must notify consumer at time of application, in writing or in same medium as application, if it intends to use credit information. If adverse action based on credit report, insurer must disclose reasons to consumer, and provide notification as required by Federal FCRA (source of report, dispute resolution procedure, etc.).
Dispute Resolution: If, after dispute resolution procedure pursuant to Federal FCRA, information in credit report is found to be incorrect, insurer must, within 30 days after notice, re-underwrite or re-rate based on corrected report. If refund is required, it must be for lesser of policy period or 12 months.
Prohibited Practices: Insurer may not use credit score based on income, gender, address, ethnic group, religion, marital status or nationality; deny, cancel, or non-renew based wholly on credit information without, another applicable

underwriting factor independent of credit information; base renewal rates solely on credit information; take adverse action based on lack of credit card; count lack of credit history as a negative factor, unless insurer can show relationship to risk; take adverse action based on credit report issued or credit score calculated more than 90 days before policy was written or renewed; use credit information if it does not recalculate every 36 months based on current credit report; treat as a negative factor collection accounts with a medical industry code, or certain credit inquiries.

Other: Insurers who use scores must file scoring model with Insurance Department.

Oregon

Child Support Debts: Or. Rev. Stat. Ann. § 25.650. The Department of Justice shall provide information on child support arrearages to consumer reporting agencies, but first both obligor and obligee parents must be notified and given opportunity to contest accuracy of information. Department of Justice shall promptly notify agency when obligor pays off previously reported arrearage.

State Credit Repair Statute: Or. Rev. Stat. Ann. §§ 646.380 to .396

Covered Activities: Improving credit record or obtaining extension of credit, in return for money or other consideration.
Exemptions: Regulated and supervised lenders; mortgage lenders approved by HUD; banks and savings associations eligible for FDIC insurance; credit unions; licensed consumer finance lenders; mortgage brokers; nonprofit organizations; licensed real estate brokers acting within scope of license; Oregon lawyers acting within scope of law practice; registered securities broker-dealers; consumer reporting agencies.
Right to Cancel? Yes (3 days).
Prohibitions: Charging before complete performance; charging for referring buyer to retail seller for credit on same terms as generally available to public; making or advising false statements to creditors or credit reporting agencies; making false statements about services offered; requiring buyer to waive rights.
Other Substantive Requirements: Disclosures.
Bond: $25,000.
Private Cause of Action: Contract voidable. A violation is a UDAP violation.

State Identity Theft Statute: Or. Rev. Stat. § 165.800.

Definition of Offense: With intent to deceive or defraud, obtains, possesses, creates, utters, or converts to person's own use the personal identification of another person.
Victim Remedies in Criminal Case: No specific provisions.
Special Record-Clearing Provisions: No specific provisions.
Duties of Private Entities: No specific provisions.
Private Right of Action: No specific provisions.

Pennsylvania

Child Support Debts: 23 Pa. Cons. Stat. Ann. § 4303. State shall report any child support arrearages provided that obligor is given notice and a period of up to twenty days to contest the accuracy of the information.

State Credit Repair Statute: Pa. Stat. Ann. tit. 73, §§ 2181 to 2192

Covered Activities: Improving credit record or obtaining extension of credit, in return for money or other consideration. The statute also has a separate but somewhat overlapping definition of "loan broker," and separate restrictions applicable to them.
Exemptions: Regulated and supervised lenders; banks and savings associations eligible for FDIC insurance; nonprofit organizations; licensed real estate brokers acting within scope of license; Pennsylvania lawyers acting within scope of law practice; registered securities broker-dealers; consumer reporting agencies.
Right to Cancel? Yes (5 days).
Prohibitions: Charging before complete performance, unless organization has posted bond; charging for referring buyer to retail seller for credit on same terms as generally available to public; making or advising false statements to creditors or credit reporting agencies; making false statements about services offered; advertising a guarantee that credit will be obtained; requiring buyer to waive rights.
Other Substantive Requirements: Disclosures.
Bond: 5% of total fees charged in previous 12 months, but not less than $5000 nor more than $25,000. (Amounts adjusted annually).
Private Cause of Action: Actual damages, not less than amount paid by buyer; attorney fees and costs; punitive damages allowed. A violation is a UDAP violation.

State Identity Theft Statute: 18 Pa. Cons. Stat. § 4120, 42 Pa. Cons. Stat. 8315, 42 Pa. Cons. Stat. § 9720.1.

Definition of Offense: Possesses or uses identifying information of another without consent to further any unlawful purpose. Enhanced penalty if victim aged 60 or above.
Victim Remedies in Criminal Case: Court may order restitution for all reasonable expenses incurred by or on behalf of the victim to investigate the theft, bring or defend criminal actions related to the theft, correct victim's credit record or negative credit reports resulting from the theft; reasonable expenses include attorney fees, fees or costs imposed by credit bureaus or incurred in private investigations, court costs and filing fees.
Special Record-Clearing Provisions: Police report by victim stating that identifying information has been lost, stolen, or used without permission is prima facie evidence that information was possessed or used without consent.
Duties of Private Entities: No specific provisions.
Private Right of Action: Greater of actual damages or $500.

Actual damages include loss of money, reputation or property. Reasonable attorney fees and court costs. Court has discretion to triple the damages.

Puerto Rico

Child Support Debts: 8 P.R. Laws Ann. § 528. Child Support Administration shall report child support arrears to consumer reporting agencies. Obligors must be notified prior to release of information and notified that they have ten days to either pay the debt or challenge the report (with opportunity to present evidence).

State Identity Theft Statute: 33 P.R. Laws Ann. § 4309.

Definition of Offense: Impersonation. Fraudulently impersonates or represents another and under this assumed character performs any act not authorized by the person falsely represented, or to the prejudice of that person or a third party.
Victim Remedies in Criminal Case: No specific provisions.
Special Record-Clearing Provisions: No specific provisions.
Duties of Private Entities: No specific provisions.
Private Right of Action: No specific provisions.

Rhode Island

State FCRA Statute: **R.I. Gen. Laws §§ 6-13.1-20 to 6-13.1-27**.

Scope: Same as the federal law.
Purposes for Which Reports May Be Issued: Same as federal law.
Consumer Access and Disclosure: Similar to federal law. Upon consumer request, an agency must disclose within four business days of the request all information in its files that pertains to the consumer at the time of the request. Any charge is not to exceed $8 per report, although the charge may increase with the Consumer Price Index. Must disclose to the consumer that the consumer has the right to request that corrected credit reports be sent to employers within two years, and to any other person within six months, when the agency has corrected information contained in the report.
Disclosures to Consumers By User: A consumer must be notified that a credit report may be requested before a report is requested in connection with an application for credit, employment, or insurance. Otherwise similar to federal law.
Restrictions on Content of Reports: No relevant provisions.
Consumer Disputes: Once a credit bureau receives notice of a dispute, it has thirty calendar days to reinvestigate the status of the information unless it has reason to believe that the dispute is frivolous or irrelevant.[45] If it is inaccurate, it must be deleted promptly. If reinvestigation does not resolve the dispute, the consumer may file a brief summary of the dispute. The bureau must then include that summary or a summary of its own with any subsequent credit report that it issues. The bureau must furnish free of charge a copy of any corrected credit report to the consumer, and if the consumer requests, furnish a copy of the corrected report to any person designated by the consumer who has received a credit report within the past two years, if for employment purposes, or within the past six months for any other purpose.
Duties of Furnishers: No relevant provisions.
Consumer Remedies: Violations constitute a deceptive trade practice for enforcement purposes. Negligent noncompliance: three working days to correct after being notified of the noncompliance or liability for $10 a day for each day in noncompliance in addition to actual damages, costs, and reasonable attorney fees.
Statute of Limitations: No relevant provisions.
Miscellaneous: Agencies must register with the office of the Secretary of State. Consumers have right to furnish a statement concerning any lapse in employment to agency, at no charge, which must be included in agency's file.

Child Support Debts: **R.I. Gen. Laws § 15-25-1 and 15-25-2**. The child support enforcement agency shall inform reporting agencies of child support arrearages, unless it determines release of information inappropriate in a particular case. Obligor must be given ten days prior notice and an opportunity to contest the accuracy of the information. State child support enforcement agency must give consumer ten days notice prior to requesting report, must make report available to consumer, and must use report solely to establish consumer's capacity to make child support payments. Department must "periodically" report to credit reporting agencies if overdue support is paid, or amount of support due is amended.

State Identity Theft Statute: **R.I. Gen. Laws § 11-49.1-1 to -5**.

Definition of Offense: Deals primarily with producing, selling or using false ID documents, but also includes knowingly transfers or uses with intent to defraud, without lawful authority, a means of identification of another person with the intent to commit, or to aid or abet, any unlawful activity that constitutes a violation of federal, state or local law.
Victim Remedies in Criminal Case: No specific provisions.
Special Record-Clearing Provisions: No specific provisions.
Duties of Private Entities: No specific provisions.
Private Right of Action: No specific provisions.

State Credit Information in Personal Insurance statute: **R.I. Gen. L. § 27-6-53**

Scope: Use of credit rating for homeowners insurance.
Dispute Resolution: At request of customer, must recalculate score every two years, based on updated insurance score. If a credit bureau determines that information is

---

45 This provision was in effect on Sept. 30, 1996, so although it regulates the time allowed an agency to reinvestigate, it is not preempted. See § 10.4.4, *supra*.

inaccurate, insurer must re-calculate, based on corrected report, within 30 days of receiving notice.

Prohibited Practices: May not decline to insure based on an insurance score, or take adverse action based on worsening of score, unless either the worsening is a result of a bankruptcy, tax lien, garnishment, foreclosure or judgment, or the worsening is confirmed by another insurance score, at least six months after the first.

Other: Insurer who wishes to use insurance scoring must demonstrate the predictive nature of its score to the insurance division.

South Carolina

Child Support Debts: **S.C. Code Ann. § 43-5-585**. Department of Social Services shall inform agencies of child support arrearages greater than $1000. Obligors must be given notice and an opportunity to contest accuracy of the information.

State Identity Theft Statute: **S.C. Code Ann. §§ 16-13-500 to -530**.

Definition of Offense: With intent to appropriate the financial resources of another for self or a third party, obtains or records identifying information which would assist in accessing financial records of another, or accesses or attempts to access the financial resources of another by use of identifying information.
Victim Remedies in Criminal Case: Court may order restitution pursuant to § 17-25-322 [general criminal restitution statute].
Special Record-Clearing Provisions: No specific provisions.
Duties of Private Entities: No specific provisions.
Private Right of Action: No specific provisions.

Other State Provisions. **S.C. Code Ann. § 38073-740.** All information, explicitly including credit reports, used by insurer in determining premium classification for automobile insurance must be kept on file for three years after date of application, and made available to applicant on request. Copies must be available, if applicant pays copying expense.

South Dakota

Child Support Debts: **S.D. Codified Laws § 28-1-69**. Department of Social Services may provide information on overdue support to consumer reporting agency at request of agency, or in the discretion of the secretary. Must notify obligor of proposed release of information, and the procedure for contesting the accuracy of the information.

State Identity Theft Statute: **S.D. Codified Laws 22-30A-3.1 to -3.3**.

Definition of Offense: Obtains, transfers, uses, attempts to obtain or records identifying information not lawfully issued for that person's use; accesses or attempts to access the financial resources of another through the use of identifying information.
Victim Remedies in Criminal Case: No specific provisions.
Special Record-Clearing Provisions: No specific provisions.
Duties of Private Entities: No specific provisions.
Private Right of Action: No specific provisions.

Tennessee

Child Support Debts: **Tenn. Code Ann. § 36-5-106**. The Department of Human Services shall report child support arrearages to agencies and also those who are current with their payments. Must provide obligor with notice and an opportunity to contest accuracy of information before release.

State Credit Repair Statute: **Tenn. Code Ann. §§ 47-18-1001 to -1011**

Covered Activities: Improving credit record or obtaining extension of credit, in return for money or other consideration.
Exemptions: Banks and savings associations eligible for FDIC insurance; lenders authorized under Tenn. or federal law; nonprofit organizations; licensed real estate brokers acting within scope of license; Tenn. lawyers acting within scope of law practice; registered securities broker-dealers; consumer reporting agencies.
Right to Cancel? Yes (5 days).
Prohibitions: Charging before complete performance; charging for referring buyer to retail seller for credit on same terms as generally available to public; making or advising false statements to creditors or credit reporting agencies; making false statements about services offered; creating new credit record under different identity; violating Consumer Credit Protection Act; requiring buyer to waive rights.
Other Substantive Requirements: Disclosures.
Bond: $100,000.
Private Cause of Action: Where willful non-compliance, the greater of actual damages or the amount paid by consumer, with punitive damages allowed; where non-compliance due to negligence, actual damages. Contract voidable. 2-year statute of limitations.

State Identity Theft Statute: **Tenn. Code Ann. §§ 39-14-150, 39-16-303, 47-18-2101 to -2106**.

Definition of Offense: Knowingly transfers or uses without authority a means of identification of another, with intent to permit, promote, carry on or facilitate any unlawful activity (means of identification broadly defined) § 39-14-150. With intent to injure or defraud another, assumes a false identity § 39-16-303. Obtains, transfers, possesses or uses, attempts to obtain, possess, transfer or use, for unlawful economic benefit, one or more identification documents or personal identification numbers of another, or otherwise obtains, transfers, possesses or uses, or attempts to obtain, transfer, possess or use, one or more financial documents of another. § 47-18-2102. Engages in any unfair, deceptive, misleading act or practice for the purpose of engaging in identity theft. § 47-18-2102.

Victim Remedies in Criminal Case: No specific provisions.
Special Record-Clearing Provisions: No specific provisions.
Duties of Private Entities: No specific provisions.
Private Right of Action: Private right of action for damages, costs, attorney fees, and "such other relief" as court considers necessary. Treble damages for willful and knowing violation. Declaratory judgment and injunction available. Plaintiff must send copy of complaint to attorney general. Violation of identity theft statute also violates the Consumer Protection Act. 2 year statute of limitations.
Other: Attorney general may sue for violation of this section, seeking restitution for ascertainable loss (plus interest) suffered by consumers, as well as for injunction, asset freeze, civil penalties, court costs, and reasonable expenses of the investigation. Restitution under this section is a set-off against any judgment obtained in private civil action.

Texas

State FCRA Statute: **Tex. Fin. Code Ann. §§ 391.001 to 391.002 & 392.001 to 392.404**.

Scope: Applies to credit reporting bureaus, i.e. persons who assemble or report credit information about individuals, for purposes of furnishing that information to third parties.
Purposes for Which Reports May Be Issued: No relevant provisions.
Consumer Access and Disclosure: All information in agency files must be disclosed to consumer within 45 days.
Disclosures to Consumer by User: No relevant provisions.
Restrictions on Content of Reports: No relevant provisions.
Consumer Disputes: No relevant provisions.[46]
Duties of Furnishers: If consumer disputes the accuracy of a debt being collected by a third party debt collector, consumer shall notify the debt collector. Debt collector must make written record of the dispute, and cease collection efforts until it makes an investigation. Within 30 days debt collector must respond to consumer, admitting or denying accuracy of debt, or stating that it has not has sufficient time to complete investigation. If information is inaccurate, collector must cease collection efforts and, within five days, notify every person who has previously received notice of the debt. If it has not had sufficient time, it must change item as requested by the consumer, send copy of changed report to all persons who received report, and cease collection efforts. If information found accurate, collector may report information and resume collection efforts.
Consumer Remedies: No liability for bona fide errors which result despite agency maintaining reasonable procedures to avoid errors. Injunctive relief, actual damages, statutory damages of $100 per violation of provisions concerning disputed accuracy, reasonable attorney fees and costs available. Fine of $200 for knowingly furnishing false information about a person's credit record. Remedies are also available under the state deceptive practices statute.
Statute of Limitations: No relevant provisions.
Miscellaneous: Credit bureau must post bond for $10,000 and file copy with secretary of state before doing business in Texas.

Child Support Debts: **Tex. Fam. Code Ann. § 231.114**. Amount of child support owed and amount paid shall be reported to consumer reporting agencies, after thirty days notice and an opportunity to contest the accuracy of the information is given to the obligor.

State Credit Repair Statute: **Tex. Fin. Code Ann. §§ 393.001 to .505**

Covered Activities: Improving credit record or obtaining extension of credit, in return for money or other consideration.
Exemptions: Lenders authorized under Texas or federal law; mortgage lenders approved by HUD; banks and savings associations eligible for FDIC insurance; credit unions; nonprofit organizations; licensed real estate brokers and mortgage brokers acting within scope of license; Texas lawyers acting within scope of law practice; registered securities broker-dealers; consumer reporting agencies; persons whose primary business is making loans secured by liens on realty; an authorized e-file provider who negotiates a refund anticipation loan on behalf of a bank, savings bank, savings and loan association or credit union..
Right to Cancel? Yes (3 days).
Prohibitions: Charging before complete performance, unless organization has posted bond; charging for referring buyer to retail seller for credit on same terms as generally available to public; making or advising false statements to creditors or credit reporting agencies; making false statements about services offered; fraudulent or deceptive practices; requiring buyer to waive rights.
Other Substantive Requirements: Disclosures.
Bond: $10,000.
Private Cause of Action: Actual damages, not less than amount paid by buyer; attorney fees and costs; punitive damages allowed. A violation is a UDAP violation. Injunctive relief. 4-year statute of limitations.

State Identity Theft Statute: **Tex. Penal Code Ann. § 32.51**.

Definition of Offense: Obtains, transfers, possesses, or uses identifying information of another without consent and with intent to harm or defraud another.
Victim Remedies in Criminal Case: Court may order restitution, including lost wages and other expenses—except attorney fees—incurred as a result of the offense.
Special Record-Clearing Provisions: No specific provisions.

---

46 *Reserved.*

Duties of Private Entities: No specific provisions.
Private Right of Action: No specific provisions.

Utah

***State FCRA Statute*: Utah Code Ann. § 70C-7-107.**

Scope: Applies to creditors who furnish negative information to credit reporting agencies.
Purposes for Which Reports May Be Issued: No relevant provisions.
Consumer Access and Disclosures: No relevant provisions.
Disclosures to Consumer by User: No relevant provisions.
Restrictions on Content of Reports: No relevant provisions.
Consumer Disputes: No relevant provisions.
Duties of Furnishers: Notice of negative credit report to be sent in writing by mail, or given in person, to last known address within thirty days after transmission of the information to the reporting agency.[47]
Consumer Remedies: Actual damages, court costs, and attorney fees for failure to provide notice of a negative credit report. Punitive damages of no more than twice actual damages for willful violations. Maintenance of reasonable procedures to avoid errors are a defense to liability.
Statute of Limitations: No relevant provisions.
Miscellaneous: No relevant provisions.

***State Credit Repair Statute*: Utah Code Ann. §§ 13-21-1 to -9**

Covered Activities: Improving credit record or obtaining extension of credit, in return for money or other consideration.
Exemptions: Regulated and supervised lenders for which at least 35% of income is derived from credit transactions; depository institutions; licensed real estate brokers acting within scope of license; Utah lawyers acting within scope of law practice; registered securities broker-dealers; consumer reporting agencies.
Right to Cancel? Yes (5 days).
Prohibitions: Charging before complete performance; charging for referring buyer to retail seller for credit on same terms as generally available to public; making or advising false statements to creditors or credit reporting agencies; making false statements about services offered; disputing credit report entry without factual basis and without buyer's written statement of belief in entry's inaccuracy; requiring buyer to waive rights.
Other Substantive Requirements: Disclosures.
Bond: $100,000.
Private Cause of Action: Actual damages, not less than amount paid by buyer; attorney fees and costs; punitive damages allowed.

***State Identity Theft Statute*: Utah Code Ann. §§ 76-6-1101 to 1104; see also § 13-11-4.5.**

Definition of Offense: Knowingly or intentionally, without authorization, obtains personal identifying information of another and uses or attempts to use it with fraudulent intent, including to obtain credit, goods, services, other thing of value, or medical information, or employment, in the name of another without consent.
Victim Remedies in Criminal Case: If thief commits a crime under a false name, court must make "appropriate findings" that theft victim did not commit that crime.
Special Record-Clearing Provisions: No specific provisions.
Duties of Private Entities: No specific provisions.
Private Right of Action: Violation of this section violates the Consumer Protection Act.
Other: Division of Consumer Protection, as well as law enforcement agencies, may investigate violations.

***Other State Provisions*: Utah Code Ann. § 31A-22-320.** Motor vehicle insurers may not use credit report or credit score [defined—does not include driving record or insurance claims history] to determine renewal, non-renewal, termination, eligibility, underwriting or rating, of motor vehicle related insurance, or except in determining initial underwriting, if risk factors other than credit information are also considered, and in determining eligibility for certain discounts. **Utah Code Ann. § 31A-22-1307.** Insurer who uses credit reports in connection with residential dwelling liability insurance must establish and adhere to written procedures which identify the circumstances under which it will request and the purposes for which it will use consumer reports; give prior notice to consumers of the use or possible use; assure compliance with Federal FCRA. Must maintain evidence of compliance, and submit it to commissioner upon request.

Vermont

***State FCRA Statute*: Vt. Stat. Ann. tit. 9, §§ 2480a–2480g; Code Vt. Rules 06 031 012 Rule CF 112.**

Scope: Same as the federal law.
Purposes for Which Reports May Be Issued: Only purposes consented to by the consumer. No exception made for sharing of information between affiliates.[48]
Consumer Access and Disclosure: All available information including credit score or predictor. Free once per year; $7.50 maximum for each additional copy. Written summary of consumer's rights under Vermont law. Agencies must be listed in the white and yellow pages under "Credit Reporting Agency."
Disclosures to Consumer by User: No relevant provisions.
Restrictions on Content of Reports: No disclosure without

---

47 Most state laws concerning the duties of furnishers of information are preempted. *See* § 10.4.4, *supra*.

48 This provision of Vermont law is explicitly not preempted. *See* § 10.4.4, *supra*.

consumer consent. No exception made for sharing of information between affiliates.[49]

Consumer Disputes: Notice to provider of information within five days of consumer dispute; reinvestigation complete within thirty days.[50] May not reinsert disputed information, if deleted, without a separate affirmation from the provider.

Duties of Furnishers: No relevant provisions.

Consumer Remedies: Injunctive relief, actual damages or $100, whichever is greater; punitive damages if willful; costs and attorney fees.

Statute of Limitations: No relevant provisions.

Miscellaneous: No relevant provisions.

Child Support Debts: Vt. Stat. Ann. tit. 15, § 793. Arrearage equal to at least one-quarter of the annual child support obligation may be reported if the obligor is given notice by first class mail or other means likely to give actual notice and given a period not to exceed twenty days to contest the accuracy of the information. Office of child support must immediately report increases or decreases in the account balance of previously reported accounts.

State Identity Theft Statute: Vt. St. Ann. title 13, § 2001.

Definition of Offense: False personation: falsely personates or represents another, and in such character receives money or other property intended to be delivered to the party so personated, with intent to convert the same to his own use.

Victim Remedies in Criminal Case: No specific provisions.

Special Record-clearing Provisions: No specific provisions.

Duties of Private Entities: No specific provisions.

Private Right of Action: No specific provisions.

Virginia

Child Support Debts: Va. Code Ann. § 63.2-1940. Child Support Enforcement Division shall report child support arrears to consumer reporting agencies. Obligors must be notified prior to release of information and given a reasonable opportunity to contest accuracy of information.

State Credit Repair Statute: Va. Code Ann. §§ 59.1-335.1 to .12

Covered Activities: Improving credit record or obtaining extension of credit, in return for money or other consideration.

Exemptions: Lenders authorized under Va. or federal law; banks and savings associations eligible for FDIC insurance; nonprofit organizations; licensed real estate brokers acting within scope of license; Va. lawyers acting within scope of law practice; registered securities broker-dealers; consumer reporting agencies; seller of consumer goods who, in connection with sale of goods, assists consumer in obtaining loan or extension of credit, or extends credit to consumer.

Right to Cancel? Yes (3 days).

Prohibitions: Charging before complete performance; charging for referring buyer to retail seller for credit on same terms as generally available to public; making or advising false statements to creditors or credit reporting agencies; making false statements about services offered; requiring buyer to waive rights.

Other Substantive Requirements: Disclosures.

Bond: 100 times standard fee charged to consumer, not less than $5000 or more than $50,000.

Private Cause of Action: Where willful non-compliance, actual damages and punitive damages allowed. Where non-compliance due to negligence, actual damages. Contract voidable. 2-year statute of limitations. Violation is a UDAP

State Identity Theft Statute: Va. Code Ann. §§ 18.2-186.3 through 186.5.

Definition of Offense: Without authority and with intent to defraud, for own use or that of a third person: obtains, records or accesses identifying information not available to the general public, that would assist in accessing financial resources, or obtaining benefits or identification documents of another; obtains goods or services by use of identifying information of another; obtains identification documents in the name of another. Penalty enhanced if victim is arrested or detained.

Victim Remedies in Criminal Case: Court must order restitution, which may include actual expenses incurred in correcting errors in victim's credit report or other identifying information.

Special Record-Clearing Provisions: Any person whose name or identification has been used without authority by another who has been charged or arrested under the stolen name, may petition the court for an order of expungement, pursuant to § 19.2-392.2. Upon receipt of the order, the Attorney General may issue an "Identity Theft Passport."

Duties of Private Entities: If a consumer submits a police report to a consumer reporting agency, the agency shall, within 30 days of receipt of the report, block any information alleged to result from the identity theft. Agency may refuse to block or rescind a block, if it reasonably and in good faith believes that block resulted from fraud, or that consumer knowingly received goods and services as a result of the blocked transaction, or if agency has specific, verifiable reasons to doubt the report. If information is unblocked, consumer must be notified as provided for in Federal FCRA. Agency must accept consumer's version, if backed by documentation from source of the item, or from public records.

Private Right of Action: No specific provisions.

---

49 This provision of Vermont law is explicitly not preempted. See § 10.4.4, *supra*.

50 This provision was in effect on Sept. 30, 1996, so although it regulates the time agency allowed for reinvestigation, it is not preempted. See § 10.4.4., *supra*.

Washington

State FCRA Statute: Wash. Rev. Code §§ 19.182.005 to 19.182.902.

Scope: Similar to Federal.

Purposes for Which Reports May Be Issued: Similar to federal law, except no authorization for provision to potential investors or servicers, or current insurers, in connection with evaluation of the credit or prepayment risks associated with existing credit obligations. In addition, if a report is procured for employment purposes, the consumer must be an employee at the time it is procured unless there is written disclosure that the report will be used in consideration for employment, or unless the consumer authorizes.

Consumer Access and Disclosure: All information in file, but only required to reveal medical information to consumer's health care provider. Otherwise similar to federal law. Must provide consumer with summary of rights under Washington FCRA. Must disclose all users who obtained report for employment purposes within two years, or for any other purpose (including a credit transaction not initiated by consumer) within six months. May charge $8 (to be adjusted for CPI) for disclosure of consumer's file, unless consumer has been subject to adverse action within sixty days, in which case disclosure is free.

Disclosures to Consumers By User: Employers must disclose in writing that consumer reports may be used for employment purposes. Prior to any adverse action based on a report, an employer must provide the name, address, and telephone number of the reporting agency; the description of consumer rights under Washington law pertaining to consumer reports for employment purposes; and a reasonable opportunity to respond to any information in a report that is disputed by the consumer. If adverse action is taken by any user, the consumer must be provided with written notice and the name, address, and telephone number of the reporting agency. Verbal notice may be given involving businesses regulated by state utilities and transportation commission, or involving an application for rental or leasing of residential real estate if it does not impair a consumer's ability to obtain a credit report without charge, and the consumer is provided with the name, address, and telephone number of the consumer reporting agency. Must inform consumer of intent to obtain an investigative consumer report. On consumer's request, must disclose the scope of the proposed investigation.

Restrictions on Content of Reports: Same as federal law, except criminal records more than seven years after date of disposition, release or parole.[51] If consumer provides copy of police report regarding identity theft, agency must notify furnisher of information, and block information resulting from the theft.

Consumer Disputes: If the accuracy of an item is disputed by a consumer, the consumer reporting agency must reinvestigate and record the status of the disputed information before the end of thirty business days with no charge.[52] If agency determines the dispute is frivolous it must notify consumer in writing of its reasons within five days. Before the end of five business days after notice of a dispute by the consumer, the agency shall notify any person who provided an item of information in the dispute. If the information is found to be inaccurate, it must be deleted promptly. If reinvestigation does not resolve the dispute, the consumer may file a brief statement of contentions. The agency must inform the consumer of the right to request a corrected notification to all users within six months, and employers within two years; notification must be within thirty days at no charge. If the agency operates on a nationwide basis, it must have a toll free telephone number that the consumer can use in case of a dispute.

Duties of Furnishers: No relevant provisions.

Consumer Remedies: Knowingly and willfully obtaining information under false pretenses: fine of up to $5000, imprisonment for up to one year or both. Violation is an unfair or deceptive act in trade or commerce and an unfair method of competition under state deceptive practices statute. Remedies available for negligent violations: actual damages, costs, and reasonable attorney fees. For willful noncompliance: actual damages, $1,000, costs, and reasonable attorney fees.

Statute of Limitations: Two years from violation or time of discovery.

Miscellaneous: Every agency must maintain reasonable procedures to avoid misuse of reports; agencies must require prospective users to identify themselves, to certify the purposes for which information is sought, and to certify that the information will be used for no other purpose. Agencies must also use reasonable efforts to verify the identity of a new user. If an agency has reasonable grounds for believing that a consumer report will not be used for the above purposes then it is prohibited from furnishing the report. May issue consumer's name, address, former addresses, places of employment or former places of employment to a governmental agency. Cannot provide prescreened information if the consumer precludes it in writing.[53]

State Credit Repair Statute: Wash. Rev. Code §§ 19.134.010 to .900

Covered Activities: Improving credit record or obtaining extension of credit or preventing or delaying foreclosure, in return for money or other consideration.

---

51 This provision was in effect on Sept. 30, 1996, so even if it could be said to be otherwise preempted by 15 U.S.C. § 1681c, it is not preempted. *See* § 10.4.4, *supra*.

52 This provision was in effect on Sept. 30, 1996, so although it regulates the time agency allowed for reinvestigation, it is not preempted. *See* § 10.4.4, *supra*.

53 State law provisions concerning prescreening lists are now preempted. *See* § 10.4.4, *supra*.

Exemptions: Regulated and supervised lenders; mortgage lenders approved by HUD; banks and savings associations eligible for FDIC insurance; credit unions; nonprofit organizations; licensed real estate brokers, collection agencies, and mortgage brokers acting within scope of license; Washington lawyers acting within scope of law practice; registered securities broker-dealers; consumer reporting agencies.

Right to Cancel? Yes (5 days).

Prohibitions: Charging before complete performance, unless organization has posted bond; charging for referring buyer to retail seller for credit on same terms as generally available to public; making or advising false statements to creditors or credit reporting agencies; making false statements about services offered; requiring buyer to waive rights.

Other Substantive Requirements: Disclosures.

Bond: $10,000.

Private Cause of Action: An amount not less than that paid by buyer; attorney fees and costs; punitive damages allowed. A violation is a UDAP violation.

State Identity Theft Statute: **Wash. Rev. Code §§ 9.35.001 to .902, § 19.182.160**.

Definition of Offense: Uses false statement, or fraudulent or fraudulently obtained document to obtain financial information of another from various sources (financial institution, merchant, etc.). Obtains, possesses, uses or transfers, financial information or means of identification of another with intent to commit, aid or abet any crime. Uses means of identification or financial information of another to solicit undesired mail for purposes of harassing another.

Victim Remedies in Criminal Case: If means of identification or financial information used without authority to commit a crime, court shall issue necessary orders to correct any public record which contains false information resulting from identity theft.

Special Record-Clearing Provisions: An identity theft victim may request that his or her fingerprints be filed, along with a statement about the theft. (Law enforcement agency may charge $5 for this service) A copy the statement may be presented to businesses when the victim requests copies of application, etc. records. (See Duties of Private Entities, above).

Duties of Private Entities: Entity (merchant, financial institution, financial information repository, etc.) that deals with thief must, upon victim's request, provide all relevant transaction and application information. Violation of this section violates the Consumer Protection Act. Credit reporting agency must permanently block information added to credit report as a result of identity theft within thirty days of receiving copy of police report. May unblock only if block resulted from fraud by consumer, or consumer agrees block was erroneous, or consumer knowingly received goods or services as a result of the blocked transaction.

Private Right of Action: Improperly obtaining financial information—greater of $500 or actual damages plus reasonable attorney fees. Identity theft—same, including costs incurred to repair credit record. Identity crime violates the Consumer Protection Act, and these provisions for private action do not limit a victim's ability to seek treble damages under the act.

Other: State has banned the use of Social Security Numbers as college ID numbers. Legislative findings note that this was done because identity theft is becoming more common, and widespread use of Social Security numbers facilitates the crime.

West Virginia

Child Support Debts: **W. Va. Code § 48-18-121**. Those in arrears for child support payments must be provided procedural due process, including notice and a reasonable opportunity to contest accuracy of information, prior to state reporting such arrearages to consumer reporting agencies. State child support enforcement agency must give consumer ten days notice prior to requesting report and must use report solely to establish consumer's capacity to make child support payments.

State Credit Repair Statute: **W. Va. Code §§ 46A-6C-1 to -12**

Covered Activities: Improving credit record or obtaining extension of credit, in return for money or other consideration.

Exemptions: Regulated and supervised lenders; lenders making loans secured by liens on realty; banks and savings associations eligible for FDIC insurance; credit unions; nonprofit organizations; public accountants and licensed real estate brokers acting within scope of license; W. Va. lawyers acting within scope of law practice; registered securities broker-dealers; consumer reporting agencies.

Right to Cancel? Yes (10 days).

Prohibitions: Charging before complete performance, unless organization has posted bond; charging for referring buyer to retail seller for credit on same terms as generally available to public; making or advising false statements to creditors or credit reporting agencies; making false statements about services offered; unfair and deceptive acts; requiring buyer to waive rights.

Other Substantive Requirements: Disclosures.

Bond: $15,000.

Private Cause of Action: An amount not less than that paid by buyer; attorney fees and costs; punitive damages allowed. A violation is a UDAP violation.

State Identity Theft Statute: **W. Va. Code § 61-3-54**.

Definition of Offense: Knowingly takes the name or other identifying information of another, without authority, in order to fraudulently represent self as that person, for purpose of making financial or credit transactions in that person's name.

Victim Remedies in Criminal Case: No specific provisions.
Special Record-Clearing Provisions: No specific provisions.
Duties of Private Entities: No specific provisions.
Private Right of Action: No specific provisions.

Wisconsin

Child Support Debts: **Wis. Stat. § 49.22(11)**. Department of Public Assistance shall report child support arrearages, but must give twenty business days prior notice to obligor and disclose methods available to contest accuracy of information. Department must report any errors or payments within thirty days and reporting agency must correct consumer files within thirty days.

State Credit Repair Statute: **Wis. Stat. Ann. §§ 422.501 to .506**

Covered Activities: Improving credit record or obtaining extension of credit, in return for money or other consideration.
Exemptions: Regulated and supervised lenders; banks and savings associations eligible for FDIC insurance; nonprofit organizations; licensed real estate brokers, adjustment service companies, mortgage bankers, loan originators, or mortgage brokers acting within scope of license; Wisconsin lawyers acting within scope of law practice; registered securities broker-dealers; consumer reporting agencies.
Right to Cancel? Yes (5 days).
Prohibitions: Charging for referring buyer to retail seller for credit on same terms as generally available to public; making or advising false statements to creditors or credit reporting agencies; making false statements about services offered; requiring buyer to waive rights.
Other Substantive Requirements: Disclosures.
Bond: $25,000.
Private Cause of Action: A violation is a UDAP violation.

State Identity Theft Statute: **Wis. Stat. §§ 943.201 and 895.80**.

Definition of Offense: Uses or attempts to use any personal identifying information or personal identification document of another, without authorization, to obtain credit, goods, money, services or anything of value by misrepresenting self as that other person, or as acting with that person's authority.
Victim Remedies in Criminal Case: No specific provisions.
Special Record-Clearing Provisions: No specific provisions.
Duties of Private Entities: No specific provisions.
Private Right of Action: Civil action for treble damages, plus all reasonable costs of investigation and litigation. Criminal conviction not a prerequisite.

Other State Provisions: **Wis. Stat. §§ 186.53, 214.507, 215.26(8)(a)(3), 224.26**. A customer, loan applicant or credit applicant of a bank, credit union, savings and loan or other banking institution may request a free copy of any written credit report on them held by the institution, for which a fee was imposed.

Wyoming

State Identity Theft Statute: **Wyo. Stat. Ann. §§ 1-1-128 and 6-3-901**.

Definition of Offense: Willfully obtains personal identifying information of another and uses it without authority for any unlawful purpose, including to obtain money, credit, goods, services or medical information in the name of the other person.
Victim Remedies in Criminal Case: May include any costs incurred by victim, including attorney fees, in clearing credit rating or credit history, or in any civil or administrative proceeding to satisfy debt, lien or other obligation resulting from the theft. If thief commits another crime under victim's name, court records shall reflect that victim did not commit that crime.
Special Record-Clearing Provisions: No specific provisions.
Duties of Private Entities: No specific provisions.
Private Right of Action: Civil action for damages, costs and attorney fees. Injunction may also be available. Criminal conviction not a prerequisite.

Appendix E — FTC and FRB Model Forms

Page 653

Replace Appendix E's introductory text with:

This appendix contains various forms developed by the Federal Trade Commission and the Federal Reserve Board. The Consumer Credit Report Reform Act of 1996[1] required the Federal Trade Commission to develop model forms for credit reporting agencies to use. The final forms were published on July 1, 1997[2] and are reprinted below as Appendices E.1, E.2 and E.3.

This appendix also contains sample adverse action notices developed by the Federal Reserve Board. These forms are reprinted in Appendix E.4, *infra*.

The Federal Trade Commission also developed sample opt-out notices under Gramm-Leach-Bliley.[2.1] These sample opt-out notices are reprinted in Appendix E.5, *infra*.

Finally, Appendix E.6, *infra* contains a sample identity theft affidavit, including instructions on how to complete the affidavit.[2.2] These documents were also prepared by the FTC.

 1 Pub. L. No. 104-208, 110 Stat. 3009 (Sept. 30, 1996).
 2 62 Fed. Reg. 35586 (July 1, 1997).
 2.1 16 C.F.R. part 313, app. A.
 2.2 Available at www.consumer.gov/idtheft/affidavit.htm.

Page 672

Add new subsections after E.4:

E.5 Sample Opt-Out Notices

Financial institutions must provide to consumers with opt-out notices under Gramm-Leach-Bliley. In light of this requirement, the FTC developed sample opt-out notices or clauses that are intended to provide guidance to financial institutions concerning the level of detail the FTC believes is appropriate under Gramm-Leach-Bliley. Financial institutions may use different language and may include as much detail as they deem appropriate.

16 C.F.R. part 313, app. A

Appendix A to Part 313—Sample Clauses

Financial institutions, including a group of financial holding company affiliates that use a common privacy notice, may use the following sample clauses, if the clause is accurate for each institution that uses the notice. (Note that disclosure of certain information, such as assets and income, and information from a consumer reporting agency, may give rise to obligations under the Fair Credit Reporting Act, such as a requirement to permit a consumer to opt out of disclosures to affiliates or designation as a consumer reporting agency if disclosures are made to nonaffiliated third parties.)

A-1—Categories of Information You Collect (All Institutions)

You may use this clause, as applicable, to meet the requirement of § 313.6(a)(1) to describe the categories of nonpublic personal information you collect.

Sample Clause A-1

We collect nonpublic personal information about you from the following sources:

- Information we receive from you on applications or other forms;
- Information about your transactions with us, our affiliates, or others; and
- Information we receive from a consumer reporting agency.

A-2—Categories of Information You Disclose (Institutions That Disclose Outside of the Exceptions)

You may use one of these clauses, as applicable, to meet the requirement of § 313.6(a)(2) to describe the categories of nonpublic personal information you disclose. You may use these clauses if you disclose nonpublic personal information other than as permitted by the exceptions in §§ 313.13, 313.14, and 313.15.

Sample Clause A-2, Alternative 1

We may disclose the following kinds of nonpublic personal information about you:

- Information we receive from you on applications or other forms, such as [provide illustrative examples, such as "your name, address, social security number, assets, and income"];
- Information about your transactions with us, our affiliates, or others, such as [provide illustrative examples, such as "your account balance, payment history, parties to transactions, and credit card usage"]; and
- Information we receive from a consumer reporting agency, such as [provide illustrative examples, such as "your creditworthiness and credit history"].

Sample Clause A-2, Alternative 2

We may disclose all of the information that we collect, as described [describe location in the notice, such as "above" or "below"].

A-3—Categories of Information You Disclose and Parties to Whom You Disclose (Institutions That Do Not Disclose Outside of the Exceptions)

You may use this clause, as applicable, to meet the requirements of §§ 313.6(a)(2), (3), and (4) to describe the categories of nonpublic personal information about customers and former customers that you disclose and the categories of affiliates and nonaffiliated third parties to whom you disclose. You may use this clause if you do not disclose nonpublic personal information to any party, other than as permitted by the exceptions in §§ 313.14, and 313.15.

Sample Clause A-3

We do not disclose any nonpublic personal information about our customers or former customers to anyone, except as permitted by law.

A-4—Categories of Parties to Whom You Disclose (Institutions That Disclose Outside of the Exceptions)

You may use this clause, as applicable, to meet the requirement of § 313.6(a)(3) to describe the categories of affiliates and nonaffiliated third parties to whom you disclose nonpublic personal information. You may use this clause if you disclose nonpublic personal information other than as permitted by the exceptions in §§ 313.13, 313.14, and 313.15, as well as when permitted by the exceptions in §§ 313.14, and 313.15.

Sample Clause A-4

We may disclose nonpublic personal information about you to the following types of third parties:

- Financial service providers, such as [provide illustrative examples, such as "mortgage bankers, securities broker-dealers, and insurance agents"];
- Non-financial companies, such as [provide illustrative examples, such as "retailers, direct marketers, airlines, and publishers"]; and

- Others, such as [provide illustrative examples, such as "non-profit organizations"].

We may also disclose nonpublic personal information about you to nonaffiliated third parties as permitted by law.

A-5—Service Provider/Joint Marketing Exception

You may use one of these clauses, as applicable, to meet the requirements of § 313.6(a)(5) related to the exception for service providers and joint marketers in § 313.13. If you disclose nonpublic personal information under this exception, you must describe the categories of nonpublic personal information you disclose and the categories of third parties with whom you have contracted.

Sample Clause A-5, Alternative 1

We may disclose the following information to companies that perform marketing services on our behalf or to other financial institutions with whom we have joint marketing agreements:

- Information we receive from you on applications or other forms, such as [provide illustrative examples, such as "your name, address, social security number, assets, and income"];
- Information about your transactions with us, our affiliates, or others, such as [provide illustrative examples, such as "your account balance, payment history, parties to transactions, and credit card usage"]; and
- Information we receive from a consumer reporting agency, such as [provide illustrative examples, such as "your creditworthiness and credit history"].

Sample Clause A-5, Alternative 2

We may disclose all of the information we collect, as described [describe location in the notice, such as "above" or "below"] to companies that perform marketing services on our behalf or to other financial institutions with whom we have joint marketing agreements.

A-6—Explanation of Opt Out Right (Institutions that Disclose Outside of the Exceptions)

You may use this clause, as applicable, to meet the requirement of § 313.6(a)(6) to provide an explanation of the consumer's right to opt out of the disclosure of nonpublic personal information to nonaffiliated third parties, including the method(s) by which the consumer may exercise that right. You may use this clause if you disclose nonpublic personal information other than as permitted by the exceptions in §§ 313.13, 313.14, and 313.15.

Sample Clause A-6

If you prefer that we not disclose nonpublic personal information about you to nonaffiliated third parties, you may opt out of those disclosures, that is, you may direct us not to make those disclosures (other than disclosures permitted by law). If you wish to opt out of disclosures to nonaffiliated third parties, you may [describe a reasonable means of opting out, such as "call the following toll-free number: (insert number)"].

A-7—Confidentiality and Security (All Institutions)

You may use this clause, as applicable, to meet the requirement of § 313.6(a)(8) to describe your policies and practices with respect to protecting the confidentiality and security of nonpublic personal information.

Sample Clause A-7

We restrict access to nonpublic personal information about you to [provide an appropriate description, such as "those employees who need to know that information to provide products or services to you"]. We maintain physical, electronic, and procedural safeguards that comply with federal regulations to guard your nonpublic personal information.

E.6 FTC Identity Theft Affidavit

The FTC developed an I.D. Theft Affidavit to assist victims who dispute fraudulent debts and accounts opened by an identity thief. The FTC's I.D. Theft Affidavit is intended to simplify this process. Instead of completing different forms, consumers can use the I.D. Theft Affidavit to alert companies where a new account was opened in the I.D. theft victim's name. The company can then investigate the fraud and decide the outcome of the consumer's claim.

DO NOT SEND AFFIDAVIT TO THE FTC OR ANY OTHER GOVERNMENT AGENCY

Instructions for Completing the ID Theft Affidavit

To make certain that you do not become responsible for the debts incurred by the identity thief, you must provide proof that you didn't create the debt to each of the companies where accounts where opened or used in your name.

A working group composed of credit grantors, consumer advocates and the Federal Trade Commission (FTC) developed this ID Theft Affidavit to help you report information to many companies using just one standard form. Use of this affidavit is optional for companies. While many companies accept this affidavit, others require that you submit more or different forms. Before you send the affidavit, contact each company to find out if they accept it.

You can use this affidavit where a **new account** was opened in your name. The information will enable the companies to investigate the fraud and decide the outcome of your claim. (If someone made unauthorized charges to an **existing account**, call the company to find out what to do.)

This affidavit has two parts:

- **ID Theft Affidavit** is where you report general information about yourself and the theft.

- **Fraudulent Account Statement** is where you describe the fraudulent account(s) opened in your name. Use a separate Fraudulent Account Statement for each company you need to write to.

When you send the affidavit to the companies, attach copies (**NOT** originals) of any supporting documents (for example, drivers license, police report) you have. Before submitting your affidavit, review the disputed account(s) with family members or friends who may have information about the account(s) or access to them.

Complete this affidavit as soon as possible. Many creditors ask that you send it within two weeks of receiving it. Delaying could slow the investigation.

Be as accurate and complete as possible. You *may* choose not to provide some of the information requested. However, incorrect or incomplete information will slow the process of investigating your claim and absolving the debt. Please print clearly.

When you have finished completing the affidavit, mail a copy to each creditor, bank or company that provided the thief with the unauthorized credit, goods or services you describe. Attach to each affidavit a copy of the Fraudulent Account Statement with information only on accounts opened at the institution receiving the packet, as well as any other supporting documentation you are able to provide.

Send the appropriate documents to each company by certified mail, return receipt requested, so you can prove that it was received. The companies will review your claim and send you a written response telling you the outcome of their investigation. **Keep a copy of everything you submit for your records**.

If you cannot complete the affidavit, a legal guardian or someone with power of attorney may complete it for you. Except as noted, the information you provide will be used only by the company to process your affidavit, investigate the events you report and help stop further fraud. If this affidavit is requested in a lawsuit, the company might have to provide it to the requesting party.

Completing this affidavit does not guarantee that the identity thief will be prosecuted or that the debt will be cleared.

If you haven't already done so, report the fraud to the following organizations:

1. Each of the three **national consumer reporting agencies**. Ask each agency to place a "fraud alert" on your credit report, and send you a copy of your credit file. When you have completed your affidavit packet, you may want to send them a copy to help them investigate the disputed accounts.

   ■ **Equifax Credit Information Services, Inc.**
   (800) 525-6285/ TDD 1-800-255-0056 and ask the operator to call the Auto Disclosure Line at 1-800-685-1111 to obtain a copy of your report.
   P.O. Box 740241, Atlanta, GA 30374-0241
   www.equifax.com

   ■ **Experian information Solutions, Inc.**
   (888) 397-3742/ TDD (800) 972-0322
   P.O. Box 9530, Allen, TX 75013
   www.experian.com

   ■ **TransUnion**
   (800) 680-7289/ TDD (877) 553-7803
   Fraud Victim Assistance Division
   P.O. Box 6790, Fullerton, CA 92634-6790
   www.transunion.com

2. The **fraud department at each creditor, bank, or utility/service** that provided the identity thief with unauthorized credit, goods or services. This would be a good time to find out if the company accepts this affidavit, and whether they require notarization or a copy of the police report.

3. Your local **police department**. Ask the officer to take a report and give you a copy of the report. Sending a copy of your police report to financial institutions can speed up the process of absolving you of wrongful debts or removing inaccurate information from your credit reports. If you can't get a copy, at least get the number of the report.

4. The FTC, which maintains the Identity Theft Data Clearinghouse – the federal government's centralized identity theft complaint database – and provides information to identity theft victims. You can visit **www.consumer.gov/idtheft** or call toll-free **1-877-ID-THEFT (1-877-438-4338)**.

The FTC collects complaints from identity theft victims and shares their information with law enforcement nationwide. This information also may be shared with other government agencies, consumer reporting agencies, and companies where the fraud was perpetrated to help resolve identity theft related problems.

Name _____ Phone number _____ Page 1

ID Theft Affidavit

Victim Information

(1) My full legal name is _____
                   (First)   (Middle)   (Last)   (Jr., Sr., III)

(2) (If different from above) When the events described in this affidavit took place, I was known as

_____
(First)   (Middle)   (Last)   (Jr., Sr., III)

(3) My date of birth is _____
                     (day/month/year)

(4) My Social Security number is _____

(5) My driver's license or identification card state and number are _____

(6) My current address is _____

    City _____ State _____ Zip Code _____

(7) I have lived at this address since _____
                                (month/year)

(8) (If different from above) When the events described in this affidavit took place, my address was

_____

    City _____ State _____ Zip Code _____

(9) I lived at the address in Item 8 from _____ until _____
                                (month/year) (month/year)

(10) My daytime telephone number is (____)_____

     My evening telephone number is (____)_____

Name _____ Phone number _____ Page 2

How the Fraud Occurred

Check all that apply for items 11 - 17:

(11) ❑ I did not authorize anyone to use my name or personal information to seek the money, credit, loans, goods or services described in this report.

(12) ❑ I did not receive any benefit, money, goods or services as a result of the events described in this report.

(13) ❑ My identification documents (for example, credit cards; birth certificate; driver's license; Social Security card; etc.) were ❑ stolen ❑ lost on or about _____.
(day/month/year)

(14) ❑ To the best of my knowledge and belief, the following person(s) used my information (for example, my name, address, date of birth, existing account numbers, Social Security number, mother's maiden name, etc.) or identification documents to get money, credit, loans, goods or services without my knowledge or authorization:

_____   _____
Name (if known)   Name (if known)

_____   _____
Address (if known)   Address (if known)

_____   _____
Phone number(s) (if known)   Phone number(s) (if known)

_____   _____
Additional information (if known)   Additional information (if known)

(15) ❑ I do NOT know who used my information or identification documents to get money, credit, loans, goods or services without my knowledge or authorization.

(16) ❑ Additional comments: (For example, description of the fraud, which documents or information were used or how the identity thief gained access to your information.)

_____
_____
_____
_____
_____

(Attach additional pages as necessary.)

FTC and FRB Model Forms / 2004 Supplement   **Appx. E.6**

Name _____ Phone number _____ Page 3

Victim's Law Enforcement Actions

(17) (check one) I ❑ am ❑ am not   willing to assist in the prosecution of the person(s) who committed this fraud.

(18) (check one) I ❑ am ❑ am not   authorizing the release of this information to law enforcement for the purpose of assisting them in the investigation and prosecution of the person(s) who committed this fraud.

(19) (check all that apply) I ❑ have ❑ have not   reported the events described in this affidavit to the police or other law enforcement agency. The police ❑ did ❑ did not   write a report. *In the event you have contacted the police or other law enforcement agency, please complete the following:*

_____	_____
(Agency #1)	(Officer/Agency personnel taking report)
_____	_____
(Date of report)	(Report number, if any)
_____	_____
(Phone number)	(email address, if any)
_____	_____
(Agency #2)	(Officer/Agency personnel taking report)
_____	_____
(Date of report)	(Report number, if any)
_____	_____
(Phone number)	(email address, if any)

Documentation Checklist

Please indicate the supporting documentation you are able to provide to the companies you plan to notify. Attach copies (NOT originals) to the affidavit before sending it to the companies.

(20) ❑   A copy of a valid government-issued photo-identification card (for example, your driver's license, state-issued ID card or your passport). If you are under 16 and don't have a photo-ID, you may submit a copy of your birth certificate or a copy of your official school records showing your enrollment and place of residence.

(21) ❑   Proof of residency during the time the disputed bill occurred, the loan was made or the other event took place (for example, a rental/lease agreement in your name, a copy of a utility bill or a copy of an insurance bill).

Name _____ Phone number _____ Page 4

(22) ❑ A copy of the report you filed with the police or sheriff's department. If you are unable to obtain a report or report number from the police, please indicate that in Item 19. Some companies only need the report number, not a copy of the report. You may want to check with each company.

Signature

I declare under penalty of perjury that the information I have provided in this affidavit is true and correct to the best of my knowledge.

_____   _____
(signature)   (date signed)

Knowingly submitting false information on this form could subject you to criminal prosecution for perjury.

_____
(Notary)

[Check with each company. Creditors sometimes require notarization. If they do not, please have one witness (non-relative) sign below that you completed and signed this affidavit.]

Witness:

_____   _____
(signature)   (printed name)

_____   _____
(date)   (telephone number)

FTC and FRB Model Forms / 2004 Supplement   **Appx. E.6**

Name _____ Phone number _____ Page 5

Fraudulent Account Statement

> **Completing this Statement**
> - Make as many copies of this page as you need. **Complete a separate page for each company you're notifying and only send it to that company.** Include a copy of your signed affidavit.
> - List only the account(s) you're disputing with the company receiving this form. **See the example below.**
> - If a collection agency sent you a statement, letter or notice about the fraudulent account, attach a copy of that document (**NOT** the original).

I declare (check all that apply):

❏ As a result of the event(s) described in the ID Theft Affidavit, the following account(s) was/were opened at your company in my name without my knowledge, permission or authorization using my personal information or identifying documents:

Creditor Name/Address *(the company that opened the account or provided the goods or services)*	Account Number	Type of unauthorized credit/goods/services provided by creditor *(if known)*	Date issued or opened *(if known)*	Amount/Value provided *(the amount charged or the cost of the goods/services)*
Example Example National Bank 22 Main Street Columbus, Ohio 22722	01234567-89	auto loan	01/05/2002	$25,500.00

❏ During the time of the accounts described above, I had the following account open with your company:

Billing name _____

Billing address _____

Account number

313

Appendix H
replacement title

Enforcement Orders Against Consumer Reporting Agencies, Resellers, Credit Repair Agencies, and Users

Page 721

Add to text after last paragraph of appendix's introduction:

Section H.6 reprints a consent order the FTC obtained against a user of a credit report that allegedly failed to provide "adverse action" notices pursuant to the Fair Credit Reporting Act (FCRA). The FTC alleged that Quicken Loans failed to comply with the provisions of the FCRA that require credit grantors who take adverse action—for example, denial of credit, insurance, employment, or certain other benefits—to notify the consumer when the action is based wholly or partly on the consumer's credit report. The notice is designed to give consumers the opportunity to dispute the accuracy or completeness of the information in the credit report. The consent agreement requires Quicken Loans provide to the applicant the notice specified in section 1681m of the FCRA whenever it takes any adverse action with respect to an application for credit, either in whole or in part because of information contained in a credit report.

Section H.7 is a Stipulated Final Order for Permanent Injunction against an identity thief who allegedly used hijacked corporate logos and deceptive spam to con consumers out of credit card numbers and other financial data. The FTC alleged that the scam, called "phishing," had the thief posing as America Online, and sending consumers e-mail messages claiming that there had been a problem with the billing of their AOL account. The e-mail warned consumers that if they did not update their billing information, they risked losing their AOL accounts and Internet access. The message directed consumers to click on a hyperlink in the body of the e-mail to connect to the "AOL Billing Center," an AOL look-alike web page that directed consumers to enter credit card numbers they had used for charges on their AOL account. It then asked consumers to enter numbers from a new card to correct the problem. The phony AOL web page also asked for consumers' names, mothers' maiden names, billing addresses, social security numbers, bank routing numbers, credit limits, personal identification numbers, and AOL screen names and passwords. The FTC charged the defendant's practices were deceptive and unfair, in violation of the FTC Act. In addition, the FTC alleged that the defendant's practices violated provisions of the Gramm-Leach-Bliley Act designed to protect the privacy of consumers' sensitive financial information.

The stipulated judgment and permanent injunction bars the defendant from future violations of the FTC Act and the Gramm-Leach-Bliley Act. It also bars the defendant from sending spam in the future.

Section H.8 is a Joint Motion for Modification of Consent Decree between the FTC and Equifax Credit Information Services, Inc. Equifax agreed to pay $250,000 to settle Federal Trade Commission charges that its blocked-call rate and hold times violated provisions of an FTC consent decree that settled a 2000 lawsuit for violations of the Fair Credit Reporting Act.[26.1] That lawsuit alleged that that Equifax did not have sufficient personnel available to answer the toll-free phone number provided on consumers' credit reports. Equifax failed to meet the specific performance standards in the consent decree for blocked calls and hold times for certain periods in 2001.

26.1 *See* Appx. H.2.5, *supra*.

Add new subsections after H.5:

H.6 FTC Consent Order Against Quicken

UNITED STATES OF AMERICA BEFORE FEDERAL TRADE COMMISSION

In the Matter of QUICKEN LOANS, INC., a corporation.

DOCKET NO. 9304

AGREEMENT CONTAINING CONSENT ORDER

This Agreement Containing Consent Order ("Consent Agreement"), by and between Quicken Loans Inc., a corporation ("Respondent"), by its duly authorized officer and its attorney, and counsel for the Federal Trade Commission ("Commission"), is entered into in accordance with the Commission's Rules governing consent order procedures. In accordance therewith the parties hereby agree that:

1. Respondent Quicken Loans Inc. is a Michigan corporation with its principal office or place of business at 20555 Victor Parkway, Livonia, Michigan 48152.

2. Respondent has been served with a copy of the Complaint issued by the Commission charging it with violations of Section 615(a) of the Fair Credit Reporting Act, 15 U.S.C. § 1681m(a), and Section 5(a)(1) of the Federal Trade Commission Act, 15 U.S.C. § 45(a)(1).

3. Respondent admits all the jurisdictional facts set forth in the Complaint.

4. Respondent waives:
   a. Any further procedural steps;
   b. The requirement that the Commission's Decision and Order contain a statement of findings of fact and conclusions of law;
   c. All rights to seek judicial review or otherwise to challenge or contest the validity of the Order entered pursuant to the Consent Agreement; and
   d. Any claim under the Equal Access to Justice Act.

5. This Consent Agreement shall not become a part of the public record of the proceeding unless and until it is accepted by the Commission. If this Consent Agreement is accepted by the Commission, it will be placed on the public record for a period of thirty (30) days and information about it publicly released. The Commission thereafter may either withdraw its acceptance of this Consent Agreement and so notify Respondent, in which event it will take such action as it may consider appropriate, or issue and serve its Decision and Order, in disposition of the proceeding.

6. This Consent Agreement is for settlement purposes only and does not constitute an admission by Respondent that the law has been violated as alleged in the Complaint, or that the facts as alleged in the Complaint, other than the jurisdictional facts, are true. Respondent denies that it has violated the law and denies all allegations in the Complaint, other than the jurisdictional facts.

7. This Consent Agreement contemplates that, if it is accepted by the Commission, and if such acceptance is not subsequently withdrawn by the Commission pursuant to the provisions of Section 3.25(f) of the Commission's Rules, 16 C.F.R. § 3.25(f), the Commission may, without further notice to Respondent, (1) issue its Decision and Order containing the following Order to cease and desist in disposition of the proceedings, and (2) make information about it public. When final, the Order to cease and desist shall have the same force and effect and may be altered, modified, or set aside in the same manner and within the same time provided by statute for other Commission Orders issued on a litigated or stipulated record. The Order shall become final upon service. Delivery of the Decision and Order containing the agreed-to Order to Respondent's address as stated in this Consent Agreement by any means specified in Section 4.4(a) of the Commission's Rules, 16 C.F.R. § 4.4(a), shall constitute service. Respondent waives any right it might have to any other manner of service. The Complaint may be used in construing the terms of the Order, and no agreement, understanding, representation, or interpretation not contained in the Order or in the Consent Agreement may be used to vary or to contradict the terms of the Order.

8. Respondent has read the Order contemplated hereby. Respondent understands that once the Order has been issued, it will be required to file one or more compliance reports showing that it has fully complied with the Order. Respondent further understands that it may be liable for civil penalties in the amount provided by law and other appropriate relief for each violation of the Order after it becomes final.

ORDER

DEFINITIONS

For purposes of this order, the following definitions shall apply:

1. "Consumer," "consumer report" and "consumer reporting agency" shall be defined as provided in Sections 603(c), 603(d) and 603(f) respectively, of the Fair Credit Reporting Act ("FCRA"), 15 U.S.C. §§ 1681a(c), 1681a(d) and 1681a(f).

2. "Application" shall be defined as provided in Sections 202.2(f) of Regulation B, 12 C.F.R. § 202.2(f), or as amended in the future.

3. "Adverse action" shall be defined as provided in Section 603(k) of the FCRA, 15 U.S.C. § 1681a(k), Section 701(d)(6) of the Equal Credit Opportunity Act, 15 U.S.C. § 1691(d)(6), and Section 202.2(c) of Regulation B, 12 C.F.R. § 202.2(c), or as those provisions are amended in the future.

4. "Respondent" shall mean Quicken Loans Inc., a corporation, its successors and assigns, and its officers, agents, representatives, and employees.

5. "Preapproval" shall mean a written or electronic statement by Respondent, after receiving a request from a consumer and analyzing the consumer's creditworthiness, that the consumer appears to be eligible for a loan from Respondent in a stated amount and on stated terms, subject to conditions. If Regulation B or any appropriate final findings, decisions, commentary, or orders issued under section 701(d)(6) of the Equal Credit Opportunity Act by the

Board of Governors of the Federal Reserve System are hereafter amended to include a definition of or a reference to "preapproval" that is inconsistent with this definition, then that definition or reference shall be substituted for this definition to the extent of the inconsistency.

I.

IT IS ORDERED that Respondent, directly or through any corporation, subsidiary, division, or other device, in connection with any application by a consumer for credit, whenever Respondent takes any adverse action with respect to such application, either wholly or partly because of information contained in a consumer report from a consumer reporting agency, unless alternative credit is offered to and accepted by the applicant, shall, as required by Section 615 of the FCRA, 15 U.S.C. § 1681m, provide to the applicant at the time such adverse action is communicated to the applicant or within thirty (30) days thereafter, orally, in writing, or electronically (1) notice of the averse action; (2) the name, address, and telephone number of the consumer reporting agency (including a toll-free telephone number established by the agency if the agency compiles and maintains files on consumers on a nationwide basis) that furnished the report to the person; (3) a statement that the consumer reporting agency did not make the decision to take the adverse action and is unable to provide the consumer the specific reasons why the adverse action was taken; and (4) notice of the consumer's right

    (A) to obtain, under Section 612 of the FCRA, 15 U.S.C. § 1681j, a free copy of a consumer report on the consumer from the consumer reporting agency referred to at (2) above, which notice shall include an indication of the 60-day period under that section for obtaining such a copy; and

    (B) to dispute, under Section 611 of the FCRA, 15 U.S.C. § 1681i, with a consumer reporting agency the accuracy or completeness of any information in a consumer report furnished by the agency.

Provided that, Respondent's failure to grant a request for preapproval that is initiated online shall not be considered an adverse action for purposes of this Part, if Respondent satisfies all of the following requirements:

A. At the time it offered the preapproval, Respondent disclosed, clearly and conspicuously and in close proximity to the offer, that (i) preapproval may be granted online or offline, and (ii) the failure to obtain preapproval online would not prevent the consumer from obtaining preapproval offline;

B. Respondent's online system has not determined, based on the information available online, whether to approve the request for preapproval; and

C. Respondent provides a clear and conspicuous online notice in response to the request for preapproval stating that:

1. The consumer's request for preapproval has not been declined;
2. Respondent requires additional information from the consumer, including the specific type or types of information required, to the extent it is feasible for Respondent to identify such information, given the technological limitations of Respondent's online system and the loan products that are available on that system, before determining whether to grant the request for approval;
3. The manner by which that additional information may be provided;
4. After obtaining the additional information, Respondent will determine whether to grant or decline the request for preapproval, but if, within seven (7) days or a longer time designated by Respondent, the consumer does not provide the requested information, the consumer will have to submit a new request for preapproval if the consumer would like Respondent to give the request further consideration; and
5. If, after receiving the additional information, Respondent determines to deny the request for preapproval based in whole or in part on information in the consumer's credit file at a consumer reporting agency, Respondent will communicate this fact to the consumer.

In the event that Respondent takes adverse action against a consumer after providing the foregoing notice and obtaining a completed application from that consumer, Respondent shall comply with all the applicable requirements of Section 615(a) of the FCRA.

II.

IT IS FURTHER ORDERED that Respondent shall, for five (5) years, maintain and upon request make available to the Federal Trade Commission for inspection and copying documents demonstrating compliance with the requirements of Part I of this order, such documents to include, but not be limited to, all credit evaluation criteria relating to consumer reports, written or electronic instructions given to employees regarding compliance with the provisions of this order, all notices or a written or electronically stored notation of the description of the form of notice and the date such notice was provided to applicants pursuant to any provisions of this order, and whom offers of credit are not made or have been withheld, withdrawn, or rescinded based, in whole or in part, on information contained in a consumer report.

III.

IT IS FURTHER ORDERED that Respondent Quicken Loans Inc. shall deliver a copy of this order to all current and future principals, officers, and directors, and to all current and future managers, employees, agents, and representatives having decision-making responsibilities with respect to the subject matter of this order, and shall secure from each such person a signed and dated statement acknowledging receipt of the order. Respondent shall deliver this order to such current personnel within thirty (30) days after the date of service of this order, and to such future personnel within thirty (30) days after the person assumes such position or responsibilities.

IV.

IT IS FURTHER ORDERED that Respondent Quicken Loans Inc. and its successors and assigns shall notify the Commission at least thirty (30) days prior to any change in the corporation that may affect compliance obligations arising under this order, including but not limited to a dissolution, assignment, sale, merger, or other action that would result in the emergence of a successor corporation; the creation or dissolution of a subsidiary, parent or affiliate that engages in any acts or practices subject to this order; the proposed filing of a bankruptcy petition; or a change in the corporate name or address. *Provided, however*, that, with respect to any proposed change in the corporation about which Respondent learns less than thirty (30) days prior to the date such action is to take place, Respondent shall notify the Commission as soon as is practicable after obtaining such knowledge. All notices required by this Part shall be sent by certified mail to the Associate Director, Division of Enforcement, Bureau of Consumer Protection, Federal Trade Commission, 600 Pennsylvania Avenue, N.W., Washington, D.C. 20580.

V.

IT IS FURTHER ORDERED that Respondent Quicken Loans Inc. shall, within sixty (60) days after the date of service of this order, and at such other times as the Federal Trade Commission may require, file with the Commission a report, in writing, setting forth in detail the manner and form in which it has complied with this order.

VI.

This order will terminate twenty (20) years from the date of its issuance, or twenty (20) years from the most recent date that the United States or the Federal Trade Commission files a complaint (with or without an accompanying consent decree) in federal court alleging any violation of the order, whichever comes later; *provided, however*, that the filing of such a complaint will not affect the duration of:

A. Any Part in this order that terminates in less than twenty (20) years;

B. This order's application to any Respondent that is not named as a defendant in such complaint; and

C. This order if such complaint is filed after the order has terminated pursuant to this Part.

Provided, further, that if such complaint is dismissed or a federal court rules that the Respondent did not violate any provision of the order, and the dismissal or ruling is either not appealed or upheld on appeal, then the order will terminated according to this Part as though the complaint had never been filed, except that the order will not terminated between the date such complaint is filed and the later of the deadline for appealing such dismissal or ruling and the date such dismissal or ruling is upheld on appeal.

[Date]
[Quicken Loan, Inc.]
[Federal Trade Commission]

H.7 FTC Enforcement Action Against Minor for Violation of Gramm-Leach-Bliley Act

UNITED STATES DISTRICT COURT
CENTRAL DISTRICT OF CALIFORNIA

FEDERAL TRADE COMMISSION Plaintiff v. [Defendant], a minor, also known as [Alias], by his parent [Parent] Defendant	STIPULATED FINAL JUDGMENT AND ORDER FOR PERMANENT INJUNCTION AND OTHER EQUITABLE RELIEF

Plaintiff, the Federal Trade Commission ("FTC" or "Commission"), filed its complaint for permanent injunction and other relief ("Complaint"), pursuant to Section 13(b) of the Federal Trade Commission Act ("FTC Act"), 15 U.S.C. § 53(b), and Section 522(a) of the Gramm-Leach-Bliley Act ("GLB Act"), 15 U.S.C. § 6822(a), charging Defendant [Defendant], also known as [Alias], a minor by his parent [Parent], with violations of Section 5(a) of the FTC Act,15 U.S.C. § 45(a), and Section 521 of the GLB Act, 15 U.S.C. § 6821.

The parties have agreed to the entry of this Stipulated Final Judgment and Order for Permanent Injunction and Other Equitable Relief ("Order") by the Court to resolve all matters of dispute between them in this action. THEREFORE, on the joint motion of Plaintiff and Defendant, **IT IS HEREBY ORDERED, ADJUDGED, AND DECREED** as follows:

FINDINGS

1. This court has jurisdiction over the subject matter and the parties.

2. Venue is proper as to all parties in the Central District of California under 28 U.S.C. § 1391(b) and 15 U.S.C. § 53(b).

3. Defendant has been properly served.

4. The Complaint states a claim upon which relief may be granted against Defendant under Sections 5(a) and 13 (b) of the FTC Act, 15 U.S.C. §§ 45(a) and 53(b), and Sections 521 and 522(a) of the GLB Act, 15 U.S.C. §§ 6821 and 6822(a).

5. The activities of Defendant are in or affecting commerce, as "commerce" is defined in Section 4 of the FTC Act, 15 U.S.C. § 44.

6. Entry of this Order is in the public interest.

7. Defendant has entered into this Order freely and without coercion, and both he and his parent, [Parent], have read and understood the provisions of this Order.

8. Defendant waives any and all rights concerning and the prosecution of this action that may arise under the Equal Access to Justice Act, 28 U.S.C. § 2412, and Defendant further waives any and all rights to attorneys fees that may arise under said provision of law.

9. The Commission and Defendant have agreed that the entry of this Order resolves all matters of dispute between them arising from the Complaint in this action, up to the date of the entry of this Order.

10. The Commission and Defendant waive all rights to seek appellate review or otherwise challenge or contest the validity of this Order, and Defendant further waives and releases any claim against the Commission or its employees, agents, or representatives.

11. This Order is for settlement purposes only and does not constitute, and shall not be interpreted to constitute, an admission by Defendant that he has engaged in violations of any law or regulation, including but not limited to violations of the FTC Act; or, except as provided in Paragraph G of Section VI below, that the facts alleged in the Complaint are true.

ORDER

DEFINITIONS

For the purposes of this Order, the following shall apply:
1. "Defendant means [Defendant], also known as [Alias].
2. "Plaintiff" means the Federal Trade Commission.
3. "Person" means any natural person, organization, or other legal entity, including but not limited to a corporation, partnership, proprietorship, association, cooperative, or any other group or combination acting as an entity.
4. A "material fact" is any fact likely to affect a person's choice of, or conduct regarding, the purchase of goods or services and/or the disclosure of personal financial information.
5. "Document" is synonymous in meaning and equal in scope to the usage of the term in Federal Rule of Civil Procedure 34(a), and includes writings, drawings, graphs, charts, photographs, audio and video recordings, computer records, and other data compilations from which information can be obtained and translated, if necessary, into reasonably usable form through detection devices. A draft or non-identical copy is a separate document within the meaning of the term.
6. "Unsolicited commercial email" means an electronic mail message that consists of or contains a communication advertising, promoting, soliciting, offering, or offering to sell any product or service, or soliciting for consumers' personal or financial information; and that is not requested by the addressee or recipient or sent pursuant to a pre-existing business or personal relationship between the sender and the addressee or recipient of the email.
7. "Customer information of a financial institution" is synonymous in meaning and equal in scope to the usage of the term in Section 527(2) if the GLB Act, 15 U.S.C. § 6827(2).
8. The words "and" and "or" shall be understood to have both conjunctive and disjunctive meanings.

I.
BAN REQUIREMENTS

IT IS THEREFORE ORDERED that in connection with the solicitation of consumers for personal or financial information or in the promotion, advertising, marketing, sale, or offering for sale of any product or service, Defendant is hereby permanently restrained and enjoined from the sending of unsolicited commercial email.

II.
INJUNCTION AGAINST MISREPRESENTATIONS

IT IS FURTHER ORDERED that in connection with the solicitation of consumers for personal or financial information or in the promotion, advertising, marketing, sale, or offering for sale of any product or service, Defendant and his agents, assigns, servants, employees, salespersons, and all other persons or entities in active concert or participation with him who receive actual notice of this Order by personal service or otherwise, whether acting directly or through any corporation, subsidiary, division, or other device, are hereby permanently restrained and enjoined from:

A. Making, or materially assisting in the making of, any statement or representation of material fact that is false or misleading, whether directly or by implication, orally or in writing, including, but not limited to, any false or misleading representation that:

1. Defendant or his agents are affiliated with, are agents of, or are authorized to act on behalf of any person or entity, including, but not limited to any representation that Defendant or his agents are affiliated with, are agents of, or are authorized to act on behalf of a consumer's Internet service provider, such as America Online, Inc. or a provider of any Internet account, including any provider of online payment services or online auction services, such as PayPal, Inc. and/or Ebay, Inc.;

2. Defendant or his agents have any kind of pre-existing relationship with a consumer;

3. A consumer's Internet service account or any other Internet accounts held by a consumer may be terminated if the consumer does not respond to a solicitation from Defendant or his agents;

4 A consumer must provide personal and/or financial information to Defendant or his agents to avoid termination of the consumer's Internet service account or any other Internet account;

5. Defendant or his agents have authorization to place orders for goods or services using another person's credit card, debit card, and/or other financial information; and

6. Defendant or his agents have authorization to establish credit card or other accounts using another person's name.

B. Sending or causing to be sent any email or other electronic message via the Internet that misrepresents the identity of the sender (*e.g.*, falsifying information in the "from" line of an email) or the subject of the email or message (*e.g.*, falsifying the information contained in the "subject" line of the email).

C. Creating, registering, promoting, operating, posting, and/or maintaining any web page, website, chat room, Internet Relay Chat Channel, or other source of information on the Internet that misrepresents the identity of its host, sponsor, creator, or operator.

D. Using another person's personal and/or financial information to purchase goods or services and/or establish credit card and/or other financial accounts in a consumer's name without that person's express authorization.

III.
INJUNCTION AGAINST GLB ACT VIOLATIONS

IT IS FURHTER ORDERED that in connection with the solicitation of consumers for personal or financial information or in the promotion, advertising, marketing, sale, or offering for sale of any product or service, Defendant and his agents, assigns, servants, employees, salespersons, and all other persons or entities directly or indirectly under his control, and all other persons or entities in active concert or participation with him who receive actual notice of this Order by personal service or otherwise, whether acting directly or through any corporation, subsidiary, division, or other device, are hereby permanently restrained and enjoined from obtaining or attempting to obtain "customer information of a financial institution" including, but not limited to, credit or debit card account numbers, bank account numbers, bank routing numbers, personal identification numbers ("PIN numbers"), and/or the three-digit card verification numbers on the back of credit and debit cards ("civ/cvv numbers"), by making false, fictitious, and/or fraudulent statements or representations to financial institutions or customers of financial institutions.

IV.
COOPERATION PROVISIONS

IT IS FURTHER ORDERED that Defendant hereby agrees to cooperate fully, truthfully, and completely with the Commission in the identification and location of individuals or entities involved in the acts and practices alleged in the Commission's Complaint. this cooperation includes, but is not limited to, the production of such information and documents as will allow the Commission to identify and locate those individuals or entities and to determine the extent of their involvement.

V.
CUSTOMER INFORMATION

IT IS FURTHER ORDERED that:

A. Defendant, and his agents, assigns, servants, employees, salespersons, and all other persons or entities directly or indirectly under his control, and all other persons or entities in active concert or participation with him who receive actual notice of this Order by personal service or otherwise, whether acting directly or through any corporation, subsidiary, division, or other device, are hereby permanently restrained and enjoined from directly or indirectly using, selling, renting, leasing, transferring, or otherwise disclosing any personal or financial information, including the name, address, telephone number, social security number, date of birth, driver's license number, mother's maiden name, credit or debit card account number, bank account number, bank routing number, bank name, email address, PIN number, civ/cvv numbers, or password of any person other than Defendant that was in Defendant's possessions at any time prior to the entry of this Order; **PROVIDED,** however, that Defendant shall transfer a true, correct, and complete copy of all such personal or financial information in his or his agents' possession to the Commission within five (5) business days after receipt of this Order as entered by the Court; **PROVIDED FURTHER** that nothing in this order shall prevent Defendant from transferring a true, correct, and complete copy of such identifying information to other law enforcement agencies as permitted or required by any law, regulation, judicial process, or court order.

B. Defendant shall destroy all originals and all copies in his or his agents' possession of such personal or financial information described in Paragraph A of this Section, no later than five (5) business days after receipt of this Order as entered by the Court.

VI.
EQUITABLE MONETARY RELIEF

IT IS FURHTER ORDERED that:

A. Judgment is hereby entered against Defendant and in favor of Plaintiff in the amount of seven thousand nine hundred and thirty-two dollars and eighty-three cents ($7,932.83), for consumer redress pursuant to Section 13(b) of the FTC Act, 15 U.S.C. § 53(b), and Section 522(a) of the GLB Act, 15 U.S.C. § 6822(a). However, this judgment shall be stayed and the Commission shall consider this judgment satisfied provided that Defendant pays the Commission three thousand and five hundred dollars ($3,500.00). Defendant hereby forfeits all rights to and agrees to make no attempt to obtain the Sager laptop computer seized from his residence at [Address] on December 19, 2002, by the Federal Bureau of Investigation. This forfeiture thereby results in a $2,100.00 credit toward the payment required to satisfy the judgment, leaving a payment balance due of one thousand and four hundred dollars ($1,400.00) to the Commission.

B. Defendant has placed one thousand and four hundred dollars ($1,400.00) into a Trust Account at the Law Offices of Mark J. Werksman, 801 South Figueroa Street, 11th Floor, Los Angeles, CA 90017, to be held and transferred to the Commission within three (3) days after entry of this Order in satisfaction of the amount due stated above. Any additional payments required by this Section shall be made in U.S. funds by certified or cashier's check, made payable to the Federal Trade Commission, and delivered to the Associate Director of Marketing Practices, Federal Trade Commission, 600 Pennsylvania Avenue, NW, Room 238, Washington, D.C. 20580.

C. All funds paid pursuant to this Section shall be deposited into a fund administered by the Commission or its agent to be used for equitable relief, including but not limited to consume redress and any attendant expenses for the administration of any redress fund. In the event that direct redress to consumers is wholly or partially impracticable or that funds remain after redress is completed, the Commission may apply any remaining funds for such other equitable relief (including consumer information remedies) as it determines to be reasonably related to the Defendant's practices alleged in the Complaint. Any funds not used for such equitable relief shall be deposited into the United States Treasury as disgorgement. Defendant shall have no right to challenge the Commission's choice of remedies under this Section.

D. The Commission's agreement to this Order providing that Defendant not have to pay the judgment amount is expressly, reasonably, and materially premised upon the truthfulness, accuracy, and completeness of the financial statements submitted to the Commission and signed under penalty of perjury by Defendant and [Parent], in his capacity as Defendant's father, dated June 10, 2003.

E. If, upon motion by the Commission, this Court finds that Defendant has failed to disclose any material asset or materially misrepresented the value of any asset, or has made any other material misrepresentation or omission, in the financial statements described in this Section, or makes any attempt to obtain the computer forfeited in this Section, the stay shall be lifted and Defendant shall immediately pay the full redress amount of $7,932.83, less any actual payments made.

F. In accordance with 31 U.S.C. § 7701, Defendant is hereby required, unless he has done so already, to furnish the commission all his taxpayer identifying numbers, including his Social Security and employer identification numbers, which shall be used for purposes of collecting and reporting on any delinquent amount arising out of Defendant's relationship with the government.

G. Defendant agrees that the facts as alleged in the Complaint filed in this action and the amount of consumer harm represented by the amount of the consumer redress award in this Section shall be taken as true in any subsequent litigation filed by the commission to enforce its rights pursuant to this Order, including but not limited to a non-dischargeability complaint arising in any bankruptcy case to which Defendant is a party, and Defendant expressly waives any and all rights to contest such allegations in such litigation.

H. Proceedings instituted under this Section are in addition to, and not in lieu of, any other civil or criminal remedies that may be provided by law, including any other proceedings that the Commission may initiate to enforce this Order.

VII.
COMPLIANCE BY DEFENDANT

IT IS FURTHER ORDERED that, in order that compliance with the provisions of this Order may be monitored:

A. For a period of five (5) years from the date of entry of this Order, Defendant shall notify the Commission of the following:

1. Any changes in Defendant's residence, mailing address, and telephone numbers, within ten (10) days of the date of such change;

2. Any changes in Defendant's employment status (including self-employment) within ten (10) days of the date of such change. Such notice shall include the name and address of each business that Defendant is affiliated with, employed by, or performs services for; a statement of the nature of the business; and a statement of Defendant's duties and responsibilities in connection with the business; and

3. Any changes in Defendant's name or use of any aliases or fictitious names;

B. One hundred eighty (180) days after the date of entry of this Order, Defendant shall provide a written report to the FTC, sworn to under penalty of perjury, setting forth in detail the manner and form in which he has complied and is complying with this Order. This report shall include, but not be limited to:

1. Any changes required to be reported pursuant to Paragraph A above;

2. A copy of each acknowledgment of receipt of this Order obtained by Defendant pursuant to Section IX;

3. A list of all electronic mail or instant message addresses he has created, registered, or used since the entry of the Order and all websites and/or domain names he has registered, created, posted or maintained since the entry of the Order;

C. For the purposes of this Order, Defendant shall, unless otherwise directed by the Commission's authorized representatives, mail all written notifications to the Commission to:

Associate Director
Division of Marketing practices
Federal Trade Commission
600 Pennsylvania Avenue, N.W., H-238
Washington D.C. 20580
RE: *FTC v. [Defendant]*

D. For purposes of the compliance reporting required by this Section, the Commission is authorized to communicate directly with Defendant.

VIII.
RECORD-KEEPING PROVISIONS

IT IS FURTHER ORDERED that, for a period of eight (8) years from the date of entry of this Order, Defendant, when acting in an individual capacity, or in connection with any entity in which Defendant has an ownership interest, or is a director, officer (or comparable position with a non-corporate entity), or is a person who formulates policies or procedures, in connection with the offering for sale, sale, or marketing of any product or service or the solicitation of information from consumers, is hereby restrained and enjoined from failing to create and retain the following records:

A. Accounting records that reflect the cost of goods or services sold, any revenues generated, and the disbursement of such revenues;

B. Personnel records accurately reflecting: the name, address, and telephone number of each person employed in any capacity, including as an independent contractor, that person's job title or position, the date upon which the person commenced work, and the date and reason for the person's termination, if applicable;

C. Records containing the names, addresses, phone numbers, any dollar amounts paid, the quantity of any items or services purchased, and a description of items or services purchased, to the extent such information is obtained in the ordinary course of business;

D. Complaints and refund requests (whether received directly, indirectly or through any third party) and any responses to those complaints or requests;

E. Domain registration and website and/or web page registration records accurately reflecting: all domain names and websites and/or web pages registered or maintained, and the name and address of the Domain Name Registrars and/or the companies hosting such websites and/or pages;

F. Records relating to all ventures undertaken that involve the sale of goods or services on the Internet and/or the solicitation of consumers for personal and/or financial information on the Internet, including, but not limited to, copies of all contracts or agreements with any sales company, Internet service provider, web hosting company, telephone company, or other person or entity that advertises or promotes goods or services, as well as copies of all advertisements, web pages, websites, commercial electronic mail, or promotional materials utilized in such ventures.

IX.
DISTRIBUTION OF ORDER BY DEFENDANT

IT IS FURTHER ORDERED that, for a period of three (3) years from the date of entry of this order, Defendant shall deliver a copy of this order to, and obtain a signed and dated acknowledgment of receipt of the Order from i) his supervisor and/or manager, and/or ii) each agent or employee under Defendant's control, or any business that employs or contracts with Defendant where such employment or contractual relationship permits Defendant to have access to any customer information, whether personal or financial. Defendant shall secure from each such person a signed and dated statement acknowledging receipt of the Order within thirty (30) days after the date of service of the Order or the commencement of the employment relationship. Defendant shall maintain for a period of five (5) years after creation, and upon reasonable notice make available to representatives of the Commission, the original signed and dated acknowledgements of receipt of copies of this Order, as required in this Section.

X.
ACKNOWLEDGMENT OF RECIEPT OF ORDER

IT IS FURHTER ORDERED that, for the purpose of monitoring and investigating compliance with any provision of this Order,

A. Within ten (10) days of receipt of written notice from a representative of the Commission, Defendant shall submit additional written reports, sworn to under penalty of perjury; produce documents for inspection and copying; appear for deposition; and provide entry during normal business hours to any business location in Defendant's possession or direct or indirect control to inspect the business operation;

B. In addition, the Commission is authorized to monitor compliance with this Order by all other lawful means, including by not limited to the following:

1. Obtaining discovery from any person, without further leave of court, using the procedures prescribed by Fed. R. Civ. P. 30, 31, 33, 34, 36, and 45;

2. Posing as consumers and suppliers to: Defendant, Defendant's employees, or any other entity managed or controlled in whole or in part by Defendant, without the necessity of identification or prior notice;

PROVIDED that nothing in this Order shall limit the Commission's lawful use of compulsory process, pursuant to Sections 9 and 20 of the FTC Act, 15 U.S.C. §§ 49, 57b-1, to obtain any documentary material, tangible things, testimony, or information relevant to unfair or deceptive acts or practices in or affecting commerce (within the meaning of 15 U.S.C. § 45(a)(1)).

C. Defendant shall permit representatives of the Commission to interview any employer, consultant, independent contractor, representative, agent, or employee who has agreed to such an interview, relating in any way to any conduct subject to this Order. The person interviewed may have counsel present.

XII.
AFFECT OF EXPIRATION OF PARTS OF THE ORDER

IT IS FURTHER ORDERED that the expiration of any requirement imposed by this Order shall not affect any other obligation arising under this Order.

XIII.
RETENTION OF JURISDICITION

IT IS FURTHER ORDERED that this Court shall retain jurisdiction of this matter for the purposes of construction, modification and enforcement of this Order.

SO ORDERED, this _____ day of _____ 2003, at _____.

_____
United States District Judge

The parties hereby stipulate and agree to the terms and conditions of the Order, as set forth above, and consent to the entry thereof.

Dated: _____

_____
[Attorney for the Commission]

Dated: _____

_____
[Attorney for Parent]

Dated: _____

_____
[Attorney for Defendant]

H.8 United States of America v. Equifax Information Services, Inc.

UNITED STATES DISTRICT COURT
FOR THE NORTHERN DISTRICT OF GEORGIA
ATLANTA DIVISION

UNITED STATES OF AMERICA,)	
Plaintiff,)	
)	
v.)	
)	CIVIL ACTION NO.
EQUIFAX CREDIT)	1:00-CV-0087-MHS
INFORMATION SERVICES,)	
INC.,)	
Defendant.)	

JOINT MOTION FOR MODIFICATION OF CONSENT DECREE

Plaintiff, the United States of America, and defendant Equifax Credit Information Services, Inc. (the "Parties"), jointly move to amend and modify the Consent Decree filed in this action on January 13, 2000, pursuant to judgment entered on January 26, 2000 (the "Consent Decree"). In support of this Motion, the Parties state:

1. The Consent Decree provides, in relevant part:

Defendant, and its officers, agents, servants, employees, and representatives, and all persons in active concert or participation with any one or more of them who receive actual notice of this Consent Decree by personal service or otherwise, are hereby enjoined from violating, directly or through any corporation, subsidiary, division, or other device, Section 609(c)(1)(B) of the FCRA, 15 U.S.C. § 1681g(c)(1)(B) as amended, or as Section 609(c)(1)(B) may be amended hereafter.

Consent Decree, ¶ 17.

2. In addition, the Consent Decree provides:

For a period of five (5) years commencing on January 17, 2000, defendant shall maintain the following levels of service which, for that five year period and solely for purposes of this Consent Decree, also shall be deemed to satisfy defendant's obligations under paragraph 17 of this

Consent Decree for all telephone numbers printed on consumer disclosures pursuant to Section 609(c)(1)(B) of the FCRA, 15 U.S.C. § 1681g(c)(1)(B): (a) a blocked call rate of no greater than ten percent (10%); (b) an average speed of answer of no greater than three (3) minutes and thirty (30) seconds.

Consent Decree, ¶ 18.

3. The Consent Decree further states:

Defendant shall not be deemed in violation of paragraph 17 or paragraph 18 of this Consent Decree if circumstances beyond defendant's reasonable control (such as acts of God, telecommunications interruptions, equipment malfunctions, labor shortages caused by illness or organized labor action, or significant increases in call volume due to unforeseen circumstances) preclude it from complying with paragraph 17 or paragraph 18, provided that the defendant takes reasonable steps to minimize the impact of these events on its toll-free telephone number service and promptly restores service to levels that comply with this Consent Decree.

Consent Decree, ¶ 21.

4. Finally, the Consent Decree provides:

Defendant shall be deemed to be in compliance with paragraph 18 of this Consent Decree if it meets the levels of service stated in paragraph 18 during twelve (12) or more of the thirteen (13) measurement periods in each audit interval.

Consent Decree, ¶ 23.

5. The Consent Decree defines an Audit Interval as a set of thirteen contiguous measurement periods. A measurement period means normal business hours during each contiguous two week interval. Consent Decree, Definitions, 13 and 8, respectively.

6. During Audit Interval 3 (January 15, 2001 through July 13, 2001), Defendant acknowledges it exceeded: (1) the blocked call rate for measurement periods 4, 5, 6, 7, and 8; and (2) the average speed of answer for measurement periods 5 and 6.

7. Plaintiff alleges that Defendant violated the Consent Decree by exceeding the blocked call rate in four measurement periods and the average speed of answer rate in one measurement period.

8. Defendant specifically denies Plaintiff's allegations that it violated the Consent Decree as alleged by Plaintiff or otherwise.

9. The Parties have agreed to settlement of the foregoing allegations without adjudication of any issue of fact or law.

10. The Parties stipulate to an entry of an order that modifies the Consent Decree to provide that Defendant shall pay to Plaintiff the amount of Two Hundred Fifty Thousand Dollars ($250,000), as payment for alleged remedial relief to disgorge unjust enrichment, which shall be deemed to satisfy completely Plaintiff's claim for violation of the Consent Decree, such payment to be made within five business days of the date of entry of the Order by electronic fund transfer in accordance with instructions provided by the Office of Consumer Litigation, Civil Division, U.S. Department of Justice, Washington, D.C. 20530, for appropriate disposition.

11. The parties further stipulate that this Joint Motion for Modification of the Consent Decree is for settlement purposes only and neither its execution by the Parties nor its entry by the Court constitutes an admission by Defendant that the Consent Decree was violated as alleged by the Plaintiff.

12. The parties further stipulate that the Consent Decree, as so modified, shall remain in full force and effect in accordance with its terms.

Dated: _____, 2003.

FOR THE UNITED STATES
PETER D. KEISLER
Assistant Attorney General
Civil Division
U.S. Department of Justice

WILLIAM S. DUFFEY, JR.
United States Attorney
Northern District of Georgia

By: _____

Assistant United States Attorney
Northern District of Georgia
600 U.S. Courthouse
75 Sping Street, S.W.
Atlanta, GA 30303-3361

EUGENE M. THIROLF
Director
Office of Consumer Litigation

I hereby certify that this document was prepared in Times New Roman font _____ (14 point), in accordance with Local Rules 5.1B and 7.1D.

ELIZABETH STEIN

Attorney
Office of Consumer Litigation
Civil Division
U.S. Department of Justice
950 Pennsylvania Avenue, N.W.
Washington, D.C. 20530-0001
(202) 307-0486 (voice)
(202) 514-8742 (fax)

_____

Joel Winston
Associate Director for Financial Practices
Federal Trade Commission

_____

Annemarie Scanlon Harthun, Attorney
Division of Financial Practices
Federal Trade Commission
Washington, DC 20580

FOR THE DEFENDANT:

EQUIFAX CREDIT INFORMATION SERVICES, INC.
1550 Peachtree Street
Atlanta, Georgia 30309

Kent E. Mast, Esq.
General Counsel
1550 Peachtree Street
Atlanta, Georgia 30309
(404) 885-8000

UNITED STATES DISTRICT COURT
FOR THE NORTHERN DISTRICT OF GEORGIA
ATLANTA DIVISION

_____)
UNITED STATES OF AMERICA)
   Plaintiff,)
)
v.   )
) CIVIL ACTION NO.
EQUIFAX CREDIT   ) 1:00-CV-0087-MHS
INFORMATION SERVICES,)
INC.,   )
   Defendant.)
_____)

ORDER MODIFYING CONSENT DECREE

Upon consideration of the Joint Motion for Modification of Consent Decree submitted by the parties and for such cause shown, the Court being fully advised in the premises,

IT IS HEREBY ORDERED that the motion be GRANTED.

The Consent Decree is hereby modified to require the payment by Defendant Equifax, within five business days of entry of this order, in the amount of two hundred fifty thousand dollars ($250,000) as complete satisfaction of the claim for violation of the Consent Decree.

The Consent Decree, as so modified, shall remain in full force and effect in accordance with its terms.

So Ordered this _____ day of _____, 2003.

       MARVIN H. SHOOB
    UNITED STATES DISTRICT JUDGE

CERTIFICATE OF SERVICE

I hereby certify that I caused a true copy of the foregoing Joint Motion for Modification of Consent Decree and proposed Order to be served by Federal Express this _____ day of _____, 2003, upon:

Kent E. Mast, Esq.
General Counsel
Equifax Credit Information Services, Inc.
1550 Peachtree Street
Atlanta, Georgia 30309

_____

Appendix I Sample Pleadings and Other Litigation Documents

Page 805

I.1 Sample Complaints

Replace subsection's first paragraph with:

This appendix contains several sample FCRA related pleadings and case excerpts. These include four sample complaints (I.1.1–I.1.4); four sample sets of interrogatories (I.2.1–I.2.4); three sample requests for production of documents(I.3.1–I.3); a sample subpoena (I.4.1); and two sample notices of deposition (I.4.2–I.4.3). Also included is a sample confidentiality order (I.4.4). Finally, Appendix I includes jury case excerpts and sample jury instructions (I.5.1–I.5.6).

I.2 Sample Interrogatories

Page 823

Add new subsection after I.2.3:

I.2.4 Interrogatories–Reinvestigation (to Furnisher)

UNITED STATES DISTRICT COURT
IN AND FOR THE DISTRICT OF _____

_____)	
Plaintiff,)	
)	
v.)	
)	
TRANS UNION, ET AL)	
_____)	

**INTERROGATORIES
TO DEFENDANT, CORP.**

To: XYX CORP.
through its attorneys of record:

PLEASE TAKE NOTICE that you are hereby notified and required to respond to the following Interrogatories and produce the requested information to Plaintiff herein, through his attorney of record, _____, within thirty (30) days from service hereof in accordance with the provisions of Rule 33, et. seq., of the Federal Rules of Civil Procedure.

You are further placed on notice that these requests are deemed continuing, requiring supplemental responses thereto in the event requested information changes or otherwise becomes known, if not currently known after proper inquiry, or otherwise becomes available which would require amendment or supplementation of your responses in order that they would be proper and truthful, become known to you.

INSTRUCTIONS

In answering these requests, please furnish all information which is available to you, including, without limitation, all information in the possession of your attorneys, accountants, affiliates, auditors, agents, employees, officers, directors, shareholders, contractors, or other personnel, and not merely such information as is in your possession.

If you cannot respond to any of the following requests in full, after exercising due diligence to secure information to do so, please so state, and respond to the extent possible, specifying all reasons why you are unable or unwilling to respond to the remainder, stating whatever information you have concerning the unproduced information, and what efforts you made to secure information sufficient to allow you to respond fully to the particular request.

Although one or more of the following requests may not appear to be applicable to or directed to you, please respond to each and every one of them to the extent that you are able to provide any response thereto whether such response consists of information within your own knowledge or what you have obtained from others. However, for every response in which you include information received from others, please provide the name, any known address, and any known phone number of the person from whom you so received such information. And, in every such instance please state that you cannot verify such of your own personal knowledge, identifying particularly the information for which you cannot vouch. Further, these requests contain words or phrases which require you to refer to the "Definitions" section of this document provided herein below.

Unless otherwise stated, each request pertains to the time period beginning January, 2000, through the present date. Thus, your responses should be fully answered as they pertain to information, recordings or information within that time frame. Further, each request should identify the appropriate time frame, if your response requires same.

DEFINITIONS

1. "You" includes XYX Corp., the company, entity, institution, agency, subsidiary(ies), parent corporation(s) and/or any of its branches, departments, employees, agents, contractual affiliates, or otherwise connected by legal relationship, in the broadest sense. "You" includes any of your sister companies or related entities and their connected companies, whether or not separately incorporated. You may also be referenced herein simply as "XYZ"

2. "Document(s)" shall mean and include any printed, typewritten, handwritten or otherwise recorded matter of whatever character, including specifically, but not exclusively, and without limiting the generality of the foregoing, letters, diaries, desk and other calendars memoranda, telegrams, posters, cables, reports, charts, statistics, envelopes, studies, newspapers, news reports, business records, book of account(s) or other books, ledgers, balance sheets, journals, personal records, personal notes, any piece of paper, parchment, or other materials similarly used with anything written, typed printed, stamped, engraved, embossed, or impressed upon it, accountants statements, accounting records of any kind, bank statements, minutes of meetings or other minutes, labels, graphics, notes of meetings or conversations or other notes, catalogues, written agreements, checks, announcements, statements, receipts, returns invoices, bills, warranties, advertisements, guarantees, summaries, pamphlets, prospectuses, bulletins, magazines, publications, photographs, work-sheets, computer printouts, telex transmissions or receipts, teletypes, telefaxes, file folders or other folders, tape recordings, and any original or non-identical (whether different from the original by reason of any notation made on such copies or otherwise), carbon, photostatic or photograph copies of such materials. The term "documents" shall also mean and include every other recording of, or means of recording on any tangible form, any form of information, data, communication, or representation, including but not limited to, microfilm, microfiche, any records stored on any form of computer software, audio or video tapes or discs, digitally recorded disks or diskettes, or any other medium whatsoever.

For each "document" responsive to any request withheld from production by you on the ground of any privilege, please state:
  (a) the nature of the document (e.g., letter, memorandum, contract, etc.);
  (b) the author or sender of the document;
  (c) the recipient of the document;
  (d) the date the document was authored, sent, and/or received; and
  (e) the reason such document is allegedly privileged

3. "Audit Trail" means complete, detailed listings of each and every alteration, deletion, inquiry into, modification or other change to the credit report or profile as maintained in recorded form, in the broadest sense, by "you." The listing should include the identity, address, employer and title of the person(s) taking the action, the identity, address, employer and title of the person(s) authorizing the action, a detailed explanation of the action taken, the date of the action, the means used to effect such action, the location of origin of the action and the reason the action was taken. The term "audit trail" also includes the definition provided for the phrase in the FederBush, Federal Trade Commission and Formal Staff Opinion Letter, March 10, 1983.

4. "Data" means the physical symbols in the broadest sense that represent information, regardless of whether the information is oral, written or otherwise recorded.

5. "Data field" means any single or group of character(s), number(s), symbol(s) or other identifiable mark(s) maintained in a permanent or temporary recording which represent, in any way, an item or collection of information. "Data field" includes all types of data whether maintained in integer, real, character or Boolean format.

6. "Database" or "databank" means any grouping or collection of data field(s) maintained, in any format or order, in any permanent or temporary recorded form.

7. "Computer" means any and all programmable electronic devices or apparatuses, including hardware, software, and other databanks, that can store, retrieve, access, update, combine, rearrange, print, read, process or otherwise alter data whether such data maintained in that device or at some other location. The term "computer" includes any an all magnetic recording or systems, systems operating on or maintaining data in digital, analog, or hybrid format, or other mechanical devices, or other devices capable of maintaining writings or recording, of any kind, in condensed format, and includes any disk, tape, recording, or other informational source, regardless of its physical dimension or size.

8. "Identify" means that you should state:
  (a) any and all names, legal, trade or assumed;
  (b) all addresses used;
  (c) all telephone and telefax numbers used; and, if applicable:
  (d) brand, make, manufacturer's name, address, phone number and the manufacturer's relationship to any and all Defendants in the above captioned action; and
  (e) employer's name, address, phone number and the employer's relationship to any and all Defendants in the above captioned action.

9. "Explain" mean to elucidate, make plain or understandable, to give the reason for or cause of, and to show the logical development or relationships thereof.

10. "Describe" means to represent or give an account of in words.

11. "Plaintiff" refers to _____.

12. "Other Defendant[s]" mean any Defendants(s) in the above entitled and captioned action except you, jointly or separately.

13. "Program" means the following: (1) a plan for solving a problem; (2) to devise a plan for solving a problem; (3) a computer routine (i.e., a set of instructions arranged in proper sequence to cause a computer to perform a particular process), (4) to write a computer routine.

14. "Header record" means a machine readable record at the beginning of a file containing data identifying the file and data used in file control.

INTERROGATORIES

INTERROGATORY NO. 1

Please state the full name, present address, employer, title and occupation of all persons providing information and documents responsive to these requests.

ANSWER:

INTERROGATORY NO. 2

Please identify all individuals known to you or your attorney who are witnesses to the events described in plaintiff's complaint or to any event which is the subject of any defense you have raised to this lawsuit. For each such person, please provide a brief summary of facts to which each might or could testify. Also for each such person, please state the following:
   (a) Please state whether each such person is affiliated with, or related to, or employed by any party (or its agents, servants, officers, or employees) to this lawsuit;
   (b) If any of the persons so listed in response to this interrogatory do not fit the characterization in subpart A above, please describe the nature of their involvement in this lawsuit;
   (c) Please explain and describe your understanding of their knowledge of such facts.

ANSWER:

INTERROGATORY NO. 3

Please list, explain and describe documents known to you or believed by you to exist concerning any of the events described in plaintiff's complaint or concerning any of the events which are the subject[s] of any defense[s] you have raised to this lawsuit.

ANSWER:

INTERROGATORY NO. 4

Please identify each expert witness, whether your employee or otherwise, that you believe may have formed any opinion or consulted with you about the facts or basis of this lawsuit or any defense or allegation you have raised in this lawsuit.

ANSWER:

INTERROGATORY NO. 5

Please identify all individuals known to you or your attorney who are not witnesses, but who you have reason to believe have knowledge pertinent to the events at issues as alleged in plaintiff's complaint, and provide a brief summary of the *facts* to which each such person could testify. For each person, please state the following:
   (a) Please state whether each such person is affiliated with, or related to, or employed by any party (or its agents, servants, officers, or employees) to this lawsuit;
   (b) If any of the persons so listed in response to this interrogatory do not fit the characterization in subpart A above, please describe the nature of their involvement in this lawsuit;
   (c) Please explain and describe your understanding of their knowledge of such facts.

ANSWER:

INTERROGATORY NO. 6

Please state whether any of the individuals listed in the answers to the preceding interrogatories have given any statement[s] to you and, if so, please identify the individual giving the statement, identify the individual to whom the statement was given, the date of the statement, and whether or not the statement was written or recorded and, if it was written or recorded, identify the individual presently in possession of it.

ANSWER:

INTERROGATORY NO. 7

Please list each exhibit which you may attempt to introduce as evidence at the trial of this case, or which has been used or referred to by any expert witness on your behalf [as called for in interrogatory no. 4].

ANSWER:

INTERROGATORY NO. 8

For each paragraph of plaintiff's complaint for which you deny the allegations, please explain and describe any facts which you believe may support each denial.

ANSWER:

INTERROGATORY NO. 9

Please explain and describe when, how and under what circumstances you archive, retain or capture consumer credit data in any file bearing any of plaintiff's personal identifiers. List the dates of each such archived data report wherein any personal information about plaintiff or attributed to any of plaintiff's personal identifiers, including the date such data was captured, retained and/or archived, who has possession of those reports, the manner in which the reports are maintained, and the retention policy[ies] regarding those reports. Please explain and describe each category and type of data field in each such report or recording.

ANSWER:

INTERROGATORY NO. 10

Please state whether you have authorized by each of your co-defendants/credit reporting agencies to report account data about your alleged customers on and by way of any or all of their credit reporting systems and affiliate networks during the years, 1998, 1999, 2000, 2001, 2002, 2003. If so, state whether you authorized each of your co-defendants/credit reporting agencies to report your credit data about plaintiff on and by way of any or all of their credit reporting systems and affiliate networks during the years, 1998, 1999, 2000, 2001, 2002, 2003. Please list each co-defendants/credit reporting agencies separately and indicate your answers. Please explain and describe the terms of your authority and all reciprocal duties and obligations arising between you and your co-defendants/credit reporting agencies.

ANSWER:

INTERROGATORY NO. 11

Please state your net income for the preceding twenty-four (24) quarters.

ANSWER:

INTERROGATORY NO. 12

Please state the dates and exact content of each of your reportings, which bore any of plaintiff's personal identifiers, which you made to any person which contained any of the disputed account[s] data or account[s] reportings, as identified in plaintiff's complaint. Please fully identify the recipient.

ANSWER:

INTERROGATORY NO. 13

Please explain and describe any disputes you received from plaintiff or from any other source which concerned or pertained to plaintiff. Please explain and describe what actions you took as a result of the dispute and the disposition of your actions in connection with each contact or communication.

ANSWER:

INTERROGATORY NO. 14

Please explain and describe the audit trail of your records regarding credit reportings you made in connection with each disputed account, as identified in plaintiff's complaint.

ANSWER:

INTERROGATORY NO. 15

Please list, explain and describe each and every code contained in each of your computerized records which you have produced. For each such code, please also explain and describe, in detail, the purpose of such code, the content of such action, the duration of such action, and the reason you permitted such action or entry.

ANSWER:

INTERROGATORY NO. 16

Please list, explain and describe each and every the header record which you reported to the credit reporting agencies in connection with each account bearing your subscriber name on plaintiff's credit reports as issued by the credit reporting agencies and as already produced to you in this lawsuit.

ANSWER:

INTERROGATORY NO. 17

Please list, explain and describe each and every contact or communication you received from your co-defendants which, in any way, referenced plaintiff. This request would include any GEIS [General Electric Information Services]-based and E-Oscar communications, UDFs, AUDFs, CDVs, ACDVs, tape transfers, system to system transfers, phone calls and other means of communication.

ANSWER:

INTERROGATORY NO. 18

For each credit reporting you issued to any third person in the two years preceding the filing of this lawsuit and since the filing of this lawsuit, please list, explain and describe, in the greatest detail you are able, each and every negative item of data appearing in the reporting and how you sought the reported item to be factored in the credit scores generated and issued about plaintiff.

ANSWER:

INTERROGATORY NO. 19

If you deny your credit reportings about plaintiff, as complained of in his lawsuit, were false, please explain and describe, in the greatest degree of detail, what facts you believe exist to support your belief and identify any witnesses who you believe will support or testify in support of your belief.

ANSWER:

INTERROGATORY NO. 20

Did you authorize the co-defendants/credit reporting agencies to re-report to other users of credit data [subscribers] the credit data you reported to them?

ANSWER:

INTERROGATORY NO. 21

Please list, explain and describe your reinvestigation activities in response to each of plaintiff's disputes. Please identify each of your employees involved in each notice, transaction or event, as well as any supervising employee overseeing such each notice, transaction or event.

ANSWER:

INTERROGATORY NO. 22

For each employee witness or proposed expert witness which you may call as a witness as trial, please list each and every lawsuit in which each respective person has published a such a written or otherwise recorded report, proposed expert report, affidavit, deposition testimony and/or trial testimony, and explain and describe the nature of the employee witness's or proposed expert witness's testimony and the complete caption, including court name and location, of the case where such a written or otherwise recorded report was rendered, where the proposed expert report was rendered, where the affidavit was filed or exchanged, where deposition testimony and/or trial testimony was taken.

ANSWER:

INTERROGATORY NO. 23

Does any account exist in your records bearing a party listing a social security number of _____? If so, please state the account number associated with any consumer listing a social security number of _____ and fully identify each responsible party on such account, the account number and the complete set of Metro Tape data fields you have reported about such an account since its inception. Similarly, please explain and describe all facts known to you as to whether you have received notice of any fraud alerts or other report flags or alerts in connected with the a social security number of _____.

ANSWER:

INTERROGATORY NO. 24

Does any account exist in your records bearing a party listing a name of "_____," and/or any of the following address(es): "_____" and "_____?" If so, please state the account number associated with the consumer[s] shown as responsible parties and fully identify each responsible party on such account, the account number and the complete set of Metro Tape data fields you have reported about such an account since its inception. Similarly, please explain and describe all facts known to you as to whether you have received notice of any fraud alerts or other report flags or alerts in connected with the name "_____," or any of the following address(es): "_____" and "_____."

ANSWER:

Respectfully submitted:

[Attorney]

I.3 Sample Requests for Production

Page 825

Add new subsection after I.3.2:

I.3.3 Request for Production of Documents to Furnisher

UNITED STATES DISTRICT COURT
IN AND FOR THE DISTRICT OF

_____)
)
v.   )
)
TRANS UNION, ET AL   )
_____)

REQUESTS FOR PRODUCTION OF DOCUMENTS TO DEFENDANT, UNITED RESOURCE SYSTEMS

To: UNITED RESOURCE SYSTEMS
through its attorneys of record:
David J. Minkin
McCorriston Miller Mukai MacKinnon
P.O. Box 2800
Honolulu, HI 96803
Counsel for UNITED RESOURCE SYSTEMS

PLEASE TAKE NOTICE that you are hereby notified and required to respond to the following Requests For Production of Documents and produce the following documents requested to Plaintiff herein, through his attorney of record, _____, within thirty (30) days from service hereof in accordance with the provisions of Rule 34, et. seq., of the Federal Rules of Civil Procedure.

You are further placed on notice that these requests are deemed continuing, requiring supplemental responses thereto in the event requested documents become available which would require amendment or supplementation of your responses in order that they would be proper and truthful, become known to you.

INSTRUCTIONS

In answering these requests, please furnish all information, documents which are available to you, including, without limitation, all documents in the possession of your attorneys, accountants, affiliates, auditors, agents, employees, officers, directors, shareholders, contractors, or other personnel, and not merely such documents as are in your possession.

If you cannot respond to any of the following requests in full, after exercising due diligence to secure documents to do so, please so state, and respond to the extent possible, specifying all reasons why you are unable or unwilling to respond to the remainder, stating whatever documents you have concerning the unproduced documents, and what efforts you made to secure documents sufficient to allow you to respond fully to the particular request.

Although one or more of the following requests may not appear to be applicable to or directed to you, please respond to each and every one of them to the extent that you are able to provide any response thereto whether such response consists of documents within your own knowledge or what you have obtained from others. However, for every response in which you include documents received from others, please provide the name, any known address, and any known phone number of the person from whom you so received such documents. And, in every such instance please state that you cannot verify such of your own personal knowledge, identifying particularly the documents for which you cannot vouch. Further, these requests contain words or phrases which require you to refer to the "Definitions" section of this document provided herein below.

Unless otherwise stated, each request pertains to the time period beginning January, 2000, through the present date. Thus, your responses should be fully answered as they pertain to information, recordings or documents within that time frame. Further, each request should identify the appropriate time frame, if your response requires same.

DEFINITIONS

1. "You" includes UNITED RESOURCE SYSTEMS, the company, entity, institution, agency, subsidiary(ies), parent corporation(s) and/or any of its branches, departments, employees, agents, contractual affiliates, or otherwise connected by legal relationship, in the broadest sense. "You" includes any of your sister companies or related entities and their connected companies, whether or not separately incorporated. You may also be referenced herein simply as "URS."

2. "Document(s)" shall mean and include any printed, typewritten, handwritten or otherwise recorded matter of whatever character, including specifically, but not exclusively, and without limiting the generality of the foregoing, letters, diaries, desk and other calendars, memoranda, telegrams, posters, cables, reports, charts, statistics, envelopes, studies, newspapers, news reports, business records, book of account(s) or other books, ledgers, balance sheets, journals, personal records, personal notes, any piece of paper, parchment, or other materials similarly used with anything written, typed printed, stamped, engraved, embossed, or impressed upon it, accountants statements, accounting records of any kind, bank statements, minutes of meetings or other minutes, labels, graphics, notes of meetings or conversations or other notes, catalogues, written agreements, checks, announcements, statements, receipts, returns invoices, bills, warranties, advertisements, guarantees, summaries, pamphlets, prospectuses, bulletins, magazines, publications, photographs, work-sheets, computer printouts, telex transmissions or receipts, teletypes, telefaxes, file folders or other folders, tape recordings, and any original or non-identical (whether different from the original by reason of any notation made on such copies or otherwise), carbon, photostatic or photograph copies of such materials. The term "documents" shall also mean and include every other recording of, or means of recording on any tangible form, any form of information, data, communication, or representation, including but not limited to, microfilm, microfiche, any records stored on any form of computer software, audio or video tapes or discs, digitally recorded disks or diskettes, or other medium whatsoever.

For each "document" responsive to any request withheld from production by you on the ground of any privilege, please state:

(a) the nature of the document (e.g., letter, memorandum, contract, etc);
(b) the author or sender of the document;
(c) the recipient of the document;
(d) the date the document was authored, sent, and/or received; and
(e) the reason such document is allegedly privileged.

3. "Audit Trail" means a complete, detailed listing of each and every alteration, deletion, inquiry into, modification or other change to the credit report or profile as maintained in recorded form, in the broadest sense, by "you." The listing should include the identity, address, employer and title of the person(s) taking the action, the identity, address, employer and title of the person(s) authorizing the action, detailed explanation of the action taken, the date of the action, the means used to effect such action, the location of origin of the action and the reason the action was taken. The term "audit trail" also includes the definition provided for the phrase in the FederBush, Federal Trade Commission and Formal Staff Opinion Letter, March 10, 1983.

4. "Data" means the physical symbols in the broadest sense that represent information regardless of whether information is oral, written or otherwise recorded.

5. "Data field" means any single or group of character(s), numbers(s), symbols(s) or other identifiable mark(s) maintained in a permanent or temporary recording which represent, in any way, an item or collection of information. "Data field" includes all types of date whether maintained in integer, real, character or Boolean format.

6. "Database" or "databank" means any grouping or collection of data field(s) maintained, in any format or order, in any permanent or temporary recorded form.

7. "Computer" means any and all programmable electronic devices or apparatuses, including hardware, software, and other databanks, that can store, retrieve, access, update, combine, rearrange, print, read, process or otherwise alter data whether such data maintained in that device or at some other location. The term "computer" includes any and all magnetic recordings or systems, systems operating on or maintaining data in digital, analog, or hybrid format, or other mechanical devices, or other devices capable of maintaining writings or recordings, of any kind, in condensed format, and includes any disk, tape, recording, or other informational source, regardless of its physical dimension or size.

8. "Identify" means that you should state:
(a) any and all names, legal, trade or assumed;
(b) all addresses used;
(c) all telephone and telefax numbers used; and, if applicable:
(d) brand, make, manufacturer's name, address, phone number and the manufacturer's relationship to any and all Defendants in the above captioned action; and
(e) employer's name, address, phone number and the employer's relationship to any and all Defendants in the above captioned action.

9. "Explain" means to elucidate, make plain or understandable, to give the reason for or cause of, and to show the logical development or relationships thereof.

10. "Describe" means to represent or give an account of in words.

11. "Plaintiff" refers to _____.

12. "Other Defendant[s]" means any Defendant(s) in the above entitled and captioned action except *you*, jointly or separately.

13. "Program" means the following: (1) a plan for solving a problem; (2) to devise a plan for solving a problem; (3) a computer routine (i.e., a set of instructions arranged in proper sequence to cause a computer to perform a particular process); (4) to write a computer routine.

14. "Header record" means a machine readable record at the beginning of a file containing data identifying the file and date used in file control.

REQUESTS FOR PRODUCTION OF DOCUMENTS
REQUEST FOR PRODUCTION NO. 1

Please produce a copy of each and every document involving communication(s) or contact(s) between you and the following persons, which in any way references Plaintiff, any of his personal identifiers or any allegation or defense asserted in this action:

(a) Equifax Information Services, LLC and CSC Credit Services, Inc. and Credit Bureau of the Pacific and any other "Equifax" affiliate;
(b) Trans Union LLC;
(c) Experian Information Solutions, Inc.;
(d) Any state or federal governmental entity;
(e) Any other consumer reporting agency;
(f) Any other defendant in this case.

RESPONSE:

REQUEST FOR PRODUCTION NO. 2

Please produce a copy of each and every document involving communications or contacts between you and any of the other defendants, which in any way references the disputed account reportings, as listed in the complaint, reported to you, or by dispute made to you, as shown in the complaint.

RESPONSE:

REQUEST FOR PRODUCTION NO. 3

Please produce your policy manuals, procedure manuals, or other documents, which address your policies, practices or procedures in the investigation or reinvestigation of disputed credit data.

RESPONSE:

REQUEST FOR PRODUCTION NO. 4

Please produce a copy of each and every document involving communications or contacts between you and the other defendants, which in any way references Plaintiff or any of his personal identifiers or any other defendant in this suit.

RESPONSE:

REQUEST FOR PRODUCTION NO. 5

Please produce your data file maintenance manuals and any decoding manuals used to interpret the various items of data appearing in your reinvestigation records.

RESPONSE:

REQUEST FOR PRODUCTION NO. 6

Please produce your statistics compiled on an annual basis regarding the number of disputes and types of disputes you received complaining or disputing, as inaccurate, your credit reportings to the respective credit reporting agencies.

RESPONSE:

REQUEST FOR PRODUCTION NO. 7

Please produce your statistics compiled on an annual basis regarding the responses you made to the respective credit reporting agencies as a result of disputes you received complaining or disputing, as inaccurate, your credit reportings.

RESPONSE:

REQUEST FOR PRODUCTION NO. 8

Please produce your complete set of records regarding any account bearing plaintiff's name or other personal identifiers. This request includes any application, billing records and invoices, payments if any, credit reportings, letters, electronic communications or other documents pertaining to plaintiff or any account bearing of his personal identifiers.
RESPONSE:

REQUEST FOR PRODUCTION NO. 9

Please produce all of your computer screens showing any information regarding plaintiff, any of his personal identifiers, or any of his disputes.

RESPONSE:

REQUEST FOR PRODUCTION NO. 10

Please produce any and all policy manuals, procedure manuals, or other documents, which are training manuals for you employees, in the following areas: consumer relations, application processing, credit approval guidelines, credit issuance guidelines, point of sale procedures, dispute investigation, credit reporting reinvestigation, handing of CDVs, ACDVs, AUDFs and UDFs, account reporting removal and deletion mechanisms, credit reporting retraction procedures, and data reporting suppression functions and deletion functions.

RESPONSE:

REQUEST FOR PRODUCTION NO. 11

Please produce any and all CDVs, ACDVs, AUDFs and UDFs which bear any of the personal identifiers of plaintiff, as well as the complete log of all investigation activities in any file, report or other record bearing any of plaintiff's personal identifiers.

RESPONSE:

REQUEST FOR PRODUCTION NO. 12

Please produce copies of your annual reports to shareholders for each of the preceding four (4) years.

RESPONSE:

REQUEST FOR PRODUCTION NO. 13

Please produce copies of your quarterly profit and loss statements for each of the preceding twenty-four (24) quarters.

RESPONSE:

REQUEST FOR PRODUCTION NO. 14

Please produce copies of your balance sheets for each of the preceding twenty (20) quarters.

RESPONSE:

REQUEST FOR PRODUCTION NO. 15

Please produce your documents discussing the Metro Tape Format and the Metro Tape 2 credit reporting formats.

RESPONSE:

REQUEST FOR PRODUCTION NO. 16

Please produce your documents discussing research or studies by Associated Credit Bureaus [ACB], or Consumer Data Industry Association [CDIA], or other third parties concerning the accuracy of data contained in your consumer credit database.

RESPONSE:

REQUEST FOR PRODUCTION NO. 17

Please produce any and all policy manuals, procedure manuals, or other documents, which address the minimal amount and type of information required of any consumer disputing any item of information on a consumer report, in order to cause you to initiate your correction, update, modification and/or deletion of the disputed data.

RESPONSE:

REQUEST FOR PRODUCTION NO. 18

Please produce your policy manuals, procedure manuals, or other documents, which address instructions or directions, provided to you by any consumer reporting agency, with regard to the means, methods and guidelines for communicating corrections of credit data.

RESPONSE:

REQUEST FOR PRODUCTION NO. 19

Please produce your policy manuals, procedure manuals, or other documents, which address instructions or directions, provided to you by any consumer reporting agency, with regard to application processing and inquiry formatting.

RESPONSE:

REQUEST FOR PRODUCTION NO. 20

Please produce your policy manual, procedure manuals, or other documents, which address any of the following programs used by you:
(a) any credit scoring models used by you:
(b) required inquiry input to receive consumer credit reports;
(c) scorecard development programs used in your credit scoring models.

RESPONSE:

REQUEST FOR PRODUCTION NO. 21

Please produce copies of any and all credit reports received by you concerning Plaintiff or which bear any of his personal identifiers. This request includes all data reports, archived reports, current, on-line reports, off-line reports, and any credit score and adverse action codes [denial codes] which you believe were attributed to Plaintiff or which bear any of his personal identifiers. In connection therewith, please identify the source(s) of each document.

RESPONSE:

REQUEST FOR PRODUCTION NO. 22

Please provide a complete audit trail of any document(s), computer(s), or other data held by you which, in any degree, address or discuss Plaintiff, any of his personal identifiers and/or any of the data identified, as false, by Plaintiff in this action.

RESPONSE:

REQUEST FOR PRODUCTION NO. 23

Please provide copies of your subscriber contracts with any of the other defendants which were in effect in the two year period preceding the date of the filing of this lawsuit.

RESPONSE:

REQUEST FOR PRODUCTION NO. 24

Please produce a complete copy of your consumer dispute verification processing and handling manual.

RESPONSE:

REQUEST FOR PRODUCTION NO. 25

Please produce your policy manuals, procedure manuals, or other documents, which address the particular architecture of your consumer credit database or other system which electronically captures account data at a given point in time.

RESPONSE:

REQUEST FOR PRODUCTION NO. 26

Please produce copies of any and all correspondence, documents or other recordings from you, or your attorneys, to any other defendant in this action, or their attorneys.

RESPONSE:

REQUEST FOR PRODUCTION NO. 27

Please produce copies of any and all correspondence, documents or other recordings to you, or to your attorneys, from any other defendant in this action, or their attorneys.

RESPONSE:

REQUEST FOR PRODUCTION NO. 28

Please produce copies of all of the internal notations made by your employees regarding contacts with plaintiff, his attorneys, or any other defendant in this lawsuit, with regard to plaintiff, any of his personal identifiers and/or the disputed account reportings.

RESPONSE:

REQUEST FOR PRODUCTION NO. 29

Please produce copies of any and all documents bearing credit scoring assessments in connection with any report or data bearing Plaintiff's names or any of his personal identifiers.

RESPONSE:

REQUEST FOR PRODUCTION NO. 30

Please produce copies of any and all documents with contain any data about complaints, assessments, audits, reports or studies of improperly reported data made by you in the years: 1997, 1998, 1999, 2000, 2001 and/or 2002.

RESPONSE:

REQUEST FOR PRODUCTION NO. 31

Please produce copies of any and all documents which provides explanations and descriptions about the various coded or encrypted data appearing on any of the records you are producing in this litigation.

RESPONSE:

REQUEST FOR PRODUCTION NO. 32

Please produce copies of any and all documents which contain any data about and/or constitute a listing, explanation and description of your consumer dispute codes.

RESPONSE:

REQUEST FOR PRODUCTION NO. 33

Please produce copies of any and all documents which contain any data about internal, self audits or external audits of the accuracy of credit data you maintain and disseminate, in the years: 1998, 1999, 2000, 2001, and/or 2002.

RESPONSE:

REQUEST FOR PRODUCTION NO. 34

Please produce any and all work papers, notes, and documents in the file of any expert witness who is expected to testify, or in the file of the expert who has written a report which is or will be relied upon, in whole or in part, by a testifying expert.

RESPONSE:

REQUEST FOR PRODUCTION NO. 35

Please produce any and all expert reports which have been prepared in connection with this lawsuit or the incident giving rise to this lawsuit, if the expert is expected to or may testify in this cause.

RESPONSE:

REQUEST FOR PRODUCTION NO. 36

Please produce any and all expert reports that were or will be relied upon, in whole or in part, or which were produced by any expert retained or engaged by you.

RESPONSE:

REQUEST FOR PRODUCTION NO. 37

Please produce copies of any statements you have taken or received from any third person in any way connected with the allegations contained in this lawsuit.

RESPONSE:

REQUEST FOR PRODUCTION NO. 38

Please produce any and all documents which contained data listing or otherwise identifying each of your operators or other employees, their corresponding office descriptions and numbers, and their corresponding badge and identification numbers, who communicated with Plaintiff, any person concerning any account, dispute, report, or other document(s) made subject of and/or requested in any of the foregoing requests by Plaintiff to you.

RESPONSE:
[Attorney for Plaintiff]

I.5 Sample Litigation Documents

Page 841

Add new subsection after I.5.5:

I.5.6 Transcript of Jury Instructions[7.1]

THE COURT: Ladies and gentlemen, now that you have heard the evidence and argument of counsel, it becomes my responsibility to instruct you on the law applicable to this case. I give a general charge in all civil cases, and then after I give a general charge, I will instruct you on the substantive law that governs this case.

On the assumption all you of you aren't so gifted you can remember verbatim what the substantive law is, you will have a copy of that to take back in the jury room, and I will give you further guidance as we go along.

You aren't to single out any one of my instructions as being controlling, but you are to consider them as a whole. And irrespective of any thoughts that you might have as to what the law ought to be, it would be a violation of your oath if you disregarded what The Court had to say and applied some law that you thought would be more appropriate.

You have been chosen as jurors, and you took an oath that you would try the issues that have been raised by the pleadings and the evidence, and the public expects you to do your duty without bias or prejudice and to render justice in the case between these litigants.

Also, under our system all entities that appear in a court of law are entitled to be treated equally, and it doesn't make any difference whether it is a corporation that is organized in Delaware or Virginia, or it is an individual against a corporation or an individual against a partnership. They are all entitled to the same even-handed justice at the hands of a jury.

The burden is on the plaintiff in a civil action such as this to prove every essential element of her claim by a preponderance of the evidence. Now, preponderance of the evidence is a quantitative concept. All of you have seen the blind lady holding the scales of justice. As she holds those scales they are always in perfect balance. And whenever someone has the burden of proving something by preponderance of the evidence, it means that they have, their evidence tilts that perfect balance every so slightly in their favor. And that is a preponderance.

There are generally speaking two types of evidence from which a jury may properly find the truth as to the facts of the case. One is direct evidence, such as the testimony of an eye witness. And the

---

7.1 This transcript of jury instructions is from the case of Johnson (aka Slater) v. MBNA, Docket No. 3:02 CR 000523 (U.D.C. Va. Jan. 21, 2003). MBNA challenged the instructions regarding the standards for determining liability, however these instructions were upheld by the 4th Circuit Court of Appeal. *See* Johnson v. MBNA America, 2004 WL 24304 (4th Cir. Feb. 11, 2004).

other is independent or circumstantial evidence, which is the proof of a chain of circumstances pointing to the existence or nonexistence of certain facts. As a general rule, the law makes no distinction between direct and circumstantial evidence. And, ladies and gentlemen, bear in mind that the system recognizes that the eight of you bring to the jury box your accumulated common sense of a lifetime, and we expect you to use your common sense in reaching a decision in this case, just as you do on a daily basis in making other important decisions.

Exhibits are considered direct forms of evidence. Arguments and statements of counsel are not evidence, unless the attorneys enter into a stipulation, and if they enter into a stipulation you can accept that stipulation as a fact in the case.

From time to time in their arguments the lawyers may have stated what law was applicable to the case. If what they made reference to differs from what The Court said, disregard what they had to say altogether and literally apply the law as stated by The Court. Also, the lawyers from time to time may have made reference to what the witnesses testified to. If their recollection differs from yours, then ignore entirely what they said and make your own determination. But we have so much confidence in the jury system that we rely a hundred percent upon you to make a determination of the facts in the case.

You as jurors are the sole judges of the credibility of the witnesses and the weight that their testimony deserves. You may be guided by the appearance and conduct of the witness or by the manner in which the witness testifies, or by the character of the testimony given. You should carefully scrutinize all the testimony, the circumstances under which each witness has testified, and every matter in evidence which tends to show whether a witness is worthy of belief. Consider each witness' intelligence, motive, and state of mind and demeanor and manner while on the stand. Consider the witness' ability to observe the matter to which the witness testifies, and whether the witness impresses you as having an accurate recollection of these matters. Consider, also, any relation each witness may bear to each side of the case, the manner in which each witness might be affected by your verdict, and the extent to which, if at all, each witness is either supported or contradicted by other evidence in the case.

Inconsistencies or discrepancies in the testimony of a witness or between the testimony of different witnesses may or may not cause you to discredit such testimony. Two or more persons witnessing an incident or transaction may see or hear it differently. And innocent misrecollection, like failure of recollection, is not an uncommon experience. In weighing the effect of the discrepancy, always consider whether it pertains to matters of importance or an unimportant detail and whether the discrepancy results from innocent error or intentional falsehood. After making up your own judgment, you will give the testimony of each witness such weight, if any, as you think it deserves.

On occasion it was suggested that a witness may have given a prior inconsistent statement when the witness' deposition was taken in a prior situation. If such is shown, it could be considered for purposes of impeaching the witness' testimony. Before discounting a witness' testimony for this reason you ought to consider whether the inconsistency was of a minor, insignificant nature, or something material to the case.

A verdict cannot be based upon surmise, speculation, or sympathy for either party, but must be based solely upon the evidence and the instructions of The Court.

Now, that concludes my general charge, and while you breathe a collective sigh of relief I will take a drink of water, and then I will instruct you on the substantive law.

The plaintiff, Linda Johnson, is suing the defendant, MBNA America Bank, N.A., for damages alleging that the defendant negligently and willfully violated the Fair Credit Reporting Act, 15 U.S.C. section 1681. The plaintiff claims that the defendant violated the Fair Credit Reporting Act because she claims that after receiving notice from three credit reporting agencies that the plaintiff was disputing the identity and balance of an MBNA account. The defendant failed to review all of the information provided by the credit reporting agencies, failed to investigate the plaintiff's disputes, and failed to report back to the agencies the result its investigation. The defendant denies that it violated any provision of the Fair Credit Reporting Act. The defendant claims that it reviewed all of the information provided by the credit reporting agencies, investigated the plaintiff's disputes, and reported back to the these agencies the results of an investigation. The plaintiff claims first, that the defendant negligently failed to comply with the Fair Credit Reporting Act in failing to review all of the information provided by Experian, Equifax and TransUnion; failing to conduct a reasonable investigation of her disputes, and failing to accurately report back to these agencies the result of its investigation. To establish her claim that the defendant negligently failed to comply with the Fair Credit Reporting Act the plaintiff must establish the following elements by a preponderance of the evidence: One, that the defendant negligently failed to, A, conduct an investigation with respect to the disputed information B, review all relevant information provided by the consumer reporting agencies; or C, report the results of the investigation to the consumer reporting agencies; and two, that the plaintiff was damaged; and three, that the negligence of the defendant proximately caused the damage suffered by the plaintiff.

Your verdict will be for the defendant if you find that the plaintiff fails to establish any one of the three elements.

Negligence as used in these instructions means the failure to do something which a reasonably prudent person would do, or the doing of something which a reasonably prudent person would not do under the circumstances which you find existed in this case.

It is for you to decide what a reasonably prudent person would do or not do under the circumstances as they existed in this case. In other words, you must determine whether the defendant's investigation of the disputed information was reasonable. The term "proximate cause" as used in these instructions means that there must be a connection between the conduct of the defendant that the plaintiff claims was negligent and the damage complained of by the plaintiff, and that the act that is claimed to have produced the damage was a natural and probable result of the negligent conduct of the defendant.

If your verdict is for the plaintiff on the claim of negligent non compliance, then your duty is to determine the amount of money that reasonably, fairly, and adequately compensates her for the damage that you decide resulted from the defendant's failure to comply. Whether the element of damages has been proved by the plaintiff is for you to decide based upon evidence and not upon speculation, guess or conjecture. Damages for embarrassment, humiliation and mental anguish will not be presumed to have occurred, but the plaintiff must prove that they did occur, and the plaintiff, while it is not obligated to prove it with mathematical precision, they must give you sufficient raw material so that you can make an intelligent estimate of it. And, also, the burden is on the plaintiff to mitigate her damages, and if you feel that any evidence shows that she had an opportunity to lessen those damages and she didn't take advantage of it, then you can take that into consideration, also.

The plaintiff's second claim is that the defendant willfully failed to comply with the Fair Credit Reporting Act in failing to review all of the information provided by Experian, Equifax and TransUnion. Failing to investigate her disputes and failing to report back to these agencies the result of its investigation to establish her claim that the defendant willfully failed to comply with the Fair Credit Reporting Act the plaintiff must establish the following elements by a preponderance of the evidence. Bear in mind we are now talking about willfully doing something, whereas the first claim was negligently doing something. That the defendant willfully failed to, A, conduct an investigation with respect to the disputed information; B, review all relevant information provided by the computer reporting agencies; or C, report the results of the investigation to the consumer reporting agency. If the plaintiff fails to prove one of these three, A, B or C, you should find your verdict for the defendant.

The term "willfully" as used in these instructions means that the defendant knowingly and intentionally committed an act in conscious disregard for the rights of the consumer and not by mistake or accident or other innocent reason. A showing of malice or evil motive is not required to prove willfulness. MBNA was required to conduct a reasonable investigation. Factors to be considered in determining whether MBNA has conducted a reasonable investigation include whether the consumer has alerted MBNA that its information may be unreliable; and two, the cost of verifying the accuracy of the information versus the possible harm of reporting inaccurate information. The standard for such an investigation is what a reasonably prudent person would do under the circumstances. And evaluating the reasonableness of MBNA's investigation involves weighing the potential harm from inaccuracy against the burden of safeguarding such inaccuracy. The damage that Mrs. Johnson may recover for MBNA's alleged failure to investigate a claim of inaccuracy of the record or to report the results of its investigation may not include any damages that were caused by the inaccuracy of the information itself.

Damages to be recoverable are limited to those, if any, arising from a willful or negligent failure to conduct any investigation or to report the results. Damages recoverable for willful noncompliance with the fair credit reporting act are two kinds. First, there are damages that are actually suffered by reason of the wrong complained of. Second, there are punitive damages, which means damages over and above the actual damages, if any, suffered by the plaintiff. These are damages that may be awarded by you in your discretion for the purpose of punishing the defendant for the wrong done. Punitive damages also serve as an example to others not to engage in such conduct. If you find that MBNA willfully failed to follow reasonable procedures in its investigation of the plaintiff's dispute, you must award her the actual damage she sustained as a result of the defendant's failure. If you find that MBNA willfully failed to follow reasonable procedures in its investigation, and also find that the plaintiff suffered no actual damage or actual damages of less than a hundred dollars, then you must award the plaintiff at least a hundred dollars, but not more than one thousand dollars.

If you as a juror further find that the acts or omissions of the defendant that proximately caused the actual injury or damage to the plaintiff were willfully done, then you may, if in the exercise of your discretion, you unanimously chose to do so, add to the award of actual damages such amount as you shall unanimously agree to be proper as punitive damages. Whether or not to make any award punitive damages in addition to actual damages is a matter exclusively within your province.

You should bear in mind not only the conditions under which and the purpose for which the law permits an award of punitive damages to be made, but also the requirement of the law that the amount of such punitive damages must be fixed with calm discretion and sound reason, and must never be either awarded or fixed in amount because of any sympathy, bias or prejudice with respect to any party. You may consider the defendant's net worth in connection with punitive damages, and I believe their net worth at 12/31/01 was 7.7 million. And also under the law there should be a rational relationship between punitive damages, if you elect to award any, and the plaintiff's actual damages.

The Fair Credit Reporting Act is not required, does not require that credit card account records, including original applications, be kept in any particular form; however, the law does prohibit MBNA from maintaining its record in such manner as to consciously avoid knowing that information it is reporting is accurate.

A corporation may act only through natural persons as its agents or employees, and in general any agent or employee of a corporation may bind the corporation by his acts and declarations made while acting within the scope of his authority delegated to him by the corporation, or within the scope of his duties as an employee of the corporation.

If a corporation has established a standard of procedure for the accomplishment of an act, it is relevant to proving that it acted in a specific instance in conformance with that standard of procedure. And here again, you have heard evidence that everybody is getting electronic now days, and it is up to you to decide whether that is a reasonable way to conduct your business or not.

Now, that concludes my substantive charge.

MR. GETCHELL: May we approach?

BENCH CONFERENCE

MR. BENNETT: It is 7.7 billion.

THE COURT: Did I say million? I meant billion.

MR. GETCHELL: I think on instruction number 12 you said "accurate" instead of "inaccurate."

THE COURT: Okay.

MR. GETCHELL: And you had something that was not here, not printed, but you put in something, if the "plaintiff," sounded like "the defendant," had failed to prove. If you will instruct the plaintiff has the burden on everything.

THE COURT: I told them that the plaintiff failed to prove.

IN OPEN COURT

THE COURT: On my instruction number 12, ladies and gentlemen—you will have a copy of it—counsel tells me that I used the word "reporting is accurate," and it should have been "inaccurate." You will have it in printed form.

Isn't that your complaint, counsel?

MR. GETCHELL: Yes, Your Honor.

THE COURT: All right.

Your first order of business when you go back in your room is to select a foreperson. It is that individual's responsibility to preside over your deliberations and see that each juror is given full opportunity to express their views and participate in your verdict. The verdict must ultimately be unanimous. The foreperson's vote counts no more than any other. You will have in addition to the charge a verdict form. It says, we, the jury, unanimously find as follows. Did the defendant MBNA negligently fail to comply with the reporting act? It has, yes, no. If you answer yes, proceed to question two. If the answer is no, proceed to question three. And then, did the defendant's conduct proximately cause plaintiff's damage? If yes, you plug in a number. And then you would go to whether MBNA willfully failed to comply with the Fair Credit Act. And then you have the same sort of questions after that.

Now, from time to time during the course of your deliberations you may need to communicate with The Court. If you do, Mr. Winn will be sitting outside the jury room. Knock on the door and he will come in. And if you have a question, that should be in writing and signed by the foreperson. If it's something I can help you with, I will bring you back in and give you further guidance. Also, after you have reached a verdict, the foreperson has to sign it and date it. Knock on the door and let Mr. Winn know you have reached a verdict. I will bring you back in and receive it and send you home. I leave it up to jurors to determine their work hours after they start deliberating, but I will tell you now that if you haven't reached a verdict by 6:30 or 7:00 I will send you home for the evening because they close down here at night, and I don't want you to freeze up there in the jury room.

Everyone remain seated while the jury departs. And see that you take your handouts with you because you will now need those.

I will get you the instructions back in due course.

(Jury withdrew)

THE COURT: Before you put anything else on the record, let me warn you that I am about to go into some arrangements, and I would hate to mistake you for one of the defendants in the case. So do you have anything further to put on the record, Mr. Bennett?

MR. BENNETT: No, Your Honor.

THE COURT: Mr. Getchell.

MR. BENNETT: Although I didn't do it.

THE COURT: All right.

MR. GETCHELL: No, Your Honor, just so the record is clear that I was complaining about a minor mistake, that my main objections to the instructions were preserved.

THE COURT: Right. And you renew those for purposes of the record.

MR. GETCHELL: Right.

THE COURT: All right, fine.

Recess court for five minutes, and just leave your things in place, counsel. They don't need to be displaced.

Tell them we are ready to proceed with the arraignment.

(Recess)

THE COURT: Counsel, I have a question from the jury. What is the total amount of the outstanding credit debt in dispute as of 1/21/03? That is a simple question. What is the number? But what is the last dun you got from the parasitic outfit that buys this kind of paper?

MR. BENNETT: $20,300.

THE COURT: Okay. Is your client being dunned for that by whoever bought the paper?

MR. BENNETT: Yes.

THE COURT: Huh?

MR. BENNETT: Yes.

THE COURT: Okay. Bring the jury in. I will tell them the number is—

MR. GETCHELL: I want to object to answering that question.

THE COURT: Fine. Your objection is now a matter of record.

MR. GETCHELL: This is not a collection action. We don't even own the debt. So obviously if they are going to use that number for something, it would be to do a quotient verdict on something that is irrelevant.

THE COURT: That is fine.

MR. GETCHELL: I object to answering the question.

(Jury took its place in the well of the court)

THE COURT: Who is the foreperson? All right. Fine.

I have your question. What is the total amount of the outstanding credit debt in dispute as of 1/21/03? That figure is $20,300. But let me tell you the MBNA sold that to one of these outfits that pays a certain sum, and then I guess they are the ones that take over, sort of in a parasitic way. You pay a small sum for it, and then you try to collect the whole thing. But, bear in mind any action that is brought against her, she has defenses to it, that they still have to prove that she is liable for it on the account. That would be the burden of the purchaser of the paper for MBNA. Does that answer your question?

THE FOREPERSON: Yes.

THE COURT: Right.

Because they are doing their own collecting work. If they think somebody owes it, they get to sell it to one of these discounts, and then that outfit goes after them.

A JUROR: Thank you.

THE COURT: Okay.

(Jury withdrew)

Mr. Bennett, put any dissatisfaction that you have to The Court's instructions on the record, if you like.

MR. BENNETT: We do not have any objection.

THE COURT: All right.

Mr. Getchell, do you want to renew yours?

MR. GETCHELL: I would renew the one I made before they were brought in. And then I would add that I object to the general explanation of things being beyond the scope of this case.

THE COURT: All right. Fine.

Adjourn court awaiting furthered word from the jury.

(A recess was taken)

(Jury took its place in the jury box)

THE CLERK: Mr. Foreperson, has the jury reached a verdict in this matter?

THE FOREPERSON: Yes, we have.

THE CLERK: Please hand it to the Marshal.

THE COURT: Publish the verdict.

THE CLERK: Linda Johnson, plaintiff, versus MBNA America Bank, N.A., defendant. Civil action number 3:02 CV 523. Verdict form. We, the jury, unanimously find as follows:

Number one, did the defendant, MBNA, negligently fail to comply with the Fair Credit Reporting Act?

Yes.

Number two. Did the defendant's conduct proximately cause the plaintiff to suffer damage?

Yes

If yes, what amount of actual damage did the plaintiff suffer?

$90,000.300.

THE COURT: $90,300.

THE CLERK: 90,300.

Number three. Did the defendant fail to comply with the Fair Credit Reporting Act?

No.

Number four. Do you find that punitive damages are warranted under these facts?

No.

Signed by the foreperson, [Jury Foreperson], January 21st, 2003.

Ladies and gentlemen, was this your unanimous verdict?

THE COURT: Any motion while the jury is in the box?

MR. GETCHELL: Would you poll the jury?

THE COURT: Poll the jury.

THE CLERK: Ladies and gentlemen of the jury, if this was your verdict, please respond by saying "yes."

Juror number two, [Juror 2].

A JUROR: Yes.

THE CLERK: Juror number 3, [Juror 3]?

A JUROR: Yes.

THE CLERK: Juror number 6, [Juror 6]?

A JUROR: Yes.

THE COURT: Juror number 8, [Juror 8]?

A JUROR: Yes.

THE COURT: Juror number 10, [Juror 10]?

A JUROR: Yes.

THE COURT: Juror number 17 [Juror 17]?

A JUROR: Yes.

THE COURT: Juror number 20, [Juror 20]?

A JUROR: Yes.

THE COURT: Juror number 24, [Juror 24]?

A JUROR: Yes.

THE COURT: Ladies and gentlemen, that completes your assignment, but before I discharge you I want to express The Court's appreciation for your services, and also commend you for the conscientious manner in which you accepted your responsibilities and discharged them.

[Jury Foreperson], I want to single you out for special thanks, because you accepted the added responsibility of being foreperson, and you kept your forces together and deliberating until such time as they reached a verdict.

Leave all of your handouts in the jury room. My staff will see they are put in a shredder and, that will be the end of them.

Thank you for your services, and now that you have some experience under your belt, don't beg off if you get notified that I need more jurors in the future. All right.

Everyone remain seated while the jury departs.

Thank you for a job well done.

(Jury withdrew)

THE COURT: Judgment will be entered on the verdict. I want to thank counsel for your cooperation and helping to expedite the case so that the jury had it presented in a reasonable period of time and you didn't convert it in to a marathon sort of operation.

Cumulative Index

This is a cumulative index. Only use this index, not the one in the main volume which is now superseded. When a section is referenced in this index, turn to that section in both the main volume and this Supplement. Section references followed by "S" are found only in the Supplement.

ACCIDENT REPORTING BUREAUS
see also DRIVING RECORDS
FCRA, application, 2.6.8

ACCOMMODATION PARTIES
see also COSIGNERS
adverse action, disclosure, 6.4.2.3.6, 6.4.4.1
adverse information, reporting, 7.8.4.10.2
reasonable agency procedures, 7.8.4.10.2

ACCOUNTANTS
see also TAX PREPARATION SERVICES
GLB Act, application, 16.4.1.2

ACCOUNTS
bank account information
  pretexting, 12.2.1, 16.4.2.3
  number sharing, 16.4.1.9
checking accounts, see FINANCIAL SERVICES
credit accounts, see CREDIT ACCOUNTS

ACCURACY
see also ERRORS; INACCURATE INFORMATION
agency liability, 7.8
copies of previous reports, 7.8.4.10.3
credit scores, 14.8
definition, 7.1aS
duty to report accurately, 3.4.2
furnisher liability, 3.4.1, 3.14
investigative consumer reports, 9.4.1
Metro 2 format, 3.3.3.2, 3.3.3.7, 3.4.2
missing accounts, 13.6.4.2
standards
  affiliate information sharing, 13.5.2.1
  FTC Commentary, Appx. C
  furnishers of information, 3.4, 13.5.2.1
  inaccurate information, 7.8.3
  legislative history, 1.4.2, 1.4.3, 1.4.6
  maximum possible accuracy, 7.8.4.1, Appx. C.3
  reasonable procedures, 7.8.4
  reinvestigations, 3.11.2

ACTIONS
see also DISCOVERY; JURY TRIALS; LEGAL PROCEEDINGS; LITIGATION; PLEADINGS
burden of proof, see BURDEN OF PROOF
case selection, 10.8
civil rights, see CIVIL RIGHTS ACTIONS
claim selection, 10.6

class actions, see CLASS ACTIONS
collection suits, see COLLECTION SUITS
credit repair violations
  CROA violations, 15.2.6.2
  state law violations, 15.3.6
  telemarketing statutes, 15.4
damages, see DAMAGES
defamation, see DEFAMATION
defenses, see DEFENSES
evidence, see EVIDENCE
FCRA violations, see FCRA CLAIMS
identity theft, 13.5.5.4, 16.6.3
invasion of privacy, see INVASION OF PRIVACY
jurisdiction, see JURISDICTION
liability, see LIABILITY
libel, see DEFAMATION
limitations, see STATUTE OF LIMITATIONS
negligence, see NEGLIGENCE
parties, see PARTIES
reporting, see PUBLIC RECORD INFORMATION
reporting limitations, 8.3.4
reports on wrong consumer, 7.8.4.6
RESPA violations, 3.3.4.4, 13.5.2.2
state law, see STATE CLAIMS
successful action, 11.6.1

ACTS
see STATUTES

ACTUAL DAMAGES
see DAMAGES, ACTUAL

ADDRESS VERIFICATION SYSTEMS (AVS)
FCRA, application, 2.3.3

ADDRESSES
consumer reporting agency, disclosure, 6.4.3.2
ECOA notice requirements, 6.4.5
furnishers of information, error complaints, 3.4.4, 13.5.2.1
investigating agencies, disclosure, 6.6.3, 9.2.1.7
Medical Information Bureau, 4.5.5
major credit bureaus, 4.4.2.3
public record information users, 7.8.5.2

ADMINISTRATIVE ORDERS
child support enforcement, permissible use, 5.2.4.2

ADMINISTRATIVE SUMMONS OR SUBPOENAS
consumer reports, obtaining, 5.2.1

ADOPTION *Fair Credit Reporting / 2004 Supplement*

References are to sections; references followed by "S" appear only in this Supplement

ADOPTION AGENCIES
see also GOVERNMENT AGENCIES; SOCIAL SERVICE AGENCIES
FCRA, application, 2.3.6.8, 2.5.2

ADVERSE ACTION
see also CREDIT, denial
affiliates, by, 6.4.4.4, 10.2.3.4
blemished credit records, 13.6.2
check writing privileges, 6.4.2.3.5, 6.4.2.7.1
collectors affiliated with reporting agency, 13.4.3
consumer report, basis, 5.1.7, 6.4
consumer's account, review, 6.4.2.7.2
cosigner's credit history, 6.4.2.3.6, 6.4.4.1
credit card authorizations, 2.4.4
credit transactions, 6.4.2.3, 6.4.2.7.2
counteroffer acceptance, 6.4.2.3.2aS
definition, 6.4.2.3.1
   denial of credit, defined, 6.4.2.3.2
ECOA obligations, 6.4.5
   model form, Appx. E.4
   record retention, 10.11.4
employment purposes, 6.4.2.4
file disclosure, fees, 4.4.5.1.1
FTC interpretations, Appx. C
government benefits and licenses, 6.4.2.6
impermissible purpose situations, 5.1.7
information other than consumer report, basis, 6.4.4
insufficient credit history, 13.6.2
insurance purposes, 5.2.6, 6.4.2.5
investigative reports, 9.2.1.7
investment opportunities, 6.4.2.7.1
leases, 6.4.2.3.3, 6.4.2.7.1
notice, *see under* NOTICE
prescreening exclusion, 6.4.2.3.7
property sale, 6.4.2.3.4, 6.4.2.7.1
reasons for, 6.4.4.3, 6.4.5
reporting by agency, 13.2.6, 13.7.8.2
reporting by creditor, 2.6.3
state law preemption, 10.4.4
third party credit requests, 2.4.5
third party information, 6.4.4.1
transactions initiated by consumer, 6.4.2.7.1

ADVERSE INFORMATION
affiliate sharing, 6.4.4.4
checks as basis for, identification, 4.5.6
consumer reporting agency obligations
   investigative reports, 9.4.2
   obsolete information, 13.2.5, Ch. 8
consumer's file
   deleting from, 8.1.3
   examining, 4.2.2
cosigners, 3.3.5.4.1
credit repair organizations, concealing, 15.2.5.2
disputed debts, 3.3.4, 3.5.3, 13.5.2.2
ECOA restrictions, 3.3.5.2, 13.5.2.2
explaining, 13.6.8
home mortgages, guidelines, 13.7.2.1
identifying information to governmental agencies, 5.2.3
inaccurate, *see* INACCURATE INFORMATION
insufficient credit history as, 13.6.1
investigative reports, verification, 9.4.2.3, 10.2.2.5
irrelevant information, *see* IRRELEVANT INFORMATION
notice

consumer report, 6.4
cosigners, 3.3.5.4.1
other than consumer report, 6.4.4
overview, 6.2
public record information, 6.6.2, 7.8.5.2, 13.3.4
receipt by reporting agency, 13.2.3
state law, 6.5.6, 13.2.3
student loans, 13.5.2.3
obsolete information, *see* OBSOLETE INFORMATION
public record information, *see* PUBLIC RECORD INFORMATION
source, disclosure, 6.4.4.3
student loans, 13.5.2.3
third party, obtaining from, 6.4.4
updating, 13.6.8
use, *see* ADVERSE ACTION
verification, reasonable procedures, 10.2.2.1

ADVERSE USE
see ADVERSE ACTION

ADVERTISEMENTS
credit repair, 15.2.2.7

AFFILIATE SHARING OF INFORMATION
see also AFFILIATES
accuracy standards, 3.4.6, 13.5.2.1
adverse action, notice, 4.5.8, 6.4.4.4
disclosures
   adverse action, notice, 6.4.4.4
   form of disclosures, 4.4.1.5
   lack of standards, 4.5.8
FCRA application, 2.4.2, 3.2.2.1
   federal standards, Appx. A.6
FCRA liability, 10.2.3.4
GLB Act, application, 16.4.1.5
legislative history, 1.4.6
notice to consumer, 6.5.4
state law preemption, 10.4.4

AFFILIATES
adverse action, 6.4.4.4, 10.2.3.4
collection and reporting agencies, 13.4.2, 13.4.3
consumer files, disclosure, 4.4.1.5
disputing debts with, 3.4.6, 13.5.2.1
information sharing, *see* AFFILIATE SHARING OF INFORMATION

AGE
credit headers, inclusion, 2.3.4
information re, consumer report status, 2.3.3

AGENCIES
adoption, *see* ADOPTION AGENCIES
child support, *see* CHILD SUPPORT ENFORCEMENT AGENCIES
credit reporting, *see* CONSUMER REPORTING AGENCIES
federal, *see* FEDERAL AGENCIES
government, *see* GOVERNMENT AGENCIES
law enforcement, *see* LAW ENFORCEMENT AGENCIES
local government, *see* LOCAL GOVERNMENT AGENCIES
social service, *see* SOCIAL SERVICE AGENCIES
state, *see* STATE AGENCIES
welfare, *see* WELFARE AGENCIES

AGENTS
consumer reports, obtaining, 5.1.4

340

Cumulative Index / 2004 Supplement

References are to sections; references followed by "S" appear only in this Supplement

AGREEMENTS
see also CONTRACTS
disputed debts, settlement
    breach of agreement, 13.5.4.3
    model agreements, 13.5.4.4, 13.5.4.5
    selecting correct language, 13.5.4.3
FTC consent agreements, *see* CONSENT AGREEMENTS (FTC)
repayment, *see* REPAYMENT AGREEMENTS

ALIMONY
see also CHILD SUPPORT; DIVORCE PROCEEDINGS
consumer reports, use, 5.3.2, 13.3.7.5
reliance for credit, 13.2.7.2.2

APARTMENT LEASES
see RESIDENTIAL LEASES

APARTMENT MANAGERS
consumer reports, obtaining, 5.1.4

APPLIANCE LOANS
what to avoid, 13.7.7

APPRAISAL REPORTS
right to copy, 6.4.5

ARBITRATION CLAUSES
enforceability, 10.14
    credit repair contracts, 15.2.6.1

ARRESTS
see PUBLIC RECORD INFORMATION

ASSIGNEES
CROA, application, 15.2.2.5, 15.2.2.6

ASSOCIATED CREDIT BUREAUS, INC.
see CONSUMER DATA INDUSTRY ASSOCIATION, INC. (CDIA)

ATTORNEY FEES AND COSTS
CROA claims, 15.2.6.2
FCRA claims
    bad faith, 11.1, 11.6.1
    establishing, 11.1
    liability for, 11.6.1
    maximizing awards, 11.6.3
    prevailing party, 11.1, 11.6.1
    right to, 11.1
    standards, 11.6.2
federal fee shifting standards, 11.6.2.2
lodestar approach, 11.6.2.2
published awards, quick reference, 11.7
Rule 68, 11.6.5
settled cases, 11.6.4
settlement agreements, breach, 13.5.4.3
successful action, 11.6.1
tort claims, 11.6.3

ATTORNEYS
consumer files
    power of attorney disclosures, 4.4.3.2
    reinvestigation requests, 7.3.2.2
consumer reports
    certification of permissible use, 5.4.2.2
    impermissible use, 5.3.4
    obtaining, 5.1.4, 5.2.1, 10.11.3.4
    permissible user, 5.2.4.2
    prospective clients, 5.3.4
CROA, application, 15.2.2.4

FCRA, application, 2.6.7
fees, *see* ATTORNEY FEES AND COSTS
legal directories, *see* LEGAL DIRECTORIES
litigation aids, *see* LITIGATION AIDS
practice tips, *see* PRACTICE TIPS
subpoenas issued by, court order status, 5.2.1, 10.11.3.4

AUDIT TRAIL
disclosure, 4.5.7.3
inaccurate information, 7.8.4.2

AUTOMOBILE DEALERS
see also DEALER PAPER
credit repair laws, application
    CROA, 15.2.2.7
    state law, 15.3.4
disclosure obligations, 6.4.4.1
GLB Act, application, 16.4.1.2
used car loans, 13.7.5

AUTOMOBILE INSURANCE
see INSURANCE

AUTOMOBILE LEASES
see also PERSONAL PROPERTY LEASES
blemished credit record, impact, 13.7.5
fraud lists, 13.2.2, 13.3.6
return of car, advertised rewards, 13.3.7.4

BAD CHECK LISTS
see CHECK CASHING LISTS

BAD DEBT LISTS
see also CONSUMER LISTS
publication, 13.3.7.4

BAD DRIVING LISTS
see also CONSUMER LISTS
specialized agencies, 13.2.2

BANKRUPTCY
advantages, 13.6.9
discharge, time, 13.7.2.1
Metro 2 format reporting, 3.3.3.13
mortgage applications, impact, 13.7.2.1
reporting limitations, 8.3.7, 13.2.5
reporting standards, 7.8.4.10.2
risk scoring, 14.2.2.3
student loans, impact, 13.6.11, 13.7.9
utility services, effect, 13.7.4

BANKS
see also FINANCIAL INSTITUTIONS; FURNISHERS OF INFORMATION
accounts, *see* FINANCIAL SERVICES
FCRA, application, 2.6.3
GLB Act, application, 16.4.1

BENEFITS
see GOVERNMENT BENEFITS; INSURANCE BENEFITS

BILLINGS
see also ACCOUNTS
disputed amounts, *see* CREDIT DISPUTES
errors
    definition, 3.3.4.3, 13.5.2.2
    FCBA, regulation, 3.3.4.3, 13.5.2.2
    home mortgages, 3.3.4.4, 13.5.2.2
    open-end credit, 3.3.4.3
records, disclosure, 4.5.7.3

BONDS
credit repair organizations, posting, 15.3

BOUNCED CHECKS
see RETURNED CHECKS

BROKERS
information brokers, see RESELLERS
loan brokers, see LOAN BROKERS
real estate brokers, see REAL ESTATE AGENTS

BULK SALES
consumer files, 5.1.5

BULLETINS
see LAW ENFORCEMENT BULLETINS

BURDEN OF PROOF
see also EVIDENCE
FCRA violations
   actual damages, 11.2.1
   attorney fees, 11.6.2.2
   negligence, 10.2.2.3, 10.2.4.2
   punitive damages, 11.4.1.1
   reasonable procedure violations, 7.8.4.2
   reasonable procedures as defense, 10.2.4.2
   willful noncompliance, 11.4.1.2
tort claims, 10.3.6

BUSINESS CREDIT
see also COMMERCIAL TRANSACTIONS; CREDIT
consumer reports
   impermissible use, 5.1.7, 5.2.9.2
   permissible purpose, 5.2.4.3
denial, notice, 6.4.2.7.1
ECOA, application, 6.4.5, 13.6.4.5
FCRA, application, 2.3.3, 2.3.6.5
reports for, see COMMERCIAL REPORTS

BUSINESS DEBTS
collection, consumer report, permissible use, 5.2.4.3

BUSINESS INSURANCE
see also INSURANCE
consumer reports, use, 5.2.6, 5.2.9.2
denial, notice, 6.4.2.7.1

BUSINESS PURPOSES
see BUSINESS CREDIT

BUSINESS REPORTS
see COMMERCIAL REPORTS

BUSINESS TRANSACTIONS
see also COMMERCIAL TRANSACTIONS
consumer reports
   adverse use, notice obligations, 6.4.2.7.1
   impermissible use, 5.1.7
   permissible purposes, 2.3.6.10.1, 5.2.4.3, 5.2.9
definition, 5.2.9.1
FCRA, application, 2.3.6.1, 2.3.6.10
insurance benefit issuance, status, 2.3.6.7.2
lease transactions, status, 2.3.6.10.3
litigation, status, 2.3.6.10.1

BUSINESSES
see also CORPORATIONS; PARTNERSHIPS; SOLE PROPRIETORSHIPS
affiliated, see AFFILIATES
consumer reports, impermissible use, 5.3.9

credit, see BUSINESS CREDIT
FCRA, application, 2.3.3, 2.3.6.5.1
insurance, see BUSINESS INSURANCE
owners, consumer reports on, 5.2.4.3
transactions, see BUSINESS TRANSACTIONS

CASE LAW
unreported, copies, 1.1.3

CDIA
see CONSUMER DATA INDUSTRY ASSOCIATION, INC. (CDIA)

CDV
see CONSUMER DISPUTE VERIFICATION (CDV) FORM

CERTIFICATION
see also VERIFICATION
consumer reports, permissible use
   blanket certification, 7.7.1
   electronic communication, 5.4.4
   generally, 5.4.2
   obsolete information, 8.5.4
   violations, 10.2.4.1
investigative reports, 9.2.1.6, 10.2.4.3
resellers, 2.6.2, 10.2.2.8

CHARGES
see FEES

CHECK APPROVAL COMPANIES
see also CONSUMER REPORTING AGENCIES
described, 13.2.2
FCRA, application, 2.3.6.3, 2.6.1
GLB Act, application, 16.4.1.2
lists issued by, see CHECK CASHING LISTS

CHECK CASHING LISTS
see also CHECK APPROVAL COMPANIES; CONSUMER LISTS
adverse use, notice, 6.4.2.3.5
blemished report, implications, 13.3.6
coding schemes, 5.3.8.2, 13.3.6
consumer report status, 2.3.3, 2.3.6.3
obsolete information, 13.3.6
privacy issues, 13.3.6
publication, 13.3.7.4

CHECK CASHING REPORTS
see CHECK CASHING LISTS

CHECK GUARANTEE BUSINESSES
see CHECK APPROVAL COMPANIES; CHECK CASHING LISTS

CHECKS
see also CHECK APPROVAL COMPANIES; CHECK CASHING LISTS
adverse characterizations, identification disclosure, 4.5.6
credit, status as, 5.2.4.1, 6.4.2.3.5
payment by
   consumer report, permissible use, 5.2.9.1
   denial, notice requirements, 6.4.2.3.5, 6.4.2.7.1
returned checks, see RETURNED CHECKS

CHILD CUSTODY
see CHILD SUPPORT; DIVORCE PROCEEDINGS

CHILD SUPPORT
see also DIVORCE PROCEEDINGS

References are to sections; references followed by "S" appear only in this Supplement

CHILD SUPPORT (*cont.*)
consumer report
  impermissible uses, 13.3.7.5
  permissible uses, 2.3.6.12, 5.2.11
enforcement, *see* CHILD SUPPORT ENFORCEMENT AGENCIES
overdue, inclusion in consumer report, 3.3.5.4.2, 5.3.2
reliance for credit, 13.2.7.2.2

CHILD SUPPORT COLLECTION UNITS
see CHILD SUPPORT ENFORCEMENT AGENCIES

CHILD SUPPORT ENFORCEMENT AGENCIES
see also CHILD SUPPORT
computer linkups with reporting agencies, 5.4.4
consumer reports, permissible users, 5.2.4.2, 5.3.2
determination of support levels, 2.3.6.12, 5.2.11
disclosure notice, 6.5.5
information, provision to reporting agency, 3.3.5.4.2, 5.3.2
state plans, 5.2.11

CITY DIRECTORIES
consumer report status, 2.3.3, 2.3.5.3

CIVIL RIGHTS ACTIONS
credit reporting abuses, 10.5
privacy from governmental intrusion, 16.2

CIVIL SUITS
see ACTIONS; COLLECTION SUITS; LITIGATION

CLASS ACTIONS
credit reporting violations, 10.7.2

CLEARINGHOUSE NUMBERS
see also NATIONAL CENTER ON POVERTY LAW
unreported cases, 1.1.3

CODING SCHEMES
check cashing lists, 5.3.8.2, 13.3.6
consumer files, 4.8.1

COLLECTION AGENCIES
see also DEBT COLLECTORS
accounts placed with, reporting, 8.3.3
affiliated with reporting agency
  credit rating, notice of adverse effect, 4.4.5.1.1
  dealing with, 13.4.2
  disclosure obligations, 13.4.3
bad debt lists, publication, 13.3.7.4
consumer report, permissible use, 5.2.4.2
FCRA, application, 2.6.4
Metro 2 format, use, 3.3.3.9
name restrictions, 13.4.4
threats to report debt, 13.4

COLLECTION SUITS
see also CREDITORS
consumer reports, use, 13.3.7.5
court orders covering reporting issues, 13.5.4.7
credit card disputes, 3.3.4.3, 13.5.2.2
reporting limitations, 8.3.4
settlement, resolving reporting issues, 13.5.4

COLLEGE PLACEMENT OFFICES
FCRA, application, 2.6.6

COMMERCIAL REPORTS
accuracy standards, 7.8.4.1
compilation and use, 5.2.9.2
consumer report status, 2.3.5.2, 2.3.5.4, 2.3.6.5
false pretenses, obtaining under, 5.6.4
litigation, use, 5.3.4
tort claims, 10.3.1

COMMERCIAL TRANSACTIONS
see also BUSINESS CREDIT; BUSINESS TRANSACTIONS
consumer reports, use, 5.2.9.2

COMMON LAW
privacy protections, 16.3, 16.5
torts, *see* TORT CLAIMS

COMMUNITY PROPERTY STATES
spouses, credit information, 13.2.7.2.2

COMPANIES
affiliated, *see* AFFILIATES
businesses, *see* BUSINESSES
check approval companies, *see* CHECK APPROVAL COMPANIES
consumer reporting companies, *see* CONSUMER REPORTING AGENCIES
corporations, *see* CORPORATIONS
credit reporting companies, *see* CONSUMER REPORTING AGENCIES
landlord reporting companies, *see* TENANT SCREENING COMPANIES
tenant screening, *see* TENANT SCREENING COMPANIES

COMPLAINTS
see PLEADINGS

COMPUTER DATING SERVICES
see DATING SERVICES

COMPUTER ERRORS
see also ELECTRONIC COMMUNICATION; ERRORS
creditors' files, 7.2.2
legislative response, 1.4.3
mismerged reporting files, 7.2.4, 7.8.4.6
transcription errors, 7.2.6, 7.8.4.8

COMPUTER FRAUD AND ABUSE ACT
see also COMPUTER FRAUD LAWS
financial information, protections, 16.4.2.1

COMPUTER FRAUD LAWS
FCRA application, 12.3
federal statute, *see* COMPUTER FRAUD AND ABUSE ACT
financial information, protections, 16.4.2.1

COMPUTER HOOKUPS
see ELECTRONIC COMMUNICATION

CONDITIONAL PRIVILEGE
defense to tort action, 10.3.7, 10.3.9

CONFIDENTIALITY
see also PRIVACY
consumer files, legislative history, 1.4.2, 1.4.3
credit score calculations, 14.5.4
discovery requests and, 10.11.3.2
financial information, 16.5
investigative reports, sources, 4.5.3, 9.2.2.3, 9.2.3
litigation, sample order, Appx. I.6
Metro 2 format, 3.3.3.1
purpose of FCRA, 5.1.1

CONSENT
see also WAIVER
consumer reports
  business purposes, 5.2.6, 5.2.9.2
  consumer's, effect, 5.2.2
FCRA disclosures, presence of another person, 4.4.1.3

CONSENT AGREEMENTS (FTC)
see also FEDERAL TRADE COMMISSION (FTC)
credit repair agencies, Appx. H.5
Equifax, Appx. H.2, Appx. H.8S
Experian, Appx. H.1
Gramm-Leach-Bliley violation, Appx. H.7S
Quicken Loans, Appx. H.6S
resellers, Appx. H.4
Trans Union, Appx. H.3

CONSOLIDATION SERVICES
see RESELLERS

CONSUMER
see CONSUMERS

CONSUMER CREDIT INFORMATION
see CONSUMER REPORTS

CONSUMER CREDIT PROTECTION ACT (CCPA)
see also EQUAL CREDIT OPPORTUNITY ACT (ECOA); FAIR CREDIT BILLING ACT (FCBA); FAIR CREDIT REPORTING ACT (FCRA); FAIR DEBT COLLECTION PRACTICES ACT (FDCPA)
rights under, exercise, discrimination, 3.3.5.2, 3.14.4, 13.5.2.2

CONSUMER CREDIT TRANSACTIONS
see CREDIT TRANSACTIONS

CONSUMER DATA INDUSTRY ASSOCIATION, INC. (CDIA)
Metro 2, creation, 3.3.1
professional liability insurance, 10.11.3.5
website, 3.3.2

CONSUMER DISPUTE VERIFICATION (CDV) FORM
electronic (ACDV) communication, 3.10, 3.12.3
Metro 2 alternative, circumstances, 3.3.2
notification of furnisher, 3.10

CONSUMER FILES
see also CONSUMER REPORTING AGENCIES; CONSUMER REPORTS; CREDIT HISTORY; CREDIT RECORD
additional information, rights, 7.6.1.3, 7.8.3.2, 7.8.4.10.4, 7.8.4.11, 13.6.4
adverse information, *see* ADVERSE INFORMATION
ancillary information, 4.5.7.3
audit trail, 4.5.7.3
authorized users, 13.2.8.1
bankruptcy, effect, 13.6.9
billing records, 4.5.7.3
bulk sales, 5.1.5
business reports, commingling, 2.3.5.4
coded information, 4.8.1
computer access, 5.4.4
consumer relations information, 4.5.7.3
consumer report distinguished, 2.3.1
contents
  checks, identifying information, 4.5.6
  examining, 4.2.2, 13.2.1
  FCRA rights, 4.3, 4.5
  fees, 4.4.5, 6.2, 13.2.1, 13.4.3
  obsolete information, 13.2.5
  obtaining, procedures, 4.4
  restrictions, 13.2.3, 13.2.4, 13.2.7.2.1
  third party information, 13.2.7.2.1
  unreasonable preconditions, 4.4.4
copies, provision, 4.4.2.3, 4.5.1
credit scores, *see* CREDIT SCORES
dating of information, 8.5.3
disclosure of rights by credit repair organizations, 15.2.3
disclosure rights, 4.1, 4.3, 4.4.2.1, 4.5, 9.2.3, 13.4.3
disclosure violations, 10.2.2.9
disclosures, obtaining, 4.4.2.3
disputed information
  cleaning up after resolution, 13.5.4.8
  cloaking procedures, 7.4.2
  correction, 3.5.4, 7.4.2, 7.4.3, 7.8.3.2, 13.5.4.5, 13.5.4.7
  expedited dispute resolution, 7.3.4.2
  furnishers, notification, 7.3.5.2
  irrelevant information, 7.3.3
  missing accounts, 13.6.4.2
  monitoring after resolution, 13.5.4.9
  numerous inquiries, 7.3.3
  past users, notification, 7.4.3
  procedures, 7.3
  public record information, 13.6.10
  reinsertion notice, 6.7, 7.5
  reinvestigation, *see* REINVESTIGATIONS
  removal, 13.5.4.1, 13.5.4.4
  rights, 7.3.1
  statement of dispute, *see* STATEMENTS OF DISPUTE
  verification, 7.4.2
errors, *see* INACCURATE INFORMATION
explanations, inclusion, 13.6.8.2, 7.8.4.10.5
guarantors, special notation, 7.8.4.10.2
historical information, removal through negotiation, 13.6.7
identifying information, 7.8.4.6
  furnishing to government agencies, 5.2.3
illogical files, 7.2.7, 7.8.4.9
inaccurate, *see* INACCURATE INFORMATION
incomplete files, 7.2.8, 7.3.2.1, 7.6.1.3, 7.8.3.2, 7.8.4.10.1, 13.6.4
information collected, purpose, 2.3.5
information not considered part of file, 4.5.7.3
insufficient credit history, dealing with, 13.6.2–13.6.4
insurance purposes, segregation, 13.3.3
irrelevant information, *see* IRRELEVANT INFORMATION
medical information, 4.5.5
mismerged files, 7.2.4, 7.8.4.6
missing accounts, adding, 13.6.4
negative information, *see* ADVERSE INFORMATION
new files or information
  agency discretion, 7.8.4.10.5, 7.8.4.11, 13.6.4.2
  consumer requests, 7.6.1.3, 13.6.4.3
no file, adverse action based on, 6.4.2.2, 13.6.1
obsolete information, *see* OBSOLETE INFORMATION
past due accounts, currency, 7.8.4.10.3
power of attorney for disclosure requests, 4.4.3.2
prior use, effect, 2.3.5.2
purging of information, 8.1.3, 13.6.4.4, 13.2.5
reasons for credit denial, inclusion, 7.8.4.10.5
reinsertion notice, 6.7, 7.5
reinvestigation of information, *see* REINVESTIGATIONS
reliability standards, 7.8.4.4

CONSUMER FILES (*cont.*)
repayment schedules, reporting, 13.6.6
restrictions on information gathered, 13.2.3
sales between agencies, 2.3.1, 5.1.5
segregation technique, 13.6.12
sources of information, *see* FURNISHERS OF INFORMATION
spouses
    ECOA requirements, 13.6.4.5
    information on, FCRA restrictions, 13.2.7.2.1
standards, legislative history, 1.4.2
statements, inclusion, 7.6, 13.6.8.2
    see also STATEMENTS OF DISPUTE
supplementing information, 13.6.4
tenant screening companies, 13.7.3
transcription errors, 7.2.6, 7.8.4.8
updating, 4.5.1, 7.8.4.10.3–7.8.4.10.5, 13.2.3, 13.2.5, 13.2.7.1, 13.4.2, 13.5.2.1, 13.5.4.8, 13.5.4.9
virtually every American, 4.2.1
withdrawing information, 13.5.4.1

CONSUMER FINANCIAL PROTECTION ACT
pending legislation, 16.7

CONSUMER LISTS
bad debts, *see* BAD DEBT LISTS
bad driving, *see* BAD DRIVING LISTS
blemished report, implications, 13.3.6
check cashing, *see* CHECK CASHING LISTS
coded, 5.3.8.2, 13.3.7.3
consumer report status, 2.3.3, 5.3.8.2, 5.3.8.5
credit guides, *see* CREDIT GUIDES
FCRA, application, 2.3.3
fraud lists, 13.2.2, 13.3.6
identifying information, consumer report status, 5.2.3
impermissible use, 5.3.8
insurance claims, *see* INSURANCE CLAIM LISTS
judgment debtors, 13.3.7.4
law enforcement agencies, *see* LAW ENFORCEMENT BULLETINS
mailing lists, *see* MAILING LISTS
prescreened, *see* PRESCREENED REPORTS
skip tracing, 2.3.6.3
specialized lists, 13.2.2
target marketing, *see* TARGET MARKETING LISTS
worker's compensation, *see* WORKER'S COMPENSATION LISTS

CONSUMER RELATIONS INFORMATION
disclosure, 4.5.7.3

CONSUMER REPORTING AGENCIES
see also CHECK APPROVAL COMPANIES; CREDIT BUREAUS; INSPECTION BUREAUS; MEDICAL INFORMATION AGENCIES; RESELLERS; TENANT SCREENING COMPANIES
accident reporting bureaus, status, 2.6.8
account numbers, information sharing, 16.4.1.9
address, disclosure, 6.4.3.2
agents, status, 5.1.4
attorneys, status, 2.6.7
bad debt lists, publication, 13.3.7.4
banks, status, 2.6.3
check approval companies, status, 2.3.6.4, 2.6.1
collection agencies affiliated with, *see under* COLLECTION AGENCIES
collection agencies, status, 2.6.4
college placement offices, status, 2.6.6
computer fraud, liability, 12.3
consumer reports, interdependence, 2.3.2, 2.5.1
consumer's guide, Appx. J
consumer's written instructions, effect, 5.2.2
contracts, sample, Appx. G.1
cooperative loan exchanges, status, 2.5.4
credit bureau collection departments, status, 2.6.4
credit bureaus, status, 2.6.1
credit header information, 2.3.4, 16.4.1.11
credit repair agencies, dealing with, 15.1, 15.2.1
credit scores, 14.2.2.1
creditors, receipt of information from, Ch. 3, 13.4
creditors, status, 2.5.4, 2.6.3
data entry, 7.8.4.8
definition, 2.1, 2.5.1
detective agencies, status, 2.6.5
disclosure obligations, 4.1, 4.3–4.6, 6.2
discovery, informal, 10.11.2
discretion to furnish reports, 5.1.2, 5.1.4, 5.2.2
disputed debts
    expedited dispute resolution, 7.3.4.2
    formal dispute process, 3.9
    notice to furnisher, 3.10
    obligations, 13.5.3
    reinsertion notice, 6.7, 7.5
electronic communications, 3.3.1, 5.4.4
    Metro 2 Format, 3.3.2, 3.3.3
    see also METRO 2 FORMAT
employees' liability, 5.5, 12.3
employees providing disclosure, 4.4.1.4, 4.8.1
employers
    certification of notice, 5.2.5.3
    permissible use, 5.2.5.2
    status, 2.6.5
    Summary of Rights, providing, 5.2.5.4, 13.3.4
employment agencies, status, 2.6.5
Equifax, *see* EQUIFAX
errors
    duty to correct, 7.3.2.2
    prevalence, 7.2.1
exclusions, 2.5.5, 2.5.6
Experian, *see* EXPERIAN (TRW)
FBI security clearances, 4.5.7.2, 5.2.12
FCRA, application, 2.1, 2.5
FCRA violations
    disclosure violations, 4.3, 10.2.2.9
    generally, 5.4.1
    impermissible reports, 5.4.1, 5.5, 10.2.2.3
    improper handling of disputes, 10.2.2.10
    inaccurate reports, 10.2.2.1
    investigative reports, 10.2.2.5
    liability, 10.2.1
    notice violations, 6.9
    obsolete reports, 10.2.2.2
    per se UDAP violation, 10.4.2
    public record information, 10.2.2.6
    reasonable procedures, failure to maintain, 5.4.1
    testers, use, 10.11.2
federal agencies, status, 2.5.6
fees, *see* FEES
files, *see* CONSUMER FILES
finance companies, status, 2.6.3
financial institution status, 2.3.4

CONSUMER REPORTING AGENCIES (cont.)
financial institutions, status, 2.6.3
FTC commentary, Appx. C
FTC consent agreements, Appx. H
furnishers of information, see FURNISHERS OF INFORMATION
GLB Act, application, 2.3.4, 16.4.1.2, 16.4.1.5, 16.4.1.9
government agencies, status, 2.5.6, 2.5.7
identification requests, 4.4.3.1, 5.4.3
identity of agency, disclosure, 6.4.3.2
identity theft
　blocking of information, 16.6.1a.4.1S
　notification of, 7.8.4.7
inaccurate information, see INACCURATE INFORMATION
independent contractors, status, 2.5.4
information collected by, see CONSUMER FILES
information furnished by, see CONSUMER REPORTS; INVESTIGATIVE CONSUMER REPORTS
information furnished to, Ch. 3
　see also FURNISHERS OF INFORMATION
inspection bureaus, status, 2.6.1
insurance claim compilers, status, 2.6.8
insurance claim exchanges, status, 2.3.6.7.2
investigative reports
　see also INVESTIGATIVE CONSUMER REPORTS
　disclosure obligations, 9.2.3
　preparation, 9.1.1
joint lenders or users, status, 2.4.5, 2.5.5
liability, see under LIABILITY
loan companies, status, 2.6.3
local government agencies, status, 2.5.7
location, disclosure, 6.4.3.2
management policies, improper, 7.8.4.3
medical information agencies, status, 2.6.1
missing accounts, obligations, 13.6.4.2
motor vehicle departments (state), status, 2.5.7, 2.6.8
nationwide reporting agencies
　see also EQUIFAX; EXPERIAN (TRW); TRANS UNION
　automated reinvestigation system, 3.12.2
　defined, 2.5.8
　prescreening opt-out notification system, 5.3.8.4.4
　special provisions, 2.5.8
　toll-free number, disclosure, 6.4.3.2
notice obligations
　disputed debts, 13.5.2.1
　employment purposes, 6.4.2.4, 6.5.2S
　expedited dispute resolution, 7.3.4.2
　overview, 6.2
　prescreening, 6.6.4
　public record information, 6.6.2
　reinsertion of information, 6.2, 6.7, 7.5
　reinvestigation results, 3.12.2, 7.4.1
　violations, 6.9
number of inquiries, reporting, 7.8.4.10.2
overview, 1.2
police departments, status, 2.6.8
prescreening, see PRESCREENED REPORTS
public record information, reporting, 6.6.2
reasonable procedures, see REASONABLE PROCEDURES
record retention, 10.11.4
　request records, 5.4.5
refusal to issue report, 5.1.2
refusal to provide report to litigant, 7.2.9
regulation, 1.3.1

reinsertion of information
　certification from furnisher, 7.5
　notice, 6.2, 6.7, 7.5
　standards, 7.5
reinvestigation of information, see REINVESTIGATIONS
reports, see CONSUMER REPORTS
resellers, status, 2.6.2
sample contract, Appx. G.1
security procedures, 7.8.4.8
sheriff's departments, status, 2.6.8
social service agencies, status, 2.5.2
sources
　see also FURNISHERS OF INFORMATION
　described, 13.2.3
　disclosure, 4.5.3
　insuring accuracy, 7.8.4.4
　withdrawal of information, 13.5.4.1
specialized agencies, 13.2.2
state agencies, status, 2.5.7
state law, application, 10.4.1, 10.4.4
statements of dispute, obligations, 7.6.1.1, 7.7.1
student loan defaults, report receipt, 13.5.2.3
suits against, 10.7.3
summary of consumer rights
　form described, 4.6
　employment purposes, providing, 5.2.5.2, 13.3.4
　provision, 6.3
superbureaus, status, 2.6.2
telephone companies, status, 2.6.9
telephone number, disclosure, 6.4.3.2
tenant screening companies, status, 2.6.1
third party authorizations, 4.4.3.2
Trans Union, see TRANS UNION
TRW, see EXPERIAN (TRW)
UDAP violations, 10.4.2
Universal Data Form
　sample, Appx. G.2
　use by creditors, 3.3.2
　use for corrections, 3.5.4
unsolicited reports, 5.1.2

CONSUMER REPORTS
see also CONSUMER REPORTING AGENCIES; CONSUMER FILES; CREDIT BUREAUS; EMPLOYMENT REPORTS; INSURANCE REPORTS; INVESTIGATIVE CONSUMER REPORTS
accuracy standards, 7.8.3, 7.8.4
additional information, 7.6.1.3, 13.6.4
administrative summons, 5.2.1
adverse information, see ADVERSE INFORMATION
adverse use, see ADVERSE ACTION
affiliate information sharing, status, 2.4.2, 10.2.3.4
agencies affiliated with collectors, 13.4.3
agents, obtaining, 5.1.4
authorized users, 13.2.8.1
bankruptcy, special procedures, 7.8.4.10.2
between agencies, 5.1.5
blemished, implications, 13.3
blocking access to litigants, 7.2.9
business reports, status, 2.3.5.2, 2.3.5.4, 2.3.6.5
check approval companies, information from, status, 2.3.6.3
check cashing lists, status, 2.3.6.3
child support debts, inclusion, 5.3.2, 13.2.3
city directories, status, 2.3.5.3

CONSUMER REPORTS (*cont.*)
closed accounts, voluntary, 3.8, 13.2.8.4
commercial reports, status, 2.3.5.2, 2.3.5.4, 2.3.6.5
confidentiality, 5.1.1
consent of consumer
　business purposes, 5.2.6, 5.2.9.2
　employment purposes, 6.5.2S
　medical information, 6.5.3
　written instructions, 5.2.2
consumer reporting agencies, interdependence, 2.3.2, 2.5.1
consumer's guide, Appx. J
contents, restrictions, 10.4.4, 13.2.3, 13.2.4, 13.2.5
continuing reports, 5.4.2.3
copies, 4.4.2.2, 4.4.2.3, 4.5.1, 4.7, 6.4.3.1, 7.8.4.10.3
corrections
　disputed debts, 13.5.4.9
　notification of previous users, 7.7
cosigners, 7.8.4.10.2
court orders, 5.2.1
credit card authorizations, status, 2.4.4
credit headers, status, 2.3.4
definition, 2.1, 2.3, 2.4
deletion of information by agency, 13.6.4.4
denial of credit, 7.8.4.10.5, 13.2.6
disclosure, *see* DISCLOSURE
discrimination, prohibition, 3.3.5.2
disputed debts
　effect, 13.5.1
　notation, 13.5.2.1
　reinsertion notice, 6.7
　restrictions, 3.3.4, 13.5.2.2
disputed information, notation, 7.6.2, 7.7.1
driving records, status, 2.3.3, 2.5.7
drug tests, status, 2.3.6.6
electronic communication, 5.4.4
employment reports, status, 2.3.6.6, 2.4.3
erroneous information, *see* INACCURATE INFORMATION
evidentiary issues, 10.11.3.3
exemptions, 2.4
explanation from consumer, inclusion, 13.6.8.2
false pretenses, obtaining under, 5.2.2, 5.6.3, 5.6.4, 10.2.4.1, 12.3
FACTA, application, 8.3.10S
FBI access, 1.4.8, 4.5.7.2, 5.2.1, 5.2.12
FCRA enforcement authorities, subpoenas, 5.2.1
FCRA scope, 2.1, 2.3, 2.4
federal law summaries, Appx. B.2
file, distinguished, 2.3.1
financially troubled consumers, 13.2
first-hand experience, 2.4.1
follow-up reports, 5.4.2.3
FTC Commentary, Appx. C
FTC subpoenas, 5.2.1
GLB Act exemption, 16.4.1.5
governmental use, 13.3.5
grand jury subpoenas, 5.2.1
guarantors, 7.8.4.10.2
home mortgages, use, 2.3.6.9, 5.2.8, 13.7.2.1, 13.7.2.3
identity theft, *see* IDENTITY THEFT
identifying information, status, 5.2.3
impermissible purposes
　alimony, 5.3.2, 13.3.7.5
　blemished report, impact, 13.3.7
　business credit, 5.2.4.3, 5.2.9.2
　child support, 5.3.2, 13.3.7.5
　collection suits, 13.3.7.5
　consumer's objection, obtaining despite, 5.1.2
　criminal liability, 12.3
　curiosity, 13.3.7.3
　discovering, 5.1.7
　generally, Ch. 5
　immigration matters, 13.3.7.5
　insurance claims, 5.3.7
　investigators, 5.3.5
　liability, 5.4.1, 5.5, 5.6, 10.2.2.3
　lists, 5.3.8, 13.3.7.4
　litigation, 5.3.4, 13.3.7.5
　marketing research, 5.3.8.3
　obtaining for, 2.3.5.3
　other uses, 5.3.9
　paternity proceedings, 5.3.3
　prescreening, 5.3.8.4
　preventative procedures, 5.4
　prosecutions, 5.3.4, 13.3.7.5
　relatives, 5.3.6, 13.3.7.2
　spouses, 5.3.6, 13.2.7.2.1, 13.3.7.2
　tax collection, 5.3.3
　testers, restrictions, 10.11.2
　third parties, 5.3.6, 13.3.7.2
　use, effect on status, 5.1.6
　use for, 2.3.5.1, 2.3.6.5.5
　vicarious liability, 5.6.5
inaccurate, *see* INACCURATE INFORMATION
incomplete, 7.1, 7.2.8, 7.8.3.2, 7.8.4.10.1, 13.2.5
information based on interviews, 13.2.4
information gathered for, *see* CONSUMER FILES
insurance reports, status, 2.3.6.7, 2.6.8
intended purpose, effect, 2.3.5
investigative reports, *see* INVESTIGATIVE CONSUMER REPORTS
IRS summons, 5.2.1
joint accounts, 5.3.6
law enforcement bulletins, status, 2.3.5.4, 2.3.6.10.3
law enforcement requests, 5.2.1, 5.2.12
legal directories, status, 2.3.3
legislative history, 2.3.6.1, 2.3.6.5.3
lists of consumers, status, 5.3.8.2, 5.3.8.5
military personnel, 13.2.8.3
misidentification, 7.8.4.6
misleading, 7.8.3.2, 7.8.4.10.1, 7.8.4.10.3, 7.8.4.11
new accounts, adding, 7.8.4.11, 13.6.4
nonderogatory information, deleting, 7.8.4.11
notice requirements, *see* NOTICE
obsolete information, *see* OBSOLETE INFORMATION
open-end account customers, 5.4.2.3
overview, 1.2
permissible purposes
　account reviews, 2.3.6.11, 5.2.10
　agents, 5.1.4
　business credit, 5.2.4.3
　business transactions, 2.3.6.10, 5.2.9
　certification, *see* CERTIFICATION
　check cashing lists, 2.3.6.3
　child support, 2.3.6.12
　consumer's permission, 5.2.2
　counterintelligence, 5.2.12
　court order, 5.2.1
　credit transactions, 2.3.6.2, 5.2.4

CONSUMER REPORTS *(cont.)*
permissible purposes *(cont.)*
  debt collection purposes, 2.3.6.2, 5.2.4.2
  employment agencies, 2.4.3, 6.4.2.4
  employment purposes, 2.3.6.6, 5.2.5.2
  exceptions, 2.3.6.5
  expected use, 2.3.5.3
  FBI purposes, 5.2.12
  generally, 2.3.5.1, 2.3.6.1, Ch. 5
  government agencies, 2.3.6.12, 5.2.3, 5.2.12
  government licenses or benefits, 2.3.6.8, 5.2.7
  information collected for, 2.3.5
  insurance purposes, 2.3.6.7, 5.2.6
  original purpose, 2.3.5.4
  personal credit, 2.3.6.2
  prescreening lists, 2.3.3, 5.3.8.4
  prospective clients, 5.3.4
  requirement for release, 5.1.2
  risk assessment, 2.3.6.9, 5.2.8
  skip tracing, 2.3.6.2, 5.2.4.2
  spouses, 5.3.6, 13.6.4.5, 13.2.7.2.1
  tenant reports, 2.3.6.4
  terrorism protection, 5.2.12
  third parties, 5.3.6
  verification, 5.4.1
  waiver of rights, 5.2.2
prescreened reports, *see* PRESCREENED REPORTS
previous recipients or inquiries
  disclosure to consumer, 4.4.2.1, 4.5.4, 5.4.5
  reporting, 7.8.4.10.1, 13.2.6
prior report, partial use, 2.3.5.2
protective bulletins, status, 5.3.8.5
public record information, 2.3.3
reading, 4.8.2
release
  agent of user, 5.1.4
  between agencies, 5.1.5
  discovering impermissible use, 5.1.7
  FCRA violations, 5.4.1
  impermissible purpose, 5.1.6
  objection, effect, 5.1.2
  reasonable procedures, *see* REASONABLE PROCEDURES
  refusal, 5.1.2
  restrictions, 5.1.2
  written instructions of consumer, 5.2.2
requests for, 4.4.2.3aS, 4.4.5.1.5S
resellers, *see* RESELLERS
sample explanations, Appx. F.2
sample reports, Appx. F.1
scope, 2.3, 2.3.6.1
settlement negotiations
  impermissible purpose, 5.3.4
  issues, resolving, 13.5.4
sole proprietorships, status, 2.3.6.5.1
sources, restrictions, 13.2.4
spouses of consumers, restrictions, 13.2.7
state law preemption, 10.4.4
state law summaries, Appx. B.3
statement from consumer, inclusion, 7.6.2, 13.6.8.2
technically accurate, 7.8.3.2
telephone directories, status, 2.3.5.3, 5.3.8.5
tenant reports, status, 2.3.6.4
third party credit requests, exemption, 2.4.5
tort claims, 10.3

trimerger reports, 10.11.2
unfavorable, policies encouraging, 7.8.4.3
unsolicited, restrictions, 5.1.2
updating, 7.7.1, 7.8.4.10.4, 13.2.3, 13.4.3
use
  actual use, 2.3.5.2, 5.1.7
  adverse use, *see* ADVERSE ACTION
  business purposes, effect, 2.3.5.4, 2.3.6.5.5
  disclosure, *see* DISCLOSURE; NOTICE
  expected uses, 2.3.5
  impermissible, *see* CONSUMER REPORTS, impermissible purposes
  landlords, 13.7.3
  permissible, *see* CONSUMER REPORTS, permissible purposes
  prior use, 2.3.5.2
  reasonable procedures, *see* REASONABLE PROCEDURES
  restrictions, 5.1.2
  utilities, 13.7.4
users, *see* USERS OF REPORTS
workplace drug tests, status, 2.3.6.6
wrong consumer, 7.8.4.6

CONSUMER TRANSACTIONS
see also CONSUMERS; CREDIT TRANSACTIONS
billings, *see* BILLINGS
FCRA, application, 2.3.6.10
permissible purpose, requirement, 5.2.9.1

CONSUMERS
see also CONSUMER TRANSACTIONS
business transactions involving, 2.3.9.5
credit record, *see* CREDIT HISTORY; CREDIT RECORD
credit reporting rights, generally, 1.3.1
dealer paper sales, notice, 6.4.4.1
definition, 2.2, 15.2.2.1
  GLB Act, 16.4.1.3
disclosure rights, *see* DISCLOSURE; NOTICE
disputing debts, *see* CREDIT DISPUTES
disputing information, *see* STATEMENTS OF DISPUTE
FACTA, application, 6.3S, 6.3aS
FCRA, application, 2.2
financially troubled, 13
GLB Act, application, 16.4.1.3
guide to credit reporting, Appx. J
identification
  see also IDENTIFYING INFORMATION
  alteration, 15.2.5.3
identity theft, *see* IDENTITY THEFT
information on, *see* CONSUMER REPORTS; INFORMATION ON CONSUMERS
medical information, *see* MEDICAL INFORMATION
payment of debts, priorities, 13.4.1
proof of identification or authorization, 4.4.3
receipt of consumer report from user, 4.7, 6.4.3.1
rights, summary of, 6.3S, 6.3aS
spouses, *see* SPOUSES
stabilizing income and debt obligations, 13.6.3
summary of rights, *see* SUMMARY OF CONSUMER RIGHTS

CONTRACTS
see also AGREEMENTS
credit repair organizations
  disclosure requirements, 15.2.3
  required terms, 15.2.4

CONTRACTS (*cont.*)
credit repair organizations (*cont.*)
　state regulation, 15.3
　void contracts, 15.2.6.1, 15.3.6
sample credit bureau contracts, Appx. G.1

CONVICTIONS
see PUBLIC RECORD INFORMATION

COOPERATIVE LOAN EXCHANGES
see also LOAN EXCHANGES
FCRA, application, 2.5.4

CORPORATIONS
see also BUSINESSES
affiliated, *see* AFFILIATES
FCRA, application, 2.3.3, 2.3.6.5.1, 2.6.1
officers, consumer reports, permissible purposes, 5.2.4.3

COSIGNERS
see also ACCOMMODATION PARTIES
adverse action, disclosure, 6.4.2.3.6, 6.4.4.1
adverse information reporting, 3.3.5.4.1
blemished credit history, option, 13.7.1
car loans, 13.7.5

COSTS
see ATTORNEY FEES AND COSTS

COUNTERCLAIMS
FCRA claims, to, 10.13

COURT ORDERS
see also COURTS; PUBLIC RECORD INFORMATION
attorney-issued subpoenas, status, 5.2.1, 10.11.3.4
consumer reports, permissible purpose, 5.2.1, 5.3.5, 10.11.3.4
disputed debts
　reporting issues, 13.5.4.7
　settlement approval, 13.5.4.6
grand jury subpoenas, status, 5.2.1
law enforcement agencies, consumer report requirement, 5.2.1

COURT RECORDS
see PUBLIC RECORD INFORMATION

COURTS
credit reporting claims, selection, 10.9
federal, *see* FEDERAL COURTS
jurisdiction, *see* JURISDICTION
orders, *see* COURT ORDERS
state, *see* STATE COURTS

CREDIT
see also CREDIT TRANSACTIONS
accounts, *see* CREDIT ACCOUNTS
adverse action, *see* ADVERSE ACTION
applications for, *see* CREDIT APPLICATIONS
billings, *see* BILLINGS
business credit, *see* BUSINESS CREDIT
cards, *see* CREDIT CARDS
checks, status, 5.2.4.1, 6.4.2.3.5
consumer reports, permissible uses
　business credit, 5.2.4.3
　collections, 5.2.4.2
　generally, 5.2.4.1
　review of accounts, 2.3.6.11, 5.2.10
　risk assessment, 2.3.6.9, 5.2.8
definition, 5.2.4.1, 6.4.2.3.1, 15.2.2.1
denial
　see also ADVERSE ACTION; CREDIT APPLICATIONS, rejection
　blemished credit record, 13.6.2
　consumer report, use, 6.4, 13.7.1
　credit record, consideration, 13.7.1
　definition, 6.4.2.3.2
　insufficient credit history, 13.6.2
　reasons, reporting, 7.8.4.10.5
　reporting on future reports, 13.2.6, 13.7.8.2
disputes, *see* CREDIT DISPUTES
extension, consumer report, permissible use, 5.2.4.1
FCBA, application, 3.3.4.3, 13.5.2.2
identity theft, obtaining by, 7.2.5, 7.8.4.7
incidental, spousal information, 13.2.7.2.2
information, *see* CONSUMER REPORTS; CREDIT INFORMATION
leases, status, 6.4.2.3.3
personal credit, defined, 5.2.4.3
public utility credit, *see* PUBLIC UTILITY CREDIT
reporting agencies, *see* CONSUMER REPORTING AGENCIES; CREDIT BUREAUS

CREDIT ACCOUNTS
see also BILLINGS; CREDIT CARDS
account numbers, information sharing, 16.4.1.9
charged off, reporting, 8.3.3
closed voluntarily, reporting, 3.8, 13.2.8.4
collection, *see* COLLECTION AGENCIES, COLLECTION SUITS, DEBT COLLECTORS
delinquent
　bringing up-to-date, 13.6.6
　reporting limitations, 3.7, 8.3.2, 8.3.3, 13.5.4.1
disputes, *see* CREDIT DISPUTES
FCBA, application, 3.3.4.3
missing from consumer file, adding, 13.6.4
new accounts, establishing, 13.6.5, 13.7
open-end accounts, 5.4.2.3
permissible purposes
　account reviews, 2.3.6.11, 5.2.10
　collections, 5.2.4.2
　open-end accounts, 5.4.2.3
　risk assessment, 2.3.6.9, 5.2.8
placed for collection, reporting, 8.3.3
spouses, designation, 13.6.4.5
unlisted, inserting in credit record, 13.6.4

CREDIT APPLICATIONS
see also CREDIT TRANSACTIONS
automated underwriting systems, 14.2.2.4
blemished record
　impact on relatives, 13.3.7.2
　implications, 13.3.2, 13.7
cosigners, disclosures, 6.4.2.3.6
home mortgages, 13.7.2.3
obsolete information, reporting, 13.2.5
rejection
　see also ADVERSE ACTION; CREDIT, denial
　consumer report, inclusion, 13.7.1, 13.7.8.2
　FCRA, application, 2.6.3
scoring systems, 14.2.2.4

CREDIT BUREAUS
see also CONSUMER REPORTING AGENCIES
addresses and phone numbers, 4.4.2.3
collection departments, FCRA, application, 2.6.4

CREDIT BUREAUS (cont.)
credit scores, 14.2.2.1
disclosure requests, 4.4.2.2
disclosures, reading, 4.8.2
dispute forms, 7.3.2.3
errors, prevalence, 7.2.1, 7.3.1
Equifax, *see* EQUIFAX
Experian, *see* EXPERIAN (TRW)
FCRA application, 2.6.1
files, *see* CONSUMER FILES
information processing, 4.5.1, 13.2.3
overview, 1.2, 4.4.2.2
reports, *see* CONSUMER REPORTS
sample contracts, Appx. G.1
sources of information, 13.2.3
Trans Union, *see* TRANS UNION
TRW, *see* EXPERIAN (TRW)

CREDIT CARDS
see also CREDIT ACCOUNTS
authorized users, 13.7.8.2
billing errors, reporting, 3.3.4.3, 13.5.2.2
blemished reports, implications, 13.3.2
Consumer Action fact sheet, 13.7.8.2
defenses, 3.3.4.3, 13.5.2.2
FCBA, application, 3.3.4.3, 13.5.2.2
home appliances, purchasing with, 13.7.7
identity theft, *see* IDENTITY THEFT
obtaining, 13.7.8.2
pros and cons, 13.7.8.1
secured credit cards, 13.7.8.2
transaction authorizations, FCRA, application, 2.4.4
using to build credit history, 13.6.5

CREDIT CLINICS
see CREDIT REPAIR AGENCIES

CREDIT COUNSELORS
contacting, 13.6.6
repair organizations, *see* CREDIT REPAIR AGENCIES

CREDIT DISPUTES
see also STATEMENTS OF DISPUTE
agency obligations, 7.3.5, 13.5.3
billing errors, 3.3.4.3, 13.5.2.2
CCPA rights, 13.5.2.2
collection of disputed debts, 3.3.4.2
complaint address, 3.4.4, 13.5.2.1
court orders covering reporting issues, 13.5.4.7
credit card defenses, 3.3.4.3, 13.5.2.2
credit scores and, 14.8.2
debt consolidators, 13.7.10S
ECOA, application, 13.5.2.2
FCBA, application, 3.3.4.3
FCRA violations, 13.5.2.2
frivolous disputes, 7.6.2
furnishers
 notice of dispute, 3.3.4, 7.3.5.2, 13.5.2.1, 13.5.2.2
 notification of dispute, 3.10
 obligations, 3.11
 reporting restrictions, 3.3.4, 3.5.3, 13.5.2.2
generally, 13.7.10S
home equity loans and mortgages, 3.3.4.4, 13.5.2.2
inaccurate information, 3.5.2, 7.3, 10.2.2.10, 13.5.2.1
 correcting, 3.5.4
 practical advice, 3.4.5

injunctive relief, 13.5.2.2
litigation aids, 13.5.4, 13.5.4.7
open-end credit, 3.3.4.3
procedures
 disputing with agency, 13.5.3
 disputing with creditor, 3.9, 13.5.2
 formal process, 3.9
reinvestigations, *see* REINVESTIGATIONS
reporting implications, 13.5.1
settlement
 breach of agreement, 13.5.4.3
 cleaning up file after, 13.5.4.8
 court approval, 13.5.4.5
 model agreements, 13.5.4.4, 13.5.4.5
 monitoring file after, 13.5.4.9
 negotiating, 13.5.4.2
 resolving credit reporting issues, 13.5.4.1
 selecting correct language, 13.5.4.3
types, 13.5.1

CREDIT FILES
see CONSUMER FILES

CREDIT GUIDES
see also CONSUMER LISTS
prohibition, 5.3.8.2

CREDIT HEADER INFORMATION
disclosure, 2.3.4, 16.4.1.11
GLB Act, application, 2.3.4, 16.4.1.11
FCRA, application, 2.3.4
pending legislation, 16.7

CREDIT HISTORY
see also AUDIT TRAIL; CONSUMER FILES; CREDIT RECORD
blemished, *see* CREDIT RECORD, blemished
building, 13.6.5
consumer files, reflection, 13.6.4.1
ECOA, application, 13.6.4.5, 13.6.4.6.1, 13.6.4.6.2
identity theft, 7.2.5, 7.8.4.7, 13.5.5
insufficient
 adding missing accounts, 13.6.4
 adverse action based on, 6.4.2.2
 establishing new accounts, 13.6.5
 generally, 13.6.1
 identifying, 13.6.2
 notice of adverse action, 13.6.2
joint accounts, 13.6.4.6.2
repair agencies, *see* CREDIT REPAIR AGENCIES
spouses
 application to consumer, 13.2.7.1
 avoiding, 13.6.4.6.3
 building, 13.6.4.5
 ECOA reporting requirements, 13.6.4.5, 13.2.7.1
 explanation to creditor, 13.6.8.4
 requests to consider, 13.6.4.6.2
 use by creditor, 13.2.7.2
unreported, alerting creditors to, 13.6.4.6

CREDIT INFORMATION
see also CREDIT HISTORY; INFORMATION ON CONSUMERS
adverse, *see* ADVERSE INFORMATION
communication by other than agency, 2.3.2
consumer reporting agencies, *see* CONSUMER REPORTS

CREDIT INFORMATION (cont.)
false pretenses, obtaining by, 5.2.2, 5.6.3, 5.6.4, 10.2.4.1
FBI access, 1.4.8, 5.2.12
spouses, obtaining, 13.6.4.5, 13.2.7.2

CREDIT MONITORING SERVICES
generally, 4.4.2.2

CREDIT RATING
see CREDIT RECORD; CREDIT SCORES

CREDIT RECORD
see also CONSUMER FILES; CREDIT HISTORY
blemished records
  automobile loans and leases, impact, 13.7.5
  coping with, 13.7
  credit card applications, impact, 13.7.8.2
  dealing with, Ch. 13
  disputing debts, 13.5
  home mortgages, impact, 13.7.2
  identifying, 13.6.2
  implications, 13.3
  improving, 13.6
  insufficient history as, 13.6.1
  insurance, impact, 13.7.6
  residential leases, impact, 13.7.3
  spouses, 13.3.7.2, 13.6.4.6.3, 13.6.8.4
  stabilizing income and debt obligations, 13.6.3
  student loans, impact, 13.7.9
  utilities, impact, 13.7.4
contents, 13.2.3
court orders, 13.5.4.7
financially troubled consumers, 13.1
examining, 13.2.1
explaining, 13.6.8
identity theft, 7.2.5, 7.8.4.7, 13.5.5
inaccurate, see INACCURATE INFORMATION
incomplete, 7.2.8, 13.6.4
insufficient, see CREDIT HISTORY, insufficient
publication in the community, 13.3.7.3, 13.3.7.4
rating, see CREDIT SCORES
repair agencies, see CREDIT REPAIR AGENCIES
settlement negotiations, protecting, 13.5.4
spouses, effect on consumer, 13.2.7, 13.6.4.6.3
students, 13.6.11
threats to damage, 13.4

CREDIT REPAIR AGENCIES
see also CREDIT REPAIR ORGANIZATIONS ACT (CROA)
cancellation rights, 15.2.4
contract terms, 15.2.4
  arbitration clauses, 15.2.6.1
  noncomplying contracts void, 15.2.6.1
CROA
  application, 15.2.2
  violations, remedies, 15.2.6
defined, 15.2.2
disclosure requirements, 15.2.3
fraud and deception, 15.2.5.5
FTC consent agreement, Appx. H.5
FTC Telemarketing Rule, application, 15.4.1
overview, 15.1
misrepresentations regarding services, 15.2.5.4
payments for services, restrictions, 15.2.5.6, 15.4
prohibited practices, 15.2.5
regulation, 15.2

reinvestigation requests, 7.3.3
schedule of services, 15.2.4
state law, see STATE CREDIT SERVICES (REPAIR) STATUTES
Telephone Consumer Protection Act, application, 15.4.3

CREDIT REPAIR ORGANIZATIONS ACT (CROA)
see also CREDIT REPAIR AGENCIES
contract terms, 15.2.4
disclosure requirements, 15.2.3
enforcement, 15.2.8
exemptions, 15.2.2.2, 15.2.2.6
overview, 15.2.1
private remedies, 15.2.6
  damages, 15.2.6.2
  voiding of contract, 15.2.6.1
prohibited practices, 15.2.5
scope, 15.2.2
state law relationship, 15.2.7
summary of Act, Appx. B.2.2
text, Appx. A.4

CREDIT REPORTING
see also CONSUMER REPORTING AGENCIES; CONSUMER REPORTS; FAIR CREDIT REPORTING ACT (FCRA); STATE CREDIT REPORTING STATUTES
consumer's guide, Appx. J
current developments, 1.1.4
legislative history, see LEGISLATIVE HISTORY
overview, 1.2
regulation, 1.3.1
summary of federal and state laws, Appx. B

CREDIT REPORTING AGENCIES
see CONSUMER REPORTING AGENCIES; CREDIT BUREAUS

CREDIT REPORTING RESOURCES GUIDE
Metro 2 manual, 3.3.2

CREDIT REPORTS
see CONSUMER REPORTS

CREDIT SCORES
see also CREDIT RECORD
accuracy concerns, 14.8
  disputed debts, 14.8.2
  inaccurate information, 14.8.1, 14.8.3
  lack of validation and re-validation, 14.8.5
  lender misuse, 14.8.6
  unreported information, 14.8.4
actual damages calculations, use, 11.2.2
automated underwriting systems, 14.2.2.4
basics of, 14.2.1
calculations, 14.5
  black box, 14.5.1
  confidentiality, 14.5.4
  FICO scores, 14.5.2
  Freddie Mac, 14.5.3
credit applications, 14.2.2.4
credit bureau scores, 14.2.2.1
credit reports, inclusion, 13.2.3
custom versus generic, 14.2.2.2
definition, 14.2.3
disclosure
  FCRA exception, 4.3.2, 4.5.7.1, 14.4.1
  obtaining, fees, 14.4.2

CREDIT SCORES (cont.)
discrimination, 14.9
  disparate impact, 14.9.1
  thresholds or overrides, 14.9.2
disputed information, rating, 7.6.2
FICO scores, 14.2.2.1, 14.5.2
free reports, 4.4.5.3AS
improving
  additional advice, 14.6.2
  industry advice, 14.6.1
  personalized analysis, 14.4.2
  re-scoring, 14.6.3
insurance scores, 14.10
key factor, notice, 6.8aS
missing information, 7.2.8, 7.6.1.3
objective standard, 3.3.3.2
overview, Ch. 14
policy concerns, 14.7
  lack of flexibility, 14.7.2
  lack of transparency, 14.7.1
  risk-based pricing, 14.7.3
specialty scores, 14.2.2.3
variations, 14.2.2
widespread use, 14.3

CREDIT SELLERS
information on consumers, see CONSUMER REPORTS

CREDIT SERVICES ORGANIZATIONS
see CREDIT REPAIR AGENCIES

CREDIT SOLICITATIONS
prescreening, 5.3.8.4.1

CREDIT TRANSACTIONS
see also CREDIT APPLICATIONS
adverse action, notice and disclosure
  consumer report, 6.4.2.3
  overview, 6.2
consumer credit transaction, defined, 15.2.2.1
consumer reports
  see also CONSUMER REPORTS
  obsolete information, 13.2.5, 8.4
  permissible use, 5.2.4.1
ECOA, application, 3.3.5.2, 13.6.4.5
FCRA, application, 2.3.3, 2.3.6.2
information concerning, see CONSUMER REPORTS
lease, status, 5.2.4.1, 6.4.2.3.3
medical information, 4.5.5
spouses, consumer reports, 13.2.7

CREDITORS
see also FURNISHERS OF INFORMATION
address for error complaints, 13.5.2.1
affiliates, see AFFILIATES
billings, FCBA, regulation, 3.3.4.3, 13.5.2.2
computer errors, 7.2.2
consumer reports, permissible use, 2.3.6, 5.2.4, 5.2.8, 5.2.10, 13.3.7.5
credit card transactions, 2.4.4
credit scoring systems, misuse, 14.8.6
CROA, application, 15.2.2.6
dealer paper sales, notice obligations, 6.4.4.1
definition, 15.2.2.6
disputed debts, see CREDIT DISPUTES
ECOA, application, 2.4.4, 2.4.5, 3.3.5.2, 6.4.5, 13.6.4.5, 13.5.2.2

FACTA, application, 16.6.1a.6S
FCRA, application, 2.4, 2.5.4, 2.6.3, 3.2.2.2
first-hand experience, 2.4.1, 2.5.4
  adverse action based on, 6.4.4.1
  direct selling of information, 3.2.2.2
friendly, use as testers, 10.11.2
FTC Commentary, Appx. C
inaccurate information, see INACCURATE INFORMATION
information obtained from non-reporting agency, 6.4.4
information supply to reporting agency, see FURNISHERS OF INFORMATION
joint lenders, FCRA, application, 2.4.5, 2.5.5
judgment creditors, see JUDGMENT CREDITORS
landlords, status, 9.1.3.3
law suits, see COLLECTION SUITS
negotiating removal of historical information, 13.6.7
negotiating repayment plans with, 13.6.6
notice obligations
  adverse action, 2.4.4, 2.4.5, 6.4.2.3, 6.4.4, 6.4.5
  adverse credit report, 6.6.4
  disputes, 3.6, 13.5.2.1, 13.5.2.2
  open-end accounts, closure, 5.4.2.3
  past due accounts, payment or discharge, 7.8.4.10.3
prospective creditors, alerting to unreported history, 13.6.4.6
record retention, 10.11.4
spouses of debtor
  ECOA reporting obligations, 13.6.4.5, 13.2.7.1
  use of file, restrictions, 13.2.7.2
third party credit requests, 2.4.5
threats to report debt, 13.4
tort liability, 3.14.5

CRIMINAL CONVICTIONS
see CRIMINAL RECORDS; PUBLIC RECORD INFORMATION

CRIMINAL OFFENSES
alleged criminals lists, see LAW ENFORCEMENT BULLETINS
arrests, see PUBLIC RECORD INFORMATION
Computer Fraud and Abuse Act, 16.4.2.1
convictions, see CRIMINAL RECORDS; PUBLIC RECORD INFORMATION
FCRA violations, 12.3
Financial Information Privacy Act, 16.4.2.2
Identity Theft and Assumption Deterrence Act, 16.6.2
indictments, see PUBLIC RECORD INFORMATION
investigations, consumer reports, use, 5.3.5
prosecutions, see PROSECUTIONS

CRIMINAL RECORDS
see also CRIMINAL OFFENSES; PUBLIC RECORD INFORMATION
reporting limitations, 8.3.6

DAMAGES
see also ATTORNEY FEES AND COSTS
actual, see DAMAGES, ACTUAL
class actions, 10.7.2
CROA claims, 15.2.6.2
FCRA claims, 11.1–11.4
multiple, see DAMAGES, MULTIPLE
nominal, see DAMAGES, NOMINAL
plaintiff's direct testimony, Appx. I.5.1
published awards, quick reference, 11.7
punitive, see DAMAGES, PUNITIVE

DAMAGES (*cont.*)
reinvestigations, failure to comply, 7.3.6
state claims
    credit repair, 15.3.6
    credit reporting, 11.1
statutory, *see* DAMAGES, STATUTORY
Telephone Consumer Protection Act, 15.4.3

DAMAGES, ACTUAL
see also DAMAGES
class actions, 10.7.2
CROA violations, 15.2.6.2
definition, 11.2.1
FCRA violations
    generally, 11.2.1
    intangible damages, 11.2.3
    mitigation, 11.2.1
    negligent violations, 11.1
    pecuniary loss, 11.2.2
nominal damages alternative, 11.2.4
punitive damages prerequisite, 11.4.1.3
tort claims, 11.1, 11.2.1

DAMAGES, MULTIPLE
see also DAMAGES
credit reporting claims, 11.1, 11.3

DAMAGES, NOMINAL
recovering, 11.2.4

DAMAGES, PUNITIVE
see also DAMAGES
class actions, 10.7.2
CROA violations, 15.2.6.2
FCRA violations
    actual damages, no need, 11.4.1.3
    amount, determination, 11.4.2
    determination by judge or jury, 11.4.3
    purpose, 11.4.1.1
    prerequisites, 11.4.1
    willful noncompliance, 10.2.1, 11.1, 11.4.1.1, 11.4.1.2
financial standing of defendant, discovery, 10.11.3
jury trials, 10.12
obsolete information reporting, 8.5.1
tort claims, 11.1, 11.4.1.1

DAMAGES, STATUTORY
see also DAMAGES
credit reporting violations
    FBI provision, 5.2.12
    FCRA claims, 11.3
    state law claims, 11.3

DATA COMMUNICATION
see also ELECTRONIC COMMUNICATION
reasonable procedures, 7.8.4.8

DATA MANAGEMENT COMPANIES
use by creditors, 3.3.1

DATING SERVICES
consumer report, permissible use, 5.2.9.1
FCRA, application, 2.3.6.10.3

DEALER PAPER
see also AUTOMOBILE DEALERS
sales, disclosure requirements, 6.4.4.1

DEALERS
see AUTOMOBILE DEALERS; CREDITORS; MERCHANTS

DEBT COLLECTION IMPROVEMENT ACT
reporting of federal government debts, 13.5.2.3

DEBT COLLECTORS
see also COLLECTION AGENCIES
bad debt lists, publication, 13.3.7.4
consumer reports, permissible user
    business debts, 5.2.4.3
    generally, 5.2.4.2
credit bureau, creating false impression as, 13.4.4
CROA, application, 15.2.2.3, 15.2.2.5
disputed debts, reporting and collection restrictions, 3.3.4.2, 13.5.2.2
FACTA, requirements, 3.3.4.2aS, 3.3.4.2bS, 16.6.1a.3.2S
false threats or information, 13.4.4
FCRA, application, 2.6.4
FDCPA requirements, 13.5.2.2
Metro 2 format, use, 3.3.3.9
name restrictions, 13.4.4

DEBTS
see also BAD DEBT LISTS
date of first delinquency, 3.7
delinquent, reporting limitations, 3.7, 8.3.2, 8.3.3, 13.5.4.1
discharging through bankruptcy, 8.3.7, 13.6.9
disputing, *see* CREDIT DISPUTES
payment, priorities, 13.4.1
purchasers of debt, *see* ASSIGNEES
repayment, effect on reporting limitations, 8.3.3
repayment plans, 13.6.6
stabilizing obligations, 13.6.3

DECEPTIVE ACTS OR PRACTICES
see UNFAIR OR DECEPTIVE ACTS OR PRACTICES (UDAP)

DECLARATORY JUDGMENT ACT (DJA)
FCRA violations, application, 11.5

DECLARATORY RELIEF
FCRA violations, 11.5

DEFAMATION
see also TORT CLAIMS
actual damages, 11.2.1
conditional privilege defense, 10.3.7
false reports, 10.3.1, 10.3.7
FCRA qualified immunity, 3.14.5, 10.3.2, 10.4.4
inaccurate reports, 10.3.7

DEFENSES
conditional privilege, 10.3.7
credit cards, 3.3.4.3, 13.5.2.2
defamation claims, 10.3.7
disputed debts, *see* CREDIT DISPUTES
ECOA violations, 6.9
FCRA claims, 10.13
impermissible reports, 10.2.2.3
inadvertent error, 6.9
mitigation, 11.2.1
notice violations, 6.9, 10.2.4.2
obsolete reports, 10.2.2.2
reasonable procedures, 6.9, 7.8.4.1, 9.2.4, 10.2.4.2, 10.2.4.3
student loans, raising, 13.5.2.3, 13.6.11
technical accuracy, 7.8.3.2

DEFINITIONS *Fair Credit Reporting / 2004 Supplement*

References are to sections; references followed by "S" appear only in this Supplement

DEFINITIONS
actual damages, 11.2.1
assemble, 2.5.3
assure, 10.2.2.1
billing error, 3.3.4.3, 13.5.2.2
business transaction, 5.2.9.1
consumer, 2.2, 15.2.2.1, 16.4.1.3
consumer credit transaction, 15.2.2.1
consumer report, 2.1, 2.4
consumer reporting agency, 2.1, 2.5.1
credit, 5.2.4.1, 6.4.2.3.1, 15.2.2.1
credit repair organization, 15.2.2.1
credit score, 14.2.3
creditor, 15.2.2.6
customer relationship, 16.4.1.3
denial, 6.4.2.3.2, 6.4.2.4
employment purposes, 5.2.5.2, 6.4.2.4
evaluate, 2.5.3
family purposes, 5.2.4.3
federally related mortgage loans, 13.5.2.2
furnisher of information, 3.2.1
governmental agency, 5.2.3
household purposes, 5.2.4.3
investigative consumer report, 9.1.2
malice, 10.3.6
medical information, 10.2.2.4S
negligence, 10.2.1
person, 2.5.2, 9.2.1.1
personal purposes, 5.2.4.3
privacy, 10.3.8
user, 5.1.2, 6.4.1

DENIAL
see ADVERSE ACTION

DEPARTMENT OF HOUSING AND URBAN DEVELOPMENT (HUD)
insured home mortgages, see FEDERAL HOUSING ADMINISTRATION (FHA)

DETECTIVE AGENCIES
consumer reports
    certification of permissible use, 5.4.2.2
    obtaining, 5.1.4
    use, 5.3.5
electronic communication with reporting agencies, 5.4.4
FCRA, application, 2.6.5
identifying information, obtaining, 5.2.3
investigative consumer reports, preparation, 9.1.1

DIRECT MARKETING TRANSACTIONS
medical information, 4.5.5

DIRECTORIES
city, see CITY DIRECTORIES
legal, see LEGAL DIRECTORIES
telephone, see TELEPHONE DIRECTORIES
trade, see TRADE DIRECTORIES

DISCLOSURE
see also NOTICE
adverse action, information used, 6.4.4.3
affiliate information sharing, 4.5.8, 6.4.4.4, 6.5.4
analyzing information, 4.8
audit trail, 4.5.7.3
authorization proof, 4.4.3.2
collectors affiliated with reporting agency, 13.4.3

consumer files
    affiliates, 4.4.1.5
    all information, 4.5.2
    check identification, 4.5.6
    cleaning up after a dispute, 13.5.4.8
    differences in information, 4.3.2
    electronic, 4.4.1.3
    FCRA violations, 10.2.2.9
    fees, 4.4.5
    form, 4.8.1
    in-person, 4.4.1.3
    insufficient credit history, 13.6.2
    making the request, 4.4.2
    obsolete information, 13.2.5
    other persons in consumer's file, 4.5.2.3
    presence of another person at disclosure, 4.4.1.3
    previously reported information, 4.5.2.2
    rights, 4.2, 4.3, 4.5, 6.2, 7.7.2
    scope, 4.4.2.1, 4.5.2
    sources, 4.5.7.3, 9.2.2.3
    telephone, 4.4.1.3
    timing, 4.4.1.1, 4.4.2.4
    written disclosure, 4.4.1.2, 4.8.1
consumer reporting agencies
    employees providing, 4.4.1.4
    FCRA liability, 10.2.2.9
    fees, 4.4.5
    identity, 6.4.3.2
    location, 4.4.1.3
    obligations, 4.3, 7.7.2
    overview, 6.2
    public record information, 6.6.2
    tort liability, 4.1, 4.3.1
    unreasonable preconditions, 4.4.4
    which agency, 4.4.2.2
consumer reports
    adverse action, 6.4.3
    contents by users, 4.7, 6.4.3.1
    copies, 4.4.2.2, 4.4.2.3, 4.5.1
    fees, 4.4.5
    past user, notification rights, 7.7.2
    recipients, 4.5.4
    rights, 4.1, 4.5.1, 6.2, 6.4.3.2
    use to consumer, 4.7, 6.4.3.1
consumer rights summary, inclusion, 4.5.2.2
credit card rejections, 2.4.4
credit repair organizations, 15.2.3
credit scores, 4.3.2, 4.5.2.1, 4.5.7.1, 14.4
ECOA relationship, 6.4.4.3, 6.4.5
Equifax, 4.4.2.3.1, 4.8.2.2, Appx. F.3.1
Experian, 4.4.2.3.2, 4.8.2.3, Appx. F.3.2
FBI security clearances, 4.5.7.2, 5.2.12
FCRA rights
    generally, 4.1, 4.3.1, 4.5
    overview, 6.2
form of disclosure, 4.8.1
FTC Commentary, Appx. C
identification proof, 4.4.3.1
impermissible purpose, Ch. 5
insurance claims reports, 4.5.7.3
investigative consumer reports
    additional disclosures, 9.2.2
    nature of report, 9.2.3
    reasonable procedures defense, 9.2.4

DISCLOSURE (cont.)
investigative consumer reports (cont.)
  requests for report, 9.2.1
  rights, 6.6.3, 9.2.1.3
  sources, 9.2.2.3
  time, 9.2.2.4
  waiver of rights, 9.2.5
medical information, 4.5.5
misrepresentations, limitations, 10.10.1.2
obtaining, 4.4.2.3
permissible purpose, Ch. 5
power of attorney requests, 4.4.3.2
prescreening lists
  notice from users, 6.6.4
  recipients, 4.5.4
prior to information request, 6.5
qualified immunity, 3.14.5, 10.3.2, 10.3.3
reading disclosures, 4.8.2
sample disclosure, Appx. F.3.1
sources of information, 4.5.7.3, 9.2.2.3
state law requirements, 6.5.6
tenant screening reports, 13.7.3
third party credit rejections, 2.4.5
tort claims, effect, 4.1, 4.3.1
Trans Union, 4.4.2.3.3, 4.8.2.1, Appx. F.3.3
utilizing disclosures
  limits on utility, 4.8.3.1
  uses of information, 4.8.3.2

DISCOVERY
see also ACTIONS; LITIGATION
accuracy statistics, 7.8.4.2
attorney fee rates, 11.6.3
audit trail, 4.5.7.3
consumer reports, determination of use, 5.1.7, 5.3.4
credit scores, 14.5.4
formal discovery, 10.11.3
generally, 10.11.1
informal discovery, 10.11.2
investigative consumer reports, sources, 4.5.3, 9.2.2.3, 9.2.3
sample interrogatories, Appx. I.2
sample notice of deposition, Appx. I.4.2, Appx. I.4.3
sample requests for production, Appx. I.3

DISCRIMINATION
credit scores, 14.9
ECOA protections, 3.3.5.2, 3.14.4, 13.5.2.2

DISPUTES
see CREDIT DISPUTES; STATEMENTS OF DISPUTE

DISTRESS
see EMOTIONAL DISTRESS

DIVORCE PROCEEDINGS
see also ALIMONY; CHILD SUPPORT
consumer reports, use, 5.3.2, 5.3.4, 13.3.7.5
impact on credit record, 13.2.7.2.1

DOCTORS
see FURNISHERS OF INFORMATION; MEDICAL INFORMATION

DRIVER PRIVACY PROTECTION ACT
privacy protections, 16.2

DRIVING RECORDS
see also ACCIDENT REPORTING BUREAUS
bad driving lists, 13.2.2
FCRA, application, 2.3.3, 2.5.7

DRUG TESTS
workplace, FCRA application, 2.3.6.6

ELECTRONIC COMMUNICATION
see also COMPUTER ERRORS; DATA COMMUNICATION
computer fraud law, application, 12.3
consumer reports, 5.4.4
furnishing of information, 3.3.1
  Metro 2 format, see METRO 2 FORMAT
reasonable procedures, 7.8.4.8
reinvestigations
  ACDV, 3.10, 3.12.3
  notice to furnisher, 3.10
  results, 3.12.2, 3.12.3
transmission, 5.2.2

ELECTRONIC DATA SYSTEMS, INC.
data management services, 3.3.1

EMOTIONAL DISTRESS
damages for, 11.2.3

EMPLOYEES
see also EMPLOYMENT PURPOSES
consumer reporting agencies
  criminal liability, 5.5, 12.3
  disclosures, providing, 4.4.1.4, 4.8.1, 5.2.5.5S
information concerning, see EMPLOYMENT REPORTS
FCRA violations, employer liability, 5.6.5

EMPLOYERS
see also EMPLOYMENT PURPOSES; FURNISHERS OF INFORMATION
adverse action, notice requirements, 5.2.5.5S, 6.4.2.4
  exemptions, 5.2.5.5S, 6.4.2.4
consumer reports
  certification of notice, 5.2.5.3
  generally, 13.3.4
  impermissible purpose, vicarious liability, 5.6.5
  notice requirements, 5.2.5.5S, 6.5.2S
  permissible use, 5.2.5.2, 5.2.5.5S
  Summary of Rights, providing, 5.2.5.4
FACTA, application, 5.2.5.5S
FCRA, application, 2.3.6.6, 2.6.5
former employers, provision of information, 5.2.5.2
information requests, see EMPLOYMENT REPORTS
investigative reports, notice requirements, 13.3.4
workers' compensation lists, use, 13.2.2

EMPLOYMENT
adverse action, see ADVERSE ACTION
agencies, see EMPLOYMENT AGENCIES
denial, see ADVERSE ACTION
income, see INCOME AND EMPLOYMENT
purposes, see EMPLOYMENT PURPOSES
reports, see EMPLOYMENT REPORTS

EMPLOYMENT AGENCIES
FCRA, application, 2.4.3, 2.6.5, 6.4.2.4
investigative reports
  certification to agency, 9.2.1.6
  exclusions, 2.4.3
  notice to consumer, 9.2.1.5

EMPLOYMENT *Fair Credit Reporting / 2004 Supplement*

References are to sections; references followed by "S" appear only in this Supplement

EMPLOYMENT PURPOSES
blemished credit record
  impact on relatives, 13.3.7.2
  implications, 13.3.4
certification of authorization, 5.2.5.3, 6.5.2S, 9.1.3.2
definition, 2.3.6.6, 5.2.5.2, 6.4.2.4
disclosures
  adverse action, 5.2.5.5S, 6.4.2.4
  investigative reports, 5.2.5.5S, 9.2.1.5, 9.2.1.6, 13.3.4
  prior to obtaining report, 6.5.2S
FACTA, application, 5.2.5.5S
FCRA, application, 2.3.6.6
FTC Commentary, Appx. C
investigative reports, 9.1.3.2, 9.2.1.5, 9.2.1.6, 13.3.4
jurors, reports on, status, 2.3.6.6, 5.2.5.2
permissible purpose, 5.2.5.2
public record information, 6.2, 6.4.2.4, 6.6.2.2, 10.2.2.6
reports, *see* EMPLOYMENT REPORTS
self-employment, status, 2.3.6.6
Summary of Rights, providing, 5.2.5.4, 9.1.3.2, 13.3.4
workplace drug tests, status, 2.3.6.6

EMPLOYMENT REPORTS
see also CONSUMER REPORTS; EMPLOYMENT PURPOSES
authorization, 6.5.2S
blemished reports, implications, 13.3.4
certification, 5.2.5.3, 6.5.2S, 9.1.3.2
consumer report status, 2.3.6.6, 2.4.3
employment agency exclusion, 2.4.3
FTC Commentary, Appx. C
investigative, *see* INVESTIGATIVE CONSUMER REPORTS
notice obligations
  adverse use, 6.4.2.4, 13.3.4
  certification, 6.5.2S
  corrections, 7.7.1
  investigative reports, 13.3.4
  overview, 6.2
  prior to information request, 6.5.2S
  public record information, 6.6.2, 13.3.4, 13.6.10
  state law, 6.5.6, 13.3.4
obsolete information, 8.4, 13.2.5
permissible use, 5.2.5.2
public record information, protections, 6.6.2, 7.8.5, 13.6.10
recipients, disclosure, 4.5.4
spouses and relatives, restrictions, 13.2.7
workers' compensation lists, *see* WORKERS' COMPENSATION LISTS
workplace drug tests, 2.3.6.6

EQUAL CREDIT OPPORTUNITY ACT (ECOA)
see also CONSUMER CREDIT PROTECTION ACT (CCPA)
adverse action notices, 6.4.5
  model form, Appx. E.4
  record retention, 10.11.4
codes, use in Metro 2 format, 3.3.3.3
credit discrimination, prohibition, 13.5.2.2
credit reporting, application, 3.3.5.2
  improperly reported information, 10.2.3.3
credit score definition in Regulation B, 14.2.3
disclosure standards, FCRA relationship, 6.4.4.3
disputed debts, application, 13.5.2.2
federal agency interpretations, 1.1.3
furnishers of information, application, 3.14.4
identity theft suits under, 13.5.5.4
insufficient credit history, application, 13.6.2, 13.6.4.6.1

spouses
  credit reporting requirements, 13.6.4.5, 13.2.7.1, 13.6.8.4
  inquiry restrictions, 13.2.7.2.2
  Regulation B, 13.6.4.5, 13.2.7.2.1
  statements of explanation, application, 13.6.8.3, 13.6.8.4

EQUIFAX
see also CONSUMER REPORTING AGENCIES; CREDIT BUREAUS; NATIONWIDE REPORTING AGENCIES
credit reports
  reading, 4.8.2.2
  sample explanation, Appx. F.2.1
  sample report, Appx. F.1.1
credit scores
  FICO score, 14.2.2.1
  obtaining, 14.4.2
disclosure requests, 4.4.2.2, 4.4.2.3.1
disputed information, accepting consumer's version, 7.3.4.3
FCRA, application, 2.6.1
fees, 4.4.2.3.1, 4.4.2.5
FTC consent orders, Appx. H.2
investigative consumer reports, specialization, 9.1.1
liability insurance, 10.11.3.5
overview, 1.2
prescreening lists, exclusion requests, 5.3.8.4.4
sample contract, Appx. G.1.3
Summary of Rights, sample, Appx. F.3.1

EQUITABLE RELIEF
FCRA violations, 11.5

ERRORS
see also ACCURACY
agency liability, 7.8.1, 7.8.4.1
billing errors, *see under* BILLINGS
computer errors, 7.2.2
consumer files, prevalence, 4.2.2, 7.2.1
disputing, *see* CREDIT DISPUTES
inaccurate information, *see* INACCURATE INFORMATION
Metro 2 format, 3.3.3.7
spousal reporting requirements, failure to comply, 13.6.4.5
transcription errors, 7.2.6, 7.8.4.8

EVIDENCE
see also BURDEN OF PROOF
consumer reports, use as, 5.3.4, 10.11.3.3
damages
  intangible damages, 11.2.3.2
  pecuniary loss, 11.2.2
  plaintiff's direct testimony, Appx. I.5.1
denial based on erroneous information, 11.2.2
joint accounts, credit history, 13.6.4.6.2
reasonable procedures, non-utilization, 7.8.4.2
willfulness, 11.4.1.2

EXPERIAN (TRW)
see also CONSUMER REPORTING AGENCIES; CREDIT BUREAUS; NATIONWIDE REPORTING AGENCIES
consent order, Appx. II.1
credit reports
  reading, 4.8.2.3
  sample report, Appx. F.1.2
credit scores
  FICO score, 14.2.2.1
  obtaining, 14.4.2
disclosure requests, 4.4.2.2, 4.4.2.3.2

EXPERIAN (TRW) *(cont.)*
disputed information, accepting consumer's version, 7.3.4.3
FCRA, application, 2.6.1
fees, 4.4.2.3.2, 4.4.5
illogical information, detecting, 7.8.4.9
liability insurance, 10.11.3.5
overview, 1.2
prescreening lists, exclusion requests, 5.3.8.4.4
subscriber service agreement, sample, Appx. G.1.1
Summary of Rights, sample, Appx. F.3.2

EXPLANATIONS
see also STATEMENTS OF DISPUTE
adverse information, 7.6.1.2, 13.6.8
consumer file, inclusion, 7.6.1.2, 7.8.4.10.5, 13.6.8.2
consumer rights, 7.6.1.2
creditors, provision, 13.6.8.3
ECOA requirements, 13.6.8.3, 13.6.8.4
extenuating circumstances, 7.8.4.10.5
spouse or third party fault, 13.6.8.4
summarizing in reports, 13.6.8.3

FAIR AND ACCURATE TRANSACTIONS ACT OF 2003 (FACTA)
consumer files
　blocking information, 6.8cS
consumer reports, 8.3.10S
　notice requirements, 5.2.5.5S
　permissible use, 5.2.5.5S
　requests for, 4.4.2.3aS, 4.4.5.1.5S
credit scores, 6.8aS–6.8eS, 8.3.10S
credit restoration, 16.6.1aS
debt collectors, 3.3.4.2aS, 3.3.4.2bS, 16.6.1a.3.2S
effective dates, Appx. A.2.4S
employee investigations, 5.2.5.5S
FCRA, amending, 16.4.2.3aS
financial information, integrity, 16.6.1aS
fraud alerts, 16.6.1a.2S, 16.6.1a.2.4S
furnishers of information, 3.4.4aS, 3.11.1aS, 3.11.1bS, 3.16S, 16.6.1a.4.2S, 16.6.1a.6.1S
identity theft, 6.3aS, 16.6.1a.3S–16.6.1a.6S
key provisions, 1.4.9.2S
legislative history, 1.4.9.1S
notice obligations
　adverse action, 5.2.5.5S
　consumer reporting agencies, 5.2.5.5S
　exemptions, 5.2.5.5S
　key factor, 16.6.1a.6S
　users of reports, 6.4aS
privacy, 16.6.1aS
private enforcement, 11.1aS
qualified immunity, 11.1a.1S
redline version of FCRA, Appx. A.2.2S
resellers, 3.15S
summary of consumer rights, 6.3S, 6.3aS
text, Appx. A.2.3S

FAIR CREDIT BILLING ACT (FCBA)
see also CONSUMER CREDIT PROTECTION ACT (CCPA)
improperly reported information, application, 10.2.3.3
scope, 3.3.4.3, 13.5.2.2

FAIR CREDIT REPORTING ACT (FCRA)
see also CONSUMER CREDIT PROTECTION ACT (CCPA); CONSUMER REPORTING AGENCIES; CONSUMER FILES; CONSUMER REPORTS; FAIR AND ACCURATE CREDIT TRANSACTIONS ACT OF 2003 (FACTA)
actions under, *see* FCRA CLAIMS
administrative enforcement, 12.1, 12.2.1
affiliate exemption, 2.4.2
　proposed FTC interpretations, Appx. A.6.1
　proposed OCC regulations, Appx. A.6.2
application
　consumer reports, 2.3
　consumers, 2.2
　credit header information, 2.3.4
　furnishers of information, 3.2
　generally, 1.3.1, 2.1
　investigative consumer reports, 9.1.2
compliance
　FTC Commentary, Appx. C
　reasonable procedures, 6.9, 8.5
computer fraud law, application, 12.3
consumer's guide, Appx. J
criminal enforcement, 12.3
cross-reference table, section numbers, Appx. A.1
ECOA notice obligations, comparison, 6.4.5
enforcement
　administrative, 12.1
　consumer reports, subpoena, 5.2.1
　FTC consent decrees, Appx. H
　private attorneys general, 11.6.2.1, 11.6.2.2
　state enforcement, 12.4
FACTA, *see* FAIR AND ACCURATE CREDIT TRANSACTIONS ACT OF 2003 (FACTA)
federal agency interpretations, 1.3.3
FTC interpretations
　generally, 1.3.3, 12.2.3
　informal staff opinion letters, Appx. D
　Official Commentary, Appx. C
FTC jurisdiction, 12.2.1
GLB Act impact, 16.4.1.10
legislative history, *see* LEGISLATIVE HISTORY
NCLC manual, using, 1.1
　updates, 1.1.4
old Act, text, Appx. A.3
overview, 1.3.1
preemption of state law
　general standard, 10.4.3
　specific preemptions, 10.4.4
prescreening provisions, 5.3.8.4.1
privacy protections, 5.1.1, 16.1
published awards, quick reference, 11.7
purpose, 1.3.1, 5.1.1
recent developments, 1.1.4
regulations, 1.3.3, 12.2.3, Appx. A.6.1
rights under, waiver, 5.2.2
scope, 2.1
summary of Act, Appx. B.2.1
Summary of Rights, *see* SUMMARY OF CONSUMER RIGHTS
text of Act, Appx. A.2
trade regulation rules, 12.2.3
under-utilization, 1.3.2
user notice, 5.1.3
violations
　actual damages, 11.2
　attorney fees and costs, 11.6
　civil rights claims, 10.5
　civil suits, 10.2

FAIR — *Fair Credit Reporting / 2004 Supplement*

References are to sections; references followed by "S" appear only in this Supplement

FAIR CREDIT REPORTING ACT (FCRA) *(cont.)*
violations *(cont.)*
  consumer reporting agencies, 5.4.1
  continuing violations, 10.10.1.1
  criminal penalties, 12.3
  deceptive practices claims, 10.4.2
  declaratory relief, 11.5
  defenses, 6.9
  false pretenses, 5.2.2, 5.6.3
  injunctive relief, 11.5
  knowing non-compliance, 5.6.2
  liability, 5.6, 10.7.3, 10.10.1.1
  limitations, 10.10.1S
  negligent, 10.2.1
  obsolete information, 8.5.1
  private remedies, 11.1
  punitive damages, 11.4
  reasonable procedures, failure to maintain, 5.4.1, 8.5.1
  state enforcement, 12.4
  statements of dispute, 7.6.1.1
  statutory damages, 11.3
  systematic practices, 10.7.2
  testers, 10.11.2
  uncertified use, 5.6.2
  unfair or deceptive practice, as, 10.4.2, 12.1
  vicarious liability, 5.6.5
  willful noncompliance, 10.2.1, 11.3, 11.4.1.1, 11.4.1.2

FAIR DEBT COLLECTION PRACTICES ACT (FDCPA)
see also CONSUMER CREDIT PROTECTION ACT (CCPA)
bad debt lists, restrictions, 13.3.7.4
disputed debts, 3.3.4.2
federal agency interpretations, 1.1.3
improperly reported information, application, 10.2.3.3
overview, 13.5.2.2

FAIR, ISAAC & CO. (FICO)
see also CREDIT SCORES
credit bureau scores, development, 14.2.2.1
credit scores, obtaining from, 14.4.2
scorecards, 14.5.2.2
scoring factors, 14.5.2.1

FALSE INFORMATION
see also INACCURATE INFORMATION
credit repair organizations, 15.2.5.2
debt collectors, reporting, 13.4.4
tort liability, 10.3.1, 10.3.6

FALSE PRETENSES
see also FRAUD
consumer reports, obtaining under
  civil liability, 5.6.3, 10.2.4.1
  criminal liability, 5.6.4, 12.3
  impermissible purpose, 5.6.3, 5.6.4
  testers, 10.11.2
  written permission, 5.2.2

FALSE THREATS
see also THREATS
credit reporting, 3.3.5.1
debt collectors, 3.3.5.1, 13.4.4
investigative consumer report, 9.2.1.2

FAMILY PURPOSES
see also CONSUMER TRANSACTIONS
defined, 5.2.4.3

FANNIE MAE
see FEDERAL NATIONAL MORTGAGE ASSOCIATION (FANNIE MAE)

FARMERS HOME ADMINISTRATION (FmHA)
see RURAL HOUSING SERVICE (RHS)

FCRA CLAIMS
see also FAIR CREDIT REPORTING ACT (FCRA)
actual damages, 11.2
affiliated companies, 10.2.3.4
attorney fees and costs, 11.6
blocking of reports by agency due to, 7.2.9
case selection, 10.8
class actions, 10.7.2
court selection, 10.9
defenses and counterclaims, 10.13
disclosure violations, 10.2.2.9
furnishers of information, 3.14, 10.2.3.2
identity theft, 13.5.5.4
illegally obtained reports, 10.2.4.1
impermissible purposes, 10.2.2.3
improper handling of disputes, 10.2.2.10
inaccurate information, 3.14.2
inaccurate reports, 7.8.1, 10.2.2.1
injunctive relief, 11.5
interest on judgments, 11.6.6
investigative reports, 10.2.2.5, 10.2.4.3
jury trials, 10.12, Appx. I.5
liability insurance, 10.11.3.5
limitations, 10.10.1S
medical information, 10.2.2.4S
negligent noncompliance, 10.2.1
notice violations, 10.2.4.2
obsolete reports, 10.2.2.2
parties, 10.7
prescreening lists
  reporting agency violations, 10.2.2.7
  user violations, 10.2.4.4
private remedies, 11.1
public record information, 10.2.2.6
published awards, quick reference, 11.7
punitive damages, 11.4
removal to federal court, 10.9.5
resellers, 10.2.2.8
sample pleadings, Appx. I
state enforcement actions, 12.4
statutory damages, 11.3
superbureaus, 10.2.2.8
under-utilization, 1.3.2
willful noncompliance, 10.2.1

FEDERAL AGENCIES
see also GOVERNMENT AGENCIES
employment reports, adverse notice exemption, 6.4.2.4
FBI, *see* FEDERAL BUREAU OF INVESTIGATIONS (FBI)
FCRA, application, 2.5.6, 3.3.5.3
FCRA enforcement agencies, 1.3.3, 12.1
furnishing of information, 3.2.1, 3.3.5.3, 13.5.2.3
IRS, *see* INTERNAL REVENUE SERVICE (IRS)
privacy protections, 2.5.6, 16.2

FEDERAL BUREAU OF INVESTIGATIONS (FBI)
see also FEDERAL AGENCIES; GOVERNMENT AGENCIES; LAW ENFORCEMENT AGENCIES
consumer reports, obtaining, 1.4.8, 4.5.7.2, 5.2.1, 5.2.12

FEDERAL BUREAU OF INVESTIGATIONS (FBI) (cont.)
counterintelligence and terrorism, 5.2.12
FCRA, application, 2.5.6
security clearances, 4.5.7.2
USA Patriot Act, 1.4.8

FEDERAL CONSUMER CREDIT PROTECTION ACT
see CONSUMER CREDIT PROTECTION ACT (CCPA)

FEDERAL COURTS
FCRA claims
   jurisdiction, 10.9.1
   removal from state court, 10.9.5
   selection of court, 10.9.4
state claims, pendent jurisdiction, 10.9.2

FEDERAL DEPOSIT INSURANCE CORPORATION
FCRA, enforcement responsibilities, 12.1

FEDERAL HOME LOAN BANK BOARD
see OFFICE OF THRIFT SUPERVISION (OTS)

FEDERAL HOME LOAN MORTGAGE CORPORATION (FREDDIE MAC)
automated underwriting system, 14.2.2.4, 14.5.3
sample contract, Appx. G.1.2
underwriting guidelines, 13.7.2.1, 14.7.2

FEDERAL HOUSING ADMINISTRATION (FHA)
joint lender exemption, 2.5.5
underwriting guidelines, 13.7.2.2

FEDERAL NATIONAL MORTGAGE ASSOCIATION (FANNIE MAE)
automated underwriting system, 14.2.2.4
underwriting guidelines, 13.7.2.1, 14.7.2

FEDERAL PREEMPTION
see PREEMPTION OF STATE LAW

FEDERAL RESERVE BOARD (FRB)
FCRA
   enforcement responsibilities, 12.1
   interpretations, 12.2.3

FEDERAL TRADE COMMISSION (FTC)
affiliate information sharing, proposed interpretations, Appx. A.6.1
consumer reports, subpoenas, 5.2.1
CROA, enforcement responsibilities, 15.2.8
FCRA
   civil actions, 12.2.1, 12.2.2
   consent decrees, 12.2.1, Appx. H
   enforcement against information furnishers, 12.2.2
   enforcement orders, Appx. H
   enforcement powers, 1.3.3, 3.14.2, 12.2.1, 12.2.2
   model forms for disclosure, 4.8.1, Appx. E
   Official Staff Commentary, 1.3.3, 12.2.3, Appx. C
   opinion letters, 1.3.3, 12.2.3, Appx. D
   public interest only, 12.2.1
   Summary of Rights, see SUMMARY OF CONSUMER RIGHTS
   trade regulation rules, 12.2.3
identity theft complaint department, 13.5.5.1, 16.6.1, 16.6.2
   Identity Theft Hotline, 13.5.5.1, 16.6.1
model forms
   Summary of Consumer Rights, Appx. E.1
   Summary of Responsibilities of Furnishers, Appx. E.3
   Summary of User Responsibilities, Appx. E.2

opinion letters
   informal letters, Appx. D
   official, Appx. C.4
Privacy Rule, see PRIVACY RULE (FTC)
Safeguard Rules, 16.4.1.1
Telemarketing Rule, see TELEMARKETING RULE (FTC)
unfair or deceptive practices, standards, 16.4.2.3

FEES
disputed reports, notification of past users, 7.7.3
explanations, insertion, 7.6.1.2
file disclosures
   allowable fees, 4.4.5.3
   FCRA prohibitions, 4.4.5.1
   maximum charge, 4.4.5.3
   state restrictions, 4.4.5.2
FICO scores, 14.4.2
major credit bureaus, 4.4.2.3, 4.4.5
new files, creation, 7.6.1.3
new information, addition to file, 7.6.1.3, 13.6.4.3
reinvestigations, 7.3.2.1
statements of dispute, 7.6.1.1, 7.6.2, 7.7.3

FICO SCORES
see CREDIT SCORES; FAIR, ISAAC & CO. (FICO)

FILES
see CONSUMER FILES

FINANCE COMPANIES
see also FINANCIAL INSTITUTIONS; LOAN COMPANIES
FCRA, application, 2.6.3

FINANCIAL INFORMATION
see INFORMATION ON CONSUMERS; FINANCIAL INFORMATION PRIVACY ACT

FINANCIAL INFORMATION PRIVACY ACT
overview, 16.4.2.2

FINANCIAL INSTITUTIONS
see also BANKS; FINANCE COMPANIES; LOAN COMPANIES
consumer reporting agencies, status, 2.3.4
customer relationships, 16.4.1.3
dealer paper purchases, disclosure obligations, 6.4.4.1
FCRA
   administrative enforcement, 12.1
   application, 2.6.3
GLB Act, application, 16.4.1.2
GLB privacy notice, 16.4.1.6
nonpublic personal information, 16.4.1.4
privacy protections
   account number sharing, 16.4.1.9
   common law, 16.3, 16.5
   GLB opt-out rights, 16.4.1.7
   governmental intrusion, 16.2
   Safeguard Rules, 16.4.1.1
   statutory protections, 16.4
   tort claims, 16.3
services provided by, see FINANCIAL SERVICES

FINANCIAL RESOURCES
information pretexting, 12.2.1, 16.4.2.3

FINANCIAL SERVICES
account information, pretexting, 12.2.1
account number sharing, 16.4.1.9

FINANCIAL SERVICES (cont.)
applications, consumer report, permissible use, 5.2.9.1
fraud lists, 13.2.2, 13.3.6
provision, FCRA, application, 2.3.6.10.3

FORECLOSURES
prior, impact on mortgage applications, 13.7.2.1

FORMS
consumer reporting agencies, sample contract, Appx. G.1
consumer reports, samples, Appx. F.1
dispute forms, 7.3.2.3
ECOA adverse action forms, Appx. E.4
FTC model forms, Appx. E

FORUM
FCRA claims
   removal, 10.9.5
   selection, 10.9.4

FRAUD
see also FALSE PRETENSES
alerts
   active military duty, 16.6.1a2S
   effects, 16.6.1a.1S
   FACTA, application, 16.6.1a2S
   notice, 6.8bS
credit repair organizations, 15.2.5.5
file disclosure, fees, 4.4.5.1.2
file segregation as, 13.6.12
identity theft, see IDENTITY THEFT
specialized fraud lists, 13.2.2, 13.3.6

FREDDIE MAC
see FEDERAL HOME LOAN MORTGAGE CORPORATION (FREDDIE MAC)

FTC
see FEDERAL TRADE COMMISSION (FTC)

FURNISHERS OF INFORMATION
see also CREDITORS
accuracy standards, 3.4
   duty to correct and update, 3.5, 13.5.2.1
   enforcement, 3.4.1, 3.14.2, 13.5.2.1
   exception, 13.5.2.1
   general duty, 3.4.2
   liability, 3.4.1, 3.4.3, 3.14
   Metro 2 format, 3.3.3.2, 3.4.2
   obligations, 13.5.2.1
   state law, 10.4.4
   transcription errors, 7.2.6
address for error complaints, 13.5.2.1
affiliate sharing of information, 3.2.2.1
child support debts, 3.3.5.4.2
closed accounts, reporting, 3.8, 13.2.8.4
contacting regarding errors, 3.4.4, 13.5.2.1
cosigner obligations, 3.3.5.4.1
date of delinquency, furnishing, 3.7
debt collectors, 3.3.4.2, 13.5.2.2
defined, 3.2.1
direct selling of information, 3.2.2.2
disclosure, 4.3.1, 4.4.2.1, 4.5.3
discrimination, 3.3.5.2, 3.14.4
disputed information
   billing errors, 3.3.4.3
   duty to correct and update, 3.5, 13.5.2.1

notation of dispute, 3.6, 13.5.2.1
notification of dispute, 3.10
obligations, 3.9–3.12, 13.5.2.2
reinvestigation, 3.11, 10.2.3.3, 13.4.6, 13.5.2.2
reporting restrictions, 3.3.4
student loans, 13.5.2.3
withdrawal of information, 13.5.4.1
duty to correct and update, 3.5, 13.5.2.1
duty to report accurately, 3.4.2
ECOA, application, 3.3.5.2
electronic provision of information, 3.3.1
   Metro 2 format, see METRO 2 FORMAT
FACTA, application, 3.4.4aS, 3.16S, 16.6.1a.6.1S, 16.6.1a.4.2S
false threats, 3.3.5.1
FCRA
   application, 2.1, 3.2.1
   claims against, 10.2.3
   enforcement against, 3.4.1, 12.4.2
federal agencies, 3.3.5.3
financial institutions, GLB Act application, 16.4.1
generally, 1.2, 1.3.1, 3.2.1, 13.2.3
GLB Act exemption, 16.4.1.5
inaccurate information
   address to contact, 3.4.4, 13.5.2.1
   correcting, 3.5, 10.2.3.3
   disputing, 3.4.5, 3.5.2
   liability, 3.4.1, 3.4.3, 3.14, 10.2.3
legislative history, 1.4.6
liability
   accuracy standards, 3.4.1, 3.14, 10.2.3.2
   reinvestigation, 3.14.3, 10.2.3.3
manual reporting, 3.3.2
notice of dispute, 3.6, 3.10, 13.5.2.1, 13.5.2.2
notice of FCRA obligations, 3.2.1
   Summary of Responsibilities, FTC model form, Appx. E.3
objective standard, 3.3.3.2
overview, 3.1
qualified immunity, 3.14.5, 10.3.2, 10.4.4
reinsertion of information, certification, 7.5
reinvestigation
   conducting, 3.11, 13.4.6, 13.5.2.2
   liability, 3.14.3
   FACTA, requirements, 3.11.1aS, 3.11.1bS
   notice of results, 3.12, 7.4.1
   reporting to nationwide credit agencies, 3.12.2
reliability standards, 7.8.4.4
reporting delinquencies, limitations, 3.7, 8.3.3
segregating, 13.2.4
state law preemption, 3.2.2.3, 3.3.5.4.1
state law restrictions, 3.3.5.4
tort liability, 3.14.5, 10.3.5
UDAP violations, 10.4.2
unintentional reporting errors, 7.2.2
Universal Data Form, use, 3.3.2, 3.5.4
updating information, 3.5, 3.11.3S, 13.5.2.1

FURNITURE LOANS
what to avoid, 13.7.7

GOSSIP
consumer report users, 13.3.7.3
legislative response, 1.4.3

GOVERNMENT AGENCIES
see also FEDERAL AGENCIES; LOCAL GOVERNMENT AGENCIES; STATE AGENCIES
adverse actions, notice, 6.4.2.6
child support, *see* CHILD SUPPORT ENFORCEMENT AGENCIES
consumer reports
 child support purposes, 5.2.11, 5.3.2
 disclosure notice, 6.5.5, 6.8, 13.5.2.3
 obtaining, 5.2.3, 5.2.12, 13.3.7.5
 permissible use, 5.2.4.2, 5.2.7
 tax collection, 5.3.3
defined, 5.2.3
FCRA application
 federal, 2.5.6
 generally, 2.3.6.8
 joint-use exception, 2.5.5
 state and local, 2.5.7
furnishing of information, 3.2.1
 information selling, 13.2.3
GLB Act enforcement, 16.4.1.11
identifying information, obtaining, 5.2.3
law enforcement, *see* LAW ENFORCEMENT AGENCIES
loan guarantee programs
 FCRA, application, 2.5.5
 reporting of defaults, 13.5.2.3
 student loans, *see* STUDENT LOANS
privacy protections, 2.5.6, 16.2
social service, *see* SOCIAL SERVICE AGENCIES

GOVERNMENT BENEFITS
see also WELFARE AGENCIES
blemished report, implications, 13.3.5
consumer reports
 adverse actions, notice, 6.4.2.6
 impermissible use, 5.1.7
 permissible use, 5.2.7, 13.3.5
eligibility, FCRA, application, 2.3.6.8, 5.2.7, 13.3.5
over-payments, consumer report, permissible use, 2.3.6.10.3, 5.2.9.1

GOVERNMENT LICENSES
see LICENSES

GRAMM-LEACH-BLILEY (GLB) ACT
account number sharing restrictions, 16.4.1.9
credit headers, application, 2.3.4
enforcement, 16.4.1.11
exempt disclosures, 16.4.1.5
 redisclosure and reuse restrictions, 16.4.1.8
FCRA, impact on, 16.4.1.10
FTC rules, Appx. A.5.2S
notice requirements, 16.4.1.6
opt-out rights, 16.4.1.7
 exemptions, 16.4.1.5
 exercise, 16.4.1.7.3
 generally, 16.4.1.7.1
 notice, 16.4.1.7.2
overview, 16.4.1.1
rules, *see* PRIVACY RULE (FTC)
scope
 consumers, 16.4.1.3
 customers, 16.4.1.3
 exemptions, 16.4.1.6
 financial institutions, 16.4.1.2

information, 16.4.1.4
text, selected provisions, Appx. A.5.1
weaknesses, 16.4.1.11

GRAND JURY
governmental agency status, 5.2.3
subpoenas, consumer report, permissible purpose, 5.2.1

GUARANTORS
see ACCOMMODATION PARTIES; COSIGNERS

HIGHER EDUCATION ACT
student loan defaults, application, 8.3.9, 13.6.11

HOME APPLIANCE AND FURNITURE LOANS
what to avoid, 13.7.7

HOME EQUITY LOANS
see HOME MORTGAGES

HOME IMPROVEMENT CONTRACTORS
credit repair laws, application, 15.3.4

HOME MORTGAGES
applying for, 13.7.2.3
bankruptcy, effect on eligibility, 13.6.9
blemished report, implications, 13.3.2, 13.7.2
consumer explanations, consideration, 13.6.8.3
credit cards secured by, 13.7.8.2
credit disputes, 3.3.4.4, 13.5.2.2
credit reports, *see* RESIDENTIAL MORTGAGE CREDIT REPORTS
Fannie Mae and Freddie Mac standards, 13.7.2.1
government-insured, joint lender exemption, 2.5.5
pre-approval, 13.7.2.3
RESPA, application, 3.3.4.4, 13.5.2.2
risk assessment, 2.3.6.9, 5.2.8
varying standards amongst lenders, 13.7.2.2

HOME SAVERS AND FINDERS
credit services organization status, 15.3.2

HOUSEHOLD PURPOSES
see also CONSUMER TRANSACTIONS
defined, 5.2.4.3

HUD-MORTGAGES
see FEDERAL HOUSING ADMINISTRATION (FHA)

IDENTIFICATION
see also VERIFICATION
consumer reports
 consumer, 7.8.4.6
 users, 5.4.2
FCRA disclosures
 consumer, 4.4.1.3
 person accompanying consumer, 4.4.1.3
identity theft, *see* IDENTITY THEFT

IDENTIFYING INFORMATION
changing to confuse reporting agency, 13.6.12, 15.2.5.3
checks, adverse characterizations, 4.5.6
consumer files, reasonable procedures, 7.8.4.6
consumer list, status as consumer report, 5.2.3
governmental agencies, obtaining, 5.2.3
private investigators, obtaining, 5.3.5
social security numbers, 7.8.4.6

IDENTITY THEFT
coping with, 13.5.5, 16.6.1

IDENTITY

IDENTITY THEFT (*cont.*)
FACTA, application, 6.3aS, 16.6.1aS federal statute, 16.6.2
filing suit, 13.5.5.4
furnisher responsibilities, 16.6.1a.4.2S
FTC, complaints to, 13.5.5.1, 16.6.1, 16.6.2
   FTC hotline, 13.5.5.1, 16.6.1
inaccurate reports due to, 7.2.5, 7.8.4.7
monitoring after correction, 13.5.5.3
nature of identity theft, 13.5.5.1, 16.6.1
pending legislation, 16.7
prevention, 16.6.1aS, 16.6.1a.5S
reporting agency procedures, 7.8.4.7, 16.6.1a.4.1S
state law, 7.8.4.7, 10.4.2S, 16.6.3
   summaries, Appx. B.3
steps to correct, 13.5.5.2, 16.6.1a.6S
tort claims, 16.3
transactional information, 16.6.1a.3S
   access to, 16.6.1a.3.1S
   debt collectors, 16.6.1a.3.2S

IDENTITY THEFT AND ASSUMPTION DETERRENCE ACT
overview, 16.6.2

IMMIGRATION MATTERS
credit issues, 13.8S
consumer reports, use, 13.3.7.5

IMMUNITY
see LIABILITY; QUALIFIED IMMUNITY

IMPERMISSIBLE PURPOSES
alimony, 5.3.2, 13.3.7.5
blemished report, impact, 13.3.7
business credit, 5.2.4.3, 5.2.9.2
child support, 5.3.2, 13.3.7.5
collection suits, 13.3.7.5
consumer's objection, obtaining despite, 5.1.2
criminal liability, 12.3
curiosity, 13.3.7.3
discovering, 5.1.7
immigration matters, 13.3.7.5
impermissible use, Ch. 5
insurance claims, 5.3.7
investigators, 5.3.5
liability, 5.4.1, 5.5, 5.6, 10.2.2.3
lists, 5.3.8, 13.3.7.4
litigation, 5.3.4, 13.3.7.5
marketing research, 5.3.8.3
obtaining for, 2.3.5.3
other uses, 5.3.9
paternity proceedings, 5.3.3
permissible use, Ch. 5
prescreening, 5.3.8.4
preventative procedures, 5.4
prosecutions, 5.3.4, 13.3.7.5
relatives, 5.3.6, 13.3.7.2
spouses, 5.3.6, 13.2.7.2.1, 13.3.7.2
tax collection, 5.3.3
testers, restrictions, 10.11.2
third parties, 5.3.6, 13.3.7.2
use, effect on status, 5.1.6
use for, 2.3.5.1, 2.3.6.5.5
vicarious liability, 5.6.5

INACCURATE INFORMATION
see also ACCURACY; CREDIT DISPUTES; FALSE INFORMATION; FURNISHERS OF INFORMATION
agency liability, 7.8, 10.2.2.1
cloaking procedures, 7.4.2
complaints re, 13.5.2.1
   address to contact, 3.4.4
correcting
   consumer necessity, 4.2.2
   creditor, 3.5, 13.5.2.1
   reporting agency, 7.3, 7.4, 13.5.3
   Universal Data Form, 3.5.4
credit repair organizations, 15.2.5.2
credit scores, effect, 14.8
defamation claims, 10.3.7
disputing, *see* CREDIT DISPUTES
FCRA claims, 10.2.2.1
furnisher liability, 3.4.3, 3.14, 10.2.3.2, 13.5.2.1
fraud, fees for file disclosure, 4.4.5.1.2
incomplete information, 7.8.3.2, 7.8.4.10.1, 7.8.4.10.2
legislative history, 1.4.3, 7.8.2
management policies encouraging, 7.8.4.3
missing information, 7.8.4.11
new information, consumer offers, 7.6.1.3
obsolete information, 7.8.4.10.3–7.8.4.10.5, 8.1.3, 13.2.5
overview, 7.1
practical advice, 3.4.5
prevalence, 4.2.2, 7.2.1
reinvestigation, *see* REINVESTIGATIONS
reporting, prohibition, 3.4.3
state law preemption, 10.4.4
statement of dispute, *see* STATEMENTS OF DISPUTE
technically accurate information as, 7.8.3.2
tests of accuracy
   first test, 7.8.3
   second test, 7.8.4
tort claims, 3.14.5, 10.3.1
types of inaccurate information
   creditor errors, 7.2.2
   illogical files, 7.2.7, 7.8.4.9
   incomplete files, 7.2.8, 7.8.3.2, 7.8.4.10.1, 7.8.4.10.2
   legislative discussion, 7.8.2
   mismerged files, 7.2.4, 7.8.4.6
   public record information, 7.2.3, 7.8.4.5
   transcription errors, 7.2.6, 7.8.4.8

INCOME AND EMPLOYMENT
stabilizing consumer debt load, 13.6.3

INDEMNIFICATION
impleading a third party, 10.13

INDEPENDENT CONTRACTORS
consumer reports, obtaining, 2.5.4, 5.1.4
FCRA, application, 2.5.4, 2.5.5

INDICTMENTS
see PUBLIC RECORD INFORMATION

INDIVIDUALS
see CONSUMERS; PERSONS

INFORMATION BROKERS
see RESELLERS

INFORMATION FURNISHERS
see FURNISHERS OF INFORMATION

INFORMATION ON CONSUMERS
see also CONSUMER FILES; CONSUMER LISTS; CONSUMER REPORTS; CREDIT INFORMATION
adverse, see ADVERSE INFORMATION
assemble, definition, 2.5.3
characteristics, 2.3.3
communication by other than agency, 2.3.2
confidentiality, 16.5
credit header information, disclosure, 2.3.4
direct selling of information, 3.2.2.2
disputed information, see CREDIT DISPUTES
evaluate, definition, 2.5.3
false, see FALSE INFORMATION
false pretenses, obtaining under, 5.2.2, 5.6.3, 5.6.4, 10.2.4.1
favorable information, 8.1.2
FCRA, scope 2.1–2.4
Financial Information Privacy Act, 16.4.2.2
first-hand experience, 2.4.1, 2.5.4, 3.2.2.2
furnishing, see FURNISHERS OF INFORMATION
GLB Act, application, 16.4.1
identifying information, 5.2.3, 5.3.5
improper use, 2.1
inaccurate, see INACCURATE INFORMATION
irrelevant, see IRRELEVANT INFORMATION
joint users, sharing, 2.4.5, 2.5.5
legislative history, 1.4.3
nonpublic personal information, 16.4.1.4
not consumer-specific, FCRA, application, 2.3.3
number of inquiries, 7.8.4.10.1
personally identifiable financial information, 16.4.1.4
pretexting, 12.2.1, 16.4.2.3
privacy protections
  common law protections, 16.5
  governmental intrusion, 16.2
  identity theft, 16.6
  overview, 16.1
  statutory protections, 16.4, 16.7
  tort claims, 16.3
purpose, 2.3.5
release for impermissible purpose, 5.1.6
reporting, see CONSUMER REPORTS; INVESTIGATIVE CONSUMER REPORTS
spouses, ECOA restrictions, 13.6.4.5, 13.2.7.2.2
suppliers, tort liability, 10.3.5

INJUNCTIVE RELIEF
credit reporting violations, 11.5

INJURIES
see DAMAGES; DAMAGES, ACTUAL

INQUIRIES
notation of, 13.2.3
reporting of, 13.2.6

INSPECTION BUREAUS
see also CONSUMER REPORTING AGENCIES
FCRA, application, 2.6.1
insurance reports, preparation, 9.1.3.1

INSURANCE
adverse action, see ADVERSE ACTION
benefits, see INSURANCE BENEFITS
business insurance, see BUSINESS INSURANCE
claims, see INSURANCE CLAIM EXCHANGES; INSURANCE CLAIM LISTS; INSURANCE CLAIMS
companies, see INSURANCE COMPANIES
denial, see ADVERSE ACTION
liability insurance, see LIABILITY INSURANCE
life insurance, see LIFE INSURANCE
marketing lists, see PRESCREENED REPORTS
purposes, see INSURANCE PURPOSES
reports, see INSURANCE REPORTS
underwriting, see INSURANCE UNDERWRITING

INSURANCE BENEFITS
FCRA, application, 2.3.6.7.2
issuance, status as business transaction, 2.3.6.7.2

INSURANCE CLAIM EXCHANGES
see also INSURANCE CLAIMS
FCRA, application, 2.3.6.7.2

INSURANCE CLAIM LISTS
see also CONSUMER LISTS; INSURANCE CLAIMS
compilers, FCRA, application, 2.6.8

INSURANCE CLAIMS
exchanges, see INSURANCE CLAIM EXCHANGES
lists, see INSURANCE CLAIM LISTS
reports, 2.3.6.7.2, 5.2.6, 5.3.7, 13.3.3

INSURANCE COMPANIES
see also FURNISHERS OF INFORMATION
FCRA, application, 2.3.6.7, 2.5.4
information requests, see INSURANCE REPORTS
Medical Information Bureau, membership, 4.5.5
notice obligations, 6.4.2.7.1

INSURANCE PURPOSES
blemished credit record
  impact on relatives, 13.3.7.2
  implications, 13.3.3, 13.7.6
credit scores, 14.10
FCRA, application, 2.3.6.7
impermissible purposes, 5.3.7
investigative reports, 9.1.3.1
medical information, 4.5.5
permissible purposes, 2.3.6.7, 2.3.6.9, 5.2.6, 5.2.8
prescreening, 5.3.8.4.1
reports for, see INSURANCE REPORTS
underwriting purposes, see INSURANCE UNDERWRITING

INSURANCE REPORTS
see also CONSUMER REPORTS
adverse use, notice requirements, 6.4.2.5
blemished reports, implications, 13.3.3
claims reports, 2.3.6.7.2, 5.2.6, 5.3.7, 13.3.3
consumer report, status, 2.3.6.7, 2.6.8, 5.3.7
disclosure, 4.5.7.3
FTC Commentary, Appx. C
investigative, see INVESTIGATIVE CONSUMER REPORTS
obsolete information, 13.2.5
permissible purposes, 5.2.6
preparation by inspection bureaus, 9.1.3.1
underwriting reports, 2.3.6.7.1, 5.2.6, 13.3.3

INSURANCE UNDERWRITING
consumer report, permissible use, 2.3.6.7.1, 5.2.6, 5.2.8, 13.3.3
credit risks, 5.2.8, 13.7.6
credit scores, 14.10
described, 5.2.6
medical information, 4.5.5
obsolete information, using, 8.4, 13.2.5

INTER-FACT   *Fair Credit Reporting / 2004 Supplement*

References are to sections; references followed by "S" appear only in this Supplement

INTER-FACT
see also RESELLERS
FTC consent agreement, Appx. H.4.1

INTERNAL REVENUE SERVICE (IRS)
see also FEDERAL AGENCIES; GOVERNMENT AGENCIES
consumer reports
    administrative summons, 5.2.1, 5.3.3
    impermissible use, 5.3.3
    permissible user, 5.2.4.2

INTERNET
see ELECTRONIC COMMUNICATION; WEBSITES

INTERVIEWS
see PERSONAL INTERVIEWS

INVASION OF PRIVACY
see also PRIVACY; TORT CLAIMS
check cashing lists as, 13.3.6
common law tort, overview, 16.3
consumer reporting agencies, liability, 10.3.8
elements of claim, 10.3.8
FCRA qualified immunity, 3.14.5, 10.3.2, 10.3.6, 10.3.8, 10.4.4, 16.3
federal agencies, 2.5.6
identity theft, *see* IDENTITY THEFT

INVESTIGATING AGENCIES
see CONSUMER REPORTING AGENCIES; DETECTIVE AGENCIES; INSPECTION BUREAUS

INVESTIGATIONS
consumers, *see* INVESTIGATIVE CONSUMER REPORTS
disputes, *see* REINVESTIGATIONS

INVESTIGATIVE CONSUMER REPORTS
see also CONSUMER REPORTING AGENCIES; CONSUMER REPORTS
additional obligations, 9.1.4
adverse action based on, 9.2.1.7
contents, 9.1.2.3
copy to consumer, 9.2.2.2
description, 9.1.1
disclosure requirements
    additional disclosures, 9.2.2, 9.3.2
    address of reporting agency, 9.2.1.7
    nature of report, 9.2.3
    notice of request for report, 9.2.1
    reasonable procedures defense, 9.2.4
    user certification, 9.2.1.6
    violations, 10.2.4.3
    waiver of rights, 9.2.5
employment agencies, 2.4.3
employment purposes, 9.1.3.2, 9.2.1.5, 13.3.4
    employee consent, 9.3.1
false threats, 9.2.1.2
FCRA definition, 9.1.2
FCRA violations, 10.2.4.3
FTC Commentary, Appx. C
identifying investigator, 9.2.3
insurance purposes, 9.1.3.1
notice
    adverse action, 9.2.1.7
    employment purposes, 9.2.1.5, 13.3.4
    overview, 6.2, 6.6.3
    user request, 6.6.3, 9.2.1

utilization of notices, 9.3
permissible purposes, 9.1.3.4
personal interviews
    confirmation of information, 9.4.2.2
    requirement, 9.1.2.3
procedures, 9.4
public record searches, status, 9.1.3.1
reinvestigation, 9.3.2
re-use, 9.4.2.4, 10.2.2.5
sources of information
    confidentiality, 4.5.3, 9.2.2.3, 9.2.3
    notice of potential discovery of identity, 9.2.3
    segregation, 13.2.4
stoppage of investigation, 9.3.1, 9.3.2
subject matter, 9.1.2.2
tenant screening purposes, 2.3.6.4, 9.1.3.3
updating, 9.3.2
use, 13.2.4
user certification, 9.2.1.2, 9.2.1.6
verification
    adverse information based on public records, 9.4.2.3
    personal interviews, 9.4.2.2
    reverification of information, 9.4.2.4, 10.2.2.5

INVESTIGATORS
see DETECTIVE AGENCIES

INVESTMENTS
see also REAL ESTATE INVESTMENTS
consumer reports, permissible use, 5.2.9.1

IRRELEVANT INFORMATION
see also INFORMATION ON CONSUMERS
consumer file, inclusion, 7.8.4.10.3
disputing, 7.3.3
legislative response, 1.4.3

JOINT ACCOUNTS
see also CREDIT ACCOUNTS; SPOUSES
ECOA reporting requirements, 13.6.4.5, 13.6.4.6.2, 13.2.7.1
evidence of credit history, 13.6.4.6.2

JOINT LENDERS
consumer reporting agency status, 2.4.5, 2.5.5
third party information, sharing, 2.4.5

JUDGMENT CREDITORS
see also CREDITORS
consumer reports, permissible use, 5.2.4.2

JUDGMENT DEBTORS
lists for locating, 13.3.7.4

JUDGMENTS
see also PUBLIC RECORD INFORMATION
discharged through bankruptcy, reporting, 8.3.7
reporting limitations, 8.3.4, 13.2.5

JURISDICTION
CROA claims, 15.2.6.2
FCRA claims
    court selection, 10.9.1
    personal jurisdiction, 10.7.3, 10.9.3
FTC enforcement powers, 12.2.1
state claims
    pendent jurisdiction, 10.9.2
    removal to federal court, 10.9.5

Cumulative Index / 2004 Supplement — **LIABILITY**

References are to sections; references followed by "S" appear only in this Supplement

JURORS
see also JURY TRIALS
reports on, FCRA application, 2.3.6.6, 5.2.5.2, 5.3.4

JURY TRIALS
see also JURORS
closing arguments, Appx. I.5.2
CROA claims, 15.2.6.2
instructions to jury, Appx. I.5.3–Appx. I.5.5
punitive damages, determination, 10.12, 11.4.3
right to, 10.12
sample complaint with request for trial by jury, Appx. I.1.2
testimony concerning damages, Appx. I.5.1

LANDLORD REPORTING COMPANIES
see TENANT SCREENING COMPANIES

LANDLORDS
see also FURNISHERS OF INFORMATION
creditor status, 9.1.3.3
FCRA application
   joint-use exception, 2.5.5
   tenant reports, 2.3.6.4
tenant reports
   notice of adverse use, 6.4.2.3.3
   prior landlords, investigative status, 9.1.3.3
   use, 2.3.6.4, 13.7.3

LANGUAGE
dispute settlements
   model agreements, 13.5.4.4, 13.5.4.5
   selecting, 13.5.4.3

LAW ENFORCEMENT AGENCIES
see also GOVERNMENT AGENCIES
consumer reports
   court order requirement, 5.2.1
   impermissible use, 5.3.5
   permissible use, 4.5.7.2, 5.2.7, 5.2.12
FBI, see FEDERAL BUREAU OF INVESTIGATIONS (FBI)
lists used by, see LAW ENFORCEMENT BULLETINS
police departments, see POLICE DEPARTMENTS
sheriff's departments, see SHERIFF'S DEPARTMENTS

LAW ENFORCEMENT BULLETINS
see also LAW ENFORCEMENT AGENCIES
consumer report status, 2.3.5.4
FCRA, application, 2.3.5.4, 2.3.6.10.3, 5.3.8.5

LAWSUITS
see ACTIONS; COLLECTION SUITS; LITIGATION

LAWYERS
see ATTORNEYS; FURNISHERS OF INFORMATION

LEASES
see also LANDLORDS; TENANT REPORTS
business transaction status, 2.3.6.10.3
credit transaction status, 5.2.4.1, 6.4.2.3.3
denial, notice obligations, 6.4.2.3.3, 6.4.2.7.1
FCRA, application, 2.3.6.10.3
personal property leases, see PERSONAL PROPERTY LEASES
residential leases, see RESIDENTIAL LEASES

LEGAL DIRECTORIES
FCRA, application, 2.3.3, 5.3.8.5

LEGAL PROCEEDINGS
see also ACTIONS; LITIGATION
bad debts published pursuant to, 13.3.7.4

LEGISLATIVE HISTORY
see also FAIR CREDIT REPORTING ACT (FCRA)
accuracy, 7.8.2, 7.8.3.2
conference committee bill, 1.4.4
confidentiality, 5.1.1
Consumer Credit Reporting Reform Act of 1996, 1.4.6
disclosure, 4.5.1
early history, 1.4.2
FCRA, 1.4
insurance purposes, 2.3.6.7.1
intent, 2.3.6.5.3
introduction, 1.4.1
passage of FCRA, 1.4.4
qualified immunity, 10.3.2
reasonable procedures, 7.8.2
recent changes, 1.4.7
Senate Bill 823, 1.4.3
subsequent amendments, 1.4.5–1.4.7

LENDERS
see CREDITORS; JOINT LENDERS

LIABILITY
"any person," 11.1
consumer reporting agencies
   employees, 5.5
   failure to reverify investigative reports, 10.2.2.5
   FCRA violations, 10.2.1
   impermissible reports, 5.5, 10.2.2.3
   improper handling of disputes, 10.2.2.10
   inaccurate reports, 7.8, 10.2.2.1
   inadequate procedures, 7.8.4.1
   insurance coverage, 10.11.3.5
   nondisclosure, 10.2.2.9
   obsolete information, 10.2.2.2
   officers or employees, 5.5
   public record information, 10.2.2.6
credit repair fraud, 15.2.5.5, 15.2.6.2
defenses, see DEFENSES
FCRA violations
   attorney fees and costs, 11.6.1
   civil liability, generally, 10.2.1
   criminal penalties, 12.3
   furnishers of information, 3.14, 10.2.3
   reporting agencies, 10.2.2
   users, 10.2.4
   vicarious liability, 5.6.5
furnishers of information
   accuracy standards, 3.14, 10.2.3.2
   reinvestigation, 3.14.3, 10.2.3.3
identity theft, 16.6.3
legislative history, 1.4.3
limitation periods, see LIMITATIONS; STATUTE OF LIMITATIONS
users
   FCRA violations, 10.2.1, 10.2.4
   illegally obtained reports, 10.2.4.1
   impermissible purposes, 5.6, 10.2.4.1
   investigative report violations, 10.2.4.3
   notices, failure to provide, 10.2.4.2
   prescreening lists, 10.2.4.4

LIABILITY INSURANCE
consumer reporting agencies, 10.11.3.5

LIBEL
see DEFAMATION

LICENSES
see also STATE LICENSING BOARDS
adverse actions, notice obligations, 6.4.2.6
consumer report, permissible use, 5.2.5.2, 5.2.7
eligibility, FCRA application, 2.3.6.8, 5.2.5.2
employment purpose, inclusion, 5.2.5.2

LIENS
see also PUBLIC RECORD INFORMATION
reporting limitations, 8.3.5
tax liens, see TAX LIENS

LIFE INSURANCE
see also INSURANCE PURPOSES; INSURANCE UNDERWRITING
obsolete information, reporting exemption, 8.4, 13.2.5

LIMITATIONS
see also STATUTE OF LIMITATIONS; TIME
adverse information reporting, 3.7, 8.1.1, 8.3, 13.2.5, 13.5.4.1
   bankruptcies, 8.3.7, 13.2.5, 13.6.9
   criminal records, 8.3.6
   delinquent accounts, 8.3.2, 8.3.3, 13.5.4.1
   disputing, 7.7.3
   exemptions, 8.4
   home mortgage loans, 13.5.2.2
   judgments, 8.3.4, 13.2.5
   obsolete information, 8.1.1, 8.1.2, 8.3, 13.2.5
   public record information, 8.3.4–8.3.6
   repayment agreements, effect, 8.3.3
   student loans, 8.3.9, 13.5.2.2
   suits, 8.3.4
   tax liens, 8.3.5

LISTS
see CONSUMER LISTS

LITIGATION
see also ACTIONS; DISCOVERY; JURY TRIALS; LEGAL PROCEEDINGS; PLEADINGS
aids, see LITIGATION AIDS
business transaction status, 2.3.6.10.1, 5.2.9.1
consumer reports
   impermissible use, 5.3.4, 13.3.7.5
   permissible use, 5.2.4.2
   refusal to provide to litigants, 7.2.9
criminal, see PROSECUTIONS

LITIGATION AIDS
see also PRACTICE TIPS
court orders covering reporting issues, 13.5.4.7
discovery, see DISCOVERY
follow-up after dispute resolution, 13.5.4.8, 13.5.4.9
generally, 10.11.1
jury trial excerpts, Appx. I.5
negotiating credit settlements, 13.5.4
pleadings, see PLEADINGS
record retention, 10.11.4
sample documents, Appx. I

LOAN BROKERS
adverse action, disclosure requirements, 6.4.4.1
credit services organization status, 15.3.2
joint-use exception, 2.5.5

LOAN COMPANIES
see also FINANCE COMPANIES; FINANCIAL INSTITUTIONS
FCRA, application, 2.6.3

LOAN EXCHANGES
FCRA, application, 2.5.4

LOAN GUARANTY AGENCIES
FCRA, application, 2.5.5
student loan reporting, 13.6.11

LOAN VERIFIERS
disclosure obligations, 6.4.4.1

LOANS
see also CREDIT
appliances and furniture, what to avoid, 13.7.7
blemished report, implications, 13.3.2
car loans, standards, 13.7.5
home equity, see HOME MORTGAGES
small loans, pros and cons, 13.7.8.1
spouses, designation on, 13.6.4.5
student loans, see STUDENT LOANS

LOCAL GOVERNMENT AGENCIES
see also GOVERNMENT AGENCIES
FCRA, application, 2.5.7

LOCATION
see ADDRESSES

LODESTAR FORMULA
attorney fee awards, application, 11.6.2.2

MAILING LISTS
prescreening, 6.4.2.3.7

MALICE
see also WILLFUL INTENT
defamation claims, 10.3.7
definition, 10.3.6
invasion of privacy claims, 10.3.8
negligence claims, 10.3.9
tort liability, 10.3.6

MARKETING LISTS
see PRESCREENED REPORTS

MARKETING RESEARCH
account number information sharing, 16.4.1.9
consumer reports, impermissible use, 5.3.8.3

MEDICAL INFORMATION
consumer consent, 4.5.5, 6.5.3
consumer file disclosure, 4.5.5
defined, 10.2.2.4S
FCRA claims, 10.2.2.4S
furnishers of, see FURNISHERS OF INFORMATION
insurance implications, 4.5.5, 13.3.3
reporting agencies, see MEDICAL INFORMATION AGENCIES
requests, notice prior to, 6.5.3

MEDICAL INFORMATION AGENCIES
see also CONSUMER REPORTING AGENCIES; MEDICAL INFORMATION
disclosure obligations, 4.5.5
FCRA application, 2.6.1
FCRA violations, 10.2.2.4S
MIB, see MEDICAL INFORMATION BUREAU (MIB)

MEDICAL INFORMATION BUREAU (MIB)
see also MEDICAL INFORMATION AGENCIES
address, 4.5.5
disclosures from, 4.5.5
reporting agency status, 2.6.1
specialized information collection, 13.2.2

MEDICARE
see GOVERNMENT BENEFITS

MERCHANTS
see also CREDITORS
check cashing lists, adverse use, 6.4.2.3.5
credit card authorizations, 2.4.4
credit card disputes, 3.3.4.3, 13.5.2.2
credit repair laws, application
  CROA, 15.2.2.7
  state law, 15.3.4
FCRA, application, 2.6.3
GLB Act, application, 16.4.1.2
third party credit requests, 2.4.5, 2.5.5

METRO 2 FORMAT
accuracy standards, 3.4.2
associated consumers segment, 3.3.3.4
base segment, 3.3.3.3
bankruptcy and, 3.3.3.13
closed accounts, 3.8
common errors, 3.3.3.7
date of first delinquency, 3.7
debt collectors and, 3.3.3.9
disputes, noting, 3.6
objective standard, 3.3.3.2
other specialized segments, 3.3.3.6, 3.3.3.8
overview, 3.3.3.1
returned checks and, 3.3.3.12
standard automated data reporting format, 3.3.1, 3.3.2
student loans and, 3.3.3.10
transfers of accounts segment, 3.3.3.5
utility bills and, 3.3.3.11

MILITARY PERSONNEL
identity theft
  active military duty alerts, 16.6.1a.2.4S
special protections, 13.2.8.3

MISLEADING INFORMATION
see INACCURATE INFORMATION

MISREPRESENTATION
see also FALSE PRETENSES
actions, limitations, 10.10.1.2
credit repair organizations, 15.2.5.2, 15.2.5.4
  pleading, 15.2.6.2

MOBILE HOME LEASES
see RESIDENTIAL LEASES

MORTGAGES
see HOME MORTGAGES

MOTOR VEHICLE DEPARTMENTS (STATE)
FCRA, application, 2.5.7, 2.6.8

MOTOR VEHICLE REPORTS
consumer report status, 2.5.7

MULTIPLE DAMAGES
see DAMAGES, MULTIPLE

NAMES
collection agencies, restrictions, 13.4.4
theft of identity, see IDENTITY THEFT

NATIONAL CENTER ON POVERTY LAW
see also CLEARINGHOUSE NUMBERS
document ordering information, 1.1.3

NATIONAL CLEARINGHOUSE FOR LEGAL SERVICES
see NATIONAL CENTER ON POVERTY LAW

NATIONAL CREDIT UNION ADMINISTRATION
FCRA enforcement, 12.1

NATIONWIDE REPORTING AGENCIES
see also CONSUMER REPORTING AGENCIES
automated reinvestigation system, 3.12.2
defined, 2.5.8
Equifax, see EQUIFAX
Experian, see EXPERIAN (TRW)
prescreening opt-out notification system, 5.3.8.4.4
special provisions, 2.5.8
toll-free number, disclosure, 6.4.3.2
Trans Union, see TRANS UNION

NECESSARIES
state law doctrine, 13.2.7.2.1

NEGATIVE INFORMATION
see ADVERSE INFORMATION

NEGLIGENCE
common law elements, 10.3.9
conditional privilege defense, 10.3.9
definition, 10.2.1
disclosure violations, 10.2.2.9
dispute procedures, failure to follow, 10.2.2.10
FCRA qualified immunity, 3.14.5, 10.3.2, 10.3.6, 10.3.8, 10.4.4
FCRA violations
  liability, 10.2.1
  limitations, 10.10.1S
impermissible reports, 10.2.2.3
inaccurate reports, 10.2.2.1
investigative reports, disclosure, 10.2.4.3
notice violations, 10.2.4.2
obsolete information reporting, 8.5.1, 10.2.2.2
prescreening violations, 10.2.2.7, 10.2.4.4
reasonable procedures
  accuracy assurance, 10.2.2.1
  failure to follow, evidence, 8.5.1
  impermissible reports, 10.2.2.3
  obsolete information, 10.2.2.2
  reseller obligations, 10.2.2.8
tort actions, see TORT CLAIMS

NOMINAL DAMAGES
see DAMAGES, NOMINAL

NON-SUFFICIENT FUNDS
see RETURNED CHECKS

NOTICE
see also DISCLOSURE
accommodation parties, 6.4.2.3.6, 6.4.4.1
adverse action
  affiliate sharing, 6.4.4.4
  check cashing reports, 6.4.2.3.5
  circumstances, 6.4.1, 6.4.4.1
  consumer report as basis, 6.4.3

NOTICE (*cont.*)
adverse action (*cont.*)
  consumer's account, review, 6.4.2.7.2
  contents, 6.4.3, 6.4.4.2
  cosigners, 6.4.2.3.6, 6.4.4.1
  credit transactions, 6.4.2.3
  ECOA obligations, 6.4.5, 10.11.4
  employment purposes, 6.4.2.4, 6.6.2, 9.2.1.5
  failure to send, 10.2.4.2, 11.2.2
  free disclosures, 4.4.5.1
  government benefits and licenses, 6.4.2.6
  insufficient credit history, 13.6.2
  insurance purposes, 5.2.6, 6.4.2.5
  leases, 6.4.2.3.3
  overview, 6.2, 6.4.1
  prescreening, 6.4.2.3.7
  property sale, 6.4.2.3.4
  tenant report as basis, 13.7.3
  third party information as basis, 6.4.4
  time, 6.4.5
  transactions initiated by consumer, 6.4.2.7.1
  written form, 6.4.3.3, 6.4.4.2
adverse information, reporting, 3.3.5.4.1, 7.8.5.2, 13.2.3
affiliate information sharing, 6.2
billing errors, creditor's obligations, 13.5.2.2
child support debts
  government agencies, 6.5.5
  reporting, 3.3.5.4.2
consumer files
  deletion of favorable information, 8.1.2
  disclosure request, 4.4.1.1
  inaccuracy, statement of dispute, 7.6.1.1, 7.7.1
  reinsertion of deleted information, 6.7
consumer reporting agencies, obligations, 6.6.2, 7.6.1.1
consumer reports
  corrections, 7.7.1
  expedited dispute resolution, 7.3.4.2
  statements of dispute, 7.6.2, 7.7.1
  use, 6.4.3
  written permission, effect, 5.2.2
cosigners, 6.4.2.3.6, 6.4.4.1
credit disputes
  CDV or "611" notice, 3.10
  expedited dispute resolution, 7.3.4.2
  notation of dispute, 3.3.4.2, 13.5.2.1
  settlement, 13.5.4.3, 13.5.4.4, 13.5.4.5
  statements in files, 7.6.2, 7.7.1
credit scores
  home loan applicant, 6.8dS
  key factor, 6.8aS
dealer paper purchases, 6.4.4.1
ECOA, 6.4.5
employers, 6.2, 6.5.2S
FCRA rights, generally, 6.2
FCRA violations, user liability, 10.2.4.2
fraud alerts, 6.8bS
furnishers of information
  disputed debts, by, 3.3.4.2
  disputed debts, to, 3.10
  FCRA obligations, 3.2.1
  negative information, reporting, 6.8eS
  Summary of Responsibilities, FTC model form, Appx. E.3
GLB Act requirements, 16.4.1.6
  opt-out notice, 16.4.1.7.2

government agencies, child support purposes, 6.5.5
identity theft
  block information about, 6.8cS
investigative consumer reports
  contents, 9.2.1.3
  form, 9.2.1.3
  overview, 6.2, 6.6.3
  requirement, 9.2.1.5
  right to disclosure, 9.2.1.3
  sources, potential discovery of identity, 9.3.2
  time, 9.2.1.2
  user requests, 9.2.1
loan brokering, 6.4.4.1
medical information, 6.2, 6.5.3
overview, 6.2
prescreening purpose, 6.6.4
public record information
  employment purposes, 6.6.2, 7.8.5.2
  overview, 6.2
reasonable procedures defense, 6.9, 9.2.4, 10.2.4.2
reinsertion, 6.2, 6.7
reinvestigations
  denials, 7.3.3
  investigative sources, 9.3.2
  past users, 7.4.3, 7.7.1
  nationwide reporting agencies, 3.12.2
  results, 3.12, 7.4.1
  requests, 7.3.2.2
state law requirements, 6.5.6
student loan defaults, 13.5.2.3
Summary of Rights, *see* SUMMARY OF CONSUMER RIGHTS
time, 6.4.5, 6.6.3
users of reports
  FCRA responsibilities, 5.1.3, 6.5.1S, 6.6.1
  post request, 6.6
  prior to a request, 6.5

NSF CHECKS
see RETURNED CHECKS

OBSOLETE INFORMATION
see also CONSUMER FILES; INFORMATION ON CONSUMERS
agency liability, 10.2.2.2
dating, 8.5.3
deletion, 8.1.3, 8.5.3, 13.2.5
existence, reporting, 8.2
favorable information, 8.1.2, 8.1.3, 13.6.4.4
FCRA claims, 10.2.2.2
FTC Commentary, Appx. C
inaccurate information as, 8.1.3, 13.2.5
investigative consumer reports, 9.4.1, 9.4.2.4
purging from file, 8.1.3
reasonable procedures, 7.8.4.10.3–7.8.4.10.5, 8.5
reliance on, 8.2
reporting exemptions, 8.4
reporting limitations
  accounts charged off, 8.3.3
  adverse items, 8.3.2
  bankruptcy reports, 8.3.7
  collection accounts, 8.3.3
  criminal records, 8.3.6
  existence of information, 8.2
  judgments, 8.3.4

OBSOLETE INFORMATION (*cont.*)
reporting limitations (*cont.*)
   paid tax liens, 8.3.5
   structure of FCRA, 8.3.1
   student loans, 8.3.9
   suits, 8.3.4
reporting restrictions, 13.2.5, 8.1.1, 8.2
retention, 8.1.1, 8.3, 8.4, 13.2.5
standards, legislative history, 1.4.2
verification, 8.4, 13.2.5

OFFENSES
see CRIMINAL OFFENSES

OFFICE OF COMPTROLLER OF THE CURRENCY (OCC)
affiliate information sharing, proposed regulations, Appx. A.6.2
FCRA enforcement responsibilities, 12.1

OFFICE OF PERSONNEL MANAGEMENT
FCRA application, 2.5.6

OFFICE OF THRIFT SUPERVISION (OTS)
FCRA enforcement responsibilities, 12.1

OFFICES
location, *see* ADDRESSES

OFFICIAL STAFF COMMENTARY (FTC)
see also FEDERAL TRADE COMMISSION (FTC)
status, 1.3.3, 12.2.3
text, Appx. C
weight, 1.3.3, 12.2.3

OPEN-END CREDIT
see CREDIT ACCOUNTS; CREDIT CARDS

PARTIES
credit reporting claims
   class actions, 10.7.2
   defendants, 10.7.3
   plaintiffs, 10.7.1

PARTNERSHIPS
see also BUSINESSES
consumer reports, permissible purposes, 5.2.4.3
FCRA, application, 2.3.3, 2.3.6.5.1

PATERNITY PROCEEDINGS
see also CHILD SUPPORT ENFORCEMENT AGENCIES
consumer reports, use, 5.3.2

PATRIOT ACT
see USA PATRIOT ACT

PENDENT JURISDICTION
see also JURISDICTION
FCRA actions, 10.9.2

PERMISSIBLE PURPOSES
account reviews, 2.3.6.11, 5.2.10
agents, 5.1.4
business credit, 5.2.4.3
business transactions, 2.3.6.10, 5.2.9
certification, *see* CERTIFICATION
check cashing lists, 2.3.6.3
child support, 2.3.6.12
consumer's permission, 5.2.2
counterintelligence, 5.2.12
court order, 5.2.1
credit transactions, 2.3.6.2, 5.2.4
debt collection purposes, 2.3.6.2, 5.2.4.2
employment agencies, 2.4.3, 6.4.2.4
employment purposes, 2.3.6.6, 5.2.5.2
exceptions, 2.3.6.5
expected use, 2.3.5.3
FBI purposes, 5.2.12
generally, 2.3.5.1, 2.3.6.1
government agencies, 2.3.6.12, 5.2.3, 5.2.12
government licenses or benefits, 2.3.6.8, 5.2.7
impermissible use, Ch. 5
information collected for, 2.3.5
insurance purposes, 2.3.6.7, 5.2.6
original purpose, 2.3.5.4
permissible use, Ch. 5
personal credit, 2.3.6.2
prescreening lists, 2.3.3, 5.3.8.4
prospective clients, 5.3.4
requirement for release, 5.1.2
risk assessment, 2.3.6.9, 5.2.8
skip tracing, 2.3.6.2, 5.2.4.2
spouses, 5.3.6, 13.6.4.5, 13.2.7.2.1
tenant reports, 2.3.6.4
terrorism protection, 5.2.12
third parties, 5.3.6
verification, 5.4.1
waiver of rights, 5.2.2

PERSONAL CREDIT
see also CREDIT
defined, 5.2.4.3

PERSONAL INFORMATION PRIVACY ACT
pending legislation, 16.7

PERSONAL INTERVIEWS
investigative consumer reports
   confirmation, 9.4.2.2
   contents, 9.1.2.3
   reinvestigation, 9.3.2
   requirement, 9.1.2.3

PERSONAL JURISDICTION
see also JURISDICTION
FCRA actions, 10.7.3

PERSONAL PROPERTY LEASES
see also AUTOMOBILE LEASES; LEASES
credit transaction status, 6.4.2.3.3
denial, notice obligations, 6.4.2.3.3
FCRA, application, 2.3.6.10.3
home appliances and furniture, 13.7.7

PERSONAL PURPOSES
see also CONSUMER TRANSACTIONS
defined, 5.2.4.3

PERSONAL REPRESENTATIVES
see POWER OF ATTORNEY

PERSONNEL
see EMPLOYEES

PERSONS
see also CONSUMERS; CONSUMER REPORTING AGENCIES
"any person," liability, 11.1
definition, 2.5.2, 9.2.1.1

PLEADINGS · Fair Credit Reporting / 2004 Supplement

References are to sections; references followed by "S" appear only in this Supplement

PLEADINGS
see also LITIGATION
credit repair deception, 15.2.6.2, 15.3.6
sample complaints, Appx. I.1
sample interrogatories, Appx. I.2
sample notice of deposition, Appx. I.4.2, Appx. I.4.3

POINT SCORES
see CREDIT SCORES

POLICE DEPARTMENTS
see also LAW ENFORCEMENT AGENCIES
FCRA, application, 2.6.8

POWER OF ATTORNEY
see also ATTORNEYS
consumer files, disclosure requests, 4.4.3.2
proof of authorization, 4.4.3.2

PRACTICE TIPS
discovery, see DISCOVERY
disputing inaccurate information, 3.4.5
FCRA, utilization, 1.3.2
guide to credit reporting, Appx. J
litigation aids, see LITIGATION AIDS
pleadings, see PLEADINGS
reinvestigation requests, 7.3.2.3, 7.3.6, 7.4.3
settlement, see SETTLEMENT

PREEMPTION OF STATE LAW
credit repair laws, 15.2.7, 15.3.7
credit reporting laws
　general preemption, 10.4.3
　specific preemptions, 10.4.4
　temporary preemption, 10.4.4
furnishers of information, 3.2.2.3, 3.3.5.4.1, 10.4.4
more protective supplementary legislation, 3.3.5.4.1, 10.4.4
tort claims, 3.14.5

PRESCREENED REPORTS
see also CONSUMER LISTS
account number information, 16.4.1.9
adverse action, notice, 6.4.2.3.7
consumer report status, 2.3.3, 5.3.8.4.2
described, 5.3.8.4.2, 8.3.8
disclosure requirements, 8.3.8, 10.2.4.4
exclusion requests, 5.3.8.4.4
FCRA application, 2.3.3
FCRA violations
　reporting agencies, 10.2.2.7
　users, 10.2.4.4
"firm offer" of credit or insurance, 5.3.8.4.3, 10.2.2.7
misuse, 10.2.4.4
notification system for consumers, 5.3.8.4.4, 10.2.2.7
"opt out" rights, 5.3.8.4.4, 10.2.2.7
permissible purposes, 5.3.8.4.1
recipients, disclosure, 4.5.4
record of inquiries, time period, 8.3.8
state law preemption, 10.4.4
target marketing, 1.4.6, 5.3.8.4.2, 5.3.8.5
users
　differentiation from report users, 5.1.7
　disclosure notices, 6.6.4
　"firm offer", 5.3.8.4.3

PRIVACY
see also CONFIDENTIALITY
common law protections, 16.3, 16.5
definition, 10.3.8
FCRA purpose, 1.4.1
FTC rule, see PRIVACY RULE (FTC)
GLB notice, 16.4.1.6
governmental intrusion, 16.2
legislative response, 1.4.3
overview, 16.1
statutory protections
　Computer Fraud and Abuse Act, 16.4.2.1
　FCRA, 5.1.1, 16.1
　Financial Information Privacy Act, 16.4.2.2
　FTC Act, 16.4.2.3
　Gramm-Leach-Bliley (GLB) Act, 16.4.1
　interests impeding, 16.7
　pending legislation, 16.7
　state law, 16.4.2.4
tort claims, see INVASION OF PRIVACY

PRIVACY ACT
federal agencies, protections, 2.5.6, 16.2

PRIVACY RULE (FTC)
account number sharing, 16.4.1.9
customer relationship, 16.4.1.3
exempt disclosures, 16.4.1.5
financial institutions, 16.4.1.2
nonpublic personally identifiable financial information, 16.4.1.4, 16.4.1.6
opt-out notices, 16.4.1.7.2
opt-out rights, exercise, 16.4.1.7.3
selected provisions, Appx. A.5.2

PRIVATE INVESTIGATORS
see DETECTIVE AGENCIES

PRIVILEGE
see CONDITIONAL PRIVILEGE

PROOF
see BURDEN OF PROOF; EVIDENCE

PROPERTY MANAGERS
consumer reporting agency status, 9.1.3.3
consumer reports, obtaining, 5.1.4

PROPERTY SETTLEMENTS
see DIVORCE PROCEEDINGS

PROSECUTIONS
see also CRIMINAL OFFENSES
consumer reports, use, 5.3.4, 5.3.5, 13.3.7.5
identity theft, 13.5.5.4

PROTECTIVE BULLETINS
see LAW ENFORCEMENT BULLETINS

PROTECTIVE ORDERS
discovery requests, 10.11.3.2

PUBLIC AGENCIES
see GOVERNMENT AGENCIES

PUBLIC ASSISTANCE
see GOVERNMENT BENEFITS

PUBLIC RECORD INFORMATION
clearing up blemished report, 13.6.10
consumer report status, 2.3.3
consumer reports, inclusion, 13.2.3

PUBLIC RECORD INFORMATION (cont.)
consumer reporting agencies
  FCRA violations, liability, 10.2.2.6
    furnishing, 6.6.2
    special procedures, 6.6.2, 7.8.4.5, 7.8.5
employment purposes, notice, 2.3.6.6, 6.2, 6.6.2, 13.3.4, 10.2.2.6
FTC Commentary, Appx. C
inaccurate reports, 7.2.3
notice of release, 7.8.5.2
reinvestigations, 7.3.4.3
reporting limitations
  criminal records, 8.3.6
  judgments, 8.3.4
  suits, 8.3.4
  tax liens, 8.3.5
searches by inspection bureaus, 9.1.3.1
state law restrictions, 13.2.8.2
up-to-date, 6.6.2.2, 7.8.5.3

PUBLIC UTILITY CREDIT
see also UTILITY SERVICES
ECOA, application, 13.6.4.5
Metro 2 format reporting, 3.3.3.11

PUBLICATION
bad debt lists, 13.3.7.4
credit record, 13.3.7.3

PUNITIVE DAMAGES
see DAMAGES, PUNITIVE

QUALIFIED IMMUNITY
disclosure prerequisite, 10.3.3
exceptions, 10.3.6
FACTA, application, 11.1a.1S
information to nonreporting agency, 10.3.5
tort liability, 3.14.5, 10.3.2, 10.3.4, 16.3

RACKETEERING INFLUENCED AND CORRUPT ORGANIZATIONS ACT (RICO)
credit repair organizations, application, 15.3

REAL ESTATE AGENTS
consumer reports, obtaining, 5.1.4

REAL ESTATE INVESTMENTS
consumer report, permissible use, 5.2.9.1
personal credit, inclusion, 5.2.4.3

REAL ESTATE SETTLEMENT PROCEDURES ACT (RESPA)
scope, 3.3.4.4, 13.5.2.2

REAL PROPERTY LEASES
see LEASES; RESIDENTIAL LEASES

REASONABLE PROCEDURES
see also CONSUMER REPORTING AGENCIES; CONSUMER REPORTS
accuracy assurance, 7.8.1, 10.2.2.1
additional information, 7.8.4.11
bankruptcy reports, 7.8.4.10.2
consumer identification, 7.8.4.6
data communication, 7.8.4.8
defense, as, 6.9, 10.2.4.2, 10.2.4.3
discovery, 10.11.3.1
electronic communication of reports, 5.4.4
employee access to files, 5.5
extenuating circumstances, 7.8.4.10.5

FCRA purpose, 1.3.1
FCRA requirements, 5.4.1
FTC Commentary, Appx. C
guarantors of debts, 7.8.4.10.2
identity theft, 7.8.4.7
illogical information, 7.8.4.9
impermissible purposes, avoiding, 10.2.2.3
inaccurate sources, 7.8.4.4
incomplete information, 7.8.4.10.1
interpretation, 7.8.4.8
investigative reports
  disclosure obligations, 9.2.4, 10.2.4.3
  preparation, 9.4.1
legislative history, 7.8.2
maximum possible accuracy, 7.8.4.1
mismerged information, 7.8.4.6
missing accounts, 7.8.4.11
new files, 7.8.4.11
notice violations, 6.9, 10.2.4.2
obsolete information, 7.8.4.10.3, 8.5, 10.2.2.2
policies encouraging unfavorable reports, 7.8.4.3
proof issues, 7.8.4.2
public record information, 7.8.4.5, 7.8.5
reinvestigations, 7.3.4.3, 7.3.4.4
retention of request records, 5.4.5
standards, 7.8.4.1
systematic violations, 10.7.2
transcription, 7.2.6, 7.8.4.8
updating procedures, 7.8.4.10.3–7.8.4.10.5
user identification and certification
  blanket certifications, 5.4.2.2
  child support, 5.2.11
  continuing reports, 5.4.2.3
  employment purposes, 5.2.5.3
  follow-up reports, 5.4.2.3
  investigative consumer reports, 9.2.1.6, 10.2.4.3
  nature of certification, 5.4.2.1
verification procedures, 5.4.3
violations, 5.4.1

RECORDS
consumer reporting agencies, obligations, 5.4.5. 10.11.4
consumer reports, users, 5.4.5
credit record, *see* CREDIT RECORD
criminal records, *see* CRIMINAL RECORDS; PUBLIC RECORD INFORMATION
public, *see* PUBLIC RECORD INFORMATION

REINSERTION OF INFORMATION
agency obligations, 7.5
disputed debts, breach of settlement, 13.5.4.3
failure to handle properly, FCRA claims, 10.2.2.10
furnisher obligations, 7.5
legislative history, 1.4.6
notice to consumer, 3.12.1, 6.7, 7.5
obsolete but favorable information, 13.6.4.4

REINVESTIGATIONS
see also REVERIFICATION
agency obligations, 3.13, 7.3.2.1, 7.3.5, 7.8.4.10.1
automated reinvestigation system, 3.12.2, 3.12.3
consumer requests
  direct requests, 7.3.2.2
  expedited dispute resolution, 7.3.4.2
  follow-up steps, 7.4.3, 7.7

371

REINVESTIGATIONS (cont.)
consumer requests (cont.)
   frivolous requests, 7.3.3
   identity theft victims, 7.8.4.7
   practical tips, 7.3.2.3
   results, notification, 3.13, 7.4.1
correction or deletion after, 7.4.2, 7.7
deadline for response, 3.12.1, 7.3.6
failure to handle properly, FCRA claims
   actual damages calculations, 11.2.2
   furnisher of information, 3.11.2, 10.2.3.3
   reporting agency, 10.2.2.10
fees, 7.3.2.1
formal dispute process, 3.9
furnisher obligations
   conducting, 3.11, 13.5.2.2
   generally, 3.9
   involvement, 3.10, 7.3.5
   liability, 3.11.2, 3.14.3, 10.2.3.3
   reporting results, 3.12
incomplete investigations, 7.3.4.3
incomplete or inaccurate information, 7.3.2.1, 13.5.2.1
investigative reports, 9.3.2, 9.4.2.4, 10.2.2.5
irrelevant information, 7.3.3
notification
   consumer, 3.12.2, 3.13, 7.4.1
   electronic, 3.12.3
   furnishers, 3.10, 7.3.5.2
   nationwide reporting agencies, 3.12.2
   previous users, 7.7
   results, 3.12
reasonable procedures standard, application, 7.3.4.4
reporting agency obligations, 7.3.1, 7.3.2.1, 7.3.5, 7.8.4.7, 7.8.4.10.1
state law preemption, 10.4.4
statement of dispute, filing, 7.6.1.1
time, 3.12.1, 7.3.6
type of reinvestigation required, 7.3.4.3

RELATIVES
see also SPOUSES
blemished credit records, implications, 13.3.7.2
consumer reports, restrictions on use, 5.2.5.2, 5.3.6, 13.2.7

REMOVAL
see JURISDICTION

RENT-TO-OWN TRANSACTIONS
see PERSONAL PROPERTY LEASES

RENTAL AGREEMENTS
see LEASES

RENTAL APPLICATIONS
consumer report, permissible use, 5.2.9.1

RENTAL CLEARANCE AGENCIES
see TENANT SCREENING COMPANIES

RENTAL SCREENING REPORTS
see TENANT REPORTS

RENTERS
see TENANTS

REPAYMENT AGREEMENTS
negotiating, 13.6.6
reporting limitations, effect, 8.3.3

REPORTERS
consumer reports, impermissible use, 5.3.9

REPORTS
business, *see* COMMERCIAL REPORTS
consumers, *see* CONSUMER REPORTS; INVESTIGATIVE CONSUMER REPORTS
credit, *see* CONSUMER REPORTS
employment purposes, *see* EMPLOYMENT REPORTS
insurance purposes, *see* INSURANCE REPORTS
investigative reports, *see* INVESTIGATIVE CONSUMER REPORTS
residential mortgage, *see* RESIDENTIAL MORTGAGE CREDIT REPORTS
tenant screening, *see* TENANT REPORTS

RESEARCH
see MARKETING RESEARCH

RESELLERS
see also CONSUMER REPORTING AGENCIES; INTER-FACT
certifications, 2.6.2, 10.2.2.8
consumer reporting agency status, 2.6.2
FACTA, application, 3.15S
FCRA, application, 2.6.2
FCRA violations, 10.2.2.8
FTC consent decree, Appx. H.4
permissible purpose requirement, 5.1.2
trimerger reports, 10.11.2
verification, 10.2.2.8

RESIDENTIAL LEASES
see also LANDLORDS; LEASES; TENANTS
blemished reports, implications, 13.3.2, 13.7.3
credit transaction status, 6.4.2.3.3
denial, notice requirements, 6.4.2.3.3, 6.4.2.7.1
FCRA, application, 2.3.6.4

RESIDENTIAL MORTGAGE CREDIT REPORTS
see also HOME MORTGAGES
use by lenders, 13.7.2.1

RETAILERS
see CREDITORS; MERCHANTS

RETURNED CHECKS
consumer report, permissible use, 5.2.4.2
Metro 2 format reporting, 3.3.3.12

REVERIFICATION
see also REINVESTIGATIONS; VERIFICATION
investigative reports, subsequent reports, 9.4.2.4, 10.2.2.5

RICO
see RACKETEERING INFLUENCED AND CORRUPT ORGANIZATIONS ACT (RICO)

RIGHT TO FINANCIAL PRIVACY ACT
privacy from governmental intrusion, 16.2

RIGHT TO PRIVACY
see PRIVACY

RISK SCORES
see CREDIT SCORES

RULE 68 OFFERS
attorney fee considerations, 11.6.5

RURAL HOUSING SERVICE (RHS)
joint lender exemption, 2.5.5
underwriting guidelines, 13.7.2.2

SAFEGUARD RULES
financial information, 16.4.1.1

SALES
consumer files, 5.1.5
resellers of information, *see* RESELLERS

SCHOLARSHIP LOCATION SERVICES
credit services organization status, 15.3.2

SECRETARY OF AGRICULTURE
FCRA enforcement, 12.1

SECRETARY OF TRANSPORTATION
FCRA enforcement, 12.1

SECURED CREDIT CARDS
see also CREDIT CARDS
Consumer Action fact sheet, 13.7.8.2
described, 13.7.8.2

SECURITIES TRANSACTIONS
personal credit, inclusion, 5.2.4.3
spouses' credit information, 13.6.4.5, 13.2.7.2.2

SECURITY AGREEMENTS
see DEALER PAPER

SECURITY CLEARANCES
adverse notice exemption, 6.4.2.4
employment purpose status, 2.3.6.6, 5.2.5.2
FBI, 4.5.7.2

SECURITY PROCEDURES
consumer reporting agencies, 7.8.4.8

SELF-EMPLOYMENT
see INDEPENDENT CONTRACTORS; SOLE PROPRIETORSHIPS

SELLERS
see MERCHANTS

SETTLEMENT
see also LITIGATION
attorney fee awards, 11.6.4
consumer reports, use, 5.3.4
credit disputes
　breach of agreement, 13.5.4.3
　cleaning up file after, 13.5.4.8
　court approval, 13.5.4.6
　credit rating, protecting, 13.5.4.1
　model agreements, 13.5.4.4, 13.5.4.5
　monitoring file after, 13.5.4.9
　negotiating reporting issues, 13.5.4.2
　selecting correct language, 13.5.4.3
delinquent accounts, repayment plans, 13.6.6
FTC consent decrees, 12.2.1
insurance liability coverage, 10.11.3.5
mortgage disputes, 13.5.2.2
Rule 68 offers, 11.6.5

SHERIFF'S DEPARTMENTS
see also LAW ENFORCEMENT AGENCIES
FCRA, application, 2.6.8

SKIP TRACING
consumer reports, permissible purpose, 2.3.6.2, 5.2.4.2, 5.3.5

SOCIAL SECURITY NUMBER PRIVACY AND IDENTITY THEFT PREVENTION ACT
pending legislation, 16.7

SOCIAL SERVICE AGENCIES
see also ADOPTION AGENCIES; CHILD SUPPORT ENFORCEMENT AGENCIES; GOVERNMENT AGENCIES; WELFARE AGENCIES
FCRA, application, 2.3.6.8, 2.5.2

SOLDIERS AND SAILOR'S CIVIL RELIEF ACT
military personnel protections, 13.2.8.3

SOLE PROPRIETORSHIPS
see also BUSINESSES
consumer reports, permissible purpose, 5.2.4.3
FCRA, application, 2.3.6.5.1, 2.3.6.6
self-employment reports, 2.3.6.6

SPOUSES
blemished credit records
　avoiding, 13.6.4.6.3
　implications, 13.3.7.2, 13.6.8.4
car loans, 13.7.5
consumer reports
　bankruptcy notations, 7.8.4.10.2
　ECOA restrictions, 13.2.7.2.2
　FCRA restrictions, 13.2.7.2.1
　permissible purposes, 5.3.6
　separate files, 13.2.7.1
credit history
　application to consumer, 13.2.7.1
　avoiding, 13.6.4.6.3
　consideration by request, 13.6.4.6.2
　ECOA reporting requirements, 13.6.4.5, 13.2.7.1
　explanation to creditor, 13.6.8.4
　relying on, 13.6.4.5, 13.7.1
　use by creditor, 13.6.4.5, 13.2.7.2
doctrine of necessaries, 13.2.7.2.1
utility services, 13.7.4

STANDARDS
accuracy
　affiliates, 13.5.2.1
　consumer reports, 7.8.3, 7.8.4
　FTC Commentary, Appx. C
　furnishers, *see under* FURNISHERS OF INFORMATION
　legislative history, 1.4.2, 1.4.3, 1.4.6
car loans, 13.7.5
consumer files
　legislative history, 1.4.2
　reinsertions, 7.5
ECOA disclosures, 6.4.4.3
home mortgages, 13.7.2
reasonable procedures, 7.8.4.1
reliability, 7.8.4.4

STANDING
credit repair organizations, suits against, 15.2.6.2

STATE AGENCIES
see also GOVERNMENT AGENCIES
FCRA, application, 2.5.7
privacy protections, 16.2

STATE CLAIMS
damages
  generally, 11.1
  nominal damages, 11.2.4
  statutory damages, 11.3
generally, 10.4.1
injunctive relief, 11.5
jury trials, 10.12
limitations, 10.10.2
pendent jurisdiction, 10.9.2
private remedies, 11.1
removal to federal court, 10.9.5
selecting claims to utilize, 10.6
unfair and deceptive practices, 10.4.2

STATE COURTS
FCRA claims
  jurisdiction, 10.9.1
  removal to federal court, 10.9.5
  selection of court, 10.9.4

STATE CREDIT REPAIR STATUTES
see STATE CREDIT SERVICES (REPAIR) STATUTES

STATE CREDIT REPORTING STATUTES
see also STATE LAW
claims under, see STATE CLAIMS
collection agencies, reporting restrictions, 13.4.2
cosigners, reporting of adverse information, 3.3.5.4.1
disclosure fees, 4.4.5.2
employment reports, 13.3.4
false threats, 13.4.4
furnishing of information, 3.3.5.4
generally, 10.4.1
investigative reports
  disclosure, 9.2.1.3
  insurance purposes, 9.1.3.1
  landlord and tenant purposes, 9.1.3.3
obsolete information, reporting, 13.2.5
preemption, see PREEMPTION OF STATE LAW
public record information, restrictions, 3.3.5.4, 13.2.8.2
reinvestigations
  denials, notice, 7.3.3
  response deadline, 7.3.6
summary, Appx. B.3

STATE CREDIT SERVICES (REPAIR) STATUTES
see also CREDIT REPAIR AGENCIES; STATE LAW
federal preemption, 15.2.7, 15.3.7
overview, 15.3.1
private causes of action, 15.3.6
retailers, application, 15.3.4
scope
  coverage, 15.3.2
  exemptions, 15.3.3
substantive prohibitions, 15.3.5
summaries, Appx. B.3

STATE ENFORCEMENT
CROA, 15.2.8
generally, 12.4.1
information furnishers, 12.4.2
investigator powers, 12.4.3
limitations, 12.4.4
notification of federal regulators, 12.4.3

STATE LAW
child support plans, 5.2.11
claims under, see STATE CLAIMS
consumer file disclosure, fees, 4.4.5.2
credit repair statutes, see STATE CREDIT SERVICES (REPAIR) STATUTES
credit reporting statutes, see STATE CREDIT REPORTING STATUTES
deceptive practices statutes, 10.4.2
doctrine of necessaries, 13.2.7.2.1
furnishers of information, 3.2.2.3, 3.3.5.4
identity theft
  generally, 7.8.4.7, 16.6.3
  suits under, 13.5.5.4
  summaries, Appx. B.3
medical information disclosure, 4.5.5
preemption, see PREEMPTION OF STATE LAW
privacy protections, 16.4.2.4
telemarketing, 15.4.2
utility services, 13.7.4

STATE LICENSING BOARDS
see also LICENSES
consumer report, permissible use, 5.2.5.2

STATEMENTS OF DISPUTE
see also EXPLANATIONS
consumer rights
  explanations, 7.6.1.2
  incomplete or inaccurate items, 7.6.1.1
  offers of new information, 7.6.1.3
frivolous or irrelevant, 7.6.2
improper handling by agency, 10.2.2.10
inaccuracy or incompleteness, 7.6.1.1, 13.6.8.2
investigative consumer reports, 9.3.2
length, 7.6.1.1
notification of previous users
  consumer request, 7.7.1
  disclosure of rights, 7.7.2
  payment for notification, 7.7.3
public record information, 13.6.10

STATISTICS
reporting agencies, requirements to keep, 7.8.4.2

STATUTE OF LIMITATIONS
see also LIMITATIONS
CROA violations, 15.2.6.2
FCRA violations, 10.10.1S
  reinvestigation provisions, 3.14.3
state claims, 10.10.2
suits and judgments, effect on reporting limitations, 8.3.4
tort claims, 10.10.2

STATUTES
CCPA, see CONSUMER CREDIT PROTECTION ACT (CCPA)
CROA, see CREDIT REPAIR ORGANIZATIONS ACT (CROA)
ECOA, see EQUAL CREDIT OPPORTUNITY ACT (ECOA)
FCBA, see FAIR CREDIT BILLING ACT (FCBA)
FCRA, see FAIR CREDIT REPORTING ACT (FCRA)
FDCPA, see FAIR DEBT COLLECTION PRACTICES ACT (FDCPA)
GLB, see GRAMM-LEACH-BLILEY (GLB) ACT
Higher Education Act, see HIGHER EDUCATION ACT
Privacy Act, see PRIVACY ACT

STATUTES (cont.)
RESPA, see REAL ESTATE SETTLEMENT PROCEDURES ACT (RESPA)
soldiers, see SOLDIERS AND SAILOR'S CIVIL RELIEF ACT
state, see STATE CREDIT REPORTING STATUTES; STATE LAW
telemarketing, see TELEMARKETING AND CONSUMER FRAUD ABUSE PREVENTION ACT
UDAP, see UNFAIR OR DECEPTIVE ACTS OR PRACTICES (UDAP)

STATUTORY DAMAGES
see DAMAGES, STATUTORY

STUDENT LOANS
blemished reports, implications, 13.3.2, 13.7.9
defaults
 clearing up, 13.6.11
 reporting, 8.3.9, 13.2.3, 13.5.2.3, 13.6.11
defenses, raising, 13.5.2.3, 13.6.11
Higher Education Act, application, 8.3.9, 13.6.11
joint lender exemption, application, 2.5.5
Metro 2 format reporting, 3.3.3.10
reporting limitations, 8.3.9

SUBPOENAS
consumer reports, obtaining by, 5.2.1, 10.11.3.4

SUITS
see ACTIONS; COLLECTION SUITS; LEGAL PROCEEDINGS; PUBLIC RECORD INFORMATION

SUMMARY OF CONSUMER RIGHTS
disclosure inclusion, 4.5.2.2
employment reports, 5.2.5.4, 13.3.4
entitlement, 4.6, 6.2, 6.3
FTC model form, Appx. E.1
overview, 6.3
sample credit bureau forms, Appx. F.3
state law, preemption by FCRA, 10.4.4

SUMMARY OF RESPONSIBILITIES OF FURNISHERS
FTC model form, Appx. E.3

SUMMARY OF USER RESPONSIBILITIES
FTC model form, Appx. E.2

SUPERBUREAUS
see RESELLERS

SURETIES
see ACCOMMODATION PARTIES

TARGET MARKETING LISTS
FCRA, application, 1.4.6, 2.3.3
FCRA violations, 10.2.2.7, 10.2.4.4
impermissible purpose, 5.2.9.1
permissible purpose, 5.1.7

TAX COLLECTION
see also INTERNAL REVENUE SERVICE (IRS)
consumer reports, use, 5.3.3

TAX LIENS
see also PUBLIC RECORD INFORMATION
consumer report, permissible purpose, 5.3.3
reporting limitations, 8.3.5
tainted data, 7.2.3

TAX PREPARATION SERVICES
credit services organization status, 15.3.2
GLB Act, application, 16.4.1.2

TELEMARKETING
credit card offers, 13.7.8.2
federal statute, see TELEMARKETING AND CONSUMER FRAUD ABUSE PREVENTION ACT
FTC rule, see TELEMARKETING RULE (FTC)
state law, 15.4.2
Telephone Consumer Protection Act, application, 15.4.3

TELEMARKETING AND CONSUMER FRAUD ABUSE PREVENTION ACT
overview, 15.4.1

TELEMARKETING RULE (FTC)
see also FEDERAL TRADE COMMISSION (FTC); TELEMARKETING
advance fee credit card offers, 13.7.8.2
credit repair agencies
 application, 15.4.1
 enforcement against, 15.2.8
violations, 15.4.1

TELEPHONE
companies, see TELEPHONE COMPANIES
consumer reports via, statements of dispute, reading, 7.6.2
directories, see TELEPHONE DIRECTORIES
FCRA disclosures via
 consumer file, 4.4.1.3
 fees, 4.4.5.1.1, 4.4.5.3

TELEPHONE COMPANIES
FCRA application, 2.6.9

TELEPHONE CONSUMER PROTECTION ACT
credit repair clinics, application, 15.4.3

TELEPHONE DIRECTORIES
consumer report status, 2.3.3, 2.3.5.3, 5.3.8.5

TELETYPE HOOKUPS
see ELECTRONIC COMMUNICATION

TENANT REPORTS
adverse use, notice, 13.7.3
blemished report, implications, 13.3.6, 13.7.3
consumer report status, 2.3.3, 2.3.6.4
financially troubled consumer, 13.2.2, 13.3.5
FTC Commentary, Appx. C
inaccuracy, 13.2.2, 13.7.3
investigative consumer report, status, 9.1.3.3
notice of adverse use, 6.4.2.3.3
permissible use, 5.2.9.1
rental payment subsidies, 5.2.7, 13.3.5
use by landlords, 13.7.3

TENANT SCREENING COMPANIES
see also CONSUMER REPORTING AGENCIES
abuses, 13.2.2
consumer reports, obtaining, 5.1.4
FCRA, application, 2.3.6.4, 2.6.1
identification, 13.7.3
reports by, see TENANT REPORTS

TENANTS
see also LANDLORDS; LEASES; TENANT REPORTS
denial of lease, notice, 6.4.2.3.3

375

TESTERS
FCRA violations, use, 10.11.2

THEFT
see FRAUD; IDENTITY THEFT

THREATS
false threats
   debt collectors, 3.3.5.1, 13.4.4
     investigative consumer report, 9.2.1.2
reporting debt to credit bureau, 3.3.5.1, 13.4

TIME
see also LIMITATIONS
investigative consumer reports
   disclosure, 9.2.2.4
   notice of investigation, 9.2.1.2
reinvestigations, 3.12.1, 7.3.6

TORT CLAIMS
appropriation, 16.3
attorney fees, 11.6.3
collection practices, 13.4.4
consumer files, disclosure, effect, 4.1, 4.3.1
consumer reporting issues, 10.3
consumer reports
   disclosure, effect, 4.1
   inaccurate information, 10.3.1
defamation, see DEFAMATION
false light, 16.3
inaccurate information, furnishing, 3.14.5
intrusion, 16.3
invasion of privacy, see INVASION OF PRIVACY
limitations, 10.10.2
negligence, see NEGLIGENCE
public disclosure, 16.3
punitive damages, 11.4.1.1
qualified immunity, 3.14.5, 10.3.2–10.3.6, 10.4.4
utilizing, 10.6

TRADE DIRECTORIES
consumer report status, 2.3.3, 2.3.5.3, 5.3.8.5

TRADE EXPERIENCE
exchanging, FCRA exemption, 2.4.1

TRANS UNION
see also CONSUMER REPORTING AGENCIES; CREDIT BUREAUS; NATIONWIDE REPORTING AGENCIES
consent orders, Appx. H.3
credit reports
   reading, 4.8.2.1
   sample report, Appx. F.1.3
credit scores
   FICO score, 14.2.2.1
   obtaining, 14.4.2
disclosure requests, 4.4.2.2, 4.4.2.3.3
FCRA, application, 2.6.1
fees, 4.4.2.3.3, 4.4.5
liability insurance, 10.11.3.5
overview, 1.2
prescreening lists, exclusion requests, 5.3.8.4.4
Summary of Rights, sample, Appx. F.3.3

TRANSCRIPTION ERRORS
see also ERRORS
consumer files, 7.2.6, 7.8.4.8

TRANSFERS
see SALES

TRIALS
see ACTIONS; DISCOVERY; JURY TRIALS; LITIGATION; WITNESSES

TRUCKER'S AMENDMENT
employment reports
   adverse use, exemptions, 6.4.2.4
   oral disclosures, 6.5.2S

TRW
see EXPERIAN (TRW)

UNEMPLOYED PERSONS
consumer file disclosure, fees, 4.4.5.1.3

UNFAIR OR DECEPTIVE ACTS OR PRACTICES (UDAP)
actions, forum, 10.9.5
credit repair organizations, 15.3.6, 15.4.1
false threats, 13.4.4
FCRA violations, 10.4.2, 12.1
FTC Act, 16.4.2.3
injunctive relief, 11.5
limitations, 10.10.2
nominal damages, 11.2.4
non-FCRA violations, 10.4.2
state law, 10.4.2
statutory damages, 11.3
waiver of rights, 9.2.5

UNIVERSAL DATA FORM
sample, Appx. G.2
use by creditors, 3.3.2
   correcting inaccuracies, 3.5.4

USA PATRIOT ACT
FBI access to credit information, 1.4.8, 5.2.12

USERS OF REPORTS
see also CONSUMER REPORTS
certification, 5.4.1, 5.4.2, 9.2.1.6
computer fraud, liability, 12.3
definition, 5.1.2, 6.4.1
disclosure restrictions, 4.7, 6.4.3.1
disputed information, notification, 7.7
employers, see EMPLOYERS
employment agencies, obligations, 6.4.2.4
false pretenses, 5.6.3, 5.6.4, 10.2.4.1
FCRA requirements, notice to user, 5.1.3
   FTC model form, Appx. E.2
FCRA violations
   defenses, 6.9, 10.2.4.2
   liability, 5.6, 10.2.4.2
gossip, 13.3.7.3
identification, 5.4.1, 5.4.2
investigative reports, 10.2.4.3
joint users, 2.4.5, 2.5.5
liability, see under LIABILITY
medical information, 6.5.3
notice obligations
   adverse action, 6.4
   defenses, 6.9, 10.2.4.2
   failure to provide, 6.9, 10.2.4.2
   post request, 6.6
   prior to information request, 6.5
   risk-based pricing, 6.4aS

USERS OF REPORTS (cont.)
past users, updated reports, 7.4.3, 7.7.1
prescreening lists, differentiation, 5.1.6, 6.6.4
regulation, 1.3.1
request records, retention, 5.4.5
restrictions, 5.1.2
sharing report with consumer, 4.7, 6.4.3.1
Summary of Responsibilities, FTC model form, Appx. E.2
verification of, 5.4.1, 5.4.2
written permission, 5.2.2

UTILITY SERVICES
see also PUBLIC UTILITY CREDIT
blemished report, implications, 13.3.2, 13.7.4

VENUE
removal to federal court, 10.9.5

VERIFICATION
see also CERTIFICATION; IDENTIFICATION; REINVESTIGATIONS
adverse information, reasonable procedures, 10.2.2.1
consumer files, information, 7.8.4.6
consumer reports, users, 5.4.3, 8.5.4
delinquent debts, 13.6.7
disputed debts, 13.5.4.1
disputed information, 7.4.2, 13.5.4.9
investigative consumer reports, information
   personal interviews, 9.4.2.2
   public record information, 9.4.2.3
   re-use, 9.4.2.4, 10.2.2.5
obsolete information, 8.4, 13.2.5
obsolete information exemption, 8.5.4
public record information, 7.8.5.3, 13.6.10
resellers, 10.2.2.8
reverification, 9.4.2.4, 10.2.2.5
superbureaus, 10.2.2.8

VETERANS ADMINISTRATION (VA)
joint lender exemption, 2.5.5

underwriting guidelines, 13.7.2.2

WAIVER
see also CONSENT
consumer reports, written permission, effect, 5.2.2
credit repair contracts, statutory provisions, 15.2.6.1
investigative reports, rights, 9.2.5

WEBSITES
CDIA, 3.3.2
related websites, Appx. K

WELFARE AGENCIES
see also GOVERNMENT AGENCIES; GOVERNMENT BENEFITS; SOCIAL SERVICE AGENCIES
consumer reports, permissible users, 5.2.7, 13.3.5
FCRA, application, 2.3.6.8

WELFARE RECIPIENTS
consumer file disclosure, no charge, 4.4.5.1.4

WILLFUL INTENT
see also MALICE
FCRA noncompliance, 11.3, 11.4.1.1
invasion of privacy claims, 10.3.8
misrepresentation, limitations, 10.10.1.2
proving, 11.4.1.2
punitive damages, 11.1, 11.4.1.1
tort liability, 10.3.6

WITNESSES
see also EVIDENCE; JURY TRIALS
consumer reports re, impermissible purpose, 5.3.4

WORKERS' COMPENSATION LISTS
see also CONSUMER LISTS
described, 13.2.2
privacy issues, 13.3.6

WORKPLACE DRUG TESTS
FCRA application, 2.3.6.6

Quick Reference to the Consumer Credit and Sales Legal Practice Series

References are to sections in *all* manuals in NCLC's Consumer Credit and Sales Legal Practice Series. References followed by "S" appear only in a supplement.

This Quick Reference pinpoints where to find specific consumer law topics analyzed in the NCLC manuals. References are to individual manual or supplement sections from NCLC's Consumer Credit and Sales Legal Practice Series. For more information on other volumes, see *What Your Library Should Contain* at the beginning of this volume.

This Quick Reference is a speedy means to locate key terms in the appropriate NCLC Manual. More detailed indexes are found at the end of the individual NCLC volumes. The detailed contents pages at the beginning of each volume provide further elaboration once the appropriate manual is identified by use of this Quick Reference. Both the detailed contents pages and the detailed indexes are also available at www.consumerlaw.org.

Pleadings, statutes, regulations, agency interpretations, legislative history, and other appendix material are also found on the CD-Roms that are included with the specified volume. In addition, everything found on the sixteen individual CD-Roms is also included on NCLC's *Consumer Law in a Box* CD-Rom. **NCLC strongly recommends that those searching for pleadings refer to the *Index Guide* that accompanies *Consumer Law Pleadings on CD-Rom*, and not to this *Quick Reference*.**

Another search option can be found on our web site at **www.consumerlaw.org/keyword**. There, users can search all sixteen of NCLC's manuals for a case name, party name, statutory or regulatory citation, or any other word or phrase. The search engine provides the title and page number of every occurrence of that word or phrase within all of our manuals. Further instructions and tips are provided on the web site.

Abbreviations		
AUS	=	Access to Utility Service (2d ed. 2001 and 2003 Supp.)
Auto	=	Automobile Fraud (2d ed. 2003 and 2004 Supp.)
Arbit	=	Consumer Arbitration Agreements (3d ed. 2003)
CBPL	=	Consumer Banking and Payments Law (2d ed. 2002 and 2004 Supp.)
Bankr	=	Consumer Bankruptcy Law and Practice (6th ed. 2000 and 2003 Supp.)

CCA	=	Consumer Class Actions: A Practical Litigation Guide (5th ed. 2002 and 2004 Supp.)
CLP9	=	Consumer Law Pleadings Number Nine (2003)
CLP8	=	Consumer Law Pleadings Number Eight (2002)
CLP7	=	Consumer Law Pleadings Number Seven (2001)
CLP6	=	Consumer Law Pleadings Number Six (2000)
CLP5	=	Consumer Law Pleadings Number Five (1999)
CLP4	=	Consumer Law Pleadings Number Four (1998)
CLP3	=	Consumer Law Pleadings Number Three (1997)
CLP2	=	Consumer Law Pleadings Number Two (1995)
CLP1	=	Consumer Law Pleadings Number One (1994)
COC	=	The Cost of Credit (2d ed. 2000 and 2004 Supp.)
CD	=	Credit Discrimination (3d ed. 2002 and 2004 Supp.)
FCR	=	Fair Credit Reporting (5th ed. 2002 and 2004 Supp.)
FDC	=	Fair Debt Collection (5th ed. 2004)
Repo	=	Repossessions and Foreclosures (5th ed. 2002 and 2003 Supp.)
Stud	=	Student Loan Law (2d ed. 2002 and 2003 Supp.)
TIL	=	Truth in Lending (5th ed. 2003)
UDAP	=	Unfair and Deceptive Acts and Practices (5th ed. 2001 and 2003 Supp.)
Warr	=	Consumer Warranty Law (2d ed. 2001 and 2004 Supp.)

Abandonment of Apartment Building in Bankruptcy—Bankr § 17.8.2
Abbreviations Commonly Used by Debt Collectors—FDC App G.4
Abuse of Process—UDAP § 5.1.4; FDC § 10.6
Acceleration—COC §§ 5.6.2, 5.7.1; Repo § 4.1
Accessions—Repo § 3.5.3.2
Accord and Satisfaction—CBPL § 1.7.3
Account Aggregation—CBPL § 4.10
Accountants—UDAP § 5.12.8
Accrediting Agencies, Student Loans—Stud § 9.4.1.2
Accurate Information in Consumer Reports—FCR § 7.8
ACH—*See* NACHA

Quick Reference to the Consumer Credit and Sales Legal Practice Series
References are to sections in *all* manuals in NCLC's Consumer Credit and Sales Legal Practice Series

Actual Damages—*See* Damages
Actuarial Rebates—COC § 5.6.3.4
Adhesion Contracts—UDAP § 5.2.3
Adjustable Rate Mortgages—TIL § 4.6.4; COC § 4.3.6
Administration of Lawsuit, Class Action—CCA Ch 13; CLP1
Admissibility of Other Bad Acts—Auto § 9.8.1
Advertisements as Warranties—Warr § 3.2.2.5
Advertising by Attorneys on the Internet—CLP4 Ch 10
Advertising Credit Terms—TIL §§ 5.4, 10.4
Affordability Programs, Utilities—AUS Ch 9, App F
After-Acquired Property—Repo § 3.4.5.2
Age Discrimination re Credit—CD § 3.4.2
Airline Fare Advertising—UDAP §§ 2.5, 5.4.13.1
Alteration of Checks—CBPL § 1.2
Alimony Discharged in Bankruptcy—Bankr § 14.4.3.5
Alimony, Protected Source under ECOA—CD §§ 3.4.1, 5.5.5.3
Alternative Dispute Mechanisms—Arbit; FDC § 15.4; UDAP § 7.7.2
American Arbitration Association—Arbit App B.1
Americans With Disabilities Act—CD § 1.6
Americans With Disabilities Act Complaint, Class Action—CLP4 Ch 16
Amortization Explained—COC § 4.3.1
Amortization Negative—COC § 4.3.1.2
Amount Financed—TIL § 4.6.2
Annual Percentage Rate—TIL §§ 4.6.4, 5.6.9; COC § 4.4
Antecedent Debt Clauses—Repo § 3.9
Anti-Competitive Conduct as UDAP Violation—UDAP § 4.10
Anti-Deficiency Statutes—Repo § 12.6.3
Apartment Buildings Abandoned in Bankruptcy—Bankr § 17.8.2
Apartment Leases—Bankr § 12.9; UDAP §§ 2.2.6, 5.5.2
Appeal of Order Requiring Arbitration—Arbit § 9.5
Applications for Credit—CD § 5.4
Appraisals, Right to a Copy—CD § 10.2.12
APR—*See* Annual Percentage Rate
Arbitration—Arbit; Bankr § 13.3.2.5; COC § 10.6.10S; FDC § 15.4; CLP1 Ch 1; CLP4 § 1.4; CLP5 Ch 12; CLP7 Ch 12; TIL App J; UDAP §§ 5.1.5, 7.7; Warr § 10.2;
Arbitration Agreement's Effect on UDAP Action—UDAP § 7.7
Arbitration and Class Actions—Arbit § 9.4; CCA Ch 2; UDAP § 7.7
Arbitration Fees—Arbit § 5.4
As Is—Warr Ch 5; Auto § 7.8.2
Assignee Liability—UDAP § 6.6; TIL § 7.3
Assignment of Tax Refunds—COC § 7.5.4
Assistance for the Payment of Utility Service—AUS Ch 16
Assisted Living Facilities—UDAP § 5.11.4
Assistive Device Lemon Laws—Warr Ch 16aS
ATM Cards—CBPL Ch 4
ATM machines, bank liability for robberies at—CBPL § 4.9
ATM machine payments—CBPL Ch 4
ATM machines, access for disabled—CBPL Ch 6
Attorney Advertising on the Internet—CLP4 Ch 10
Attorney as Debt Collector—FDC §§ 4.2.7, 11.5.3
Attorney Fees—TIL § 8.9; Bankr Ch 15; Auto §§ 5.8.4, 9.12; CD § 11.6.6; FCR § 11.6; FDC §§ 6.8, 11.2.5, 11.3.5; UDAP § 8.8; Warr §§ 2.7.6, 10.8; CLP1 Ch 11; CLP5 Ch 8
Attorney Fees, Class Actions—CCA Ch 15, App C
Attorney Fees for Creditors—COC § 7.3.3; FDC § 15.2
Attorney Fees, Sample Pleadings—Auto App L; FDC App K; CLP1 §§ 2.10, 4.14, Ch 11; CLP2 § 3.3.11; CLP4 §§ 4.3, 15.25
Attorney General Enforcement—UDAP Ch 10
Attorneys Liable Under FDCPA—FDC §§ 4.2.7, 4.6.3
Attorneys Liable Under UDAP—UDAP §§ 2.3.9, 5.12.1

Auctions—Repo §§ 10.7.1, 10.9.3; Auto §§ 2.5.4, 2.6.4
Authorization to Represent—CCA App C
Authorization to Sue—CCA § 1.2.4
Automatic Stay—Bankr Ch 9
Automobile Accessories—UDAP § 5.4.11
Automobile Auctions—*See* Auctions
Automobile Dealer Files—UDAP § 5.4.2
Automobile Dealer Licensing—Auto § 6.4, Appx. F
Automobile Dealers, Bonding Requirement—Auto § 9.13.4, App C
Automobile Dealers, Rebate Fraud—CLP3 § 9.2
Automobile Dealers, Registration with Auction—Auto Appx. E.3
Automobile Fraud—Auto; CLP3 Ch 9
Automobile Insurance, Force-Placed—*See* Force-Placed Auto Insurance
Automobile Leases, Article 9 Coverage—Repo § 14.2.1
Automobile Leases, Default and Early Termination—TIL Ch 10; UDAP § 5.4.8.3; Repo § 14.2; CLP1 Ch 9
Automobile Leases, Misrepresentation—UDAP § 5.4.8
Automobile Leases, Odometer Rollbacks—Auto §§ 4.6.6.5, 5.2.6; CLP1 Ch 3
Automobile Leases, Sublease Scams—UDAP § 5.4.10
Automobile Leases, Unconscionability—UDAP § 5.4.8.5
Automobile Manufacturers, List—Warr App N
Automobile Pawn Transactions—Bankr § 11.9S; COC § 7.5.2.3; Repo § 3.5.5; CLP3 §§ 4.2, 4.3
Automobile Rentals—UDAP § 5.4.9
Automobile Repairs—Warr Ch 17; UDAP § 5.4.1
Automobile Repossession—*See* Repossessions
Automobile Safety Inspection Laws—Warr § 14.9
Automobile Sales—Warr Chs 13, 14; UDAP §§ 5.4.2, 5.4.6, 5.4.7; CLP2 Chs 5, 6; CLP6 Ch 9, Ch 11
Automobile Service—Warr § 17.8; UDAP § 5.3.5
Automobile Spot Delivery Abuses—UDAP § 5.4.5; Repo § 4.5; TIL §§ 4.4.5, 4.4.6
Automobile Sublease Scams—UDAP § 5.4.10
Automobile Title—Auto §§ 2.3, 2.4, Apps. D, E; UDAP § 5.4.5; Warr § 14.5.5
Automobile Valuation—Bankr § 11.2.2.2.1
Automobiles, Theft Prevention, Federal Statutes & Regulations—Auto App B.2
Bad Checks—FDC §§ 5.6.4, 15.3
Bail (i.e. replevin)—Repo Ch 5
Bait and Switch—UDAP § 4.6.1
Balloon Payments—COC § 4.6.2, Ch 5; TIL § 2.2.4.2.2
Bank Accounts, Attachment—FDC Ch 12; CLP2 § 12.3
Bank Accounts, Closing—CBPL § 1.6
Bank Account Garnishment—CBPL § 1.10
Bank Accounts, Joint—FDC § 12.7
Bank Accounts, Set-Off—FDC § 12.6.7
Bank Fees—CBPL § 1.11
Bank Accounts, Unfair Practices—UDAP §§ 4.4.5, 5.1.15, 5.1.16
Banker's Right of Set Off—CBPL Ch 8; CLP7 Ch 13
Bankruptcy and Debt Collection—FDC §§ 2.2, 9.10; Bankr § 9.4.3
Bankruptcy and Security Interests—Repo Ch 8
Bankruptcy and Sovereign Immunity—CLP6 Ch 7
Bankruptcy and Utility Service—AUS §§ 4.5, 12.1, Bankr § 9.8
Bankruptcy, Claims Against Landlords in—Bankr § 17.8
Bankruptcy, Claims Against Creditors, Merchants in—Bankr Ch 17; UDAP § 6.8; CLP1 Ch 10; CLP7 Ch 6
Bankruptcy Code, Text—Bankr App A
Bankruptcy, Consumer Reports of—FCR §§ 13.6.9, 7.8.4.10.2, 8.3.7
Bankruptcy Court as Litigation Forum—Bankr Ch 13, CLP1 Ch 8; CLP4 Ch 14
Bankruptcy, Discharge of Credit Card Debts—CLP7 Ch 17

Quick Reference to the Consumer Credit and Sales Legal Practice Series
References are to sections in *all* manuals in NCLC's Consumer Credit and Sales Legal Practice Series

Bankruptcy, Discharge Injunction—CLP6 Ch 16
Bankruptcy Discharge of Student Loans—Stud Ch 7
Bankruptcy Official Forms—Bankr App D
Bankruptcy Petition Preparers—Bankr § 15.6
Benefit Overpayments and Bankruptcy—Bankr § 14.5.5.4
Bibliography—Bankr
Billing Errors—FDC § 5.7; Repo § 19.2.2
Billing Error Procedures, Credit Cards—CBPL § 3.5; TIL § 5.8
Bill Stuffers—Arbit § 3.8
Binding Arbitration—Arbit
Blanket Security Interests—Repo § 3.4.5.2.2
Boat, Seizure of—CLP2 § 12.2
Bond, Claims Against Seller's—UDAP § 6.8; Auto § 9.13.4, App C
Bonding Statutes—Auto App C
Book-of-the-Month Clubs—UDAP § 5.8.5
Bounced Checks—CBPL § 1.4
Bounce Loans—TIL § 3.9.3.3
Breach of Contract—UDAP § 5.2.5
Breach of the Peace and Repossession—Repo § 6.4
Breach of Warranties—Warr; UDAP § 5.2.7.1
Briefs, Class Action—CCA Ch 9
Broker Fees—COC §§ 7.4.2, 11.2.1.4
Brokers, Auto—UDAP § 5.4.10
Brokers, Loan—*See* Loan Brokers
Brokers, Real Estate—*See* Real Estate Brokers
Budget Payment Plans—AUS § 6.4
Burglar Alarm Systems—UDAP § 5.6.2
Business Credit, Discrimination re—CD § 2.2.6.5
Business Opportunities—UDAP §§ 2.2.9.2, 5.13.1
Buy Here, Pay Here Car Sales—UDAP § 5.4.6.13
Buy Rate—UDAP § 5.4.7.6
Buying Clubs—UDAP § 5.10.6
Calculating Interest Rates—COC Ch 4
Campground Resort Memberships—UDAP §§ 2.2.8, 5.10.5; CLP1 Ch 6
Cancellation Rights—TIL Ch 6; UDAP §§ 5.2.6, 5.8.2, 9.5
Cardholders' Defenses—TIL § 5.9.5
Carfax—Auto § 2.3.2, Appx. E.2
Cars—*See* Automobile
Case Selection—CCA § 1.2
Case Summaries, FDCPA—FDC App L
Cash Discounts—TIL § 5.9.6.4
Cashier's Checks—CBPL § 1.1.8.1
Chapter 7 Bankruptcy—Bankr Ch 3
Chapter 11 Bankruptcy—Bankr §§ 6.3.3, 17.7
Chapter 12 Bankruptcy—Bankr Ch 16
Chapter 13 Bankruptcy—Bankr Ch 4
Charge Cards—TIL § 5.2.4.2
Charitable Contributions—Bankr § 1.1.1.5S
Charitable Solicitations—UDAP § 5.13.5
Check 21—CBPL § 1.15S, App IS
Check Advancement Loans—*See* Payday Loans
Check Approval Companies—FCR §§ 2.3.6.3, 2.6.1, 6.4.2.3.5, 13.2.2, 13.3.6
Check Cards—CBPL § 4.1.4.2
Check Cashing Services—UDAP §§ 5.1.15, 5.1.16
Check Cashing Regulation—CBPL § 1.14
Check Guarantee Companies—FDC § 4.2.3
Checklist, Automobile Fraud Litigation—Auto § 1.4
Checklist, Debt Collection—FDC App G
Checklist, Truth in Lending—TIL §§ 1.6, 3.11
Checklist, Usury—COC § 1.6
Checks—CBPL Ch 1
Checks, Bad—FDC §§ 5.6.4, 15.3

Checks, Preauthorized Draft—UDAP §§ 5.1.15, 5.1.16
Child Support, Credit Reports—FCR § 5.3.2
Child Support Discharged in Bankruptcy—Bankr § 14.4.3.5
Children in Household, Discrimination Based On—CD § 3.5.1
Choice of Laws—COC § 9.2.9; Repo § 2.18
Churning Repossession Schemes—Repo § 10.9.4
Civil Rights Act—CD § 1.5
Class Actions—CCA; AUS § 15.5.1; Auto § 9.7, App H; FCR § 10.7.2; FDC §§ 6.2.1.3, 6.3.5, 6.6; TIL §§ 6.9.9, 8.8; UDAP § 8.5; CLP1–5
Class Actions and Arbitration—Arbit § 9.4; CCA Ch 2; CLP1 Ch 1; CLP4 Ch 1; CLP5 Ch 12; UDAP § 7.7
Class Actions, Evaluating a Potential Lawsuit—CLP4 § 9.1
Class Actions Guidelines for Settlement, NACA—CCA App B; CLP4 § 12.2
Class Actions in Bankruptcy Court—Bankr §§ 13.7, 17.4.2
Class Definitions—CCA Ch 3; CLP4 § 9.2
Class Notices—CCA Ch 10, App N
Client Authorization to Represent—CCA App C
Client Authorization to Sue—CCA § 1.2.4
Client Contacts with Other Parties—CCA §§ 1.2.6, 5.3
Client Forms—CLP4 §§ 15.7–15.21
Client Handout on Bankruptcy—Bankr App I
Client Handout on Credit Discrimination—CD App H
Client Handout on Credit Reporting—FCR App J
Client Interview Checklist, Bankruptcy—Bankr App H
Client Interview Checklist, Debt Collection Harassment—FDC App G
Client Interview Sheet, Warranties—Warr App I
Client Retainer Forms, Sample—CLP4 Ch 8
Closed-End Auto Leases—TIL Ch 10; Repo § 14.2; CLP1 Ch 9
Closed-End Credit—TIL Ch 4
Closed School Discharge—Stud § 6.2
Coercive Sales Techniques—UDAP § 4.8
Collateral—Repo
Collection Fees—FDC § 15.2; Stud § 4.4
Collection of Student Loans—Stud Ch 4
College Transcripts and Bankruptcy—Bankr §§ 9.4.3, 14.5.5.2
Collision Damage Waiver (CDW)—UDAP § 5.4.9
Common Law Contract Defenses—UDAP § 9.5
Common Law Fraud, Misrepresentation—Warr § 11.4; UDAP § 9.6.3; Auto Ch 7
Common Law Right to Utility Service—AUS § 3.1
Common Law Violations and Credit Reporting—FCR § 10.2
Common Law Warranties—Warr § 17.4
Communications to Client from Other Attorney—CCA § 5.3; FDC § 5.3.3
Community Reinvestment Act—CD § 1.9
Compensating Balances—COC § 7.4.4
Complaint Drafting, Class Actions—CCA Ch 4
Complaints—*See* Sample Complaints
Compound Interest—COC § 4.6.1
Computers, Sale of—UDAP § 5.7.6
Condominiums—UDAP § 5.5.4.5
Condominium Warranties—Warr Ch 16
Consignment—Repo § 9.6.3.3
Consolidation Loan—Stud § 8.2
Conspiracy in Odometer Case—Auto § 4.7
Constitutionality of Arbitration Agreement—Arbit Ch 8
Contract Formation of Arbitration Agreement—Arbit Ch 3
Constructive Strict Foreclosure—Repo §§ 10.5.2, 12.5
Consumer Class Actions—CCA; CLP4 Ch 9
Consumer Complaints to Government Agencies—UDAP § 9.7
Consumer Credit Reporting Reform Act of 1996—FCR § 1.4.6

Quick Reference to the Consumer Credit and Sales Legal Practice Series

References are to sections in *all* manuals in NCLC's Consumer Credit and Sales Legal Practice Series

Consumer Guide to Credit Reporting—FCR App J
Consumer Leasing Act—TIL Ch 10, App I.1
Consumer Recovery Funds—Auto § 9.13.5
Consumer Reporting Agencies—FCR; CLP2 Ch 10
Consumer Reporting Agencies, Enforcement Agreements—FCR App H
Consumer Reporting Agency, Sample User Agreement—FCR App G.1
Consumer Reports, Disputing and Right to Use—FCR Ch 7
Consumer Reports, Keeping Credit Disputes Out of—FCR § 13.5.2
Consumer Reports for Business Transactions—FCR §§ 2.3.5.4, 2.3.6, 5.2.4.3, 5.2.9
Consumer Reports for Employment Purposes—FCR §§ 2.3.6.6, 5.2.5
Consumer Reports for Government Benefits—FCR §§ 2.3.6.8, 5.2.7
Consumer Reports for Insurance Purposes—FCR §§ 2.3.6.7, 5.2.6
Consumer Reports from Non-Reporting Agencies—FCR § 6.4.4
Consumer Resources Lists—UDAP App G
Consumer/Seller Liability under Odometer Act—Auto § 4.8.13
Contests—UDAP §§ 4.6.6, 5.13.4
Contract Defenses—UDAP § 9.5
Contractual Misrepresentations—UDAP § 5.2.4
Cooling Off Periods—*See* Cancellation
Correspondence Schools—Stud Ch 9
Cosigners—Bankr § 9.4.4; CD § 5.6; Repo § 12.9; TIL §§ 2.2.2.2, 8.2; UDAP § 5.1.3.1.9
Counseling the Debtor—Bankr Ch 6
Coupon Settlement, Class Actions—CCA § 11.6; CLP4 Ch 12
Cramming—AUS § 2.7.5S
Credit Abuses—COC; UDAP §§ 2.2.1, 5.1.9; CLP1
Credit Accident and Health Insurance—COC § 8.3.3; TIL §§ 3.7.9, 3.9.4
Credit Balances—TIL § 5.6; UDAP § 5.1.7
Credit Cards—CBPL Ch 3; CLP7 Ch 17; TIL Ch 5
Credit Card Finders—UDAP § 5.1.18
Credit Card Issuers, Raising Seller-Related Claims Against—UDAP § 6.6
Credit Card Issuer's Security Interest in Goods Purchased—Repo § 3.6
Credit Card Surcharges—TIL § 5.9.6.4
Credit Card Unauthorized Use—TIL § 5.9.4; CLP2 Ch 9
Credit Cards—TIL Ch 5; UDAP § 5.1; FDC § 4.2.3
Credit Cards, Reporting Services for Lost—UDAP § 5.1.19
Credit Charges—COC Ch 5; UDAP § 5.1.9.2; CLP6 Ch 6
Credit Denial, Notice—CD § 10.2.4; FCR § 6.2
Credit Disability Insurance—COC §§ 8.3.3, 8.5.2.3; Repo § 16.7.5; TIL §§ 3.7.9, 3.9.4
Credit Evaluation—CD §§ 6.2, 6.3
Credit File, Disputing and Right to See—FCR Chs 4, 7
Credit Insurance—COC Ch 8; TIL §§ 3.7.9, 3.9.4; Repo § 4.4; UDAP § 5.3.10 ; CLP7 Ch 16
Credit Life Insurance—COC §§ 8.3.2, 8.5.3.1.2; TIL §§ 3.7.9, 3.9.4; CLP7 Ch 16
Credit Math—COC Ch 4
Credit Property Insurance—COC §§ 8.3.5, 8.5.3.1.4, 8.5.3.3.3, 8.5.4.4; TIL §§ 3.9.4.4, 3.9.4.6, 4.9.8
Credit Rating, Injury to—FCR § 13.4; FDC §§ 5.5.2.9, 8.3.8; UDAP § 8.3.3.6; CLP2 Ch 10
Credit Regulation, History of—COC Ch 2
Credit Repair Organizations—FCR Ch 15; UDAP § 5.1.17
Credit Reporting Agencies, Contacting—FCR § 4.4.2
Credit Reports—FCR; TIL § 5.9.4.5; CLP2 Ch 10; CLP4 Ch 7; CLP6 Ch 2, Ch 10

Credit Reports, Affiliate Sharing—FCR §§ 2.4.2, 4.4.1.5, 4.5.8, 6.4.4.4, 6.5.4
Credit Reports, Furnishers of Information Obligations—FCR Ch 3, § 13.5.1
Credit Reports, Keeping Credit Disputes Out of—FCR § 13.5.2
Credit Reports from Non-Reporting Agencies—FCR § 6.4.4
Credit Reports, Student Loans—Stud § 3.3
Credit Scams—UDAP §§ 5.1.10–5.1.13
Credit Scoring—CD § 6.4; FCR § 6.6.4
Credit Terms—COC; UDAP § 5.1.8
Creditor Remedies—FDC Chs 12, 13, 15; UDAP § 5.1.3
Creditors' Overcharges in Bankruptcy—CLP3 Ch 7
Creditors, Types of—COC Chs 2, 9
Creditors Filing Bankruptcy—CLP7 Ch 6
Creditworthiness—Bankr § 6.2.2.2
Criminal Prosecution Threats—FDC § 15.3
Cross-Collateral—Repo § 3.7.2
Cross Metering, Utility Service—AUS § 5.2
Cruise Line Port Charges—UDAP § 5.4.13.2
Cure of Default—Repo §§ 4.8, 13.2.4.4
Cy Pres—CCA § 11.7; CLP1 Ch 12; CLP3 Ch 3; CLP5 Ch 11
Daily Accrual Accounting—COC § 4.6.8S
Damages—FDC §§ 2.5.2, 6.3, Ch 10; FCR Ch 11; Repo Ch 13; TIL Ch 8; UDAP § 8.3; Warr §§ 10.4–10.6; CLP1
Damage to Credit Rating—UDAP § 8.3.3.6; CLP2 Ch 10
Dance Studios—UDAP § 5.10.4
Daubert Doctrine—Warr § 10.1.7.5
Dealer's Only Auto Auctions—Repo § 10.9.3
Debit Cards—CBPL Ch 4
Debt Cancellation Agreements—TIL §§ 3.7.10, 3.9.4.7
Debt Collection—FDC; UDAP §§ 2.2.2, 5.1.1; CLP2 Ch 11; CLP3 Ch 3; CLP4 Ch 6
Debt Collection and Bankruptcy—FDC § 2.2.5
Debt Collection by Arbitration—FDC § 15.4; UDAP § 5.1.5
Debt Collection Case Preparation—FDC Ch 2
Debt Collection Procedures Act—FDC § 13.2.1.1
Debt Collection Scams—UDAP § 5.1.12
Debt Collectors—FDC § 1.2, Ch 4
Debt Collector's Common Abbreviations—FDC App G.4
Debt Harassment, How to Stop—FDC § 2.3
Debtor in Possession under Chapter 12—Bankr § 16.3
Debt Pooling—FDC § 1.5.5
Deceit—Warr § 11.4; UDAP § 9.6.3
Deception—UDAP § 4.2; FDC § 5.5
Deceptive Practices Statutes—*See* UDAP
Deceptive Pricing—UDAP § 4.6.3
Defamation—FDC § 10.5; FCR § 10.3.7
Defamatory Use of Mail—FDC § 9.1
Default—Repo Ch 4
Default Insurance—TIL § 3.7.7
Defective Automobile Title—Auto
Defenses as Grounds for Nonpayment—Repo § 4.6
Defenses to Credit Card Charges—CBPL Ch 3
Deferment of Student Loan—Stud § 2.2
Deferral Charges—COC § 4.8.2
Deferred Payment Plans—AUS § 6.5
Deficiency Actions—Repo Ch 12, App C.1; CLP6 Ch 4
Deficiency Judgments—Repo § 21.3
Delay—UDAP § 4.9.2
Delaying Tactics, Opposing—CCA Ch 6
Delinquency Charges—*See* Late Charges
Deliverable Fuels—AUS § 1.6S
Demonstrator Vehicles—Auto §§ 1.4.8, 2.1.6
Denial of Credit, Notice—FCR § 6.2

382

Quick Reference to the Consumer Credit and Sales Legal Practice Series

References are to sections in *all* manuals in NCLC's Consumer Credit and Sales Legal Practice Series

Department of Housing and Urban Development (HUD)—CD § 12.3.1, App D; Repo Chs 16, 17, § 18.2
Department of Motor Vehicles—Auto Appx. D
Deposit, Consumer's Right to Return When Seller Files Bankruptcy—Bankr § 17.5
Deposition—Auto § 9.5.5
Depositions in Class Actions—CCA § 7.4.4, Ch 8
Depository Creditors—COC Ch 2; FDC Ch 12
Deregulation of Utilities—AUS Ch 1S
Detinue—Repo Ch 5
Digital Divide—CD § 3.8.2
Direct Deposits—CBPL Ch 4, §§ 5.1–5.3
Disabilities, Discrimination Based On—CD § 3.5.2
Disability Discharge—Stud § 6.6
Disabled Access to ATM machines—CBPL Ch 6
Discharge in Bankruptcy—Bankr Ch 14
Discharging Student Loan Obligations—Stud Ch 6, § 7.2.2S
Disclaimers, Warranties—Warr Ch 5
Disclosure and UDAP—UDAP § 4.2.14
Disclosure of Credit Terms—TIL
Disconnection of Utility Service—AUS Chs 11, 12
Discovery—Auto § 9.5, App H; *see also* Sample Interrogatories; Sample Document Requests
Discovery, Arbitration—Arbit § 9.1, App C
Discovery, Class Actions—CCA Ch 7, App E; CLP1
Discovery, Motions to Compel—CCA Apps F, G, H
Discrimination in Collection Tactics—FDC § 9.8
Discrimination re Credit—CD
Disposition of Repo Collateral—Repo Chs 9, 10
Dispute Resolution Mechanisms—Warr §§ 2.8, 13.2.9
Disputing Information in Consumer Report—FCR § 13.5.2
Document Preparation Fees—TIL § 3.9.6; UDAP § 5.4.3.7
D'Oench, Duhme Doctrine—COC § 10.7; Repo §§ 12.10, 16.7.7; UDAP § 6.7.5
Door-to-Door Sales—UDAP § 5.8.2; Warr § 17.6
Dragnet Clauses—Repo § 3.9
Driver Privacy Protection Act—Auto § 2.2.4, App A.2
Driver's Licenses and Bankruptcy—Bankr §§ 14.5.4, 14.5.5.1
Drunk Driving Debts in Bankruptcy—Bankr § 14.4.3.9
Dunning, How to Stop with Sample Letters—FDC § 2.3
Duress—UDAP § 9.5.12; AUS § 6.1.9
Duty of Good Faith and Fair Dealing—COC § 11.8
Early Termination Penalties in Auto Leases—TIL § 10.5
Earned Income Tax Credit—Bankr § 2.5.2
EBT—CBPL Ch 6
E-Commerce, Jurisdiction—COC § 9.2.9.4
Educational Loans—*See* Student Loans
EFT 99—CBPL § 5.1
Elder Financial Exploitation—CLP3 Ch 1
Elderly, Special Foreclosure Problems—Repo § 16.10
Election of Remedy Statutes—Repo § 12.4
Electric Service—AUS § 1.2.2S; UDAP § 5.6.8
Electric Industry Restructuring—AUS § 1.4S
Electronic Banking—CBPL Ch 4; FDC § 12.6.6
Electronic Benefit Transfers—CBPL Ch 6, App F.2
Electronic Credit Transactions—COC § 9.2.10S
Electronic Disclosure—TIL §§ 4.2.9, 5.3.6, 9.3.9; UDAP § 4.2.14.3.6
Electronic Funds Transfer—CBPL § 1.4S, Chs 4, 5
Electronic Repossession—Repo § 6.4
Electronic Signatures and Records—CBPL Ch 9
Electronic Transaction Fraud—UDAP § 5.9.4
Electronic Transfer Account (ETA)—CBPL § 5.5
Employer Bankruptcy—Bankr § 17.7.11S
Employment Agencies—UDAP § 5.13.2
Encyclopedia Sales—UDAP § 5.7.1
Endorsements—UDAP § 4.7.7
Energy Savings Claims—UDAP § 5.6.6
Enforceability of Arbitration Clause—Arbit
Equal Credit Opportunity Act—CD; AUS § 3.7.2; FCR §§ 6.4.5, 13.2.7; CLP7 Ch 1
Equal Credit Opportunity Act Regulations—CD App B
E-Sign—CBPL Ch 9; COC § 9.2.10S, 11.3.1.8a
ETAs (Electronic Transfer Accounts)—CBPL § 5.3
Ethnic Discrimination—CD § 3.3.3
Evictions—AUS § 12.4; UDAP § 5.5.2.10; CLP2 §§ 1.2, 1.3, 1.4, 2.1; FDC § 1.5.2
Evidence Spoilation—Warr § 10.1.2.5
Evidentiary Issues in Automobile Litigation—Auto § 9.8
Exempt Benefits and Bankruptcy—Bankr § 10.2.2.11
Exempting Interest Rates—COC Ch 3S
Exemption Laws, Liberal Construction—FDC § 12.2
Exemption Planning—Bankr § 10.4.1
Exemptions, Benefits, Earnings, Due Process Protections—FDC Ch 12
Expert Inspection—Warr § 10.1.5.1
Experts, Attorney Fee Award for—UDAP § 8.8.7.3
Expert Witnesses—FDC § 2.4.14; Warr § 10.1
Expert Witnesses, Sample Questions—Auto App I
Exportation of Interest Rates—COC Ch 3S
Express Warranties—Warr Ch 3
Expressio Unius Est Exclusio Alterius—COC § 9.3.1.2
Extended Warranties—*See* Service Contracts
Extortionate Collection—FDC § 9.5
FACT Act—FCR Supp
Fair Credit Billing Act—CBPL § 3.5; TIL § 5.8; FCR § 13.5.2.2.1.1; AUS § 11.3.5
Fair Credit Reporting Act—FCR; FDC § 9.6; CLP2 Ch 10; CLP3 Ch 5; CLP6 Ch 17
Fair Debt Collection Practices Act—FDC Chs 3–7, Apps A, B, L; CLP2 Ch 11; CLP3 Ch 3; CLP4 Ch 6; CLP6 Ch 12, Ch 14; CLP7 Chs 3, 4, 7, 8, 9, 14
Fair Housing Act—CD; AUS § 8.3
Fair Housing Act Regulations—CD App D
False Certification Discharge—Stud § 6.3
False Pretenses, Obtaining Consumer Reports—FCR § 5.6
Family Expense Laws—FDC § 14.6; CD § 9.3
Farm Reorganizations, Bankruptcy—Bankr Ch 16
Farmworker Camps—UDAP §§ 2.2.7, 5.5.4
Faxes, Junk—UDAP § 5.9.2.2
Federal Agency Collection Actions—FDC Ch 13
Federal Arbitration Act—Arbit Ch 2, App A; UDAP § 7.7
Federal Benefit Payments, Electronic—CBPL §§ 5.1–5.3
Federal Civil Rights Acts—CD; AUS § 3.7.1
Federal Direct Deposit of Benefits—CBPL §§ 5.1–5.3
Federal Direct Student Loans-Stud
Federal Energy Regulatory Commission (FERC)—AUS § 1.2.2.2S
Federal False Claims Act—UDAP § 9.4.13
Federal Family Education Loans—Stud
Federal Preemption—FDC §§ 2.2, 6.14; UDAP § 2.5
Federal Preemption of State Usury Laws—COC Ch 3S; CLP7 Ch 10
Federal Racketeering Statute—*See* RICO
Federal Reserve Board—*See* FRB
Federal Trade Commission—*See* FTC
Federally Insured Student Loans—Stud § 9.5
Fees—TIL § 3.7; COC § 7.2.1; FDC § 15.2
FHA Mortgage Foreclosure—CLP2 § 3.2
Fiduciary Duty—COC §§ 8.7.2, 11.9
Fifth Amendment Privilege—Auto § 9.8.6.7

383

Quick Reference to the Consumer Credit and Sales Legal Practice Series

References are to sections in *all* manuals in NCLC's Consumer Credit and Sales Legal Practice Series

Filed Rate Doctrine—UDAP § 5.6.9.1
Film Developing Packages—UDAP § 5.7.10
Finance Charge—TIL Ch 3; COC § 4.4
Finance Charges, Hidden—COC Ch 7; TIL § 3.10
Finance Companies—COC Ch 2; UDAP §§ 2.2.1, 5.1.9
Flipping—COC § 6.1; UDAP § 5.1.9; CLP3 Ch 2
Flood Damage to Vehicle—Auto § 2.1.3
Food Advertising—UDAP § 5.11.2
Food Stamps, Electronic Payment—CBPL Ch 6
Forbearance of Student Loans—Stud § 2.3
Force-Placed Auto Insurance—UDAP § 5.3.11; COC § 8.3.5.4.2; TIL § 3.9.4.4.2; CLP1 Ch 2; CLP5 Ch 5
Foreclosure—Repo; CLP2 Ch 3
Foreclosure, False Threat—CLP6 Ch 3
Foreclosure, Government-Held Mortgages—Repo Ch 18
Foreclosure, Preventing Through Bankruptcy—Bankr Ch 9, §§ 10.4.2.6.4, 11.5, 11.6; Repo Ch 20; CLP1 Ch 8; CLP2 § 3.3; CLP4 Ch 14
Foreclosure, Preventing Through Refinancing—COC § 6.5; Repo § 17.9.2
Foreclosure, Preventing Through Rescission—TIL Ch 6; Repo § 16.7.3.1; CLP3 Ch 8; CLP4 Ch 14
Foreclosure, Preventing Through Workouts—Repo Ch 17
Foreclosure, Setting Aside—Repo § 21.1
Foreclosure, Special Problems for Elderly—Repo § 16.10
Foreclosure, Summary of State Laws—Repo App I
Foreclosures and UDAP—UDAP § 5.1.2; Repo § 16.7.1.1
Forged Signatures, Indorsements—CBPL § 1.2
Forms—*See* Sample Forms
Franchises—UDAP §§ 2.2.9.2, 5.13.1
Fraud—UDAP; Warr § 11.4
Fraud and Arbitration—Arbit Ch 4
FRB Official Staff Commentary on Reg. B—CD App C
FRB Official Staff Commentary on Reg. M—TIL App I.3
FRB Official Staff Commentary on Reg. Z—TIL App C
Free Offers—UDAP § 4.6.4
Freezer Meats—UDAP § 5.7.2
FTC (Federal Trade Commission)—UDAP
FTC Act, No Private Action Under—UDAP § 9.1
FTC Cooling Off Period Rule—UDAP § 5.8.2, App B.3
FTC Credit Practices Rule—Repo § 3.4.2; UDAP § 5.1.3.1, App B.1; FDC § 8.4.2
FTC Debt Collection Law—FDC Ch 8
FTC FCR Enforcement Actions—FCR App H
FTC FCR Official Staff Commentary—FCR App C
FTC FDCPA Official Staff Commentary—FDC § 3.2.6, App C
FTC Funeral Rule—UDAP § 5.11.5, App B.5
FTC Holder Rule—UDAP § 6.6, App B.2; CLP1 Chs 3, 4, 6
FTC Mail or Telephone Order Merchandise Rule—UDAP § 5.8.1.1, App B.4
FTC Staff Letters on FCR—FCR App D
FTC Staff Letters on FDCPA—FDC § 3.2.5, App B
FTC Telemarketing Sales Rule—UDAP App D.2.1
FTC Telephone and Dispute Resolution Rule—UDAP App D.2.2
FTC Used Car Rule—UDAP § 5.4.3.2, App B.6; Warr § 14.7, App D
Funds Availability—CBPL § 1.8
Funerals—UDAP § 5.11.5
Furniture Sales—UDAP § 5.7.3; CLP2 § 7.2
Future Advance Clauses—Repo § 3.9
Future Service Contracts—UDAP § 5.10
GAP Insurance—TIL §§ 3.7.10, 3.9.4.7
Garnishment—FDC § 5.5.7, Ch 12, App D; CLP2 § 12.3
Garnishment of Bank Account—CBPL § 1.10
Garnishment to Repay Student Loans—Stud § 5.3, App B.1.2A

Gas Service—AUS § 1.2.1S; UDAP § 5.6.8
Gasoline, Price Gouging—UDAP § 5.6.7.5
Government Benefits—FCR §§ 2.3.6.8, 5.2.7
Government Checks—CBPL § 1.1.8.4, Ch 5
Government Collection Practices—FDC Ch 13; Stud Ch 4
Gramm-Leach-Bliley Act—COC §§ 3.10S, 8.4.1.5.2; FCR § 1.5.3
Gray Market Sales—Auto § 1.4.11; Warr § 13.7
Guaranteed Student Loans—Stud
Guarantees—UDAP § 5.2.7.3
Guarantors—*See* Cosigners
Handguns—UDAP § 5.7.9
Handicapped, Discrimination Against—CD § 3.5.2
Handouts for Client—*See* Client Handouts
Health Care Bills—FDC Ch 14; Bankr § 6.2.2.3.1; CLP2 Ch 15
Health Care Plans, Misrepresentations—UDAP § 5.11.6
Health Care Treatment, Discrimination In—CD § 2.2.2.6
Health Cures, Misrepresentations—UDAP § 5.11
Health Maintenance Organizations—CLP6 Ch 5
Health Spas—UDAP § 5.10.3
Hearing Aids—UDAP § 5.11.1
Heating Fuel—AUS §§ 1.2S, 1.6S; UDAP § 5.6.7
HELC—TIL § 5.11
Hidden Interest—COC Ch 7; TIL § 3.10
High Pressure Sales—UDAP § 4.8
Hill-Burton Act Compliance—UDAP § 5.11.5; CLP2 § 15.4
Holder in Due Course—UDAP § 6.6; COC §§ 10.6.1, 10.7.2.3
Home Builders—UDAP § 5.5.5.2; CLP5 Ch 7
Home Equity Lines of Credit—TIL § 5.11
Home Equity Loans—TIL Ch 9
Home Foreclosure—*See* Foreclosure
Home Heating Fuel—AUS §§ 1.2S, 1.6S; UDAP § 5.6.7
Home Improvement Practices—TIL § 6.5.3; UDAP § 5.6.1; Warr § 17.7, Apps I.3, K.4; CLP2 §§ 4.2, 4.3; CLP3 §§ 1.1, 1.2; CLP4 Ch 1
Home Mortgage Disclosure Act—CD § 4.4.5
Home Mortgage, Rescission of—TIL Ch 6, App E.3
Home Owners' Loan Act—COC § 3.5S
Home Owners Warranty Program—UDAP § 5.5.5.2
Home Ownership & Equity Protection Act—TIL Ch 9, App E.4; COC § 11.3.2; Repo §§ 16.7.3.5, 14.11.3.2; CLP4 Ch 2; CLP6 Ch 1
Homes and UDAP—UDAP §§ 2.2.5, 5.5.5
Homes, Warranties—Warr § 1.4.3
Homestead Exemptions, Bankruptcy—Bankr § 10.2.2.2
Horizontal Privity—Warr § 6.3
Hospital Bills—FDC Ch 14; CLP2 Ch 15; CLP6 Ch 8
House Warranties—Warr Ch 16
Household Goods, Bankruptcy Exemption—Bankr §§ 10.2.2.4, 10.4.2.4
Household Goods Security Interest—Repo § 3.4; UDAP §§ 5.1.2, 5.1.3.1; TIL § 4.6.7
Household Goods Security Interest, Credit Property Insurance on—COC § 8.5.4.4
Houses and UDAP—UDAP §§ 2.2.5, 5.5
HOW Program—UDAP § 5.5.5.5.2
HUD—*See* Department of Housing and Urban Development
Identity Theft—FCR § 13.5.5; CLP3 Ch 5; CLP5 Ch 1
Illegal Conduct—UDAP §§ 4.3.9, 9.5.8
Illegality as Contract Defense—UDAP § 9.5.8
Immigrant Consultants, Deceptive Practices—UDAP § 5.12.2
Immigrant Status, Discrimination Based On—CD § 3.3.3.3
Implied Warranties—Warr Ch 4
Improvident Extension of Credit—UDAP § 5.1.9.3
Incomplete Information in Consumer Reports—FCR Ch 7

Quick Reference to the Consumer Credit and Sales Legal Practice Series

References are to sections in *all* manuals in NCLC's Consumer Credit and Sales Legal Practice Series

Inconvenient Venue—*See* Venue
Indian Tribal Law, Bankruptcy Exemptions—Bankr § 10.2.3.1
Industrial Loan Laws—COC Ch 2
Infancy—*See* Minority
Infertility Programs, Deceptive Practices—CLP4 Ch 13
Infliction of Emotional Distress—FDC § 10.2
In Forma Pauperis Bankruptcy Pilot Program—Bankr § 13.6.1
In Forma Pauperis Filings in Bankruptcy—Bankr §§ 13.6, 17.6
Informal Dispute Resolution—Warr § 2.8
Injunctions—UDAP § 8.6; FDC §§ 6.12, 12.6.2, 13.3
Insecurity Clauses—Repo § 4.1.6
Inspection by Experts—Warr § 10.1.5.1
Installment Sales Laws—COC §§ 2.3.3.4, 9.3.1.1
Insurance and Arbitration—Arbit § 2.3.3
Insurance and UDAP—UDAP §§ 2.3.1, 5.3
Insurance Consumer Reports—FCR §§ 2.3.6.7, 2.6.8, 5.2.6
Insurance, Credit—COC Ch 8; TIL §§ 3.7.9, 3.9.4; UDAP § 5.3.10
Insurance, Illusory Coverage—UDAP § 5.3.6
Insurance Packing—COC § 8.5.4; UDAP § 5.3.12
Insurance Redlining—CD § 7.3
Insurance, Refusal to Pay Claim—UDAP § 5.3.3; CLP7 Ch 15
Intentional Infliction of Emotional Distress—FDC § 10.2
Intentional Interference with Employment Relationships—FDC § 10.4
Interest Calculations—COC §§ 4.2, 4.3
Interest, Hidden—COC Ch 7; TIL § 3.10
Interest Rates, Federal Preemption of—COC Ch 3S
Interference with Employment Relationships—FDC § 10.4
International Money Orders and Wires—CBPL § 2.2
Internet Banking—CBPL Ch 4
Internet, Fraudulent Schemes—UDAP § 5.9
Internet, Invasion of Privacy—UDAP § 4.11
Internet Service Providers—UDAP § 5.6.9.7
Interrogatories—*See* Sample Interrogatories
Interstate Banking and Rate Exportation—COC § 3.4.5S
Intervenor Funding—AUS § 9.5
Interview Checklist for Debt Collection—FDC App G
Interview Form, Bankruptcy—Bankr App H
Interview Form for Clients, Warranties—Warr App I
Invasion of Privacy—FCR §§ 1.5, 10.3.8; FDC § 10.3
Investigative Reports—FCR Ch 9
Investments—UDAP §§ 2.2.9, 5.13
Involuntary Bankruptcy Cases—Bankr §§ 13.8, 16.1.2
Irrelevant Information in Consumer Reports—FCR § 7.8.4.10.3
JAMS—Arbit App B.3
Joint Bank Accounts, Seizure—FDC § 12.7
Joint Checking Accounts—CBPL §§ 1.6.8, 1.10
Judicial Liens, Avoiding in Bankruptcy—Bankr § 10.4.2.3
Jury, Disclosure to, that Damages Will Be Trebled—UDAP § 8.4.2.8; Auto § 9.9.7
Jury Instructions—*See* Sample Jury Instructions
Jury Trial, Class Action—CCA Ch 14
Jury Trial, Preparing FDCPA Case—FDC § 2.5.7
Land Installment Sales—CLP3 Ch 10; Repo § 16.11
Land Sales—UDAP §§ 2.2.5, 5.5.4.7
Land Trusts—TIL §§ 2.2.1.1, 2.4.3
Landlord Evictions—FDC § 1.5.2.2
Landlord's Removal of Evicted Tenant's Property—Repo § 15.7.4; FDC § 1.5.2.4
Landlord's Requested Disconnection of Utility Service—AUS § 12.4
Landlord's Termination of Utility Service—AUS Ch 4
Landlord-Tenant—Bankr §§ 12.9, 17.8; UDAP §§ 2.2.6, 5.5.2; CLP2 Ch 1; FDC § 1.5.2

Landownership, Utility Service Conditioned on—AUS Ch 4
Late Charges—COC §§ 4.8, 7.2.4; TIL §§ 3.9.3, 4.7.7; UDAP §§ 5.1.3.1.8, 5.1.9.2
Late Charges, Utility Bills—AUS §§ 6.2, 6.3
Late Posting of Payments and Interest Calculation—COC § 4.6.3.5
Law, Unauthorized Practice of—FDC §§ 4.2.7.7.3, 11.5; Bankr § 15.6S; CLP7 Ch 3
Lawyer—*See* Attorney
Layaway Plans—UDAP § 4.9.1
Lease-Back of Home—COC § 7.5.2.1; TIL § 6.2.4.1; CLP3 § 1.1
Leases—Repo Ch 14; TIL § 2.2.4.2, Ch 10; UDAP §§ 2.2.6, 5.4.8, 5.5.2; Warr Ch 19; Auto §§ 4.6.2.3, 4.6.6.5, 5.2.6; Bankr § 12.9; CD § 2.2.2.2; COC § 7.5.3; *see also* Rent to Own
Lease Terms for Residence—UDAP §§ 5.5.2.2, 5.5.2.3; CLP2 § 1.1
Leased Vehicle Damages—Auto § 9.10.1.2
Legal Rights, Misrepresentation of—UDAP § 5.2.8
Lemon Cars Being Resold—Auto §§ 1.4.6, 2.1.5, 2.4.5.5, 6.3, App C; Warr § 14.5.3; UDAP § 5.4.6.7
Lemon Laws—Warr § 13.2, App F; CLP4 Ch 15
Lender Liability Claims—COC Ch 11; CLP1
Liability of Agents, Principals, Owners—UDAP Ch 6; FDC § 2.8
Licenses to Drive and Bankruptcy—Bankr § 14.5.5.1
Liens—Repo Ch 15
Life Care Homes—UDAP § 5.11.3
Life Insurance, Excessive Premiums for—UDAP § 5.3.9
Lifeline Assistance Programs—AUS § 2.3.2S
LIHEAP—AUS Ch 7, App D
Limitation of Remedies Clauses—Warr Ch 9
Living Trusts—UDAP § 5.12.3
Loan Brokers—UDAP §§ 2.2.1, 5.1.11; COC § 7.3.2; CLP1 Ch 7
Loan Flipping—*See* Flipping
Loan Rehabilitation—Stud § 8.4
Long Arm Jurisdiction—COC § 9.2.9.6; UDAP § 7.6.2
Lost Checks—CBPL § 1.3
Lost Credit Card Reporting Services—UDAP § 5.1.19
Low Balling—UDAP § 4.6.5
Low Income Home Energy Assistance Program—AUS Ch 7, App D
Magazine Sales—UDAP § 5.7.1
Magnuson-Moss Warranty Act—Warr Ch 2, Apps A, B; Auto § 8.2.5; CLP4 Ch 15
Magnuson-Moss Warranty Act Relation to Federal Arbitration Act—Arbit § 5.2.2, App F; UDAP § 7.7
Mail Fraud—UDAP § 9.2.4; FDC § 9.1
Mail Order Sales—UDAP § 5.8.1
Malicious Prosecution—FDC § 10.6.2
Managed Care, Misrepresentations—UDAP § 5.11.6
Manufacturer Rebates—UDAP § 4.6.3
Marital Status Discrimination—CD § 3.4.1
Master Metering—AUS § 5.5
Math, Credit—COC Ch 4
McCarran-Ferguson Act—Arbit § 2.3.3; COC § 8.5.2.5.3; TIL § 2.4.9.5; UDAP § 7.7
Mechanical Breakdown Insurance—*See* Service Contracts
Mediation—Auto § 9.11.1.3
Medical—*See* Health Care
Medicare, Medicaid Applications Not Processed by Hospital—CLP2 § 15.6
Mental Anguish Damages—FDC §§ 2.5, 6.3, 10.2
Mental Incompetence—UDAP § 9.5.7.3
Meter Tampering—AUS Ch 5
Migrant Farmworker Camps—UDAP §§ 2.2.7, 5.5.4
Mileage Disclosure—Auto §§ 2.4.5.8, 4.6.6
Military Personnel and Credit Protection—FDC § 9.12; FCR § 13.2.8.3; Repo §§ 6.3.5.1, 16.6

385

Quick Reference to the Consumer Credit and Sales Legal Practice Series
References are to sections in *all* manuals in NCLC's Consumer Credit and Sales Legal Practice Series

Mini-FTC Laws—*See* UDAP
Minority—UDAP § 9.5.7
Misrepresentation—UDAP § 4.2; Warr § 11.4; Auto § 8.4
Mistaken Undercharges, Utility Bills—AUS § 5.1.2
Mobile Home Defects—Warr § 15.1.3
Mobile Home Foreclosure—Repo § 16.12
Mobile Home Park Conversions—CLP2 § 2.2
Mobile Home Parks—UDAP §§ 2.2.6, 5.5.1; CLP2 Ch 2
Mobile Homes, Federal Statutes—Warr App C
Mobile Homes and Interstate Rate Deregulation—COC Ch 3S
Mobile Homes and Repossession—Repo §§ 2.2.2, 3.5, 4.8.3, 5.2, 6.3.3, 7.1
Mobile Homes, Sale by Consumer—Repo § 9.6.3
Mobile Homes and UDAP—UDAP §§ 2.2.5, 5.4.12
Mobile Homes, Utility Service—AUS § 5.6
Mobile Homes, Warranties—Warr Ch 15; CLP2 § 4.1; CLP5 Ch 4
Model Pleadings—*See* Sample Complaints, Sample Interrogatories, etc.
Money Orders—CBPL § 2.1
Mortgage Assistance Scams—UDAP § 5.1.12; Repo §§ 16.7.6, 15.10
Mortgage Assistance, State Programs—Repo § 17.9.4
Mortgage Fees—TIL § 3.9.6; COC Ch 7
Mortgage Loans—UDAP § 5.1.9
Mortgage Servicers—Repo § 17.2.4.3, Ch 19; CLP3 § 7.1; CLP7 Ch 11
Mortgage Servicing, Summary of State Laws—Repo App MS
Most Favored Lender—COC § 3.4.3S
Motor Vehicle Information and Cost Savings Act—Auto Chs 4, 5, App A.1
Motor Vehicle Installment Sales Act—COC § 2.3.3.5; Repo § 2.1
Multiple Damages—UDAP § 8.4.2; Auto § 5.8.1
Municipal Utilities (MUNIs)—AUS §§ 1.5S, 12.2
NACA Class Actions Guidelines for Settlement—CCA App B; CLP4 § 12.2
NACHA—CBPL Ch 4S
National Arbitration Forum—Arbit App B.2, App G
National Origin Discrimination—CD § 3.3.3
"Nationwide" Reporting Agencies—FCR § 2.5.8
Native Americans and Repossession—Repo § 6.3.5.2
Necessities Laws—FDC § 14.6; CD § 9.3
Negative Equity—COC § 11.2.2.3
Negative Option Plans—UDAP § 5.8.5
Negligence—Warr Ch 12; FCR § 10.3.9; FDC §§ 10.2, 10.7
Negotiations, Class Actions—CCA Ch 11
New Car Lemon Laws—Warr § 13.2, App F; CLP2 Ch 5
New Cars, Sales—Warr Ch 13; UDAP § 5.4.7; CLP2 Ch 5
New Cars, Undisclosed Damage to—Auto §§ 1.4.5, 6.2.3
New House Warranties—Warr Ch 16
900 Numbers—UDAP §§ 5.9.3, 6.9, Apps D, E
Nonattorney Legal Service Providers, Deceptive Practices—UDAP § 5.12.2
Nondisclosure and UDAP—UDAP § 4.2.14
Non-English Speaking—UDAP § 5.2.1
Nonfiling Insurance—COC § 8.5.4.5
Nonpayment of Loans, When Excused—Repo § 4.6
Non-Signatories Rights and Obligations—Arbit §§ 6.3, 6.4
Notario Fraud—UDAP § 5.12.2
Notice to Class—CCA Ch 10
Notice to Quit, Deceptive—UDAP § 5.5.2.9
Not Sufficient Funds (NSF) Checks—CBPL § 1.4
Nursing Homes, Deceptive Practices—UDAP § 5.11.3; CLP4 Ch 3
Obsolete Information in Consumer Reports—FCR Ch 8
Odometers—Auto; Warr § 14.5.2; UDAP § 5.4.6.5

Odometer Tampering—Auto §§ 4.3, 4.4; CLP5 Ch 3
Offer of Judgment—FDC § 2.4.13; CCA § 6.3.1
Official Bankruptcy Forms—Bankr App D
Oil, Home Heating—AUS § 1.6S; UDAP § 5.6.7
On-Line Fraud—UDAP § 5.9.4
On-Line Disclosures—UDAP § 4.2.14.3.6
On Us Checks—CBPL § 1.1.7
Open-End Credit—TIL Ch 5; COC § 2.3.2.3
Open-End Credit, Spurious—TIL § 5.2.3
Outdated Information in Consumer Reports—FCR Ch 8
Overcharges by Creditor in Bankruptcy—Bankr § 13.4.3.3S; CLP3 Ch 7
Pain and Suffering Damages—FDC § 2.5; UDAP § 8.3.3.9
Paralegals, Attorney Fees for—UDAP §§ 8.6.11.6, 8.8.7.2
Parol Evidence—UDAP § 4.2.15.4; Warr § 3.7
Partial Prepayment—COC § 8.2
Pattern and Practice Evidence—Auto § 9.8
Pawnbrokers—COC §§ 2.3.3.9, 7.5.2.3; UDAP § 5.1.14
Payday Loans—COC § 7.5.5, App F; CLP3 § 4.1
Payment Holidays for Interest-Bearing Loans—COC § 4.8.3
Payment Packing—COC § 11.2.2.4
Payment Plans, Utility Bills—AUS Ch 6
Pay Phones—AUS § 2.6S
Pensions in Bankruptcy—Bankr §§ 2.5.1, 10.2.2.11
Percentage of Income Payment Plans—AUS § 9.2.3
Perkins Loans—Stud
Personal Injury Suits—UDAP § 2.2.11
Personal Property Seized with Repo—Repo Ch 7
Pest Control Services—UDAP § 5.6.3
Petroleum Products, Price Gouging—UDAP § 5.6.7.5
Photoprocessing Packages—UDAP § 5.7.10
Plain English—UDAP § 5.2.2
Pleadings—*See* Sample Complaints, Sample Answer, etc.
Point of Sale (POS) Electronic Transfers—CBPL Ch 4
Points—COC §§ 4.7, 6.4.1.3, 7.2.1, 8.3.2; TIL § 3.7.5
Postal Money Order—CBPL § 2.3
Postdated Checks—CBPL § 1.5
Preauthorized Drafts—CBPL § 1.9
Precomputed Interest—COC § 4.5
Precut Housing—UDAP § 5.5.5.6
Preemption of State Usury Laws—COC Ch 3S; CLP7 Ch 10
Preexisting Debt Clauses—Repo § 3.9
Prepayment—TIL § 4.7.6; COC Ch 5
Prepayment Penalties—COC § 5.8
Prescreening Lists—FCR § 5.3.8.4
Preservation of Documents, Class Actions—CCA § 5.2
Price Gouging in an Emergency—UDAP § 4.3.11
Pricing—UDAP § 4.6
Privacy, Invasion of—FCR § 10.3.8; FDC § 10.3
Privacy, Restrictions on Use of Consumer Reports—FCR § 1.5, Ch 5
Private Mortgage Insurance (PMI)—Repo § 16.7.8.7; COC § 8.3.6; UDAP § 5.3.13
Private Sale of Collateral—Repo § 10.5.7
Privity—Warr Ch 6; UDAP § 4.2.15.4
Prizes—UDAP § 5.13.4
Procedural Unconscionability—Warr § 11.2; COC § 11.7
Proceeds—Repo § 3.3.2
Progress Payments—COC § 4.9
Propane—AUS § 1.6S; UDAP § 5.6.7
Protective Orders—CCA § 5.2, App H
Public Assistance Status, Discrimination Based on—CD § 3.4.3
Public Housing, UDAP Coverage—UDAP §§ 2.3.3.3, 2.3.6
Public Housing, Utility Service—AUS Ch 8
Public Records—FCR § 7.2.3

Quick Reference to the Consumer Credit and Sales Legal Practice Series

References are to sections in *all* manuals in NCLC's Consumer Credit and Sales Legal Practice Series

Public Sale of Collateral—Repo § 10.7
Public Utilities—AUS
Public Utility Credit—TIL § 2.4.6
Punitive Damages—Auto § 7.10; CD § 11.6.4; FCR § 11.4; FDC § 2.6, Ch 10; UDAP § 8.4.3; CLP1 Ch 5
Pyramid Sales—UDAP § 5.13.3
Pyramiding Late Charges—COC § 7.2.4.3; AUS § 6.2.6
Race Discrimination re Car Sales—CLP3 § 9.2
Race Discrimination re Credit—CD § 3.3.1
Racketeering Statute—*See* RICO
Reachback Periods—Bankr § 6.5.2.4S
Reaffirmations and Bankruptcy—Bankr § 14.5.2; CLP5 Ch 2
Real Estate—UDAP §§ 2.2.5, 5.5.5
Real Estate Brokers—CLP2 § 4.4
Real Estate Settlement Procedures Act—COC § 11.3.1
Real Estate Tax Abatement Laws—Repo App J
Reassembled Cars from Parts—Auto §§ 1.4.3, 2.1.4; UDAP § 5.4.6.6
Rebates from Manufacturer—UDAP § 4.6.3.2; TIL § 3.7.5.2
Rebates of Interest—COC Ch 5, §§ 6.3, 6.4; TIL §§ 2.7, 3.7.2.2
Recoupment Claims—TIL §§ 6.3.3, 7.2.5; Bankr § 13.3.2.4S; CLP3 Ch 8
Redemption and Repo—Repo § 9.3
Redemption, Foreclosures—Repo §§ 16.2.6, 21.2
Redlining—CD §§ 7.1, 7.2
Referral Sales—UDAP § 5.8.3
Refinancings—COC Ch 6; Repo § 3.8; TIL § 4.9; UDAP § 5.1.9; CLP3 Ch 2
Refund Anticipation Loans—COC § 7.5.4
Refunds—UDAP § 5.2.6
Regulation B, Text—CD App B
Regulation E—CBPL Ch 4, App D
Regulation M, Text—TIL App I.2
Regulation Z, Text—CBPL Ch 3, App C; TIL App B
Regulation CC—CBPL § 1.8
Regulation DD—CBPL § 1.11.2
Rejection—Warr Ch 8
Reliance—TIL §§ 8.5.4.2, 8.5.5.7; UDAP § 4.2.12
Religious Discrimination re Credit—CD § 3.3.2
Rent and Bankruptcy—Bankr §§ 12.9, 14.5.5.3, 17.8
Rent to Own—UDAP § 5.7.4; Bankr § 11.8; COC § 7.5.3; Repo § 14.3; CLP2 Ch 8; CLP4 Ch 11
Rent, Utility Service—AUS Chs 4, 8
Rental Cars—UDAP § 5.4.9; Auto § 2.4.5.6
Rental Housing, Substandard—UDAP §§ 5.5.2.4, 5.5.2.5
Repairs—UDAP § 4.9.7
Repairs, Automobile—Warr § 17.8; UDAP § 5.4.1
Repayment Plan for Student Loans—Stud § 8.3
Replevin—Repo Ch 5
Reporting Agencies—FCR
Repossessions—Repo; UDAP § 5.1.2; FDC § 4.2.5; CLP2 Ch 12; CLP3 § 9.3; CLP4 Ch 4; CLP5 Ch 3; CLP6 Ch 4, Ch 13
Repossessions, Stopping—Bankr Ch 9
Requests for Admissions—CCA § 7.5; Repo App E.5; CLP1–5
Resale of Utility Service—AUS §§ 5.5, 5.6
Rescission—TIL Ch 6, App E.3; Auto § 7.11; Repo § 16.7.3.1; UDAP §§ 8.7, 9.5.2; CLP5 Ch 10
Rescission by Recoupment—TIL § 6.3.3
Resisting Repossession, Liability for—Repo § 6.2.4.3
RESPA—COC § 11.3.1; Repo §§ 16.7.8.8, 17.2.4.3, 17.2.7.6, Ch 19; TIL §§ 4.1.1, 4.3.4; CLP3 Ch 6; CLP6 Ch 15
Retail Installment Sales Acts (RISA)—COC § 2.3.3.5; Repo § 2.5
Retail Sellers—COC §§ 2.3.1.3.2, 9.2.3.2
Retaliation for Exercise of TIL, CCPA Rights—CD § 3.4.4

Retroactive Statutes—UDAP § 7.4; COC § 9.3.2
Reverse Metering—AUS § 5.1
Reverse Redlining—CD §§ 8.2, 8.3
Review of Arbitration Decision—Arbit Ch 10
Revocation of Acceptance—Warr Ch 8
Revolving Repossessions—Repo § 10.9.4
RICO—UDAP §§ 9.2, 9.3, App C.1.1; COC § 11.6; FDC § 9.5; Auto § 8.5; CLP3 § 9.3
Right to Cure Default—Repo § 4.8, App B; Bankr § 11.6.2
Right to See Consumer Reports—FCR § 4.3
Right to Utility Service—AUS Ch 3
RISA—COC § 2.3.3.5; Repo § 2.5
Rooker Feldman—FDC § 7.6.4
RTO Contracts—*See* Rent to Own
Rule of 78—COC § 5.6.3.3; TIL § 3.7.2.2.3; Repo § 11.3.2.2.2
Rural Electric Cooperatives (RECs)—AUS §§ 1.5S, 12.2
Rustproofing—UDAP § 5.4.3.3
Safety—UDAP § 4.7.4
Sale and Lease-Back—COC § 7.5.2.1; TIL § 6.2.5; CLP3 § 1.3
Sale of Collateral—Repo Ch 10
Salvage Auctions—Auto § 2.6.4.2
Salvage Vehicles, Sale of—Auto §§ 1.4.3, 2.1.4, 2.4.5.4, 6.2.1; Warr § 14.5.4; CLP5 Ch 6
Salvaged Parts—UDAP § 5.4.6.6
Sample Answer and Counterclaims—Repo Apps D.1, O.2.1S; COC App E; CLP2
Sample Briefs, Class Action—CCA Apps L, M; CLP1–5
Sample Client Retainer Forms—CLP4 Ch 8
Sample Closing Arguments—Auto App I; FCR App I.2
Sample Complaints—Arbit App C; Auto App G; CD App F; CCA App D; COC Apps E, F; FCR App H; FDC App H; Repo Apps D.3, O.3.1S, O.4S; Warr App K; TIL Apps D, E; CLP1–8
Sample Consumer Reporting Agency User Agreement—FCR App G.1
Sample Deposition Questions—FCR App I.4.2; CLP1; CLP3
Sample Discovery—*See* Sample Interrogatories; Sample Document Requests
Sample Document Requests—Arbit App D; Auto App F; CCA App E; CD App G; FDC App I.2; Repo Apps E.2, O.2.2S; TIL App F.3; Warr App L.3; CLP1–8
Sample Forms, Bankruptcy—Bankr Apps D, E, F, G
Sample Forms, Credit Reporting—FCR App F
Sample Interrogatories—Arbit App D; Auto App F; CCA App E; CD App G; COC App E; FCR App I.2.1; FDC App I.1; Repo Apps E, O.2.2S, O.3.3S, O.3.4S; Warr App L; TIL App F.2; CLP1–8
Sample Interview Forms—Warr App I
Sample Jury Instructions—CCA Ch 14; Auto App G.6S; FDC App J.2; FCR App I.3; TIL App G
Sample Letter to Debt Collector—FDC § 2.3
Sample Motion in Limine—Auto App I; FDC App J.5
Sample Motions for Class Certification—CCA App K; CLP1–8
Sample Notice for Rescission—TIL App D; CLP1 Ch 8
Sample Notice of Deposition—CLP2 §§ 8.3, 15.3.1; CLP3 § 5.1.2
Sample Notice of Revocation—Warr App J.1
Sample Notice That Consumer Is Deducting Damages From the Outstanding Balance—Warr App J.2
Sample Objection to Document Requests—CCA App J
Sample Opening and Closing Statement—Auto App I
Sample Pleadings—*See* Sample Answer; Sample Complaint
Sample Requests for Admissions—COC App E; FDC App I.3; Auto App F.1.4; Repo App O.2.2S; CLP1–8
Sample Summary Judgment Briefs—FDC App J.1; CLP1–5

Quick Reference to the Consumer Credit and Sales Legal Practice Series

References are to sections in *all* manuals in NCLC's Consumer Credit and Sales Legal Practice Series

Sample Trial Brief—FDC App J.4
Sample Trial Documents—Auto App I; FDC App J; Warr App M
School-Related Defenses to Student Loans—Stud § 9.5
Schools, Vocational—Stud Ch 9
Scope of Arbitration Agreement—Arbit Ch 6
Scrip Settlements, Class Actions—CCA § 11.6; CLP4 Ch 12
Second Mortgage, Rescission of—TIL Ch 6
Secret Warranties—UDAP § 5.4.7.10.2; Warr § 13.5.3.2
Securities Law—UDAP § 9.4.10
Securitization of Consumer Paper—COC § 2.4.2
Security Deposits, Consumer's Rights to Reform Where Seller in Bankruptcy—Bankr § 17.8.4
Security Deposits, Tenant's—UDAP §§ 5.5.2.2, 5.5.2.3; FDC § 1.5.2.5
Security Deposits, Utility § 3.7
Security Interest Charges—TIL § 3.9
Security Interests—Repo Ch 3; TIL § 4.6.7
Security Interests, Avoiding in Bankruptcy—Bankr § 10.4.2.4, Ch 11
Security Systems—UDAP § 5.6.2
Seizure of Collateral—Repo
Self-Help Repossession—Repo Ch 6
Service Contracts—Warr Ch 18, App G; UDAP §§ 5.2.7.2, 5.4.3.5; Auto §§ 2.5.10, 2.6.2.11
Service Contracts, When Hidden Interest—COC §§ 7.2.3, 7.3.1; TIL § 3.6.5
Servicemembers Civil Relief Act—*See* Soldiers' and Sailors's Civil Relief Act
Services and Warranties—Warr Ch 17
Set Off, Banker's—CBPL Ch 8
Set-Offs—TIL §§ 5.9.3, 8.4; FDC § 12.6.7
Settlement, Auto Case—Auto § 9.11; CLP4 Ch 15; Warr § 10.1.6
Settlement, Class Actions—CCA Chs 11, 12, Apps O, P; CLP3 §§ 3.5, 7.2.7; CLP4 Ch 12
Settlement, Class Actions, Objections—CCA § 12.8, App Q; CLP4 Ch 12
Settlement, Individual Prior to Class Action—CCA § 1.2
Settlements and Consumer Reports—FCR § 13.5.2
Sewer Service—AUS § 1.2.3S
Sex Discrimination re Credit—CD § 3.3.4
Sexual Orientation, Discrimination Based On—CD § 3.7
Shell Homes—UDAP § 5.5.5.6
Single Document Rule—COC § 11.2.2.8S
Slamming, Telephone Service—AUS § 2.7.5.1S; UDAP § 5.6.10
Small Loan Laws—COC § 2.3.3.2
Smart Cards—CBPL § Ch 7
Social Security Benefit Offset to Repay Student Loan—Stud § 5.4
Social Security Payments, Electronic—CBPL §§ 5.1–5.3
Soldiers' and Sailors' Civil Relief Act—FDC § 9.12; FCR § 13.2.8.3; Repo § 6.3.5.1
Spendthrift Trusts in Bankruptcy—Bankr § 2.5.1
Spoilation of Evidence—Warr § 10.1.2.5
Spot Delivery of Automobiles—UDAP § 5.4.5; Repo § 4.5; TIL §§ 4.4.5, 4.4.6; COC § 11.2.2.5; CLP7 Ch 5
Spouses, Consumer Reports on—FCR §§ 13.2.7, 13.3.7.2
Spreader Clauses—TIL § 4.6.7.6
Spurious Open-End Credit—TIL § 5.2.3
Stafford Loans—Stud
Standard Form Contracts, Unfair—UDAP § 5.2.3
State Arbitration Law—Arbit Ch 2
State Bonding Laws—Auto App C
State Cosigner Statutes—Repo § 12.9.6.2
State Credit Discrimination Laws—CD § 1.6, App E
State Credit Repair Laws—FCR App B
State Credit Reporting Laws—FCR § 10.4.1, App B

State Debt Collection Statutes—FDC § 11.2, App E
State Foreclosure Laws—Repo App I
State Home Improvement Statutes and Regs—Warr § 17.7.4
State Leasing Disclosure Statutes—TIL § 10.5.2.2
State Lemon Buyback Disclosure Laws—Auto App C
State Lemon Laws—Warr § 13.2, App F
State Lending Statutes—COC App A
State 900 Number Laws—UDAP App E
State Odometer Statutes—Auto App C
State Real Estate Tax Abatement Laws—Repo App J
State RICO Statutes—UDAP § 9.3, App C.2
State Right to Cure, Reinstate and Redeem Statutes—Repo App B
State Salvage Laws—Auto App C
State Service Contract Laws—Warr App G
State Telemarketing Laws—UDAP App E
State TIL Laws—TIL § 2.6
State Title Transfer Laws—Auto § 6.5, App C
State UDAP Statutes—UDAP App A
State Usury Statutes—COC App A
Statute of Limitations—Stud § 3.2; TIL § 7.2
Statute of Limitations as Consumer Defense to Collection Action—Repo § 12.7
Statutory Damages—TIL § 8.6; FDC §§ 6.4, 11.2; Repo § 13.2; UDAP § 8.4.1
Statutory Liens—Repo Ch 15
Statutory Liens, Avoiding in Bankruptcy—Bankr § 10.4.2.6.2
Staying Foreclosure—Bankr Ch 9
Stolen Checks—CBPL § 1.3
Stolen Vehicles—Auto §§ 1.4.10, 2.1.7, 8.2.2
Stop Payment on Checks, Credit and Debit Cards—CBPL §§ 1.6, 3.5, 4.4.4
Storage of Consumer Belongings—CLP2 § 7.1
Storage of Evicted Tenant's Property—Repo § 15.7.4; UDAP § 5.5.2.5
Stored Value Cards—CBPL Ch 7, App G
Straight Bankruptcy—Bankr Ch 3
Strict Liability in Tort—Warr Ch 12
Student Loan Collection Abuse—Stud Ch 4; CLP2 Ch 14
Student Loan Repayment Plans—Stud Ch 8
Student Loan Regulations—Stud App B
Student Loans—Bankr § 14.4.3.8; FCR §§ 8.6.9, 13.5.2.3, 13.6.11, 13.7.9; Stud; TIL § 2.4.5; CLP2 Chs 13, 14; CLP5 Ch 9
Student Loans and Bankruptcy—Stud Ch 7
Student Loans, Private Loans—Stud § 1.9S
Student Loans, Reinstating Eligibility—Stud Ch 8
Surety for Consumer Debtor—Repo § 12.9
Surety Liability for Seller's Actions—Auto § 9.13.4
Survey Evidence—FDC § 2.9.3
Surveys, Use in Litigation—CCA § 7.6
Target Marketing Lists—FCR §§ 2.3.3, 5.2.9.1, 5.3.8.4.2
Tax Abatement Laws, State Property, Summaries—Repo App J
Tax Consequences, Bankruptcy Discharge—Bankr § 14.6S
Tax Intercept—Bankr § 9.4.3S
Tax Liens—Repo Ch 22
Tax Refund Intercepts—Stud § 5.2
Tax Refunds—COC § 7.5.4
Tax Refunds in Bankruptcy—Bankr § 2.5.2
Tax Sales—Repo Ch 22
Taxis, Undisclosed Sale of—Auto § 2.4.5.6
Telechecks—UDAP §§ 5.1.15, 5.1.16
Telecommunications Act of 1996—AUS Ch 2S, App C
Telemarketing, Payment—CBPL § 1.9.4
Telemarketing Fraud—UDAP § 5.9; FCR § 15.4
Telemarketing Fraud, Federal Statutes—UDAP App D

Quick Reference to the Consumer Credit and Sales Legal Practice Series

References are to sections in *all* manuals in NCLC's Consumer Credit and Sales Legal Practice Series

Telephone Companies as Credit Reporting Agencies—FCR § 2.6.9
Telephone Harassment—FDC § 9.3
Telephone Inside Wiring Maintenance Agreements—UDAP §§ 5.2.7.2, 5.6.9
Telephone Rates, Service—AUS Ch 2S, App C; CLP7 Ch 2
Telephone Service Contracts—UDAP §§ 5.2.7.2, 5.6.9
Telephone Slamming—AUS § 2.7.5.1S; UDAP § 5.6.10
Teller's Checks—CBPL § 1.1.8
Tenant Approval Companies—FCR §§ 2.3.6.4, 2.6.1, 6.4.2.3.3, 13.3.2, 13.7.3
Tenant Ownership in Chapter 7 Liquidation—Bankr § 17.8.2S
Tenant's Property Removed with Eviction—Repo § 15.7.4
Tenant's Rights When Landlord Files Bankruptcy—Bankr § 17.8; AUS § 4.5
Termination of Utility Service—AUS Chs 11, 12
Termite Control Services—UDAP § 5.6.3
Testers, Fair Housing—CD §§ 4.4.4, 11.2.2
Theft at ATM machines, bank liability—CBPL § 4.9
Theft of Identity—FCR § 13.5.5; CLP3 Ch 5
Third Party Liability Issues—AUS §§ 11.4, 11.5
Threats of Criminal Prosecution—FDC § 15.3
Tie-In Sale Between Mobile Home and Park Space—CLP2 § 2.2; UDAP § 5.5.1.2
TIL—*See* Truth in Lending
Time Shares—UDAP § 5.5.5.8
Tire Identification—Auto § 2.2.3
Title, Automobile—Auto §§ 2.3, 2.4, Ch 3, Apps. D, E; UDAP § 5.4.5; Warr § 14.3.5
Tobacco—UDAP § 5.11.7
Tort Liability—FDC Ch 12
Tort Liability, Strict—Warr Ch 12
Tort Remedies, Unlawful Disconnections—AUS § 11.7.2
Tort Remedies, Wrongful Repossessions—Repo § 13.6
Towing—UDAP § 5.4.1.8; Repo Ch 15
Trade-in Cars—UDAP § 5.4.4.4
Trade Schools—Stud Ch 9; UDAP § 5.10.7
Trading Posts—UDAP § 5.1.14
Transcripts and Bankruptcy—Bankr § 14.5.5.2
Traveler's Checks—CBPL § 1.1.8.3
Travel Fraud—UDAP § 5.4.13; CLP4 Ch 5
Travelers Checks—UDAP § 2.2.1.3
Treble Damages—UDAP § 8.4.2
Trebled, Disclosure to Jury that Damages Will Be—UDAP § 8.4.2.7.3
Trustees in Bankruptcy—Bankr §§ 2.6, 2.7, 16.4.2, 17.7
Truth in Lending—TIL; COC §§ 2.3.4, 4.4.1; FDC § 9.4; Repo § 2.11
Truth in Mileage Act—Auto Chs 3, 4, 5
Truth in Savings—CBPL § 1.11.2
Tuition Recovery Funds-Stud § 9.6
Typing Services—Bankr § 15.6
UCC Article 2—Warr
UCC Article 2 and Comments Reprinted—Warr App E
UCC Article 2A—Repo §§ 2.3, 14.1.3.1; Warr Ch 19, App E.4; UDAP § 5.4.8.5
UCC Articles 3 and 4—CBPL Ch 1, App A
UCC Article 9—Repo
UCC Article 9, Revised—Repo App A
UCC Article 9 and Comments Reprinted—Repo App A
UDAP—UDAP; AUS § 1.7.2S; Auto § 8.4; COC §§ 8.5.2.5.2, 11.5; FDC § 11.3; FCR § 10.4.2; Repo §§ 2.7, 13.4.3; Warr § 11.1
Unauthorized Card Use—TIL § 5.9.4
Unauthorized Practice of Law—FDC §§ 4.2.7.7, 5.6.2, 11.5; Bankr § 15.6; UDAP § 5.12.2

Unauthorized Use of Checks, Credit and Debit Cards—CBPL §§ 1.2, 3.3, 4.5
Unauthorized Use of Utility Service—AUS § 5.3
Unavailability of Advertised Items—UDAP § 4.6.2
Unconscionability—Warr §§ 11.2, 19.2.6; COC §§ 8.7.5, 11.7; UDAP §§ 4.4, 5.4.6.5; Auto § 8.7
Unconscionability of Arbitration Clauses—Arbit §§ 4.2, 4.3, 4.4; UDAP § 7.7
Unearned Interest—COC Ch 5
Unemployment Insurance—COC § 8.3.4
Unfair Insurance Practices Statutes—UDAP § 5.3; COC § 8.4.1.4
Unfair Practices Statutes—*See* UDAP
Unfairness—UDAP § 4.3
Uniform Commercial Code—*See* UCC
United States Trustee—Bankr §§ 2.7, 17.7.2
Universal Telephone Service—AUS Ch 2S
Unlicensed Activities—UDAP § 4.9.8; COC § 9.2.4.5
Unpaid Refund Discharge of Student Loan—Stud § 6.4
Unsolicited Credit Cards—TIL § 5.9.2
Unsolicited Goods—UDAP § 5.8.4; FDC § 9.2
Unsubstantiated Claims—UDAP § 4.5
Used as New—UDAP § 4.9.4
Used Car Lemon Laws—Warr § 14.8
Used Car Rule—Warr § 14.7, App D; UDAP § 5.4.6.2, App B.6
Used Cars—Auto; Warr Ch 14, App K.3, App L.6; UDAP § 5.4.6; CLP2 Ch 6
Used Cars, Assembled from Salvaged Parts—Auto §§ 1.4.3, 2.1.4; CLP2 § 6.2
Used Cars, Financing—COC § 11.2.2
Used Cars, Undisclosed Sale of Wrecked Cars—Auto §§ 1.4.4, 2.1.4
Users of Consumer and Credit Reports—FCR Ch 5
Usury, Trying a Case—COC Ch 10
Utilities—AUS; CD §§ 2.2.2.3, 2.2.6.2; TIL § 2.4.6; UDAP §§ 2.3.2, 5.6.8
Utilities and Bankruptcy—AUS §§ 4.5, 12.1; Bankr § 9.8
Utilities as Credit Reporting Agencies—FCR § 2.6.9
Utility Commission Regulation—AUS § 1.3S, App A
Utility Service Terminated by a Landlord—AUS § 12.4
Utility Subsidies in Subsidized Housing—AUS Ch 8
Utility Termination, Remedies—AUS § 11.7; UDAP § 5.6.8.1; CLP2 § 1.3; FDC § 1.5.6
Utility Terminations, Stopping—AUS Chs 11, 12; Bankr Ch 9
VA Mortgage Foreclosures and Workouts—Repo §§ 17.5.2, 18.3; CLP2 § 3.1
Variable Rate Disclosures—TIL § 4.8
Variable Rates, Calculation—COC § 4.3.6
Vehicle Identification Number—Auto § 2.2.4
Venue, Inconvenient—FDC §§ 6.12.2, 8.3.7, 10.6.3, 11.7; UDAP § 5.1.4
Vertical Privity—Warr § 6.2
Vocational Schools—Stud Ch 9
Voluntary Payment Doctrine—UDAP § 4.2.15.5aS
Wage Earner Plans—Bankr Ch 4
Wage Garnishment—FDC Ch 12, App D
Waiver of Default—Repo § 4.3
Waiver of Right to Enforce Arbitration Clause—Arbit Ch 7
Wage Garnishment of Student Loans—Stud § 5.3, App B.1.2A
Warehouseman's Lien—Repo § 15.7.4; CLP2 § 7.1
Warranties—Warr; Auto § 8.2; UDAP § 5.2.7
Warranties, Secret—Warr § 13.5.3.2; UDAP § 5.4.7.10.2
Warranty Disclaimers—Warr Ch 5
Warranty of Habitability, Utility Service—AUS § 4.4.1
Water Quality Improvement Systems—UDAP § 5.6.4

389

Quick Reference to the Consumer Credit and Sales Legal Practice Series
References are to sections in *all* manuals in NCLC's Consumer Credit and Sales Legal Practice Series

Water Service—AUS § 1.2.3S; UDAP § 5.6.10
Weatherization Assistance—AUS Ch 10
Web Sites, Consumer Advocacy—UDAP § 1.3
Welfare Benefits, Bankruptcy—Bankr §§ 10.2.2.11, 14.5.5
Welfare Benefits, Credit Discrimination—CD §§ 3.4.3, 5.5.5.5
Welfare Benefits, Credit Reporting—FCR §§ 2.3.6.8, 5.2.2, 13.3.5
Welfare Benefits, Exemptions—FDC § 12.5
"Wheelchair" Lemon Laws—Warr Ch 16aS
Wire Fraud—UDAP § 9.2.4.4
Wires—CBPL § 2.2
Withholding Credit Payments—Repo § 4.6.3; Warr § 8.5

Women's Business Ownership Act of 1988—CD § 1.3.2.4
Workers Compensation and Bankruptcy—Bankr § 10.2.2.1
Workout Agreements—TIL § 4.9.7
Workout Agreements, Foreclosures—Repo Ch 17
Wraparound Mortgages—COC § 7.4.3
Writ of Replevin—Repo Ch 5
Yield Spread Premiums—CD § 8.4; COC §§ 4.7.2, 7.3.2, 11.2.1.4.3, 11.2.2.6; CLP3 Ch 6; UDAP §§ 5.1.11.3, 5.4.3.4
Yo-Yo Delivery of Automobiles—UDAP § 5.4.5; Repo § 4.5; TIL §§ 4.4.5, 4.4.6; COC § 11.2.2.5; CD § 10.2.3.3; CLP Ch 5

NOTES

NOTES

NOTES

NOTES

NOTES

NOTES

NOTES

NOTES

About the Companion CD-Rom

CD-Rom Supersedes All Prior CD-Roms

This CD-Rom supersedes the CD-Rom accompanying *Fair Credit Reporting* (2002) and its 2003 Supplement. Discard the prior CD-Roms. This 2004 CD-Rom contains everything found on the earlier CD-Roms and contains much additional material.

What Is on the CD-Rom

For a detailed listing of the CD's contents, see the CD-Rom Contents section on page xxiii of this book. Highlights and new additions include:

- A redlined version of the Fair Credit Reporting Act with FACT Act amendments, the FACT Act and its legislative history, the Consumer Repair Organizations Act, sections of Gramm-Leach-Bliley, and summaries of state credit reporting and identity theft laws;
- 30 sample complaints and over 40 discovery requests and discovery documents, and a sample deposition transcript;
- Plaintiff's direct testimony on damages, closing arguments, jury instructions, 20 briefs and memos, and other trial documents;
- A universal data form, FTC model credit reporting forms, sample credit reports, explanations of credit reports, summary of rights, sample contracts between credit bureau and retailers, and other forms;
- The full text of *all* FTC Staff Opinion Letters on the FCRA with a sectional index, and the FTC Official Staff Commentary;
- Over 20 enforcement orders against the major reporting agencies and others; and
- Consumer's guide to credit reporting and numerous other consumer education brochures.

How to Use the CD-Rom

The CD's pop-up menu quickly allows you to use the CD—just place the CD into its drive and click on the "Start NCLC CD" button that will pop up in the middle of the screen. You can also access the CD by clicking on a desktop icon that you can create using the pop-up menu.[1] For detailed installation instructions, see *One-Time Installation* below.

All the CD-Rom's information is available in PDF (Acrobat) format, making the information:

- Highly readable (identical to the printed pages in the book);
- Easily navigated (with bookmarks, "buttons," and Internet-style forward and backward searches);
- Easy to locate with keyword searches and other quick-search techniques across the whole CD-Rom; and
- Easy to paste into a word processor.

While much of the material is also found on the CD-Rom in word processing format, we strongly recommend you use the material in PDF format—not only because it is easiest to use, contains the most features, and includes more material, but also because you can easily switch back to a word processing format when you prefer.

Acrobat Reader 5 and 6.0.1 come free of charge with the CD-Rom. **We strongly recommend that new Acrobat users read the Acrobat tutorial on the Home Page. It takes two minutes and will really pay off.**

How to Find Documents in Word Processing Format

Most pleadings and other practice aids are also available in Microsoft Word format to make them more easily adaptable for individual use. (Current versions of WordPerfect are able to convert the Word documents upon opening them.) The CD-Rom offers several ways to find those word processing documents. One option is simply to browse to the folder on the CD-Rom containing all the word processing files and open the desired document from your standard word processing program, such as Word or WordPerfect. All word processing documents are in the D:\WP_Files folder, if "D:" is the CD-Rom drive,[2] and are further organized by

---

1 Alternatively, click on the D:\Start.pdf file on "My Computer" or open that file in Acrobat—always assuming "D:" is the CD-Rom drive on your computer.

2 The CD-Rom drive could be any letter following "D:" depend-

399

book title. Documents that appear in the book are named after the corresponding appendix; other documents have descriptive file names.

Another option is to navigate the CD in PDF format, and, when a particular document is on the screen, click on the corresponding bookmark for the "Word version of..." This will automatically run Word, WordPerfect for Windows, or *any other word processor* that is associated with the ".DOC" extension, and then open the word processing file that corresponds to the Acrobat document.[3]

Important Information Before Opening the CD-Rom Package

Before opening the CD-Rom package, please read this information. Opening the package constitutes acceptance of the following described terms. In addition, the *book* is not returnable once the seal to the *CD-Rom* has been broken.

The CD-Rom is copyrighted and all rights are reserved by the National Consumer Law Center, Inc. No copyright is claimed to the text of statutes, regulations, excerpts from court opinions, or any part of an original work prepared by a United States Government employee.

You may not commercially distribute the CD-Rom or otherwise reproduce, publish, distribute or use the disk in any manner that may infringe on any copyright or other proprietary right of the National Consumer Law Center. Nor may you otherwise transfer the CD-Rom or this agreement to any other party unless that party agrees to accept the terms and conditions of this agreement. You may use the CD-Rom on only one computer and by one user at a time.

The CD-Rom is warranted to be free of defects in materials and faulty workmanship under normal use for a period of ninety days after purchase. If a defect is discovered in the CD-Rom during this warranty period, a replacement disk can be obtained at no charge by sending the defective disk, postage prepaid, with information identifying the purchaser, to National Consumer Law Center, Publications Department, 77 Summer Street, 10th Floor, Boston, MA 02110. After the ninety-day period, a replacement will be available on the same terms, but will also require a $20 prepayment.

---

ing on your computer's configuration.

3 For instructions on how to associate WordPerfect to the ".DOC" extension, go to the CD-Rom's home page and click on "How to Use/Help," then "Word Files."

The National Consumer Law Center makes no other warranty or representation, either express or implied, with respect to this disk, its quality, performance, merchantability, or fitness for a particular purpose. In no event will the National Consumer Law Center be liable for direct, indirect, special, incidental, or consequential damages arising out of the use or inability to use the disk. The exclusion of implied warranties is not effective in some states, and thus this exclusion may not apply to you.

System Requirements

Use of this CD-Rom requires a Windows-based PC with a CD-Rom drive. (Macintosh users report success using NCLC CDs, but the CD has been tested only on Windows-based PCs.) The CD-Rom's features are optimized with Acrobat Reader 5 or later. Acrobat Reader versions 5 and 6.0.1 are included free on this CD-Rom, and either will work with this CD-Rom as long as it is compatible with your version of Windows. Acrobat Reader 5 is compatible with Windows 95/98/Me/NT/2000/XP, while Acrobat Reader 6.0.1 is compatible with Windows 98SE/Me/NT/2000/XP. If you already have Acrobat Reader 6.0, we *highly* recommend you install version 6.0.1 from this CD because a bug in version 6.0 interferes with optimum use of this CD-Rom. The Microsoft Word versions of pleadings and practice aids can be used with any reasonably current word processor (1995 or later).

One-Time Installation

When the CD-Rom is inserted in its drive, a menu will pop up automatically. (Please be patient if you have a slow CD-Rom drive; this will only take a few moments.) If you do not already have Acrobat Reader 5 or 6.0.1, first click the "Install Acrobat Reader" button. Do not reboot, but then click on the "Make Shortcut Icon" button. (You need not make another shortcut icon if you already have done so for another NCLC CD.) Then reboot and follow the *How to Use the CD-Rom* instructions above.

[*Note*: If the pop-up menu fails to appear, go to "My Computer," right-click "D:" if that is the CD-Rom drive, and select "Open." Then double-click on "Read_Me.txt" for alternate installation and use instructions.]